ARCHAIC POTTERY OF CHIOS

TEXT

Oxford University Committee for Archaeology
Monograph No. 30

ARCHAIC POTTERY OF CHIOS

The Decorated Styles

Volume I   Text

ANNA A. LEMOS

Oxford University Committee for Archaeology
1991

Published by
Oxford University Committee for Archaeology
Institute of Archaeology
Beaumont Street
Oxford

Distributed by
Oxbow Books
Park End Place, Oxford OX1 1HN

© Anna A. Lemos, 1991

ISBN 0 947816 30 5

Typeset by Oxbow Books at Oxford University Computing Service
Printed in Great Britain
at the S&S Press
Abingdon

Μνήμη
Ἀνδρέα καί Μαρίας Λαιμοῦ

Κάποτε μὲς στὰ ὄνειρά μας ὁμιλοῦνε
κάποτε μὲς στὴν σκέψι τὲς ἀκούει τὸ μυαλό.
Κ.Π.Καβάφη, *Φωνές*.

CONTENTS

PREFACE	vii
ABBREVIATIONS	ix
INTRODUCTION	1
1 THE PATTERNED CHALICES OF THE SEVENTH CENTURY	7
2 THE WILD GOAT STYLE	14
SHAPES	14
DECORATION	25
A. ANIMALS	26
B. BIRDS	37
C. HYBRIDS	38
D. COMPOSITION	43
E. ORNAMENTS	43
STYLE	64
EARLY WILD GOAT STYLE	64
MIDDLE I WILD GOAT STYLE	67
MIDDLE II WILD GOAT STYLE	70
LATE WILD GOAT STYLISTIC GROUPS	76
3 THE RESERVING STYLES OF THE SIXTH CENTURY	79
WORKSHOPS	79
SHAPES	80
STYLES	88
1. THE ANIMAL CHALICE STYLE	88
2. THE GRAND STYLE	94
I. Shapes	95
II. Iconography	95
1. Men	96
2. Women	98
3. Scenes from everyday life	100
4. Architectural Elements	104
5. Landscape Elements	107
6. Mythological scenes	107
III. Ornamental decoration	108
IV. Style	109
V. Connections with free painting	114
VI. Place of manufacture	117
2A. LIGHT ON DARK DECORATION	118
3. THE CHALICE STYLE	125
A. Vases with no filling ornament	125
B. Patterned sixth-century vases	131
D. Vases with floral decoration	132

4 THE BLACK-FIGURE STYLES — 133
   1. THE SPHINX AND LION STYLE — 133
      I. Shapes — 133
      II. Decoration — 140
         A. Animals and Birds — 140
         B. Human Figures — 142
         C. Ornaments — 142
         D. Composition — 145
      III. Style — 145
   2. THE BLACK-FIGURE GRAND STYLE — 154
      I. Shapes — 154
      II. Subjects — 155
      III. Style — 158
      IV. Place of manufacture — 160
   3. THE BLACK-FIGURE CHALICES — 163
      I. Shapes — 163
      II. Subjects — 163
      III. Style — 169
         1. Komast chalices — 169
         2. Animal chalices — 173
   4. THE BLACK-FIGURE KANTHAROI — 175
   5. LATE BLACK-FIGURE GROUPS — 177

5 DATING — 181
   RESERVING STYLES — 181
   BLACK-FIGURE STYLES — 186

6 DISTRIBUTION — 191
   A. EGYPT AND CYRENAICA — 192
   B. THE WEST — 195
   C. MAINLAND GREECE AND THE AEGEAN ISLANDS — 197
   D. NORTH GREECE AND THE BLACK SEA — 200
   E. EAST GREECE AND ANATOLIA — 203
   F. THE EASTERN MEDITERRANEAN — 206

7 A CHIAN WORKSHOP IN THRACE? — 209

8 THE CHARACTER OF CHIAN VASE PAINTING — 223

CATALOGUE

EXPLANATORY NOTE — 227
ABBREVIATIONS — 228
CONTENTS — 229
CATALOGUE — 231

PREFACE

Archaic Pottery of Chios, The Decorated Styles has its origins in my doctoral thesis submitted at the University of Oxford in 1984; it was further updated and reworked during 1989.

The aim pursued was to collect the known material, as well as that which, during my travels in Greece, Turkey and Italy and visits to various museums in Europe, was drawn to my attention by observation or the kind information of other people. With excavations going on all over the Mediterranean it would be difficult, if not impossible, to claim to be able to draw together here an exhaustive corpus of Archaic Chian Painted Pottery. However, if any of the published fragments have escaped my attention and are not here included, their omission will hopefully not much affect the overall picture of an interesting and productive Vase Painting School of Archaic Greece.

Plain and Patterned Chian Wares will constitute a separate study, which will appear in conjunction with the publication of the material from Rizari.

In the catalogue of my debts of thanks the first mention goes to the late Professor Nikolaos M. Kontoleon, whose inspiring teaching led me to study Classical Archaeology; his excavated material from Rizari, Chios provided the initiative for my involvement with Chian pottery which ultimately directed me to Oxford.

Here it was my very good fortune to study under the stimulating guidance of Professor Sir John Boardman. Not only did he most generously organize access for me to the key material from Naucratis in the British Museum, but he opened his personal archives too. Furthermore, his constructive criticism and encouragement, which included the thorough review of the book in draft, have saved me from many an error. Without his invaluable help this work would have inevitably been the poorer; it is difficult to express the depth of my gratitude for his all-encompassing assistance.

Help has come to me too from other sources: Professor R.M. Cook gave me the benefit of fruitful discussions and advice. I owe him great thanks. Professor F. Brommer provided me with copies of his photographs both from museums in Germany, of sherds from Naucratis mostly lost in the war, and from Egyptian ones too: a most valuable addition to the record for which I am deeply grateful.

Material from Naucratis is now dispersed all over the world. Many scholars and institutions have granted me permission to study and publish the pieces in their care. I am indebted to them all: the Trustees of the British Museum, and Drs. B.F. Cook and D. Williams; Dr. A.W. Johnston, University College, London; Professor A.M. Snodgrass, Museum of Classical Archaeology, Cambridge; Dr. R. Lang, Liverpool Museum; Dr. J.R. Mertens, the Metropolitan Museum of Art, New York; Dr. J.W. Hayes, Royal Ontario Museum, Toronto; Dr. D. Said, Graeco-Roman Museum of Alexandria.

For providing me with photographs, or allowing me to take my own, and for scholarly assistance I am obliged to: Prof. E. Akurgal (Ankara), Prof. P. Alexandrescu (Bucarest), Dr. A. Andreiomenou (Thebes), The Managing Committee of the Archaeological Society at Athens, Mrs. A. Archontidou (Chios), Dr. G. Beckel (Würzburg), The British School at Athens (Managing Committee and Mr. G. Sanders), Dr. J. Bourriau (Cambridge, Fitzwilliam Museum), The Department of Antiquities at the Museum of Fine Arts (Boston), Dr. T. Bro (Copenhagen), The Department of Antiquities at the Musées Royaux d'Art et d'Histoire (Brussels), Prof. A. Cambitoglou (Sydney), Dr. A. Collinge (University College, Dublin), Prof. J.M. Cook (Edinburgh), Prof. K. de Vries (Philadelphia), Mrs. J. Diamant (Athens, The Agora Excavations), Dr. C.A. Di Stefano (Palermo), Prof. P. Dupont (Lyon), Miss J.F. Gardner (Reading University), Dr. E. Goring (Edinburgh), Dr. H. Gropengiesser (Heidelberg), Dr. P.P. Guzzo (Tarentum), Prof. F. Giudice (Catane), Prof. J.J. Jully (Agde), Miss J. Ilyina (Leningrad), Prof. L. Kahil (Paris), Dr. V. Karageorghis (Cyprus), Mr. P. Kontos (Athens University), Dr. Ch. Koukouli-Chrysanthaki (Kavala), Ass. Prof. N. Kourou (Athens University), Prof. H. Kyrieleis and Mrs. N. Lazaridou (Athens, DAI), Prof. V. Lambrinoudakis (Athens University), The Department of Antiquities of the Louvre and M. Chuzeville, Prof. L.B. v.d. Meer (Leiden, Rijksuniversiteit), Dr. F. Nicosia (Florence), Dr. A. Pasinli (Istanbul Archaeological Museum), Prof. E. Paul (Leipzig), Dr. P. Pelagatti (Rome, Villa Guilia), Prof. B.B. Piotrovskiy (Leningrad), Miss A. Porter (University of Vermont, Burlington), Dr. K. Rhomiopoulou (Athens, National Archaeological Museum), Dr. I.I. Saverkina (Leningrad), Prof. G.P. Schaus (Waterloo, Ontario), Ass. Prof. E. Simantoni-Bournia (Athens University), Mr. C. Simon (Cambridge, Fitzwilliam Museum), Prof. M. Tiverios (Thessaloniki), Dr. G. Voza (Syracuse), Dr. Ph. Zapheiropoulou (Athens, Ephoreia for the Cyclades), Dr. E. Zervoudaki (Athens, National Archaeological Museum), Dr. G. Zimmer (Berlin, Staatliche Museen), and Prof. E Walter-Karydi (Munich).

Special thanks are due and happily acknowledged to all my colleagues and friends at the Department of Archaeology and History of Art in the University of Athens.

I am especially grateful to D. Evely for the line drawings, help with editorial aspects and for minimizing my maltreatment of the English language; above all for profitable suggestions and sustained support that have seen the work through to completion.

Concerning details of preparation, St. Piscardelis executed both the vase profiles in the Archaeological museum of Chios and the distribution maps, C. Unwin drew up from my originals the ornamental motifs. The late Sp. Tsavdaroglou, E. Eliades, J. Burrage, B. Wilkins and D. Plantzos between them produced the photographs; C. Brocklehurst and P. Everest organized the transfer of script to computer. To all, my warmest thanks are extended.

The book was wholly written in Oxford, courtesy of the extensive holdings of the Ashmolean Library; to the authorities and staff of which I am most obliged. The opportunity to work here has been supported by the University of Athens, to which I am deeply grateful.

Finally, I wish also to thank the Committee for Archaeology, Oxford University, for undertaking this publication in their series of monographs.

ABBREVIATIONS

AA	*Archäologischer Anzeiger*
AASyrie	*Les Annales archéologiques de Syrie. Revue d'archéologie et d'histoire*
ABV	Beazley J.D., *Attic Black-figure Vase-painters*, 1956
Acta X Inter. Congr. Class. Arch.	*Acta of the X International Congress of Classical Archaeology*, 1973
Acta XI Inter. Congr. Class. Arch.	*Acta of the XI International Congress of Classical Archaeology*, 1978
ADelt.	*Archaiologikon Deltion*
AE	see *Arch. Eph*
Aegina	Furtwängler A., *Aegina, Das Heiligtum der Aphaia*, 1906
Agora VIII	Brann E.T.H., *Late Geometric and Protoattic Pottery, The Athenian Agora*, Vol. VIII, 1962
Agora XII	Sparkes B.A. and Talcott L., *Black and Plain Pottery of the 6th, 5th and 4th centuries B.C., The Athenian Agora*, Vol. XII, 1970
Agora XXIII	Moore M.B. and Philippides M.Z.P., *Attic Black-figured Pottery, The Athenian Agora*, Vol. XXIII, 1986
AGSP	*Antichnye Goroda Severnogo Prichernomor'ya*, 1955
Akurgal, Bayrakli	Akurgal E., 'Bayrakli Kazisi On Rapor', *Ankara Universitesi Dil ve Tarih Cografya Fakultesi Degisi* 8:1, 1950
Akurgal, *Alt Smyrna* I	Akurgal E., *Alt Smyrna I, Wohnschichten und Athenatempel*, 1983
Akurgal, *Anatoliens*	Akurgal E., *Die Kunst Anatoliens von Homer bis Alexander*, 1961
Akurgal, *Türkei*	Akurgal E., *Griechische und römische Kunst in der Türkei*, 1987
AJA	*American Journal of Archaeology*
Alt-Ägina II.1	*Alt-Ägina*, Band II. 1, 1982
Ametos	*Ametos, Festschrift for Professor Manolis Andronikos*, 1987
Amyx, *CorVP*	Amyx D.A., *Corinthian Vase-Painting of the Archaic Period*, 1988
AnatSt	*Anatolian Studies*
Ancient Macedonia, Catalogue	*Ancient Macedonia, Catalogue of the Exhibition of Macedonian Finds in Australia*, 1988
AntCl	*L'antiquité classique*
AntK	*Antike Kunst*
Äol. Kunst	Walter-Karydi E., *Äolische Kunst*, *AntK*. 7 Beiheft, 1970, 3ff
ArchCl	*Archaeologia classica*
Arch. Eph	*Archaiologike Ephemeris*
Arch. Reports	*Archaeological Reports*
ASAtene	*Annuario della Scuola archeologica di Atene e delle Missioni italiane in Oriente*
AttiMGrecia	*Atti e memorie della Società Magna Grecia*
Austin, Greece and Egypt	Austin M.M., 'Greece and Egypt in the Archaic Age', *Proceedings of the Cambridge Philological Society*, Suppl. 2, 1970
BABesch	*Bulletin antieke Beschaving. Annual Papers on Classical Archaeology*
BAdd[2]	*Beazley Addenda*[2], compiled by T.H. Carpenter, 1989
Ballu, *Olbia*	Ballu E. Bellin de, *Olbia, Cité antique du littoral nord de la mer noire*, 1972, reviews in: *JHS* 94, 1974, 251-2 and *Gnomon* 1977, 617-622

BCH	*Bulletin de correspondance hellénique*
Belleten	*Belleten. Türk tarih kurumu*
Bernard, *Le Delta égyptien*	Bernard A., *Le Delta égyptien d'après les textes grecs*, 1970
BICS	*Bulletin. Institute of Classical Studies, University of London*
Boardman, *ABFH*	Boardman J., *Athenian Black Figure Vases, a Handbook*, 1974
Boardman, *AGG*	Boardman J., *Archaic Greek Gems*, 1968
Boardman, CN	Boardman J., 'Chian and Naucratite', *BSA* 51, 1956, 55–62
Boardman, *GA*[2]	Boardman J., *Greek Art* ed. 2, 1973
Boardman, *GO*[3]	Boardman J., *The Greeks Overseas* ed. 3, 1980
BolldArte	*Bollettino d'arte*
Boreas	*Boreas, Münstersche Beitrage zur Archäologie*
Bothmer, *Amasis*	Bothmer D. von, *The Amasis Painter and his world*, 1985
Brijder, *SCI*	Brijder H.A.G., *Siana Cups I and Komast Cups*, 1983
Brown, *Etruscan Lion*	Brown W.L., *The Etruscan Lion*, 1960
BSA	*The Annual of the British School at Athens*
Bull. Inst. Arch. Bulg.	*Bulletin de l'Institut archéologique bulgare*
Buschor, *Gr. Vasen*	Buschor E., *Griechische Vasen*, 1940
Buschor, *Satyrtänze*	Buschor E., *Satyrtänze und frühes Drama*, 1943
CAH	*Cambridge Ancient History* III 2 and 3
Catalogue Istanbul, 1983	The Council of Europe, XVIIIth European Art Exhibition: *THE ANATOLIAN CIVILISATIONS II Greek, Roman, Byzantine*. St. Irene, Istanbul, May 22 – October 30, 1983
CGED	*Les Céramiques de la Grèce de l'Est et leur Diffusion en Occident.* Colloques Internationaux du Centre National de la Recherche Scientifique. N569. Sciences Humaines, 1978
Charbonneaux-Martin-Villard	Charbonneaux J., Martin R. and Villard F., *La Grèce archaique*, 1968
Chiaka Meletemata I	Stephanou A., *Chiaka Meletemata* I, 1958
Chios Conference	*Chios, A Conference at the Homereion in Chios 1984*, ed. J. Boardman and C.E. Vaphopoulou-Richardson, 1986
ClPh	*Classical Philology*
ClRh	*Clara Rhodos, Studi e Materiali Pubblicati a cura dell' Istituto Storico-Archeologico di Rodi*, 1–11, 1928–1938
Cook, *Claz. Sarc.*	Cook R.M., *Clazomenian Sarcophagi*. Forschungen zur Antiken Keramik. II Reihe, Kerameus 3, 1981
Cook, Distribution	Cook R.M., 'Distribution of Chiot Pottery', *BSA* 44, 1949 154–161
Cook, Fikellura	Cook R.M., 'Fikellura Pottery', *BSA* 34, 1933–34, 3–98
Cook-Woodhead	Cook R.M., and Woodhead A.G., 'Painted Inscriptions on Chiot Pottery', *BSA* 47, 1952, 159ff
Cook, *Ionia and East*	Cook J.M., *The Greeks in Ionia and the East*, 1962
Corinth VII.1	Weinberg S.S., *The Geometric and Orientalizing Pottery*, Corinth VII.1, 1943
Coulson and Leonard, *Naucratis*	Coulson W.D.E. and Leonard A. Jr., *Cities of the Delta I, NAUCRATIS*, American Research Centre in Egypt, Reports, 1981
CVA	*Corpus Vasorum Antiquorum*

Délos X	*Exploration archéologique de Délos*, Dugas Ch., *Les vases de l'Héraion*, 1928
Délos XV	*Exploration archéologique de Délos*, Dugas Ch. and Rhomaios C., *Les vases préhélleniques et géométriques*, 1934
Délos XVII	*Exploration archéologique de Délos*, Dugas Ch., *Les vases orientalisants de style non melien*, 1935
Délos XX	*Exploration archéologique de Délos*, Robert F., *Trois Sanctuaires sur le Rivage Occidental*, 1952
Ducat, *Vases plastiques*	Ducat J., *Les Vases plastiques rhodiens archaïques en terre cuite*, 1966
EAA	*Enciclopedia dell'Arte Antica Classica e Orientale*, 1958–66
Edgar, *Catal. Caire*	Edgar C.C., *Catalogue General des Antiquités égyptiennes du Musée du Caire, Greek Vases*, 1911
Eirene	*Eirene, Studia Graeca et Latina.*
Emporio	Boardman, J., *Excavations in Chios 1952–1955, Greek Emporio, BSA* Suppl. 6, 1967
Epitymbion Tsountas	*Epitymbion Christou Tsounta*, 1941
Eretria VI	*Eretria VI, Ausgrabungen und Forschungen*, 1978
Et. thas. VII	*Etudes thasiennes* VII, L. Ghali-Kahil, *La Céramique grecque*, 1960
Et. thas. XI	*Etudes thasiennes* XI, Weill N., *Plastique archaïque de Thasos, Figurines et statues de terre cuite de l'Artemision. I. Le Haut Archaïsme*, 1985
Fabritsius, *Arch. Karta* I	Fabritsius I.V., *Arkheologicheskaya karta Prichernomor'ya Ukrainskoy SSR*, 1951
Fairbanks, *Catal.*	Fairbanks A., *Catalogue of Greek and Etruscan Vases in the Museum of Fine Arts*, Boston, 1928
GGP	Coldstream, J.N., *Greek Geometric Pottery*, 1968
Gjerstad, *Cyprus*	Gjerstad E. et al., *Greek Geometric and Archaic Pottery found in Cyprus*, 1977
GO[3]	See Boardman, *GO*[3]
GPP[2]	Cook R.M., *Greek Painted Pottery* ed. 2, 1972
Graef-Langlotz	Graef B. and Langlotz E., *Die antiken Vasen von der Akropolis zu Athen*, I–II, 1925–1933
Greenewalt, Diss. 1966	Greenewalt C.H. Jr., *Lydian Pottery of the sixth century B.C.: The Lydion and marbled ware*, Ph.D. University of Pennsylvania, 1966
Greenewalt in *Stud. Hanfmann*	Greenewalt C.H. Jr., 'An Exhibitionist from Sardis', 29–46 and pls. 8–15 in *Studies presented to George M.A. Hanfmann*, 1971
Hanfmann, *Sardis*	Hanfmann G.M.A., *Sardis from Prehistoric to Roman times. Results of the Archaeological Exploration of Sardis, 1958–1975*, 1983.
Helbig, *Führer*	Helbig, W., *Führer durch die öffentlichen Sammlungen klassischer Altertümer in Rom*, I–IV, 1963–1972
Hemelrijk, *Caeretan Hydriae*	Hemelrijk J.M., *Caeretan Hydriae*, Forschungen zur Antiken Keramik. II Reihe, Kerameus 5, 1984
Himera I	Adriani A. et al., *Himera I, Campagne di scavo 1963–1965*, 1970
Himera II	Allegro N. et al., *Himera II, Campagne di scavo 1966–1973*, 1976
Histria I	Condurachi E. et al., *Histria I*, Monografie Archeologica I, 1954
Histria II	Condurachi E., *Histria II*, 1966

Histria IV	Alexandrescu P., *Histria IV, La Céramique d'époque archaique et classique VIIe–Ve s.*, 1978
Homann-Wedeking, *Vasenornamentik*	Homann-Wedeking E., *Archaische Vasenornamentik in Attika, Lakonien und Ostgriechenland*, 1938
Hopper, Addenda	Hopper R.J., 'Addenda to Necrocorinthia', *BSA* 44, 1949, 162–257
Horos	Ὅρος. Ἕνα Ἀρχαιογνωστικό περιοδικό
Jackson, *East Greek Influence*	Jackson D.A., *East Greek Influence on Attic Vases*, Suppl. Paper 13 of the *Society for the Promotion of Hellenic Studies*, 1976
JdI	*Jahrbuch des deutschen Archäologischen Instituts*
Jeffery, *AG*	Jeffery L.H., *Archaic Greece*, 1977
JHS	*Journal of Hellenic Studies*
Johnston, *Exhibition* 1978	Johnston A.W., *Pottery from Naukratis. An exhibition on the occasion of the eleventh International Congress of Classical Archaeology, 1st–10th September 1978*, UCL
Johnston, Ireland	Johnston A.W., 'A Catalogue of Greek Vases in Public Collections in Ireland', in the *Proceedings of the Royal Irish Academy*, 73, Section C, 1973, 339–506
Jones, *Review*	Jones, R.E., *Greek and Cypriot Pottery. A Review of Scientific Studies*, 1986
Jully, *Languedoc*	Jully J.J., *Céramiques grecques ou de type grec et autres céramiques en Languedoc, Méditerranéen, Roussillon et Catalogne VIIe–IVe s. avant notre ère*, Partie I, 1982
ILN	*The Illustrated London News*
IstMitt	*Istanbuler Mitteilungen*
Kardara, *Rhodiake*	Kardara Ch., *Rhodiake Angeiographia*, 1963
Karouzou, *Anagyrountos*	Karouzou S., *Aggeia tou Anagyrountos*, 1963
Kerameikos VI.2	Kübler K., *Die Nekropole des späten 8. bis früher 6. Jahrhunderts, Kerameikos* VI.2, 1970
Kinch, *Vroulia*	Kinch K.F., *Fouilles de Vroulia*, 1914
Kocybala, Diss. 1978	Kocybala A.X., *Greek Colonization on the north shore of the Black Sea in the Archaic Period*, Ph.D. University of Pennsylvania, 1978
Kornysova, *Olbia*	Kornysova B.N., *Olbia* (Russian), 1987
Körte, *Gordion*	Körte G. and A., *Gordion, Ergebnisse der Ausgrabung im Jahre 1900*, 1904
LA	*Libya Antiqua*
Labraunda II.3	Jully J.J., *Archaic Pottery, Labraunda* II.3, 1981
Lamb, Phana	Lamb W., 'Excavations at Kato Phana in Chios', *BSA* 35, 1934–35, 138–164
Lamb, *Thermi*	Lamb W., *Excavations at Thermi in Lesbos*, 1936
Lambrino, *Vases*	Lambrino M.F., *Les Vases archaiques d'Histria*, 1938
Lane, Lakonian	Lane A., 'Lakonian Vase-Painting', *BSA* 34, 1933–34, 99–198
Langmann in *Fest. Eichler*	*Festschrift für Fritz Eichler*, 1967. Langmann, 'spätarchaische Nekropole unter dem Staatsmarkt zu Ephesos'
Larisa am Hermos III	Boehlau J. and Shefold K., *Larisa am Hermos, Die Ergebnisse der Ausgrabungen, 1902–1934*, Band III: *Die Kleinfunde*, 1942
Lazaridis, *Guide*	Lazaridis D., *Guide of the Kavala Museum*, 1969, in Greek

ABBREVIATIONS

LIMC	*Lexicon Iconographicum Mythologiae Classicae*
Locri Epizefiri I	Bagnasco M.C. et al., *Locri Epizefiri* I, 1977
Longpérier, *Musée*	Longpérier A. de, *Musée Napoléon* III, 1882
MA	see *MonAnt*
Materiale	*Materiale și cercetàri archeologice*, Bucarest
Mégara Hyblaea II	Vallet G. and Villard Fr., *Mégara Hyblaea* II, *La céramique archaique*, 1964
MIA	*Materiali y issledovaniya po arkheologii SSSR*, Moscow
MonAnt	*Monumenti antichi*
MüJb	*Münchner Jahrbuch der bildenden Kunst*
Naukratis I	Petrie W.M.F., *Naukratis*, Part I, 1886
Naukratis II	Gardner E.A., *Naukratis*, Part II, 1888
NC	Payne H.G.G., *Necrocorinthia*, 1931
Neugebauer, *Führer*	Neugebauer K.A., *Führer durch das Antiquarium*, II *Vasen*, 1932
NSc	*Notizie degli scavi di antichità*
OpRom	*Opuscula romana*
PAE	*Praktika tes Archaiologikes Hetaireias*
Papers on the Amasis Painter	Robertson M. et al., *Papers on the Amasis Painter and his World*, 1987
Payne-Young, *AMS*	Payne H.G.G. and Young G.M., *Archaic Marble Sculpture from the Acropolis*, 1936
Perachora II	*Perachora, the Sanctuaries of Hera Akraia and Limenia* II, ed. by Dunbabin T.J., 1962
Perrot-Chipiez, IX	Perrot G. and Chipiez C., *Histoire de l'Art dans l'Antiquité*, Vol. IX: *La Grèce archaique*, 1882–1914
Pfuhl, *MuZ*	Pfuhl E., *Malerei und Zeichnung der Griechen*, 1923
Pottier, *Vases*	Pottier E., *Vases antiques du Louvre*, 1897–1922
Price	Price E.R., 'Pottery of Naucratis', *JHS* 44, 1924, 180–222
Price, *EGP*	Price E.R., 'East Greek Pottery' in *Classification des Céramiques antiques*, Union Académique Internationale, 1928
Prins de Jong, *Scherben*	Prins de Jong E.F., *Scherben aus Naukratis*, 1925
RA	*Revue archéologique*
Rayonnements	*Les Rayonnements des Civilisations Grecque et Romaine*. VIIIème Congrés International d'Archéologie Classique, 1963
RDAC	*Report of the Department of Antiquities of Cyprus*
REG	*Revue des études grecques*
Richter, *Korai*	Richter G.M.A., *Korai, Archaic Greek Maidens*, 1968
Robertson, *HGA*	Robertson M., *A History of Greek Art*, 1975
Roebuck, *Ionian Trade*	Roebuck C., *Ionian Trade and Colonization*, 1959
Rumpf, *MuZ*	Rumpf A., *Malerei und Zeichnung*, Handbuch der Archäologie IV 1, 1953
Salzmann, *Camiros*	Salzmann A., *La Nécropole de Camiros*, 1875
Samos IV	Isler H.P., *Das archaische Nordtor und seine Umgebung im Heraion von Samos. Samos* IV, 1978
Samos V	Walter H., *Frühe Samische Gefässe, Chronologie und Landschaftsstile, Ostgriechischer Gefässe. Samos* V, 1968
Samos VI.1.	Walter-Karydi E., *Samische Gefässe des 6. Jahrhunderts v. Chr., Samos* VI.1, 1973

SCE	*The Swedish Cyprus Expedition*
Schaus, *Dem. Sanct., Cyrene* II	Schaus G.P., *The Extramural Sanctuary of Demeter and Persephone at Cyrene, Libya. Final Reports Vol. II. The East Greek, Island and Laconian Pottery*, 1985
Schiering, *Werkstätten*	Schiering W., *Werkstätten orientalisierender Keramik auf Rhodos*, 1957
Seeberg, *Corinthian Komos*	Seeberg A., *Corinthian Komos Vases*. *BICS* Suppl. 27, 1971
Shtitelman, *Antique Art*	Shtitelman F.M., *Antique Art, Works of World Art in the Museums of Ukraine*, 1977
Skudnova, *Olbia*	Skudnova B.M., *The ancient necropolis of Olbia* (Russian), 1988
SovArch.	*Sovetskaya Arkheologiya*
StEtr.	*Studi etruschi*
Stibbe, *LV*	Stibbe C.M., *Lakonische Vasenmaler des sechsten Jahrhuderts v. Chr.*, 1972
Stucchi, *Agorà di Cirene* I	Stucchi S., *L'agorà di Cirene I*, in Monographie di archeologia libica 7, 1965
Stucchi, *Cirene 1957–1966*	Stucchi S., *Cirene 1957–1966*, 1967
Sūkās II	Ploug G., *Sūkās II, The Aegean, Corinthian and Eastern Greek Pottery and Terracottas*, 1973
Tarsus III	Goldman H., *Excavations at Gözlü Kule, Tarsus* III, 1963
Tocra I	Boardman J. and Hayes J., *Excavations at Tocra 1963–1965, The Archaic Deposits I*, *BSA* Suppl. 4, 1966
Tocra II	Boardman J. and Hayes J., *Excavations at Tocra 1963–1965, The Archaic Deposits II and Later Deposits*, *BSA* Suppl. 10, 1973
TürkAD	*Türk arkeoloji dergisi*
Vasseur, *Marseille*	Vasseur G., *L'origine de Marseille*, 1914
Venit, *Egypt. Museums*	Venit M.S., *Greek Painted Pottery from Naukratis in Egyptian Museums*, American Research Center in Egypt. Catalogue, Volume 7, 1988
Villard, *Marseille*	Villard Fr., *La Céramique grecque de Marseille, VIe–Ve siècle*, 1960
Wiel, *Leiden*	Wiel van de W.H., *Verzameling Ceramiek en Terracotta's van het Archaeologisch Instituut der Rijksuniversiteit Leiden*, 1968
Zervos, *Rhodes*	Zervos S., *Rhodes*, 1920

INTRODUCTION

Chian figure-decorated pottery of the Archaic period begins around the middle of the seventh century; its floruit can be placed in the last third of the seventh and the first half of the sixth century and production continues well on into the second half of the century.

Plain chalices have also been included for two reasons: the finesse of their manufacture qualifies them as fine wares, and they are produced in the same workshops that decorated sixth-century figured vases.

Inscribed vases,[1] mainly kantharoi, but also chalices, phialai and bowls, are included only when they bear figure decoration.

Amphorae and generally all vessels with linear decoration are excluded. There are unpublished intact amphorae from Rizari, in Chios town, which head the later famous series of Chian wine-jars, and quite a number of plain and patterned intact vases too in a variety of shapes, which will form the nucleus of the publication of Rizari.[2]

FABRIC

The clay of Chian fine ware is quite hard, sometimes chalky in texture and well-levigated containing only small amounts of mica.[3] It is easily distinguished, with the help of the slip which covers it, from other East Greek wares. The colour of the clay is pink or reddish brown with a greyish core, particularly obvious on thick vessels—to give an example, picked at random, the black-figure lekane from Chios town, **1419***.

In terms of the Munsell Chart[4] the colour of Chian clay starts from 2.5YR 6/4 "light reddish brown" to 10YR 7/4 "very pale brown", and it normally ranges between 5YR 7/2 "pinkish grey" and 5YR 7/3 and 7/4 "pink" to 5YR 7/6 "reddish yellow" and 7.5YR 7/4 "pink" or 7.5YR 7/6 "reddish yellow". Unfortunately, owing mainly to the ancient process of firing, the "chroma"[5] of soil colours in the Munsell chart does not fully and in all circumstances correspond to the actual colours of the clay.[6]

---

[1] *BSA* 47, 1952, 159 ff., the basic study on them, covers all aspects. Amendments in *BSA* 51, 1956, 57 notes 1 and 4 and 58 notes 1, 7–9. Also *BSA* 65, 1970, 3 pl. 1b and *Emporio* 243 ff. Inscribed vases from the Aphaia Temple on Aegina, in *AA* 1983, 170–7 and 183–6, where fresh material enabled D. Williams to piece together the dedicators' names and thus amend old hypotheses.

[2] See Preface.

[3] *Emporio* 102; also *GPP*² 128 and 249; *BSA* 60, 1965, 140 and *CGED* 288 (Boardman) and 28 (Bayburtluoğlu) for pottery found in sites of Western Anatolia.

[4] *Munsell Soil Color Charts*, 1975.

[5] In the sense given on p. 16 of the booklet, "A color notation" accompanying the *Munsell Chart*.

[6] See, Schaus, *Dem. Sanct., Cyrene* II, for the Chian material from the sanctuary of Demeter and Persephone at Cyrene, where nearly all his identifications accord with ours. These last were mainly taken from the material from Rizari in Chios town, Kavala, Naucratis in the British Museum, Oxford, Cambridge, Reading and University College London, and other available pieces. Cf. also Descoeudres in *Eretria* VI, 11, no. 36, pl. 2, for a fragment from an early chalice, here **109***.

The consistency of Chian clay has been proven by clay analyses undertaken by the Oxford Laboratory by optical emission spectroscopy.[7] Recently, R.E. Jones of the Fitch Laboratory in the British School at Athens undertook a major survey of the clays of ancient Greek and Cypriot pottery.[8] Chemical analysis was performed on clays of Chian sherds, mainly from Emporio, Naucratis and samples taken from clay beds in various parts of the island, including one from Chios town. It has been concluded that the Chian vases from Naucratis are definitely made of Chian clay[9] and that the Emporio material tested seems generally to vary from that from Chios town. This seems to suggest that workshops on the island were provided with clays and slips from different clay beds.[10]

Clay samples of Chian vases unearthed on the coastal sites of Eastern Macedonia and Thrace have not yet undergone clay analysis; they have been claimed to be Chian but of local—Thasian[11]—manufacture on various other grounds.[12] Boardman is of the opinion, however, that clay analyses are not necessarily conclusive evidence for the place(s) of manufacture, since clays could be transported.[13]

The characteristically Chian slip is usually white, but again its colour can range from yellowish to milky white. These tonal divergences, from a dull pale cream, yellowish or beige to a paler cream, white or even brilliant white do not seem to me to be chronological.[14] There are workshops which used a brilliant white slip at an early stage, as shown in a small group of fragments from oenochoai and lekanai unearthed at Rizari, decorated in Late Wild Goat patterns of a rather debased style.[15] This group reinforces the view that these differentiations are due to the various workshops where the vases were produced.[16]

The slip is hard, usually thick in texture and tends to flake off very easily. It is used to cover vases from Late Geometric times onwards and it is applied on the inside of open shapes as well. Thus, it provides a finely smoothed and light surface which contrasts vibrantly with the dark decoration executed largely in dull black, but sometimes in grey, brown or red paint.

Paint used for the outline of figures in the reserving styles of the sixth century had been diluted into golden brown or yellow to accentuate certain details, e.g. the network manes of lions.

Polychromy is used for a category of vases, chalices for the main, unfortunately fragmentary: these derive mostly from Naucratis, as well as Aegina, the Athenian Acropolis, Kavala, Pitane[17] and Berezan, all of which provided outstanding pieces. Chios

---

[7] *CGED* 287–8. For analyses of Chian clays see also P. Dupont in *Dacia* 27, 1983, 24 with note 11, 30–31 and mainly 41.

[8] Jones, *Review*, 282–288 with Table 3.21 and fig. 3.54.

[9] *Ibid.* (Boardman), 662–4.

[10] *CGED* 288.

[11] By F. Salviat in *CGED* 87–92.

[12] See Chapter 7 and A.A. Lemos, *BCH*, Supplement forthcoming.

[13] *BSA* 51, 1956, 56, Boardman in Jones, *ibid.* 663 and in *Chios Conference* 252, 258 and n.14.

[14] They are generally thought to be of chronological value, see *Emporio* 102 and *BSA* 60, 1965, 140. Also *GPP*² 248 and *Tocra* I, 25.

[15] **270*–2*** and **324*–339***.

[16] Evidently workshops in Chios town used different clay beds from those of other workshops in other parts of the island, see Jones, *ibid.* 285–6 and fig. 3.54.

[17] The two better known Pitane chalices in the Grand style are executed in a somewhat restrained variant. Here **800*** and **801***.

INTRODUCTION

proper has not as yet yielded any example,[18] and this has given rise to inevitable speculation.[19]

In the black-figure technique added colours are at first confined to red, mostly fired purple. White is used only later—after the middle of the sixth century—usually on unslipped vases influenced by Clazomenian and Athenian wares.

Red and white on the dark background are used for the decoration—mostly floral and a few figurative—on the inside of open vases, usually chalices, kantharoi, and phialai. This decoration lies over the inevitable slip and is practised only by Chian vase painters of the Archaic period.

Finally, black or brown paint covers the outside of handles and feet on chalices.

TECHNIQUES OF DECORATION

Chian fine wares employ three different techniques of decoration:

1. **The Reserving Technique** is used on Late Geometric categories of bird-bowls and bird-oenochoai and continues with a more extensive use of outline in the Wild Goat style and in a few categories of the sixth century. It is clearly the favourite technique of the School since three quarters of the known output is rendered in it.
2. **The Polychrome Technique** appears in two different manners:
    a) In the Grand style, where generally four to six, sometimes even more, colours are employed.
    b) The light on dark technique is met on the inside of open vases of the sixth century; it is also encountered on the outside of a few pieces. The method employed is as follows: on top of the slip the surface is painted dark brown or black, and then the decoration is added in red and white. The decoration is mostly floral, but on the most elaborate pieces of the Grand style chalices, figures appear as well; in this case, yellow is also used and incisions are applied to emphasize outlines and a few details. The technique is well rooted in the white-on-dark decoration met on kantharoi (Pl. 240.3) and tall cups, and it goes back to the end of the eighth century.[20]
3. **The Black-Figure Technique** in Chian pottery was employed in various categories influenced by the wares of Mainland Greece, mainly Corinthian, subsequently Laconian and finally Athenian. Some isolated pieces betray a Clazomenian influence and others which dispense with the slip and Atticise in the extreme were only identified as Chian by an expert eye.[21] These classes run on to about the end of the sixth century and are the very last specimens of Chian figure-decorated pottery.

What has been claimed as a fourth Chian technique[22] will be discussed in Chapter 7 and forms a category of vases deriving from a Chian workshop operating outside the

---

[18] The pieces from Greek Emporio claimed by D. Williams, in *AA* 1983, 182 note 35, to be of the Grand style are so mutilated that they do not prove anything: nos. 275–7 are Wild Goat chalices and their handle patterns are very common in that style; as for nos. 731–734, rim, handle and interior patterns are of the Animal Chalice style; their wall decoration, which would have been decisive in this matter, has flaked away.

[19] Boardman, CN 55 with note 5 and *Chios Conference* 251 ff.

[20] *Emporio* 102, and especially nos. 199–204, pl. 32 (kantharoi) and nos. 298–302, pl. 37 (tall cups).

[21] *Emporio* 168, 169 and *CGED* 85.

[22] *Samos* VI.1, 69.

island. The peculiarity of these vases is based on two factors; first, most do not use a slip or, if they do, but a very thin one, and secondly, wherever incisions might be expected to render the vases truly black figure, there are instead reserved stripes. Outline is widely used for the rendering of faces and other parts of humans and animals according to the favoured Chian manner. At first sight they give the false impression of being in black figure, but in fact they are in the usual reserving technique, though here most are unslipped.

Finally, there are vases demonstrating mixed techniques of decoration, black figure and reserving or a combination of all three.

SHAPES

Chian potters explored their skills in a vast variety of shapes. Here, however, attention will be confined to those bearing figured decoration, or patterned fragments which suggest that in their original state they also had figured decoration.

The chalice is the shape that predominates, representing approximately 73% of the material collected here.[23] It is by far the most popular and typical form, constituting one of the principal features of this School.

When Hermippos, a fifth-century B.C. comic poet, is quoted by Athenaeus in his *Deipnosophists*:[24] Ἐπαινοῦνται δὲ καὶ αἱ Χῖαι κύλικες, ὧν μνημονεύει Ἕρμιππος ἐν Στρατιώταις· Χία δὲ κύλιξ ὑψοῦ κρέμαται περὶ πασσαλόφιν, one wonders whether he is referring to any ordinary Chian drinking cup which could be hung on a peg or a version of the chalice, which could not be hung in the usual way for kylikes—interior to the wall.

The Wild Goat style and the Sphinx and Lion style are the basic categories in Chian figurative pottery, displayed on a wider range of shapes, from dinoi, oenochoai, bowls, lekanai etc. to oddities such as phallus cups, bell-shaped or incense pots. Shapes are common to both styles but some are "largely complementary".[25]

Oenochoai are not dominant as in the southern schools of East Greece. However, some display a peculiar originality and have animals' heads on the necks. Dinoi are not rare either,[26] at least in the decorative styles.

Plastic heads, almost invariably female, decorate rims, handles and feet of certain shapes in the Wild Goat style, for example the Aphrodite bowl (**252***), but especially in the Sphinx and Lion style.[27]

The stylistic development of the various categories and the treatment of shapes, figurative and ornamental decoration and the formation of stylistic groups, are the main preoccupations of this work. The Chapters and the Catalogue are basically divided into stylistic categories taking into consideration the main chronological sequence; of course, styles and techniques of decoration largely overlap. In the discussion on dating an attempt is made to describe the development of Chian Painted pottery with the available material.

---

[23] This percentage may be somewhat statistically misleading, as patterned chalices of both centuries appear in the Catalogue, whereas other undecorated pieces, or shapes with linear decoration, have not been listed.

[24] *Deipn.* XI 480e. Cf. Eust. 1428.61. See, *Chios Conference* 233.

[25] As put by Cook, Distribution 158.

[26] Cf. *Emporio* 115.

[27] *Emporio* 194 with some additions in the present Catalogue, **1377*–1398**.

Distribution summarises the evidence and traces the passage of Chian pottery abroad, and Chapter 7 explores a category of Chian vases brought to light in recent excavations on Thasos and at certain coastal sites of East Macedonia and Thrace.

I

THE PATTERNED CHALICES
OF THE SEVENTH CENTURY

The sanctuary of Apollo at Phana in the southern part of Chios was the first site to be excavated on the island in the beginning of this century.[1] Kourouniotes' unfinished excavations were taken up by Lamb who worked for one season in 1933.[2] The limited though important material uncovered led the excavators to suggest among other things that the chalice, already known from Naucratis,[3] might have antecedents.[4] However, it was not until the fifties when the British School at Athens launched a fresh programme of research on the island[5] that the prolific material from Emporio enabled Boardman to trace in a definite manner the origin and evolution of the chalice[6] from the Late Geometric period onwards. Material published since then, including the piecemeal information on Pitane's Chian vases,[7] proved that Boardman's fundamental classification was valid.[8] A few refinements can be added for the sixth-century chalice.[9]

E. Price in 1924 dubbed the shape "chalice" in her noteworthy study of the "Pottery of Naucratis" and she has been followed by all English scholars. The word "chalice" is obviously inappropriate because of its lexical associations with the Christian sacred vessel, even despite a certain similarity of form, but using it enables us to avoid confusion with the numerous types of ancient Greek kylikes. Nevertheless, one of its ancient makers who proudly proclaims his name calls it **kylix**: ΝΙΚΗΣΕΡΜΟΣΤΗΝ[ΔΕ]ΤΗΝΚΥΛΙΚΑ ΕΠΟΙΗΣΕΝ,[10] kylix being a generic term[11] (FIG. 1).

---

[1] *ADelt* I, 1915, 64–93 and II, 1916, 189–215.

[2] *BSA* 35, 1934–5, 138–64.

[3] *Naukratis* I, 18 and mainly 51 ff with pl. X.1 and 3 and *Naukratis* II, 38 ff.

[4] *BSA* 55, 1934–5, 196–8 and *JHS* 57, 1937, 228 and note 9.

[5] For Greek Emporio see *Emporio*; for excavations in Chios town (Kofiná Ridge) see *BSA* 49, 1954 123–182; at Delphinion, *BSA* 51, 1956, 41–54; at Pindakas, *BSA* 53–54, 1958–59, 295–309; and an Underwater Survey in *BSA* 56, 1961, 102 ff; for Prehistoric Emporio, see M.S.F. Hood, *Excavations in Chios 1938–1955: Prehistoric Emporio and Ayio Gala*, *BSA* Supp. vol. 15–16, 1981–82.

[6] *Emporio* 102–3 and fig. 60 for the evolution of the shape and 119–20 for the origin, Nikesermos and the early chalices. Also *GPP*² 128, mainly 218, and 233–4; *BSA* 60, 1965, 139; *Tocra* I, 57–8 type I nos. 771–2 and *CGED* 28. Also *GGP* 294 for the very early specimens.

[7] *CGED* 27–30, with helpful profiles for the early chalices on pl 6.7 and 7.8–11. Here **100*–104**.

[8] In the publication of the excavations at Taucheira in Cyrene, in *Tocra* I and II, J. Hayes ventured his classification of the chalice shape from the material at hand—mainly of the sixth century—see, *Tocra* I, 58 ff. His type I corresponds to *Emporio* fig. 60D (late seventh century) chalice.

[9] See Chapter 3.

[10] *Emporio* 120 no. 251 and 243–4 no. 614. See also, *Samos* VI.1, 108 note 186; *AA* 1969, 382. Here **35***.

[11] See *Emporio* 120 and note 6. In Modern Greek the term κύλικα should be preserved, and defined by the epithet "Chian". I think that the use of the word "κάλυκας", however convenient, is misleading.

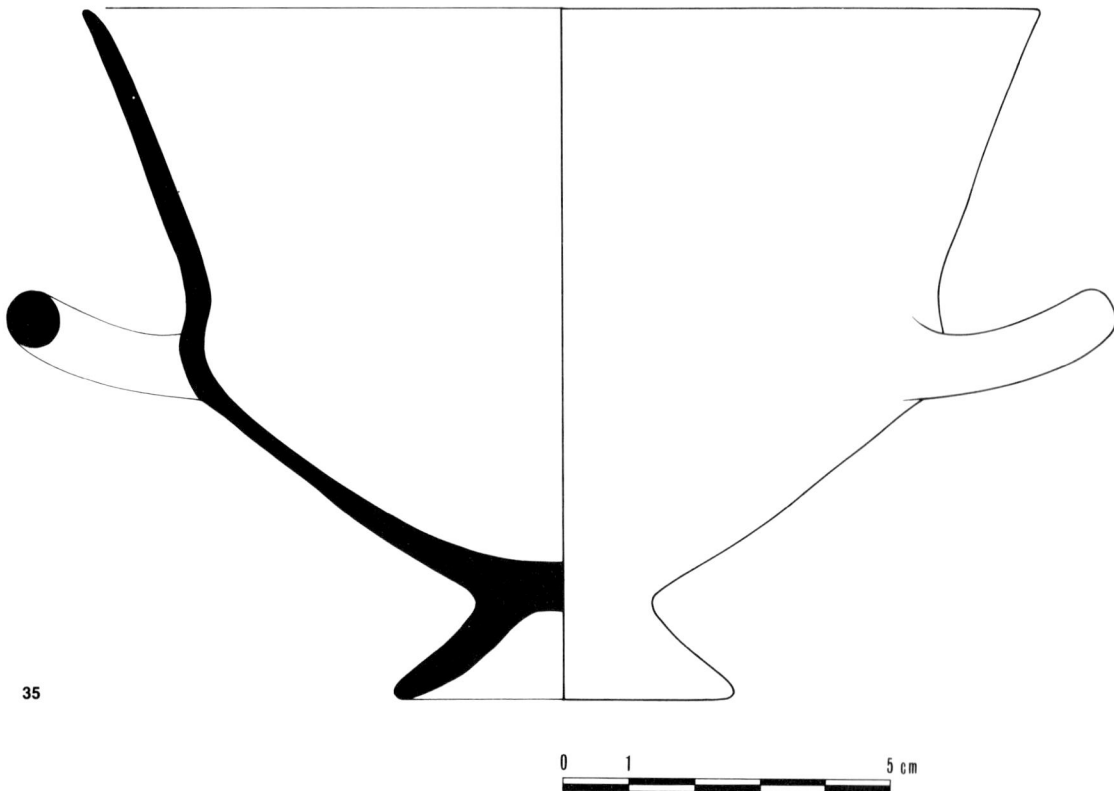

Fig. 1 The Nikesermos Chalice

SHAPE (FIG. 2)

The earliest phase of the late eighth century, represented by three fragments from Emporio[12] and scraps reported from Old Smyrna,[13] can scarcely be distinguished from the next. This and following phases are well attested in the Emporio finds as well as in the stratified levels of Old Smyrna (**96***), a stray from Tarsus (**107**) and possibly the recently reported pieces from Pitane (**100*–104**). They show a skyphos of ordinary make: that is a bowl convex in profile with a low upright lip, which gradually grows to a greater height; it presumably stands on a ring foot, though none has been preserved; the handles are set almost diagonally and gradually become horizontal. This form has been called the protochalice, the precursor of the early-chalice, whose first appearance in the new Archaic era is marked by a radical change.

In the beginning of the last third or quarter of the seventh century the new shape has a minimised bowl; the ring base develops into a low, heavy and conical foot, and what was formerly the lip is now augmented in height, thus becoming the wall to which decoration is admitted. The transition from bowl to wall is at first very marked but, by the end of the century, it has gradually diminished until it is scarcely perceptible. The curvature of the

---

[12] *Emporio* fig. 60A from Period I. Here **4***, **5***, **7***. [13] *BSA* 60, 1965, 140.

THE PATTERNED CHALICES OF THE SEVENTH CENTURY

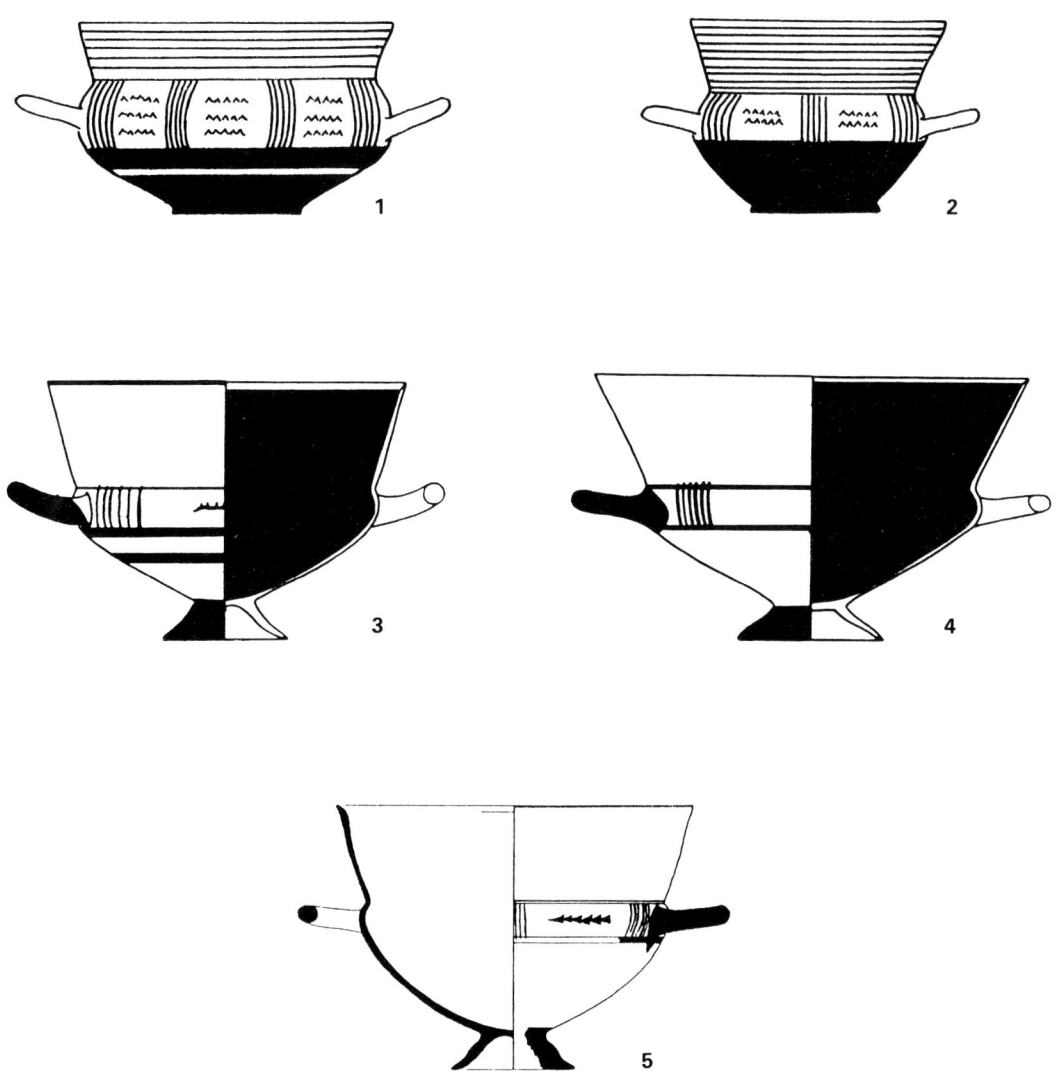

Fig. 2　1, 2 Proto-chalices (*Emporio*, fig. 60 b and c). 3–5 Early chalices (*Emporio*, fig. 74; *Tocra* I, fig. 30). (Courtesy of Professor Sir J. Boardman and Dr. J.W. Hayes)

bowl towards the foot is sharper at the beginning, whereas later on it becomes smoother and somewhat more concave. The chalices of around the end of the century, among which are those in Würzburg (**236*** and **237***),[14] already intimate future development.

The change was radical and might have been caused by many factors, one of which was perhaps competition posed from abroad by more elegant shapes. For it seems that from now on Chian chalices started travelling widely either as personal belongings and votive offerings of their owners, or as the first, isolated and diffident purchases of non-Chian travellers trading with the island—most probably both. They were used as votives in sanctuaries on Chios and elsewhere: does their good state of surface preservation make it unlikely that personal drinking cups were dedicated? They were also considered appropriate offerings to the deceased, since many were found in the necropoleis of Etruria (**76** and **77***), at Vroulia on Rhodes (**106**) and at Pitane (**100*–104**). Seventh-century plain and decorated chalices occur at Pitane, though it is commonly assumed that this necropolis was in use exclusively in the sixth century.[15]

The old view that the developed form of the chalice originated in Lydian wares[16]—a theory in accordance with the general tendency in the first half of this century to discover influences from the East in practically every aspect of Archaic Greek Art—no longer holds good. The idea of the chalice as "an Ionic reply to the early Protocorinthian drinking cups"[17] cannot be entirely excluded. Chian potters were working on the shape for a long time, but the possibility of their being influenced by "a cup of the general type" produced in Corinth in the middle of the seventh century[18] is rather remote, since so little Corinthian of an early date has been unearthed on Chios as yet and no cups at all.[19] It seems fairer to credit Chian potters with the creation and evolution of their own particular drinking vessel.[20]

It may be observed that the seventh-century chalices found no imitators, save two peculiar items in early Athenian black-figure pottery:[21]

A) A vase attributed by Beazley to Sophilos,[22] which has now been dated to the last period of the Painter,[23] is decidedly an Athenian translation of the shape. Sophilos, or his potter,[24] imitates the type of the late seventh-century chalice.[25] It is difficult, however, to understand why the Athenian artist copied a type already old-fashioned

---

[14] Profiles in *CVA* Würzburg I, 31 and 32, figs. 15 and 16.

[15] See *CGED* 27, pls. 7.9 and 10 at least are stated to be from Pitane and both are of the late seventh century form (*Emporio*—fig. 60D).

[16] *AJA* 18, 1914, 434; Price 207; Lambrino, *Vases* 299–300; Greenewalt, Diss. 1966, 133 note 97.

[17] *BSA* 60, 1965, 139.

[18] *GPP*² 128 and fig. 4B.

[19] See for Corinthian Vases on Chios in *Emporio* 153 with note 1. There are two intact Corinthian kotylai from Rizari (unpublished).

[20] For a parallel evolution of the Laconian lakaina see *BSA* 34, 1933–34, 102–3, 108, 116, 134–5, 153 and 189. And for the kantharos, in general, M.G. Kanowski, *Containers of Classical Greece* 1983, 48–51.

[21] Both were singled out in Cook, Distribution 158 and n. 10.

[22] *ABV* 39, 11; and *BAdd*² 10 (Boardman, *ABFH* 19, fig. 28 and p. 189).

[23] G. Bakir, *Sophilos, Ein Beitrag zu seinem Stil*, 1981, 28 (for the stylistic analysis of the vase), 59 (for dating the working phases of the Painter), 70 (no. A. 30) (for all previous bibliography), pl. 55 and especially fig. 29 (for the profile of the vase).

[24] According to Bakir, *ibid*. 5–7, though the painters' signatures are undoubtedly secure, the potter signatures on the dinos fragment from Pharsala and the louterion from Menidi (*Para*. 18) are not.

[25] *Emporio* 103, fig. 60D.

by then; unless we accept that knowledge of the shape dated from an earlier stage in the potter's career.

B) An even earlier vase is attributed to the Anagyrus painter.[26] The handles and the broad ring base are those of a lekane, but the deep, squat bowl and in particular the rather high walls emerging from it are vaguely reminiscent of the mid-seventh-century Chian chalice.[27]

Taking into consideration these strays and their varying degrees of imitation, it cannot be claimed that the seventh-century chalice exercised any substantial impact on other artistic centres.

DECORATION (FIG. 3)

1. PROTO-CHALICES: The decoration is entirely geometric in character. It consists almost invariably of metope patterns of rows of Vs which look like zigzags flanked by a series of vertical lines.[28] It is an unprofitable pastime to count the number of the apices on the Vs and of vertical lines: they are without exception always the same, executed by a multiple brush; its use is known from other and earlier Greek wares,[29] but on Chios it continues to be employed as the decorative pattern of the handle zone on chalices beyond the middle of the sixth century.

The seventh-century metope pattern occurs on the bowl[30] and eventually is introduced to the lip. Variety is restricted but includes examples of the broken cable, disposed horizontally or vertically, bounded or flanked by broad close-set lines. The butterfly pattern, so common on other Chian contemporary shapes and a trade mark on Rhodian oenochoai, occurs on a few chalices, again from Emporio.[31] A row of zigzags (**27***) or a dotted network (**26***) occasionally appears. There is some variety from unpublished material found in Anatolia: an original lip pattern with two rows of concentric circles (**100***); a handle zone pattern of crossed squares (**101***).[32] Meander and trapezoid patterns also exist, but the saw-edged metope pattern prevailed there too.

2. EARLY CHALICES: The repertory of the geometric patterns is now enriched. More frequently, chains of hatched triangles (**44*** and **48***), or hatched lozenges alternating with stippled ones[33] (**45***–**7*** and perhaps **41**). In a few pieces, the following patterns occur:
   1. the four-star rosette (**48***).
   2. the six-star rosette (**49***), a very common ornament in the subsequent century.

---

[26] *ABV* 21, 2; and *BAdd²* 2 Boardman, *ABFH* 19, fig. 30.

[27] *Emporio* 103, fig. 60C. Also Cook, Distribution 158 note 10 where there are references to two more, fragmentary, Athenian pots, whose resemblances are considered casual.

[28] *Emporio* 105 and fig. 61, Pattern S and 120 with pls. 32–3. Lamb calls them "multiple chevrons" in *BSA* 35, 1934–5, 157. Her pl. 37.22 is either a one-handled cup type B or a kalathos but it is not a chalice; see also *GGP* 295.

[29] *Antiquity* 34, 1960, 89 and *Emporio* 105, 120 with note 1.

[30] Examples also on Samian bowls: *Samos* V, pl. 38.212 and 40.226.

[31] For the broken cable, see *Emporio* 103–4 with fig. 61 Patterns A and B: Examples, here, **15***, **17***, **25*** and **26***. For the butterfly pattern, *ibid.* fig. 61 Pattern O. Examples **13***, **17***, **29*** and **44***.

[32] *CGED* 28.

[33] *Emporio* 104 fig. 61 Pattern H.

3. a row of dotted loops (**41** and **42**).
4. an eight-petal dotted circle (**48***).
5. a circle ringed with dots (again on **48***).

Lip pattern now admits vertical open cables and zigzags bounded by bands.

The bowl below the handle zone is usually striped with three bands and the foot painted on the outside; inside it is only slipped.

The interior of patterned chalices (and this goes also for their Wild Goat style companions) does not receive any kind of decoration. They are only painted in black, or dark brown, paint on top of the slip.

The stylistic and chronological sequence established for the Emporio seventh-century chalices[34] leads to the classification and rough dating of the chalices from Phana, Kófiná Ridge and abroad. The patterns, especially of the handle zone, strengthen the threefold division observed already on the ground of shape:[35]

a) The very early specimens correspond to Emporio HS Period I and end at approximately 690 B.C. Besides **4***, **5*** and **7*** from Emporio, **96*** from Old Smyrna and possibly **107** from Tarsus belong here.

b) The Proto-chalices correspond to Emporio HS Periods II and III, from around 690–630 B.C., and comprise, beside the Emporio pieces which were found in those strata, **59** and **61** from Phana, **100***–**103*** from ? Pitane, **108** and **109*** from Al Mina and **76** from Cerveteri.

c) The Early Chalices correspond to Emporio HS Period IV, dating from around 630–600 B.C. They can be arranged in the following chronological order, based on the handle zone patterns which are related to the breadth of the vase. They permit the formation of three subdivisions:

1. **58** from Phana, **94*** from Rheneia and **78*** and **79*** from the Athenian Agora. They display three to four saw-edged patterns on the handle zone.
2. **77*** from Cerveteri, **70*** from Tocra, **97***, **98***, **99*** from Old Smyrna, **66*** and perhaps **67*** and **68*** from Naucratis and **104** from Pitane. This is a group of chalices with broad bowls decorated on the handle zone with two saw-edged patterns and flanked by three sets of stripes, which appear also on the other side of the vessel.
3. Towards the end of the century, perhaps in the last decade, can be dated the Nikesermos chalice with its companions from Emporio, **62** and **63** from Phana and perhaps **64** and **65** from Naucratis.

It could be suggested that different workshops manufactured the patterned seventh-century chalices on the one hand and their Wild Goat companions on the other, especially as the same shape is used for both. However, the handle zone patterns offer a safe criterion in this matter, and permit a basic distinction into two workshops. The first is characterised

---

[34] *Emporio* 121–2.
[35] *Ibid.* 119–120 and fig. 60B and C. Here the distinction into B and C is taken together.

THE PATTERNED CHALICES OF THE SEVENTH CENTURY

Fig. 3 Patterns on Proto-chalices and Early chalices

by the saw-edged patterns and continues production in the sixth century with the Chalice style. The second workshop specialised in the Wild Goat style contemporary with the seventh-century patterned chalices, and continued production with the Animal Chalice and Grand styles.

2

THE WILD GOAT STYLE

The Wild Goat style on Chios is roughly dated from around the middle of the seventh to the first decades of the sixth century.[1] What has generally been called Late Wild Goat style[2] is here considered to be a renovation of the Animal style and has been dealt with separately.[3] A few other groups continue: their late date is suggested by their retarded and degenerate character.

The discussion is divided into shapes, decoration—figurative and ornamental, stylistic groups and then style in general; a pattern followed in the subsequent chapters too.

SHAPES

The variety of shapes in Chian Wild Goat style is second only to the Sphinx and Lion style, the main Chian black-figure category. It is evident at first sight that the chalice is here too the most popular shape but contrary to the common belief (which perhaps arose from the fact that the two intact examples in Würzburg had been long known and admired) that Chian Wild Goat is better demonstrated on chalices, it is now clear that less than half of the known output appears on this shape. This proportion might have been even less, had Wild Goat style been more readily recognisable and assignable to the various East Greek centres of production. Paradoxically enough the masterpieces of the style or what is here considered as such, **253*** and **255***, are both from open bowls. Nevertheless the production of chalices is considerable and exceeds in quantity the manufacture of other individual shapes. The form and its evolution have been discussed in detail above, and the decorated sort differ in no respect from the patterned or plain companions.[4] From the point of view of shape the two intact Würzburg chalices[5] still remain the most exquisite examples, because of the excellent state of their preservation.[6] To these the not altogether happily restored Emporio chalice (**114***) can be added.[7] The recent example from the Samian Heraion (**247***) seems to be one of the earlier, if not the earliest, example of a seventh-century decorated chalice, as the placing of the decoration on the handle zone and style indicate, even though it is stated that the shape is similar to

---

[1] See Chapter 5 Dating for a detailed discussion.
[2] Cook, Distribution, 158.
[3] See Chapter 3.
[4] *Emporio*, fig. 60D is the shape used for Middle II Wild Goat chalices; also Hayes' type I in *Tocra* I, 58 nos. 771–2 and fig. 30.
[5] Profiles in *CVA* Würzburg II 31 and 32, figs. 15 and 16.
[6] There are unpublished intact chalices with Wild Goat decoration from Pitane and Erythrae. Two from Pitane, **241** and **242**, are on exhibit in the Archaeological Museum in Istanbul. The profile of another from Erythrae is given by C. Bayburtluoğlu in *CGED* 29, pl. 7.11. (Here, **245**).
[7] The restoration was performed long after the excavation, by a team from the National Archaeological Museum of Athens, when the exhibits had been moved to the new Archaeological Museum in Chios town.

the Würzburg vases.[8] Chalice fragments are numerous, but it is not easy on grounds of shape alone, especially if they are wall sherds, to classify them as from the late seventh-century type of chalice or the early sixth-century one; moreover, two late Wild Goat groups continued well into the sixth century, retaining the earlier form although they now display an elementary inner decoration.

In figurative pottery, the shape, with the exception of **247***, comes in late since it has not yet been encountered in the Early and Middle I phases. This might be due to a lack of evidence, but it is more probable that potters, following the general East Greek trend, were keen on manufacturing shapes of common use and acceptance. In the beginning of the Middle II phase, however, when the renovated form of the early chalice with its better articulation appeared, vase painters took a liking to the shape which from then on was to become so characteristic as to be one of the principal distinctive features of the School. Much of the evidence still comes from Naucratis and this could be misleading.

Bowls of various types exist and are used only for a short period as indicated both by their style and number. Fragments do not permit safe reconstructions but it seems that at least three different types were favoured, one of which was a wholly Chian creation with no ancestors or parallels in plain pottery. This is an open bowl with steep straight-sided and out-turned walls: a large vessel with a low and thick ring base and a flattened, wide and thick offset rim, jutting out from the wall, on which an opposed pair of vertical, arched and triple-reeded handles are placed. The shape approximates to that of a lekane and it might be called such, had the term "lekane" not been so generic and confusing. An intact example is the Aphrodite bowl (FIG. 4; **252***) which bears an incised inscription on the upper part of the inner wall. It reads: ΣΩΣΤΡΑΤΟΣΜΑΝΕΘΗΚΕΝΤΗΦΡΟΔΙΤΗ giving the names of both deity and dedicator. Six female protomes are displayed on the rim, two between the handles and a pair flanking each handle's roots. Whilst this practice of the potter and coroplast working together, maybe even in the same person, might have been picked up from Corinthian pottery where it had a longer and earlier tradition, yet the Chian series of the female protomes,[9] headed by the Aphrodite bowl, looks to be indigenous both in respect of type and style.[10]

Fragments from open bowls are not uncommon, but unless handled, they can easily be mistaken for plates or dishes.[11] This form had no continuation in the history of Chian pottery.

The other two types of bowls are first the common type with curved walls ending in an offset rim, and second the tripod bowl from Emporio, (FIG. 5; **259***). The fragments of the common bowls are small and do not indicate whether they originally had handles. As for the tripod bowl a fragmentary one of the sixth century and the foot of another[12] suggest that the shape survived, though enjoying a restricted popularity.

---

[8] H. Kyrieleis in *Chios Conference* 192.
[9] Curiously F. Croissant, *Les Protomes féminines archaïques*, 1983, in his Chian group C, 69–93 ignores the vase protomes which are of certain Chian origin (noted by J. Boardman in his review, *The Classical Review*, 35, 1985, 154).
[10] See *Emporio*, 194. Cf. Ducat, *Vases plastiques*, 31 ff, especially series A, B and C which have nothing in common with the almost contemporary Chian plastic heads.
[11] Cf. *Samos* V, no. 615 (teller) and Johnston, *Exhibition* 1978, no. 66 (dish).
[12] **1399*** in the Sphinx and Lion style and **1400** perhaps even later.

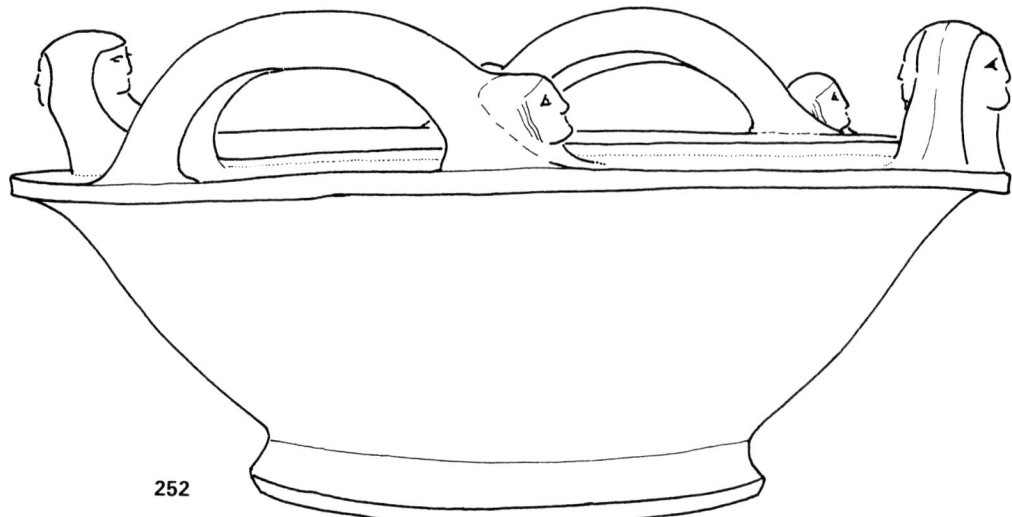

Fig. 4 The Aphrodite bowl from Naucratis

No intact plate or dish in Wild Goat style has so far been found. There are, however, rim fragments which identify certain pieces (**266*** and **268***) as plates. The rim is broad and flat inside, with a thin ribbed lip outside; the shape is not as frequent in Chian as in other East Greek schools.[13]

It is not safe to deduce Chian identity[14] for the Aegina stemmed dish (**264***) by shape alone; more joining fragments have been added[15] and help to show that the profile finds some parallels in the group of seventh-century plain dishes from Emporio,[16] where the lip is slightly upturned.

A group of large and thick pieces from Rizari are from lekanai (FIG. 6). Their decoration argues for a later date, perhaps the first quarter of the sixth century, but they are discussed here because the ornaments displayed are all in the Wild Goat manner. **270*** is a flat piece which ends in an angular lip outside and a ribbed one of two steps on the inside. On **272***, the walls are straight and out-turned, ending in a ribbed rim, on which a disc (rotelle) and the root of a double-reeded vertical handle are preserved. The variety in form and size of dishes, plates and lekanai in Chian Wild Goat style is comparable to that from other East Greek centres, especially of the following century.[17]

The fragmentary votive shield from Phana (FIG. 6—base; **273**) displays patterns of the Wild Goat style but the shape is common, with undecorated parallels coming from the same sanctuary,[18] Emporio[19] and the Heraion on Samos.[20] The Phana clay shield retains the root of the handle-grip as does another from Emporio.[21]

---

[13] Cf. Schaus, *Dem. Sanct., Cyrene* II, 84; incidentally, *Samos* VI.1, pl. 99.723 is not Chian.

[14] *Emporio* 149 and note 5.

[15] Cook, Distribution 154, pl. 41a; the publication of all the fragments in *Alt-Ägina* II.1, 15, no. 74, pl. 5 and fig. 2 where the profile is given.

[16] *Emporio*, nos. 403–410, especially no. 403, pl. 40 and fig. 80 for the profile.

[17] Cf. Schaus, *Dem. Sanct., Cyrene* II, 83–4.

[18] *ADelt* II, 1916, 200, fig. 17 top right.

[19] *Emporio*, 232–3, nos. 483–496, pl. 94 and fig. 153.

[20] *AM* 58, 1933, 118ff, pls. 36–37 and *AM* 54, 1930, 15 and 24.

[21] *Emporio*, no. 483.

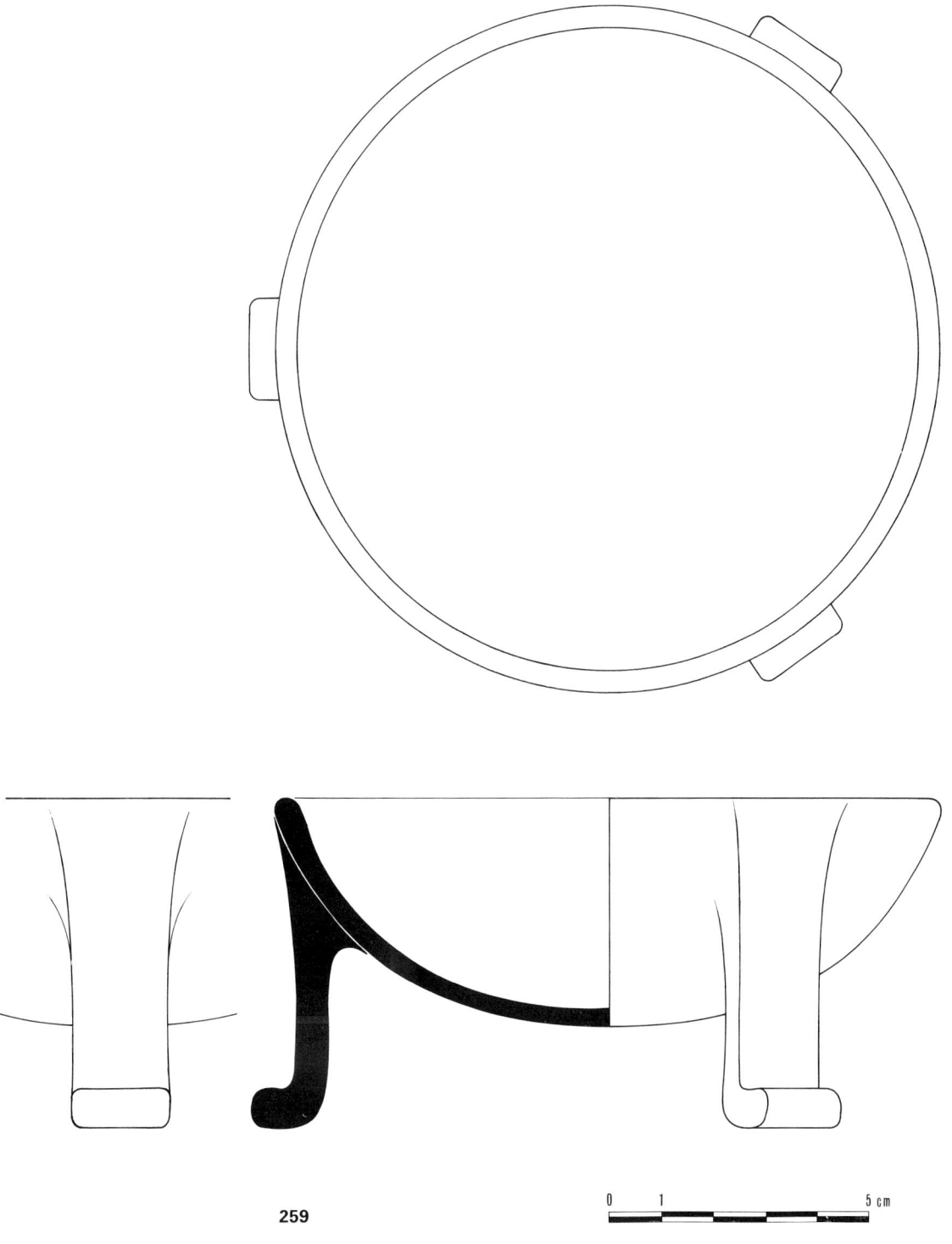

259

Fig. 5 The tripod bowl from Emporio

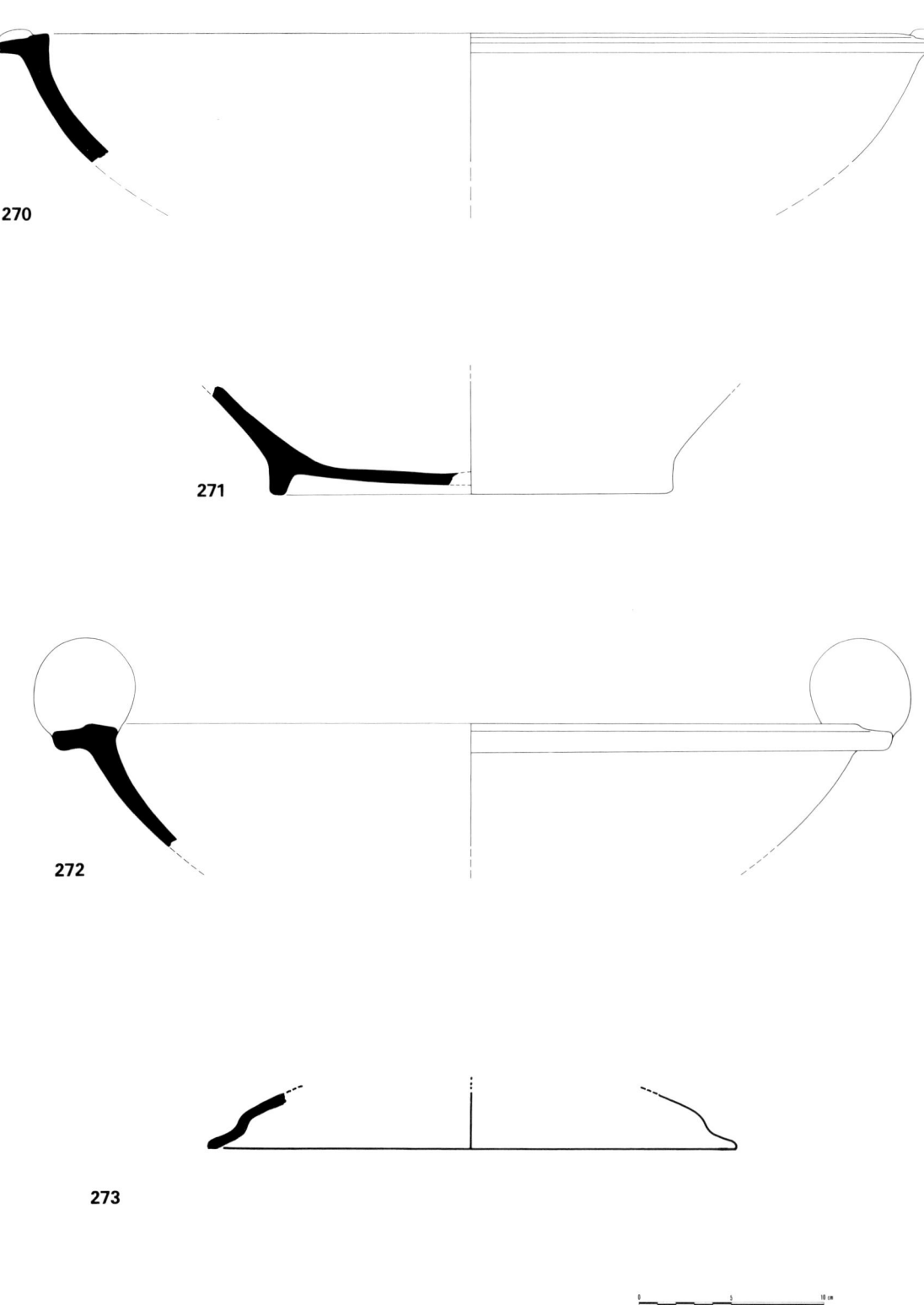

Fig. 6 **270–272** Lekanai from Rizari. **273** The Votive Shield from Phana

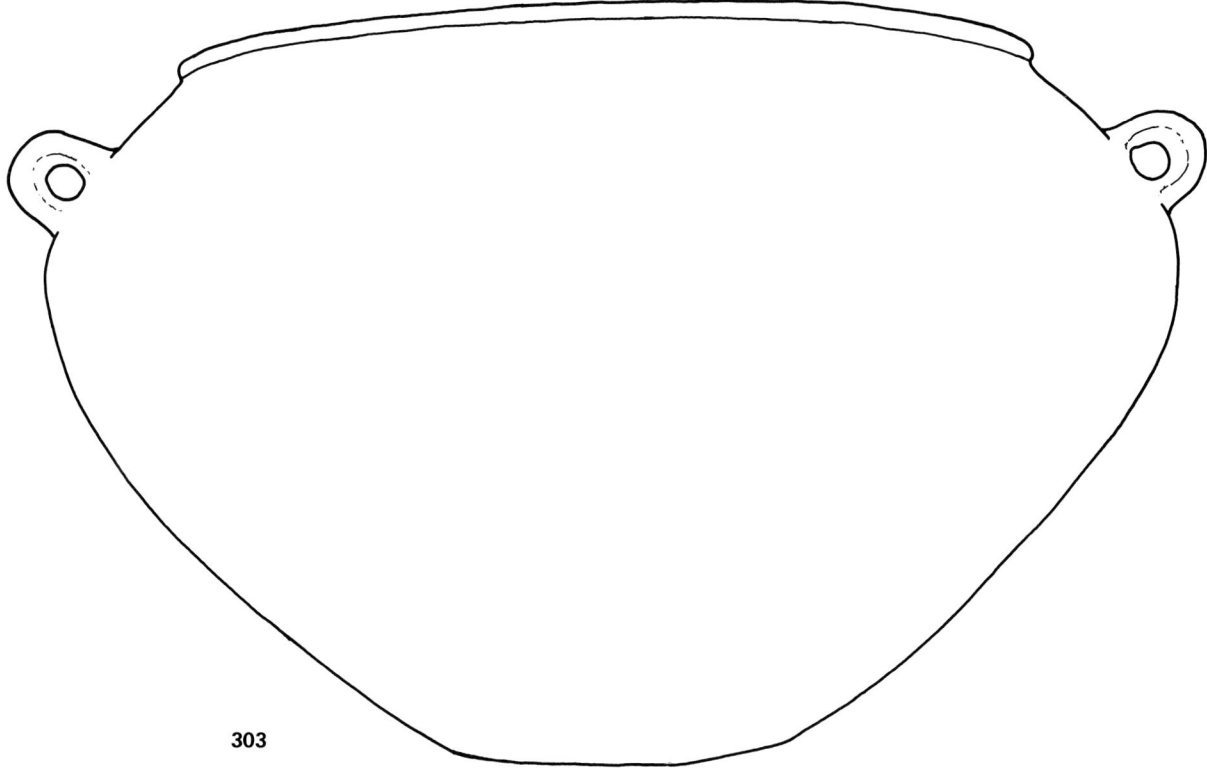

Fig. 7 The Palermo dinos from Gela

Dinoi are more frequent in Wild Goat than in plain pottery. An intact example is the one from Gela in Palermo, (FIG. 7; **303***). It is a large round vessel, with curving sides, broadest at the centre of the belly, with a wide and offset rim, and a flat base. The vase might have been fitted to a stand. Stands are not unknown,[22] yet not very frequent; a fact which may perhaps mislead one into believing that the stands were optional. Chian dinoi are not handleless; the one from Gela has two triple-reeded ring handles attached to the shoulder just below the rim and above the point where the body starts swelling.[23] An intact striped Chian dinos from Naucratis in Boston[24] (Pl. 240.1) has a rounder, more spherical body, because the swelling starts higher up and makes the vase look more symmetrical. A smaller vessel comes from Emporio (**274***) and is earlier than the Gela one.

Fragments selectively listed in the catalogue are from either rims or handles.[25] Two rim fragments from Rizari (FIG. 8; **276*** and **277***) permit the reconstruction of the circumference. The large pieces from Naucratis, (**282***, **283**, **284***, **285** and **287**), might be from dinoi, but the evidence of the single frieze on the Gela dinos and the two-frieze

[22] East Greek stands in *AntK* 13, 1970, 93 note 7 where two examples from Naucratis in Boston are cited: Fairbanks, *Catal.*, pl. 32.305.7 and pl. 37.336.

[23] For photographs of the whole vase: *MonAnt* 17, 1906, 250, fig. 188 and *CGED* pl. 55.17.a

[24] Fairbanks, *Catal.*, pl. 30.306 and *Samos* VI.1, pl. 91.689.

[25] A dozen or more handles, usually quadruple-reeded, of Chian dinoi are in the collection of the BM.

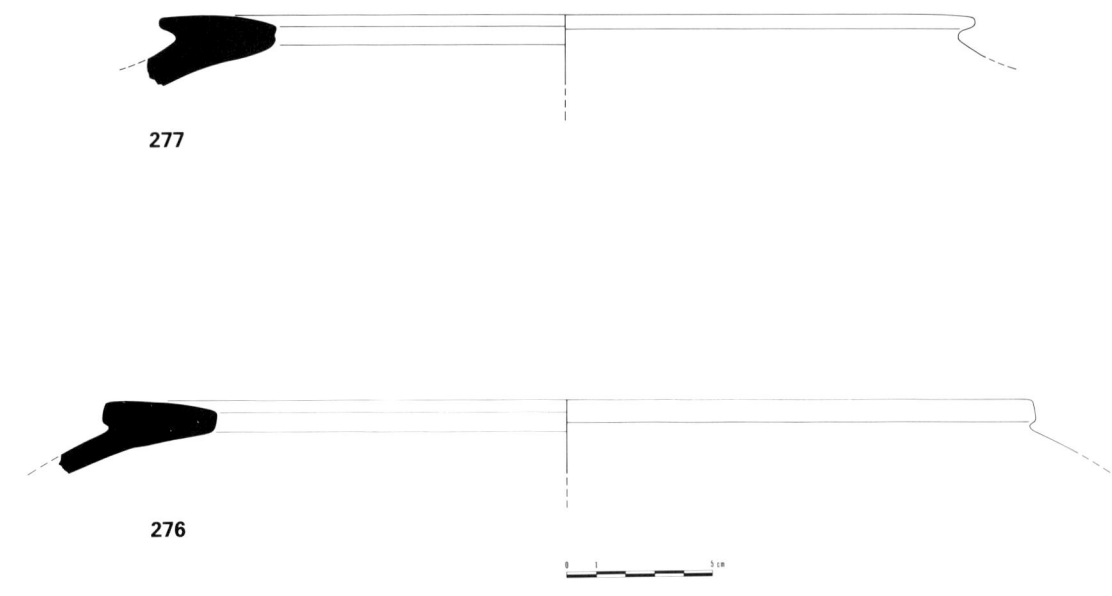

Fig. 8 Dinoi from Rizari

decoration on later Aeolian ones (which were strongly influenced by the Chian)[26] suggest that the three or four friezes seen here are not the usual disposition of the decoration on dinoi and the possibility that they are from oenochoai cannot be excluded.

Oenochoai are numerically second to chalices in Chian Wild Goat. The East Greek centres of the southern area had established this as the favoured shape in Wild Goat and the impact on Chian potters was not without results. The two almost intact oenochoai are of different type and date within the Middle phase:

1. The Emporio bull-vase (FIG. 9; **310***) is a large vessel, roughly double the size of an average Middle I "Rhodian" oenochoe.[27] It has a globular body which narrows towards the ring base; the neck is set off at a sharp angle, splaying almost imperceptibly towards the mouth which is formed as a bull's head. The quadruple-reeded vertical handle has two discs (rotelles) on either side, just behind and below the animal's ears. This type of oenochoe is not common in the pottery of the region: its contemporary East Greek companions do not compare either in general concept or in profile.[28] The bull's head finds a close parallel in one from Choperskie, in the Russian hinterland (**351***), and both have a common antecedent in a ram's head (**350***), found in Krivoroshie.[29] The ram's head is decorated with a double guilloche, a trait

---

[26] The Dinos workshop in Kardara's *Rhodiake*, 271–276 and E. Walter-Karydi, Äol. Kunst, 3–18, pls. 1–3 (with n. 6 on p. 4).

[27] The Emporio bull-vase is considered Samian in *Samos* VI.1, 2, together with the ram's head from Krivoroshie. However, there is no mention of the bull's head from Choperskie.

[28] "Rhodian" oenochoai narrow towards the bottom but in a completely different way. An example is Kinch, *Vroulia*, fig. 91. The profile of the Emporio vase is given in *Emporio*, 151, fig. 99.

[29] *Arch. Reports* for 1962–3, 41, fig. 17 (ram) and 18 (bull) and *Emporio*, 148 note 1. Also *RA* 1975, 63 ff and *GO*³ 3 244 fig. 284 and note 92. P. Alexandrescu also thinks that they are Chian in *Histria* IV, 20 and note 9.

310

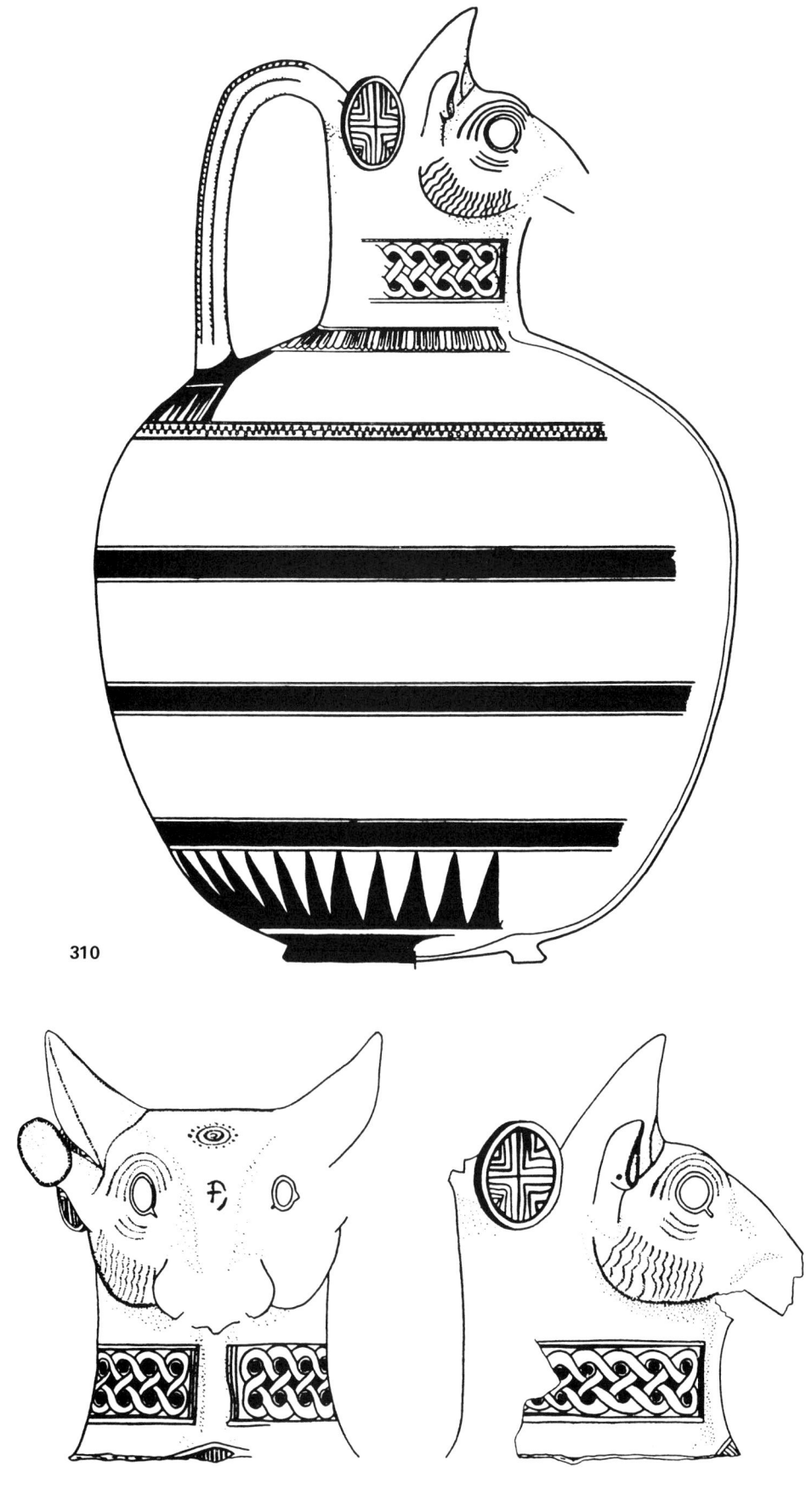

Fig. 9 The Emporio bull-vase (*Emporio*, figs. 99 and 100)
(Courtesy of Professor Sir J. Boardman)

which it has in common with the Emporio oenochoe. The list of Chian oenochoai ending in animals' heads is short and chronologically runs as follows:
1. The Krivoroshie ram-oenochoe (**350***).
2. The Choperskie bull-oenochoe (**351***).
3. The Emporio bull-oenochoe (**310***).
4. The bull's head from Naucratis in Oxford (Pl. 243.4) which decorated a lid as the knob and is much later.[30]

Common features of the Emporio and Choperskie bulls are the upright, slightly forward bent ears; the bulbous eyes, though these are more almond-like in the latter, and the flat and somewhat low cheeks which give this figure, on which they have been wholly preserved, a rabbit-like impression. The scale pattern which covers the Choperskie neck is familiar to Chian painters.[31] Finally the rotelles of the Emporio and Choperskie oenochoai share a common pattern, crossed and squared lines, which also appears in East Greek oenochoai of the Southern centres.[32]

2. The fragments of the Rizari oenochoe (FIG. 10; **324***) clearly demonstrate that they are from a trefoil oenochoe, triple-handed and with two discs at the junction between handle and lip: a canonical Middle II Wild Goat oenochoe.[33] The shoulder bears the "metope" decoration and the body must have been divided into three "friezes" with grazing goats; whereas the lower part of the vessel remained undecorated or might have been decorated with rays. In the Southern workshops it has a lotus-and-bud frieze.[34]

These nearly intact oenochoai do not demonstrate all the possible Chian types. For example, a fragment from the neck of a Late Wild Goat oenochoe from Rizari (FIG. 11; **338***) displays a bulge at the transition from neck to shoulder. One suspects that there must have been even more variety.[35]

Ring vases (or Kernoi) are common in Chian Wild Goat, the Sphinx and Lion style and undecorated pottery. An intact vase from Naucratis in Boston (**364***), though simply patterned with a network and evidently later than the Wild Goat pieces (**359** and **360**), demonstrates the shape. It is composed of a hollow ring body sitting on three feet; on the upper surface of the ring, spouts alternate with twin-reeded ring handles. On the Wild Goat examples, (**359–360** and **363***), the handles are replaced by protomes, undoubtedly female, since the base of the necks with dotted necklaces, similar to those on the Aphrodite

---

[30] *CVA* Oxford II, pl. 396.57.

[31] Though for a different purpose. It covers the body of sirens on the later Animal chalices: examples nos. **536**, **537** and **547**.

[32] *Samos* V, pls. 93 and 94. The same, as filling ornament, is met on Chian Wild Goat vases and is used to excess on those of the London Dinos workshop.

[33] *GPP*² 225.

[34] *Samos* V, pls. 119.600; 120 and 121.

[35] The Old Smyrna oenochoe, Izmir Museum 3333, which has been considered as Chian—see *Samos* V, 76, pl. 124.612 and A.A. Lemos in *Chios Conference*, 239—should be excluded. Recently R.M. Cook in *Festschrift Akurgal*, 1987, 74 note 4 was in favour of it being an import from Chios, but after the reassurance of clay analyses. I think it cannot easily be classified within the canonical Middle Wild Goat style of Chios but nonetheless it is under its strong influence. The Missouri-Columbia oenochoe 71.113, see W. Moon and L. Berge, *Greek Vase-Painting in Midwestern Collections*, 1979, 16, no. 11, in shape adheres to the norm of a Late Wild Goat oenochoe, but does not classify as Chian either. It might be of Carian origin—or generally Western Anatolian—see Schaus, *Dem. Sanct., Cyrene* II, 78 note 7 and id., *BSA* 81, 1986, 290; see also R.M. Cook in *Festschrift Akurgal*, 1987, 71–73 and mainly 74 note 8 with a list of vases of possible Milesian origin. And now E.A. Hemelrijk in *BABesch* 62, 1987, 33–55.

324

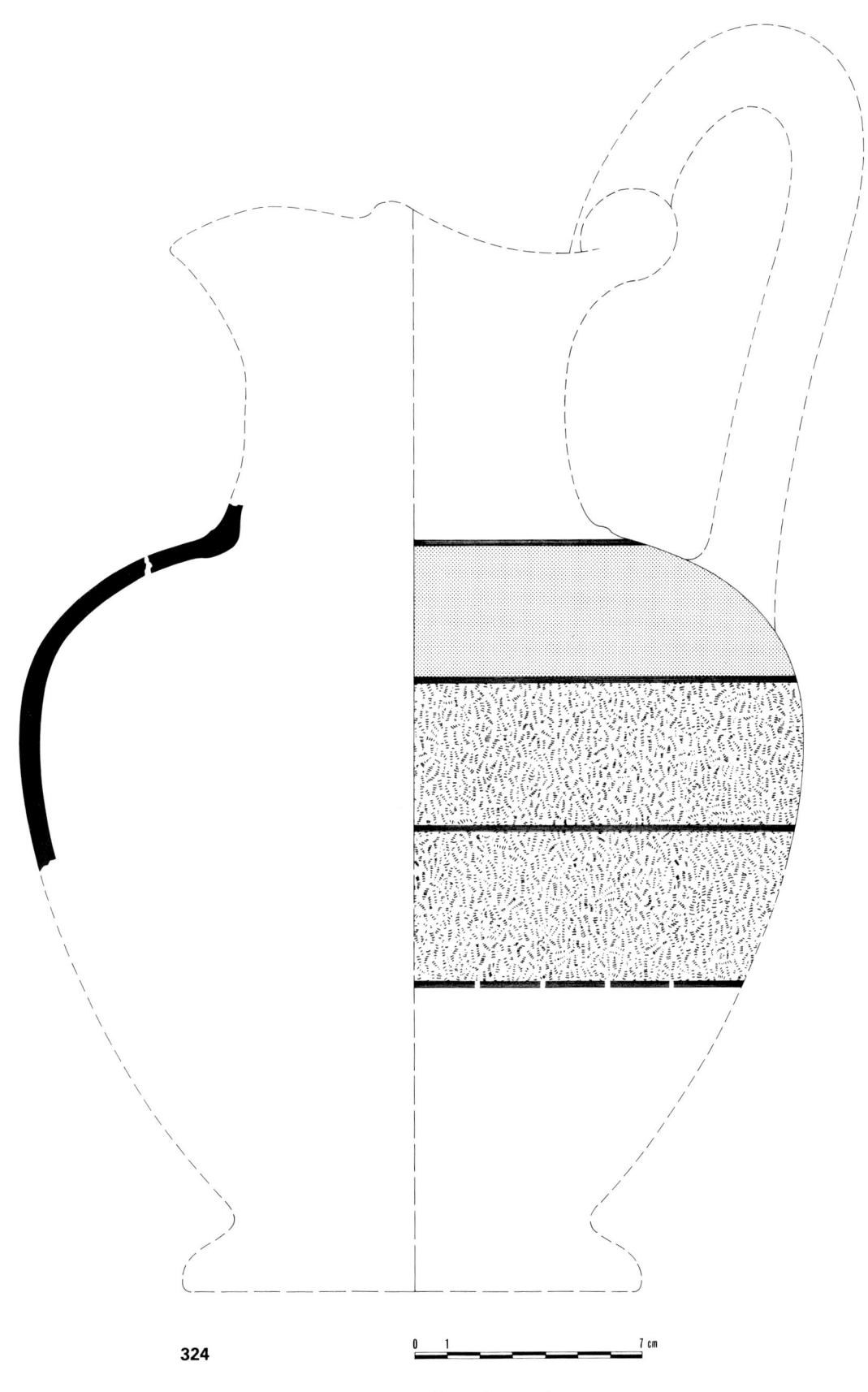

Fig. 10 The Rizari oenochoe

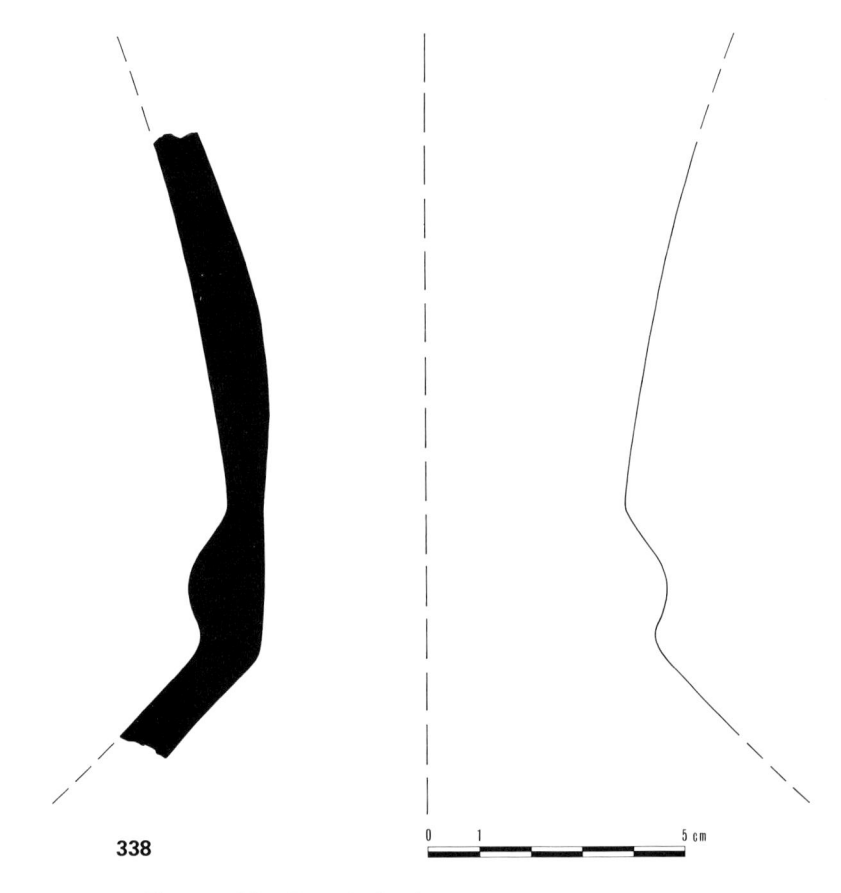

Fig. 11 The Late Wild Goat oenochoe from Rizari

bowl, have been preserved. A few ring vases listed here, (**355–359** and **361**), are a little later; in fact they might even be of the sixth century.[36]

Phallus vases have been recovered: two at Naucratis and one on the Athenian Acropolis.[37] The nearly complete one (FIG. 12; **365***) is an erect phallus in the full Wild Goat style, with a vulva placed at the opposite end of the glans which is not pierced: therefore it is not a rhyton.

An undecorated example of roughly the same time, possibly from a vase, was among the Emporio finds.[38] Phallus vases or genitals as part of plastic vases were not uncommon in East Greece and were used as perfume vases.[39] The Chian vases, however, were all recovered in sanctuaries or among votive debris, and seem to have been offerings symbolizing fertility or beseeching it.

[36] Ring vases of the fourth century and even later were recovered at Rizari in Chios town suggesting, together with seated terracotta figurines, a Demeter cult. See *Chiaka Meletemata* I, 63 ff and pl. 8.1396.

[37] Cook, Distribution 158 and note 12.1–3 and *AA* 1976, 288 and note 25. The second piece from Naucratis, (**366**), is no longer in the collection of the BM.

[38] *Emporio*, 191, pl. 77.75 and *AA* 1976, 288 and note 25.

[39] Ducat, *Vases plastiques* 158 ff. References for other East Greek in *AA* 1976, 288 notes 22–24 (for Samos, "Larisa" and Sardis). For the Lydian squatting man see now Hanfmann, *Sardis* 85 and note 32. He appears in a new reconstruction, on fig. 143, deprived of his phallus as he became a horseman.

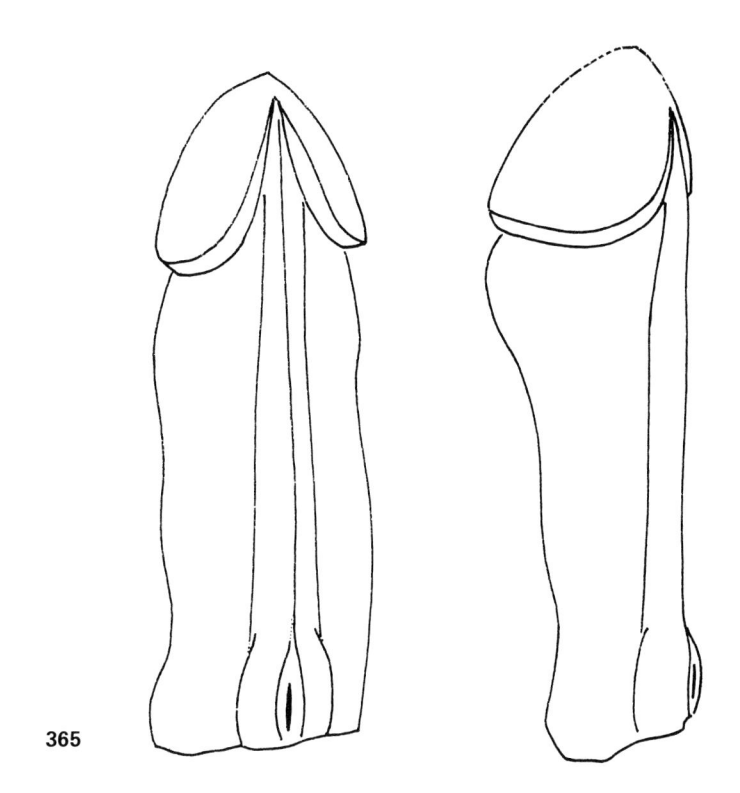

Fig. 12 Phallus vase from Naucratis

DECORATION

Animals, birds and hybrids which decorate Chian Wild Goat are also found in the other East Greek schools engaged in producing the same style. In fact in Chian Wild Goat there is less variety both of animals and birds. This paucity is probably due to insufficient material and the fragmentary state of what does exist.

It is inconvenient to separate the fauna represented in the Early and Middle phases of Wild Goat from their immediate antecedents, the Animal Chalices (whether the latter be considered as a late phase in the Wild Goat style or as a renovating phase of the old tradition). Therefore, they will be considered only here, stressing their appearance, frequency, growing sparsity and final extinction. This disappearance in some cases coincides with the end of the Middle II phase.

The Chian animal repertoire follows the same trends as in the other East Greek centres. Although they share much common subject-matter, they also demonstrate certain differences, more evident during the ripe phase, especially in the manner of applying the decoration to different shapes—Chians mainly on chalices and open bowls, Southerners on oenochoai and plates.

The list of the motifs used in the Chian animal style, which includes Wild Goat and Animal Chalice styles, but excludes the Black-figure styles, may be divided thus: A.

Animals: goat, deer and doe, dog, fox, ram, lion and panther, bull and boar; B. **Birds**: goose and water-bird; and C. **Hybrids**: sphinx, siren, griffin and perhaps a chimaera.

A. ANIMALS

Goat (FIG. 13): These are always painted in silhouette, with the head and a stripe, invariably dotted, on the belly in outline. A reserved arched line denotes the transition from neck to body and another the separation between the hindlegs. Up to the end of Middle I they usually have no added colours (**310***); afterwards, occasionally, red, almost purple, is added on the shoulder and thigh. The typical scheme has them heading right, even on fragments with three or four friezes (**282*** and **285**). Exceptions are extremely rare: **349**, where little has been preserved to suggest a reason; **255*** and **377***, where goats are facing a floral rosette and might have been part of an antithetical composition, and **303***— because of the composition. The material preserved suggests that this was not accidental, and though the reason may not be obvious, the origin for this practice may possibly lie in other media which influenced Wild Goat style.

Chian goats demonstrate all the known poses of their East Greek counterparts:
a) walking, with all four legs rendered, (**253***).
b) grazing, with head bent to ground level and again all four legs shown, (**253***).
In these two cases, the norm is to draw a triangle between the forelegs and a horseshoe roundel between the hindlegs;
c) running, in which case only two legs, those supposedly nearest to the spectator, are drawn in an attempt to produce an illusion of motion.
d) rearing, or rather jumping over a triangle or a rosette, in which case both forelegs are drawn the one next to the other, (examples are **412***, **520** and **574***).[40]
e) mounting on a floral, as does the leading goat on the reverse on the larger Würzburg chalice (**236***), and again the leading one on the obverse of the smaller Würzburg chalice (**237***).

In a few cases they turn their heads back in surprise and at times are attacked by birds (**113***).

Protomes of goats or of any other animal or bird, characteristic of Rhodian dishes, are not encountered in Chian Wild Goat.[41]

Goats are almost always in the processional composition. **376*** displays a particularly interesting scene of two antithetically poised goats.

Goats exist from the early stages of Wild Goat, though for Chian the evidence for this phase is scarce; they heavily populate the vases of the Middle II period and gradually fade away after the turn of the seventh to the sixth century. The renovated animal style rarely if ever makes use of them.

---

[40] Cf. Schiering, *Werkstätten* 93 and cf. note 719; now, however, with the addition of the unpublished fragments in the BM and the UCL it is not exceptional.

[41] Protomes in general, apart from an isolated example (the oenochoe **1284*** in the Sphinx and Lion style), are unknown in Chian vase painting; Aeolian, though influenced by Chian in other aspects, must have picked up this practice from the Southern centres.

THE WILD GOAT STYLE 27

Fig. 13 Goats

Fig. 14 Deer and Does

Deer and Doe (FIG. 14): Contrary to the Southern schools, where fallow deer come second in popularity[42] to the goat, in Chian they are very rare. Although they appear only on one intact vase and four fragments, they demonstrate two variations; the one might be earlier than the other.

The first type of doe appears on the fragments from Al Mina (**352**) and on the Emporio oenochoe (**310***). Legs, body and short antlers are drawn in silhouette with the head, the stripe on the belly (undotted on the first and dotted on the second) and circles on the body (again undotted on the first and dotted on the second) are in outline; finally a reserved line marks the separation of neck from body. There are no added colours. Only two legs are shown, to denote the running pose. Fallow deer do not survive the Middle I phase and apart from **345***, which is a walking doe, and **676***, the later animal chalice from Pitane, there are no other examples. In this last the does running round the perimeter of the vase have their bodies in silhouette and both forelegs and hindlegs are shown as if they are rearing.

The second type of deer appears only once, on **283**; he is the male companion but rendered in a different way. Neck, legs and antlers are in silhouette, whereas the whole body is in outline covered with dark spots. He is grazing in a row[43] to the right. As with

---

[42] Schiering, *Werkstätten* 48 and Kardara, *Rhodiake* 143.   [43] Both fragments now joining, Price fig. 41 and pl. 10.2.

Fig. 15 Dogs

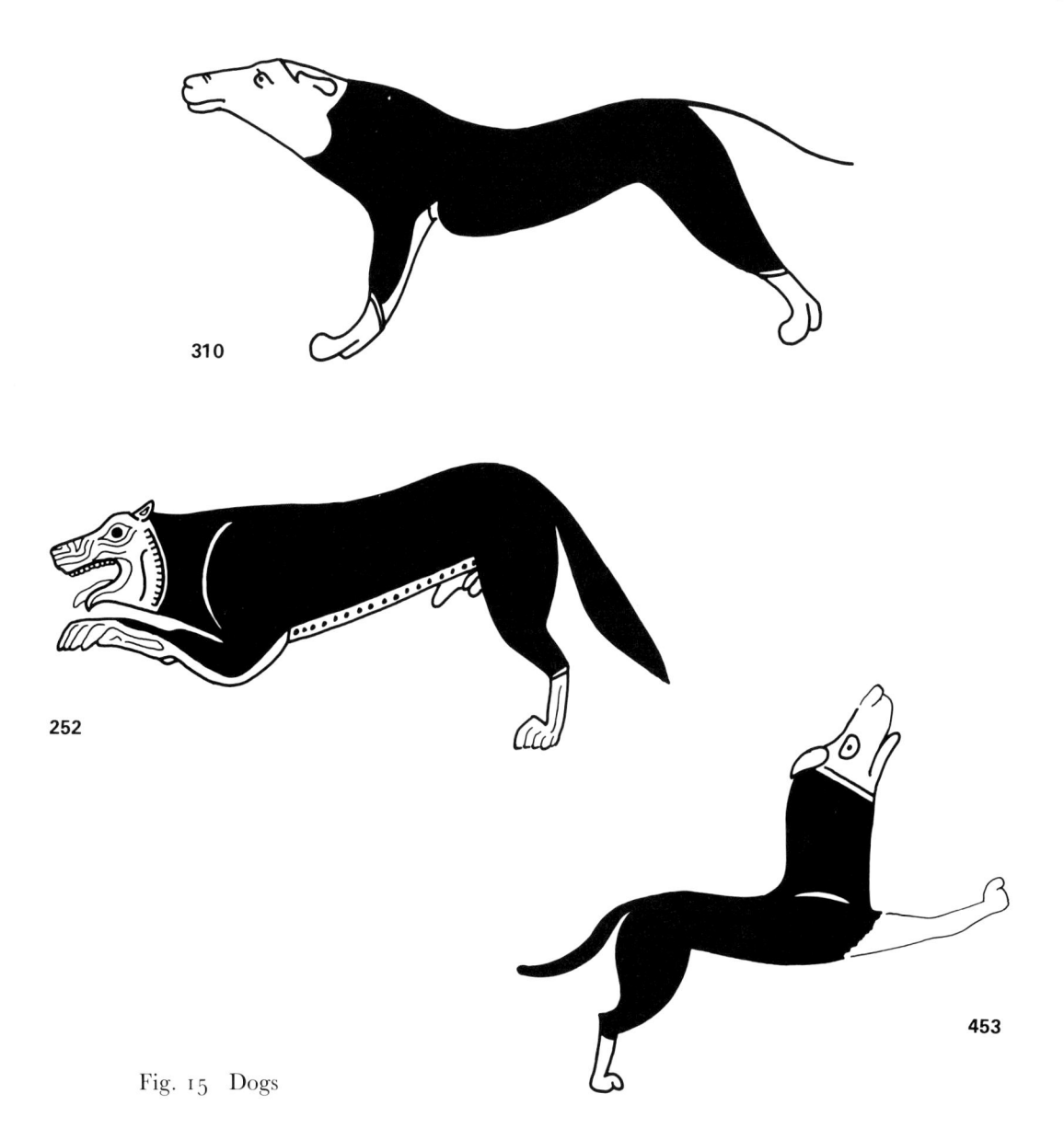

the goats this is the preferred direction. Deer do not survive the end of the century, apart from one example. On a much later fragment, (**556***), there is the head of a deer facing or turning its head to the left. Finally, on **215** the creature with the long neck and short but bushy antlers is drawn in outline, with dark patches covering neck and horns.

Dogs (FIG. 15): There are two variations, an early and a later. In Middle I the type is known from the Al Mina (**352**) and the Emporio oenochoe (**310***) and on fragment **311***. They are either running in a row or, as in the last two cases, chasing goats. They differ in no respect from their "Rhodian" counterparts: with body in silhouette, head and paws in outline; two reserved arched lines are placed between neck and body, and a further pair between foreleg and belly. Only two legs, as expected, are shown. The type survives in

Middle II with a few additions. The dogs chasing a boar in the inside of the Aphrodite bowl (**252***) are executed in the same manner but have more elongated bodies; genitals are added as well as a reserved dotted stripe on the belly following the fashion of the other animals on the vase. Two further pieces (**378***–**9***) preserve only the heads in outline with ears set back and pointed muzzles, of what most probably are dogs. In the Animal Chalice style the type is rendered somewhat differently. The whole body is in silhouette with a bushy tail wherever that is shown (**453***), the head is either in outline or silhouette, the latter on late examples (**455*** and **887***). They occasionally wear a collar rendered in a reserved and dotted line,[44] which originates from the earlier Aphrodite bowl dogs, where in place of the collar there were short parallel lines.

Fox (FIG. 16): This is as rare in Chian as it is in the Southern schools. The early representation of the animal on the Emporio dinos (**274***) shows the body, the upright ears and the thick bushy tail in silhouette; the head in outline[45] and a reserved arched line between neck and body. Red has been added on certain parts of the body. The scene is vivid, with the fox chased by a lion which has driven him into a corner. He seems to have no choice but to place his foreleg on the floral in front of him and to turn his head with open mouth in agony towards his attacker.

The smaller creatures on the Aegina plate (**264***) and the early chalice from the Samian Heraion (**247***) might be vixens[46] who, unfortunately, have not preserved their heads but whose tails speak for them. Foxes do not survive Middle I and do not reappear in the Chian animal world.

Ram (FIG. 16): The ram[47] appears twice in Chian. On **284*** of the Middle II phase in a superb drawing, the body and the twisted horns are in silhouette; head and neck in outline, with the latter covered by spots indicating the locks of the fleece; a reserved arched line denotes the separation between neck and body. Both forelegs are shown as if the ram is walking. This ram compares well with the head of oenochoe **350***; the muzzle is more pointed in the former but the difference in media and time must not be forgotten. The type of the Chian ram may be compared with its counterpart on an earlier "Rhodian" oenochoe,[48] but has nothing in common with the late Wild Goat rams of the southern region.[49]

The ram reappears in another instance (**565***) where the animal's head is drawn[50] rather hastily and in a way that is not reminiscent of its predecessor. Only the head is in outline and a striped band separates it from the neck.

Lion (FIG. 17): There are *two* types of lion in Chian figurative pottery. The Emporio type is the earlier, of *Middle I phase*: with closed mouth[51] and pointed muzzle, it bears little resemblance to the later well-known Chian type. On the Emporio dinos (**274***) only the

---

[44] **487**, but also the dogs on the boar-hunt scene of the Kavala column-crater, (Pls. 221–225).

[45] Foxes with heads in outline 1) on the Levy-oenochoe: Schiering, *Werkstätten*, 68, pl. 13.1; and 2) on the shoulder of an oenochoe in Leningrad: *Samos* V, pls. 95–96. Also *Emporio*, 148 and note 7 and *Alt-Ägina*, II.1, 15.

[46] Cf. Cook, Fikellura 63 note 2.

[47] A list of rams on East Greek vases in Cook, *Claz. Sarc.* 102 note 50.

[48] Schiering, *Werkstätten* 68 and pl. 3.1.

[49] Especially *Samos* VI.1, pl. 132.1071.

[50] Cf. *CVA* Cambridge II, 33 no. 25.

[51] Brown, *Etruscan Lion*, 98 for an Egyptian influence for the closed mouth creature.

THE WILD GOAT STYLE

Fig. 16 Fox and Rams

forepart and the head of the animal are shown; the head with pointed ears is in outline; the body is in silhouette with a reserved arched line (in the middle of which is a painted line), which marks the separation between the body and the forepart including the foreleg. The last is in silhouette with a line surrounding the contour. An arrow-like floral on the muzzle represents perhaps a hairy wart.[52] Red is added on the double-chin and shoulder. This mastiff-like lion has perhaps some descendants. **357**, earlier considered as a dog, could be a lion with a closed and pointed mouth. A more successful comparison may be with **308***, which demonstrates a not dissimilar creature to the Emporio one. The crater from Cyprus (**308***) offers a better parallel on grounds of shape and style with a lion on a column-crater in Leningrad.[53] The Cypriot and Leningrad craters share a dotted quadruple-rosette placed exactly in front of the animal's nose, as if the animal is sniffing it. This type of rosette is not found on the fragment of the Emporio dinos but appears on **314*** of the same group. Finally, the animal on plate **686*** might be a lion with closed mouth: a late derivative of the Emporio type.

[52] *Emporio*, 158 and note 6.
[53] *Samos* VI.1, pl, 118.968. The dogs on the upper frieze of the Kavala column-crater, (Pls. 224 and 225), though certainly in better style, approximate to the type of both.

The second type of Chian lion is the well-known one from the Würzburg chalice (**236***), the Aphrodite bowl (**252***) and a few pieces of the *Middle II phase*. The type is established towards the middle of this phase but continues in greater frequency in the Animal Chalice style and other categories of the sixth century, until it is finally dropped from the repertoire after the middle of the century.

It has been established that the Chian lion derives from the Assyrian prototype[54] with the wide-open mouth, the square-pointed muzzle and the heavy network-like mane; the lolling tongue, however, another inseparable feature, is that of the neo-Hittite type.[55]

The body of the Chian lion is always in silhouette, whereas the head, the mane (which is covered with a network pattern) and the paws are all in outline; on the most elaborate pieces the forelegs are drawn half in silhouette for the front part and half in outline for the rear. A reserved dotted band runs alongside the belly and an arched reserved line marks the separation between the hindquarters. The Middle II lion is always walking, showing all four legs and though the wide open mouth gives the impression that the animal is roaring, in fact it is a completely tame and innocent creature introduced into the repertory for purely decorative purposes. The lion is not frequently encountered in this period: apart from the two intact vases mentioned, it appears only on six fragments, e.g. **325***.

However, with the opening of the new century the lion with sphinx, bull and boar become the favourite motifs in the animal style. The type continues unaltered except for a few refinements, such as partial silhouette for the upper part of the foreleg and outline for the contours on the most elaborate pieces.[56] The mane is even more thoroughly worked in minute crossed lines of diluted brown, almost golden brown. Exceptions to the rule are **666*** and **696***, on which lions appear with their manes in silhouette or with added red.

Walking Middle II lions are placed at random amidst other animals. On a few chalices from the sixth century, however, they demonstrate the processional composition (**558***, **667*** and **675***), the antithetical, as well as back to back (on the rear of the Delos chalice, **643***). A favourite scene now is the lion attacking a bull or a boar. As a rule, the lion is placed to the right of the onlooker when attacking a bull or boar; only once when the creature at bay is a boar, the lion comes from the left (**438***). The lion attacking other animals is an oriental motif known to Greek art since Mycenaean times;[57] it reappears in Late Geometric art and continues thereafter perhaps not uninfluenced by prototypes from the East. In the group of the simple figure chalices, lions sitting on their haunches with upright heads (séjant) are one of the two favourite creatures that embellish them; they are almost always heading left. The iconographical type has remained the same but has been simplified to essentials, thereby losing all the refinements of the earlier ones.

Special mention should be made of the exquisitely drawn lion on a chalice of the Grand style (**762***) with lower feet and paws in outline.

---

[54] *Emporio*, 138; *NC* 68; E. Akurgal, *Späthethitische Bildkunst*, 1949, 39 ff; T.J. Dunbabin, *The Greeks and their Eastern Neighbours*, 1957, 46 ff; *AE* 1953–54, 256 ff; Brown, *Etruscan Lion* 103 ff and *GO*³ 78 with fig. 78.

[55] Salviat in *BCH* 86, 1962, 95 ff thinks that the Chian type comes from North Syria and is of Hittite origin. H. Gabelmann, *Studien zum frühgriechischen Löwenbild*, 1965, 10 ff. Kardara, *Rhodiake*, 152–3 thinks that her Classical Camiran is of the same general type as the Assyrian lion which was possibly introduced via Phoenician works or even Phoenicians inhabiting the island. Also *CGED* 68. And *BICS* 16, 1969, 4 for a Phoenician "colony" on Rhodes.

[56] Especially **438*** and **439***. The two lines denoting the eyebrows of Middle II Wild Goat lions are repeated in a lion on a Clazomenian sarcophagus from Acanthus, see Cook, *Claz. Sarc.*, H1, pl. 94.1

[57] Brown, *Etruscan Lion* 3 ff; *CGED* 68 and *GO*³ 78.

274

308

252

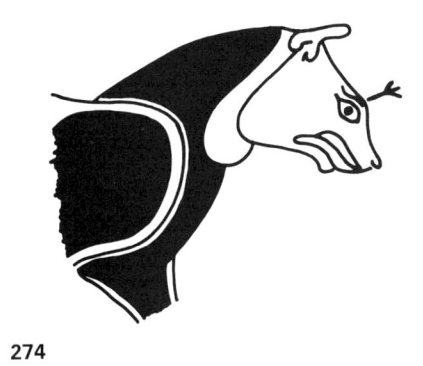

696

546

972

Fig. 17 Lions

Fig. 18 Panther

Panther (FIG. 18): The frontally facing lions without manes are still conventionally, but conveniently, called panthers.[58] In Chian the type is represented on only a few examples. Two mutilated pieces (**314*** and **354**) of the Middle I phase, show only part of the body in outline covered with dense spots executed in horizontal rows. Two further fragments (**157*** and **604***) preserve feline legs drawn elaborately; the paws are in outline, as well as the thighs, which at the top are covered with dotted circles with a calligraphic "eyebrow" above them. On **287** the whole animal, frontal head included, is in outline. A fragment of a somewhat later plate (**266***) shows the forepart of a frontal lion; head and body are in outline and, apart from the head, everything else is covered with tear-like circles ringed by three-quarter arched lines, thus giving the impression of a scaly pattern. It is a hastily executed vase and it is interesting that the painter has drawn the eyes as if they were meant to be seen in profile.

Bull (FIG. 19): The type is established in Chian Middle II Wild Goat where some complete examples exist; the increased frequency on the Animal Chalice style ranks it second only to lions and sphinxes. Body and horn—one only is shown—are in silhouette whereas head, neck and hoofs are in outline. The representation of the bull mixes vividness and stylization: on the one hand, care has been taken to depict the animal in its usual ambling stance with a naturalistic touch furthered by the wrinkles of the neck; on the other hand the body is executed partly in silhouette and partly in outline with large curved areas ending in spirals (**236*** and **298***). The wrinkles on earlier pieces are disposed horizontally and reach the separation of the forelegs, whereas on later pieces they are almost diagonally disposed and drawn below the forelegs.[59] The tail is half in silhouette and half in outline, either plaited between the hindlegs or tasseled alongside the haunches. In addition to walking and sometimes heading towards a floral, poses common in the Middle II phase, sixth-century chalices also depict apparent activity in situations where the bull is being mauled or sometimes simply encountered by a lion, as on the Delos vessel (**643***). This becomes almost the norm. However, there are two fragments, (**441*** and **519**), showing bulls in a processional row and a third (**445***) on which a bull confronts a rearing, almost upright, dog.

[58] On abandoning the name panther see Boardman in *AntK* 13, 1970, 94.

[59] Compare the bull on **236*** with **643***.

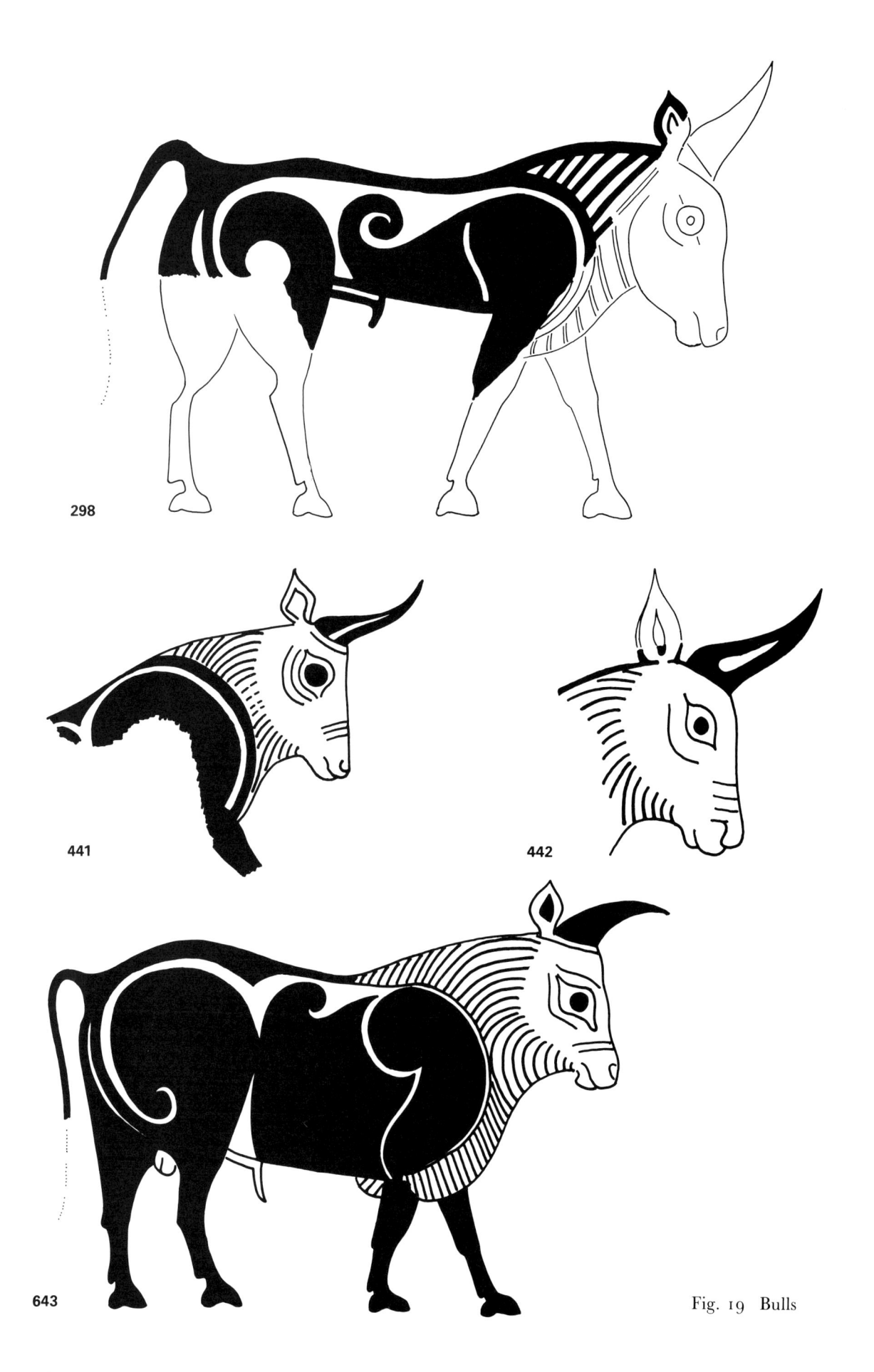

298

441
442

643
Fig. 19 Bulls

439

Fig. 20 Boar

In Chian vase painting bulls do not outlive the first quarter of the sixth century and are not found in other categories of the reserving styles. In other East Greek wares it is a very rare motif and at this same date it becomes extinct.[60]

Boar (FIG. 20): With regard to frequency the same consideration applies for the boar. It appears in the Middle II phase, becomes quite frequent, though less than the bull, on the Animal Chalice style and dies out with them. The boar on the tondo of the Aphrodite bowl (**252***) is drawn with its body in silhouette accompanied by a few details, such as a reserved stripe, with dots, alongside the belly, hoofs and striped line on the crest and finally the head in outline. This treatment of the head in outline is unique not only in Chian but in East Greek of the reserving styles. It could be due either to its date, around 600 B.C., or it may be a peculiarity of the painter's style. All subsequent boars have their heads in silhouette with a few details reserved, namely the eye-socket, first round and then almond-shaped, and the tusk. The tail, partly in outline, is short and twisted. Boars are always walking with all four legs splayed[61] and almost always attacked either by dogs (**252*** and **887***) or by a lion (**439***) or simply encountering one (**324***). Added colours are mostly red, either in patches or in spots, covering shoulder and haunches in the beginning and later on the whole body, and occasionally white is applied for the area around the eye and for the tusk, especially on a few elaborate examples (**432*** and **448*–451***).

Noteworthy for its stance is a later example on a chalice with no filling ornaments (**887***) where a boar, chased by a dog, has its forelegs drawn close together as well as its hindlegs, as if rearing.[62]

Hare: Not a single example of the species has been traced in the Chian Wild Goat style.[63]

---

[60] In Fikellura, for example, it occurs twice, see Cook, Fikellura 62 and pl. 3b and 93, fig. 19. See also Schaus in *BSA* 81, 1986, 253, no. 1, 259 and pl. 13b.

[61] On the Emporio chalice (**114***) the hindquarters of the animal are shown on the left metope.

[62] A fragmentary chalice, classified as Chian: Price 211, fig. 45 and E. Walter-Karydi in *Samos* VI.1, 138, pl. 92.692, must be Aeolian, on grounds of both drawing (heavy and flabby body) and the un-Chian filling ornaments.

[63] Though both Price in Price 212 (two fragments) and Cook in Cook, Fikellura 63 refer to "Naucratite" hares.

236   **303**

Fig. 21 Geese

A fragment of a lid[64] with a hare, believed to be Chian, does have a white slip and a dotted stripe on the belly of the animal, but so do many vessels and animals of the Middle II phase from other East Greek schools. Both shape and style are otherwise unknown to Chian Wild Goat and until other parallels turn up, this doubtful piece is better excluded.[65]

B. BIRDS

Goose (FIG. 21): Most probably geese, and not ducks, are depicted in Chian figurative pottery, as their large and long necks argue. It might have been the Nile goose which was domesticated in the third millennium.[66] This bird comes second in frequency only to the goat; it occurs on Middle I vases, becomes very common in Middle II Wild Goat and gradually peters out in the new repertoire of the renovated animal style.[67] The type is similar to the one well-established by the Southern schools, differing only in details. Head, neck and body are in silhouette; legs in outline; the long wings over the rear part of the body are reserved with feathers striped with horizontal or diagonal lines, whilst the front part is rendered with a reserved bow, crescent, or heart-like shape (the latter on the Palermo dinos **303***), with lines inside following the contour. A wide, almost vertical, band drawn in silhouette divides the upper from the lower part.[68] A reserved line denotes the lower beak; another which frequently becomes a patch indicates the separation of the neck from the head.[69] Finally a reserved circle forms the eye with a dot in the middle. A few Chian geese have a second reserved band lower down the neck which is a special feature of the school, rarely if ever encountered on other East Greek geese.

Stances are restricted in contrast to their southern counterparts. Geese are always walking—with both feet showing—to the left or to the right, in a processional composition

---

[64] BM 1888.6–1.477a.
[65] Hares: Schiering, *Werkstätten*, 51. Kardara, *Rhodiake*, 66.
[66] J. Hine, *AA* 1970, 133 note 5 and W.H. Riddell, *Antiquity* 17, 1943, 148ff on the domestication of the wild goose in Egypt.
[67] There are only two strays (**575*** and **641***), which display inner elaborate decoration.
[68] Examples **150***, **169***, 202, **205***, 207, **252*** and **275***.
[69] Cook, *Claz. Sarc.*, 98.

or in pairs, as on the Palermo dinos (**303***), the Pitane chalice (**221**) and fragments (**149***, **151***, **153*** and **173**). Other poses are with a gosling (**111***) or mixed with other animals, usually goats and lions as on the Würzburg larger chalice (**236***) and the Aphrodite bowl. They often face a floral (**236***) or a bigger filling ornament (e.g. on **150***), or are driven into a corner (e.g. on **202**). Sometimes they turn their heads backwards as if in surprise (**111***, **168*** and **275***); on one occasion a goose is pecking at a worm (**303***) and finally on **151***, the birds give the impression that they are courting.

Water-bird: This appears only once in front of the bull on the obverse of the Würzburg chalice (**236***). It is drawn wholly in outline with a long neck[70] turned backwards and the bill pecking at its feathers; the rear part of its body with the horizontal stripes is identical to that of the goose; the front part is flecked. It bears some resemblance to the bird on **123** where only the back part is shown, but has no stylistic affinities with other birds appearing in Chian vase painting either earlier, as on the Geometric bird-bowls and -oenochoai and on the Middle I bull vase from Emporio (**310***) and **318–9**, or later, as the partridge on a Grand style chalice (**777***).

C. HYBRIDS

Sphinx (FIG. 22) : The winged female sphinx is the type used in Chian Wild Goat and in the styles of the sixth century.[71] It occurs only three times in two variations and quite late in the Middle II phase. After the turn of the century, together with the lion it becomes the most favourite motif in the reserving animal styles—as well as in the Sphinx and Lion— and continues on the group of the simple figure chalices even beyond the middle of the sixth century. The earlier type is that which appears on the inside of the Aphrodite bowl (**252***), unfortunately having lost its face. The body is drawn exactly as that of the lion on the same vase. The face must have been in outline as the preserved neck and all other later fragmentary depictions dictate; the spiral seems to start from rather low at the back of the head and ends in a hook. The wings are divided into three registers; that nearest to the neck consists of a sickle-shaped feather in silhouette, outlined with a reserved line and then followed by two registers again in outline, patterned with stripes; the outer one is strongly curved. The sphinx is walking with all four legs showing. This is the common Chian type which recurs in the repertory throughout all the subsequent styles. But whereas this sphinx is walking to the left, a direction which becomes standard for the creature, her antecedents prefer to squat or crouch; only few walk. Another specimen in the Middle II Wild Goat portrays a somewhat debased sphinx (**302***), whose upper part and head have been preserved; she follows the trend set by the Aphrodite sphinx and approximates to the southern East Greek type in the modelling of the hair as a wig. The omission here of the middle register in the wing is wholly a stylistic compromise due to hasty drawing: a habit which will continue henceforth.

For the second type of sphinx, **280*** shows the upper part and head with her left raised foreleg resting on the floral in front of her. The difference lies in the treatment of the outer

---

[70] It is not long-legged as Price thought in Price 212.
[71] N.M. Verdelis, L'apparition du Sphinx dans l'art grec in *BCH* 75, 1951, 11–13. See also, A. Dessenne, *Le Sphinx, Etude Iconographique*, 1957, 199 ff and P. Bosana-Kourou, *The Sphinx in Early Archaic Greek Art*, (D. Phil., Oxford 1979) 94 ff.

THE WILD GOAT STYLE

Fig. 22 Sphinxes

wing which is now strongly curved upwards and consists of dark bands alternating with reserved lines. This sphinx heads to the right and she might indeed be part of an antithetical composition.

In the renovated animal style the creature is very common, second only to the lion. The Aphrodite bowl type has been established with but minor alterations, the principal of which are that the legs, including the lower part and paws, are in full silhouette and the dotted stripe on the belly is generally but not always abandoned. The wig-like coiffure is extremely rare, as on **459***, and the usual rendering is either in a solid mass with undulating edges on the face and neck in which case they usually wear a stephane (**559***), or in straight locks reaching but never overlapping the wing (**492***). The face in outline is that of a woman with almond eyes, eye-brows and ears, occasionally the lobe is covered with an earring.

A completely different type is demonstrated on **462*** and **582***. It is icongraphically very close to the Early Protoattic type.[72] The remnants of the Chian sphinxes have in common with the Protoattic ones the body in silhouette, the claws in outline and the single, slender and sickle wing, here dotted, whereas in Early Protoattic it is scale-patterned. These common traits—though the Protoattic are separated from the Chian examples by about a century—make the Chian specimens look like direct descendants.

The single dotted wing reappears on a most elaborately drawn sphinx[73] (**552***) with an exquisite coiffure falling in three wavy locks on the neck *and* wing; a row of saw-edged tresses ends on the forehead and facial details—eye and eye-brow in particular – are drawn twice.[74] The sphinx wears a stephane and the spiral emerges upright from the middle of the head.

A unique example of a helmeted sphinx is perhaps shown on **419***, although the decoration is much worn.[75] The head in particular is badly damaged and it would be precarious to venture any connection with the much earlier Attic and Cretan sphinxes,[76] which are completely different. This iconographical type, whose very existence is uncertain, is not repeated.

Sphinxes in the group of the simple figure chalices have retained the essentials of the species, that is the wing is always divided into an inner and an outer register, of which the latter is sickle-like in outline and striped. Occasionally the dotted line on the belly reappears on very late examples, e.g. on **938***.

The spiral seen on Chian sphinxes is never omitted.[77]

The principal stances are two:

a) The walking one which is early and then recurs on very late examples; it occurs with the sphinx of the Aphrodite bowl (**252***), continues on rare examples on the animal chalices (**462***, **487**, **488*** and **492***) and finds favour with the vase painter in the last stages of the reserving styles. In this phase it is not clear whether the sphinx is walking or merely standing stupefied;[78] however all four legs are shown.

b) The squatting one—sitting upright on her haunches with forelegs almost at a right angle and the head raised (sphinx séjant) is most characteristic of the Chian sphinx and is attested from the beginning of the sixth century in all the categories of the reserving technique. The examples are numerous: typical are **440*** for the Animal Chalice style and **822*** for the Chalice style. The pose in which she stretches out her forelegs, as befitting a feline ready to attack, is not encountered in Chian, although it appears occasionally in the schools of other East Greek centres.[79] In brief, Chian vase painting does not display the variety of poses of other schools.

Sphinxes are disposed either in processional composition, as on **440***, **552***, **615*** and many others, or antithetical, as on **458***, **470***, **901***, **910***, **927***, **928***, **968** and many

---

[72] *BSA* 35, 1934–5, 172–3, pl. 40a (Analatos painter) and 177, and note 2, pl. 46b (Mesogeia painter).

[73] I think it is a sphinx and not a siren.

[74] Either by mistake or more possibly by accident during the firing of the vase.

[75] The drawing in *Emporio*, fig. 106, shows clearly a helmet.

[76] *BSA* 56, 1961, 80 and especially note 26.

[77] Price, 213; P. Amandry in *BCH* 77, 1962, 54.

[78] Examples: **846***, **847***, **859**, **924***, **938***, **965***. There may be others still, but being fragments their inclusion is uncertain.

[79] Cf. Kardara, *Rhodiake*, 107, fig. 119.

Fig. 23 Siren, Griffen and ? Chimaera

others. They rarely mix with other animals—an example is **252*** —and in the group of the simple figure chalices (**938*** or **973***) they are set solitary in the field.

A fact much remarked on is that Chian sphinxes invariably face left. In other centres there is no rigid rule. Now, Chian lions always face right. It is possible that lions entered the repertory earlier than sphinxes. If lions were imported into Chian pottery from representations in another, perishable, medium it is possible that their pose was imported as well. If the sphinx was added late, its pose, antithetical to the lion's, could have been chosen originally for purely decorative reasons and then subsequently fixed in the tradition. This practice of facing left continued throughout Chian figurative drawing in all techniques[80] and was taken up also in the coins of the island with the emblem of a sphinx[81] from the middle of the sixth century onwards.

Siren (FIG. 23): This exists in the reserving Chian styles though unfrequently.[82] Sirens are drawn on an almost intact vase (**675***)[83] and on seven badly mutilated fragments (**?366**, **478**, **479**, **493***, **554***, **555***, **567***). The siren on the Pitane chalice (**675***) has the hair, outer wing and legs in silhouette whereas the face and neck are in outline; the body is covered with a scale pattern and the sickle-shaped inner wing is striped; the tail is drawn with bands of alternating black paint and blank spaces. The long hair is in a solid mass and the spiral is curling. The scaly body is a characteristic feature of the Chian siren which, however, is used in the Cycladic school[84] as well and might have been of an eastern origin.[85] The pose is either standing or walking with both legs shown. It is a motif that

---

[80] I do not think that this is the rule in other East Greek schools; however, the difference in shapes, mostly oenochoai and plates, might have dictated the posture there.

[81] E. Babelon, *Traité des Monnaies grecques et romaines*, 1907, Vol. I. 2, 295–302 and pl. 12.1–9 and C.M. Kraay, *Archaic and Classical Greek Coins*, 1976, 30, 35, 242–3 and pls. 2.37 and 4.91; however on pl. 3.72, a stater of electrum of around 550 B.C., the sphinx faces right.

[82] Cf. Price 213, thought that sirens occurred only in the black-figure technique.

[83] There must have been a second siren in a processional rather than an antithetical composition, to judge by the lions on the other side of the vase. The side with the sirens is the obverse of the vase; however, the reverse side with the lions faces the visitors of the Bergama Museum. The side with the sirens is badly damaged and a large part is missing; in addition it was placed very near the wall and so not much could be made out.

[84] On some Parian amphorae of the seventh century the body is identical. For example the "Melian" amphora 1287 (59) from Rheneia in *AM* 57, 1931, Beilage 31. See also, Ph. Zapheiropoulou, *Provlemata tes Meliakes Angeiographias*, 1985, 60, pl. 55 and colour plate.

[85] *AM* 57, 1932, 123. Ivory reliefs such as the siren from Ephesos (fig. 2) might have been the source of inspiration for Chian vase painters. Sirens in general come late in the other East Greek schools as well and this might be another instance of vase painting borrowing from other media.

enters the Chian animal style late, appearing in the early chalices of the sixth century but is not encountered in other categories of the reserving technique. In the black-figure categories it is more frequent in the Sphinx and Lion and appears also in the black-figure Grand style.

Griffin (FIG. 23): The hybrid, though certainly rare, exists[86] on three fragments, **218***, **437** and **456***. Body and neck are in silhouette; head, lower part of the forelegs with paws and part of the wing are in outline; a reserved line delineates the contour of the front wing; another line—dotted—runs along the belly and a third on the haunches. Added red is applied in large patches all over the body, wing and neck. The sickle-shaped wing is half reserved and half alternating in red semi-circular stripes. The neck tendril is rendered with a reserved spiral. The forehead knob consists of a circle and then a cross bending forwards, all in silhouette. The type is similar to that of the Southern schools and most probably derives from the bronze protomes decorating cauldrons,[87] which were frequent in the East Greek centres, especially in the Heraion of Samos[88] and not uncommon in the Chian sanctuaries.[89] The type of the cauldrons, that is the eagle-headed hybrid with an open beak, originated in the East.[90]

Of the fragments only part of the open beak has remained, on **218*** and **437** and part of the face on **456***. As regards stances nothing can be said with such scrappy material; the squatting pose is the more probable as is the case with its counterparts on the shoulder frieze of other East Greek oenochoai.[91] It seems that the griffin too enters the Chian repertory late;[92] though perhaps not as late as the sirens. Griffins are not encountered in other categories of the reserving styles or in Chian black figure.

Chimaera? (FIG. 23): On **384*** this mythological creature may be depicted. The remnants give the impression that this is so for the following three reasons: first, the reserved horizontal line on top of the body could be the line separating the goat neck and head from the rest of the creature; secondly, the horn reaches further left than the middle of the body and, thirdly, one thigh is drawn heavily as if implying that of a lion whereas the inner is the thin canonical goat leg. Unfortunately, only the beginning of the tail has been preserved which would have assured the animal's identity. However, these oddities could be merely due to a whimsical peculiarity or the painter's incompetence.[93]

---

[86] Cf. Price 213; P. Amandry in *AM* 77, 1962, 57 and note 138 thought of Price, fig. 31, as Chian, which now is classified as North Ionian, see *Samos* VI.1, pl. 121.983.

[87] *GO³* 67 where it is stated that certain types of bronze griffins as cauldron attachments developed in Greece.

[88] Jantzen, *Griechische Greifenkessel*, 1958, passim and *AM* 73, 1958, 26 ff.

[89] Up to now there are three: one griffin's ear from Emporio in *Emporio*, 224–5 and two protomes from Phana in *ADelt* 1, 1915, 76, fig. 13 and *BSA* 35, 1934–5, pl. 31.38.

[90] B. Goldman in *AJA* 64, 1960, 32–3 derives the creature with open beak from the Assyrian roaring lion which appears in the West on the cauldrons.

[91] The nearest would be the griffin on the Izmir oenochoe 3333, Akurgal, *Alt-Smyrna* I, 1983, 48, pls. 38–9 and Text-plates B and C.

[92] With the exception of the chalice fragment, **218***, which is black and undecorated in the inside.

[93] Chimaeras are extremely rare in the Southern Schools as well. Very late examples of the motif in *Samos* VI.1, pls. 133.1070 and 135.1082.

D. COMPOSITION

The order of the composition has already been mentioned in the relevant paragraphs on each single motif; almost always it is either processional or antithetical. The latter might not be as frequent as the former, although both seem to start contemporaneously. However, the antithetical composition continues in later use in the Chian reserving styles, in a group that is dated to around the beginning of the second quarter of the sixth century.[94] A third composition or stance is the back to back: much less common than the others, it appears towards the end of the seventh century, on the reverse of the Delos chalice (**643***).

The recently found fragmentary chalice from the Samian Heraion (**247***) with a lion and a fox or vixen flanking a primitive floral on the handle zone is exceptional and unique so far.[95] This decoration could indicate an early date, perhaps even Early or Middle I Wild Goat, as the drawing of animals and ornaments suggest.

The disposition in panels on the walls appears in Chian Wild Goat of the Middle II phase both on chalices and oenochoai. On chalice **114*** both front and back of the vase are divided into three panels and this seems to be an early feature; on **236***, **237***, **240**, **241**, **242** and **?245** one panel occupies each side and seems to be a later fashion, though still within Middle II. Panels appear also on oenochoai shoulders (**324*** and **340***) framed by inverted rays; the upper frieze of the belly bears the figurative, whereas the lower the ornamental decoration—usually a flower-and-bud frieze, which is a practice frequent on other East Greek oenochoai. On account of the fragmentary state of the material it is not possible to know the number of panels on all chalices, only that "metope" decoration certainly existed widely.[96] It is evident that the metope system fitted the seventh-century squat chalice to which it was aesthetically most suited. Apart from chalices in the transitional stage, as **624***, the renovating style abandons this system of decoration. On the sixth-century chalices the whole circumference of the vase is conceived as an unbroken unity to which the decoration is applied.

Finally, on the dinos (**303***) a frieze rather than a metope occupies the upper part of the vessel, just below the rim; it is divided by the handles. This is a late and isolated example which probably does not represent the norm. **282***, **283** and **285**—if indeed they are from dinoi—would indicate that the disposition was usually in three or even four friezes.

E. ORNAMENTS

Ornaments in the reserving styles of both seventh- and sixth-century Chian figurative pottery are, like animals and birds, considered only here (FIGS. 24–40). They comprise the two interwoven strands of "floral" and "geometric" patterns.[97]

---

[94] The group of antithetical sphinxes: **927***–**928***, **968** and **953**–**955** and a few fragments.

[95] Kyrieleis in *Chios Conference*, 192 and fig. 4.

[96] **127***, **132***, **133***, **140***, **145***, **146***, **147***, **156***, **158***, **159***, **160***, **167***, **178**, **179**, **180**, **181**, **187**, **195**, **202**, **203** and **210**.

[97] "Floral" and "geometric" correspond respectively to R.M. Cook's "vegetable" and "abstract". For Chian ornamental decoration see Homann-Wedeking, *Vasenornamentik*, 27–30.

The following classification is heavily influenced by the predominance of the chalice shape and certain formulae dictated by it. In fact the chalice per se creates the first two distinctive categories; as for the others they are mainly, yet not wholly, encountered on the same vase. In a few instances certain ornaments occur in two categories:

1. Rim patterns　　　　　　　on chalices　　　　　(FIGS. 24–25)
2. Handle zone patterns　　　on chalices　　　　　(FIGS. 26–27)
3. Friezes with floral or　　　a) on chalices　　　　(FIG. 28)
　　pattern decoration
　　　　　　　　　　　　　　b) on all shapes　　　(FIG. 28)
4. Framing ornaments　　　　a) on chalices　　　　(FIG. 29)
　　　　　　　　　　　　　　b) on other shapes　　(FIG. 30)
5. Florals　　　　　　　　　　　　　　　　　　　(FIGS. 31–32)
6. Filling ornaments　　　　　a) Pendants:
　　　　　　　　　　　　　　　1. Triangles　　　　(FIGS. 33–34)
　　　　　　　　　　　　　　　2. Roundels　　　　 (FIG. 35)
　　　　　　　　　　　　　　　3. Corner Ornaments (FIG. 36)
　　　　　　　　　　　　　　b) Field Ornaments　　(FIGS. 37–40)

1. Rim Patterns (FIGS. 24–25): Rim patterns of the Wild Goat style and its sixth-century descendants have been set out on FIGS. 24–25. The vast range of fundamentally the same patterns, either with slight variations or placed in different positions and combinations, is obvious at first sight.

Three basic remarks may be made. First, there is continuity between the end of Middle II phase and the following period. On Animal Chalices of the later stage a simplification of patterns (these are mainly collected on FIG. 47) is demonstrated, but others of the same date have heavy and complicated designs. In short, it is not safe to distinguish between early and late simply from the complexity of the rim pattern. Secondly, the meander is the most favourite pattern followed by battlement, tongue, guilloche, astragal and zigzags. Thirdly, the meander in Chian pottery, as is clearly demonstrated in the drawings, is almost always[98] running to the left.

Type 1:　　billets or dots in a row, not always discernible.
Type 1a:　 the same with billets alternating with dotted blanks.
Type 2:　　paired hook meander: simple variety.
Type 3:　　simple broken meander.
Type 4:　　billets above paired hook meander: simple variety.
Type 5:　　billets alternating with dotted blanks above simple broken meander between two lines.
Type 6:　　simple broken meander,
　　　　　　below: billets alternating with blank filled with squares.
Type 7:　　paired hook meander: simple variety between two lines.
Type 8:　　paired hook meander between lines.

---

[98] Types 22 and 23 do not count as the design dictates the direction.

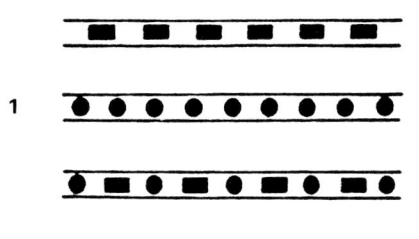

Fig. 24   Rim Patterns

Type 9:   billets alternating with dotted blanks,
            below: paired hook meander: simple variety.
Type 10:   diagonal strokes to the right between lines,
            below: paired hook meander.
Type 11:   vertical strokes between lines,
            below: paired hook meander: double variety.
Type 12:   billets alternating with dotted blanks,
            below: double broken meander.
Type 13:   paired hook meander: simple variety,
            below: smaller alternating with larger dots.
Type 14:   paired hook meander: simple variety,
            below: billets alternating with dotted blanks.
Type 15:   paired hook meander: simple variety,
            below: solid tongues outlined.
Type 16:   meander running left.
Type 17:   billets,
            below: meander running left between two parallel lines.
Type 18:   billets,
            below: meander running left between lines.
Type 19:   billets, alternating with dotted blanks,
            below: double meander running left beween lines.
Type 20:   billets,
            below: double meander running left, and then: billets alternating with dotted blanks.
Type 21:   billets alternating with dotted blanks,
            below: double meander running left, and then: billets alternating with dotted blanks.
Type 22:   billets,
            below: groups of double meander facing alternately right and left with cross squares filled with squares.
Type 23:   billets alternating with dotted blanks,
            below: groups of meander facing alternately right and left with cross squares filled with squares.
Type 24:   diagonal strokes to the left,
            below: stopt meander
            and then: zigzag.
Type 25:   billets alternating with dotted blanks,
            below: stopt meander, and then: zigzag between two lines.
Type 26:   billets alternating with dotted blanks,
            below: stopt meander, and then: billets alternating with dotted blanks.
Type 27:   three parallel lines,
            below: solid tongues outlined, and then: blanks filled with squares.
Type 28:   zigzag between lines.
Type 29:   billets alternating with dotted blanks,
            below: dotted squares flanked by two lines.
Type 30:   guilloche between two lines.

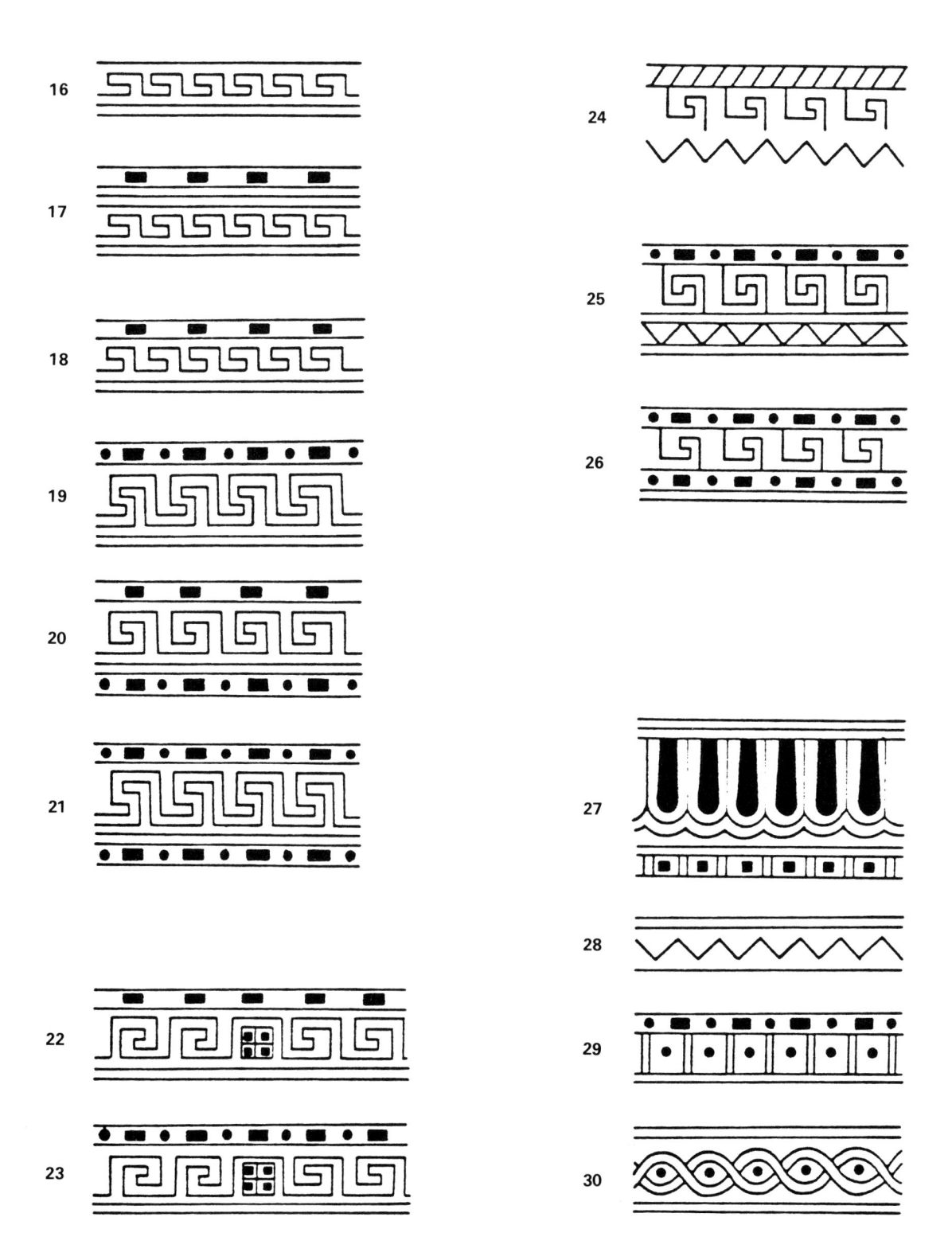

Fig. 25 Rim Patterns

2. Handle zone patterns (FIGS. 26–27): A restricted variety of patterns decorates the handle zone of chalices in the Wild Goat style and the chalices with filling ornaments, as is demonstrated on FIGS. 26–27. The double guilloche is by far the most favourite pattern. It is extremely frequent in the Middle II phase and continues in popularity both on Animal and the Grand style chalices. The side of the chalice decorated with the double guilloche is meant to be the obverse of the vase as can be deduced:

1. from the larger Würzburg chalice (**236***)—with bull and lion—and **114*** where the main decoration is placed above this pattern;
2. from the fact that this pattern is used very frequently on Grand style chalices and
3. because in the group of antithetical sphinxes (**927***–**928***, **954**–**955** and **968**) the double guilloche appears on the side of the main decoration, while a double meander below a simple rosette appears on the reverse.

The variations of the simple and triple guilloche are rare (FIG. 26); a little more frequent is the simple guilloche with eyes at the corner. Meanders show a wide variety (FIG. 26), most common of all is the triple meander running left. In chalices where the obverse is decorated with a double guilloche, almost unfailingly there is a double or triple meander on the other side.

Fig. 26 Handle zone patterns

c Dotted circles

Fig. 27 Handle zone patterns

Dotted circles (FIG. 27) in a row make up the handle zone pattern of a few late Middle II chalices uncovered both at Naucratis and Emporio, the latter in a simple variation. They always have tongues, mostly void and outlined, near the handle root.

3. Friezes with floral or pattern decoration (FIG. 28):
a) on chalices: The bowl of the squat Middle II Wild Goat chalice is always decorated with patterns of varying complexity. Three variations of basically the same ornaments are drawn on FIG. 28.1–3. They are all from intact chalices and are representative, as three fragments confirm.

1. The Emporio chalice (**114***) has a band of paired hook, simple, meander above a band of blanks filled with squares[99] placed between two broad dark bands and lines (FIG. 28.1).
2. The Würzburg chalices (**236***–**237***) and **246** have simpler decoration consisting of paired hook, simple, meander band between bands and lines (FIG. 28.2).
3. The Catane chalice (**624***) has the bowl decorated with bands of ss and meanders between bands and lines (FIG. 28.3). Late sixth-century chalices have usually only bands on the bowl, from three to six, according to the size of the vessel.

b) on all shapes: Rays are almost always placed at the base of both chalices[100] and oenochoai[101] (FIG. 28.b.2). Inverted rays are used as a decorative motif at the back metopes of **114*** (FIG. 28.b.1) where they might not have been the sole decoration.

Two types of lotus-and-bud are encountered in Chian:
1) the Middle II Wild Goat type[102] (FIG. 28.a.1), which is placed at the base of vases.[103] The well-known type with two outer and three inner outlined petals for the flower and two unified semi-petals for the bud sitting on circles and joined with tendrils; East Greek examples date from the last quarter of the seventh century which is an appropriate date for the Chian pieces as well.[104] This motif seems to replace the rays from c.625 BC as base decoration because the latter are not represented in Tarsus.[105] Rays start earlier and continue for much longer, being met on vases of the sixth century.

---

[99] Cf. Cook, *Claz. Sarc.*, fig. 53.8, calls them astragals.
[100] Examples on **136**, **137**, **189**, **236***, **237***, **246** and **624***.
[101] On **310*** and **327***.
[102] *GPP*² 122 fig. 19A.
[103] **114***, **124***, **134**, **138**, **190**, **192**, **215**, **342** and **375**.

[104] A debased version of inverted lotuses and buds, which is due to hasty execution, is shown on the two sides of the tripod bowl (**259***) and a late variant is the one that decorates the plate (**687**): (Drawing for the latter in *Samos* VI.1, 71, fig. 138).
[105] *Tarsus* III, 300; also Kardara in *AJA*, 59 1955, 49.

2) the Late Wild Goat type[106] (FIG. 28.a.2), which is definitely later, is rarely met on Chian. **338*** and **371*** are both from the late Wild Goat group from Rizari, and are most probably from the necks of oenochoai.

Finally, another ornament rarely met is the double guilloche on the neck of the Emporio oenochoe (**310*** and **350***) (FIG. 28.c).

Volutes with chevrons, solid triangles and solid or void lozenges in between, hastily drawn, form the unique floral pattern of the lower part of the dinos **303*** (FIG. 28.d).

4. Framing ornaments:
a) on chalices (FIG. 29): some of the more important framing ornaments on intact chalices have been drawn on FIG. 29. More fragments with framing ornaments exist which are so badly mutilated as not to allow a safe reconstruction. Those illustrated here are of the Middle II phase and belong to the group of the Würzburg chalices or are in their style. The ornaments framing the figurative "friezes" of the Würzburg chalices (1) are a complex consisting of four quadruple meanders juxtaposed in pairs and flanked by vertical rows of squares and dots on the inner edge and of paired hook, simple, meander on the outer.

The other types (2–8) are variations consisting of the same central meanders though differing in their direction and in the dividing bands.

The placement of the framing ornaments is invariably the same: above the handles of the squat chalices in the full Wild Goat style, thus providing for the separation of the figure-decoration into two "pictures" and covering the inevitable gap.

On **114*** vertical dividing bands, on the front side at least, create three "metopes".[107] These framing ornaments are abandoned later as the chalice shape changes and the "metope" system of decoration dies away; perhaps the last examples of this once fashionable decoration are **616*** and **696*** where the vertical dividing bands with ss are identical to the similar rim patterns.

b) on other shapes (FIG. 30): on the group of the Middle II open bowls (**252*–255***) and on the dinos (**284***) a continuous meander running left is placed above and below the figurative scene thus providing a frame for the "picture" (FIG. 30.a).

It is worth mentioning the flanking vertical rows of the Rizari oenochoe (**324***) which are similar to those on the Würzburg chalice, and the tongue pattern decorating the top of the picture, a derivative of the same vessels (FIG. 30.c.1 and 2).

Finally, several dinoi bear bands of squares and dots (**296***) (FIG. 30.b); meander (**284***) or tongues with dotted squares (**281*** and **295**) just below the rim. However others make do with a broad dark band (**274***, **303***, **304**), or merely with a line (**298***), from which the triangles are hanging, or even a loop pattern (**352**) (FIG. 30.c.3).

5. Florals (FIGS. 31 and 32): Individual florals decorate chalices, bowls and dinoi of the Middle II phase. On FIGS. 31 and 32 the surviving intact florals have been drawn together with some mutilated ones. The essential components of the Würzburg floral (FIG. 31.a.1) are the two juxtaposed pairs—the one on top of the other—of volutes with their outer band filled with dots. Above and below at the corners, two equilateral triangles are placed, subdivided into two smaller triangles and a lozenge, each filled with a dot. At the centre a

[106] *GPP*² 122 fig. 19C.   [107] See p. 43 on composition.

a Lotus-and-bud

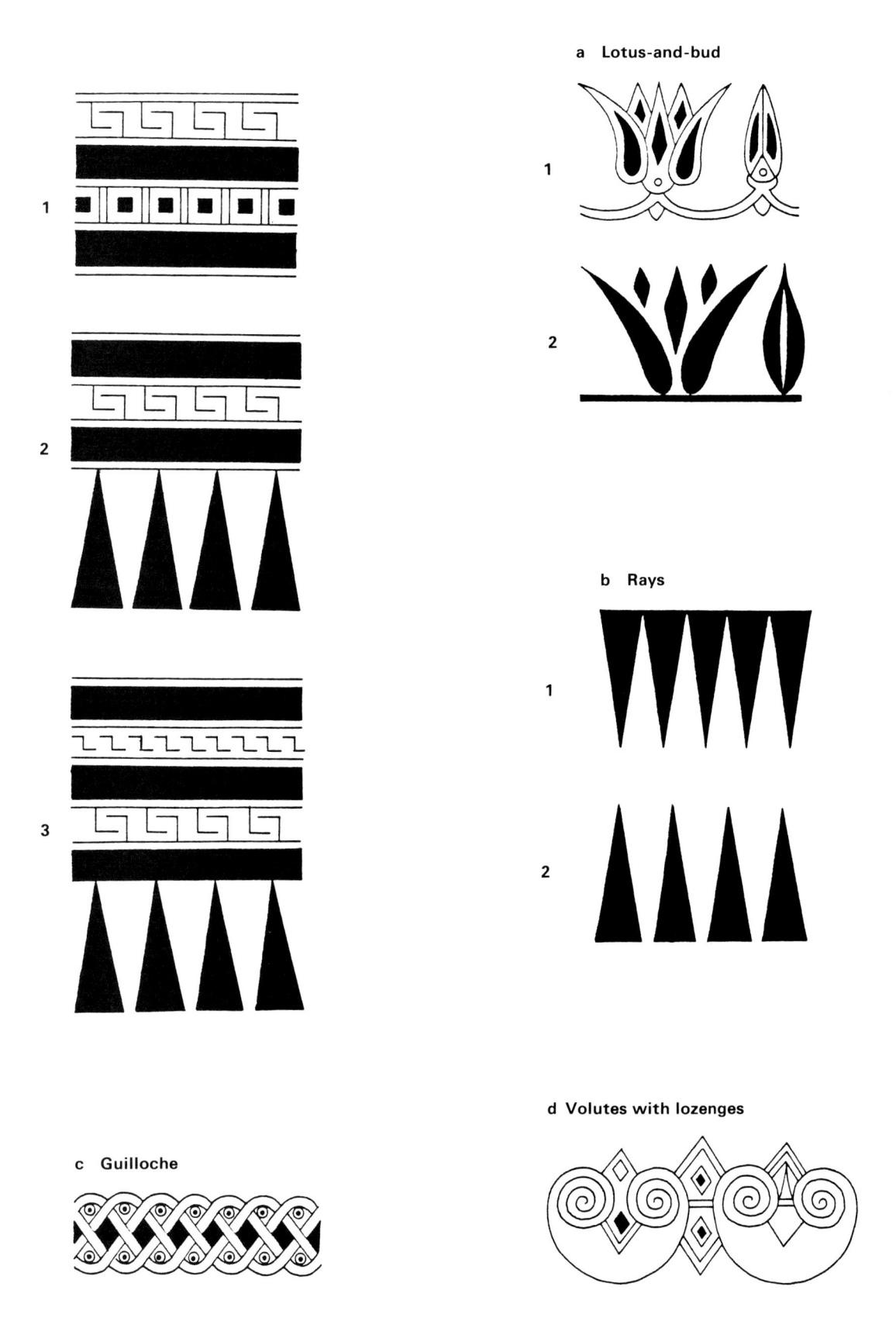

b Rays

c Guilloche

d Volutes with lozenges

Fig. 28 Friezes with floral or pattern decoration

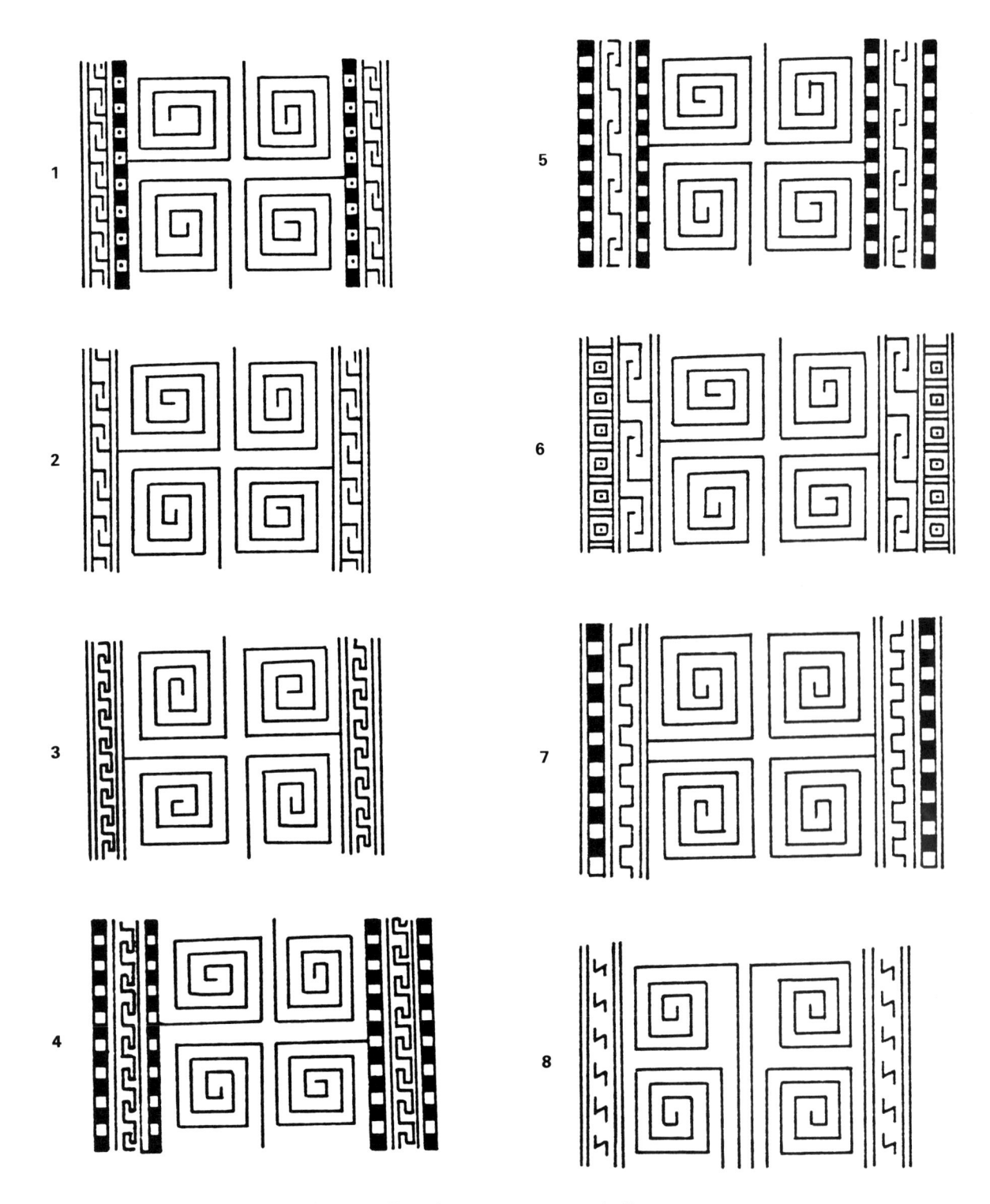

Fig. 29 Framing ornaments on chalices

a Open bowls

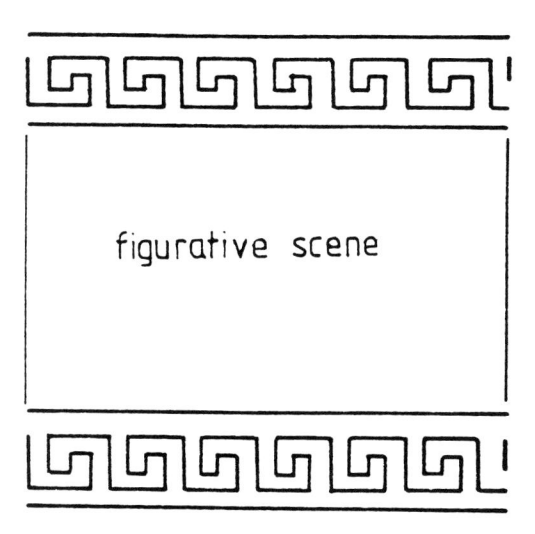

b Dinoi

c Oenochoai

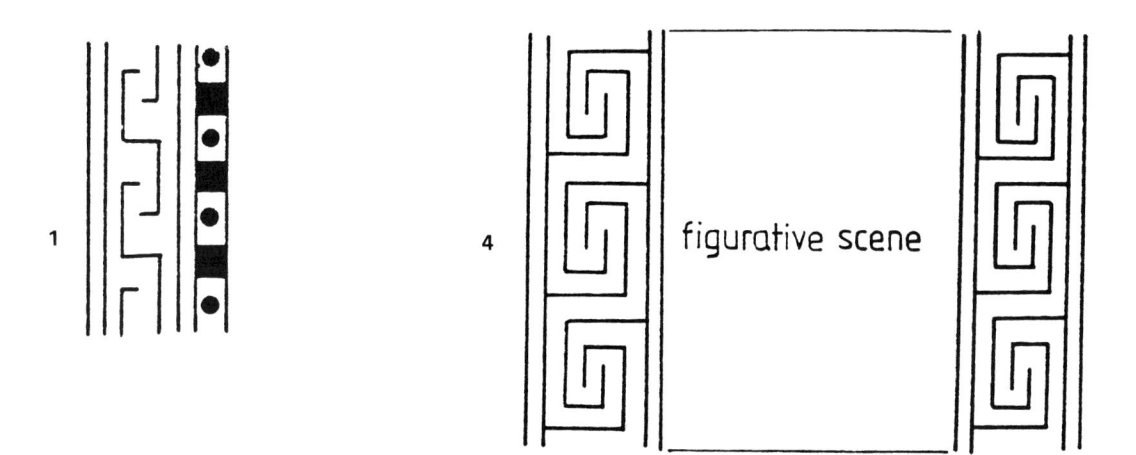

Fig. 30 Framing ornaments on other shapes

lozenge is drawn, subdivided into four smaller lozenges filled with dots. The two lateral corners are defined by a striped border within which are two horizontally disposed triangles again sub-divided into triangles, and lozenges. The florals of **219*** and a.2–4 on FIG. 31 are similar to the Würzburg one. Parallels to the Würzburg floral amongst Wild Goat style of other East Greek centres have already been discussed.[108] The tectonic form of the Würzburg floral originates in the antithetical compositions of Assyrian art and might have influenced the much later Fikellura handle ornaments and subsequently the Athenian Nicosthenic workshop.[109] However, it must be stressed that this, as well as other types of Chian florals, are restricted to the Middle II Wild Goat and do not recur on sixth-century painted vases.

Another type (FIG. 31.b.1) is that seen on the open bowl (**255***) and is composed of volutes—undoubtedly in a quadruple form—with palmettes filling up their wide-spreading angles. This type approximates to a pattern on a Samian crater[110] most closely and indicates that Chian vase painters were adapting decorative motifs from the wider repertoire of the southern East Greek centres. It is doubtful, however, whether in this particular aspect they had any influence on their Thasian colleagues.[111]

The floral (1) drawn out on FIG. 32 decorates the centre of the interior of **252***.[112] It consists of a central solid circle, outlined, out of which emerge eight, solid full buds also outlined; the circumference is closed by a band of tongues again outlined and solid. Then follows a circular band with white dotted rosettes, characteristically Chian, on the dark background. This is the earliest evidence for *the light on dark decoration* which later both occupies the outer surface of certain vases: chalices (**808*–813***) and a phiale mesomphalos (**814***), and forms the well-known interior decoration, again on open vases.

The floral at the base of **259*** is a quickly executed ornament with eleven solid petals and arched lines uniting them at the tips (FIG. 32.2).

Finally, the central floral on the dinos (**303***) consists of two flowers and one bud of inverted lotuses; they are unique in Chian and look, as does the whole decoration, like the cursory work of an incompetent artisan; in particular the inner petals of the lotus-flower are schematic (FIG. 32.3).

6. Filling ornaments (FIGS. 33–40): For convenience the filling ornaments in the Wild Goat and Animal chalice style have been divided into: A. PENDANTS: Triangles, Roundels and Corner Ornaments (FIGS. 33–36), and B. FIELD ORNAMENTS (FIGS. 37–40).

A. PENDANTS (FIGS. 33–36)

1. Triangles (FIGS. 33 and 34): Their variety is obvious. The triangle is subdivided, usually by two lines into two nearly equilateral smaller triangles and a lozenge which is twice their size. To the basic pattern, painters enjoyed adding or removing lines, solid or void triangles and lozenges, and dots or rings to the apex. The triangles hanging from the upper border (FIG. 33) are more frequently found and demonstrate a slightly wider range of designs than those standing on the lower border (FIG. 34). More than one variation can be used for the

[108] Schiering, *Werkstätten*, 72, Beil. 8.4; also *Samos* VI.1.72 with the Levy-oenochoe (*Samos* V, pl. 117.592) and still closer to the Samian crater (*Samos* V, pl. 105.556).
[109] See Jackson, *East Greek Influence*, 41.
[110] *Samos* V, pl. 105.556.
[111] *Samos* VI.1, 85 where similarities are drawn.
[112] Drawing also in *Samos* VI.1, 72, fig. 139. Fig. 141 is certainly not Chian and it is doubtful whether fig. 140 is.

THE WILD GOAT STYLE

a Chalices

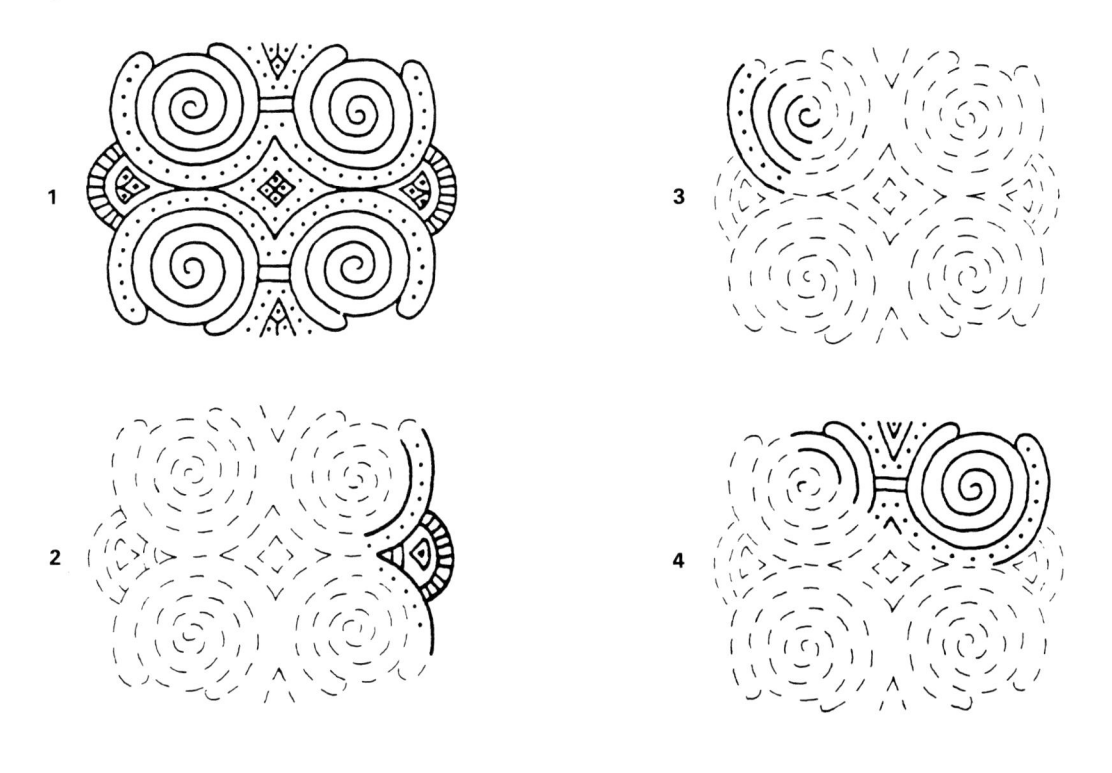

b Open bowls

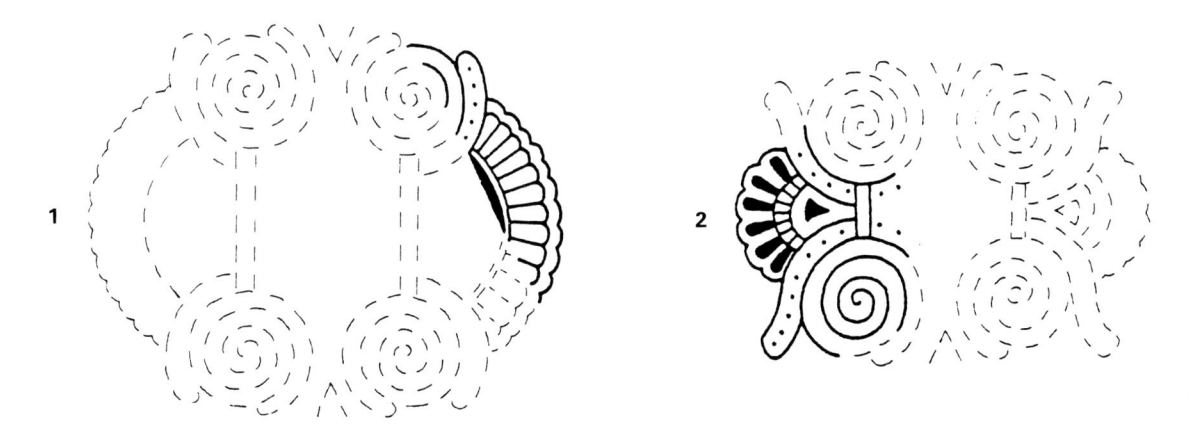

Fig. 31 Florals on chalices and open bowls

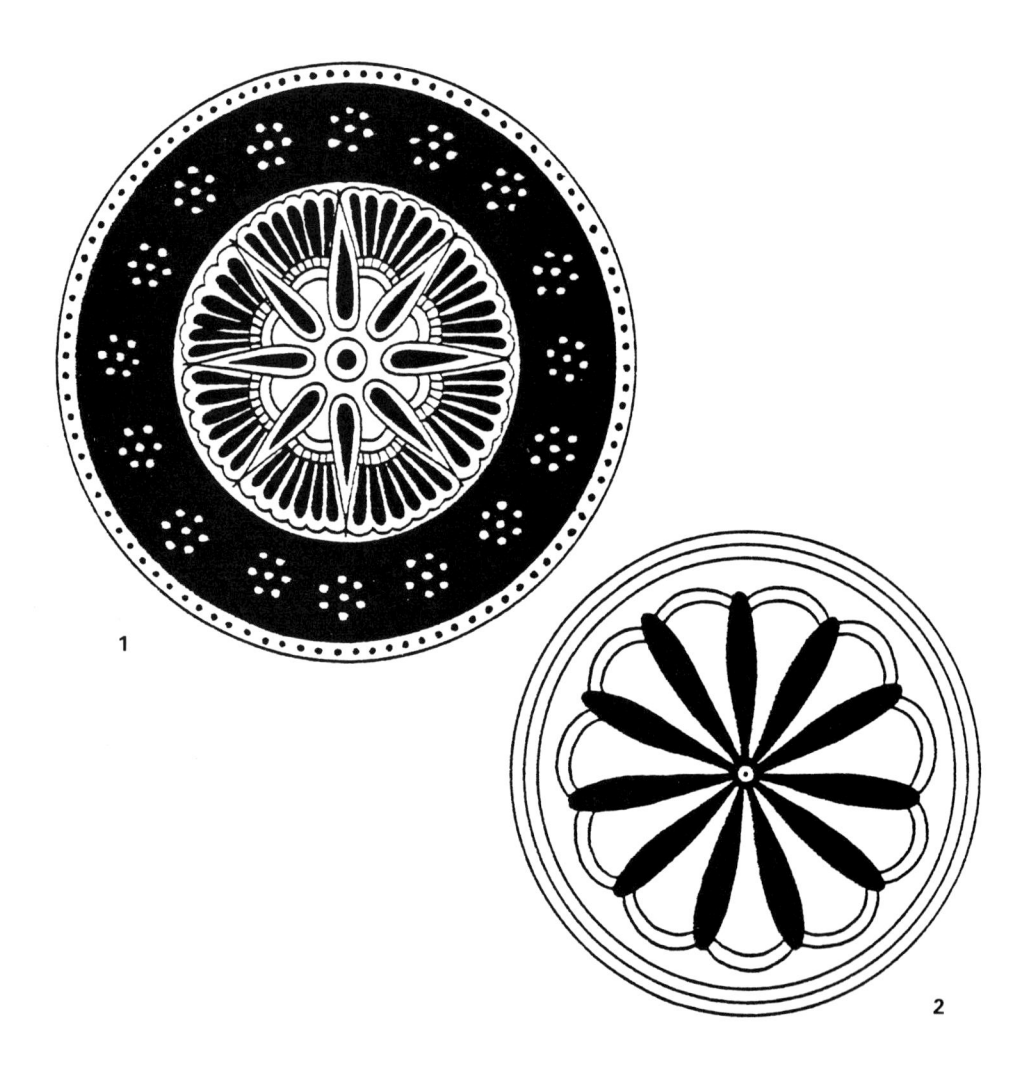

Fig. 32   Florals on bowls and on the dinos from Gela

Fig. 33　Filling ornaments: Pendants – triangles

Fig. 34 Filling ornaments: Pendants – triangles

decoration of the same vase, e.g. the smaller Würzburg chalice (**237***) bears four different variants; others make do with two or three. The practice of placing upright triangles below the *forelegs* of a wild goat in the Middle II phase[113] is perhaps in reaction to a more haphazard approach seen on earlier Chian vases[114] and in other East Greek schools at the same time.[115]

2. Roundels (FIG. 35): This is a less numerous and less varied ornament form than the triangle in Chian, although in other East Greek schools the situation is reversed.[116] In Chian, by far the commonest type is the horseshoe, both hanging and standing which consists of a solid tongue with an arched contour, always striped. On certain vases of exquisite drawing this horseshoe roundel gives the impression of a tear-drop ready to fall.[117] It is one of the principal features of Chian Middle II Wild Goat and futhermore of the school as a whole. Variants place either another or even two or three arched lines between the tongue and the outlining contour; instead of the tongue may be found a line topped by a dotted circle. None, however, has the finesse of the horseshoe type. Size may vary as well. It is rare for more than one type to be displayed on the same vase (**236***). The norm during the Chian Middle II is to place roundels below the *hindlegs* of wild goats. They gradually diminish on the later Animal Chalice style. Roundels with festooned contours are depicted on few vases: on **303*** (with a similar corner ornament), **310*** and **312**. It cannot be safely said by this criterion alone whether a vase is early or late.[118]

Roundels perhaps appear slightly later than triangles in Chian Wild Goat, as the latter are widely known to Greek art long before the Wild Goat style comes into being. Further, on the Aegina plate, (**264***), roundels are absent; nevertheless this is an isolated example. In the following group of Middle I roundels are attested in a most complex form.

Both roundels and triangles faded away simultaneously at the end of the Animal Chalice style.

3. Corner Ornaments (FIG. 36): These follow in structure the roundels and are used to fill up the corners; they mostly hang from the upper border. The core of the type consists of a triangle of simple or complex form, which is subdivided into smaller ones; the perimeter is flanked by simple lines, striped bands or even small solid tongues outlined. Needless to say corner ornaments are only appropriate to Middle II chalices with the "metope" compositions.

B. FIELD ORNAMENTS (FIGS. 37–40)

The field ornaments of the Aegina dish (**264***) and the group of Middle I oenochoai and dinoi from Emporio, have been drawn on FIGS. 37 and 38. The constant preference of Chians for two ornaments: **the swastika** and **the dotted concentric circles** is perceptible at first glance.[119]

---

[113] See p. 26; examples **124***, **236***, **237***, **252***, **324*** and others.

[114] The Emporio dinos (**274***); however on the oenochoe (**310***) they are placed haphazardly.

[115] Kardara, *Rhodiake*, 166.

[116] Kardara, *Rhodiake*, 169.

[117] There are also late examples of this type, e.g. the Emporio plate, **684***.

[118] Kardara who tackles the matter with more substantial material opposes Kinch's view, see Kardara *Rhodiake*, 167–8.

[119] Price 210, calls it "the rosette with double outline" and states that it is "by far the most common" ornament.

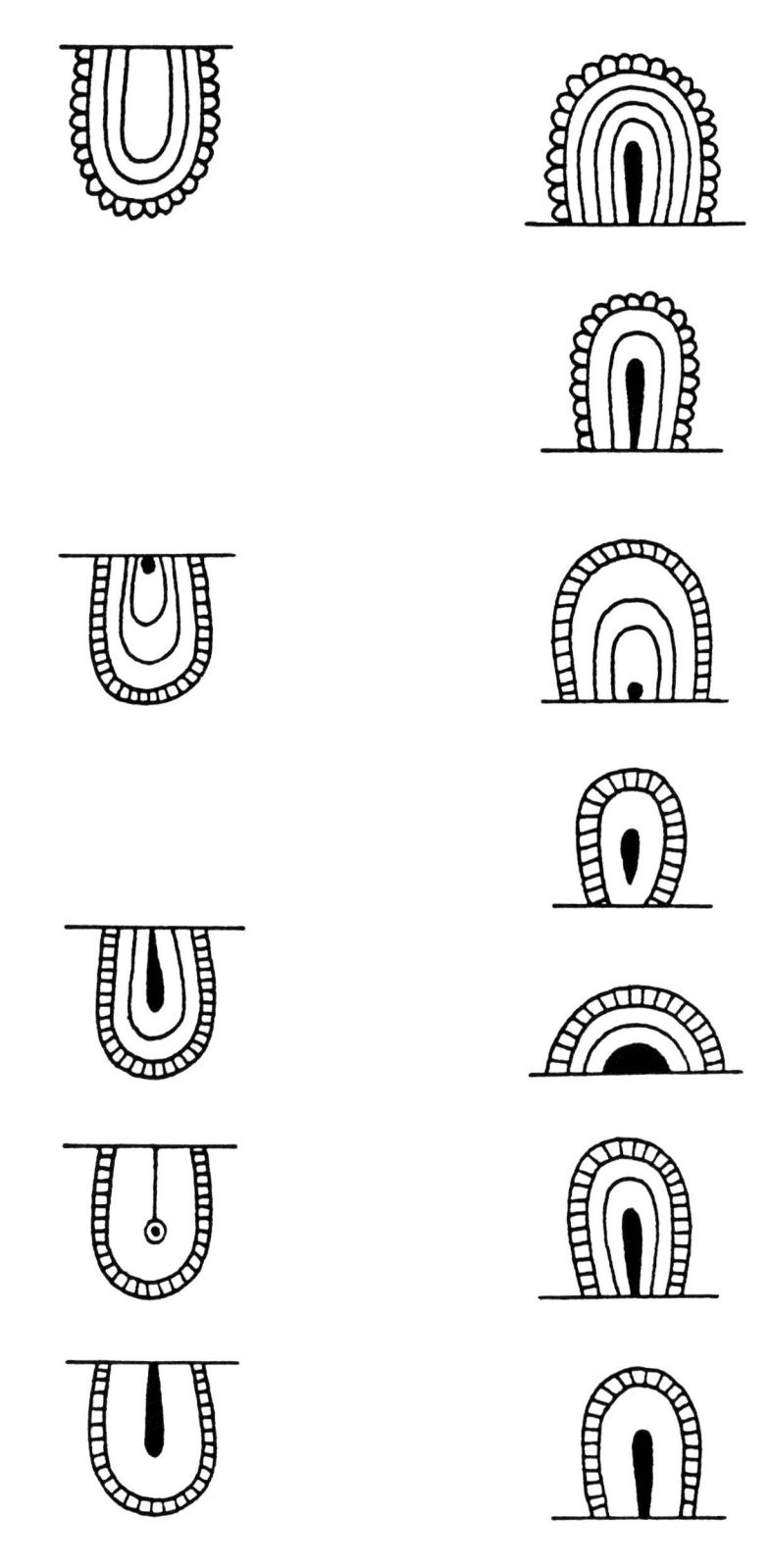

Fig. 35 Filling ornaments: Pendants – roundels

THE WILD GOAT STYLE

Fig. 36 Filling ornaments: Pendants – Corner ornaments

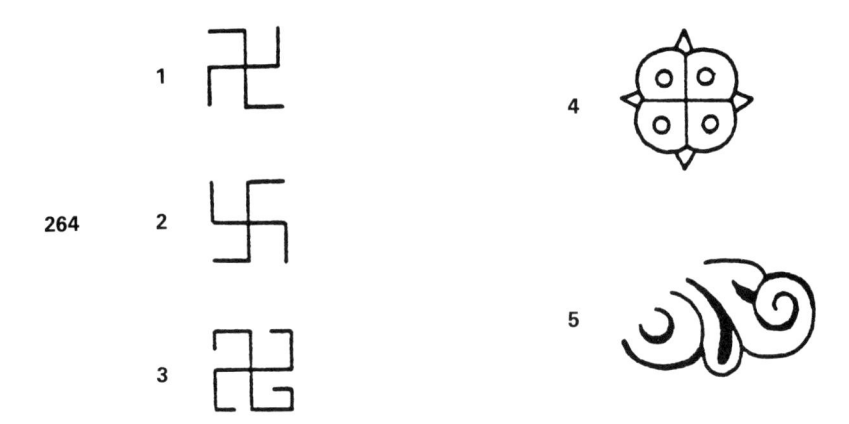

Fig. 37 Field ornaments on the Aegina plate

A few remarks on these relatively early pieces may be made:

1) **swastikas** appear from the start, inherited from the previous Late Geometric style, and remain common throughout in all forms from the simpler to the most complex. In addition swastikas with rounded edges and spikes appear in the Middle I.

2) The Aegina **volute complex**, (5) on FIG. 37, is not encountered again in Chian but is bequeathed to the North Ionian workshops;[120] it holds the same position there too, below the belly of animals, giving the impression that it may have some representational significance—perhaps the animals are jumping over an obstacle.

3) **The concentric circles ringed with inverted TT**, (4) on FIG. 38, in Middle I is common enough, but this specific form is not repeated thereafter.

The field ornaments of the Early and Middle I stages are slightly less densely positioned than those in Middle II, their range is more selective and their disposition better and more precisely judged.

Middle II Wild Goat field ornaments have been drawn on FIGS. 39 and 40.

A variety of **dotted rosettes and concentric circles** (FIG. 39 right) dominates and their constant use makes them the most favourite Chian ornaments—together with the swastikas. They have links with other Chian styles, e.g. the light-on-dark polychrome decoration, and indicate a Chian identity for the Emporio bull vase (**310***), where one decorates its forehead. **Crosses of simple and complex forms** (FIG. 39 left) are common and of great variety. The simple dotted cross is the most frequent; **the complex cross** appears on fragments of very fine drawing at the peak of the style. This form packs the later vases of the London Dinos workshop[121] and must have been taken over from Chian Middle II. It might be via Aeolian that it continued later in the Clazomenian

---

[120] Examples on North Ionian oenochoai in *Samos* VI.1, pls. 105.877, 879; 106.881, 882; 108.899, 901.
[121] Schiering, *Werkstätten* 37ff (Rhodian of the Vlastos group); Kardara, *Rhodiake* 271ff (Late Rhodian I); Äol. Kunst, 3ff and *Samos* VI.1, 88 (Aeolian); Cook, *Claz. Sarc.* 106 and note 67.

Fig. 38 Field ornaments on Middle I Wild Goat style vases

Sarcophagi workshops.[122] **Lozenges** are somewhat less common than **swastikas**. The **complex swastika** with edges indiscriminately arranged to right or left is one of the more, if not the most, favoured ornament. Now too the **spiked swastikas with rounded angles** (FIG. 40 bottom left) win favour with the vase painters and, though encountered in the Southern schools,[123] became a characteristically Chian ornament discernible by its slenderness and finesse. **Circles enrolled in crosses** (FIG. 40 middle) display a vast variety and start very early, occuring on the Aegina Plate (4 on FIG. 37) and continuing down to the end of Animal Chalice style. **Complex rosettes**, (FIG. 40 right) are shared with other Wild Goat schools. One variation, however, namely the rosette with petals alternately in dark and light—whether eight or six, with or without spikes at the corners—is an entirely Chian creation. **The complex form with triangles, circles, spikes** (FIG. 40, bottom right), by its size—c. 0.03 m—and its disposition, can be better classified as a filling ornament and not as an individual floral.

These same and related field ornaments continue into the Animal Chalice style of the sixth century (FIG. 48; with rim patterns on FIG. 47); vase painters are now more

[122] Cook, *Claz. Sarc.*, 107, believes that the Clazomenian Sarcophagi painters were mainly influenced by other media, as at the time no unified Wild Goat was in practice; this view does not exclude the possibility that they could pick up isolated patterns or ornaments from here and there in the preceding pottery styles of East Greece.
[123] Schiering, *Werkstätten*, Beil. 1, 2 and 3.

parsimonious with them. However, there are exceptions. **Concentric circles with spikes** and **rosettes with or without spikes** (FIG. 48, left) are now more common; whilst **circles enrolled in crosses** (FIG. 48, right of centre) continue to exist. **Enrolled crosses** reappear, usually with circles at their corners or sometimes with the omission of the cross (FIG. 48, bottom of the second column from left). The earlier **Würzburg rosette** (FIG. 48, penultimate in the right column) gives way to the new form of **multi-petal rosette** (FIG. 48, sixth in the right column), which occurs only once so far, on the Catane chalice (**624***).

Field ornaments follow the general trend and character of Wild Goat in that they differ but slightly from those employed at other Greek centres. Chian ornaments display the same finesse and elegance in the execution of drawing as do the figures.

Many scholarly opinions have been expressed over the years on the significance and interpretation of the filling ornaments on Orientalizing and Early Archaic pottery. Of the two most prominent views one suggests that filling ornaments represent certain elements from the natural environment amidst which the animal world of the Wild Goat style moves; the other that this practice betrays a superstitious fear of vacant space, the notorious "horror vacui". Whether either of these two views has any value at all for the origins of Wild Goat, which might lie in perishable media and whose very beginnings originate in the cultures of the East of even earlier date, is very difficult to say and controversial to argue. But it is difficult to believe that from the last third of the seventh century onwards vase painters, who employed these filling ornaments on their vessels, were not free from superstition. The more sensible and widely accepted explanation is that filling ornaments were highly decorative and simply very appropriate for such a style.

STYLE

Wild Goat style is an expression of a koine embracing the East Greek world which took separate paths in various centres and is not always easily distinguishable one from the other. More than once groups which have been defined have not readily, and in certain cases have not at all, found a home.

In Chian pottery of the Archaic period, Wild Goat is the style that occupied potters and vase painters for roughly two generations.[124] On Chios it acquires certain specific features, inbred into the island's pottery production, which distinguish local from alien manufacture, especially for the mature phase.

The early stages, or what is commonly called Early and Middle I, are in Chios more confusing and problematic because of the dearth of material.

EARLY WILD GOAT STYLE

The main problem at the beginning of Wild Goat style is first that it lacks a solid link with the previous sub-Geometric tradition—apart from certain geometric patterns that are

---

[124] Other classes of figurative pottery, i.e. the bird-bowls and -oenochoai, which were still produced until around the end of the seventh century are within the Geometric tradition.

Fig. 39 Field ornaments on Middle II Wild Goat style vases

Fig. 40 Field ornaments on Middle II Wild Goat style vases

transferred to the ornamental decoration—and then that there is no evidence for the preparatory stages. No definite Orientalizing stage can possibly be defined, as it has already been for the Southern schools. However short the evolution might have been elsewhere, in Chian pottery it is not even perceptible. An example will suffice: between the Late Geometric goats depicted on Chian craters[125] and the exquisitely drawn goats on the Emporio oenochoe (**310***) or on the Rizari oenochoe (**324***) exists a considerable gap which has not yet been filled; there must surely have been intervening stages, or at least vases. This dearth in the Early phase has been underlined by the publication of the small in quantity, albeit very significant, material on the island.[126]

Three items can be considered as Early,[127] without, however, forming a stylistic group as they have no intimate unity:
1. The dish from Aegina (**264***).
2. The votive shield from Phana (**273**).
3. The chalice from the Samian Heraion (**247***).

The fragmentary dish whose identity had been questioned[128] seems nonetheless to be Chian. The whiteness of the slip, the shape which is not unknown in Chian decorated and plain pottery[129] and the filling ornament below the dog's belly[130] on the recently added fragments argue for this identification. The dating in the recent publication has been lowered to the beginning of the sixth century[131] for reasons that could well be reversed to argue for its previous early dating. The elementary drawing of animals with the undotted bellies, and the rough and over-simplified form of the filling ornaments, in addition to the floral tree that has been compared with Middle Protoattic,[132] place the dish at the head of the Chian Wild Goat series.

The vixen on the fragmentary chalice from the Samian Heraion (**247***) stands stylistically between the creature on the Aegina plate (**264***) and that of the Emporio dinos (**274***); also the sketchy lion and the elementary floral could place this piece in the transition of Early to Middle I phase.

The patterns of simple guilloche and bands of squared blanks of the Phana votive shield (**273**) are undoubtedly in the Wild Goat style; however, they are well-attested on vases and fragments of later stages as well.

MIDDLE I WILD GOAT STYLE

A group of definitely more advanced style was recovered at Emporio.[133] A few strays from overseas which appear to be of relative stylistic proximity are here tentatively added.

---

[125] From Phana in Lamb, Phana, pl. 35.31 and from Emporio, in *Emporio* no. 124, fig. 64.
[126] By Boardman in *Emporio*, 149.
[127] The two were defined by Cook, Distribution, 154–5.
[128] *Emporio*, 149.
[129] *Emporio*, 130, nos. 403–410; especially no. 403 has an almost identical rim profile.
[130] This volute complex, unique though it may be in Chian, is a filling ornament passed on to the London Dinos Workshop, see here note 26.
[131] *Alt-Ägina* II.1, 15.
[132] Cook, Distribution 155.
[133] *Emporio*, 148–152; Boardman does not define how early "early" is, but, on p. 148, warns of the danger of updating Wild Goat style in general.

The Group of the Emporio Bull Oenochoe consists of:

310*		Oenochoe from Emporio
311*	fr.	Oenochoe from Emporio
312	fr.	Oenochoe from Emporio
313	fr.	Oenochoe from Emporio
314*	fr.	Oenochoe from Emporio
354	fr.	Oenochoe from Al Mina
315–320	frs.	Oenochoai from Emporio
321	fr.	Oenochoe from Emporio[134]
348	fr.	Oenochoe from Aegina
349	fr.	Oenochoe from Aegina[135]
322–3	frs.	Oenochoai from Emporio
260*–2*	frs.	Dishes from Emporio
274*	fr.	Dinos from Emporio
308*	fr.	Dinos from Salamis in Cyprus
309*	fr.	Crater from Salamis in Cyprus
353	fr.	Oenochoe from Al Mina
352	fr.	Oenochoe from Al Mina
350*	fr.	Ram head oenochoe from Krivoroshie
351*	fr.	Bull head oenochoe from Choperskie

The group has a loose stylistic unity.[136] Undoubtedly, however, it precedes the groups of Middle II as certain factors indicate. The mainly creamy slip differs in tonal nuances, which could be explained by its coming from different clay beds. The chalice and the trefoil oenochoe are not yet found.[137] The decoration uses the early fauna, foxes, dogs, and does in particular; and also employs the plastic heads on top of oenochoai, which feature seems to be a transitory vogue. Finally, some of the ornaments are characteristic only of this group. Stratigraphical evidence from the excavations at Emporio also assigns it to an early stage.[138]

Reasons justifying the gathering of these vases into one group may be put forward. Although not one goat head has been preserved, thus rendering the job of finding parallels a difficult one, yet wherever they appear their bellies are already dotted, and on **261** there is even a double dotted line. The same practice is followed by the does on **310*** but on **352**, where undotted fallow deer are depicted, they are very near stylistically to those on **310***. In both the contour of the head and ears are in outline, the eyes are embellished with an eye-brow and the snouts are identical. The Al Mina animals with undotted bellies and undotted patches on the body look slightly earlier than the Emporio does. Lions with mouth closed on **274*** and **308*** (the latter might be a mastiff but is iconographically close) are restricted to this group although the later example on **686*** might also show this beast. This type may provide the inspiration, though remotely, for the much later breed that

---

[134] Very close stylistically but perhaps not Chian is an oenochoe fragment from Al Mina in *JHS*, 60, 1940, pl. III.o.

[135] It has a double dotted line on the belly, as does **261** from Emporio.

[136] The three Al Mina items might not be Chian; however, they are stylistically close.

[137] An argument leading to the belief that the group possibly dates from around 630 but not later.

[138] *Emporio*, 148.

appears on certain Clazomenian sarcophagi.[139] Dogs in this group are identical, but so they are on most early Wild Goat vases from other regions. The partial outline for the back of the dogs' forelegs on the Emporio oenochoe (**310***) is intentional and is used for the rendering of lions' legs in the Middle II phase. The placing of the ear inside the outline of the head is another element that places the Emporio oenochoe slightly later than the Al Mina one. The fox on the Emporio fragmentary dinos (**274***) approximates to the vixen on the Aegina plate (**264***), sharing a bushy tail and an elastic body, though the Emporio fox is more stout. Panthers on **314*** and **354** are not dissimilar though not much can be said with so little of them remaining.

The Emporio oenochoe (**310***) has been claimed as Samian[140] on the argument that a large number of plastic vases and animal-heads, many of which decorate ring vases,[141] were dedicated in the Heraion of Samos at the end of the seventh century. Though rare as yet in Chian production, the find-place and the exquisite drawing of both animals and ornaments—which does not match any Samian vase—classify the oenochoe as Chian. The bull head, especially in profile, matches that of **351***; the double guilloche, with a double meander running left below it, decorates the neck also of the ram's head (**350***) and provides the link between them. The latter recalls instantly the later bull head from Naucratis in Oxford[142] with which it shares the flatness of the forehead.

The relative sparsity and the restricted variety of the filling ornament[143] is common to all items comprising the group. The spiked swastikas with rounded edges—a favourite Chian ornament—are already present on **352**; swastikas with rounded edges decorate both **310*** and **352** which also share quadruple lozenges: void on **352**, solid on **310***. The four-petal rosette with dots in between appears here on **308***[144] and **314***; it becomes frequent on sixth-century North Ionian vases and might have been inherited via them by the still later Fikellura.[145]

All the filling ornaments are held in common to varying degrees in the Wild Goat style of the southern East Greek centres but a particular one, which consists of four concentric circles around a dot with twelve inverted T's in their outer perimeter, is unique to the Emporio oenochoe (**310***).[146]

The group of the **Emporio Bull Oenochoe** is nearest in style to the Leningrad oenochoe from Boltishka,[147] which, together with numerous other East Greek vases recovered from the colonies, cannot readily be assigned to any specific school.[148] Points of resemblance are the animal drawing, the loop pattern framing the picture and the filling ornament.

---

[139] Cook, *Claz. Sarc.* 100 with notes 29 and 30 and fig. 43.
[140] *Samos* VI.1, 2 and note 3.
[141] *AM* 74, 1959, 29–30, Beil. 67; *AM* 76, 1961, 25–29. Beil. 11–35.
[142] *CVA* Oxford, II, pl. 396.57.
[143] See FIG. 38.
[144] Cf. *CGED* 46, where the vase is dated to the first quarter of the sixth century.
[145] Cook, Filkellura 69–70 fig. 9 type 20 which derives it from the stalked rosette. Illustrations on vases in *Samos*

VI.1, no. 94, pl. 10 and no. 613, pl. 84.
[146] A completely different form but approximating to this Type is the circle round a blob with nine inverted T's, see Kardara, *Rhodiake*, 170, fig. 141.4; she states that it is rarely encountered.
[147] Kardara, *Rhodiake*, 74–77, figs. 41–42 and *GO*[3], 244 with notes 90 and 91, fig. 283.
[148] Kardara's Late Orientalising Style, in *Rhodiake* 61ff, but cf. Cook in *Gnomon* 1965, 506 (Middle I Wild Goat style, *c.* 640–625).

Finally the characteristics of this group, however loosely its members are connected, are defined by:

1. The slip which is mostly creamy and seems to be a feature of the workshop and not of date.[149] Added colours are used, as on **274***, but are not frequent.

2. The shapes used which are oenochoai, dinoi and dishes; chalices are definitely not employed.

3. The decoration of fauna, with foxes and dogs, is that used in early Wild Goat groups and does not appear in Chian Middle II. The characteristic lion with closed mouth does not persist. Amongst the ornaments, the loop pattern is both typical of the group and not readily encountered afterwards. The festooned roundels on **312**, **313**, **261** and **353** with a semi-circular form are employed; yet no horseshoe roundels appear. In fact, filling ornament is sparingly used.

4. The composition on the central piece follows the general East Greek manner, that is in friezes.

5. The style: the most prominent feature is the calligraphy, as is elegantly exemplified by the figures and ornaments on the Emporio oenochoe (**310***). This outstanding piece alone speaks for that particular Chian sensitivity for fine line and fluent drawing.

MIDDLE II WILD GOAT STYLE

Most of the material collected in the Catalogue under the heading "Wild Goat style" belongs to the mature stage. Of course all pieces cannot be classified according to style either because they are too fragmentary to give any indication, or because a few, as the ring vases (**355–364***), are covered only with patterns.

The prolific material from Naucratis has particularly enriched knowledge of this phase[150] and when compared with material deriving from Emporio, Phana and Rizari clearly shows that it comes from the same workshop.

The groups that follow are all stylistic, apart from a typological group of late seventh-century squat chalices which has dotted concentric circles as a handle zone pattern and tongues around the handle roots, (see FIG. 27.c). Some of its members which retain a little of the decoration on the walls are also classified according to style. The **group of the chalices with dotted concentric circles** consists of:

> **115** and **117*** from Emporio
> **120**, **121** and **122** from Phana
> **133***, **162***, **163***, **196**, **197**, **198**, **201** and **231** from Naucratis and
> **243*** from Old Smyrna.

They all belong to the Middle II Wild Goat style since wherever part of the wall decoration has been preserved (**115**, **162*** and **231**), they demonstrate the typical Middle II scheme with the triangle below the forelegs of the goat. Wherever enough information is given the interior is black and undecorated.

Stylistically, however, the chalices from Phana might be earlier—as **123** with the Geometric bird and the panels covered with zigzags produced with a multiple brush

---

[149] The Aegina plate, (**264***), which is earlier, has a milky white slip.

[150] The same to a lesser degree holds good for Rizari.

suggests, whereas **162*** and **231** are of an advanced style and finally **198** looks late from the little that remains of the lower part of a goose and the semi-circular standing roundel.

The Emporio chalices group:[151] This is a group of fragmentary chalices (**110*–119***) centered around its most important piece: chalice **114***. They approximate stylistically to the following group. This connection is shown by the patterns of the bowl and the guilloche on the obverse of the handle zone. However, the complex meander on the reverse, the lotus-and-bud frieze at the base, the triangle below the hindlegs of the bull on **114*** and of a dog on **115** and above all the three-panel disposition may perhaps be of an earlier date. The potter NIKESERMOS was also a dedicator as **112** suggests[152] and perhaps the painter too.

The double saw-edged pattern on the handle zone of **111*** is perhaps a link between the two workshops of the patterned and of the decorated squat chalices.

I The Würzburg chalice group: The material permits a distinction into two main stylistic groups: that of the Würzburg chalices and that of the Aphrodite bowl. The first has more members with even more being added in a derivative group called **in the style of the Würzburg chalices**. The last has two subdivisions.

The works of **The Painter of the Würzburg chalices**[153] are:

236*		Chalice from Vulci
237*		Chalice from Vulci[154]
176*	fr.	Chalice from Naucratis[155]
275*	fr.	Dinos from Rizari
296*	fr.	Dinos from Naucratis
245		Chalice from ?Pitane[156]

The larger **group** consists of:

129	fr.	Chalice from Naucratis
139	fr.	Chalice from Naucratis
148*	fr.	Chalice from Naucratis
149*	fr.	Chalice from Naucratis
152*	fr.	Chalice from Naucratis
153*	fr.	Chalice from Naucratis
154*	fr.	Chalice from Naucratis
155*	fr.	Chalice from Naucratis
156*	fr.	Chalice from Naucratis
157*	fr.	Chalice from Naucratis
166*	fr.	Chalice from Naucratis

---

[151] *Emporio*, nos. 268–277 and pls. 35–36.

[152] *Emporio*, 244.

[153] The title has been used by M. Vickers in *JHS* 91, 1971, 114.

[154] Both Vulci chalices have been attributed to one hand by Price 216–7; Cook, Distribution 155; and Vickers, in *JHS* 91, 1971, 114–5.

[155] Apart from the same triangle below the forelegs and double guilloche as handle zone pattern, the same spiked swastika with angled edges is placed below the belly in exactly the same place as on the obverse of **237*** (last goat on the left) and also the reverse of **236*** (first goat to the right).

[156] Said to be perhaps by the same painter as the one of the Würzburg chalices in *CGED* 29, but no photograph is given and the profile that appears on pl. 7.11 shows that it might be earlier in form than the Würzburg chalices.

167*	fr.	Chalice from Naucratis
205*	fr.	Chalice from Naucratis
210	fr.	Chalice from Naucratis
219*	fr.	Chalice from Naucratis
220*	fr.	Chalice from Naucratis
222*	fr.	Chalice from Naucratis
224*	fr.	Chalice from Naucratis
226*	fr.	Chalice from Naucratis
229*	fr.	Chalice from Naucratis
281*	fr.	Dinos from Naucratis
295	fr.	Dinos from Naucratis (if not from the same vase then by the same hand as last)
162*	fr.	Chalice from Naucratis
240		Chalice from ?Pitane[157]

In the style of the Würzburg chalices: The pieces collected here are all fragmentary chalices from Naucratis with only one item from Samos. They display a pattern on the rim, handle zone, bowl, framing the figurative scene or filling ornament, which is similar to that depicted on the Würzbug chalices themselves:

127	fr.	Chalice from Naucratis
132*	fr.	Chalice from Naucratis
147*	fr.	Chalice from Naucratis
158*	fr.	Chalice from Naucratis
160*	fr.	Chalice from Naucratis
161*	fr.	Chalice from Naucratis
165*	fr.	Chalice from Naucratis
178	fr.	Chalice from Naucratis
179	fr.	Chalice from Naucratis
180	fr.	Chalice from Naucratis
181	fr.	Chalice from Naucratis
188	fr.	Chalice from Naucratis
203	fr.	Chalice from Naucratis
221	fr.	Chalice from Naucratis
223*	fr.	Chalice from Naucratis
246	fr.	Chalice from Samos.

In the style of the Würzburg chalices but **later** than them, are the following. The style of drawing is debased, and inner decoration generally has not yet appeared; where it does on occasions, it is an elementary and isolated ornament:

126	fr.	Chalice from Naucratis
128	fr.	Chalice from Naucratis
140*	fr.	Chalice from Naucratis

[157] *CGED* 29 where it is said that it is of the same size and shape as the Würzburg chalices; on pl. 7.10 only the profile is given.

142*	fr.	Chalice from Naucratis
144*	fr.	Chalice (same painter as **140***)
145*	fr.	Chalice from Naucratis
146*	fr.	Chalice from Naucratis
169*	fr.	Chalice from Naucratis
173	fr.	Chalice from Naucratis
182	fr.	Chalice from Naucratis
198	fr.	Chalice from Naucratis
202	fr.	Chalice from Naucratis
207	fr.	Chalice from Naucratis
217*	fr.	Chalice from Naucratis
218*	fr.	Chalice from Naucratis
238	fr.	Chalice from Delos
239	fr.	Chalice from Delos
282*	fr.	Dinos from Naucratis
283	fr.	Dinos from Naucratis
285	fr.	Dinos from Naucratis
212*	fr.	? Chalice from Naucratis
372*	fr.	from Naucratis
373*	fr.	from Naucratis
374	fr.	from Naucratis
375	fr.	from Naucratis
382*	fr.	from Naucratis
383*	fr.	from Naucratis
384*	fr.	from Naucratis
409*	fr.	from Naucratis

Also:

241		Chalice from Pitane
242		Chalice from Pitane

Both these two last chalices are small[158] and their decoration and style take after the Würzburg ones; the composition is unbalanced, e.g. the framing patterns are placed on the front panel and not above the handles (**242**) and the drawing of only one animal, a goat (**241**), seems to be a late habit. However, both drawings of animals and patterns with filling ornaments imitate the norm set by the Würzburg chalices.

II The group of the Aphrodite bowl: Pieces of a more advanced style belong to this group out of which emerges the personality of an anonymous vase painter, **The Painter of the Aphrodite bowl**. To him can be attributed all the known open bowls and three fragmentary chalices deriving from Naucratis:

252*		Open bowl from Naucratis[159]
253*		Open bowl from Naucratis

[158] When viewed in their case in the Istanbul Archaeological Museum they appear to measure 0.10–0.15 m in height and diameter.

[159] Price 216–7 attributed the Würzburg chalices and the Aphrodite bowl to one hand; however, Cook, Distribution, 155, seems to disbelieve this attribution but places the Aphrodite bowl at the same stage of Wild Goat Middle II; Vickers in *JHS* 91, 1971, 114 follows Price.

255*		Open bowl from Naucratis
254*		Open bowl from Naucratis
256*		Open bowl from Naucratis
?**258**		Open bowl from Naucratis[160]
211*	fr.	Chalice from Naucratis
377*	fr.	Chalice from Naucratis
412*	fr.	Chalice from Naucratis

The open bowls are but few. The unity of both shape and style combines to suggest that one person could have been the potter and indeed the inventor of this wholly Chian, short-lived shape. However, the ubiquitous chalice would not have escaped his attentions.

The style of his animals is painstaking and precise. His goats can be singled out from the rest of the production by two facial details. First they *always* have a wrinkle underlining the eye—as if it were an inverted eye-brow—and second in his best works (**253*** and **255***) he divides the goat's beard with a line thus producing a more naturalistic effect. The Aphrodite bowl (**252***) seems an earlier work of his, whereas **253*** and **255*** are pieces executed in the prime of his career and indeed the masterpieces not only of his style but of the whole Chian Wild Goat style.

The link between the Painter of the Aphrodite bowl and the Painter of the Würzburg chalices is the open bowl, **254***, with the characteristic Middle II rosette with six alternating dark and light petals. That the former painter's style is more advanced than the latter's can be clearly demonstrated in the filling ornament, which will be discussed in brief after the list of the **group of the Aphrodite bowl**, which is pieced together from:

125	fr.	Chalice from Naucratis
141*	fr.	Chalice from Naucratis
143*	fr.	Chalice from Naucratis
150*	fr.	Chalice from Naucratis
151*	fr.	Chalice from Naucratis
164*	fr.	Chalice from Naucratis
168*	fr.	Chalice from Naucratis
170*	fr.	Chalice from Naucratis
171*	fr.	Chalice from Naucratis
172*	fr.	Chalice from Naucratis
175*	fr.	Chalice from Naucratis
177*	fr.	Chalice from Naucratis
		(same meander as inside the Aphrodite bowl)
194	fr.	Chalice from Naucratis
225*	fr.	Chalice from Naucratis
231*	fr.	Chalice from Naucratis
227*	fr.	Chalice from Naucratis
		(same floral as **255***)
284*	fr.	Dinos from Naucratis
298*	fr.	Dinos from Naucratis
343	fr.	Oenochoe from Naucratis

---

[160] No photograph given in Edgar's *Catal. Caire*.

344*	fr.	Oenochoe from Naucratis
345*	fr.	Oenochoe from Naucratis
365*	fr.	Phallus cup from Naucratis
376*	fr.	from Naucratis
380*	fr.	from Naucratis
		perhaps late (same floral with **255*** but debased)
381	fr.	from Naucratis
387*	fr.	from Naucratis
390	fr.	from Naucratis

This group displays more variety in the filling ornaments and a few appear for the first time, namely:
  the dotted circle encircled by inverted T's
  the solid arched triangles forming a circle (an emblem)
  the squared crosses with all its types
  and above all, the spiked swastika with angled edges.

Finally the roundel, especially when hanging, becomes a real horseshoe, or perhaps more accurately, a teardrop—consisting of a solid tongue in silhouette surrounded by a striped tear-shaped band in outline—thus accentuating the delicacy and extreme finesse of the style and the sensitivity of its craftsmen.

The group of the Rizari oenochoe: decorated fragments from Rizari, have added another stylistic group, which approximates to the Aphrodite bowl group and the Gela dinos. Its members are yet few but significant for a variety of reasons: first comes the provenance; second is an oenochoe of *certain* origin and thirdly because it provides the closest link so far with the Gela dinos. This group consists of:

124*	frs.	Chalice from Rizari
324*	frs.	Oenochoe from Rizari
328*	fr.	Oenochoe from Rizari
329	fr.	Oenochoe from Rizari
330*	fr.	Oenochoe from Rizari
369*	fr.	Oenochoe from Rizari
370*	fr.	Oenochoe from Rizari

The typical Middle II scheme of standing triangles below the forelegs and roundels below the hindlegs of goats is kept. The little that remains of one goat's muzzle (**124***), the horseshoe form of the roundel and the rest of the filling ornaments (suffice it to mention the dotted crosses on **328*** and **329** and the cross on **370***) make this an outstanding group in Middle II. Though the peak of the style is demonstrated here, signs of "fatigue" are already obvious in the slight elongation of the goats' bodies and legs on **324***. At the same time this feature provides the closest parallel to the goats on the Gela dinos (**303***).

The Gela dinos: This vessel,[161] together with its companion, the fragment of a dinos (**304**) again from Gela, cannot be readily classified in Chian Wild Goat; the flabby geese

---

[161] Suggested as Chian by Cook, Distribution, 155 and accepted by Boardman, *Emporio*, 149; however, Schiering, *Werkstätten*, 39 classified it in his Vlastos group as a provincial work and Kardara, *Rhodiake*, 78 in her Late Orientalizing style. Orlandini, *CGED*, 95, remained neutral.

and the otherwise unknown patterns decorating the lower part of the vessel arguably distance it. Further the creamy to pale yellowish slip is somewhat discouraging to seeing it as Chian. Nevertheless, some features weigh in favour of Chios: the slender legs and dotted bellies of the goats—the labour-saving elongation must be due either to the incompetence of the artisan or perhaps to a later date, or both; the filling ornament which is all attested in the Chian repertoire (the festooned roundels still retain their horseshoe form); the dotted circles which decorate the rim of the dinos (**303***) and the head of the goose preserved on the fragmentary dinos (**304**), which has the same characteristically reserved patch at the end of the head.[162] The absence of the typical scheme below the goats' legs and the hasty work of both figures and ornaments suggest a date either on the edge between Middle II and the Late phase, or perhaps even later.

Before departing from Middle II, it is necessary to single out in brief the general features of this most productive and mature phase of Wild Goat.

The slip as a rule is whiter than in the previous phase. Shapes are now dominated by the fashionable chalice,[163] whose form causes the typical layout of the composition. Open bowls, restricted perhaps to one potter's creativity, oenochoai, dinoi and phallus cups survive the flood of chalices. The decoration prefers goats and geese, which are eventually joined by other species in order to relieve the inevitable boredom; certain hybrids, the sirens and griffins, remain rare. Patterns are dictated by the shape of the chalice and filling ornament shows here an arguably greater originality. The continuous frieze of hanging triangles and roundels becomes canonical in the group of the Würzburg chalices and their followers. The characteristic horseshoe roundel, which exists throughout the phase, becomes a little **objet de vertu** in the hand of the Painter of the Aphrodite bowl, especially in his masterpieces (**253*** and **255***). The dotted bellies of animals, the dotted bands of florals and particularly the ubiquitous dotted circles are features which although shared with other East Greek schools became predominant and in a way *the* Chian trademark.

Finally, the style of drawing of both figures and ornaments ranges from meticulous and painstaking work to the most exquisite and elegant art. It may be true that Wild Goat is a dull, repetitive and unimaginative style, but it is an excellent exercise for competent draughtsmanship which in its mature phase achieved results worth attention and appreciation.[164]

LATE WILD GOAT STYLISTIC GROUPS

The Late phase in the Chian Wild Goat style, as has already been observed,[165] takes a separate path and demonstrates certain divergencies and originalities of its own. Therefore, this Late phase which is a restatement of the animal style and straddles the turn of the century will be considered in the next chapter, where the reserving styles of the sixth century are discussed. Here, two groups will be presented, which follow the tradition set by Middle II and whose degenerate decoration manifestly shows that they must be late.

---

[162] See p. 37 and Cook, *Claz. Sarc.* 98.
[163] Approximately 90% of Chian Middle II appears on chalices.
[164] See Chapter 5 Dating.
[165] *Emporio*, 157 and *GPP*², 127.

A. The aforementioned chalice fragments under the heading **in the style of the Würzburg chalices**, especially the group singled out there as late belong here chronologically. In particular the two small intact chalices from Pitane (**241** and **242**), which are certainly late followers of the Würzburg chalices' style, depict a manner of decoration rare so far in Chian, that is the placing of a single goat (**241**) and of two isolated geese (**242**).

B. The **group of Late Wild Goat fragments from Rizari**

266*	fr.	Plate
270*	fr.	Lekane
271*	fr.	Lekane
272*	fr.	Lekane
276*	fr.	Dinos
277*	fr.	Dinos
278*	fr.	Dinos
279*	fr.	Dinos
327*	fr.	Oenochoe
338*	fr.	neck of oenochoe
340*	fr.	
371*	fr.	

The specific features of this group are: first, the unusually milky white slip, obviously a special characteristic of the particular workshop in Chios town; the variety of shapes displayed, rare in other groups; the patterns and filling ornament which are those of the Wild Goat style but of a definitely debased character.

The two badly mutilated figures—the forepart of a panther on **266*** and the muzzle of the grazing goat on **327***—are evidence of hasty work which has yet not altogether lost its freshness and bears remote reminiscences of better drawing. All these in addition to the form of the lotus-and-bud chains on **338*** and **371*** point to a date within the first quarter of the sixth century.

The Wild Goat is the first, and for at least two generations, the exclusive style in the Archaic period. The early stages on Chios still remain obscure, as the necessary links to tie them with the previous Geometric tradition—apart from certain patterns—are missing. Its more immediate origins are held to be drawn from other media, such as textiles, tapestries, or other minor arts of the Orient.

A limited influence was exercised on the island's school by the centres of the Southern region, especially during its Middle II phase; this is detected more readily in the general character of the style and the drawing of certain specific animals, such as the goats and the geese,[166] than in shape or ornamental decoration. However, the autonomy of the School does not permit one to think of the Chian Wild Goat style as a direct loan from the Southern region or merely a local refinement; it would perhaps be better to consider it as a translation on Chios of a much loved style, which the workshop offered as its own distinctive contribution to the wider "koine" of the East Greek world. Wild Goat established a tradition on the island which heavily influenced the further evolution of

---

[166] Kardara's Classical Camiran style in *Rhodiake*, 89 ff.

certain styles, whilst being ignored by others. The impact of Chian Wild Goat on other East Greek regions or categories is undoubtedly traceable first to the rest of the North-Ionian region, where Chios had a leading role,[167] and secondly to what is today generally called and accepted as Aeolian and is perhaps better defined as the work of the London Dinos workshop.[168]

The connection and interrelations with certain regions of Western Anatolia, such as Phrygia[169] or Caria,[170] are more obscure and indirect; but it seems that there too, even in an indirect manner, a certain Chian impact was felt.

It is worth enumerating the qualities and limitations of Chian Wild Goat style. The principal virtues are the finesse and elegance of the line, the relative sparsity of the filling ornament, the meticulous drawing and in addition the painters' intermittently successful attempts at naturalism. The limitations are self-evident: it is a merely decorative, least of all an imaginative style; it is rarely,[171] if ever, concerned with the human figure and as has been pithily put: '*it is a style without ambition*'.[172]

---

[167] Cf. the Wild Goat vases of the Old Smyrna workshop and specifically the Izmir oenochoe 3333: Akurgal, *Alt-Smyrna* I, 1983, 48, pls. 48–9 and Text-plates B and C.

[168] *Äol. Kunst*, 5 ff.

[169] A dinos with a ram's head on one side, and a lively scene on the upper frieze, see J.R. Mertens, *The Metropolitan Museum of Art, Greece and Rome*, 1987, 41, no. 25.

[170] A group of vases, amongst which the Missouri-Columbia oenochoe, see W. Moon and L. Berge, *Greek Vase-Painting in Midwestern Collections*, 1979, no. 18, has some vague connection with Chian Late Wild Goat style (see note 35 in this chapter).

[171] **778*** classified in the Grand style chalices depicts a goat confronting a bearded man. It is a puzzle-piece but, I think, it cannot be classified within Wild Goat. However, there are a few chalices, late in date, which bear a mixed decoration of humans and animals, mainly hybrids, as **458***, **612*** and **613***.

[172] *GPP*² 117.

3
THE RESERVING STYLES OF THE SIXTH CENTURY

It is not always possible to determine whether fragments, apparently in the Wild Goat style, of chalices or other shapes belong to the end of the seventh or the beginning of the sixth century. Some Late Wild Goat groups run well into the sixth century and the same applies for some other vases which stand at the transitional stage, that is in the beginning of the "Animal Chalice style", datable to the years around 600 B.C. The division made here between pottery of the seventh and sixth centuries is conventional to a certain extent and is dictated by reasons of convenience; it is mainly based on two fundamental factors: a) the type of the new chalice shape and b) the use on the interior of floral and occasional figurative decoration.

Only the human figure decoration which is now encountered for the first time in Archaic Chian vase painting will be discussed in detail, whereas brief references, when necessary, will suffice for the animal and ornamental decoration, which represents a continuation of the Middle II Wild Goat style.

WORKSHOPS

The reserving styles of the sixth century can be divided on stylistic grounds into three basic categories which are closely followed in the Catalogue.[1] These are the products of probably two workshops continuing their output from the previous century. From the first of these come:
1. The Animal Chalice style, which could equally well be labelled "Chalices with filling ornament", and
2. The Grand style

Both originate from the seventh-century Chian Wild Goat workshop.

From the second workshop comes the Chalice style[2] with its components
a) the chalices without filling ornament,
b) the patterned sixth-century chalices and
c) the floral chalices

All are from the workshop which manufactured the seventh-century patterned chalices.[3]

The two workshops were evidently in close contact, as the transmission of subjects, ornamental decoration and general stylistic traits show. Both are derived from existing

---

[1] Discussion here is based on the more pertinent pieces; the Catalogue itself is fuller, containing items which cannot be classified stylistically, lack decoration or are too small to be securely identified. Such have been included to enable the Catalogue to serve as a Corpus.

[2] The term is used in the sense of R.M. Cook in his Distribution, see *JHS* 44, 1949, 158 and *GPP*[2] 126.

[3] See Chapter 1 pp. 12–13.

seventh-century workshops, though that now producing the Animal Chalice and Grand styles flourished earlier than the one producing the figurative Chalice style, and naturally influences it in the spheres of decorative, figurative and ornamental schemes.

SHAPES

1. Chalices: The shape underwent a major and radical change sometime around 600 B.C.[4] The old squat type of the seventh century was abandoned to be replaced by a slenderer, almost biconical one (FIG. 41). It consists of the usual three parts, though the relative proportions have altered:

The foot becomes a truncated cone, approximately one third of the vase in height.

The bowl height is greatly reduced, corresponding roughly to one sixth of the whole. Its role is also minimized, so that it forms merely the base out of which the walls emerge. The handles spring almost horizontally from the upper part of the bowl. The transition from bowl to wall is barely perceptible in the beginning (**624***, **643***) and gradually becomes non-existent (**971***, **972*** and many others); thus the profile runs uninterrupted from the rim to the junction with the foot.

The walls now become higher; they are straight, slightly flaring and range in thickness; however, even the lightest sixth-century chalices cannot be compared in this respect with some Chian Geometric skyphoi from Emporio with egg-shell walls (Pl. 240.4).[5] The walls are half the height of the entire vase; the diameter of the rim is roughly equal to the whole height, and exactly equal in certain chalices. Two calibres of chalice were evolved: the heavy and the light-walled (FIG. 42). Both are employed indiscriminately for the Animal Chalice and Grand styles, but only the light variety survives for the later Chalice style.

No obvious reason is now detectable to explain this fundamental change in the chalice shape. One clear fact is that the successful introduction of Athenian black-figure vases, in competition with Corinthian vases, will have intensified commercial pressures at around 600 B.C. It may be that this stimulus compelled even the provincial industry on Chios to evolve its designs in order to remain fashionable and competitive.

This, the most typical Chian shape in the reserving style of the sixth century, accounts for 88% of the entire output in figurative vase painting.[6]

Towards the middle years of the century a further stage in the evolution of the shape, or to be more precise, a retrograde step, can be discerned (FIG. 43). It is represented by, in the main, undecorated examples:[7] **1007** and **1008** from Tocra; **1019*** and **1020*** from Syracuse; **938*** and **1030*** from Tarentum; **973***, **1062*** and **1063*** from Camirus.

The foot once more becomes lower and the bowl broader; the whole impression is that of an archaistic, somewhat debased, form. Apart from **938*** and **973*** all are plain with

---

[4] *Emporio* 156–158 and fig. 60E; also *Tocra* I 58–60, types II–IV.

[5] *Emporio* 118–9, nos. 197–8, pl. 31.

[6] The figure is a little misleading because patterned chalices have been included, whereas other classes of fine pottery, e.g. the numerous plain kantharoi, whether with painted inscriptions, or not, have been left aside. See D. Williams in *AA* 1983, 169 ff.

[7] It corresponds roughly to Hayes' type IV, especially his no. 799, fig. 30. The undecorated chalice recently on the London market, Charles Ede Ltd., *Corinthian and East Greek Pottery* VII, 8.3.1990, no. 25, is another example of this retrograde form from the mid sixth-century.

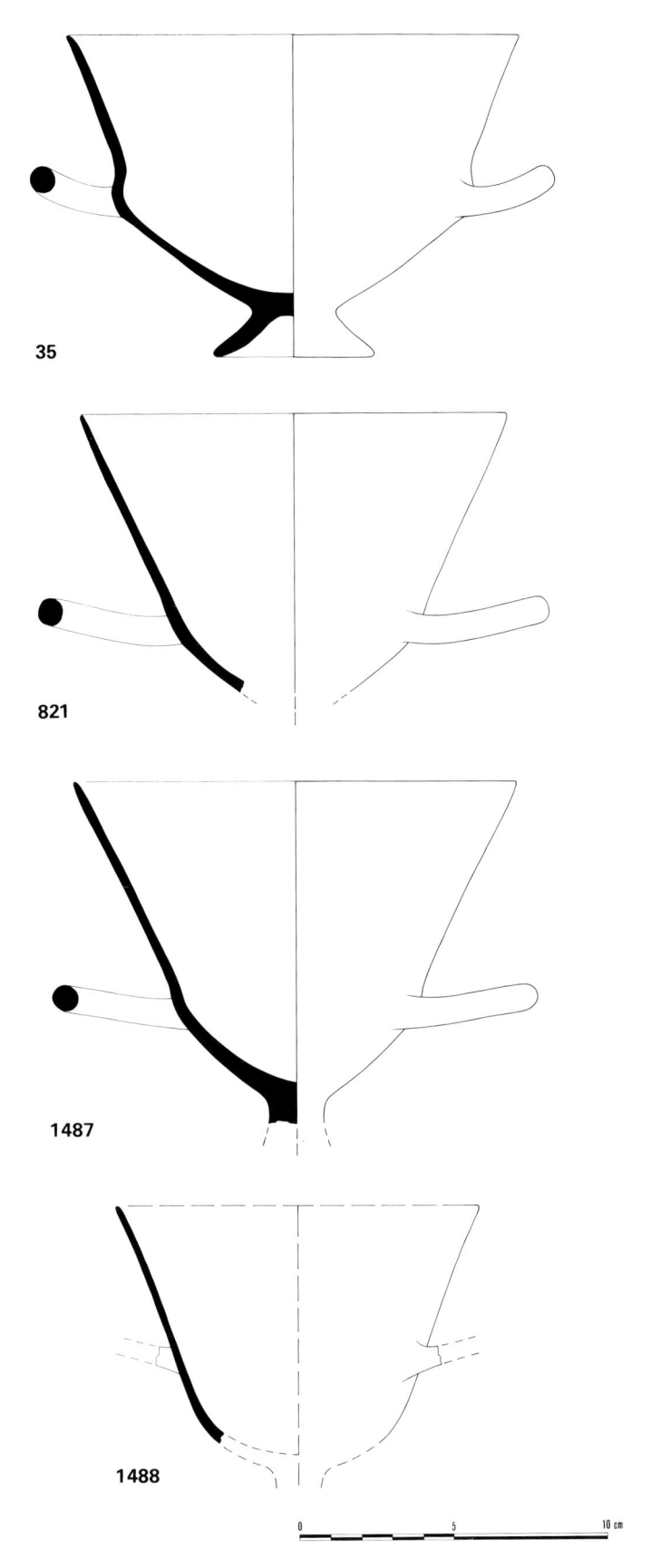

Fig. 41   The evolution of the chalice (c. 630–530 B.C.)

800

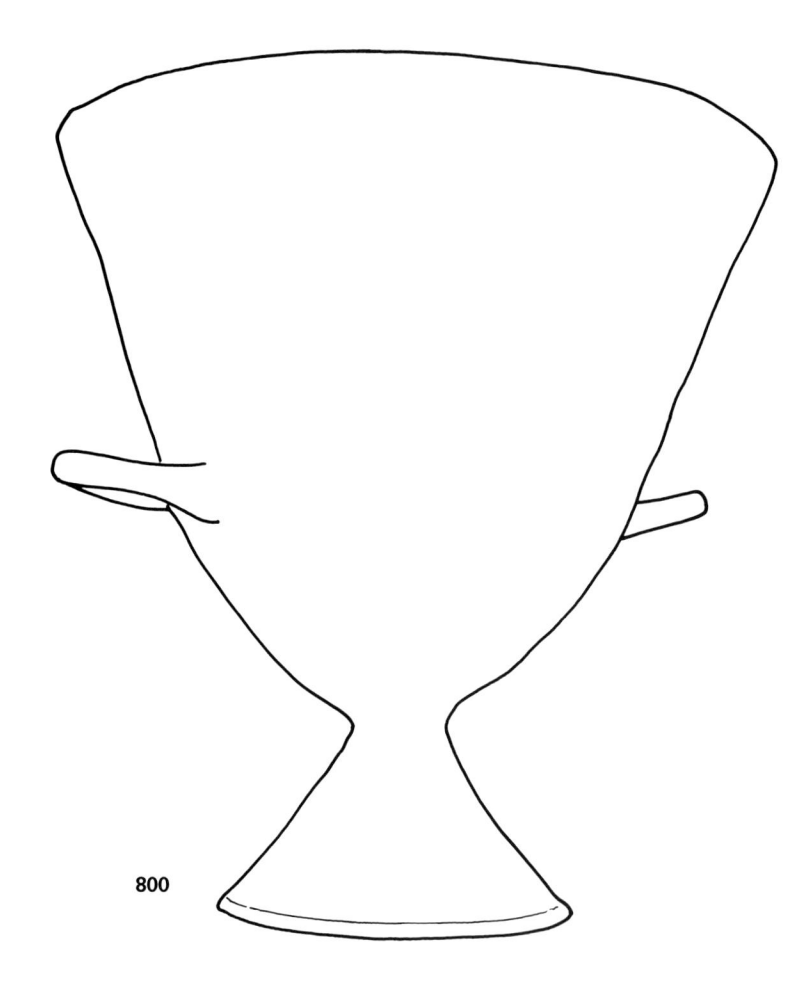

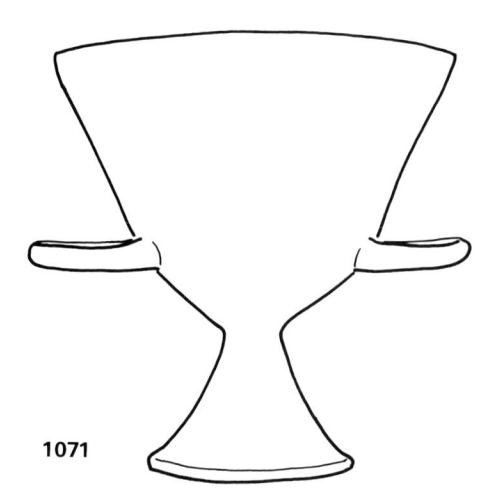

1071

Fig. 42 Heavy and light chalices

1063

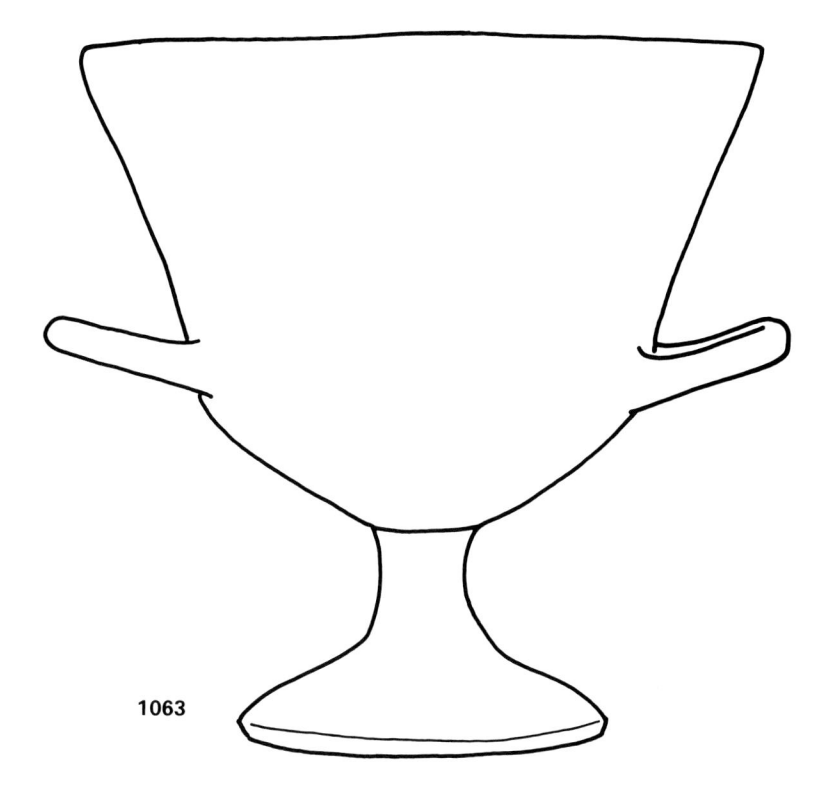

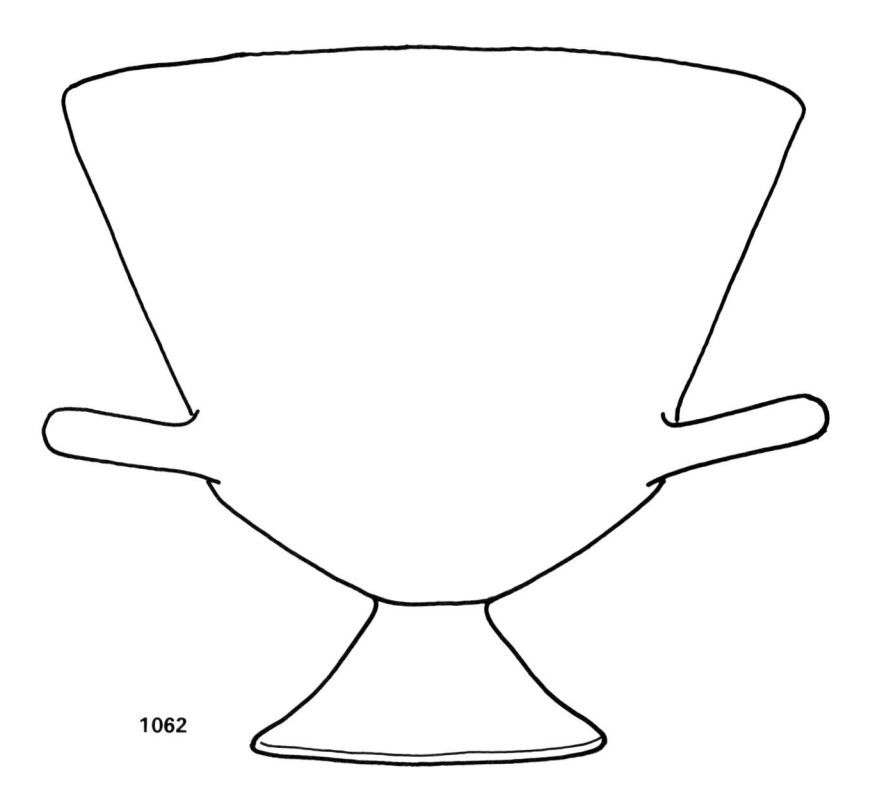

1062

Fig. 43 The sixth-century squat type of chalice

simple rim patterns and an elementary, almost minimal, inner decoration. This seems to be the very last stage of the famous Archaic chalice.[8]

The impact that the chalice exercised on other local schools from the point of view of shape was in no way compatible with its popularity. The similarity between the Athenian calyx crater and the chalice certainly reflects the common structure of both vessels:[9] they share wide bowls with high spreading walls. The view which suggests that the Athenian calyx crater—the earliest example, *c.* 530 B.C., is by Exekias who may have introduced it[10]—derives or owes much in inspiration to the Chian chalice,[11] especially to the squat seventh-century type, is well justified by the general Ionicising vogue in Athens of the last third of the century. The well-excavated Agora and the Acropolis of Athens have produced restricted quantities of Chian vases, among which are chalices of the squat seventh-century type (**78*–80**) and early sixth-century chalices (**658–661*** and **797***). The Sophilos chalice and a few other possible examples in Athenian black-figure pottery of the first quarter of the century have already been discussed in the previous Chapter.

Further instances of Chian reflections in Athenian pottery of a later date are observable. In particular, Amasis' signed cup of special type[12] with a komast holding a vase is reminiscent of the Chian early sixth-century chalice type.[13] Ure suggested that this similarity is owed to a common Egyptian link involving both the chalice, then considered to be from Naucratis, and the assumed origin of Amasis, to judge from his name.[14] Moreover, an olpe from the Agora with a symposium scene attributed to the Amasis Painter[15] shows a reclining man holding a cup very similar in shape to the Chian vessel. Both Athenian vases are dated to the last period of the artist, *c.* 520–515 B.C.[16] Almost contemporary is a bilingual fragmentary cup from the Acropolis attributed by Beazley to the Andokides painter.[17] It too recalls the Chian shape. It seems then that connections and influences can only be detected for the pottery to a limited degree, unlike the role of Chios in sculpture in the Ionicising art of Athens of the last third of the century.

2. *Other Shapes:* Apart from the overwhelming use of the chalice, other shapes with figure decoration in the reserving styles include the kantharoi, second in popularity in the plain wares. These usually, but not always, have painted inscriptions bespoke by the dedicator(s) before firing[18] and were a fashionable class of votive pottery.[19] It is difficult to distinguish whether small wall fragments are from a chalice or a kantharos.[20] Chalices— and phialai—can also bear painted dedicatory inscriptions, though most inscribed votive fragments are from kantharoi.[21] The rich series of dedicated kantharoi from the temple of

---

[8] There is further evolution and degeneration of the shape traced in the finds at Emporio; see *Emporio* 172–3, nos. 878–87, pl. 65, until the third century. An intact chalice from Rizari is similar to Emporio no. 880, see A.A. Lemos, *Chios Conference* 235, fig. 4.
[9] *GPP*² 228.
[10] Boardman, *ABFH* 187, fig. 103
[11] Robertson, *HGA* 221.
[12] Bothmer, *Amasis* no. 62. *ABV* 157.87 and *BAdd*² 46.
[13] Bothmer, *ibid.* 224.
[14] A.D. Ure in *JHS* 42, 1922, 196–197. On the implications of Amasis name see now Boardman in *Papers on the Amasis painter*, 141ff.

[15] Bothmer, *Amasis* 244 and fig. 117. *ABV* 714.31bis
[16] Bothmer, *ibid.* 225.
[17] *ARV*² 4.4 and Bothmer, *ibid.* 224. Graef-Langlotz, pl. 56. B. Cohen, *Attic Bilingual Vases and their painters* (Ph.D., New York University 1977) 1978, 509–510 is not concerned with the shape.
[18] Cook-Woodhead, 159 ff. for the main study. See also Introduction, 1 and note 1.
[19] *GO*³ 123 and fig. 141. Three such kantharoi are depicted in a banquet scene on a Grand style chalice **742***.
[20] *Emporio* 157.
[21] Boardman, CN, 57.

Aphaia in Aegina provided two main distinctions of the shape and two further subdivisions, according to differentiations in the handles.[22] Type A has striped twin-reeded handles, whereas type B1 comprises striped handles but round in section, type B2 plain handles which are flat in section. Most of the figure-decorated kantharoi from the Aphaia temple are of Williams' type A. The undecorated inscribed ones, from Naucratis as well, are almost all of his type B2. Kantharoi are also encountered in the black-figure technique.[23]

Phialai mesomphaloi, sometimes also inscribed, are another class of votive vase. The shape, a shallow rimless and handleless bowl, which ranks third in popularity, has been fully explored with the publication of a most prominent example from Marion in Cyprus (**1081***).[24] A new, almost intact example from the Parthenos sanctuary of Neapolis, modern Kavala (**814***), is very important from the point of the technique of decoration and figure drawing.

Plates and dishes[25] are not frequent in the reserving styles as they are rarely decorated. Of these shapes various forms exist. The most complete example is the plate from Emporio (**684***; FIG. 44) with a shallow and slightly curved body, heavy rim and four cylindrical lug handles. **1082** is a plate (FIG. 45) and **1083** a shallow dish (FIG. 45), both from Phana; the latter has an upturned rim and a slight ring base. Suspension holes on **684*** and **1083*** speak for their function as dedications at the relevant shrines.

A lid from Himera in Sicily (**693**) must have been the cover of a round pyxis and **688*** is part of the rim of another lid, again in the Animal Chalice style.

The dinos, a shape rare in the plain wares,[26] is not infrequent in figurative pottery, especially in the Wild Goat and the Sphinx and Lion styles. In the reserving sixth-century categories it is perhaps encountered in the Grand style (**805***).

Finally fragments **695*** and **696*** (FIG. 46) are from closed vases, probably oenochoai or hydriai. Oenochoai are rare in both figurative[27] and plain[28] sixth-century Chian pottery and the same goes for hydriai.[29] The restricted variety of shapes in the reserving sixth-century styles are overwhelmingly from open vases, which seems to demonstrate the workshop's preference. But of course our knowledge of Archaic pottery, and more specifically Chian, relies heavily on excavated material from sanctuaries and cemeteries only.

---

[22] D. Williams, *AA* 1983, 169.
[23] See Chapter 4, where detailed discussion.
[24] By Boardman in *RDAC* 1968, 12 ff. Also see J. Hayes *Tocra* II, 25 and notes 4–6 for **1075***.
[25] See also Schaus, *Dem. Sanct., Cyrene* II, 83–4. The plate from Naucratis (*Samos* VI.1 no. 733, pl. 99) is not Chian to judge from what is known about Chian sphinxes, cf. *ibid*. 84, note 43. Schaus, I think, is right in removing from the Chian output *Samos* VI.1, nos. 730–733, which might be of a North Ionian workshop, but *ibid*. no. 734 (**1076***) looks Chian to me.
[26] *Emporio* 115.
[27] See also Schaus, *Dem. Sanct., Cyrene* II, 77.
[28] See *Emporio* 165, nos. 818–820.
[29] Recently a hydria in black-figure decoration from Lithi on Chios (**1638***) was added to the repertory of shapes. For plain sixth-century hydriai see *Emporio* 166, 821–823 and there are some unpublished from Rizari.

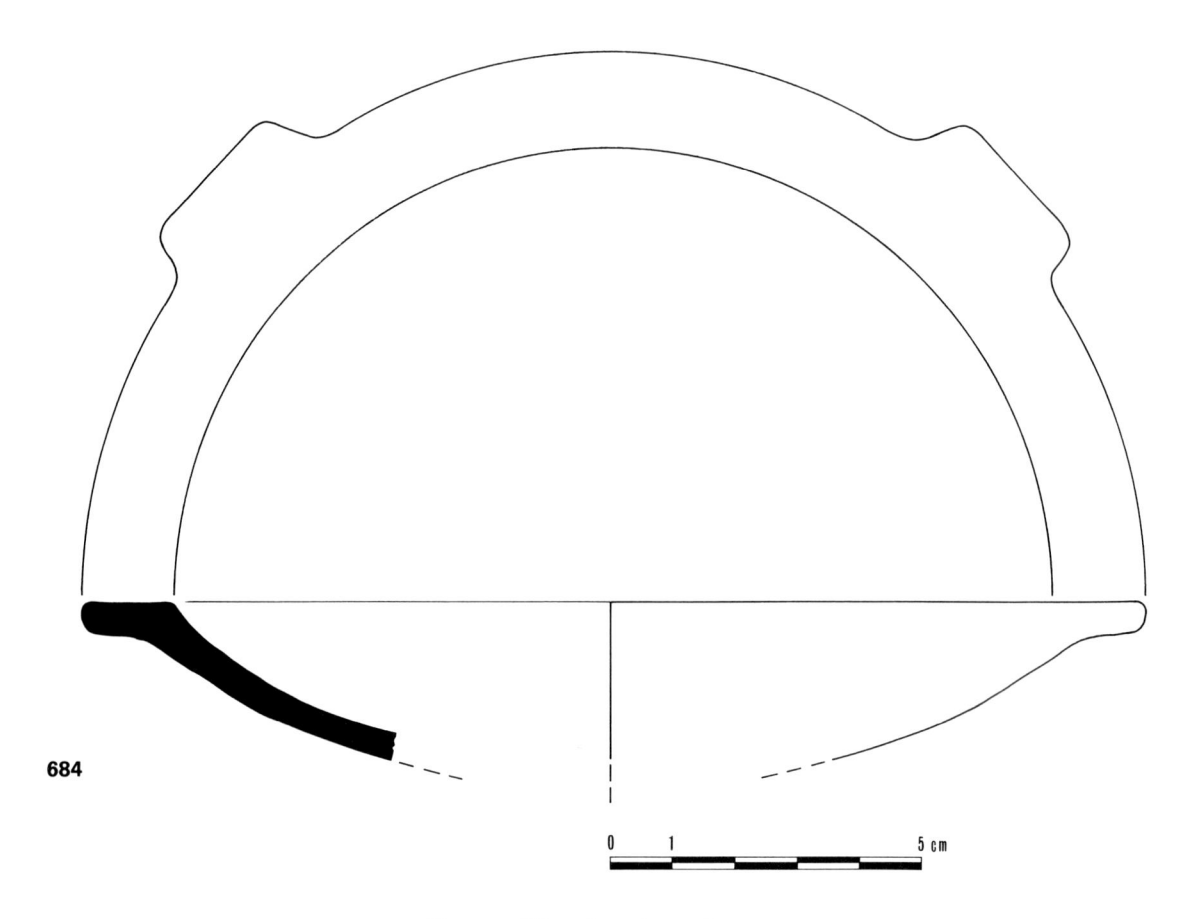

Fig. 44 The plate from Emporio

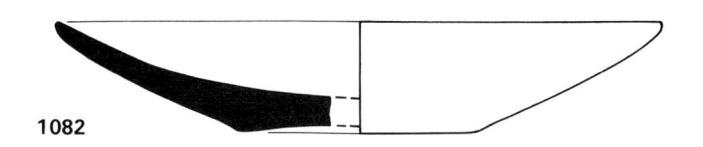

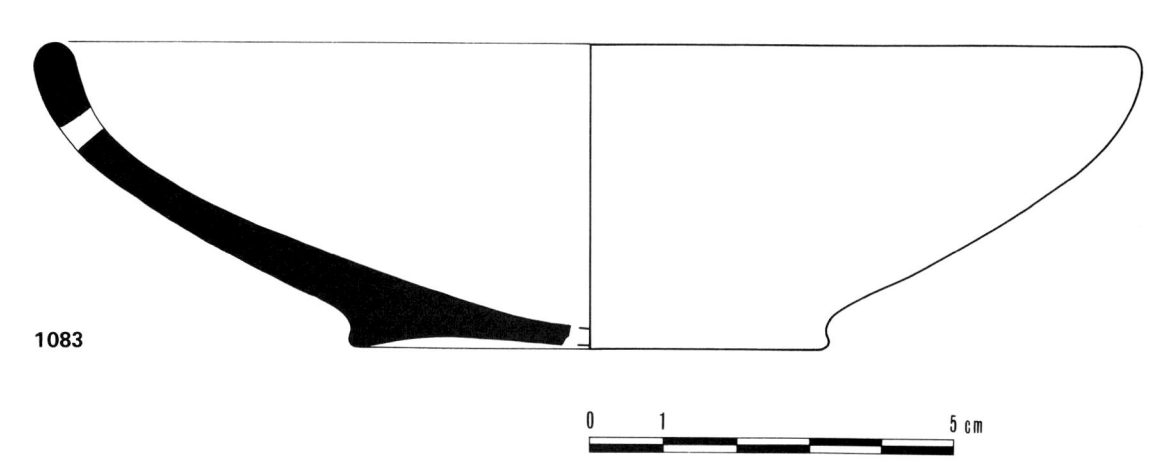

Fig. 45 Plate, **1082**, and Dish, **1083**, from Phana

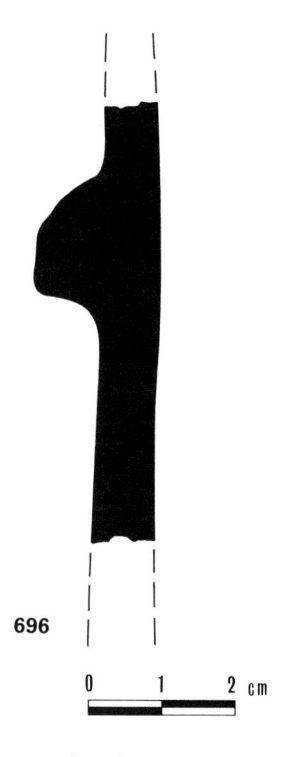

Fig. 46 Sherd from a closed vase-shape from Chios town

STYLES

1. THE ANIMAL CHALICE STYLE

The reserving technique of decoration continues in Chian figurative pottery after the turn of the seventh to the sixth century. Other East Greek schools, however, especially the Northern ones, succumb to the stronger Corinthian influence and finally compromise with an incised Corinthianising manner.[30] Chians also adopt the black-figure technique; the impact of Corinthian and Laconian,[31] as well as Athenian and Clazomenian vase painting, was felt as well, influencing Chian black-figure styles to an arguably large degree.[32] However, the technique of reservation, with which vase painters were more familiar, goes on: it is in these styles, in the first half of the sixth century, that the masterpieces of Chian vase painting are produced.

The first style can be labelled "The Animal Chalice style"[33] because it makes an almost exclusive use of chalices and the decoration is once more drawn from the animal world, with some rare exceptions, where humans appear also. The style can also be defined as "Chalices with filling ornament", as these are still crammed among the figures in contrast to the following style.

Both animals and ornament are in the tradition of the Wild Goat style and in fact the Animal Chalice style marks a continuation of its Middle II phase. It has been considered the late phase of the Wild Goat style,[34] but as there are manifest differences from Middle II Wild Goat, and a definite stylistic development, it might be better considered as a renewal of the style and not simply a decline or a degeneration, which is implied by the word "late". It seems that the change took place in the same workshops or rather, in my opinion, in one particular "atelier": the one set up by the "Painter of the Aphrodite bowl" and his followers. This trend was the more progressive, whereas a more conservative one, set by the Painter of the Würzburg chalices and his entourage, continued producing the well-known old schemes.

Thus, two different approaches can be discerned:

A. The lineage of the Painter of the Würzburg chalices has been traced at the end of the last chapter under the heading "in the style of the Würzburg chalices". The group assembled here and named after the centrepiece stands at the division between Middle II and the Animal Chalice style; it differs from the last in many ways and can therefore be isolated as an independent group.
The group of the Catane chalices consists of:
624* from Catane; **625–629*** from Catane; **616*** from Tocra (same group but much later); **662** from Apollonia Pontica.

These belated products are separated from the earliest set on several grounds. Firstly, of shape: the transition from bowl to the walls is still *barely* perceptible, but the

---

[30] *Samos* VI.1, 77–87, pl. 105–125. Also *Tocra* I, 64 ff and *Tocra* II, 28f. Jones, *Review* 664.
[31] A.A. Lemos in *Praktika of the 3rd International Congress of Peloponnesian Studies*, 1987–1988, 71–80.
[32] These will be discussed in detail in Chapter 4, though chronologically they overlap each other.
[33] The "Animal style chalices" in *Emporio* 157.
[34] Cook, Distribution 158 and cf. *GPP*² 126.

chalices already display a high conical foot;[35] they all are light-walled. Secondly, they display inner decoration, floral ornament in red and white. Furthermore, the context of the deposit in which the Catane chalices were found could be dated to the beginning of the sixth century.

616* from Tocra is certainly in a debased style and indicates that this group lasted for some time, perhaps till around 580 B.C.

The group of the Catane chalices still displays the old, restricting "metopes" as decoration, the same patterns on the bowl that have been encountered in Middle II Wild Goat (FIG. 28.3), and again the same framing patterns on the walls above the handles (FIG. 29.7). Wild goats continue to occupy the walls, if the most substantial piece, the Catane chalice (**624***), is typical. It seems that the group survived till the end of the style, as the debased framing rim pattern, as well as the feline's tail, on **616***, the Tocra chalice, indicate.[36]

This group has few members; it follows the new fashions up to a certain extent and at the same time sticks to the old tradition. It might have lasted at least as long as other groups within this style and provides a solid link between Middle II Wild Goat and the subsequent styles of the sixth century.

B. The renewed Animal style takes root in the works of the **Painter of the Aphrodite bowl** and his entourage. Slight, though decisive, innovations demonstrate the fresh orientation at the turn of the century. First, there is a noteworthy change in the *repertoire*. Goats, geese, deer and dogs are extremely rare; foxes vanish. Lions, sphinxes, bulls and boars become the favourite stock; sirens and occasionally griffins appear. Iconographically there is no difference from the Middle II Wild Goat; each animal has been considered individually in the previous chapter.

Secondly, the radical change that transformed the *chalice shape* and in particular led to the high spreading walls provides for a wider and more extended field for the decoration. The "archaic", old-fashioned, restricting "metopes" give way to an uninterrupted *composition* with figure-drawing, which embraces the whole circumference of the vessel.

Thirdly, the *inner decoration* with floral motives appears in the new chalice form, as it also does on other open vases—mainly kantharoi and phialai—for the first time. In this manner vase painters express their decorative preoccupation with detail; a predilection rarely encountered in other provincial schools at the time.

Lastly, *style*, or rather the execution of drawing, is very painstaking and can rise to the almost impeccable by general Chian or even East Greek standards of the period.

The changes point to a remarkably robust and interesting style, second to no other Chian animal category, at least in the execution of drawing. This renewed animal style can be divided into five main stylistic groups, all of which are extremely close to one another.[37]

---

[35] *BolldArte* 45, 1960, 255, where it is stated that fragments from at least twenty chalices were recovered and were being restored. Also *Emporio* 120.

[36] *Tocra* I 58.

[37] Boardman CN 61 thought of the elaborate Animal Chalices from Naucratis as another possible Chian class, manufactured locally.

1. **The group of the elaborate animal chalices**, with all its members from Naucratis, consists of:

432*; heavy[38] **438***; heavy **439***; heavy **440***; mediocre, but big **441***; **442***; **447***; **448***; **449***; **450***; **451***; light-walled, but big **458***; **471***; **477**; **517***; **518***; **519**; **520**; **536**; **544***; heavy **546***; mediocre, but very big **552**; **559**; **574**; **582***; **887*** (chalice with no filling ornament, which stylistically belongs here)

The common features of the group are that almost all are big chalices, varying in diameter at the rim from *c.* 0.30–0.40, and most are heavy-walled: they are *chalice-craters*, as are a number in the Grand style also.[39]

They display a kind of *polychromy*.[40] On a very white to creamy slip the brown paint is usually diluted to yellow or even golden yellow in parts, e.g. on the lion's manes (**439***), and added colours are used rather lavishly, red for patches on the body of boars and white for the eye-sockets of boars and sphinxes (**552***).

All the red-spotted *boars*, though executed by two or three different hands, belong to this group; the similarity to their Laconian counterparts has been singled out, as well as the slight variations in the different technique of decoration employed for each.[41] It seems that the *bulls* of the group, unlike the boars, are all by the same hand, save perhaps **442***. The *lions* are executed with the utmost care; their network mane and the careful outline on the periphery of bodies and legs both speak for the painters' skill. Strangely enough two, iconographically different, types of *sphinxes* exist: one, on **440***, is the well-known Chian séjant type and the other, on **552*** and **582***, is a fine and elaborate creature, which has a close typological, even to a certain extent a stylistic, proximity to her kin on a fragmentary chalice from Naucratis of the Grand Style (**700***).

From what can be deduced from the larger pieces, the *compositions* which embrace the walls are lively and fresh by Chian standards; a favourite scene now becomes bulls or boars held at bay.

Rim patterns are mostly heavy and complicated but at times simpler ones exist (FIG. 47), generally diagonal strokes between two lines (1) or a broken cable between two lines (2).

The double guilloche is the usual *handle zone pattern*, occasionally trimmed with other patterns on top, e.g. billets in squares, as on **439***, which form the baseline on which the figures stand.

The most common *filling ornaments* (FIG. 48) are: the six—or eight—petal dotted rosette with or without spikes; the ornament consisting of five concentric circles united by spikes and the dotted cross inscribed in a square. Naturally, dotted rosettes and swastikas of all forms, which are the most frequent field ornament in the Wild Goat style, continue in favour. Pendants, both triangles and roundels, continue to hang

---

[38] Wherever I have information on the chalice shape, I note it in front of the number.

[39] *Emporio* 157 and *Tocra* I, 58 type II; also *AA* 1983, 156 ff. Of these chalice-craters the largest, I think, is **801*** from Pitane, which must be over 0.40 in diameter, but also the Troilos chalice (**800***) has a 0.306 diam.; the Aegina chalice (**795***) 0.34 diam. and most of the "elaborate Animal chalices" of which **552*** is perhaps the largest.

[40] Cf. F. Villard, who used the term "polychromie partielle" in *ASAtene* XLIII, 1981, 133 for vases of the seventh century from Cyclades, Thasos and Megara Hyblaea, which display restricted polychromy.

[41] By Boardman in CN, 61.

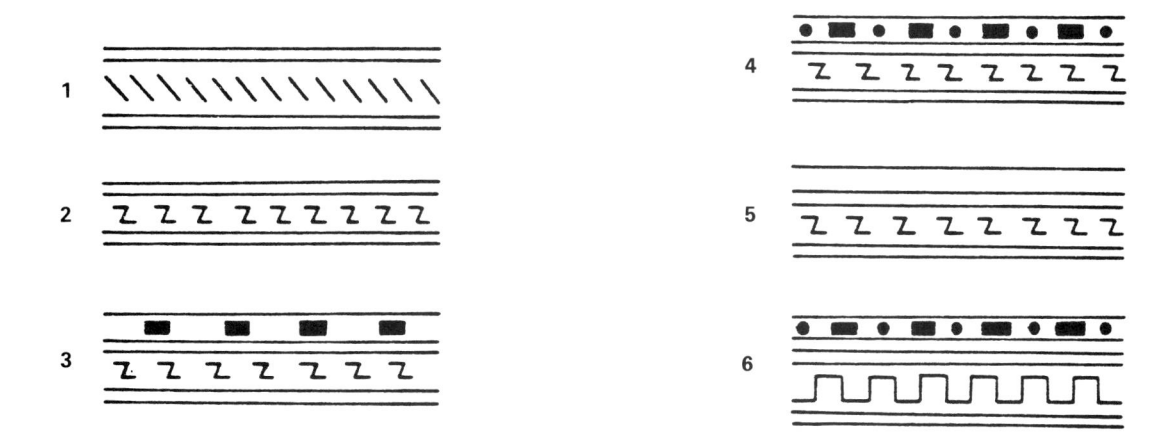

Fig. 47 Rim patterns in the Animal Chalice style

from the upper boundary, if very sparsely; but rarely, if ever, do they emerge from the base-line. The old scheme of triangles below animals' forelegs and roundels below hindlegs is now completely abandoned.

The style of drawing is exquisite; certainly the best workmanship in Chian vase painting of the Archaic, and consequently of all periods. It certainly is not an inventive, let alone an inspiring, style in conception or composition; but it is undoubtedly superb in execution. Three examples will suffice to sustain this claim:

a) the painstaking execution of the lion's mane, on **439***, with the diluted, almost golden-yellow paint in minute, parallel and crossed lines, as if it were an elaborately woven network. The same is repeated on sphinxes' wings;

b) the carefully conceived and executed reservation for the lions' upper forelegs, on the same fragmentary chalice (**439***), or the reserved lines denoting separate areas on all animals;

and c) the marvellous drawing of the eyes of both boars, e.g. on **439***, and bulls, e.g. on **441***, with the double lines outlining the eye, giving the impression of eyelids.

Besides these details the whole picture gives the impression of fine work. The group has its roots in the tradition of "the Aphrodite bowl group", not only in the professionally impeccable drawing of animals, but also in ornamental details. It continues to use either the same or developed forms of similar field ornament. **546*** can be considered as a direct successor to this group of which the British Museum and University College, London bowls (**253*** and **255***) are the most distinguished members.

As well as its predecessors, mention can be made of a few but very close links with its immediate antecedent in the Grand style. **458*** depicts two antithetically disposed sphinxes and behind them a standing female figure in black chiton and red himation. The same representation appears on **612*** and **613** from Tocra; on the latter the sphinxes are placed back to back. More significantly the woman carrying the vessels, Polyxena, on the Troilos chalice from Pitane (**800***), is drawn in the same statuesque

Fig. 48 Field ornaments in the Animal Chalice style

THE ANIMAL CHALICE STYLE

posture and in an almost identical style with the lady on **458*** from Naucratis. In fact, this last piece, where a human is found beside animals, approximates very closely stylistically to the Grand style.

2. **The group of the light-walled Naucratis animal chalices** consists of:
434; **435**; **460***; **461***; **463***; **464***; **466***; **478**; **480***; **481**; **482**; **483**; **484**; **488***; **489***; **490***; **491***; **492***; **493***; **494***; **495***; **496***; **497***; **498***; **499***; **503***; **504***; **506**; **521**; **522**; **523**; **527**; **541**; **542**; **543**; **545**; **547**.

All are *small* fragments which convey very little information. Most, if not all, are from *light-walled* chalices, this being the main distinctive feature from the previous group. Further, the standard of draughtsmanship is noticeably poorer. This is possibly due to the fact that the group stretches over a longer period; and that these, mostly later pieces, are quickly, almost carelessly, drawn. In some their simple inner decoration shows the first signs of deterioration.

3. **The group of the Tocra-Delos animal chalices** is composed of:
heavy **611*** from Tocra; heavy **612*** from Tocra (very near to **458*** from Naucratis); **613** from Tocra; **617** from Cyrene; **643*** from Delos; **644** from Delos.

This group differs from "the elaborate Naucratis animal chalices" only in that polychromy is not displayed. Subject-matter, filling ornament, composition are the same. For example, **643*** and **644** from Delos bear the pomegranate motif in their inner decoration. Style however betrays some signs of a slightly later date.

4. **The painter of the Pitane animal chalices**:
At least two of the unpublished animal chalices from the Pitane excavations[42] are by the same hand: heavy **675*** exhibited in the Bergama Museum; heavy **676*** exhibited in the Archaeological Museum in Istanbul.

On both, rim patterns, handle zone patterns and filling ornament are identical in placing and execution. Both are heavy and big: *c.* 0.25–0.30 in height and diameter at the rim. The animal drawing varies from very meticulous for **676*** and the front of **675*** with the siren—her face is very elaborately drawn, to the rather hastily drawn lions on the reverse of the latter. The paint is not well distributed over bodies; outline is used only partly for the upper foreleg and the tails spring from higher up the buttocks, almost at the end of their back.

5. **The group of the Berezan animal chalices** is composed of:
chalice, light **615*** from Tocra; chalice **665*** from Berezan; chalice, heavy **666*** from Berezan [perhaps same painter as **696***]; chalice, heavy **667*** from Berezan; chalice **668*** from Berezan; chalice **669** from Berezan; chalice **670** from Berezan; plate **684*** from Emporio; fr. from closed vase **696*** from Chios town [perhaps same painter as **666***]; lid **693** from Himera.

The group displays no polychromy.

---

[42] My impression is based on the assumption that the vases exhibited in the Archaeological Museums of Istanbul, Izmir and Bergama are the most important.

Conceivably it occupies a longer period of time, perhaps even a quarter of a century, starting with the early fragmentary chalice from Tocra (**615***) and ending with the chalice from Berezan (**666***) and the Chios piece (**696***). Both heavy and light-walled chalices remained in use until the end of this style, which might have been towards the end of the first quarter of the sixth century. Rim patterns are simpler, mostly broken cables between lines; handle zone patterns continue as guilloches for the front, and, usually, meanders for the rear. Lions are hastily, but still quite well, painted. **667***, on both fragments, displays lions with snub muzzles and the tails placed at random, and the well-worked network mane marks the continuation of the style. Other details mark the first steps in decline. This is apparent on **666*** where the lion's mane has lost the Chian network "touch", being painted solid in red with a fringed contour at the back. Again the bull, on the same fragment, has a triangular muzzle, a deformed round eye underlined with two unsteady eye-lids and an unusually solid neck: it must be one of the last bulls drawn by a Chian artist. **696*** with the lion's forepart and mane in particular rendered in the same manner as **666*** could argue for the attribution to the same hand, despite the rough and hastily drawn framing patterns, which otherwise might imply a slightly later date. Both **666*** and **696*** are of the latest stage in the late Animal Chalice style.

In brief, the Animal Chalice style is a direct continuation of the Middle II Wild Goat style and in particular of the "group of the Aphrodite bowl". It employs both heavy and light-walled chalices, and the inner decoration, which for the first time appears, is almost everywhere executed with the utmost care. The various groups distinguished here have an intimate stylistic connection, even in the last stage. They demonstrate the refinement and finesse of Chian painters as well as their predilection for the animal repertoire established by the Wild Goat tradition and here rehearsed in a fresh manner.

2. THE GRAND STYLE

This style was labelled "Grand" by Boardman[43] and indeed, though on the whole the figure drawing is of a small scale, it has a grandeur of its own and a relative monumentality. Many aspects contribute to the grandiose impression this category makes on the viewer, unique not only by Chian standards but also generally by those of East Greek vase painting at the time, with the sole exception of the Euphorbos plate.[44]

Notably, the polychrome technique of decoration[45] is used for all the vases (**697***–**807***), although it is true that the almost intact Pitane chalices (**800*** and **801***) display only a restricted polychromy.[46]

---

[43] Boardman CN 59.

[44] The Euphorbos plate in the British Museum, see E. Simon, *Die griechischen Vasen*, 1976, 54–55, no. 31, is earlier by roughly a quarter century. However, it is an isolated example from the East Dorian area, which, on grounds of certain details of its subject matter and inscription, might have been inspired by prototypes from North-East Peloponnese, or might even have been painted by an Argive immigrant to Rhodes, as Johansen claimed, see K.F. Johansen, *The Iliad in Early Greek Art*, 1967, 79–80.

[45] Cf. Schaus, *Dem. Sanct, Cyrene* II, 78 on the distinction "Grand" style and "Polychrome" style. I think the distinction is unnecessary here since all vases and fragments collected under this heading display some sort of polychromy.

[46] As has also been seen on the Animal Chalice style, on partial polychromy see F. Villard, *ASAtene* XLIII, 1981, 133–4 for seventh-century vases.

The *colours* employed range usually from four to six in number, but in some groups they rise to ten on a single piece. The fundamental colours are black, brown, red and white; in addition, there are shades of dark or light brown, beige, yellow, golden yellow, mauve. Blue is never used. The *slip* is thick and has three different tonal variations: a brilliant white, a light beige which is almost creamy white, and a grey.[47]

Other features are the original subject matter, where care is taken in the rendering of the human figure and scenes of action. Finally, the relatively high quality of the figure drawing is consonant with the more expansive and ambitious nature of the style.

I. Shapes

That most exclusively employed was the chalice in its renovated sixth-century form and in its two noteworthy variations, *the heavy* and *the light-walled*. The diameter of the rim can range from 0.306 for the Troilos chalice (**800***) to 0.34 for the Aegina one (**795***) and possibly over 0.40 for **801***, again from Pitane. On **801*** the bowl bulges out and the transition to the walls is still slightly perceptible. The thickness of the walls is remarkable and can range from 0.4–0.75 cm. on a single vase (**795***). These three vases, with many other fragments from Naucratis, resemble a crater-like vessel, appropriate for mixing liquids—presumably wine with water—and eventually, of course, for dedication at sanctuaries and to the dead. Almost all the fragments of the Grand style from Naucratis are classified in the Catalogue according to whether they are from heavy or light chalices; the latter are more numerous.

Three more shapes are used in this style: *plates* are encountered twice—both are ambiguous pieces. A fragment from Naucratis, (**803***), on grounds of the whiteness of its slip and the patterns on the drapery and couch, could be Chian; another (**804***), from the Parthenos sanctuary at Neapolis, has a Tityos scene which, if Chian, is of the Grand style.[48] From the same site is *a phiale*, possibly mesomphalos, **814***, in the light on dark technique. And finally *a dinos*, **805***, to which have been attributed three fragments,[49] of which two certainly belong.

It is therefore apparent that the Grand style was not entirely restricted to chalices but appeared on an extremely limited variety of other, popular, Chian shapes.

II. Iconography

The subject matter of the style is very interesting and instructive. Such idea as exists of the iconography of Ionian men and women and some of their activities in the first half of the century has been gained to a large extent from the Chian Grand style. Vase painters give up the monotonous animal repertory and are engaged in drawing humans and scenes from everyday life and mythology. The nearly complete scenes on the Pitane vases (**800*** and **801***) may contribute to a better understanding of certain fragments from Naucratis.

---

[47] The variations are further explained below and measured according to the Munsell Chart.

[48] Lazaridis in his *Guide*, 93, A 1103 and Hemelrijk, *Caeretan Hydriae*, 178 and note 754 consider it Chian. The plate displays a fine polychromy and very good figure drawing; however, the complicated swastika below the feet of Apollo and Artemis looks more Cycladic than Chian.

[49] By Cook in Fikellura 53 and pl. 10a and b; the Oxford sherd is Chian and most probably the Brussels one too (*CVA*, Brussels III, pl. 105.10), but the BM 1888. 6-1.780 does not look Chian to me: the drawing of the plump komast figures and the filling ornament are unparalleled in the series; however, the human head, a man, in the lower register could be near to Chian work.

However, it is mainly from the latter that the types of men and women can be most fully appreciated; a detail missing on one piece can be supplied by another.

1. Men: The convention of Archaic Greek art in depicting the male flesh with brown or red paint, picked up from Egyptian art and first apparently adopted by the Corinthians in the seventh century,[50] is also observed by the Chians. The paint ranges in colour from dark to light brown, rarely red; usually the contour of the naked parts, e.g. legs on **742***, is outlined with a darker brown or red line and frequently facial details are singled out with darker colours, black or brown, e.g. eye, eyebrow and beard, on **728***. The face, rendered strictly in profile, has an unbroken line from forehead to nose, almond-shaped eyes with closing lines at their corners, sharp and sometimes protruding nose, lips denoted by a small horizontal line and ears usually drawn in a calligraphic manner, as on **701***. Only once does a man wear an earring, on **763**, and presumably he is a reveller.[51]

Men wear a short, pointed beard and have clean-shaven upper lips; a notable exception is Heracles, on **797***, who bears a thin moustache. Hairstyles (FIG. 49) can be either long, as on **725*** and **733***, where a lock appears, or, more frequently, short; men usually wear a stephane, on **702*** and **706***, or the Lydian mitra,[52] the turban, on **726*** and possibly **728***. The protruding edge on **708*** is part of the felt hat of an archer. A hood might be the headgear of the man behind Polyxena's attendant, on **800***.[53]

Male dress (FIG. 50) is usually the long-sleeved, Ionian chiton,[54] not differing much from the female counterparts, as on **730***. On top they wear either a long (**773***), or usually a short himation, whose paryphe is perhaps sometimes misleadingly taken for a band across the chest, as on **702***, **703*** and **764***. Short chitons are usually worn when men are in some sort of action, e.g. riding on **756*** and **760***, hunting on **761*** and **765*** or striding, perhaps marching in military order, on **707***, **734***, **736*** and **738***. A loin-cloth is worn by Heracles on **741*** and **797***.

The man on **728***, presumably a komast, wears a garland across his chest. One wonders if the man on **725*** is completely nude, which would constitute an unprecedented case for the otherwise puritanical Chian morals reflected in vase painting.

Men are barefooted or have some kind of footwear. FIG. 51 shows sandals of two different types or in fewer instances boots. The discernible sandals fall into the simpler yoke-type, which is clearly demonstrable on the Aphaia chalice (**795***), and the more complicated network type.[55] Soles are not rendered by the painter. A chalice fragment from Naucratis

---

[50] The Thermon metopes, see Charbonneaux-Martin-Villard, pls. 33 and 34 and Robertson, *Greek Painting* 1959, on p. 50. The Pitsa wooden panels in *EAA* VI, 201–5, figs. 225, 226 and colour Pinax I, and in Protocorinthian and other vase painting schools. For a recent discussion on "The Beginning of Greek Polychrome Painting" see G.P. Schaus in *JHS* 108, 1988, 107 ff. and especially 109, where he argues for the dependence of polychrome pottery on "free" painting since this appears in five different wares about the mid-seventh century almost simultaneously.

[51] Cf. *Samos* VI.1, 70 and note 201: "a reclining bearded man".

[52] The basic study on the mitra is by H. Brandenburg, *Studien zur Mitra*, 1966, especially 76ff for the mitra worn by revellers and komasts. For a detailed discussion on the Lydian mitra (and earrings) worn by Chian komasts and the distinction of this headdress from the sakkos see Boardman in *AA* 1976, 284. Also D.C. Kurtz and J. Boardman in *Greek Vases in the J. Paul Getty Museum*, 3: *Occasional Papers on Antiquities*, 2, 1986, 50–51 and note 88, for the Lydian mitra en vogue in Ionia for male revellers at the time, which passed over to Athens later in the century.

[53] Cook, *Claz. Sarc.* 119 note 77.

[54] M. Bieber, *Entwicklungs Geschichte der griechischen Tracht*, 1967, 26–27.

[55] K. Dohan Morrow, *Greek Footwear and the Dating of Sculpture*, 1985, 3–5 and 23ff where no use of the iconography on vase painting is made. It is difficult to tell which way the straps join the thong on the Aphaia chalice (**795***).

THE GRAND STYLE

Fig. 49 Men – Hairstyles and headgear

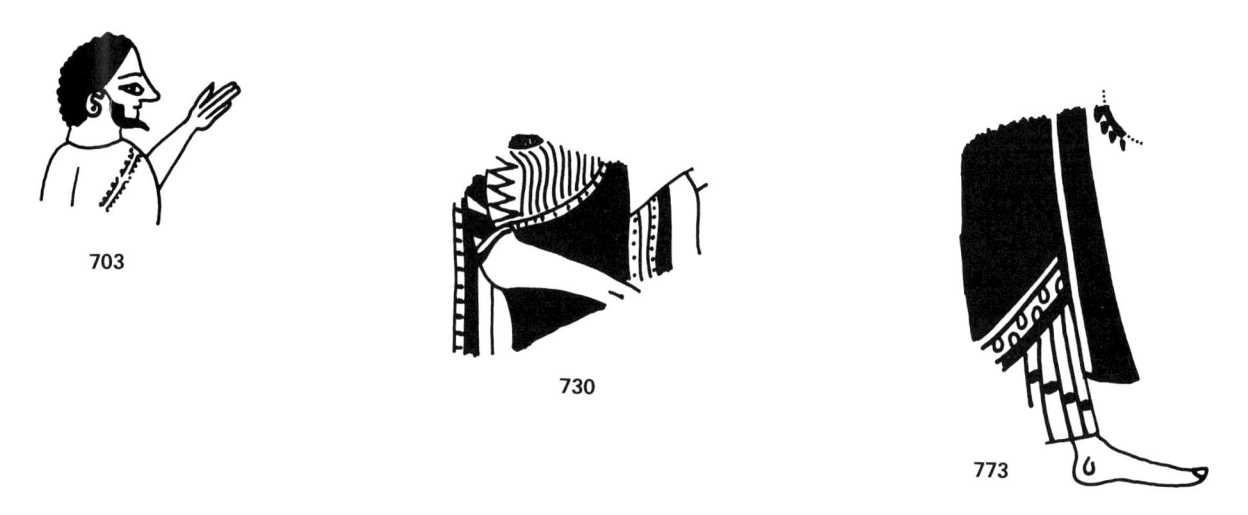

Fig. 50 Men – Dress

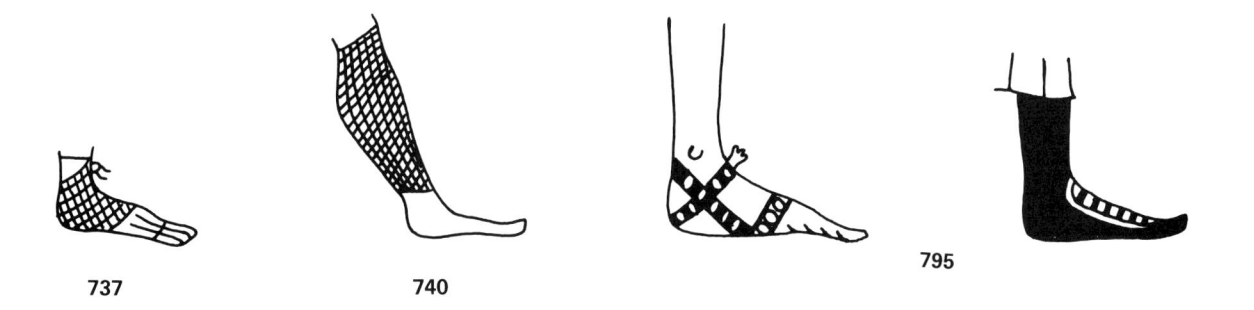

Fig. 51 Men – Footwear

(**737***) demonstrates clearly the network type with the many straps and the fastening in a bow above the ankle; on this piece (**737***) barefooted men appear also. Calf-length boots with laces, and with pointed, slightly upturned toes, are worn by other men on the same Aphaia chalice (**795***). Laced boots were a customary footwear in the Near East[56] and had penetrated the Archaic Greek world probably via East Greece. Usually men are barefooted when parading, hunting (on **732*** and **762***), riding (on **709*** and **756***) and dancing (on **742***). The left leg of the warrior of **740*** might be wearing a cross-hatched greave,[57] but the total lack of all footwear both on his comrades here and elsewhere should make one cautious about interpreting this as either a greave or a strapped sandal.

2. Women: The painter either leaves naked flesh reserved on the light-slipped background or uses added white, thus producing the effect of a "second" white, while contours are outlined with brown or red.

Women are shown in profile and have more or less similar facial details to men as regards the unbroken line from forehead to nose as well as lips, nose and necks. Eyes are almond-shaped with white for the eye and usually black for the pupil, as on **700***. Ears are calligraphically drawn in many ways, mainly snail or kidney-like, with circular earrings, as on **700***, **771*** and **901***. Dress is a long chiton, mostly sleeved and with a belt. A sleeveless chiton with belt appears on **759***. Usually a himation is worn on top of the chiton, draped obliquely from the left shoulder to the right armpit, as on **733***. This is the fashionable Ionian himation which can be either short or long, like a cloak. The paryphai are lavishly decorated with strokes or dots, sometimes in white. Examples are **716***, **718***, **719***, **720***, **721***, **723*** and **733***. Two interesting pieces are **791*** with a woman in a chiton and her companion in a chiton and long himation, and the Troilos chalice (**800***) which displays the same variety with Polyxena in long, sleeved chiton with a belt and paryphe decorated with little strokes,[58] and her attendant behind her in a chiton and a long, obliquely draped, himation.

Women are either barefooted when walking, as on **773***, or dancing, as on **784*** and **795***; alternatively they wear some sort of shoes or boots, similar to male fashion pumps as on **717***. The boots recall the footwear of the Acropolis Kore no. 683 with her upturned pointed toes[59] and also ladies' boots on the Boccanera slabs.[60]

Not many of the Chian ladies have retained their heads, but the few that do show a variety of hairstyles (FIG. 52). The hair is either worn long in a mass often with a stephane, as on **783***; or short and bound in a krobylos, as is Polyxena's on **800***. Other styles involving long hair have it falling either in separate tresses, on **759***, or in three curly strands with hairbands separating them, on **700*** and **901***, which are female heads of sphinxes. It seems clear that the curly lines on **717**[61] are from the long floating tresses which identify the figures as women.

On two heads (**775*** and **789***), most probably female and if so presumably Athena, appear two different types of helmet (FIG. 53). Neither seem to fall into known types of the

---

[56] D. Williams in *AA* 1983, 158.
[57] Johnston, *Exhibition* 1978 no. 73.
[58] This same pattern, bands with alternating bars, appears on a fragmentary bowl-crater from Thasos, as a dividing band, see *CGED* 90, pl. 52.19 and Chapter 7.
[59] Richter, *Korai*, 1968, no. 120 and figs. 381–384.
[60] BM 1889.4–10.1, see *LIMC* II.1 s.v. Athena/Minerva no. 241.
[61] See Colour Plate II.

THE GRAND STYLE

700 **759** **783**

Fig. 52 Women – Hairstyles

775 **789** **800**

Fig. 53 Types of helmet

Ionian helmet as exemplified by East Greek plastic vases or terracotta figurines.[62] The first type with a skull-cap and a high crest ending in a volute in front appears on **775***;[63] the second type, which has a pointed geison on the forehead and a low-fitted crest running vertically to the brow appears on **789***. The latter is ornamented with a reserved and dotted band which ends in a volute.

A third type of Chian helmet can now be added, worn by Achilles on the Troilos chalice (**800***) and by the warrior on the "Farewell scene" (**801***). It seems to be of a more canonical Ionian type. The brow has a central spur which develops to give full coverage of the neck, and the clearly rendered cheek pieces (especially on **800***) are arguably movable, similar to those known from the Rhodian and Samian plastic vases in the form of a warrior's head;[64] finally, the high crest ends in a rich and very long plume spreading over the back part of the head, neck and part of the shield.

[62] K.H. Edrich, *Der ionische Helm*, 1969, 2ff.
[63] *Emporio* 27 and note 12, where it is compared to a probable reconstruction (fig. 15a on p. 26) of the helmet worn by the cult statue of the goddess; also discussion for the Gordion frescoes and their iconographical connections.
[64] Edrich, *ibid.* 97ff, 105 and 128 and his figure on p. 3.

3. Scenes from everyday life: The craving for narrative is expressed in a remarkable manner in this category, to which it is mainly restricted. Following other more advanced schools and their artistic aims, Chians depict scenes from both everyday activities and mythology. It is unfortunate that only two nearly complete vases, from Pitane, have been preserved: the one with a mythological scene, the ambush of Troilos (**800***), and the other perhaps from real life showing the departure of a warrior (**801***). The rest are badly mutilated fragments that can only provide uncertain interpretations. It is not always easy to decide whether they are taken from everyday life or mythology. Nonetheless, a few can be understood with a degree of certainty and can themselves suggest an explanation for others; identification rests mainly on the attitudes of figures and the various accessories present.

Scenes from everyday life can be divided according to their *subject* into: a) Processional; b) Riding; c) Banquet and Komos; d) Hunting and Battle.

a) Processional scenes, which must have some sort of religious connotation, are probably depicted on **737***. Of course one must not exclude the possibility of their being part of a wider composition with a completely different meaning. **703***, man with raised hand; **704***, man holding a lotus flower; **725***, man holding a wreath; **735***, woman with pomegranates; and finally **712***, **721***, **743***, **785***, and **791*** and a few more with parts of garments might be from processional activities with worshippers carrying gifts. Thematically identical are vases and fragments in the Chalice style (**829***-**835***)—and specifically, the complete vessel from Berezan (**964***)—confirming the interpretation of humans as worshippers in a processional attitude.

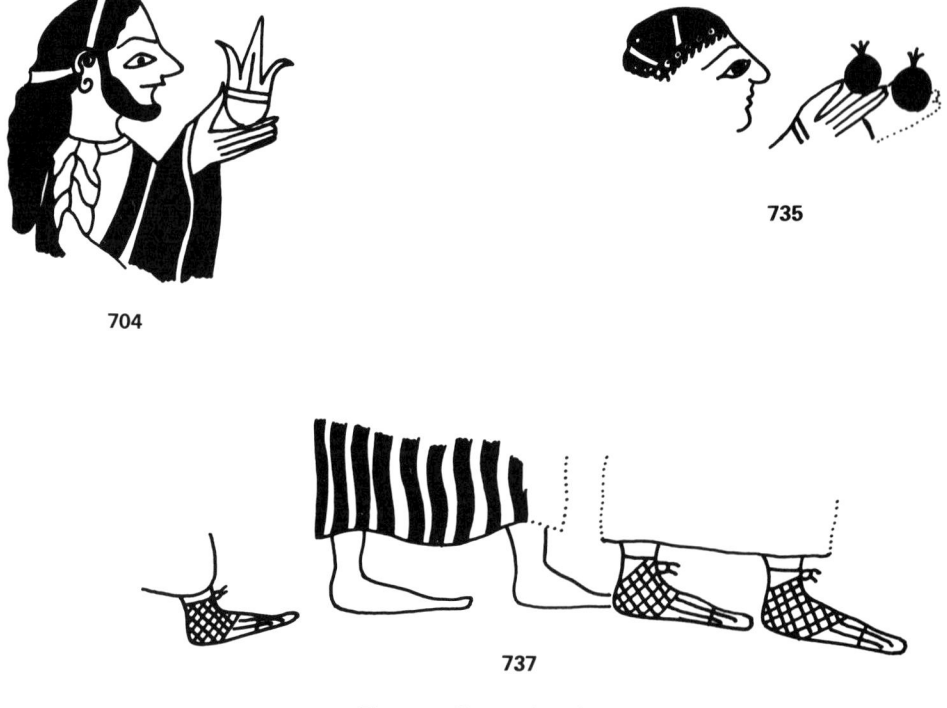

Fig. 54 Processional scenes

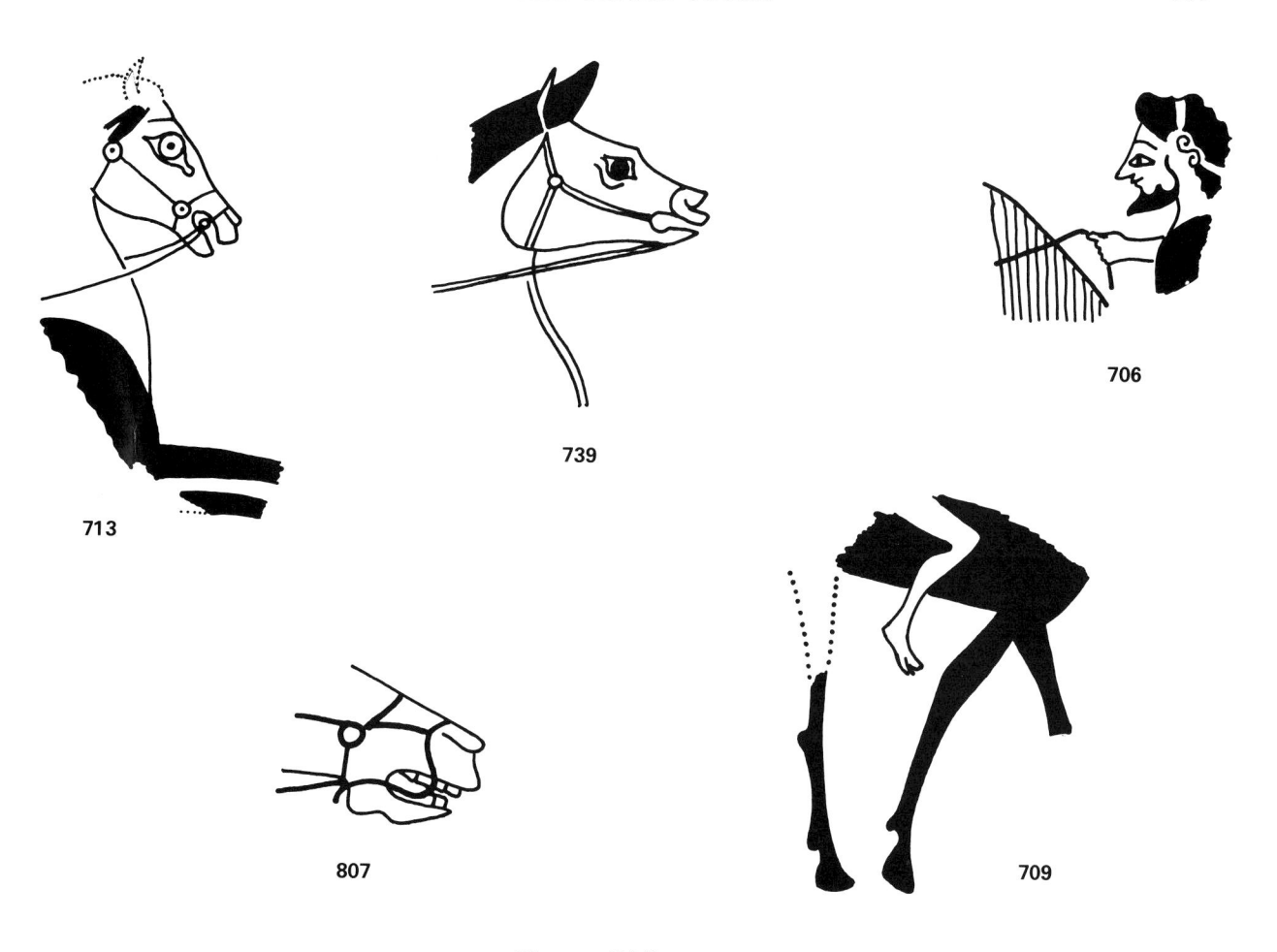

Fig. 55 Riding scenes

b) Riding scenes with horses, horsemen, chariots.

From Naucratis: **706***, with horse and horseman; **709***, with horse and horseman; **713***, with two horses; **739***, with two horses; possibly **752***, with a horseman; **756***, with horseman;[65] **757**, with horse; **768***, with hand of a charioteer and reins; **769***, with charioteer and reins; **774***, with horse's head in bridle; possibly **776***, ?horse's mane (perhaps Troilos' attendant pouring from a phiale); **781***, four horses, heads from a quadriga;[66] **790***, a mule rather than a horse with a bridle; **807***, horse's head in bridle; **810***, two horsemen in the light on dark technique.

Also, **796***, with horseman from Aegina; **798***, with a winged horse, from Neapolis; **800***, with Troilos and two horses from Pitane; **801***, with seven horsemen on the reverse chalice, from Pitane.

---

[65] See Colour Plate IV.
[66] Johnston in the publication of the UCL fragment collects seven Chian horses in BICS 29, 1982, 42 note 16. To these should now be added the above-mentioned pieces from Naucratis, Pitane and Neapolis. To the Grand style horses, two more in black figure are now added: 1. the Rizari lid, **1324*** in the Sphinx and Lion style and 2. the Leningrad dinos fragments in the black-figure Grand style (FIG. 89). In all, seventeen certain and two possible, fragments.

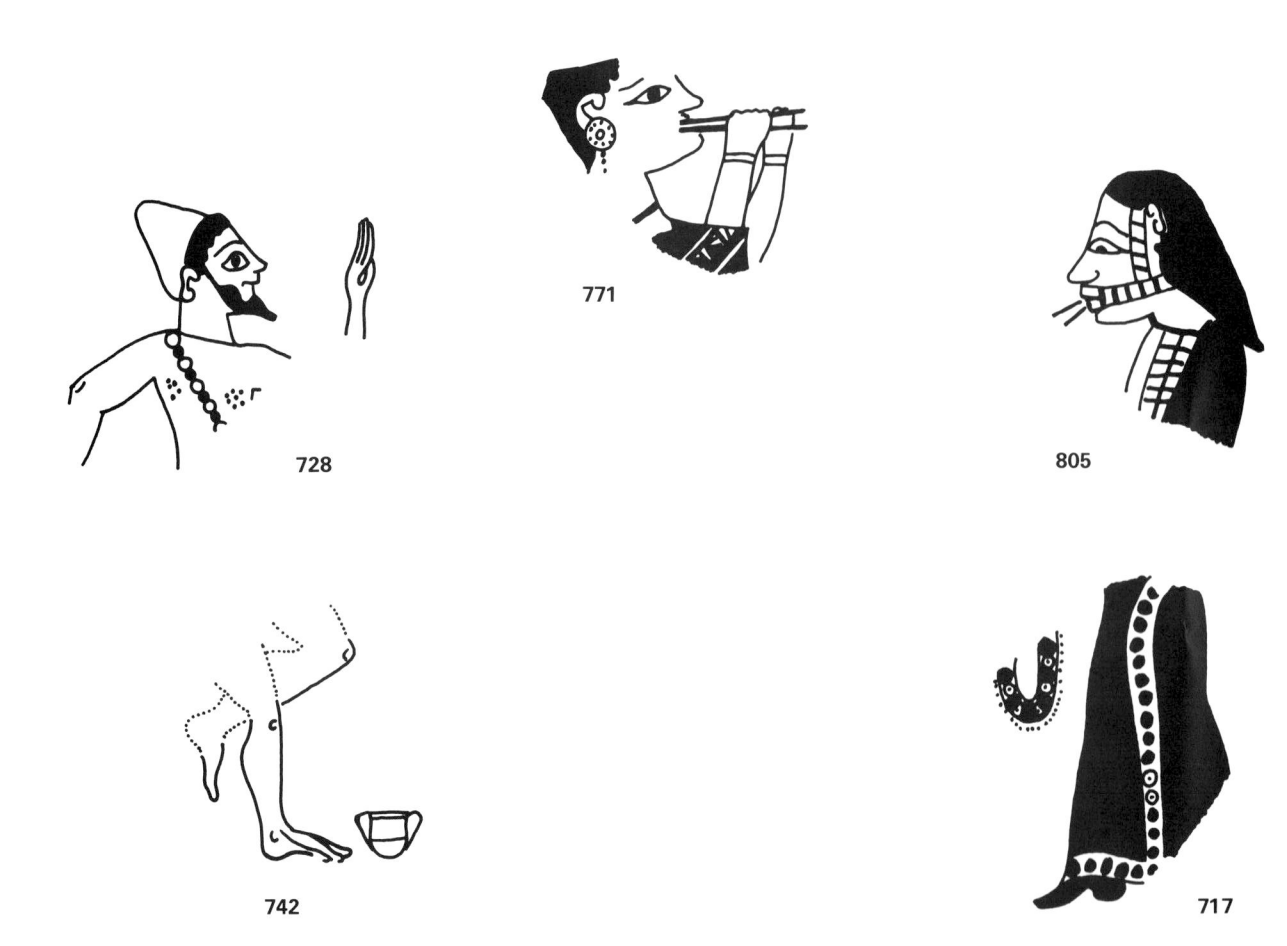

Fig. 56 Banquet and komos scenes

To these horses and horsemen, those on **800*** and **798*** — the latter presumably Pegasus — have been added, though they definitely belong to mythological scenes, in order to demonstrate that other fragments might equally be from analogous scenes and do not necessarily depict members of contemporary aristocracy. In the first half of the sixth century these subjects are rarely represented either in other Chian categories or in East Greek vase painting in general. After the middle of the century they appear on Clazomenian pottery,[67] and become frequent on the Clazomenian Sarcophagi,[68] the Caeretan hydriai[69] and other wares, as well as in Western Anatolian wall-painting,[70] but it is doubtful whether any of the above derive from the Chian "cavalier" repertory; at least their style does not permit such conjecture.

c) Banquet and Komos scenes are represented, with a varying degree of certainty, on the following: **717***, women dancing and holding garlands; **726***, perhaps a komast wearing a turban; **728***, a komast with a garland across the chest;[71] **742***, komasts' feet dancing; **763**,

---

[67] *Samos*, VI.1, pl. 119.976a & b, and *BSA* 47, 1952, pl. 31.1
[68] Cook, *Claz. Sarc.* 126 and plates, passim.
[69] Hemelrijk, *Caeretan Hydriae* IIIL1–3 (pp. 147–150).

[70] The chariot and horses in the Kizilbel tomb at Elmali, see *AJA* 77, 1973, pl. 43.
[71] See also *AA* 1983, 162 for both **726*** and **728*** but **763** is not referred to, though published in *Samos* VI.1.

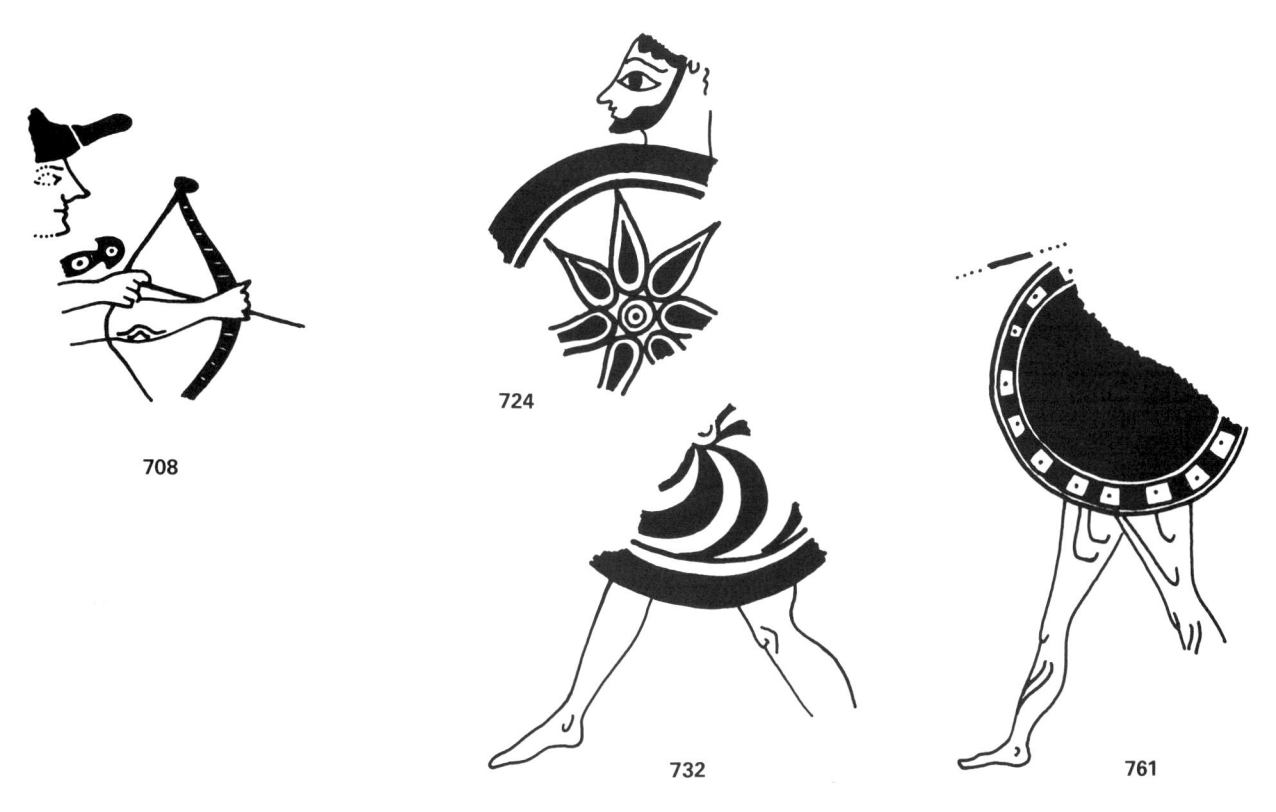

Fig. 57 Hunting and Battle scenes

man—presumably a komast—wearing earrings; **771***, flautist; **784***, female feet dancing, or fleeing Nereids?;[72] *plate*: **803***, part of a couch and feet; *dinos*: **805***, flautist and dancer.

It is not easy to distinguish the banquet from the komos scenes. However, it seems that the latter are more common and are the favourite subject also in other categories of Chian pottery, such as the black-figure komast chalices and in a mixed technique of reserving and black-figure style.

d) Hunting and Battle scenes. Hunting scenes on the Grand style fragments can be easily confused with battle scenes because men usually hold shields and spears in both. One could take the view that they are all incidents from peaceful hunting scenes, relying on the evidence provided by the upper frieze of the Kavala column-crater,[73] where the hunters use spears, tridents and shields and generally have a military air. However, two fragments (**761***, **762***)—if indeed from the same vase—depict on the one a lion and on the other two juxtaposed adversaries, ready for a duel. Thus, the evidence provided by the fuller scenes is not conclusive and unless more vases with relevant subjects come to light, hunting and battle scenes are better kept together: **698***, shield with a spiked rosette as blazon; **705***, hand holding a spear; **708***, archer drawing his bow; **710***, shield with bull's forepart as device; **724***, hunters or warriors; **732***, hunters or warriors; **736***, warrior holding shield

[72] *Samos* VI.1, 108 note 198.
[73] Kavala Museum A 985, 986 = Lazaridis, *Guide* 106.
See Chapter 7.

with eye-device; **740***, probably warriors rather than hunters; one of them wears a greave/footwear; **758***, hunters or warriors; **761***, warriors with shields; **765***, warriors or hunters; **767***, most probably spears.

With these, all from Naucratis, the scene on **801*** from Pitane should be considered, as it is thematically related. On the other side to the seven parading horsemen, there is "the farewell scene of a warrior"; this can be deduced from the martial appearance of the two men. It cannot be identified, even in a simplified Ionian version, as "Amphiaraos taking leave of Eriphyle", despite the female unveiling herself and the kneeling figures, because a few fundamental elements are missing—for one the chariot, also the necklace, though the last might have been depicted in a part of the vase not preserved.[74]

It has to be stressed once more that the dispiritingly fragmentary nature of the important material from Naucratis might lead to misinterpretation[75] of these unique and vivid scenes. However, one remains with the impression that painters engaged in this style were equally preoccupied with showing human activities that took place before their eyes in everyday life as with mythological subjects.

4. Architectural Elements

A few yet very important architectural elements are depicted on the Troilos chalice (**800***, FIG. 58), where the fountain has been represented as an Aeolic prostyle building with one column.[76] The column sits on a rectangular base; its capital with volutes has its own rectangular support; the intervening shaft is unfluted. The building has a sloping roof and palmette-acroteria crown the three corners of the gable.[77] Typologically the Aeolic column of the Troilos chalice seems to be slightly more developed than the early Archaic capitals from the Athena temple at Old Smyrna,[78] and to approximate in form to those from Klopedi[79] and Mytilene,[80] so far as comparisons between a pictorial art and architectural sculpture are permissible. That Aeolic architectural features occur on a Chian, therefore Ionian, vase need not cause any concern nor should the origin of the vase be questioned on this account.[81] "Aeolic" is, of course, a conventional form with no close geographical connotation in this case. A comparable case has recently been discovered: the clay model house from Sellada on Thera which displays an entrance and a wall on which stand columns with Aeolic capitals.[82] This piece declares its local manufacture by the typically Cycladic patterns decorating its walls.

Another architectural feature on Chian vases of the Grand style is the Ionic stepped altar,[83] which is perhaps depicted on **777*** and possibly on **780***. The latter could equally well be depicting a wall similar to the one on the Troilos chalice: the identical chequer pattern indicating in both cases the stone construction, supposedly isodomic.

[74] Both Pitane chalices (**800*** and **801***) have big areas where the surface has flaked away.

[75] E.g. Troilos with his horses might be intended in certain riding scenes.

[76] Cf. Oliver Smith, Representations of Aeolic capitals on Greek vases before 400 B.C., in *Essays in memory of Karl Lehmann* 4, 1964, 233. For two examples with Aeolic columns in Corinthian and Athenian vase painting of the second quarter of the sixth century, see *ibid.*, 234 and fig. 1.

[77] See P. Betancourt, *The Aeolic style in Architecture*, 1977, 97–98 and 153 no. 6.

[78] E. Akurgal, *ASAtene* XLIII, 1981, 127–132 and figs. 6 and 8.

[79] Betancourt, *ibid.*, pl. 49 and figs. 41 and 42.

[80] Betancourt, *ibid.*, pl. 50.

[81] Cf. *Samos* VI.1.70 and note 201 that the chalice "lokal chiotisierend ist"

[82] *Arch. Reports* 1983–84, 54–55 and figs. 98 and 99.

[83] *GO*³ 143 and mainly 120 with note 37. Also C.G. Yavis, *Greek Altars*, 1949, 115 ff.

Fig. 58 The Troilos chalice from Pitane (after Bayburtluoğlu, *JdI* 85, 1970, 48, figs. 14 and 15)

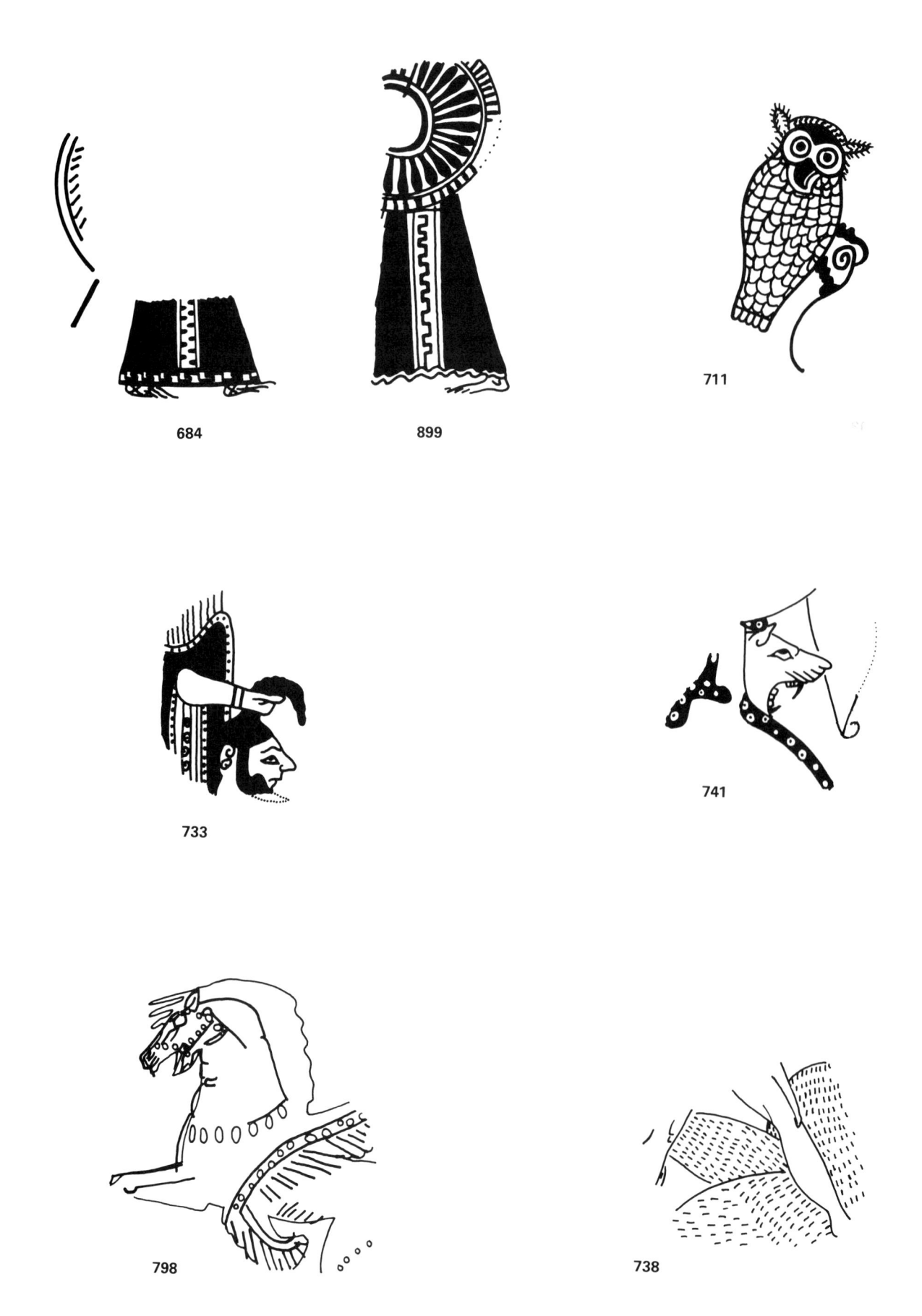

Fig. 59 Mythological figures and scenes

THE GRAND STYLE

5. Landscape Elements

The sole landscape element in all Chian vase painting is *the tree*,[84] again depicted on the Troilos chalice (**800***, FIG. 58). The surface of the vase has flaked away in the area of the branches and the tree is thus hardly identifiable.[85] It is placed between Troilos and the attendant who pours water from an oenochoe into a basin; it is an integral part of the outdoor scene of the ambush.

The owl with fluffy ears perched on *a branch* (**711***) is perhaps the only other candidate for an intentional representation of external surroundings attempted by a Chian painter.

6. Mythological scenes: These might be more in number than at present realized and some are quite unusual, even unexpected.

A list of mythological figures and subjects arranged alphabetically follows, giving the name of the scholar who identified the scene in brackets. They are in a rough chronological order.[86] Whenever mythological subjects are not in the Grand style it is stated. It is obvious that many of the scenes are puzzling and that the connoisseurs are not in agreement.

1. **Aphrodite protecting Aeneas in battle** (Il.v,315): **702*** [Price]; "the man does not look like a warrior" [Beazley]; this "might be the Greek way of depicting the Egyptian and oriental "embrace" of a king by his tutelary deity" [Boardman]; "Diomedes fighting Aeneas" (Il. v, 297ff.) [Johansen] and "the man is unarmed" [Johnston].
2. **Athena**: **775*** [Boardman]; **789***; **899*** [Price]—in the Chalice style (FIG. 59); **684*** [Boardman]—a plate in Animal Chalice style (FIG. 59).
   Athena's owl: **711*** [Walter-Karydi] (FIG. 59).
3. **Busiris scene (a negro)**: **1657*** [Hemelrijk]—in black-figure technique.
4. **Calydonian boar hunt**: [Lazaridis; Walter-Karydi; Salviat; Hemelrijk] Chian category from Thrace.[87]

---

[84] With the exception of **1648*** which might depict Apollo's shrine at Phana.

[85] It could perhaps vaguely recall the palm tree on the much later Exekias amphora in Boulogne with Ajax's suicide, see E. Simon, *Die griechischen Vasen*, 1976 pl. 76 for a photograph and L.G. Nelson, *The Rendering of landscape in Greek and South Italian Vase painting*, (State University of New York at Binghamton, Ph.D 1977) 17 for the palm tree on the vase; also on some late Athenian black-figure vases. However, the Chian tree has upright branches, judging from what little has remained.

[86] Scholars who were involved in interpreting Chian mythological scenes and the publication where they gave their opinion are here cited in alphabetical order:

Akurgal	in *Orient und Okzident*, 1980², 183.
Beazley	in L.D. Caskey and J.D. Beazley, *Attic Vase Paintings in the Museum of Fine Arts, Boston*, Part II, 1954, 20.
Boardman	in CN 60 and in *Emporio* 27 note 12.
Brommer	in *AA* 1941, 40 and 52 and in *Vasenlisten zur griechischen Heldensage*, 1973, 315.17 (Calydonian boar hunt) and 360.9 (Achilles ambush for Troilos)
Hayes	in *Tocra* I 58
Hemelrijk	in the *Caeretan Hydriae*, 195 and 178 with note 754.
Johansen	in the *Iliad in Early Greek Art*, 1967, 200 and 271–2.
Johnston	in *Exhibition* 1978, passim.
Kemp-Lindermann	in *Darstellungen des Achilleus in griechischer und römischer Kunst*, 1974, 98–99.
LIMC	s.v. Achilles, I.1 no. 254 (A. Kossatz-Deissman); s.v. Herakles, IV.1 no. 57 (J. Boardman)
Lazaridis	in *Guide* 93 and 106
Price	in "Pottery of Naucratis" in *JHS* 44, 1924, 218–9.
Salviat	in *CGED* 91
Schauenburg	in *JdI* 85, 1970, 48.
Walter-Karydi	in *Samos* VI.1, 70 and notes 196–201
Williams	in *AA* 1983, 160–1.

[87] The disposition of the dogs makes it probable that a Calydonian boar hunt scene was meant by the painter. See Chapter 7.

5. **Centauromachy**: **1440*** [Price] in the Sphinx and Lion style.
6. **Danaids carrying their husbands' decapitated heads**: **727***, **730*** and **733*** (FIG. 59) [Price], *but* "perhaps Isis reassembling Osiris?" [Boardman] *and* for **733*** "possibly Agave and Pentheus" [Johnston]. However, warriors carrying decapitated heads are encountered on a late black-figure Athenian lekythos[88] and on Etruscan seals.
7. **Hera in the Judgement of Paris**: **714*** [Price]; with Athena on **899*** [Price]. [Walter-Karydi followed her but not wholeheartedly]. The two sherds are definitely from different vases, as their inner decoration shows.
8. **Heracles**: **741*** [Price and Boardman]; **797*** [Price and Boardman].
9. **Gigantomachy (the Alcyoneus story)**: **795*** [Williams].
10. **?Pegasus**:[89] **798*** (FIG. 59). It could however be merely ornamental, as are winged horses on later Caeretan hydriai.[90]
11. **Peleus and Thetis**: **707*** [Price]; **784*** [Walter-Karydi]—fleeing Nereids.
12. **Polyphemus blinded**: **793** [Hayes; Williams; Hemelrijk]; **738*** [Walter-Karydi; Williams; Hemelrijk] (FIG. 59); **727*** [Williams]—Odysseus' companion carrying the stake; and **772***—the same.
13. **Silen**: **738*** and **760*** [Price] and [Brommer]—capture of Silenus *but* the drunken Polyphemus blinded [Williams].[91]
14. **Tityos scene**: **804*** [Hemelrijk] *but* Gigantomachy [Lazaridis].
15. **Troilos**: **800*** [Akurgal and others] (FIG. 58).

Many of the identifications and interpretations are certain—Heracles, Athena, the Troilos episode,[92] the Centauromachy; others are highly likely, as the blinding of Polyphemus on **793*** and perhaps Pegasus on **798***. The rest are disputable to varying degrees, owing to the mutilated condition of the fragments, which precludes them from telling their stories clearly.

It seems however from these "tantalizing" pieces that the Chian, and thus the Ionian, mythological repertory differs in certain aspects from the better known and preserved Corinthian and Athenian.

III. Ornamental decoration

On the vases of the Grand style ornamental decoration is of the simplest type. Priority is given to figure drawing. On the other hand it is of paramount importance because, with other factors, it places this category stylistically and chronologically between the Animal

---

[88] In *AA* 1942, 74, figs. 6–8 and Boardman, *ABFH* fig. 279. See now M. Halm-Tisserant, *BABesch* 64, 1989, 100ff. for a discussion on the iconography of decapitated heads.

[89] A marble protome of a Pegasus in Chios Museum inv. no. 250, possibly from Phana, was identified and dated to the mid-sixth century by N. Kontoleon in *AE* 1939–41, Arch. Chronicles 24–26 and figs. 1–3. Boardman in *The Antiquaries Journal* 39, 1959, 185, no. 44 pl. 27e agrees with the identification though he lowers the date and disagrees as to its function.

[90] Hemelrijk, *Caeretan Hydriae*, 123 IIIC4B and mainly note 214 on p. 211.

[91] The same figures have been interpreted as Silens, Midas story and Polyphemus. Cf. however, the camel driver on an East Greek vase from Smyrna in *GO*[3] 152, fig. 192. The composition with the human legs in front still remains unsatisfactorily interpreted for the Chian piece.

[92] Kossatz-Deissmann, *LIMC* I.1, 77, no. 254 and I.2, pl. 81. Also, D. Kemp-Lindemann, *Darstellungen des Achilleus in griechischer und römischer Kunst*, 1975, 98–99 where the building is considered as a fountain with a Doric column.

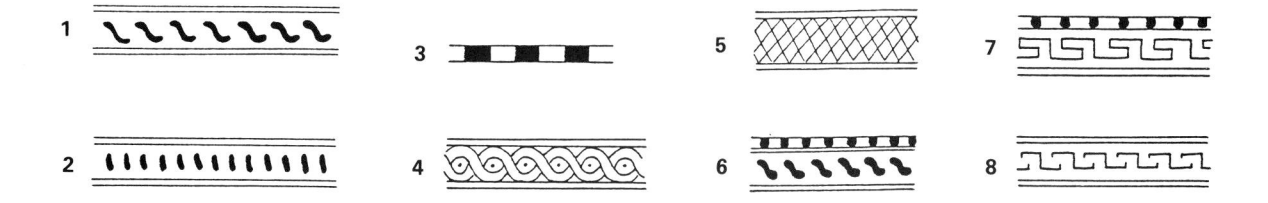

Fig. 60 Rim patterns in the Grand style

Chalice style and the Chalice style. This relative position is well demonstrated by the disappearance in some groups of filling ornament within the lifetime of the Grand style.

1. Rim patterns (FIG. 60) are mostly either mere strokes obliquely or diagonally disposed, or SS, between two lines (FIG. 60.2&1), similar to the ones on the Chalice style. Other motifs appear rarely: on **751***, a simple cable (FIG. 60.4); on the Pitane chalices—(**800***, FIG. 60.8), a broken meander between two lines, and (**801***; FIG. 60.7), a battlement pattern between two lines, below a row of billets and blanks. Finally, on **796*** (FIG. 60.6), come billets and blanks above SS between two lines.

2. Handle zone patterns are almost always a double guilloche. The double guilloche is the most favoured Chian pattern in all the categories of the reserving technique starting from Middle II Wild Goat style to the Chalice style.[93]

3. Filling ornaments (FIG. 61) are used only in the first group, and the Kiev chalice from Berezan (**799***). At first sight their derivation from and stylistic proximity to the Animal Chalice style seem clear. Indeed, there is not one single field ornament in the Grand style which has not already been encountered in the preceding style. Filling ornament is sparsely used and the motifs that prevail are the simple and spiked rosettes. Their existence in one group and their absence in the others is arguably one of the main reasons for seeing all such work as produced on Chios—the argument will be developed later.[94]

4. The bowl of chalices is decorated on the outside with five to six dark bands, to judge from **795***, **800***, and **801***. It certainly depends on the overall size of the vessel. The foot on **800*** has a pair of matt white lines on the junction with the bowl, in the middle and at the base.

IV. *Style*

All the fragments and vases classified here are in the Grand style (**697*–807***) and employ

---

[93] A double guilloche pattern on the handle zone with no preserved figure decoration is an inadequate argument for proclaiming a chalice as Grand style. Williams in *AA* 1983, 182 with note 35 identifies some Grand style fragments among the Emporio material on this basis. However, I think *Emporio* nos. 275–277 are in the Wild Goat style and *Emporio* nos. 731-4 are in the Animal Chalice style; and the fact remains that the style has not as yet been found on Chios.

[94] See below, p. 117–118.

Fig. 61 Filling ornaments in the Grand style

the polychrome technique of decoration, so it could also be called "Polychrome style".[95]

The homogeneity of the style is very strong; however, the following three factors permit division into separate stylistic groups: first, the colour of the slip, which differs greatly in each group; secondly, the existence or non-existence of the filling ornament; and thirdly the manner of figure drawing. Both types of chalices, heavy and light, are indiscriminately used in all the groups.

A. The group with the filling ornament consists of:

From Naucratis: **697*** light; **698*** light; **699*** light; **701*** light; **702*** heavy; **703*** light; **704*** light; **705*** light; **706*** light; **707*** heavy; **708*** light; **709*** light; **710*** light; **722*** light; **752*** light; **764*** light; **766*** light; **768*** heavy; **769*** heavy; **774*** light; **783*** ?light; **790*** ?light; **791*** ?light; **792*** ?light. Also: **796*** light, from Aegina (town); **799*** from Berezan.

---

[95] Cf. Schaus, *Dem. Sanct., Cyrene* II, 78 on the distinction between "polychrome" and "Grand" style which is, in my opinion, unnecessary, as both definitions cover the same category. Certainly, there are narrative scenes in other Chian styles, but only a few.

The common features of this group are: 1) *The colour of the slip* which, wherever information is available, is milky white: approximately 10YR 8/1 of the Munsell chart and even whiter; 2) The only group in the style that makes use of *filling ornament*, all of which is close to that of the Animal Chalice style and could possibly date the group at the end of the first quarter of the century; 3) The *iconography* of men, already referred to, is best illustrated by members of this group. **702***, **704***, **706***, **752*** and **764*** seem to be by the same hand, as is indicated by the rendering of facial details, especially the long hair floating at the back and bound in a hairband, and by the identical folds of the chiton sleeves, i.e. a fishbone pattern on **704*** and **764***. **703*** and **796*** betray other hands; 4) Another feature of the group is the first clumsy *endeavour to render some sort of perspective*; painters aiming at the effect of foreshortening reduce the length of the arm by a half, either both arms or more frequently the one further from the onlooker. **768***, **769*** and **774*** are from different vases but by the same hand.

The bull's forepart as a shield device, on **710***, is a firm link with the previous Animal Chalice style, as is also the filling ornament. The horse's head with the mulish expression on **790*** has a close stylistic proximity to **1324*** in the Sphinx and Lion style.

B. The Aphaia Painter and group[96] can be divided into works attributable either to the master or to his companions. All are from Naucratis, apart from the very first.

The Aphaia Painter's works are: **795*** heavy from Aegina [Williams: "the Aphaia Painter"]; **712*** light [Williams: "the Aphaia Painter"]; UCL 382 [Williams: "the Aphaia Painter"]; **714*** light; **715*** light; **716*** light; **743*** heavy; **745*** light.

The Aphaia group: in the same group but not by the same hand: **719*** light; **720*** light; **721*** light; **723*** light; **773*** light; **784*** ?light; **785*** ?light.

Members of this group present a thematic unity; all display garments, in particular the lower part of chitons and himatia. From what can be judged there is no filling ornament. The Aphaia chalice, **795***, and fragments **712***, **716***, **743*** and **745*** have *inner figure-decoration*—all are komasts—in the light on dark technique, which will be discussed further below.

C. The Naucratis Painter and group

The Naucratis Painter's works: **727*** light; **730*** light; **731*** light; **732*** heavy; **733***; **734***; **736*** light; **737***; **738***; **739*** light; **740*** heavy; **741*** light; **742*** heavy; **757*** (perhaps by his hand); **758***; **759***; **760***; and **797***, from the Athenian Acropolis.

The Naucratis Painter's group: **713*** light; **726*** light; **761*** heavy and big, crater-like and **762*** the same; **763** light; **765*** light; **771*** light; **772*** light (not same chalice as **727***); and **807***.

The colour of the slip is *a light beige, almost creamy white*. It ranges almost, but not exactly, between 10 YR 8/2 "white" to 8/3 "very pale brown" of the Munsell chart.

There is no filling ornament, and rim patterns are of the simplest. The figure drawing, on the other hand, is of the highest level: these are *the masterpieces* not only of the Grand style but of the entire Chian output. It seems this group is the work of a very few painters.

---

[96] D. Williams, *AA* 1983, named him from the centre piece, **795*** and attributed **712*** to his hand, as well as UCL 382.

Sixteen to seventeen fragments, (**727***, **730***–**734***, **736***–**742***, **?757**, **758***–**760*** and **797***), some perhaps from the same vase but not joining,[97] could be attributed to one hand. He may be labelled the '*Naucratis Painter*', since the majority of his works so far have been found at Naucratis, with only one from the Athenian Acropolis (**797***).

The drawing of garments, embellished with lavishly decorated paryphai filled up with little white dots, is painstaking. The rendering of naked human legs with the working out of knee-caps and ankle-bones on **732***, **742***, **758*** and athletic muscles in general on **734***, **738***, **740***, **758*** and **760***, are, with the slight overlapping of his figures, a remarkable feature of his work.

An error is the disproportionate, rather inflated, breast of the lady on **759***, who compensates for this with her excellent coiffure approximating to the elaborate one of the sphinxes on **700***.

The culmination of the painter's career is marked by **739***: a horse overlapping the tail of another is a masterpiece of Archaic drawing; the inner decoration with the superbly drawn palmette and lotus add to this impression. Very close stylistically to this piece are three more fragments with horses, which seem to be painted by another hand; these are **713*** and **757** possibly from the same chalice, with identical inner decoration, and **807***. The horses' muzzles recall works by Athenian red figure and white ground painters of advanced style, of at least a hundred years later.

D. The grey-slip group

724* light from Naucratis; **735*** heavy from Naucratis.

Both have a peculiarly grey slip; almost, but not exactly, ranging from 2.5Y N7 "light grey" to N6 "grey" of the Munsell chart. **724*** has white dotted circles in the inner decoration which bring it close to **717***, from a light chalice and **718***, a small fragment from a heavy chalice. Though **717*** and **724*** have a stylistic proximity, the rest are but loosely connected.

Two recently published fragments of a chalice from Berezan (**799***)[98] in the Grand style are closely related to the Naucratis fragments; thematically they belong to the riding scenes and could have formed part of a Troilos episode. The horse on **799*** approximates in style the head of the horse on **713***; the decoration on the interior, which on the top row displays pomegranates within the chain of lotus and rosette, recalls the identical pattern on the Delos Animal chalice (**643***); and finally the spiked rosette which is identical to the one on **698*** and the drawing of the warrior with the almost flat head implies that this vase should be placed within group A with the filling ornament. The Kiev chalice from Berezan (**799***) is perhaps the best example to demonstrate the solid link between Middle II Wild Goat and the Grand style; its filling ornament—in particular the horseshoe roundel—conforms to that of the former style. This implies a rather early date for the chalice, within the first quarter of the sixth century, which would mean that it is slightly earlier than the Pitane chalices (**800*** and **801***).

[97] However compare the inner decoration on **730***, **733*** and **759*** which is identical.

[98] Kornysova, *Olbia* 45, fig. 18.

These last two chalices (**800*** and **801***) definitely belong to the Grand style: first, the manner of their drawing is similar to the other fragments of this category and then they use a restricted form of polychromy: on the light, ivory-white slip, the sepia-tan paint creates a vivid contrast, supplemented by added crimson, purple and white.

Closer stylistic observations can be drawn with the Naucratis material in the rendering of horses, for example the muzzle of the white horse on the Troilos chalice (**800***) is identical to those on **774*** and **807***. Polyxena's figure and stance are similar not only to those of Grand style women, as **771*** or **783***, but also to female heads in the Chalice style, as **821***, **829*** and **835***. She wears a long belted chiton with a paryphe similar to the ones on **888***, **889*** and **895***. Achilles' device with the rosette complex approximates to the one on **698***.

As for the inner decoration, the lions of the second frieze on **800*** are very near in style to the two horsemen in the Oxford chalice (**810***) and the chain with lotus and palmettes on spiral tendrils recalls the patterns of **739*** or **774***.

Stylistically they share a number of common features: their dimensions—both are chalice-craters; the rendering of human figure and their anatomical details; as regards ornamental decoration both have very similar rim patterns (FIG. 60.7 and 8), the guilloche on both sides of the handle zone and of course no filling ornament. However, any attribution of these chalices to the same hand must await fuller publication.[99]

The three unpublished vases in polychrome style (**798***, **804*** and **814***) recovered at the sanctuary of Parthenos at Neapolis (modern Kavala) have been left intentionally to the end of the Grand style, as their allocation still seems somewhat dubious.[100] Lazaridis proclaimed them to be Chian[101] and Hemelrijk ardently accepted this assignment for the plate with the Tityos scene (**804***).[102]

The polychrome decoration of all three does indeed display typical Chian characteristics: both of the purely Grand style for **798*** and **804***, and of the light on dark technique for **814***. In addition the imaginative scene on **804*** recalls Chian iconographical practices. Finally the manner of drawing, especially of the Tityos scene (**804***) and the winged horse (**798***) are of Chian spirit and execution. The slip too looks white enough to be acceptable.

However, there are some minor but fundamental details, which are disturbing: first, the composition of the tondo with the division into two segments, upper figurative and lower animal, recalls other practices outside Chios. Secondly, and even more importantly, the ornamental decoration is not wholly Chian: the lotus-and-bud frieze encircling the tondo of the Tityos plate (**804***), though very common as an ornament on Chian vases differs in execution. In addition, the drawing of the swastika as filling ornament in the lower register of the plate looks more Cycladic and the asterisks around the winged horse (**798***) when used in Chian are never so crowded or used by themselves. These points should make one cautious about accepting their unreserved classification as purely Chian. It is therefore

---

[99] From Bayburtluoğlu's article in *CGED* 29, it seems that the Troilos chalice (**800***) was in context with an Athenian komast cup by the KX painter (or the KY painter, according to Bakir) and the Farewell chalice (**801***) with an Athenian band cup; such attributions would distance them by twenty years.

[100] I have seen the vases in the Kavala museum but still think that more material is needed to make the situation clearer.

[101] See Lazaridis, *Guide*, for **798*** and **814***, and very likely from Chios for **804***.

[102] *Caeretan Hydriae*, 178 "a Chiot plate".

proposed here that these three vases ought to be regarded either as products of a local Chian manufacturing centre outside the island,[103] but not necessarily Thasos; or as from a workshop of possibly another tradition but here working under heavy Chian influence.

At the present restricted state of knowledge, these three pieces must be considered as part of the Grand style, to whose appreciation and understanding they add greatly.

The impact of Chian polychromy and good figure work can be traced also in the output of an individual Samian artist. Fragments of a hydria in polychrome decoration with scenes of processions have recently come to light there (Pls. 241 and 242). The scenes are iconographically and stylistically so close to the Chian Grand style as to have compelled, not unjustly when fewer fragments were known, their classification within Chian production.[104] Recently, however, with the addition of more sherds their definite attribution to a Samian artist who worked under heavy Chian influence has become clear,[105] despite the two islands' hostile relations and their artistic development along completely different lines.[106]

To conclude this consideration of the Grand style, the impact it exercised on alien artists is obvious in the case of Samos, and argued to have given rise to other derivative workshops elsewhere in the North Aegean. It can be claimed that in iconography this was the most imaginative and promising style of the entire Chian vase painting school, as well as of East Greece at the time. The polychrome technique of decoration first appears in Ionia in the earlier half of the sixth century—an original achievement of this School, which went on to set a norm for East Greek styles of a painterly character in the later half of the century. Although the manner of figure drawing was completely within the well-established limits of Archaic convention, this Chian version maintained a consistently high standard of workmanship.

V. Connections with free painting

Some scholars have argued that vase painting in the Archaic period is an art independent from free painting on the grounds of differences in iconography[107] and that it should be viewed per se. Nevertheless, the commonly accepted theory is that a relation between the two does exist and can be traced.[108] Regretably no wall painting of this period has been found on Chios to give an idea of any probable connections. The impression, however, that the Grand style with its polychrome technique of decoration must have had some connection with free painting,[109] may be reasonably deduced also from other more advanced and earlier schools.[110]

---

[103] Cf. Chapter 7 concerning a Chian workshop in Thrace for another category in the reserving styles.

[104] *Samos* VI.1, no. 854, pl. 98.

[105] Inv. K.1770. A. Furtwängler in *AM* 95, 1970, 188–197, pls. 54–55 and Beil. I (in colour); also H. Kyrieleis in *Chios Conference* 194 with a colour photograph, pl. III.

[106] H. Kyrieleis, *ibid.*, 187–204, for a recent and instructive discussion mainly on the divergencies in the artistic traits of the two islands during the Archaic period.

[107] See D.A. Amyx, Archaic Vase Painting vis-a-vis "Free" Painting at Corinth, in *Ancient Greek Art and Archaeology*, ed. W.G. Moon, 1983, 37–52, where the conclusion reached for the independent course of each art, based on ample evidence, is persuasive.

[108] M. Robertson *Greek Painting* 1959, 34–81 and *BSA* 46, 1951, 151–9. Also *GPP*² 174–6.

[109] Boardman in *Chios Conference* 252–253. See also E. Walter-Karydi in *Alt-Ägina* II.1, 14–15.

[110] For a recent discussion see G.P. Schaus in *JHS* 108, 1988, 109–110.

Polychrome decoration for all East Greek vase painting of the first half of the sixth century is limited to this style;[111] it springs up suddenly after generations of good but routine drawing from an avant-garde atelier of the second main workshop, no doubt as part of a search for new horizons. Even if there was no direct borrowing or copying, at least the source of inspiration of the Grand style lies in other media. To a certain extent this notion is reinforced by the arguable, if indirect, connection that this particular Chian category has with paintings discovered recently, at the fringes of the Greek world, mainly in Asia Minor, Egypt and elsewhere.[112]

Noteworthy hints of interrelations and artistic exchanges can be drawn from the following monuments:

The Gordion frescoes[113] of the late sixth century have been thought of as betraying Chian influence and even as the possible works of a Chian artist. Their style originates in the North Ionian milieu and it is clear that iconographical similarities with Chian works exist. Rumpf in particular ardently supported the view of a Chian painter at work at Gordion.[114] More specifically, the headgear in the form of a diadem decorated by griffin protomes and worn by a lady on the Phrygian frescoes approximates to the probable reconstructions of the helmet of the Athena cult statue at Emporio; this last was also ornamented by griffin protomes found at the Emporio excavations and interpreted as such by Boardman.[115]

Polychromy, the common iconographical elements and a stylistic proximity may be argued to account for the Gordion wall paintings' relation to the Chian school.

The Elmali (Kizilbel) wall paintings[116] recall in certain aspects an East Greek approach, but it would be difficult to maintain that they are specifically connected with Chian work. What they share is much of the subject matter, but not the manner of drawing. Thus, there is the warrior's departure (in neither case to do with that of Amphiaraos); processions of warriors or hunters; horsemen; a possible Troilos episode and the Medusa story involving Chrysaor, Pegasus and the Gorgons. The banquet scene is in a purely Anatolian manner,[117] and the depictions of sea voyages, though frequent in Etruscan art, are not witnessed in East Greek art. The winged figure, thought of as female,[118] above the chariot scene, recalls a similar male figure in Chian *black-figure* Grand style (**1461***, FIG. 88) though differently intended.[119] Another minor detail is the anthemion on the mounting warrior's corselet[120] similar to the palmette acroterion on the building of the Troilos chalice (**800***).

The similarities, therefore, are vague and loose, at best restricted to details, and mostly confined to a common thematic stock known and used by other East Greek schools.

---

[111] Cook in *BSA*, 47, 1952, 147.
[112] Boardman in *Chios Conference* 252 where the case for possible production at Naucratis is presented.
[113] *AJA* 59, 1955, 9–10, pls. 4–5, figs. 16–21 and *AJA* 60, 1956, 249–266, pl. 86, figs. 20 and 21. M. Mellink, forthcoming, from *GO*³ note 243 on p. 273.
[114] *AJA* 60, 1956, 75; see also his *MuZ* 46, pl. 11.10–12.
[115] *Emporio* 27 and note 9. Also *GO*³ with notes 242–3 and fig. 105.

[116] Reports by Mellink in *AJA*, especially *AJA* 74, 1970, 245–253, pls. 55–62; *AJA* 77, 1973, pls. 43–4. Also in *RA* 1976, 21–34, where information about a Bryn Mawr Dissertation by D. Duryea, *The Kizilbel tomb near Elmali*, 1971.
[117] *GO*³ 10f.
[118] Mellink in *RA* 1976, 3.
[119] See p. 155.
[120] *AJA* 77, 1973, pl. 43.

The Saqqara wooden panel[121] depicts a processional scene of humans with a cow and a bull, which has been variously interpreted; it must have been painted by an East Greek artist, probably kin of the Caeretan hydriai painters, or the painters themselves on their way to Italy from East Greece at the beginning of the last third of the sixth century.

Chians seldom mixed humans with animals and in the rare instances that they did (**458***, **612*** and **613**), the scenes are of purely decorative character. Furthermore, the style of the two bovines on the panel, which clearly demonstrate their interrelation with the works of the Caeretan hydriai painters[122] does not relate to earlier known Chian bulls. Samian works and in particular a bronze bull[123] are stylistically closer to the animals on the Saqqara wooden panel.

The connection of the panel to Chian art, if there is any, is perhaps no more than a loose and indirect influence transferred to Egypt through the Carians from East Greek art in general.[124]

It has been stated[125] that Chian painting, apparently of the Grand style, is stylistically an ancestor to the Boccanera slabs and the Pontic Paris painter.

As regards the Boccanera slabs[126] from Caere it is true that some details in the Grand style vases come readily to mind, i.e. the conventional colours; the unveiling figures on **714*** and **801***; the pointed headdress of the archer on **708***; the boots with upturned toes on **717*** and **795***; the rendering of the male ankle-bones on **742*** and the ornaments on the paryphai of garments on **730*** and **733***. The resemblances seen in the type of head on the Boccanera plaques, which takes after the Chian as has been already pointed out,[127] together with the general composition of the processional scenes cannot be accidental and though both styles run in parallel, it is possible that the Chian had some sort of an indirect impact on the Etruscan Boccanera slabs. Of course, the claims of other East Greek schools, with their common background, must be born in mind too. The Pontic Paris painter's[128] style, however, has practically nothing to remind one of the Grand style painting. Apart from boots with upturned toes, unveiling female figures and the depiction of certain mythological episodes, such as Centaurs, the blinding of Polyphemus, the Troilos story and few more subject connections common to all Archaic art, there is nothing held in common.

This brief survey, in which some monuments have to varying degrees a disputable connection with Chian vase painting, implies that the polychrome Grand style had a relation, of some kind, to "free" painting. In the absence of direct evidence from the island, the only elements on which this speculation is based are on the one hand the palette range and on the other, derivative connections, especially with the Gordion frescoes, the Boccanera slabs and, as regards the repertory, the Kizilbel wall paintings.

[121] G.T. Martin, *The tomb of Ḥetepka* 1979, 74–8 (R.V. Nicholls), no. 284, pls. 60, 85 and frontispiece (H. Ward's watercolour). Also *CAH* III, pls. to vol. III (ed. J. Boardman) 1984, 224–5.

[122] J. Hemelrijk *Caeretan Hydriae*, 201–2; *CAH* pls. to vol. III 224–5, no. 299; J. Boardman in *Chios Conference* 252, and recently in *Papers on the Amasis Painter* 147–8 and fig. 5 where he hints at a possible connection between the Amasis potter/painter, Ionian painting (whatever medium) and Egypt.

[123] *AM* 96, 1981, 88, fig. 8 and pl. 24.1.

[124] *GO*³ 135 and recently see E.A. Hemelrijk in *BABesch* 62, 1987, 33–55 on publishing "a group of provincial East-Greek Vases from South Western Asia Minor" and mainly p. 54.

[125] Hemelrijk, *Caeretan Hydriae*, 185.

[126] F. Roncalli, *Le Lastre dipinti da Cerveteri*, 1965, pls. 13–15, M. Spenger, G. Bartoloni, *Die Etrusker, Kunst und Geschichte*, 1977, pl. 7 and Rumpf, *MuZ*, pl. 11.12.

[127] A. Akerström in *OpRom*. 1, 1954, 215 note 5.

[128] P. Ducati, *Pontische Vasen*, 1932, passim and L. Hannestad, *The Paris painter, an Etruscan Vase-painter*, 1974 passim. Cf. *GPP*² 155 where the resemblances of Pontic to East Greek vase painting are considered accidental.

VI. Place of manufacture

The British excavations at Phana and subsequently at Emporio settled once and for all the controversy over the *origin* of Chian pottery. Local production is almost unanimously accepted, but *the question of the manufacture at Naucratis* for three categories, amongst which was the Grand style, by a Chian workshop using imported clay and slip has been raised.[129] As regards this particular category the view was inevitably based on the argumentum e silentio and other reasons, that will remain valid,[130] as long as pottery of the Grand style, or of any kind of polychrome painting, is not revealed on the island.

The lack of systematic excavations and hence material on Chios over the last thirty five years, even of finds from rescue excavations in Chios town, has hampered any serious consideration of this matter.

However, a few suggestive arguments could perhaps lead towards a point of view quite different to the above:

1. Clay analyses[131] have proved that the clay and slip used are Chian. Whilst this does not preclude their importation to Naucratis, it does yet equally hold open the chance of production at home.
2. Whilst acknowledging the limited nature of excavations and the even smaller amount of deposits of the first half of the sixth century, the absence of this material category on Chios is perhaps not so surprising.[132] A similar situation exists for other ceramic groups, e.g. "the Poultry black-figure group",[133] but this has not led to claims of a centre of production outside the island.
3. Distribution of this category outside Naucratis is known at a number of places. Aegina town (**796***); Aegina, the Aphaia temple (**795***); the Athenian Acropolis (**797***); Pitane (**800*** and **801***), albeit in a more restricted version of polychromy;[134] and most recently at Berezan (**799***).[135] Again, whilst this fact does not automatically argue for a production centre on Chios, neither by the same token does it argue for a specific one elsewhere.
4. Within the Grand style four groups have been put together.[136] Group A and the Berezan chalice (**799***) with their filling ornament have close ties to the Wild Goat and Animal Chalice styles; in its first steps it follows their practices as regards ornamental decoration; i.e. rim and handle zone patterns and more specifically filling ornament. The other three groups: B, C, D and the Pitane chalices (**800*** and **801***) lose this filling ornament, but still their consistency and homogeneity of style show that this took place *within the same workshop*. Moreover, the later Chalice style, even if

---

[129] By Boardman, CN, 59–60.

[130] Boardman in *Chios Conference* 252–8, where his view is to some degree mitigated and the question is left open. However, he maintains his position with regard to the class of the inscribed kantharoi with fresh arguments.

[131] See Introduction p. 2 and notes 7–10.

[132] By analogy with the other categories I have estimated that not more than a handful of sherds should have turned up on Chios. But after all, not a single rich sanctuary, or even cemetery of the first half of the century where the category is to be dated has been excavated so far in Chios town.

[133] See Chapter 4.

[134] Other excavated coastal sites of Asia Minor, it seems, have not yielded Grand style vases (*CGED* 28). There is only brief mention of a surface sherd near Erythrae, at the Donkey site, see J.M. Cook in *BSA* 60, 1965, 141 "a scrap of chalice in what appeared to be a polychrome animal style".

[135] However, other objects, such as Greek faience produced also at Naucratis, did reach the Black Sea colonies at this time, see V. Webb *Archaic Greek Faience* 1978, 7–10.

[136] See pp. 110–4.

deriving from a separate seventh-century workshop, yet shows by its lack of filling ornament and the similarity in its figure drawing that it is closely related to the Grand style.

A reasonable interpretation of all these close interrelationships must take their integral unity into account. Since it has never been suggested that the Chalice style is anything other than Chian inspired and produced, it surely follows that the centre for the Grand style must also be so located.

5. External evidence: The connections, albeit loose and lacking full comprehension of the steps of their development, being detected between the Grand style and wall paintings from Anatolia and elsewhere, are capable of having evolved only within a metropolitan and wealthy Ionian city.

6. Furthermore, the impact of this style was more remarkable than was thought up to now. It can with certainty be traced as far apart as an artist on Samos on the one hand and in fragments unearthed at Neapolis (modern Kavala) on the other. Although the link between Naucratis and the North Aegean, possibly via Maroneia, which might have played a significant role in the trading relations, has been argued for,[137] it does not necessarily follow that these vases were imported from Naucratis.

Thus, in conclusion, the source of the clay and slip of the vases; the lack of extensive excavation on the island; the ever widening circle of proveniences; the intimate connection, by means of stylistic connotations, with accepted Chian wares; the external, if indirect, influences; and finally the impact on Samian and North Aegean artists more in keeping with a metropolitan centre than a trading port can all in conjunction tip the balance on behalf of the view that sees the production centre located in Chios town.

2A. LIGHT ON DARK DECORATION

This technique of decoration is used in Chian vase painting throughout the sixth century for the interior of open vases. Rarely, however, is it employed on the outer surface as well. The technique is the following: on the slipped surface of the vase a dark paint is applied, usually black or dark brown and once, on **810***, mauvish; on top of this the decoration is lavishly worked in red and white.[138] The effect of this limited palette is to make this decoration stand close to the polychrome Grand style and in fact it could be classified as a subdivision, though working in a contrary manner.

The light on dark decoration starts at the beginning of the sixth century and one of its earliest manifestations is *the tondo of the Aphrodite bowl*, (**252***, FIG. 32.1), where a circular

[137] C. Roebuck in *ClPh.* 46, 1951, 212 ff. and more recently in *Chios Conference* 83–84. However, cf. Austin, *Greece and Egypt*, 40, where the evidence is considered insufficient to support the triangular trading relations between Egypt, East Greece and Thrace in general. See also Chapter 7.

[138] *Emporio* 157; *GPP*² 127; *Samos* VI.1, 69 where "Schalen" are included in the shapes employing the technique.

black band decorated with Corinthianising white dot-rosettes encircles the central motif. Had this technique in a simpler form[139] (Pl. 240.2) not been long known to Chian vase painting, the skilful "Aphrodite bowl painter" could have been credited with its invention. However, it looks as if it were he who adapted it for the interior of open vases and thereby launched a long and successful career for this type of decoration.

The floruit of this is seen in the Animal Chalice style, where the interior of the radically reformed chalice is no longer left plain. The charismatic idiosyncrasy of Chian vase painters in their appreciation of colours brings them near to the art of "interior decorators". The culmination is reached in the Grand style vases where a few—mainly of the Aphaia painter and his circle—figurative works are so treated. Though ornamental patterns are always present on the slightly later Chalice style, yet on the plain sixth-century chalices they diminish in elaboration, until simple pairs of lines mark its gradual extinction.

The technique of light on dark is used on chalices, kantharoi and phialai. It is one of the fundamental characteristic features of the School employed, as already mentioned, in all its categories.[140] Furthermore it supplies a safe criterion for identifying a sherd as being from an open vase and belonging to the sixth century.

According to the repertory displayed, light on dark decoration can conventionally be divided into figurative and floral. The former seems to be always mixed with the latter and never stands alone, as **795*** and **800*** demonstrate.

1. Figurative decoration: This is exclusively, with only one exception (**899***), confined to vases in the Grand style either in the interior or occasionally on the exterior.

Chalice **810*** (FIG. 62) with the exquisite horsemen on the exterior approximates stylistically to works of the "Naucratis painter", who seems to have a liking for white dot rosettes, for example **737***;[141] it also stands close to **811***.[142]

A distinct group centres around the "Aphaia Painter" with his outstanding chalice **795***: the inside of **712***, komast with garland; the inside of **743***, komast playing the double flute; the inside of **716***, komast, and perhaps, **813***, front part of a griffin head.

The figures stand on a baseline; incision and yellow paint are added here and there for accentuating details.

These two painters succeed in making art out of this technique both by the subject matter and the elaboration of colours: to the usual red and white are added golden-brown or yellow and vermilion, together with thin incisions for the garlands on the chest, the knee-caps and toes of komasts.

Two more vases in this technique have remarkable decoration. On the interior of the Troilos chalice (**800***), the second frieze from the top is embellished with a row of lions interchanging with rosettes. The detailed work and the colours, white for the bodies, red for the manes of lions, produce the effect of an elaborate and artistic mood. It is the interior decorative scheme—style and polychromy—of this vase that are used to support the argument for the manufacture of the Grand style at Chios.

---

[139] *Emporio* 102 and pl. 47.537 (Here, Pl. 240.2).
[140] For categories in black-figure technique, i.e. the komast and animal chalices, see Chapter 4, where this decoration is again treated in detail.
[141] But also **724***.
[142] Price's attribution in *CVA*, Oxford II, 82.

810

Fig. 62 Horsemen on chalice **810**

Finally, on the Kavala phiale, (**814***, FIG. 64) the figurative frieze, again second from the top, and enclosed by a floral zone of lotus and palmette with linear patterns below, is an impressive and interesting vase. The figures are also picked out on the dark background, distinguished by a white line for their contours and elaborated with mauve and golden-yellow details, which culminates in an all-over polychrome effect. The vase could either be considered as an import from Chios, or else strongly imitating this particular Chian style and technique.

This figurative light on dark technique has been considered an independent one,[143] but it is better thought of as another version or even a subdivision of the polychrome Grand style.

[143] *Samos* VI.1, 69.

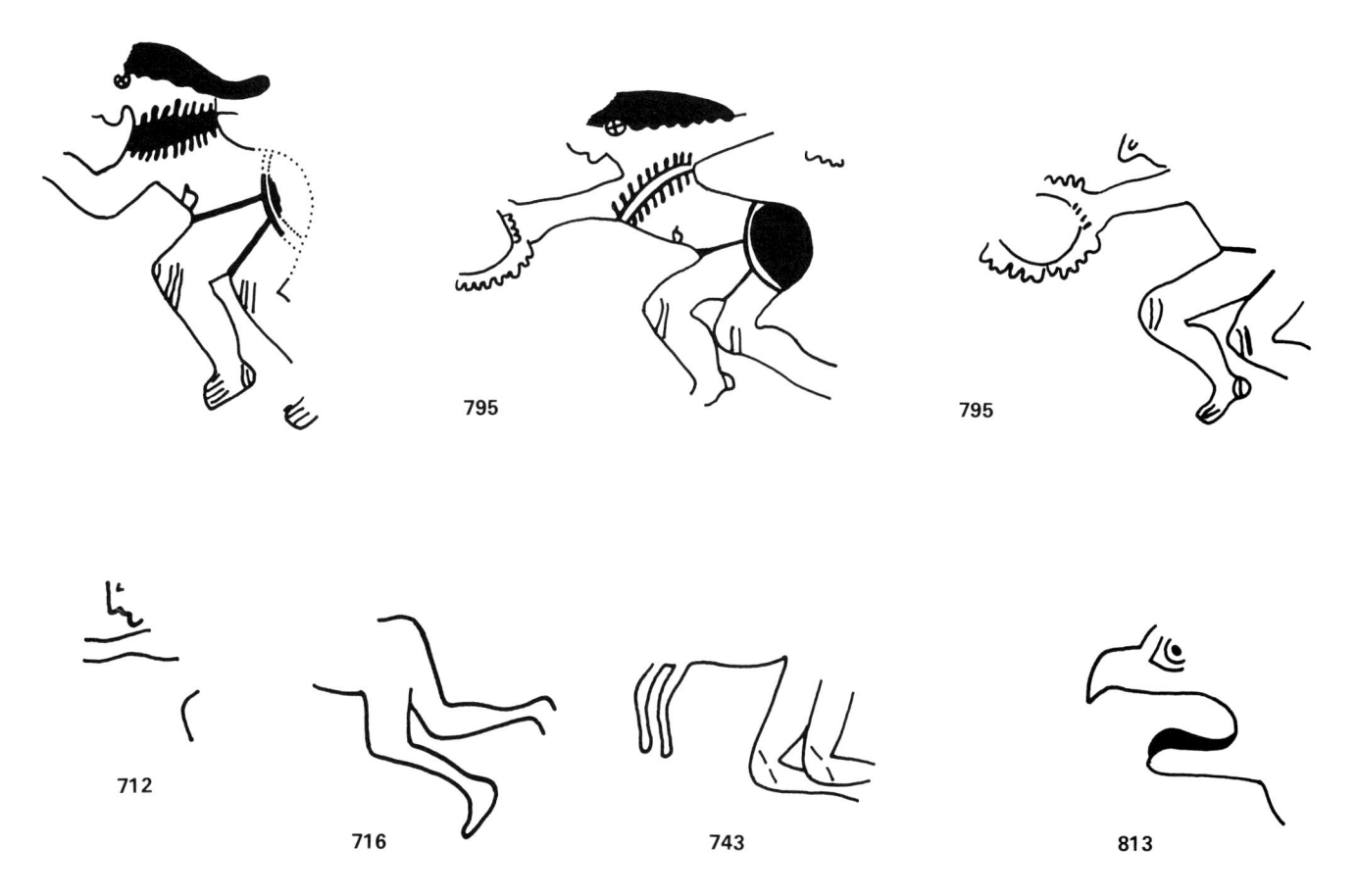

Fig. 63 Light on dark decoration: The Aphaia group

2. Floral decoration: With the exception of the outer frieze on **814***, floral decoration always occupies the inside of open vessels. It displays great variety: the main component is the *lotus flower in composition with buds, rosettes and palmettes*.[144] These motifs constitute the decoration of the upper frieze, the nearest to the rim. Quite a few linear patterns, e.g. rows of squares, zigzags and fishbone are used as dividing bands to separate friezes of floral decoration. Frequently, chains of pomegranates, dot rosettes, concentric circles, tongues and strokes are found interspersed on the primary or secondary friezes.

Amongst the most elaborate examples are the inner decoration of the Marion phiale mesomphalos, (**1081***),[145] from the acme of the series and the slightly later Tocra phiale, (**1075***).[146]

The examples on chalices are innumerable; only very brief mention can be made of the elaborate inner decoration found in certain heavy Animal style chalices (FIG. 65), e.g. **440*** with lotus and rosette linked by tendrils on the primary frieze, and buds with concentric circles below; **441*** with lotus and rosette; **469*** with lotus and rosette linked by tendrils;

---

[144] For an excellent drawing of a lotus and palmette chain united with tendril and a fishbone pattern below, see Williams in *AA* 1983, 159, fig. 5.

[145] Boardman in *RDAC* 1968, 12–15, where, among other things, this decoration is explored in full.

[146] *Tocra* II, 25.

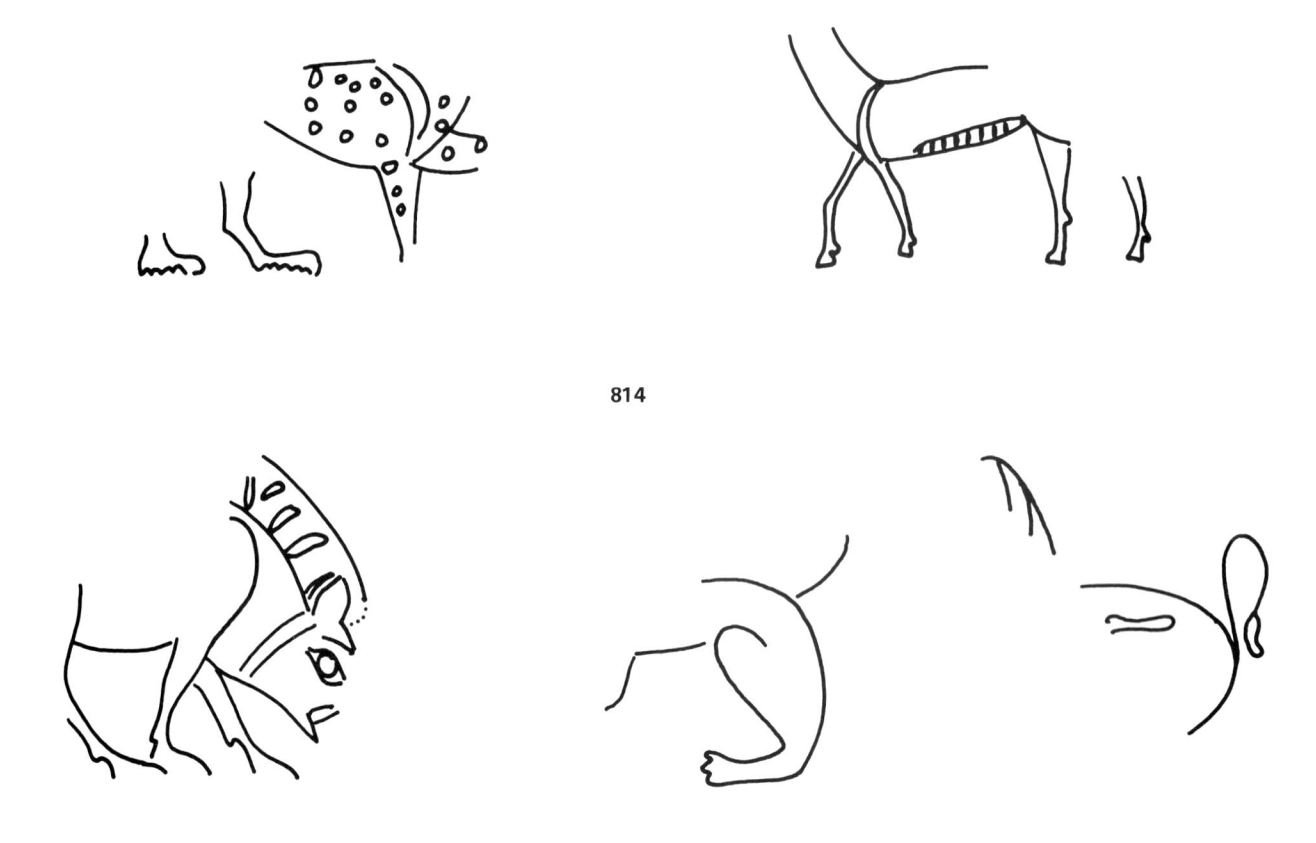

Fig. 64 Animals on the Kavala phiale **814**

471* with lotus and rosette; **552*** with lotus and rosette lined by tendrils; and **643*** with lotus and rosette linked with tendrils and with inserted pomegranates, below dot rosettes.[147]

The decoration is continued on the interior of the Chalice style vessels but wanes as time goes by to the simplest and most rudimentary types ending up as mere bands or lines.[148] Some examples, drawn on FIG. 66, are: **822*** and **922*** with lotus; **927*** with lotus and bud with tendrils; **928*** with lotus and rosette; **972*** and **1071*** with lotus and bud; **974*** with lotus and spiked swastika; **973*** and **1062*** with bands or pairs of lines.

---

[147] For an excellent drawing of the inner decoration of the Delos chalice see *Délos* X, pl. 62.

[148] *Emporio* 158.

440

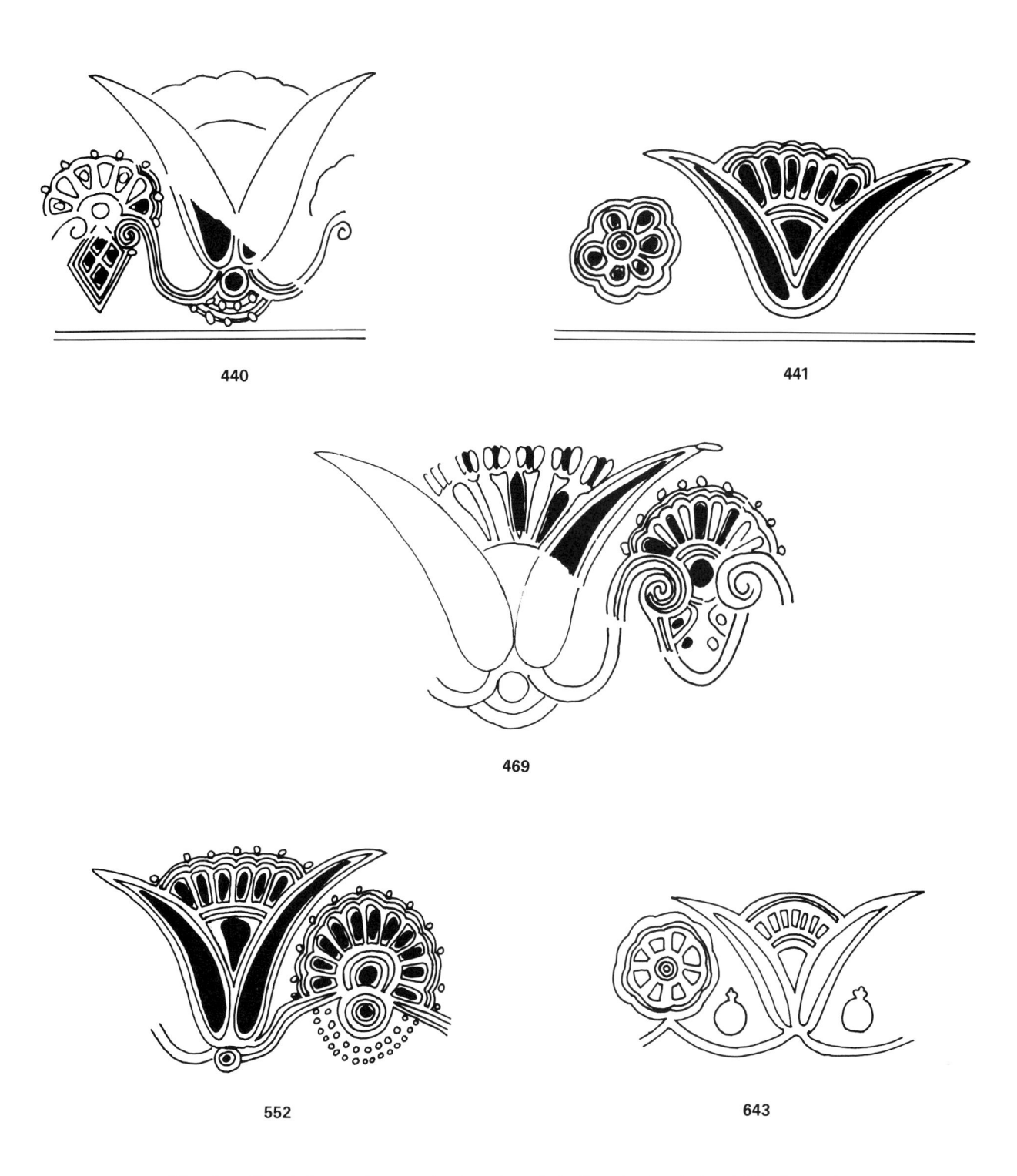

441

469

552

643

Fig. 65 Floral decoration on the interior of chalices in the Animal Chalice style

822

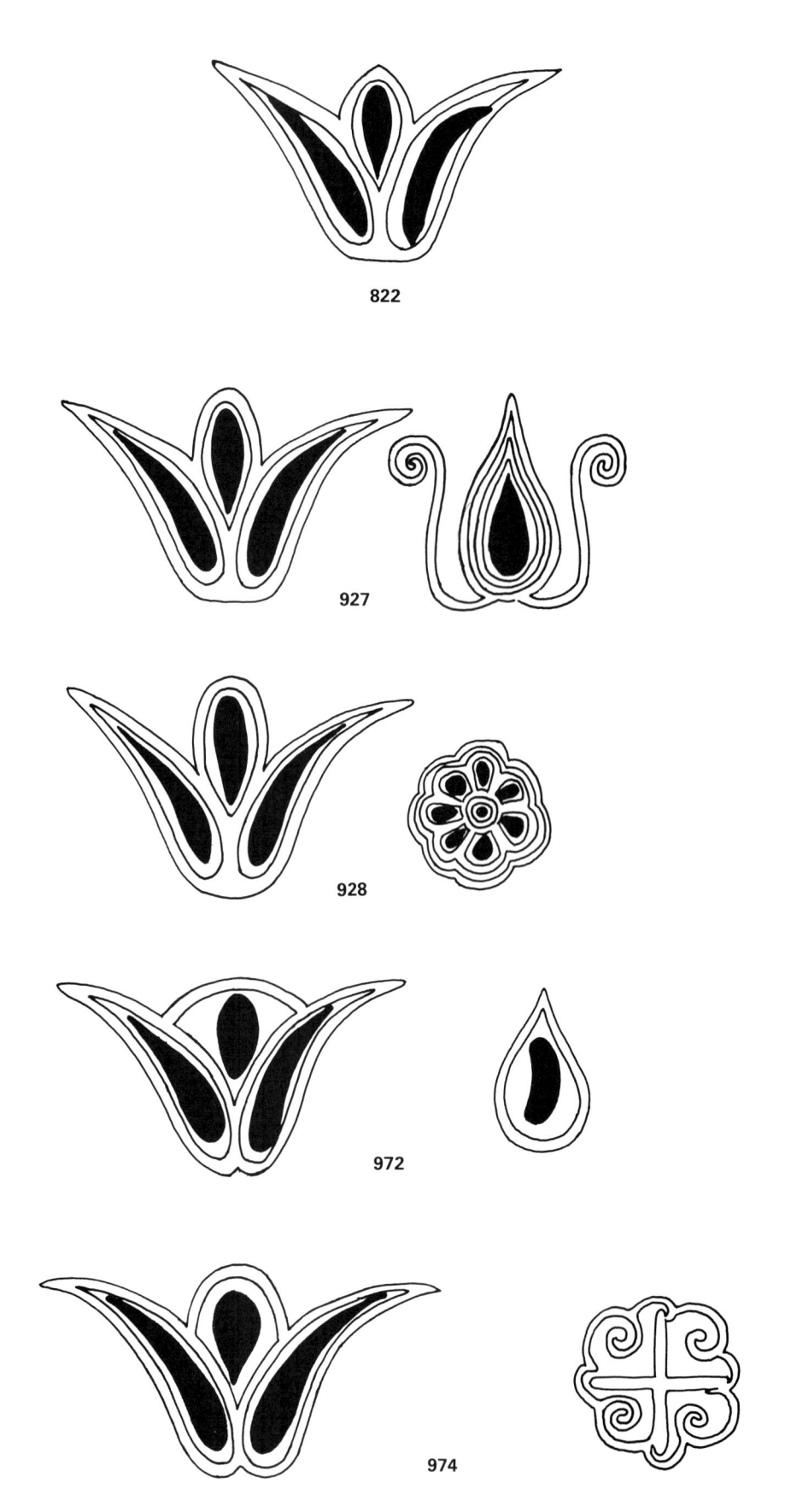

927

928

972

974

Fig. 66　Floral decoration on the interior of chalices in the Chalice style

3. THE CHALICE STYLE

The last figurative category in the reserving styles of the sixth century is separated into three main divisions as seen in the Catalogue. A. vases (chalices, kantharoi and phialai mesomphaloi) with no filling ornament; B. vases with patterned decoration; and D. vases with floral designs. To these is added a third set, C., of fragments belonging to either of the first two. In all probability this style was produced by the same workshop as that of the seventh century patterned chalices.[149] The thematic stock, however, of division A. is derived both from the preceding Animal Chalice and the almost contemporaneous Grand styles.

A. Vases with no filling ornament[150]

The lack of filling ornament, the difference in concept, composition and execution of the figure drawing and the summary inner decoration single out this category as an independent one, manifestly the last in this technique of decoration.

The characteristic features, save the slip, which follows the Chian norm of being chalky and white, could be summarised as follows:

1. The shape, commonly yet not exclusively used, is the chalice, which has light walls and is small in dimension. A typical example is the chalice from Phana (**821***, FIG. 67). All the intact examples range from around 0.13 to about 0.16 in height, the most being 0.181 for **927*** and **928***. The height corresponds in certain cases exactly to the diameter at the rim. This is the normal proportion for an average sixth-century light chalice and will be again met in the contemporary black-figure animal and komast chalices.[151] Kantharoi of Williams' type A and phialai mesomphaloi are also employed.

2. The subject matter comprises both humans and animals. The repertory of the latter is restricted to the two favourite Chian beasts: the lion (FIG. 68) and the sphinx (FIG. 69). One of the two is set solitary in the field, occupying usually the central axis of the obverse side only, whereas on the rear, either a rosette is placed, as on **927*** and **928***, or it is left completely blank, as on **971*** and **972***. The types of lion and sphinx derive from the Wild Goat style and consequently the Animal Chalice style, where they have been dealt with; suffice it to say that the rendering of the whole and of details is in a more concise manner. The standard posture is for the lions to face right and for sphinxes left, with a few exceptions, e.g. **905*** for a lion, where it must be part of an antithetical composition. On a few sherds remnants of sphinxes facing right have been preserved; in this case, they are also obviously part of an antithetical composition of confronting sphinxes, as the intact examples from Tocra, Pitane and Ayia Paraskevi, near Thessaloniki, make clear. This practice, which might have had some meaning and significance in the Wild Goat style, here has turned into mere mannerism. Sphinxes are usually squatting (séjant), but towards the end of the style, there are examples in the walking posture (passant), on **924*** and **938***. An attested but not frequent composition is that of the confronting sphinxes which

---

[149] See end of Chapter 1.
[150] Boardman in *Emporio* 157–8 dubbed them "Simple Figure Chalices", which is retained here for the labelling of the most numerous and important group.
[151] See Chapter 4.

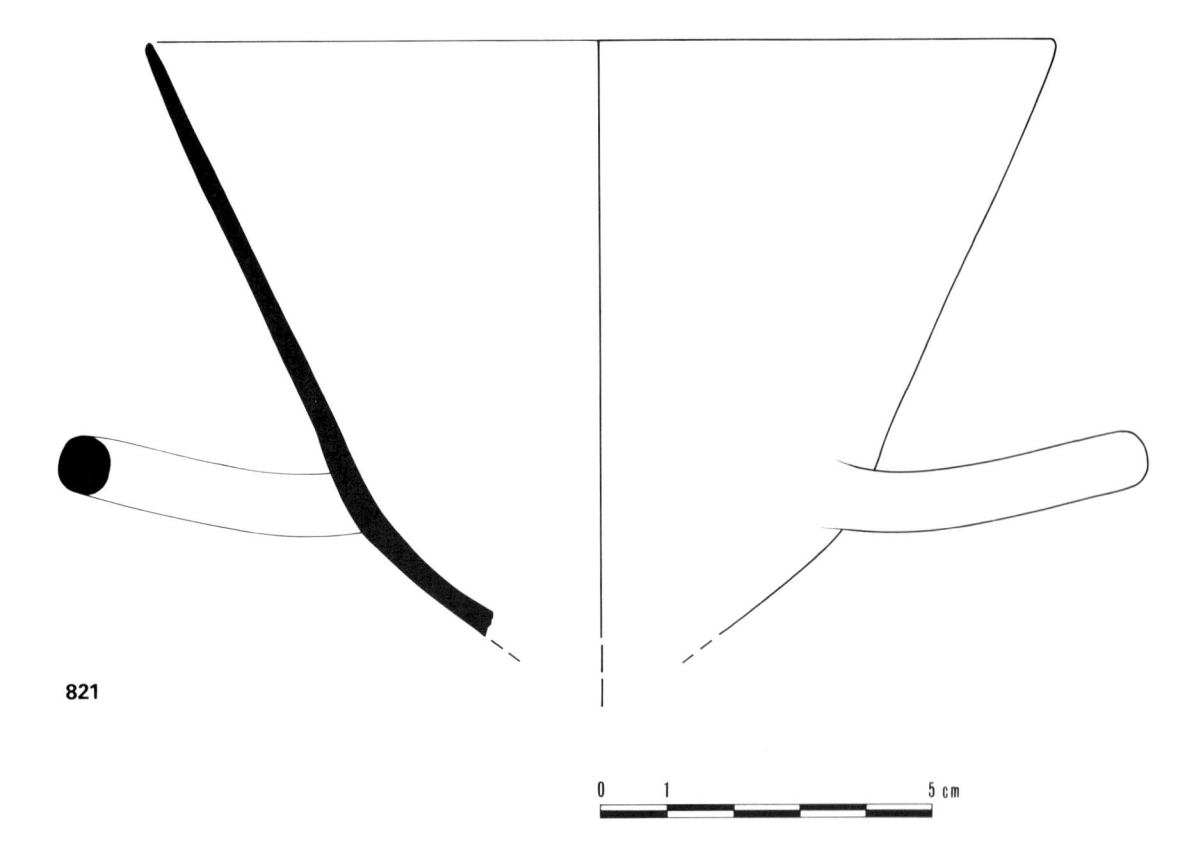

Fig. 67 The chalice from Phana in the Chalice style

decorates the obverse with the central axis separating them. It is a simple and highly decorative composition. A rosette, as usual, adorns the reverse. Intact examples are **927*** and **928*** from Tocra, the still unpublished ones both from Ayia Paraskevi **953**, **954** and **955** in the Thessaloniki Archaeological museum and from Pitane **968** in the Istanbul Archaeological museum. More fragments are added below.

Lions' manes are drawn carefully in a network pattern, save on **905***, where the solid mass ending in little horizontal bristles immediately recalls the more detailed, yet still unusual examples on its predecessors, **666*** and **696*** of the Animal Chalice style.

Human figures are portrayed in a simplified version, most similar to the ones met on Grand style, the difference being in the polychrome technique of the latter. Most figures here are female with the flesh, i.e. faces, arms, feet, and chiton paryphai reserved on the light-slipped background. They are either worshippers, **835*** and **900***, or women who take part in komos scenes usually carrying wreaths, **888*** (FIG. 70), **891*** and **895***, or pomegranates, **889***, **890*** (FIG. 70) and **896*** (FIG. 70). Their participation in komos scenes must be regarded as certain, not only because of their accessories but also from the fragmentary **896*** where the raised arm of a komast can be discerned and from the fuller scenes on **1564*** and especially **1468*** and **1487***. **939***, with the flautist, must be associated with them.

THE CHALICE STYLE

127

972

905

Fig. 68   Lions in the Chalice style

974

938

973

Fig. 69   Sphinxes in the Chalice style

Fig. 70 Human figures in the Chalice style

As has been observed[152] this group is in a mixed technique with the women drawn in silhouette and outline and the komasts in black figure. They usually appear in pairs, as the Rizari chalice, (**1487***), implies, but may also occur in fuller compositions, as on the Emporio fragmentary one (**1468***). Their restrained, almost statuesque, posture is hardly indicative of merry-making.

The solitary worshipper, on **964*** (FIG. 70), who has been thought of as a woman,[153] is most probably a man, because of his short hair and the fishbone pattern on his chiton sleeve, which is used for men in the Grand style.[154] The obscure object on his raised right hand looks like a butterfly and from his left one a lotus flower is suspended.[155]

Finally, a warrior in full armour appears on **933*** from Tocra. It is interesting to compare the eye-device of his shield with the exquisitely drawn eye-device on **736*** of the Grand style.

Mythological figures are a rarity in this category. An Athena, holding her spear is depicted on **899***—a piece already mentioned in the mythological scenes of the Grand style. Though the inside bears an elaborately drawn hand in the light on dark technique, the sherd is better classified here, since there is no polychromy on the outer surface.

The woman on **815*** is, in the absence of any attributes, unsuitable to be considered as an Athena; she might be an ordinary lady, perhaps a worshipper.

3. *Ornamental decoration* on these chalices is of the simplest type. Rims have SS between lines, **927***, **928***, **968** (FIG. 71.4 and 5), or dots between lines, **815**, **835***, **938*** and **964*** (FIG. 71.1). They often do without rim patterns, which is not always an indication of a late

---

[152] *Emporio* 158.
[153] Price 210 and 218; followed by Kocybala, Diss. 1978, 199; Hayes compares his no. 879 (here **1564***, where only the lower part of a female skirt survives) to this figure and apparently implies that this is also a woman.

[154] Compare **699***, **704***, **752*** and **764***.
[155] M. Blomberg in a letter drew my attention to this figure's resemblance to scenes on the late fifth-century Corinthian Sam Wide group, see now Amyx, *CorVP*, Vol. I, 275–6, Vol. III, pl. 125.5–6.

THE CHALICE STYLE

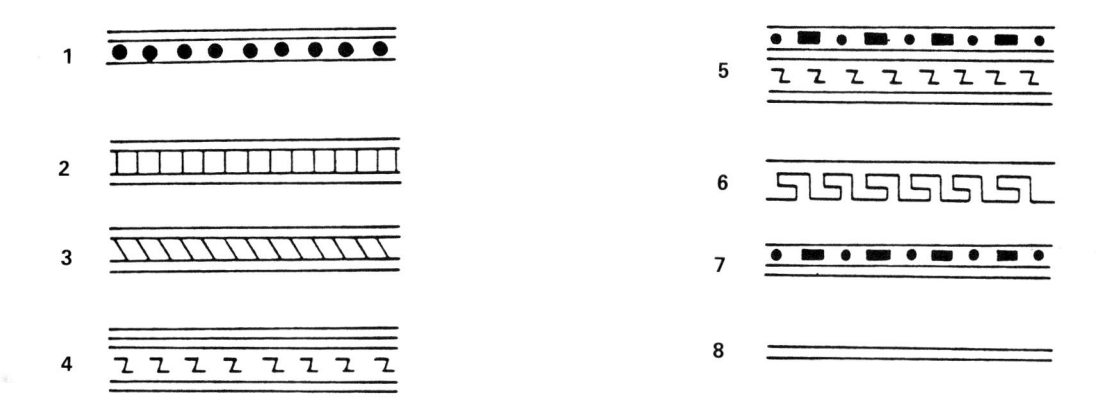

Fig. 71 Rim patterns in the Chalice style

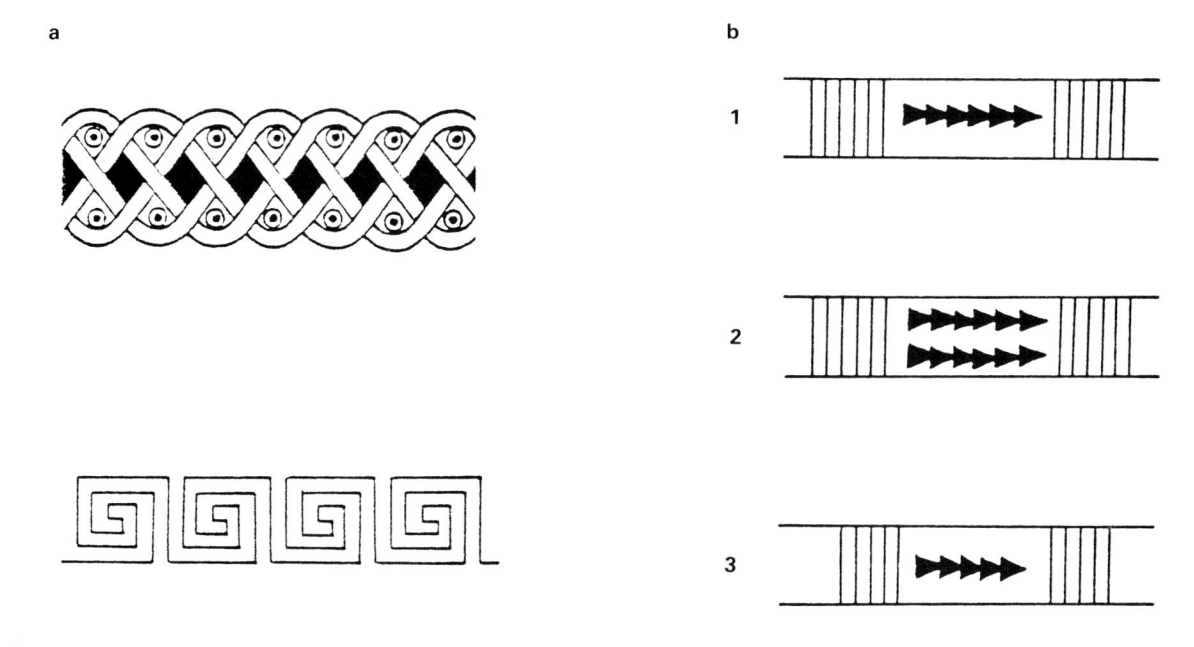

Fig. 72 Handle zone patterns in the Chalice style
a) from the 'Antithetical Sphinxes' group   b) from all other chalices

date,[156] because disorderly rim patterns recur on the latest examples of the series, **938*** from Tarentum and **973*** from Camirus.

Handle zone patterns are here considered as criteria by which this workshop's individuality may be singled out. This involves the Chian trademark: a saw-edged metope pattern flanked by groups of lines, executed by a multiple, usually sextuple, brush,[157] most commonly in one (FIG. 72.b.1) and sometimes in two rows (**952*** and FIG. 72.b.2). This design can be detected earlier in a seventh-century workshop and continues even later too;

[156] Cf. *Emporio* 158.   [157] *Emporio* 105 with note 1.

after about the middle of the sixth century. The small group of the antithetical sphinxes which used the double guilloche (**927***, **928***, **953–955** and **968**) on the obverse, and the double meander running left on the reverse (FIG. 72.a) stands at the very start of this style's development, looking also to the Animal Chalice and Grand styles, where this same combination of patterns is dominant.

The inner decoration, already mentioned in the last section, is elementary, but even on the latest examples, i.e. **973***, pairs of lines and a central rosette at the bottom, exists.

The absence of filling ornament, which is the principal feature of this style, links it to Groups B, C, and D of the Grand style and demonstrates their approximate contemporaneity.

4. Style. The manner of the figure drawing is directly descended from the Animal Chalice style. Three noteworthy fragments attest to this most effectively: **887***, from Naucratis, with a boar hunted by a dog, which belongs to the "group of elaborate animal chalices"; **963***, from Berezan, from a heavy chalice, with lions in a row; and **953** from Ayia Paraskevi, near Thessaloniki, of the "Antithetical Sphinxes group", on which the sphinxes' wings at the outer row are dotted. All three have rim patterns with diagonal strokes between two lines and furthermore no filling ornament. They stand at the very beginning of the series.

930* and **931*** with no filling ornament have been attributed by Hayes to the same hand as **615*** in the Animal Chalice style, which is awkwardly much earlier.

On the other hand the Chalice style is influenced by the Grand style, not only in the throwing off of the "oppressive" filling ornament but also in the types of man and woman that it takes over.

In brief, it follows stylistically and chronologically the two preceding styles from which it inherits a number of types and details.

The style though uniform goes through stages of evolution and, eventually, declines. Three stylistic groups might be distinguished:

1. The group of the antithetical sphinxes,[158] which stylistically and chronologically stands at the beginning of the Chalice style, consists of: **927*** and **928*** both from Tocra and by the same painter [Hayes]; **953** from Ayia Paraskevi; **954** and **955** both from Ayia Paraskevi and by the same painter; and **968** from Pitane.

2. The group of the simple figures, can be internally distinguished into four consecutive stages:

The first comprises both: **826***, **844***, **903***, **904***, **918***, **934*** and **961***; and another set, in which the double saw-edged pattern appears on the handle zone both on front and rear: **924***, **925***, **926***, **930***, **931***, perhaps **941**, **942**, **952***, **966*** and **967***.

The second stage comprises: **821***, **822***, **823*** (same painter); **965***; **969**, **970**, **971*** (same painter); **972*** and **974***.

---

[158] Confronting sphinxes are also represented on **467***, **470***, **902*** and **910***, all from Naucratis, which stylistically do not form part of this group.

THE CHALICE STYLE

The third stage is made up of: **827***, **845***, **846***, **847***, **848***, **860***, **861***, **862***, **870***, **911***, **938***, **960***. All are probably the work of a single hand. They centre around the Tarentum chalice, (**938***), which looks however to be one of his latest; the painter has a liking for "passant" sphinxes, drawn in a characteristically flat-headed manner, with their long hair falling into three separate tresses.

Finally, the fourth stage consists of: **929***, **932*** and **973***. The figure drawing by now is deteriorating. Specifically, the debased sphinx on the unpublished Florence chalice from Camirus (**973***) with its disorderly rim pattern; scribbles on the reverse and the handle zone, hardly reminiscent of the well-known metope pattern, all demonstrate perfectly the sad end of a style and of a technique of decoration.

3. The group of worshippers centres around the intact Leningrad chalice from Berezan (**964***). The other members of the group involve women: **888***–**900***—including Athena **899***, **906*** and **920***. Most of the fragments must be from chalices on which a mixed technique of decoration is being practised: outline for women and black figure for komasts. They are linked with **939*** from Marseilles and, furthermore, with **1487*** from Rizari. In fact, they are inseparable from group A of the komast chalices.[159]

To conclude, the Chalice style has a finesse and an elaboration of its own, mainly due to the impression given by the clear, light-ground field on which the solitary figures or isolated pairs stand out, undisturbed in their solemnity. They give the immediate impression that they may have been copying other more "famous" prototypes, but on the whole the absence of filling ornament, the statuesque posture and isolation of the figures are frequent traits of other schools of vase painting at the time. The manner of figure drawing rises from meticulous to elaborate but, eventually, sinks during the period of decline, especially the third and fourth stages of the second group, to hasty, routine, and hackneyed work.

B. *Patterned sixth-century vases*

The *shape* of the sixth-century chalice and its evolution, comprising a late stage of retrograde type, has been already considered at the beginning of this chapter. The intact examples **1062*** and **1063*** (FIG. 43), both from Camirus on Rhodes, make this plain.

As regards *patterns*, they are of the utmost simplicity. Rim patterns when they exist at all are mere dots or strokes between lines, disorderly in execution and occur, or rather, recur on the latest examples. Handle zones are *always* decorated with the saw-edged metope pattern, executed with a multiple, usually a sextuple, brush (FIG. 72.b.1).[160] The two late examples from Camirus, **1062*** and **1063*** have them done with a quintuple brush (FIG. 72.b.3).

Plain chalices in the sixth century were produced in the same workshop as their figured counterparts, as previously discussed. This fact is indicated by the identical form of the vessel, its size and ornamental decoration on rims. Two further arguments could strengthen this belief:

---

[159] See Chapter 4.

[160] *Antiquity* 34, 1960, 86, fig. 1 k and mainly p. 89.

a. The existence of the saw-edged metope pattern on both, and
b. The discovery in a number of places of *pairs* of sixth-century chalices—one plain and the other decorated. Examples are:

    972* from Camirus found together it seems with **1062***.

    974* from Marion in Cyprus with **1071***.

    952*, **953**, **954** and **955** recently found at Ayia Paraskevi accompanied by four plain ones **1047–1050**.

Analogous cases ought to exist in Pitane, where confirmation must await full publication, and most probably in Istros. As these cases are all connected with cemeteries, it is possible that their combination was deliberate. To interpret this burial custom is less easy; perhaps the cost of the vessels led to a compromise whereby an undecorated chalice was substituted for a more expensive decorated one.

D. *Vases with floral decoration*

Fragments pertaining to this division of the Chalice style are basically from chalices (**1256–1265***) and a few phialai, perhaps mesomphaloi (**1266–1269***). An almost intact small chalice from Pitane, **1263**, provides the nucleus in relation to which the other pieces can be interpreted. The decoration is based on the lotus and bud which can appear on different parts of the *outer* surface. On the Pitane chalice, (**1263**), the upside down lotus, flanked by dotted rosettes, is on the handle zone with a meander running left. On the Istros chalice (**1262***) the upside down lotus and bud is from a rim fragment, as is the earlier **1257** and **1259** from Naucratis. **1260** again from Naucratis[161] is however on the bowl.

Both types of lotuses are demonstrated: type 1 (FIG. 28.a.1) in a rather debased form on the Naucratis chalice fragments and the Pitane chalice; type 2 (FIG. 28.a.2; a very late type, close to Fikellura) on the Istros chalice and the phialai sherds **1266** and **1267**. Their poor quality together with the rudimentary inner decoration implies a classification and its consequent dating towards the end of the Chalice style.

---

[161] It is the photograph in this example **which is upside down**: *CVA* Oxford II, pl. 396.5.

4
THE BLACK-FIGURE STYLES

The black-figure technique starts in Chian painted pottery at about the turn of the seventh to the sixth century and continues production in various styles until roughly the end of the century.

1. THE SPHINX AND LION STYLE

The Sphinx and Lion style is the first category in black figure; it has a remarkably consistent homogeneity of style and a variety of shapes unique in the entire Chian output.

I. Shapes

The Sphinx and Lion style is at its best in the hands of its potters. If its painters cannot show any originality, its potters, on the other hand, put in a strong claim for it and deserve appreciation. Their inventiveness and ingenuity is well displayed in the number of shapes produced and, basically, in their attempts at rather unexpected creations that are generally innovating, sometimes even bizarre.

The lack of the chalice in this style is another feature which demonstrates their avoidance of the ordinary. The miniaturist character of the decoration in the Sphinx and Lion style tends to correspond with the disposition of the decoration and aims at covering the whole surface of the vase. Chalices of the early sixth century[1] demanded a special decoration restricted to a specific place: that of the walls, which have now become higher. The decoration in the Sphinx and Lion style cannot be adapted to the requirements of the chalice shape; thus, shape and decoration could not be harmonically and organically linked.[2] The material in this popular style is sufficiently well represented and since no chalice has appeared as yet, it is highly unlikely that one will. It seems that the workshop producing Sphinx and Lion vases was in strong competition with those manufacturing the contemporary Animal Chalice style.

The shapes used by the Sphinx and Lion style potters are: bowls with lids, probably on a high stem; dinoi; a kothon; plates and dishes; open vases; ?lekanai; oenochoai; incense-vases; a basket-handled bell-shaped vessel; ?basket; and ring vases.

The predominant shape is the bowl with a domed lid.[3] More than half of the material in the Catalogue is classified as such, almost all are fragments though many are substantial.

---

[1] See FIG. 41.
[2] Cf. *REA* 48, 1946, 154, 156–7 for Villard's view on the decoration on the Athenian Komast cups.
[3] *Emporio*, 166; Price 200 and Price, *EGP*, 19, calls it pyxis with lid. Hayes in *Tocra* II, 26 calls it lekane with a domed lid. Lekane would be more precise, if it had not been confused already with the (Athenian) Lekanis (*Agora* XII, pls. 40–42). I think bowl is a better term as it is practical and defines the vase, though in a generic manner.

1270   **1271**

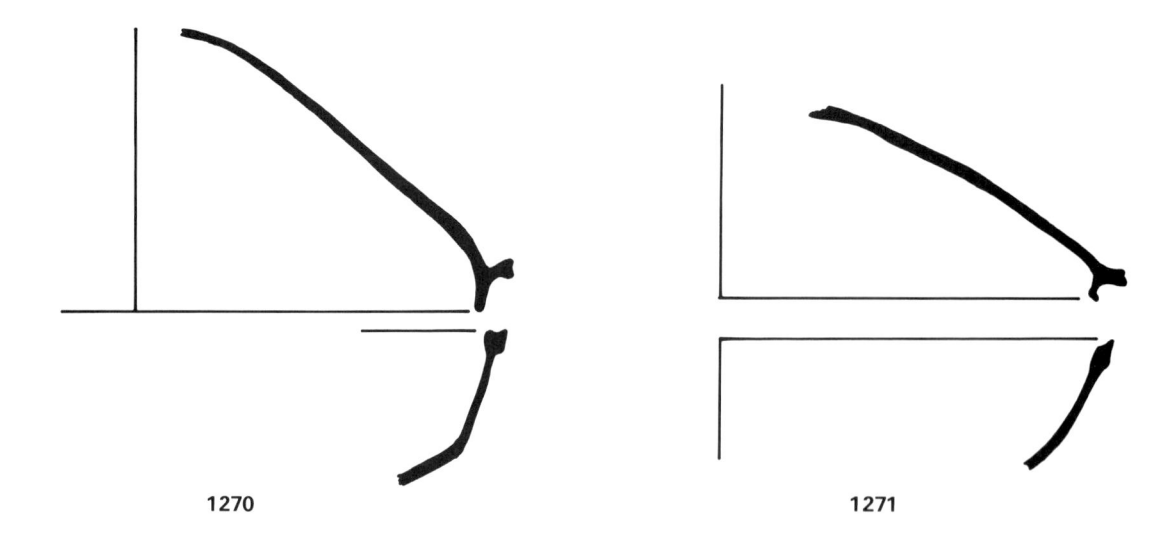

Fig. 73 Bowls with lids from Emporio and Tocra (*Emporio* no. 825, fig. 115 – courtesy of Professor Sir John Boardman; *Tocra* no. 2052, fig. 10 – courtesy of Dr. J. W. Hayes)

In addition, Pitane has provided an intact vase, **1272***, which, whatever one may call it,[4] is certainly of the same shape.

The bowl is rather shallow and could have either steep sides, as on **1271*** (FIG. 73), or a carination, as on **1270*** (FIG. 73). It always has a square-sectioned rim. It may well have sat on a tall foot with a splaying base, as is seen on the Pitane vase (**1272***), which feature may not necessarily have been repeated in all the bowls. The domed lid has a deep flange beneath its edge in order to fit the rim of the bowl. The Rizari komast rider lid (**1324***, FIG. 75) is a good example. Both bowls and lids are usually slipped inside, bearing the decoration on the outside. But it is not uncommon for the inside of both to be decorated also, as on **1273***, **1280***, **1284*** and **1334**. In size they can range from around 0.20–0.25 in diameter for the smaller examples up to *c.* 0.42 for the larger pieces, as **1270*** from Emporio.

The stemmed skyphos crater **1272*** (FIG. 74) is introduced now into the Chian repertoire. The bowl stands on a conical stem. The lid has almost the same height as the bowl and is crowned by four moulded female heads. There is a flat-topped knob above them.[5]

The nearest parallels are the earlier stemmed skyphos craters by the Athenian Nessos Painter.[6] Though the vases from Anagyrous are double the size of the Pitane vase and with more emphasis on the stem and bowl, they share the general conception of the shape, the domed lid and the conical high foot. In the Chian vase the structure is better; the three parts of the vase—stem, bowl, lid—are proportionately almost equal and this produces a strong effect of harmony. Other examples near to the shape are bowls and lids from

---

[4] Akurgal, who first presented it in *AJA* 66, 1962, 278, pl. 103.31 calls it a stemmed skyphos crater and E. Walter-Karydi in *Äol. Kunst*, 7, has classified it as Aeolian. I have seen the vase in the Archaeological Museum of Istanbul and think that it is in the canonical Sphinx and Lion style.

[5] Cf. *Kerameikos* VI.2, pls. 62–65.

[6] Karouzou, *Anagyrountos*, figs. 1–3 and pls. 1, 2, 12 and 21.

THE SPHINX AND LION STYLE

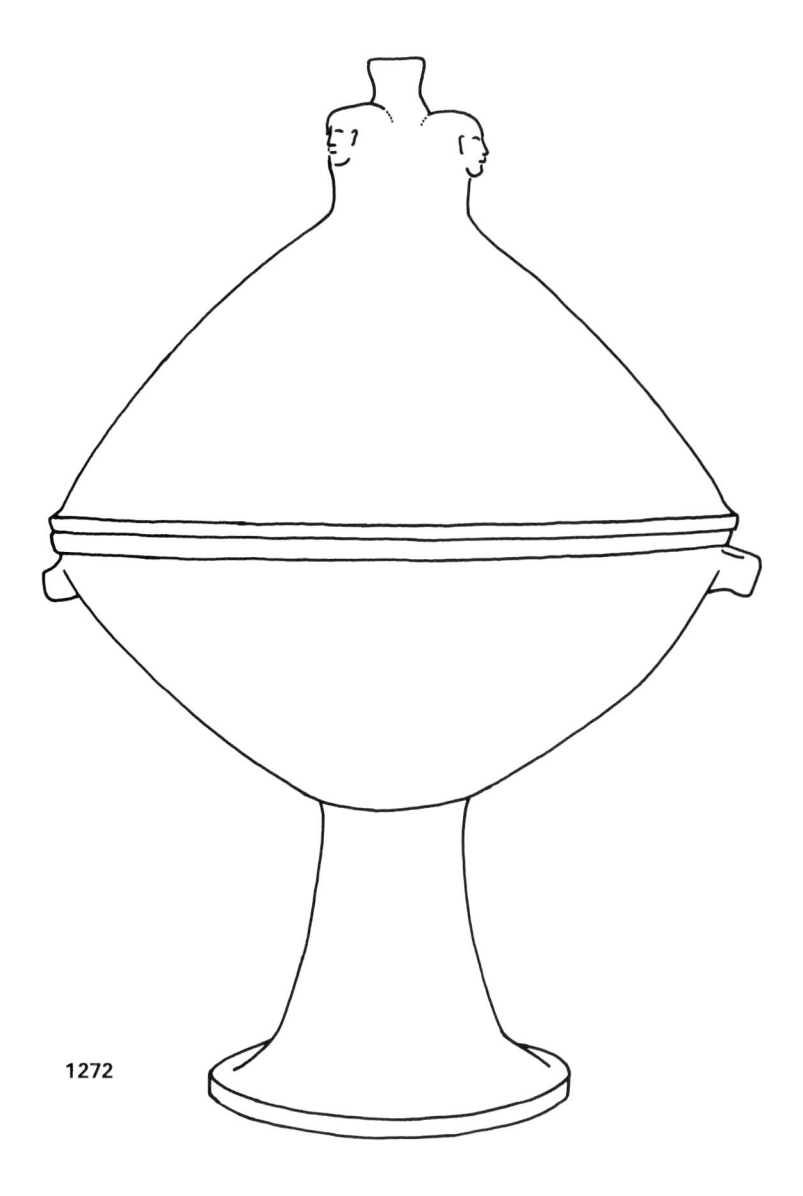

Fig. 74 The stemmed skyphos crater from Pitane

Athens[7] which, however, have not exactly the same profiles or proportions as the Chian ones.

It is now becoming clear that dinoi were not uncommon in the Chian figure-decorated wares;[8] more frequent in the Wild Goat style, here they comprise three specimens, **1401*** (FIG. 75) and **1402–3**.

1404 is perhaps a fragment from the inturning rim of a kothon, an unexpected piece for East Greek wares.[9] From such a tiny fragment details of the shape cannot be drawn.

---

[7] *Kerameikos* VI.2, pls. 4, 5 and 16.
[8] Whereas it is in plain pottery from Emporio, *Emporio* 115.
[9] *Emporio*, 166. Possible parallels from Mainland Greece: a) Corinth in *NC* 355, fig. 183 and *Corinth* VII.1, pls. 29.217 and 37.296–8; b) Athens in *Agora* XII, pl. 44.

It appears that plates are more frequent than dishes and most have flat rims (**1405*** and **1406***). Only two fragments (**1417*** and **1418***) are from dishes, the latter sits on a ring foot. These two shapes seem to have enjoyed a restricted popularity in both figurative and plain pottery.

A relatively big fragment from a heavy lekane-like vase, decorated on both sides, is **1419*** (FIG. 75). No rim or any edge has been preserved, though the thinner part has developed an upward curve reminiscent of the rim of that vase shape.

1420*, which is also decorated on both sides, is probably not from a dinos with a wide offset rim[10] as published, but rather from a vase akin in shape to the previous one: a lekane-like vase with curved short walls and of a calibre implying that it comes from a large and heavy vessel.

1433* is the only intact trefoil oenochoe, with a globular but somewhat squat body. Its tall neck, compared to the short Late Wild Goat oenochoai of East Greece, sits upon the splaying shoulders, from which the body narrows gradually towards the base ending in a ring foot.

Fragments, **1422*–1425***, **1428*–1429***, **1432** and **1434*** are from closed shapes. They could equally well be from oenochoai, or even perhaps hydriai. The latter is not an attested shape in this style; there is, however, an intact example which came to light recently (**1638***) in a related black-figure style and should perhaps date to the third quarter of the century.[11]

The intact incense vase, **1437***, is another original shape. It consists of three parts: a) *a domed top*, which is not a separate lid, and is crowned by a vertically placed arched handle like that of a basket; b) *a cylindrical body* with convex profile and a wide opening on one side to receive the incense; and c) *a bowl-like steep-sided base* sitting on a ring foot. At its top a pierced surface, as in a strainer, runs across to permit access from below to either air or heat. Two deep protruding flanges exist between a and b; and b and c.

The shape does not find ready parallels; the only one near to this but with concave walls could be the powder-pyxis in Late Protocorinthian of around the middle of the seventh century.[12] A vase analogous in shape comes from Aphrodisias.[13] These are not close parallels but imply the same spirit and concept for the shape and function of the vase.

1435* (FIG. 76) is of the same shape.[14] The surviving fragment cannot be from a lid, firstly because the wall beneath the flange, being broken, would have continued, and secondly, for this reason, the sphinx's head must have had a body. It should be further noted that the Sphinx and Lion style uses no "protomes".[15] **1436*** is most probably from the same shape.

The basket-handled, bell-shaped vase, **1438*** (FIG. 77), is another interesting and innovating shape. The vase has a cylindrical neck with two slightly protruding flanges. It is

---

[10] *CVA* Oxford II, 182 "may be part of a dinos with a wide offset rim". (E. Price).

[11] See pp. 177–8.

[12] *NC* 295, no. 672 and 21–22; Hopper, Addenda 216–8. The earliest are from Syracuse (the Fusco cemetery) and continue for one hundred and fifty years, showing little change in shape and ornament. See also D.A. Amyx *CorVP* passim.

[13] *GO*³, 99 and note 262, fig. 113. Also compare Lamb's *Thermi*, pl. 36.382 (of Early Bronze age) and H.S. Georgiou, 'Late Minoan Incense Burners' in *AJA* 83, 1979, 427–35, pls. 61–4; neither of these last two have more than a common conception with the Chian shape.

[14] Cf. *Emporio* 166, no. 828.

[15] Apart from one exception, the oenochoe from Pitane, (**1433***).

THE SPHINX AND LION STYLE

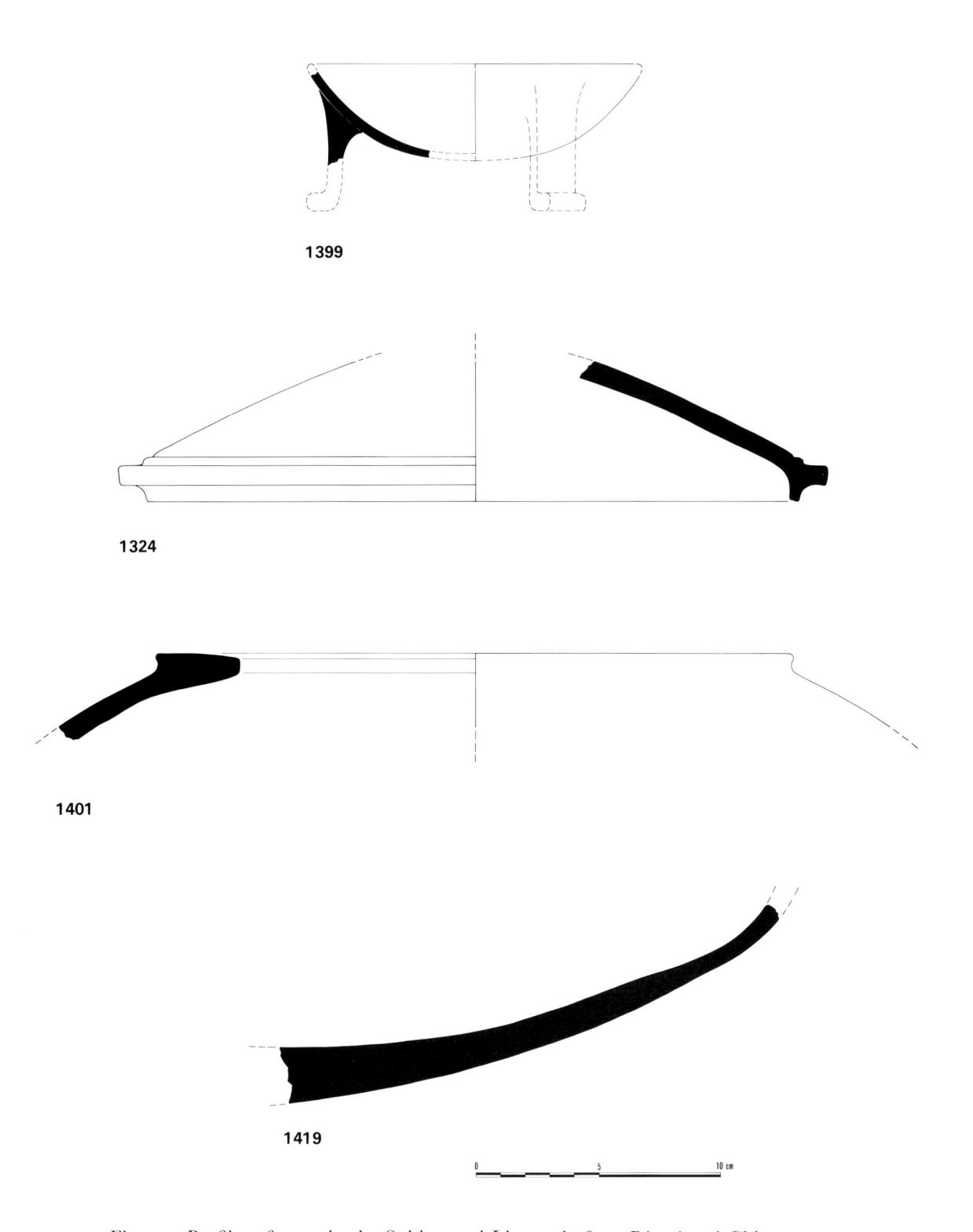

1399

1324

1401

1419

Fig. 75 Profiles of vases in the Sphinx and Lion style from Rizari and Chios town

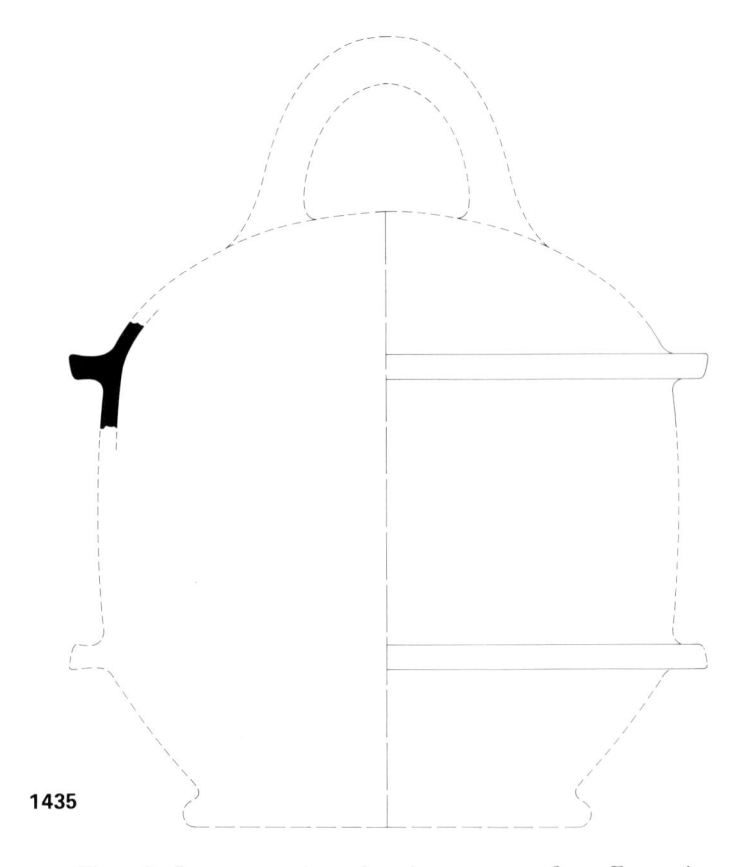

Fig. 76 Reconstruction of an incense vase from Emporio

topped by a twisted basket handle carrying two female heads at its base and on the very top two antithetically placed rams' heads. The lower profile is reconstructed, largely on the evidence of one fragment: its elongated shape and pattern of decoration has been based on the number and position of the alternating friezes of lions and sphinxes. The internal division is tentative and suggested by the presence of internal band decoration at the bottom and lack of it at the top.

1439* looks like a basket because of its upright handle. It might however have been from an oenochoe.[16]

Part of a ring vase, **1440***, very significant for its decoration, has been preserved. It is round in section, as are most East Greek ring vases, and still retains one of its spouts. Kernoi seemed to be in favour with the Chian potter from the Wild Goat style through to the Sphinx and Lion style as well as in plain pottery,[17] being produced till perhaps the third century, or even later.[18]

Special mention should be made of **1399*** and **1400**. **1399*** (FIG. 75) is part of a tripod bowl which has preserved part of its bowl and the beginning of one of its feet; in shape it is

---

[16] Kocybala, Diss. 1978, 196.

[17] Most of the examples, even when only patterned, have been collected in the Wild Goat style.

[18] Undecorated kernoi and seated terracotta figurines of Late Classical and Hellenistic time have been unearthed in Chios town, see *Chiaka Meletemata* I, 63–89 and pls. 1–8, and recently again presumably from the same deposit, which points to a Demeter sanctuary nearby.

THE SPHINX AND LION STYLE

1438

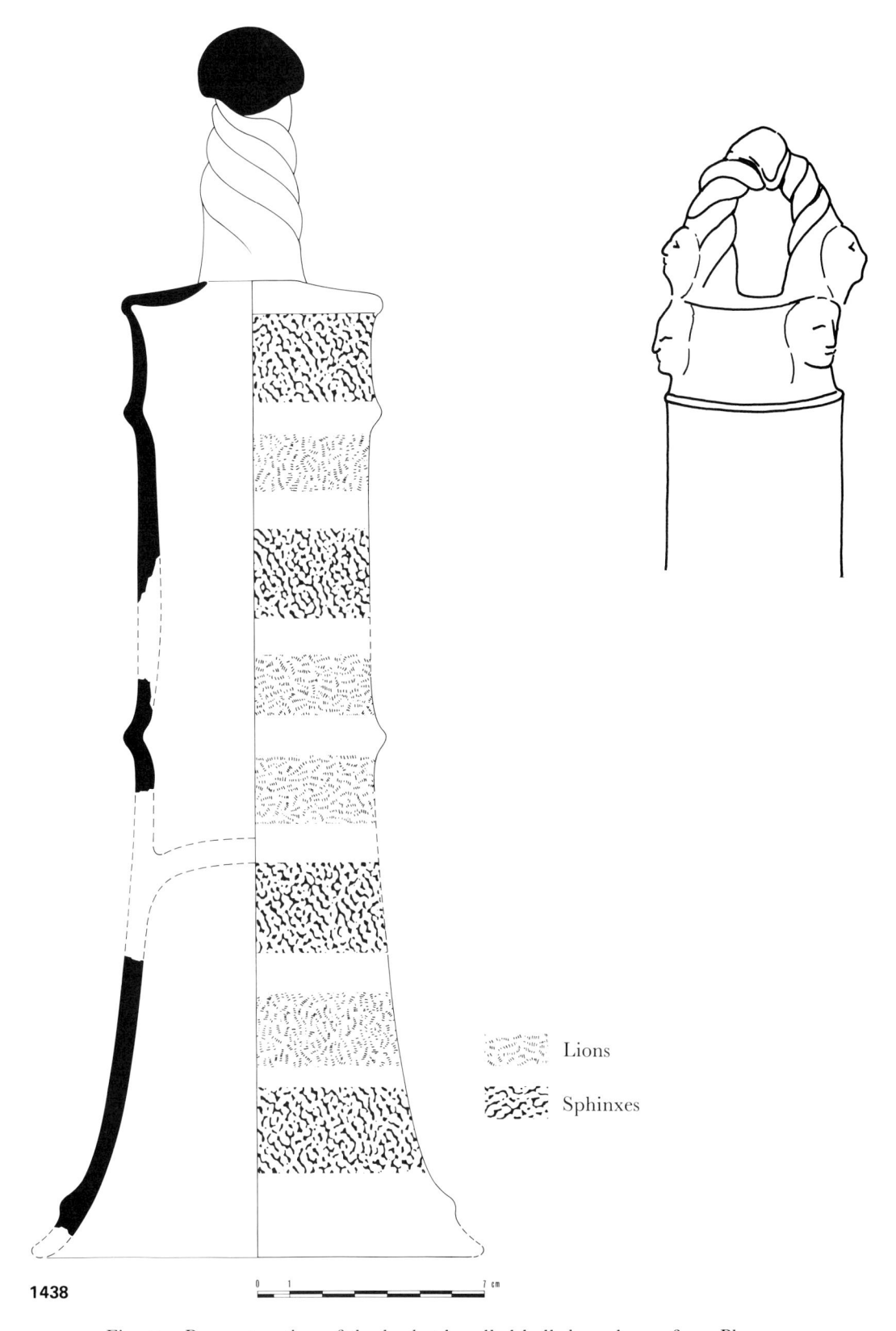

Fig. 77 Reconstruction of the basket-handled bell-shaped vase from Phana

identical with the intact **259***. It belongs to the output of the Sphinx and Lion workshop because incisions have remained on the surface and also part of a rosette.

1400 is the foot of another sixth-century tripod bowl.[19]

In short, the shapes in the Sphinx and Lion style give credit to the potters who, apart from producing the usual dinoi, oenochoai and kernoi, launched out into innovating rarities of remarkable inspiration and originality, i.e. the stemmed skyphos crater; the open vases: lekanai-like or that with the wide offset rim; the incense vase; the basket-handled bell-shaped vessel with moulded heads; and finally, the lekane-like vase, again with moulded heads, from Thasos, **1311***. The original, sometimes even bizarre, shapes are unique not only for the entire Chian output but for East Greek schools in general. This craving for the unusual could perhaps be explained as a reaction to the ever increasing predominance of the chalice at this time.

A single pottery workshop with an inventive potter and his entourage must have been responsible for the production of vases in the Sphinx and Lion style. That it was comparatively shortlived, as the style indicates, could be due to a number of reasons. It could be explained either by assuming the potter left no successors, or perhaps more plausibly by the ultimate failure of this workshop to hold off the eventually overwhelming demand of the fashionable chalice both for local consumption and export.

Almost all the *plastic heads* of the sixth century belong to the Sphinx and Lion style vases and have been drawn together in the Catalogue under a separate heading; most of them have even been illustrated. However, as they fall beyond the scope of this book, they will constitute a separate study.

II. *Decoration*

A. Animals and Birds

The comprehensive title *Sphinx and Lion style* was invented by Boardman[20] and it emphasises that sphinxes and lions predominate as subjects on the decoration of these vases. Newer evidence has not changed the picture since 1967. There is little variety; few other animals and even fewer birds appear. Human figures—men—number even less and there is only one mythological scene. All these are far outnumbered by the repetitive rows of lions and sphinxes.

Animals and birds ranked by frequency of occurrence are: lions, sphinxes, bulls, sirens, geese, other birds, boar, panther, gorgoneion and mule.

Lions: as a rule they face right,[21] but there are a few exceptions. The most noteworthy are two friezes with lions facing left on the oenochoe from Pitane, **1433***. **1286*** is an early attempt to translate Chian Wild Goat into black figure.[22] **1332*** is an ambitious piece and demonstrates a variety of animals in different poses. On **1344*** and **1367*** there is a commonplace fight between lion and bull.

Painters have a narrow repertory of poses. The favourite one is that of the lion sitting on its hindquarters with its forelegs straight, or sometimes at an oblique angle to the ground (séjant). On **1301*** and **1405*** the lions have more elongated bodies than usual and walk to

---

[19] Boardman in *Chios Conference*, 251 note 3.
[20] *Emporio*, 166.
[21] *Ibid.*, 166.
[22] For another example: **1405***, see *Emporio*, 166, note 1.

the left. A few other poses occur: on **1420*** the lion grasps with his left front paw the tail of the bull in front of him (séjant with raised forepaws); on **1297*** he grasps an indistinct object; on **1332*** there are two lions in unusual poses: on the upper frieze one places his feet on the right front leg of the sphinx coming towards him and turns his head to look away from her, whilst on the lower one, another grasps a sphinx's tail and turns his head back to roar at another much bigger lion behind him.

Sphinxes: Almost all of them face left.[23] The exceptions occur on **1326***, **1338** and **1347*** and the three vases from Pitane, **1272*** (but for one row), **1433*** and **1437***.[24]

The invariable pose is that of the squatting sphinx (séjant), with the exception of **1332*** where she decides, finally, to walk (passant).

The structure and rendering of details on the body and head, and even the red colour and incisions, vary but little from one fragment to another.

Bulls: They occur on eleven fragments and are always standing or walking in procession to the right, but for one exception, **1339**, where the bull faces left. On **1344***, **1345*** and **1367*** the bull is attacked by the lion in an antithetical composition.

Sirens: They are the fourth most popular subject and either stand or walk, mostly to the left, following the treatment of sphinxes. **1311*** is exceptional in that they have lost their spirals.

Geese: Eight pieces, **1271***, **1272***, **1324***, **1333**, **1349***, **1419***, **1427*** and **1446** present geese in procession standing or walking. They may face equally left or right. They have heavy bodies and tails and quite long necks. On **1272***, **1333**, **1349*** and **1419*** the geese have open wings in a posture ready to fly. On **1272*** and **1419*** they strongly give the impression that they might be swans and are more elaborately drawn: the difference might be a stylistic one. The goose on **1324*** is a direct copy of Chian Wild Goat style prototypes; the general structure of body and posture and rendering of details, here with incisions, are those of the geese on the Würzburg chalices (**236*** and **237***) and the Aphrodite bowl (**252***) from Naucratis, and generally on the Middle II Wild Goat vases.

Other birds: Two other birds are of rather indeterminate sort. The bird on **1270*** could fit in the series of sirens, had it not such long feet. The fragment shows a part of its wing with a row of incisions similar to that of sirens. Alternatively it could be a goose with open wings, as on **1272*** and **1419***. On **1276** it is even more difficult to make out the kind of bird; it might be a wagtail.

Boar: An unexpected piece from Chios itself, **1401*** shows part of a red-spotted boar,[25] the first known, so far, in Chian black figure. The parting of the bristles on his back are worked out in small parallel incisions and red colour in patches is added all over his hindquarters.

---

[23] *Ibid.*, 166.

[24] Some of the photographs reproduced might have been printed in reverse, therefore no safe conclusion can be drawn until the final publication.

[25] Boardman, CN, 61.

"Panther": On the fragmentary plate from Phana, **1405***, part of a "panther" is shown; he is walking to the right and has small concentric circles incised all over his body. The same animal appears on **1296*** walking back to back with a bull, their tails entangled.

Gorgoneion: On **1438***, between two of the three women's heads and just below the rim, the gorgoneion unique in this and any other Chian style is painted without the use of incision. The drawing of gorgoneia in outline was the practice in early black figure even in more advanced schools, as for example the Athenian.[26] Here the gorgoneion has turned into a purely decorative pattern.[27]

Mule: It appears only once, on **1324***, where the tail of the preceding one is also discerned. They are heading left and have long legs and tails. The animal has good proportions and incision is used to render its facial details. Perhaps a horse was meant but instead a mule was produced; iconographically, it approximates to **790*** in the Grand style.

B. Human Figures

No women appear in the Sphinx and Lion style, so far. There are only five fragments **1274***, **1278***, **1324***, **1440*** and possibly **1442** on which men are represented, which indicates that painters of this style were not keen on painting human figures.

From three fragments the type of man can be established: he is always painted in silhouette with careless incisions for details, almost identical to those of komasts. The torso is frontal and dressed. The face in profile has long hair, tied perhaps in a krobylos. A broken, wavy, incised line divides face from hair. On **1274*** and **1440*** men are facing to the right and are bearded, but without moustaches. On **1278*** the man, here beardless, moves to the right but faces left as if something has attracted his attention. On **1440*** the man carrying branches has already been interpreted as a centaur and the whole scene a Centauromachy.[28] This is the only mythological scene in the Sphinx and Lion style, so far. On **1442** only a hand holding a spear has been preserved.[29] Finally, on **1324*** the rider is a direct borrowing from the komast chalices. He is riding his horse, heading left: he holds the reins and wears the usual turban of his counterparts; however, he differs from them in that there is no incision on his body to indicate whether he is naked or not.

C. Ornaments

The ornaments and patterns that occur in the Sphinx and Lion style are: filling ornament: rosettes and half-rosettes; dividing bands; rays; tongue patterns; meanders; step patterns; lotus flowers and buds; and cable pattern.

---

[26] J.D. Beazley, *The Development of Attic Black-figure* 1951, 14 and Boardman, *AFBH*, 16 for the Nessos painter.

[27] For East Greek gorgoneia see *Samos* VI.1, 36–37, note 125 and G.P. Schaus in *BSA* 81, 1986, 275 with notes 78–80 for the sole example in Fikellura.

[28] Price 219 and 221.

[29] The subject on this piece reminds one of two Geometric Chian predecessors, the crater fragment from Emporio, see *Emporio*, 108 and 114, no. 119, fig. 64 and pl. 28 and the crater fragment from Phana, see J.N. Coldstream in *Chios Conference* 181–6, fig. 1.

[30] They have been variously named by each scholar involved in the study of this ware:
1. Price 220–1, calls them blobs.
2. Anderson, *BSA* 49, 1954, 135, "cogwheels".
3. Boardman, *Emporio*, 158, rosettes and then, discs.
4. Hayes in *Tocra* II, 2, "target" motif for a piece at the end of the style.

I think that "cogwheel" would be more accurate, had it not referred to only one type (type 1); therefore, rosette is comprehensive because it covers almost all types and disc can be used for the last phase.

THE SPHINX AND LION STYLE

Filling ornament: rosette[30] and semi-rosette (FIG. 78): this is a typical feature of the whole style. They are the only ornaments in the field. Four types of rosettes[31] could be distinguished:

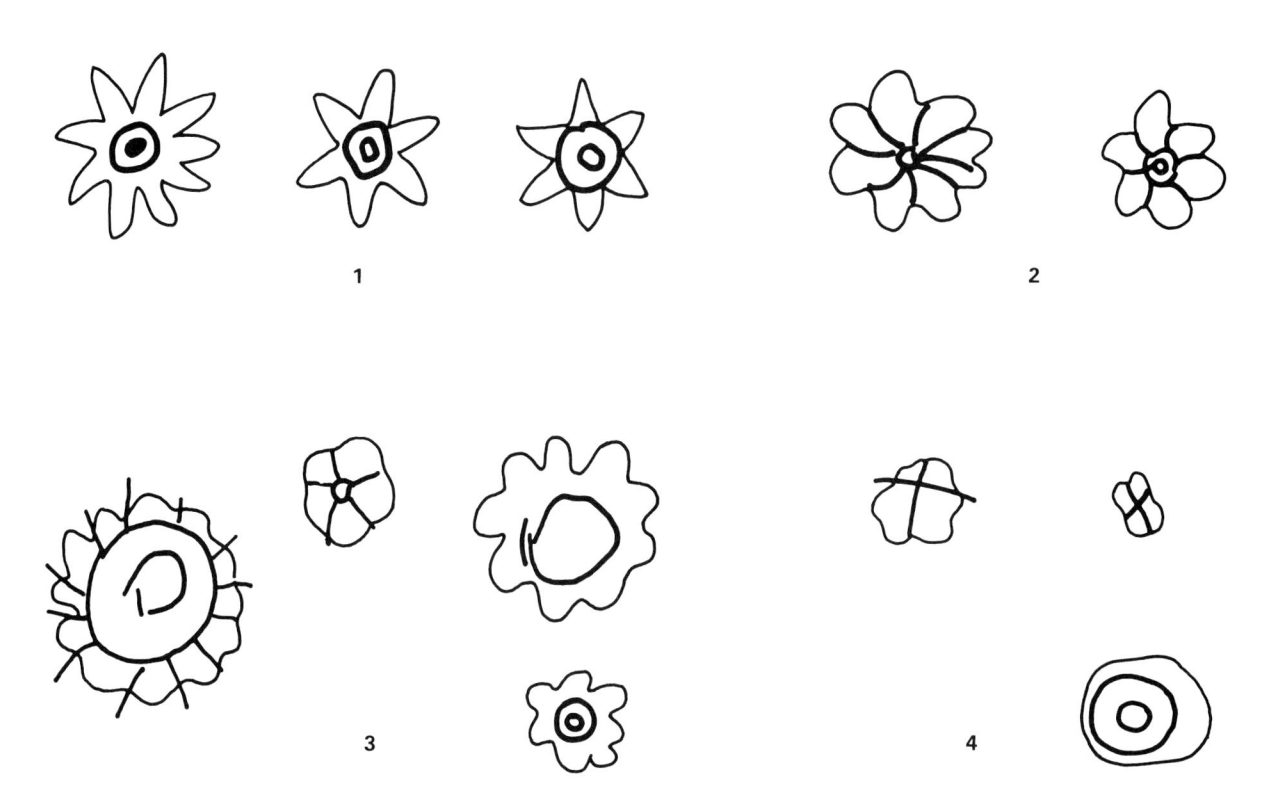

Fig. 78 Types of rosettes in the Spinx and Lion style

Half rosettes hang from the upper boundary of the field or spring from the base-line: a practice taken over from the Wild Goat style. Rosettes are one of the main links between the Sphinx and Lion style and the komast and black-figure animal chalices whenever they exist in the latter pair of styles. No other filling ornament is used in both these categories of Chian black-figure wares.

Dividing bands (FIG. 79): The most popular are the types 1 and 5, though there is a wide variety and a vast repertoire for painters to choose from. Worth mentioning is **1270*** which demonstrates six different patterns (types 4, 5, 8, 9, 10 and 12). Strangely enough **1419***, though a large fragment, goes on repeating the same pattern (type 5) in all its dividing bands on both sides.

Rays (see FIG. 28.b.1 and 2): They are triangular on the elaborate pieces. On the rest they are but elongated strokes, roughly triangular. Rays always have two positions: either at the edge of the lid, where they are painted longer in order to cover a much bigger space, or at

---

[31] *NC* 157, fig. 68A. There is some similarity of our type 2 with fig. 8 (left) and of our type 4 with fig. 69 (right).

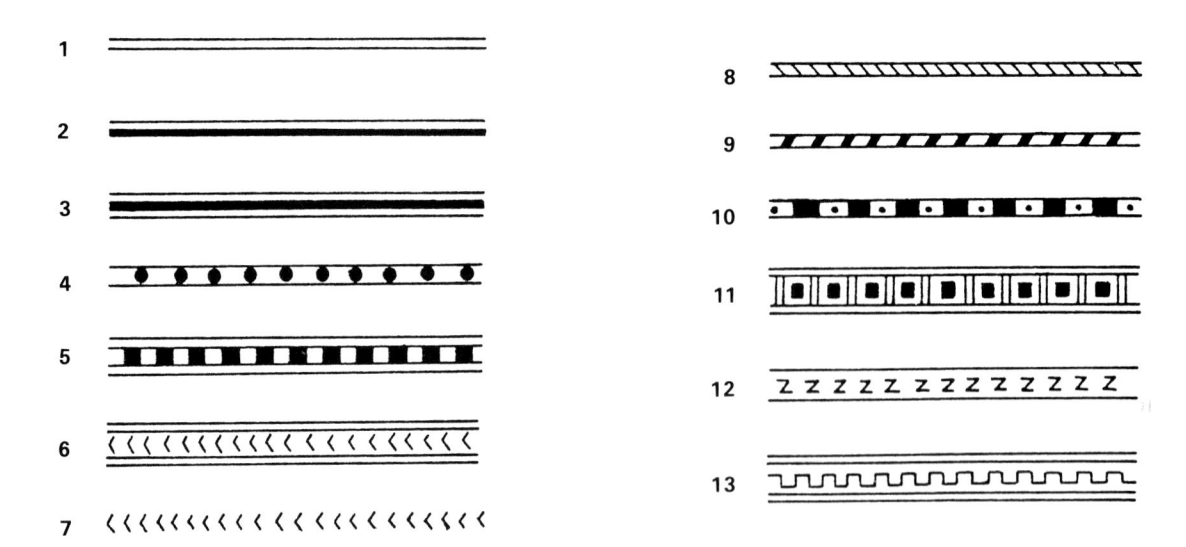

Fig. 79 Dividing bands in the Sphinx and Lion style

the rim of bowls. In brief, they are a rim pattern, occurring without a single exception on all the lids and bowls.

On two elaborate specimens, **1323*** and **1324***, above the rays an elegant row of dots framed by two lines appears. Rays are also used for the rim pattern of a dish, **1417***.

Tongue Patterns: Two types may be distinguished: the usual and the intermittent. They occur on the necks and shoulders of oenochoai: on **1433***, the intact oenochoe from Pitane, there are two rows on both neck and shoulder. They also occur on lids, mostly near the centre; e.g. **1332*** as decorative bands; at the top of a spout, **1276***; on the knob, **1318*** or below it, **1272*** of lids; on the spout of a ring vase, **1440*** and, finally, on the twisted handle of the bell-shaped vase, **1438***.

Meanders: Two different meander types appear: A) the broken type and B) the double meander running left (see FIG. 27.b.3).
A. appears twice, on **1286*** and **1287***.
B. is the commonest and is exemplified by seven pieces: **1272***, **1280***, **1399***, **1414***, **1424***, **1425** and **1437***. On **1424*** and **1425*** the meander is placed at the edge of the neck of the oenochoai, just below the rim. On **1406** and **1414*** it is the rim pattern of a plate. On **1437*** the meander is placed vertically in order to decorate the crowning handle. On **1272*** it decorates the penultimate frieze. On **1280*** and **1287*** it has the function of a decorative zone of the stem. And on **1399*** it decorates the foot of a tripod bowl.

Step patterns:[32] They occur twice and are flanked by two parallel lines. Once horizontally at the rim of a plate, **1405***; and once vertically bordering the frieze of decoration of a basket, **1439***.

[32] Or battlement pattern used more recently, e.g. *CVA* Great Britain XIV, 26.

Lotus and bud: Two types, which appear in Wild Goat style vases, are also represented in the Sphinx and Lion style. However, the flowers and buds are somewhat thinner now; a possible indication that these vases are chronologically slightly later.

Type A (FIG. 28.a.1) appears only twice, on **1279*** and **1281***, as decorative zones of a bowl, probably from near the centre of the vase.

In type B (FIG. 28.a.2) where a reserving line in the middle of the bud divides it into two equal parts. Type B occurs on the lowest frieze of both the oenochoe (**1433***) and the incense vase (**1437***) from Pitane; at the outermost frieze of the inside of lid **1334**, and on three bowls (**1273***, **1282*** and **1287***) at the centre.

Cable Pattern: The cable pattern (see FIG. 28.c) of the reserved Chian styles is also used here. It occurs three times: once on the neck of the trefoil oenochoe (**1433***) and twice as the ordinary rim pattern of dinoi (**1401*** and **1402**).

In conclusion, it must be stressed that all the ornaments of the Sphinx and Lion style vases are executed in silhouette and outline; nowhere is there any use of incision, except, of course, in the filling ornament: the rosette and the semi-rosette.

D. Composition

The Sphinx and Lion style is arranged in friezes; it is clear, despite the fragmentary material, that the processional arrangement is the usual one. One animal follows another with hardly any variation of pose. On **1296***, **1332*** and **1405*** some variety is displayed and the placing changes; various animals are intermingled in various poses. Only three times does the antithetical composition occur: on **1302***, **1344*** and **1345*** a bull is, or rather will be, attacked by a lion. Finally, on **1331***, there are two heraldically placed sphinxes with an elaborate rosette in between.

III. *Style*

The Sphinx and Lion style is the basic and the earliest Chian style in black figure,[33] which can be defined by these features:

A. The characteristically Chian creamy or white, or even milky white, porcelain-like slip, which is never absent.
B. The black-figure technique itself: figures are always painted in silhouette with incision used for details and added red. Added white does not occur.
C. The shapes used: chalices are not used, skyphos craters and bowls with lids are the commonest shapes, but there are also some freaks, not met in other black figure, nor in any other Chian technique of decoration.
D. Its subject repertory: lions and sphinxes, mostly crouching, predominate, outnumbering all other animals and the scarce human figures.
E. The rendering of the lions' necks in the characteristically incised "ham-frilled" manes.[34]
F. The filling ornament: rosettes and half-rosettes which are the sole ornament in the field.

[33] *Emporio*, 166. [34] Price 221 and Price *EGP*, 19.

The workshop owes a few elements to Corinthian vase painting:[35]

First, its *technique of decoration* which appears for the first time in Chian art.

Second, the *manner of drawing*, which is distinctive in two respects: both the miniature conception and the execution of the figures, lions and sphinxes in the main, and in their arrangement, i.e. in repetitive processional, and rarely antithetical, rows which fill the vase from top to bottom. The processional placing of figures is not new in Chian; it is inherited from the Middle Wild Goat style and is also the commonest practice in the contemporary Animal Chalice style. But, here the whole character alters: the pots have more rows and the animals, whose scale is reduced, are crammed into them. This practice is equally dictated by the different shapes and the larger size of the vessels.

Thirdly, *the filling ornament: the incised rosette* comes from Corinthian vase painting;[36] yet it is used somehow more sparingly. In Middle Corinthian rosettes are stuffed into the picture creating a feeling of confusion. In the Sphinx and Lion style, though the drawing is less imaginative, rosettes are not so densely packed and tend to produce a somewhat neater picture. Half-rosettes, not encountered in Middle Corinthian, pendant or emerging from the dividing zones in the Chian style, are again a legacy from the Middle Wild Goat.

From this it may be deduced that the Chians, even when adopting a foreign technique, do not completely surrender themselves to it and imitate obsequiously; they adapt it to their own artistic tradition and to some degree retain their individuality. In this, they differ considerably from the other North-Ionian black-figure schools, where the Corinthian influence has overwhelmed local approaches.[37]

The consistent unity of this style made Price think that it must be "... if not the work of one single hand ... at least the output of one workshop".[38] Though the picture has changed a great deal since 1924, the second part of her statement is still valid.

New fragments and nearly complete vases which have since been recovered, help towards a classification into stylistic groups and the tracing of an evolution. The formation of these stylistic groups relies heavily upon the execution and evolution of the filling ornament. Facial details, mainly of sphinxes and some other animals, are also taken into consideration. It must however be pointed out that, though the rosette seemed a reliable criterion, the rendering of details of the animals is not always a safe one. The most obvious case is that of lions, where the same vase can display different renderings, e.g. on the exterior of lekane **1419*** from Phana, the lions' necks are given the characteristic saw-edged mane. On the interior of the very same vase, the lions' necks have instead an elaborately incised wavy line. The lions on **1371*** and **1311*** also display this same specific handling.

The stylistic groups are five:

Group A (FIG. 80): This group comprises the most elaborate work in the Sphinx and Lion style. These are: **1270***; **1277***; **1280***; **1284***; **1292***; **1294***; **1296***; **1301***; **1311**; **1315***;

[35] A.A. Lemos in *Praktika of the 3rd International Congress of Peloponnesian Studies*, 1987–88, 71–74 and figs. 1–4.
[36] *NC*, figs. 68 left and 69 right.
[37] See *Samos* VI.1, pls. 105–125, especially the black-figure vases.
[38] Price 221. Of course, the meaning of the word "workshop" is here employed in the Beazleyan sense, see *BAdd*², Preface (M. Roberton), p. XVI–XVII.

THE SPHINX AND LION STYLE

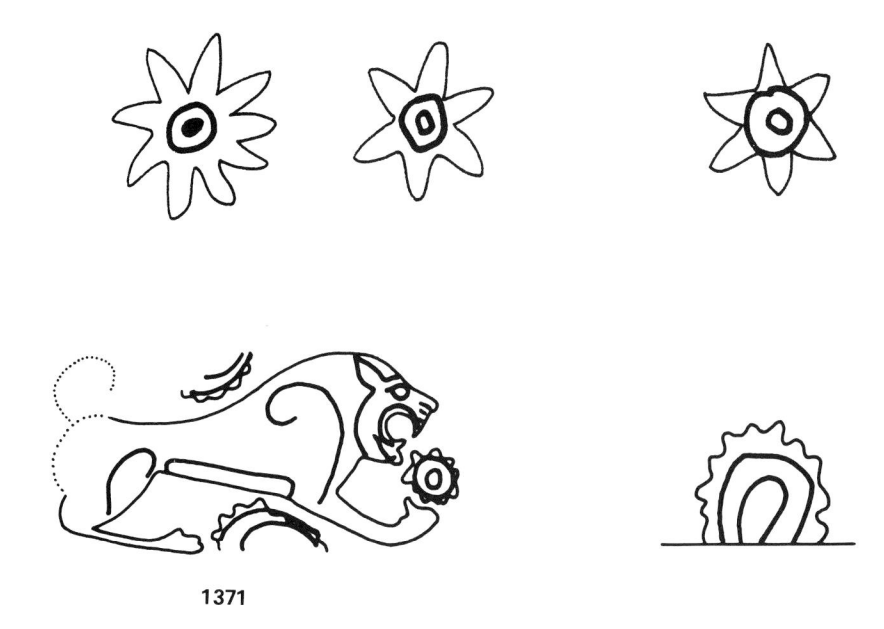

Fig. 80   Stylistic Group A

1319*; **1321***; **1325***; **1326***; **1327***; **1329***; **1333***; **1334**; **1335**; **1336**; **1337**; **1356***; **1358***; **1367***; **1371*** (FIG. 80); **1375***; **1401***; **1406**; **1408***; **1409***; **1413***; **1414***; **1418***; **1419***; **1426***; **1438***; **1447*** and **1457***.

The rosette is of a cogwheel shape consisting of two concentric circles carefully incised after the silhouette has been painted on with its almost triangular petals. Figures are well drawn and details incised most carefully. Good incised parallel lines are used for dividing the sphinxes' wings and their ears are rendered like earrings with an elaborate S-spiral.

The pieces are not of equal quality, but almost all are among the best examples of this style. **1447*** has a semi-rosette hanging like a tear drop pendant which is a direct loan from Chian Middle Wild Goat style.

Group B (FIGS. 81 and 82): This group comprises the following pieces: **1286***; **1340**; **1347*** (FIG. 82); **1376** (FIG. 81); **1405***; **1407*** (FIG. 82) and **1444*** (FIG. 82).

It is not an altogether coherent group, but this might be due to its early date and problems of adaptation to the new technique. There are, though, two elements that unite it, however loosely: the elongated bodies of the animals and the type of the rosette which has the shape of a daisy rendered with two incised concentric circles (sometimes only one circle is used) and incised lines radiating from the circle; the petals are almost realistic.

1444* from Naucratis has three locks for its sphinx's hair, as do black-figure sphinxes influenced by Chian found in East Macedonia. Sphinxes' ears are mostly as in Group A.

On the lid from Erythrae (**1376***, FIG. 81) the lions' manes do not have the two parallel lines to divide them from the saw-edged fringe; the latter is rendered like the sphinx's hair on **1444***.

Group C (FIG. 83): This group consists of the following vases and sherds: **1272***; **1273***; **1293***; **1300***; **1373***; **1402**; **1423***; **1427** (FIG. 83); **1433***; **1434*** (FIG. 83); **1437*** and might be the work of one hand.

The rosette is the cogwheel type, with more spikes here, which brings this set closest to Group A. They and the animals too are executed with a firmer and more decisive hand.

The sphinxes' ears on **1433*** and **1434*** are identical and rendered in a kidney shaped manner, approximating to, but not the same as, some pieces of Group A.

Group D (FIGS. 84 and 85): This is a group in a loose and careless, but lively style. The variety of animals and their postures is best manifested in the playful lions on **1332*** and **1420*** and the komast rider on **1324***.
This group may be subdivided into two stages:
Stage 1: Members are: **1278***, **1279***, **1281***, **1287***, **1288***, **1297***, **1323*** and **1324*** (FIG. 84) probably by the same hand.
Other members are: **1291***, **1312***, **1313***, **1314***, **1328***, **1339**, **1342***, **1343***, **1346***, **1348***, **1424***, **1445** and **1451***.
The rosette is executed carelessly with hasty incisions, reminiscent of children's drawings of the sun.
Stage 2: This rosette, later, becomes even more elementary, especially on **1282***, **1302***, **1305***, **1316***, **1320***, **1332*** (FIG. 85), **1338**, **1341**, **1344***, **1345***, **1349***, **1350***, **1351***, **1354***, **1368***, **1372***, **1374***, **1420*** (FIG. 85), **1421***, **1430***, **1436*** and **1446**.
1344*, **1345*** and **1351*** are by the same hand.

On this second stage of Group D the first indications hinting at the decay of the style appear; this becomes more evident on the sphinxes' and sirens' faces, especially on **1332*** and **1430***.

This group has close affinities with the komast chalices, especially **1324*** with the komast rider.

Group E (FIG. 86): This is the latest group where the decadence of the style is immediately evident. The rosettes, justifiably called discs or blobs, become mere blots: that is, a hastily painted circle in which two concentric circles or a cross are incised. **1271***, **1285***, **1295*** (FIG. 86), **1297***, **1303***, **1322***, **1352*** (FIG. 86), **1369***, **1370*** and **1422*** form this group.

The drawing of sphinxes and sirens is rough and sketchy. The lion on **1295*** (FIG. 86) is almost unrecognisable without his saw-edged mane and his un-Chian closed muzzle. But the lions on **1271*** still retain much of their old form. The type 4 rosette unites stylistically the Sphinx and Lion style with groups of komast and black-figure animal chalices.

Apart from this stylistic division there are matters of details raised by some scholars that concern points of iconography and style. They will be considered separately here.

First, it has been remarked that the tails of the animals on vases of the Chalice and black-figure styles are placed unusually high up the buttocks.[39] So far as concerns the Sphinx and Lion style this is not entirely so. There are many examples, where sphinxes'

---

[39] Ploug in *Sūkās* II, 70 note 412.

1376

Fig. 81 Fragmentary lid from Erythrae

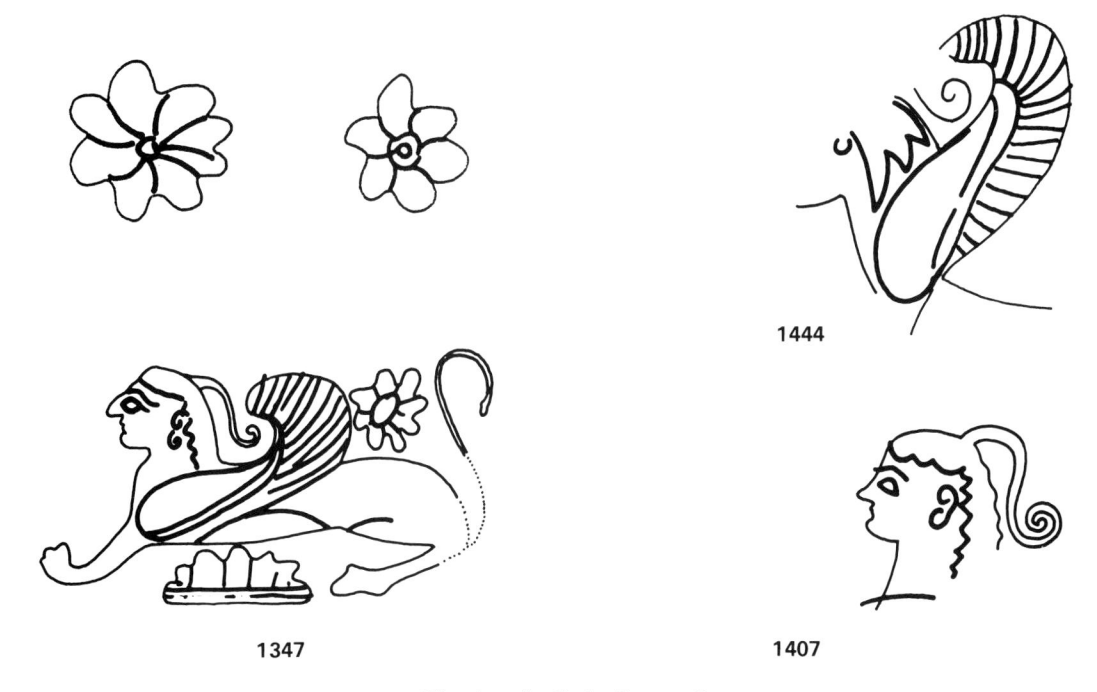

1444

1347

1407

Fig. 82 Stylistic Group B

1434 **1427**

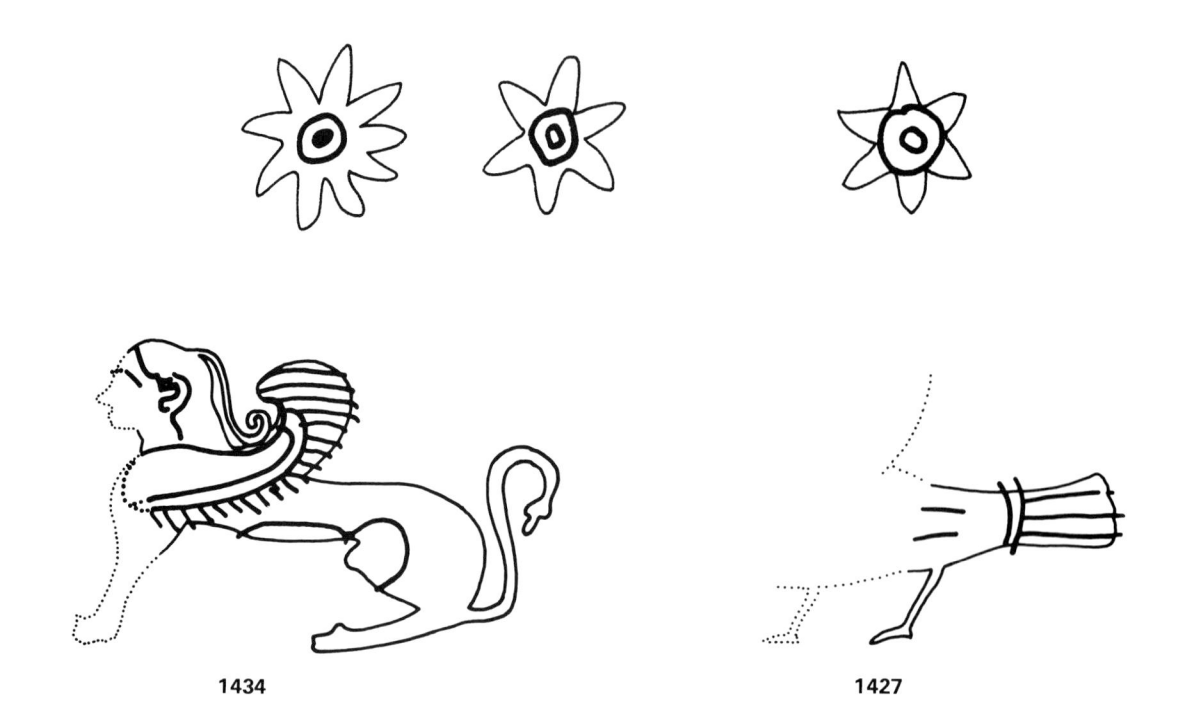

Fig. 83 Stylistic Group C

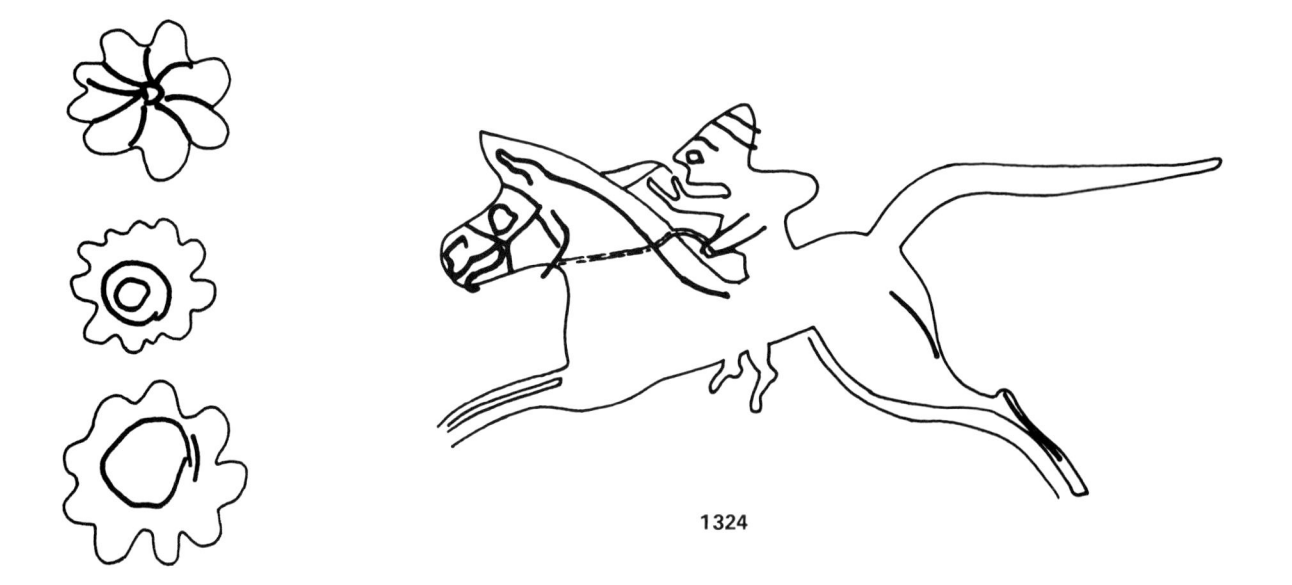

1324

Fig. 84 Stylistic Group D – stage 1

THE SPHINX AND LION STYLE

1332 **1332**

1332 **1420**

Fig. 85 Stylistic Group D – stage 2

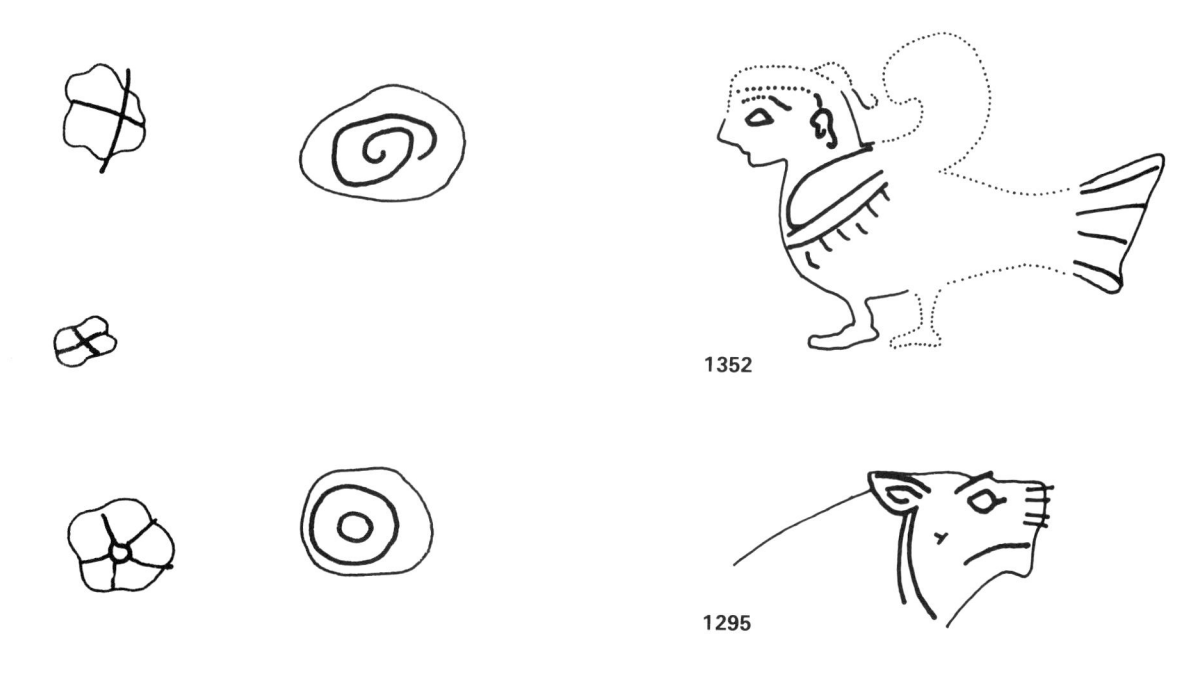

1352

1295

Fig. 86 Stylistic Group E

tails are in their normal position; e.g. **1280***, **1300***, **1317***, **1322***, **1347***, **1419***, **1433*** and **1434**. The possibility of a chronological difference or a decadence in style is ruled out by the fact that on both **1280*** from Rizari and **1419*** from Phana, sphinxes' tails are placed in their normal position on the *outside* of the vase, whereas on the *inside* they are placed higher up. This very same vase from Phana also displays, as noted above, different renderings of lions' necks, which strongly suggests the involvement of two painters. As for the Chalice style there are three examples, respectively from Phana (**822***), Delos (**940***) and Marion in Cyprus (**947***), on which tails are where they should be. This peculiarity can be ascribed either to the painter's idiosyncratic manner, especially since the usual rendering appears even on vases of decaying style, as **1322***, in black figure and the chalice from Delos, **940***, in the Chalice style; or to the possibility of a master craftsman painting the outside and his apprentice the inside of the vase.

Secondly, Chian black figure in general had been thought of as "a counterpart to the Attic Polos style";[40] a closer look, however, reveals obvious differences.

The Polos painter's work,[41]—now dated *c*. 575–565 B.C.,[42] at a period when the Sphinx and Lion style is fading away—has no close ties with the Chian ware. They both share a common repertory to a certain degree, since Corinthian is the common source of inspiration. Yet on the Polos painter vases sirens predominate, followed closely by sphinxes, then women—all three wearing cross-hatched poloi—and finally lions. In the Chian ware, lions are the most common followed by sphinxes and then, less frequently, by sirens and the rest.

Shapes used by the Polos painter are mainly the amphora, the hydria, the tripod-kothon and the lekanis, which are either not encountered or not at all frequent in the Sphinx and Lion style. The paint on his work is poor and diluted, contrary to the Chian practice. The poloi worn by his female creatures are also unknown in the style under survey.

Both styles are uninspiring but in completely different ways. The Polos painter lacks precision and his drawing is elementary, whereas the Sphinx and Lion style, though rough for the most part, displays accuracy and exact figure-drawing. In fact the animal bodies on Chian work may be regarded as true attempts at representation, whereas the figures of the Polos painter are whimsically drawn and seem to have no purpose beyond that of filling the space they occupy.

The incompetence of this painter is shown also in details, for example, his animals' tails emerge as a rule from their feet, whereas in good quality Chian work, as mentioned above, they are in their appropriate place.

Most of the Polos painter's compositions are antithetical, a practice not much favoured in the Sphinx and Lion style. When used, as on **1331*** or **1405*** (back to back), the Chian

---

[40] Cook, Distribution, 158; *GPP*², 126 and *Samos* VI.1, 68.
[41] *ABV* 43 with bibliography and J.M. Hemelrijk in *BABesch*, 4, 1971, 105–110, for further bibliography.
[42] The accepted date of the Polos Painter was about 590–570, but on stratigraphical evidence from the Tocra excavations the dating of the group was lowered to the second quarter of the century (*Tocra* I, 97 and 104–5, where twenty five pieces are cited. Two more items are added in *Tocra* II, 48); also Boardman, *ABFH*, 9.

painter succeeds in drawing identical figures which stand on the same level and have the same proportions.[43]

Incisions in the Polos works are not only hasty but coarse and disorderly. They are not used for the contours of figures but restricted to the cross-hatched poloi, the rendering of eyes and ears and for the hybrids' wings; they become dense and unsteady for the inner details, particularly on the sirens' tails and the sphinxes' hindquarters. Chian painters, however—even when their drawing is rough—take great care in incisions. Like the Polos painter they do not use them for contours, but for inner details they are executed accurately.

Finally, the filling rosette occurs on both. The Polos rosettes are coarse blobs with an incised cross in the centre and are executed in a manner which gives the impression that little effort was involved on the part of the painter. By contrast, rosettes in the Sphinx and Lion style are executed with the utmost care, except for the last group, and display great variety—a basic element which shows the painters' love for detail.

In conclusion, the common repertory is a rather misleading guide; the Polos painter's style is dreadful and suffers a great deal from comparison with the Sphinx and Lion style.

If a source of inspiration for the Sphinx and Lion style is sought, then the Dodwell painter[44] provides a most suitable candidate. The evidence for this is contained in two points: first, the rendering of the sphinxes' wings is similar, and second, his main rosette is identical to Chian type 2 (FIG. 78).

The Sphinx and Lion style, if viewed per se, is no doubt a provincial style providing for the needs of a local market, though exported widely, in limited quantities. It has been characterised as a monotonous and invariable style and as trivial work.[45] This, to a certain degree, is true; the repetitive rows with the same, invariable animals and postures are dull and tiresome.

On bigger preserved fragments and on the almost intact vases from Pitane, (**1272***, **1433*** and **1437***) this effect is more obvious. After the first impression the resulting confusion is somehow reduced, especially when seen from a certain distance; the balance between the light colour of the white-slipped background and the dark colour of the painted figures and ornaments produces an effect not altogether unpleasant. This result is even stronger on fragments. Good quality work demonstrates a precision in drawing and on it figures are quite well-proportioned. The care and patience for detailed work are indeed to the painters' credit. Their attempts, though, at drawing human figures are disappointing. Repetition is rarely avoided, but when this happens, the Sphinx and Lion style can offer unexpected originalities, thus 1) the various mingled animals and their poses, e.g. on **1332***, **1344*–1345***, **1367*** and **1420***; 2) the komast-like horseman on **1324***; 3) the centaur on **1440*** and 4) scenes with lions attacking bulls break the monotony.

---

[43] Cf. *ABV* 48, 15 of the Polos painter from Marseilles where the sphinx's head on the left confronts the bust of one opposite.
[44] M. Blomberg *Observations on the Dodwell Painter* 1983, passim, and see now, Amyx *CorVP*, 205–10, 320–1, 346–8 and mainly 346 for an appreciation of his work, pls. 86 and 87.
[45] Price 220 and *GPP*² 126.

The Sphinx and Lion style did not have an impact on other local schools; only one fragment takes after it, recently recovered at Labraunda[46] (Pl. 243.1), with a bull and lion scene.

In conclusion, the Sphinx and Lion style in the field of composition is at its best on the pieces displaying some variety. And though as a whole this miniaturist style has something of the monotony of Middle Corinthian,[47] the Chian draughtsmen retained to a certain extent some of their traditional qualities.

2. THE BLACK-FIGURE GRAND STYLE

I. Shapes

Three out of the ten fragments, (**1458***, **1459** and **1460***), are from cups of Laconian type. **1458*** is the best preserved piece; a minor but very important fragment has been added to it, giving the beginning of the broken handle, and thus, unambiguously, the shape.[48] The estimated diameter of about 18 cm is normal for Laconian cups of the same period.[49] **1459** and **1460*** are small fragments from a similar type of cup. On **1459**, the end of a handle-palmette on the exterior and the characteristic pomegranate pattern at the border of the tondo is preserved. The same applies for **1460*** which on the outside is decorated with lines alternating with bands. It must be stressed that these three pieces are unique in shape in the entire Chian output. They imitate Laconian models with which, it seems, their potters were familiar.[50]

Yet, it must be observed that the Oxford fragment, **1458***, differs a little in shape from its prototypes.[51] Its profile does not exactly match the examples which its ornamental decoration follows, because the handle springs out immediately below the rim, leaving but very little space for the lip, unlike any contemporary Laconian cup.[52]

Five sherds in this style are from chalices, (**1461***–**1464*** and **1465**) and have in the inside black paint over the slip; **1462*** and **1463*** display on it an elaborately drawn white rosette, and **1461*** a lotus. The sherds to hand are from the walls of sixth-century chalices and **1463*** has preserved the rim with its pattern.

1466* is from a bowl and **1467*** from Berezan is from an open shape.

---

[46] J.J. Jully in *CGED* 32, pl. 10, fig. 3.2 and *Labraunda*, II.3, 29, pl. 39.42.

[47] *NC* pls. 28 and 29. And now Amyx *CorVP*, passim in the relevant section on Middle Corinthian.

[48] The join does not appear in *CVA*, Oxford II, pl. 396.33. It was later added by Boardman. A photograph of the outside in Stibbe's, *LV*, pl. 60.3.

[49] E.g. no. 143 in Stibbe's *ibid.*, Catalogue, p. 235 has a diameter of 18.4 cm and is attributed to the Boreads painter to whose work our fragment has been linked.

[50] Boardman in *Chios Conference* 198 and 254.

[51] Plain cups, or cups decorated with a single band are a very common shape in Chian plain pottery. They appear early in the seventh century and continue to be produced till around the middle of the sixth. They turned up in masses in Emporio (where Boardman classified the seventh-century stock into five distinctively recognised groups according to their shape and the sixth-century into three. *Emporio*, 123–128, nos. 284–389 and 162–3, nos. 768–784 respectively) and other parts of Chios and elsewhere. Their shapes are completely different and have nothing in common with the pieces discussed above.

[52] Stibbe, *LV* nos. 140, 143, 190, but no. 11, pl. 5.5 seems to be the nearest parallel from the point of view of shape.

II. Subjects

The subjects employed together with the manner of drawing are the reasons for the title "Grand".[53] For the first time so far in *Chian black figure* are encountered figures, human and other, in a composition where too little is left for a secure interpretation. Animals or hybrids are not excluded. The homogeneity of style on the one hand and the varied repertory of subjects, as it seems, on the other, single out this category.

1. Animals: The bull appears once, on **1466***, heading to the right. Iconographically, it does not differ in the least from its counterparts in the Sphinx and Lion and in both these black-figure styles the type derives from the one established by the Middle Wild Goat.

The remains of a tail and a wing are indicative of a siren, on **1461***, below the winged feet of a flying figure.[54]

On **1465*** there might be a siren with a scale-patterned body,[55] but almost nothing of her lower part is left. On the fine piece from Oxford, (**1458***, FIG. 87), the siren[56] is facing left; a spiral is clearly visible, thus it is more likely that she wears an elaborate headband and not a polos. Her size and position of the head, in proportion to the dimension of the tondo, will not permit the elongated body of a sphinx to fit in. In addition, the arrangement of her wings[57] follows the practice for sirens.

2. Humans, winged daemon and ?deities: Above the siren on **1461*** (FIG. 88) is a pair of winged feet flying to the right, the opposite direction to the siren. It has been said that this is Perseus with the monster,[58] but the gorgons are not represented in the form of winged birds. A daemon wearing winged boots, striding away as in other East Greek vase and wall paintings,[59] would not explain the presence of the siren. The flying winged figure above the departing warrior in the wall painting from the Kizilbel tomb at Lycia has a different connotation.[60]

The winged feet are likely to belong to a flying Eros, often depicted on Laconian cups together with sirens,[61] where both these creatures are placed towards the border of the tondo above the figure scene, usually a banquet.[62] Here the fragment is from immediately

---

[53] In analogy to Boardman's Grand for the polychrome style. See Boardman CN, 59 ff and here Chapter 3, p. 94 ff.

[54] Boardman CN, 60 note 5.

[55] Kunze's article in *AM* 57, 1932, on "Sirens" for an eastern origin of the scale-pattern. In fact, the ivory relief of a siren from Ephesus, fig. 2, might have been the source of inspiration for Chian painters as well.

[56] Cf. Stibbe, *LV* 234 no. 142 thinks it is a sphinx and makes stylistic comparisons with the feathers of a bird on a Laconian fragment. However Schaus, *Dem. Sact.*, *Cyrene* II, 8, in the discussion for his catalogue entry, no. 526, thinks that she is a siren.

[57] However, sphinxes with open and drooping wings are depicted in early Athenian black figure, e.g. on the Nessos painter's skyphoid crater B, on the stem, see Karouzou, *Anagyrountos* pl. 17 (the sphinx at the right).

[58] Price 219 but Boardman, CN 60 note 5 restored the 'monster' to a siren. Harpies—linked with Boreads—could not be represented either. On the Phineus cup, Pfuhl, *MuZ* fig. 164, or in Athenian vase painting, *ABV* 5, the Nessos painter's bowl in Berlin. In Laconian they never take the shape of the bird (which could otherwise explain the tail).

[59] On a plate in Berlin, Pergamonmus. F 3917, see Kardara, *Rhodiake* 252 and fig. 200, where also references to clay reliefs with the same subject; also *Samos* VI.1, pl. 136.1121.

[60] *AJA* 77, 1973, pl. 43.

[61] The interpretation and its link with Laconian was suggested to me by Professor Boardman. Erotes, though not in connection with sirens, appear in East Greek art, e.g. on late Archaic gems see Boardman *AGG* F2–3, especially nos. 169–72; on the lid of a Clazomenian sarcophagus in the BM see Cook, *Claz. Sarc.*, 122 (G1) and pls. 40–1.

[62] Stibbe, *LV* pl. 6.1 and 58. Recently G.P. Schaus in *BSA* 81, 1986, 275 with notes 71–77 on winged daemons on East Greek vases. For a recent study on Laconian Iconography, see M. Pipili *Laconian Iconography of the Sixth Century B.C.* 1987, 71–2 and figs. 103–104a, where a detailed discussion on the appearance and interpretation of winged daemons on Laconian cups is given.

156   ARCHAIC POTTERY OF CHIOS

1458

Fig. 87 Reconstruction of a siren on the tondo of **1458***

THE BLACK-FIGURE GRAND STYLE

Fig. 88 Reconstruction of a siren and Eros on **1461***

below the rim, as its inner decoration shows and would thus be in the correct position had the decoration below been a symposion.

Two female heads occur on each of the fragments **1460*** and **1463***: on the former, one head overlaps the other, whilst on the second, one is behind the other. A strong hint that they might be goddesses are the poloi clearly preserved on the latter.[63] These heads could equally well belong to ordinary Ionian ladies in a procession similar in subject and composition to the fine polychrome fragments from Naucratis, e.g. **717***. Poloi are not a decisive proof of divinity.[64]

Identical subjects appear on the last three fragments, **1462***, **1464*** and **1467***. The lower part of a chiton worn by a (?) female figure: on **1462*** and **1464*** turned to the left; the figure on **1462*** might be seated on a throne or a diphros, as suggested by a possible stool leg on the right. However on **1467*** she is walking to the right followed by a dog at the left. This suggests a possible reconstruction for **1464***, but the strong curve of the animal's neck on **1462*** seems better explained as of a cock. Both these two last animals are *in front* of the figure and have the characteristically Chian ham-frill collar, which is missing on the dog's neck from Berezan (**1467***). Black paint for the figures' feet on **1464*** and **1467*** is not decisive for their gender, as these fragments are in black figure, where added white for naked female parts comes in only after the mid years of the century.

---

[63] Price 218, pl. 6.2 and 7 interprets them as two out of the three goddesses contesting in a Judgement of Paris scene.

[64] Cf. Payne-Young, *AMS*, 15 and especially note 2. Also Richter, *Korai*, 12. In the minor arts the examples are innumerable.

The figures on **1462*** might have been enthroned goddesses, perhaps, though not necessarily, in the manner of the Laconian funerary limestone reliefs,[65] receiving offerings amongst which first comes the cock. **1467*** depicts a mortal, who takes her dog for a walk. This last picture would have been a scene from everyday life in a highly sophisticated society, as the Archaic Chian of the earlier part of the sixth century must have been. On **1464*** a similar scene may have been depicted.

3. Patterns: Patterns in this category are rare and of two kinds: a) the well-known Chian and b) Laconian.

a) Chalice **1463*** has a rim pattern of broken cable (or SS but without dots) for long popular on Chian.[66]

Two elaborately drawn white rosettes still remain as the inner decoration on **1462*** and **1463*** and a lotus flower with lines on **1461***. And, finally, three favoured Chian patterns occur as decorative details on figures and are incised: the battlement, or step, pattern on **1458***, for the division of the upper from the lower part of the body; the zigzag flanked by two lines on the chiton's hem on **1462*** and the chequer, for the same use as the last, on **1464***.

b) On the outside of the cup, **1458***, there are bands of alternating tongues and rays, in the Laconian manner. On this and **1459** the remains of horizontal palmettes at the handle[67] and pomegranate patterns bordering the tondi[68] are Laconian features which will be discussed below.

III. Style

1458*–1467* are the best examples of Chian draughtsmanship in black figure which could well be compared with products from other more advanced schools of Archaic Greek vase painting, had they not been in such a desperately fragmentary state.

Black-figure Grand style is a separate and distinctive Chian category with strong individuality. The principal common features which speak for the coherence and homogeneity of this category are:

1. The overwhelming whiteness of the slip.
2. The shapes which are always from open vessels and mostly drinking cups of both Laconian type and chalices.
3. The subject-matter involves representations of figures or scenes, which are not met on other Chian black-figure categories, save the Centauromachy (**1440***) and the hackneyed komast scenes.
4. The style displays a unique finesse both in drawing and incision.
5. The scale of the figures which shows that it is not a miniaturist style, as is the Sphinx and Lion.
6. From what is left and can be judged filling ornament is completely avoided.

---

[65] J. Boardman, *Greek Sculpture, the Archaic Period, a Handbook*, 1978, 165 and fig. 253; H. Hausman, *Griechische Weihreliefs*, 1960, 25 and fig. 11. On the Chrysapha Laconian relief a cock is offered by the first worshipper.

[66] *Emporio*, 103 and fig. 61A.

[67] Possibly, of Stibbe's, *LV*, type no. 12 on page 92 (it might however be type no. 18).

[68] Stibbe's, *LV*, type 2 on p. 91.

Besides the above-mentioned characteristics the following elements add to its clear distinction: the Laconising features,[69] as well as the unmistakable use of an elaborately incised wavy line, applied for the rendering of details, as on sirens' heads and wings and on women's hair and chiton folds.

Laconian influence apparent in this category can be discerned in four features:

1. The kylix shape: Nowhere else in Chian wares is this shape to be met. The slight differentiation from its model has already been mentioned. It could be explained as a Chian adjustment, in that a potter, perhaps used to producing bowls with handles,[70] made his own modifications.

2. The decoration:
a) *On the outside*, bands of rays and tongues in the Laconian manner,
b) The horizontal handle palmette on the bowl of the Oxford cup (**1458***) and **1459** and
c) The pomegranate pattern at the border of the *tondo* of the same vases.

3. The style: the linear pattern forming the feathers in the birds' wings.[71] This rendering of plumage is a wholly Laconian feature,[72] not met on any other Chian example. Sphinxes' and sirens' wings in the Sphinx and Lion style or the more elaborate Chian cock of the black-figure animal chalices are portrayed in a completely different manner. Two more Laconian patterns are also common on the Chian fragments under survey:

a) The battlement pattern[73] as a dividing zone on garments.
b) The zigzag flanked by lines: again as a dividing zone on the garment appears on **1462***
for the rendering of the chiton hem.

4. Poloi: Poloi are not met on other Chian styles[74] nor generally in East Greek pottery. They are most possibly borrowed from Laconian, where examples are not very frequent, the most prominent being that of Athena on the Boreads painter's kylix in New York.[75]

The attribution of all the fragments to a single hand is based partly on identification made already,[76] taken further by these observations:

a) *The elaborate, incised, parallel wavy lines*, which are almost always present to indicate the borders of the polos on **1458***; the parting of the hair into parallel and radiating tresses on **1463*** and garment folds on **1462***, **1464*** and **1467***.
b) *The elaborate incised line*, which indicates the curls, terminating in spirals, on the forehead of **1460*** and the head of **1463***.
c) *The zigzag line flanked by two parallel lines*, which occurs both on **1460*** as the decorative pattern of the polos and on **1462*** as the decorative pattern of the chiton hem.
d) *The profiles* preserved on **1458*** and **1460*** and the little that is left of **1463*** are almost the same, with straight foreheads and protruding noses and chins. The eyes are also

---

[69] Boardman, CN 60 and note 1 and *RDAC* 1968, 13 with note 4. Stibbe, *LV*, 88–89, 234, pl. 60.2.3.

[70] Of the type, see *Emporio* 165, no. 813, fig. 113, where the handles are very near the rim.

[71] Other examples in Laconian from Stibbe's, *LV*: no. 27 pl. 14.1 for a cock's feathers; no. 98 pl. 32.2 for a cock's feathers; no. 118 pl. 36.1.2 for identical use with the Chian, i.e. for siren's wings; no. 119 pl. 37.1 for Harpies' wings; no. 339 pl. 122.3 for a cock's feathers; no. 325 pl. 116.2 for a cock's feathers.

[72] Stibbe, *LV* 234, no. 142 and pl. 45.3, which is the most representative example.

[73] Stibbe, loc. cit.

[74] Boardman, CN, 61 note 1. A sphinx on a dinos support from Thasos, *CGED*, pl. 46.4, gives a vague impression of wearing a polos, but, it could be due to the flatness of her head.

[75] *BSA* 49, 1954, pl. 50 and Stibbe, *LV* no. 10, pl. 44.1.

[76] Boardman, CN, 61 note 1.

identical on the first two though slightly smaller on the last, which could be a further elaboration and refinement of his work. Ears look quite similar in style on **1458*** and **1460***.

This Chian painter must have been a prominent artist; his works stand out among other hackneyed material in Chian black figure, such as the more trivial vases in Sphinx and Lion or the bulk of the komast chalices. Stylistically he can be compared with good Laconian, which attracted and influenced him deeply, albeit only in some strictly isolated aspects, involving curvilinear decoration: a) the line of curls, forming spirals, that occur on Heracles' forehead in his fight with the Nemean lion,[77] b) the parallel wavy lines that occur mainly on Laconian hair;[78] which are also used by the Amasis painter for the rendering of Poseidon's and Dionysos' chiton, as well as for their hair and beards on the neck amphora in the Cabinet de Médailles [79] and c) a broken cable appears in Laconian for the paryphe of men's chitons as an incised motif; a feature again paralleled by the Amasis painter, e.g. the hemlines on Dionysos' and the maenads' chitons.[80] In Chios, the pattern has a long history of use as a painted design on the rims of chalices, e.g. **1463***, one of hundreds.

The conclusion to be drawn from the above is that though this Chian painter can be argued to have been particularly influenced by certain Laconian features, it is nonetheless true that they were held in common by good quality black-figure work in Archaic Greece elsewhere.

Finally, fabric, the chalice shape, and a stylistic idiosyncrasy like the ham-frill collar on the animals' necks (on **1462*** and **1464***) are unmistakably Chian and unite this with other Chian black figure, especially in the Sphinx and Lion style, e.g. on **1407*** where the hybrid's profile and the scale could be compared to those of the black-figure Grand style.[81] Facial detail, eyes and ears and especially the receding forehead, remind one vaguely of the rendering of the best works in the Sphinx and Lion style and the komast chalices, e.g. **1468***. Furthermore, the general character and manner of drawing—the refined contours and the carefully drawn or incised lines, naturally varying in quality—are present in almost all Chian work, even at its most trivial.

IV. *Place of manufacture*

Almost all black-figure styles, even of the same stylistic groups, are met both on Chios[82] and at Naucratis.

As regards this specific category the arguments favouring its manufacture at Naucratis by a Chian workshop with imported clay and slip from the motherland are that Laconian pottery and the Laconising category have not been recovered on Chios and furthermore that the strongly Laconising features point to a cosmopolitan centre where Laconian

---

[77] Stibbe, *LV* no. 212, pl. 70.1.
[78] Stibbe, *LV* no. 196, pl. 63.1; no. 194, pl. 61.2; no. 220, pl. 78.1; no. 353, pl. 128.2 and pl. 58.e.
[79] E. Simon, *Die griechischen Vasen* 1981, pls. XXIII and 72. Also, Bothmer, *Amasis*, 23.
[80] *Ibid.* and Boardman, *ABFH* 55, figs. 85–86.

[81] On **1407***: the face has a width of 0.026, whereas the smallest in black-figure Grand style is reckoned to be *c.* 0.030.
[82] Black-figure animal chalices have not been found as yet on Chios; nine examples are from Naucratis and fourteen from other sites.

Fig. 89 Horsemen on a fragmentary dinos from Berezan (Hermitage, Leningrad)

pottery was an everyday commodity.[83] Naucratis is proposed as the most likely place where Chians met Laconians and their decorated pottery.[84]

However, hints pointing to Chios as the place of manufacture for this category also should be considered. In addition to what has already been argued[85] from the fabric and the limited excavations on the island,[86] the following deserve attention:

a) A sherd (**1467***) was found at Berezan, a factor that might seem to exclude Naucratis as the source. Trade with the Pontic colonies was in the hands of Ionians in the early part of the sixth century and even if Chians had not participated in the foundation of colonies they were nonetheless trading substantially with the region.[87] It seems reasonable that they carried pottery produced at home. Moreover, a fragmentary black-figure dinos (FIG. 89) has been found at Berezan and is now in the Hermitage. It is not of the same group but has a close proximity in style; the rim pattern, a double guilloche, together with the figure drawing of the horses and riders classify it as good quality Chian black-figure work.

---

[83] Boardman, CN 60–61; *RDAC* 1968, 13 and *GO*³ 123–4 and 274 notes 41–3. See also Lane in *BSA* 34, 1933–4, 186 and Stibbe, *LV* 89 note 1, 96 and 234. Cook in *GPP*² 126 considers the resemblances due probably to "a similar ineptitude".

[84] Boardman in *Chios Conference* 198, 254.

[85] See Chapter 3, pp. 117–8.

[86] Boardman in *CGED* 85, where he emphasizes Emporio's lack of fine pottery in the sixth century; Chios town, apart from Kontoleon's excavations at Rizari and the British excavations at Kofiná, remains unknown territory for fine wares of the Archaic period.

[87] Boardman, *GO*³ 250–1 and note 130.

Of course, faience and other products of Naucratis reached the Black Sea colonies,[88] so that the possibility of Chians and/or other traders carrying goods from Naucratis should not be completely ruled out.

b) Laconian influence, evident in this category and discussed above, is not limited to it. The red-spotted boar favoured in Laconian vase painting appears on a Sphinx and Lion style fragmentary dinos unearthed at Rizari in Chios town, **1401***. It does not differ from its Laconian counterpart, not even in execution: incision is used for inner details, as well as the parting of its bristles on the back, and the added red spots are of an irregular form.[89]

c) The pomegranate motif, a wholly Laconian feature, is present as a *pattern for inner decoration* not only on many chalices and open vases unearthed at Naucratis,[90] but also on vases recovered elsewhere, e.g. the phiale mesomphalos from Marion in Cyprus, **1081*** and the animal chalices from Delos, **643*** and **644**.[91] Thus, indirect Laconian influence exists not only on Chian black figure, including the unique fragment in the Sphinx and Lion style (**1401***), but also in other techniques of decoration.

The statement "Laconian is not found [on Chios] at all as yet"[92] is undeniably true. However, Corinthian, which obviously influenced the Sphinx and Lion style, is comparatively rare and Athenian, whose influence is detectable in many isolated works and in the second half of the sixth century in a series of Chian black figure, is even more scarce; other vases from various local Archaic schools, even of the East Greek region, are completely absent on Chios.[93] Even after the middle of the century when Chian decorated pottery is gradually declining, Chians avoided imports and mainly used plain pottery of their own.[94]

Laconian influence is traced in an indirect manner in other Chian black-figure styles—in the isolated example of the red-spotted boar (**1401***) and the pomegranate motif, present in other categories as well—and might equally account for this style. A random example for an indirect impact on other traditions would be the Samian artist working under heavy Chian influence, and that too on an island on bad terms with Chios and with no other apparent artistic links.[95]

The thesis made here in favour of Chios might not be considered conclusive and the problem of the place of manufacture for the black-figure Grand style will remain open until future excavations on the island provide the necessary evidence.

---

[88] V. Webb, *Archaic Greek Faience*, 1978, for Berezan her nos: 411, 507, 953 and for Olbia: nos. 855, 931–2.

[89] A.A. Lemos in *Praktika of the 3rd International Congress of Peloponnesian Studies*, 1987–88, 78ff.

[90] E.g. **551**, **728*** and **754**.

[91] However, both these vases were considered by Boardman as manufactured at Naucratis, see *RDAC*, 1968, 12 "might be from a local [Naucratis] Chian studio" for the Marion phiale and CN, 61 note 6 for the Delos chalice. Incidentally, worshippers, usually women, in the Chalice style and the Komast chalices hold pomegranates: again on chalices recovered at Naucratis but not claimed to be produced there: **889***, **890***, **896*** and **1538***. See also Williams *AA* 1983, 162 and note 25.

[92] Boardman, CN 60.

[93] For recent rescue excavations, see *Chiaka Chronica* 16, 1984, 107–118.

[94] This applies mainly to the sixth century, because in late fifth and fourth they imported Athenian red figure (L. Beaumont, Athenian red-figure fragments from Chios, unpublished article), but always in reduced quantities.

[95] See Chapter 3, p. 114.

3. THE BLACK-FIGURE CHALICES

I. Shapes

Intact or almost intact chalices with black-figure decoration: **1487*** (FIG. 90), **1488*** (FIG. 90), **1561***, **1562***, **1582***, **1600***, **1602***, **1603***, **1611***, **1614***, **1617***, and a number of large pieces, **1468***, **1574***, **1601***, mainly fragments of the walls, give the form of the shape used in this technique during the first three quarters of the sixth century. They all fall into Hayes' type III.[96]

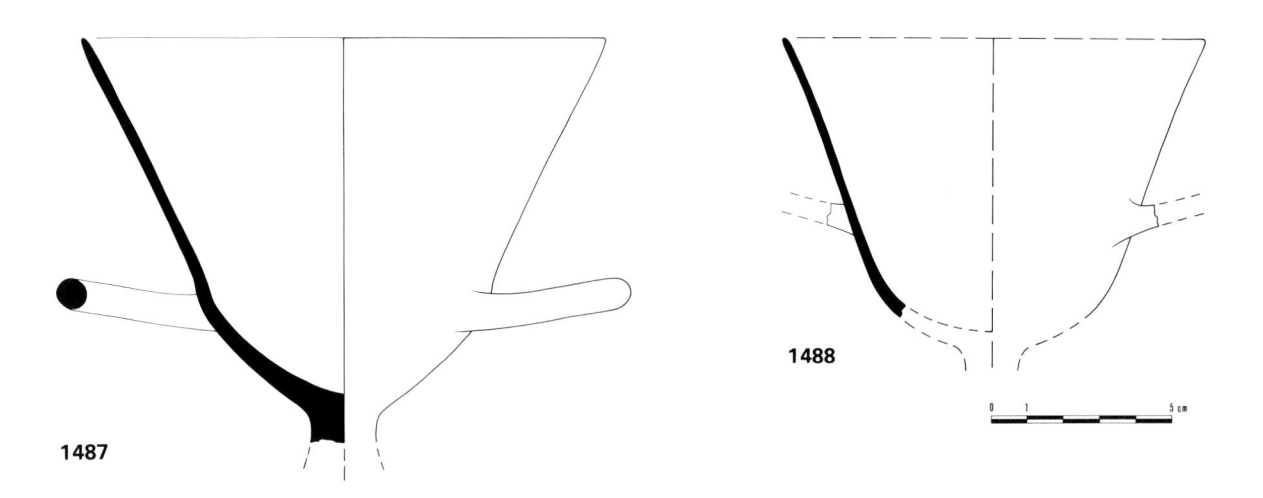

Fig. 90 Komast chalices from Rizari

The black-figure chalices vary in height from c. 11.4 to 18.3 cm and in diameter from c. 11.4 to 19.6 cm. The diameter is consistently close to the height, even exactly corresponding in many cases. Of the preserved chalices one eighth are in black figure.

Komast chalices are smaller than the black-figure animal ones, as even the fragmentary evidence from Naucratis shows.[97] In fact, many are miniatures.

II. Subjects

A. Human figures

On the komast chalices, **1468*-1591**, only komasts and occasionally women appear. The type of woman can be reconstructed from the few fragments where it has been preserved. An element missing on one sherd is supplied on another. That they are all from komos scenes is suggested by the fact that women do not appear at all on other Chian black figure, except for the black-figure Grand style. The fuller scenes are provided by **1468*** from Emporio, **1487*** (FIG. 94) from Rizari and **1564*** from Tocra where they intermingle with komasts. Women are rendered in the usual black figure; incision is used only for inner detail. Occasionally, women's flesh is left blank on the white-slipped background, thus producing a more realistic effect. Red is the only added colour.

---

[96] *Tocra* I, 58–59; also, *Emporio*, 103, fig. 60, type E.   [97] *Tocra* I, 59 and note 7.

The iconographical type is that of the standing figure; only on **1489*** (FIG. 96) does the upper part give a vague impression of a slight forward movement. Both head and torso are without exception drawn strictly in profile. They wear a long chiton, sleeved to the elbows, belted and with the paryphe decorated in well-known Chian patterns, such as vertical chequers on **1468*** (FIG. 96) and simple dots on **1487*** (FIG 94). On the last, the pattern continues on the upper part covering her left arm and on **1539*** a broken cable pattern appears at the same place.

Most of them hold wreaths which they are either offering or receiving from komasts; one is holding a pomegranate, **1538*** (FIG 98), and another plays the double flute, **1468***. Their hair is kept in a mass hanging in a queue behind, whilst above the forehead it is rendered by a coarse zigzag. On **1487*** (FIG. 94), the artist intends to show that the woman is wearing a stephane, as the reserved lines indicate. Of facial details, eyes are rendered by a small circle terminating in a small quirk and eyebrows by a slightly curved line; ears, preserved on **1468*** and **1539***, are on the first rendered as an elaborate snail-like spiral and on the second as scrawls.

Komasts are always painted in silhouette and incisions are used for specific inner details: the loin-cloth, the band on the chest and facial features, as ears, eyes, eyebrows and the headdress. The exceptions are **1468*** from Emporio, where incisions outline the contour of the legs of one of the komasts. So too do the komasts on the komast chalice from Ayia Paraskevi, **1580**.[98] Added red is frequently used; not always an indication of good work, as it is often missing on the best pieces.

Heads, hands, buttocks and legs are always in profile. The upper part of the torso is either frontal or there are rare attempts at a three-quarter view. The posture is that of the dancing man, evident from both the way the legs are bent in postures of violent movement and from the manner in which the hands are stretched out in all kinds of extravagant gestures. Sometimes they clasp or slap their buttocks. On **1487*** (FIG. 94) the komast holds a wreath; on **1496** and **1555*** a ball; and on **1562*** a pomegranate.

Genitals are not shown, since a loincloth is always worn, rendered in a conventional way with two lines forming an angle across the top of the legs and two semicircles at the point where the buttocks protrude. They all wear around their necks, and most often across their chests, a band incised in three different ways: either like a *'ham-frill'* as on the Sphinx and Lion lions' necks or an *oblique line from which small parallel fringes spring* or just *two parallel oblique lines*. These have been interpreted as amulets,[99] but they are better regarded as fringe-hems of an Ionian chiton or a shawl.[100] The type of paryphai, together with the filling ornament, helps distinguish the stylistic groups.

Facial details are roughly indicated. Eyes are incised as a circle or are sometimes rather elongated; eyebrows as a line; ears are a rough kidney shape, usually misplaced, two consecutive curly lines (**1468***), or merely scribbles. The coiffure is rendered in two different ways: either kept as a mass hanging behind the head, or bound by a taenia with some hair flying out behind, as on **1505*** (FIG. 96) and **1506*** (FIG. 96). On **1482*** it is left

---

[98] *Ametos*, 794, pl. 163.2 (upper row, right).
[99] Price 220.
[100] Buschor, *Satyrtänze*, 62; similar fringed mantles or shawls appear on the large, terracotta human idols from Ayia Eirini in *SCE*, II, pl. 208 nos. 1028 and 2077 and pl. 238 nos. 1505, 1562 and 1741.

to float free in two tresses, identical with that of a male figure on a Chian relief pithos.[101] Usually, however, no hair is shown, being completely hidden under a turban, a habit also met on the contemporary Polychrome style.[102] Attention should be drawn to the distinction between the mitra (or turban) worn by East Greeks and the Lydians[103] and which subsequently, perhaps through Anakreon, the Ionian poet, was introduced to Athenian vase painting, and the sakkos which is usually a female headdress. A line of interpretation of the iconography for these komasts was developed from the premises that these headdresses were sakkoi and that on the most elaborate pieces the komasts also wore earrings. From this a view was promoted on the possible transvestism of the participants at the Artemis festivals on Chios.[104] However, both headgears, the mitra and the *sakkos*, have recently been fully explained and documented and it is now clear that the one worn by Chian komasts is the *mitra*, the Lydian turban.[105]

Finally, it must be admitted that their composition is uninspired. Komasts are placed loosely in the field, though their distorted limbs give the impression of movement and vividness. When women are present some sort of variety is introduced into the otherwise flat komos scenes. However, even they adopt a statuesque posture, somehow frigid and remote and look as if they are not enjoying themselves, at least not as much as the komasts.

B. Animals

Cocks and hens occur in a single group, which could be named the "Poultry Group". They are always pictured standing. Cocks are either placed alone in the field or in an antithetical composition with a hen between.

Single cocks appear on **1611***, **1612**, **1605*** and **1608**. Cocks face each other with a hen on **1600***, **1601*** and **1602***. A single hen exists on the fragment **1607**: she could have been between two companions. Finally, cocks face each other with a lotus between on **1603***.

There are a few fragments, **1593–1596*** and **1613***, where details of the composition do not emerge.

Cocks have their feathers drawn in close-packed and parallel incised lines and a tail consisting of two long feathers. Their comb has added red usually ending in four to six small points: the pronounced wattles may be similarly treated. Their necks, mostly with added red as well, end in a saw-edged collar, scarcely different from lions' necks in the Sphinx and Lion style. Hens are rendered in much the same way as their partners. Middle Corinthian influence might be traced in both these creatures.[106]

Birds appear on **1614*** and are most probably swans. **1598***, though a small fragment, shows this more clearly, because of their long necks. However, from such poor drawings the possibility of their being ducks or geese cannot be excluded.

---

[101] A fragment in the Chios museum, see *AE*, 1960, 217 note 6, pl. 58A and L.H. Anderson, *Relief Pithoi from the Archaic Period of Greek Art*, 1975, Chios no. 128. W. Fuchs in *Chios Conference* 277, fig. 1. And E. Simantoni-Bournia, *La Céramique à reliefs au Musée de Chios*, forthcoming, where the creature is differently interpreted.

[102] Price pl. 6.12 and 13.

[103] *GO³*, 98.

[104] D. Williams in *AA* 1983, 162–3. To his note 31 on pp. 163–4 of the Phana fragment = *ADelt*. 1916, 199, fig. 16, another ARTEMIS inscription on a Chian vase could be added from Emporio, *Emporio* no. 615. Boardman in *Emporio* 62–3, explains the probability of an Artemis cult in Emporio.

[105] See now D.C. Kurtz and J. Boardman in *Occasional Papers on Antiquities 2, Greek Vases in the J.P. Getty Museum*, vol. 3, 1986, 50–6 on headdress and specifically p.51 on the Chian komasts' headgear.

[106] *NC* fig. 20 C-F, especially F and pp. 74–6 note 9. Amyx *CorVP*, 669.

The only fish in this category, apparently a dolphin, appears on **1597***. Others that appear on Chian are on two unslipped black-figure kantharoi, **1627*** from Emporio and **1631*** from Naucratis. The dolphin on a phiale fragment in the Grand style, **802***, does not compare closely with these pieces.

C. Ornaments

Patterns on the black-figure chalices occur on two specific parts of the vase, the rim and the handle zone, thus accentuating them.

Rim patterns (FIG. 91) are of seven types, the most popular of which is type 1.

Type 1: dots flanked by a simple line at each side, as on **1468***, **1482***, **1483***, **1485***, **1488***, **1491***, **1493***, 1504, **1534***, **1535***, **1537***, **1540***, 1542, **1545***, **1558***, **1583***, **1584***, **1587***, **1590***, **1595***, **1596***, 1608 and **1611***.

Type 2: dots flanked by a pair of lines at each side, as on **1605***.

Type 3: elongated dots slanting leftwards and flanked by a single line at each side, as on 1502 and **1530***.

Type 4: stripes slanting leftwards and flanked by a pair of lines at each side, as on **1600***, **1601***, **1616*** and **1620***.

Type 5: two parallel lines, as on 1510, **1511*** and **1614***.

Type 6: SS facing left flanked by two lines at each side, as on **1546***.

Type 7: zigzag flanked by two lines at each side, as on **1602***.

Both rim and handle zone patterns are never incised; most are identical to their counterparts in the reserving styles and are simplified versions of Middle Wild Goat patterns.

The commonest handle zone pattern (FIG. 92) is the Chian trade mark: a *metope* on both sides of the vase, in which appears a saw-edged pattern, flanked vertically by usually six stripes; it is executed with a multiple brush (FIG. 92.1).

Some variety is also displayed on isolated examples: *a double meander running left* on **1503**, **1570** and on the back side of **1600*** (FIG. 92.2); *a complex meander* with stopt key, alternately facing right and left and with dotted cross square on **1601*** (FIG. 92.3); and a simple cable pattern on **1520*** (FIG. 92.4).

A wave-pattern running left on **1600*** is unique in Chian (FIG. 92.5).

Filling ornament (FIG. 93): Rosettes are the only ornaments to appear in the field, though not all groups have them. Their evolution is the main criterion for distinguishing the stylistic groups and tracing a chronological sequence. There are three main types. On types 1 and 2 rosettes are quite carefully drawn and incised, albeit they never achieve the precision of the Sphinx and Lion rosette. Type 3 is present on a quantity of pieces. It starts as an almost circular disc or "target" motif[107] with two incised concentric circles and gradually turns into a blob placed at random. Frequently there is added red at the centre of types 1 and 2, which seldom, however, appears on type 3.

An unusual semicircle on **1530*** (FIG. 93) hangs from the rim; and another springs from below, on **1484**. Both take after the Middle Wild Goat pendants.

[107] *Emporio*, 158 and *Tocra* II, 25.

THE BLACK-FIGURE CHALICES

Fig. 91 Rim patterns on the Komast and Animal black-figure chalices

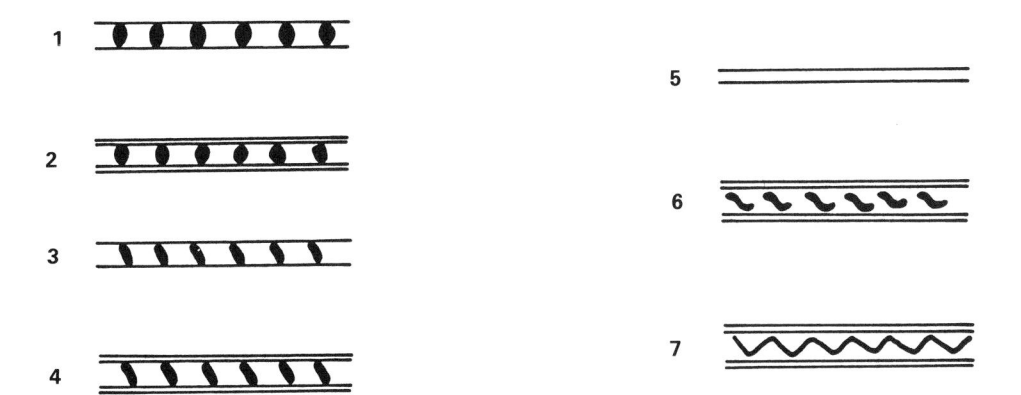

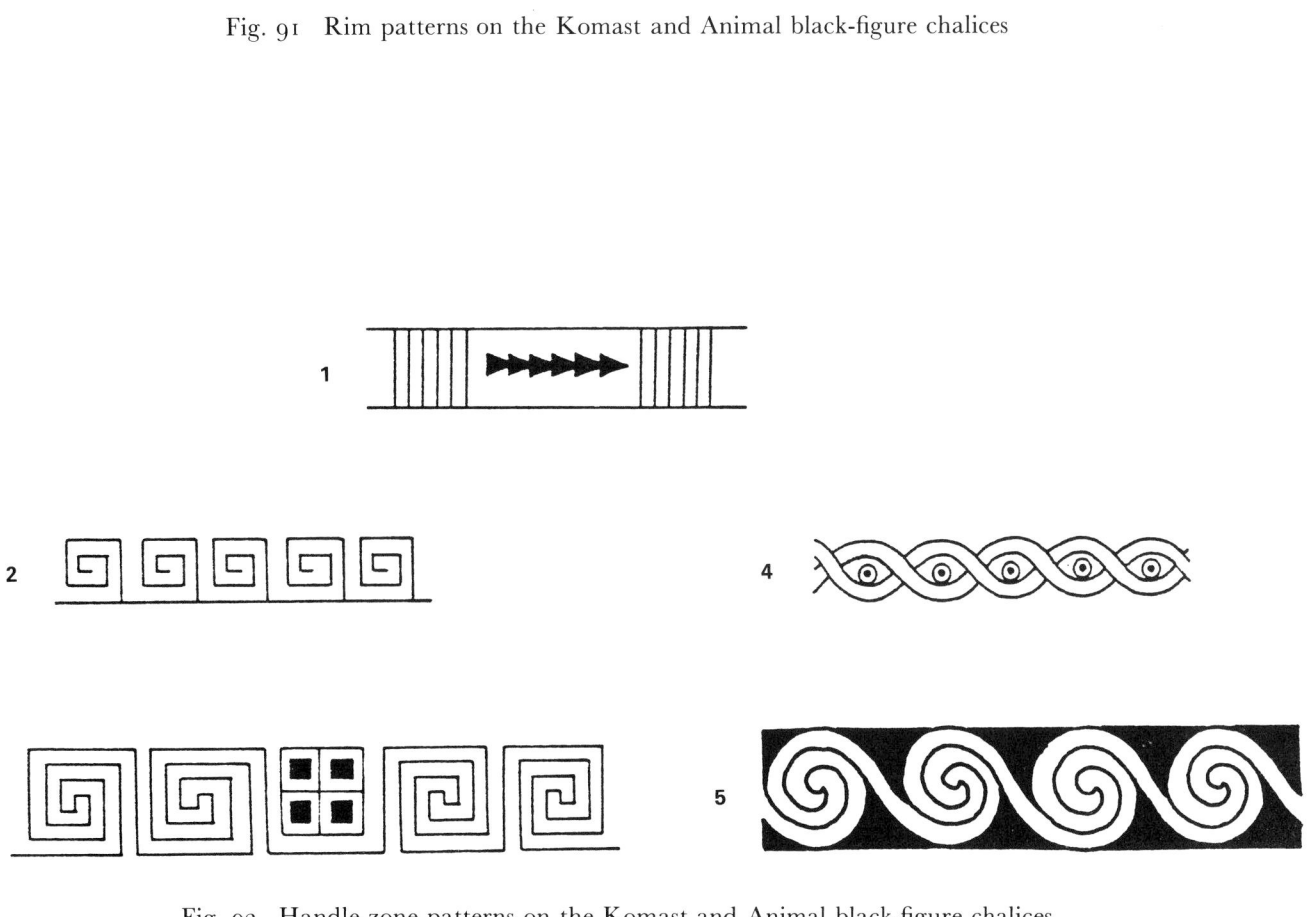

Fig. 92 Handle zone patterns on the Komast and Animal black-figure chalices

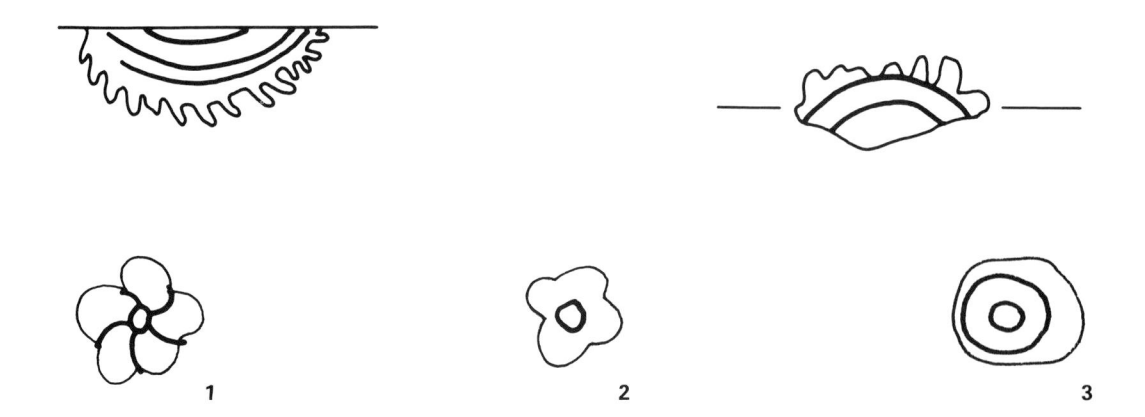

Fig. 93 Filling ornament on the Komast and Animal black-figure chalices

In almost half of the pieces, inner decoration is either not perceptible because the fragment is small and does not show it, or not stated by the publisher. That by no means implies that it is absent. Decoration, even of an elementary type, on the interior of a black-figure chalice is *never* absent.

Five different combinations, on most of which the lotus is the predominant element, can be distinguished. On certain fragments it is still very elaborate; but on most it has become perfunctory.

The simple lotus is the most common, appearing on most fragments. Decoration starts immediately below the rim where a red and white lotus—or a chain of lotuses—is depicted, then come three, or usually two, white lines and at the centre, on the floor, a simple red and white cross. There are slight variations, e.g. on **1468*** besides the lotus are three rows of white dots. The best drawn lotuses are on the finer pieces, petals are fuller and more substantial, whereas later on they gradually degenerate becoming thinner and the drawing more rough. This evolution of the lotus flower is an additional criterion for establishing the chronological sequence.

The most elaborate appearance of the *lotus and palmette* is on **1600***. A chain of red and white lotus-and-palmette bounded by a white zigzag between pairs of white lines starts below the rim; below that, come a pair of white lines; and on the floor is a large rosette composed of a white cross with red dots, surrounded by red and white petals. A slight variation is on **1601***, where at the centre of the floor is a simple cross.

The lotus and bud appears on **1561***, **1562*** and **1564***. There the ornament is of red and white lotuses and buds, pairs of white lines and a rosette at the centre.

The lotus and rosette appears on **1487***, **1488***, **1613*** and **1617*** differing both in quality of execution and the proximity of the ornaments. A very elaborate and early lotus and rosette is shown on **1505*** and **1506*** which most probably are from the same vessel. Another very well executed white rosette occurs on **1620***; above it is a cogwheel cross consisting of four petals. A much simpler rosette is that on **1595***.

1520* is unique in this category. It displays *a zigzag* flanked by a pair of white lines immediately below the rim, and then a row of tongues with a white line below it.

Inner decoration is *always* painted in red and white on top of the dark background. Nowhere do incisions occur, save the figured pieces in Grand style.[108]

III. Style

The black-figure chalice style is an easily recognisable and coherent class[109] and can be defined by the following characteristics:

A. The whitish porcelain-like slip present in all.
B. The black-figure technique itself: figures are always in silhouette and incision is used for inner details; red, but never white, on the outside, supplements them.
C. The shape.
D. The subjects, which are komasts and animals.
E. The filling ornament which, when present, is the rosette, of a slightly different type to the one in the Sphinx and Lion style.
F. The inner decoration, which is present also on late examples, even in the simplest form.[110]

In the treatment of style it is necessary to divide the black-figure chalices according to their subject-matter:

1. Komast chalices

They are the more frequent and owe their inspiration to Corinth, the first centre in Archaic art to depict komasts. Corinthian komos scenes start at about the beginning of the Early Corinthian period and fade out after the beginning of the Late Corinthian, c. 630–550 B.C.[111] This favoured subject spreads all over the major Archaic schools of vase painting, e.g. in Athenian from around 585,[112] in Boeotian from about 580,[113] in Laconian from early in the second quarter of the century[114] and remains en vogue for some time. The subject of komasts enters Chian art from Corinth appreciably later than the introduction of the black-figure technique. However, no more than the subject was borrowed.

Stylistically, as well as iconographically, Chian komasts are completely different. From the start the slender Chian komasts have nothing in common with Corinthian or other companions.

From what can be judged from the intact vases and the larger fragments, komasts in Chian are placed isolated in the field, e.g. on the Olbia chalice, **1582*** (where four komasts are placed on the walls: one each above the handles and one each on the front and back); in threes, as on the Ayia Paraskevi example, **1580**; or in pairs, e.g. on the Tocra chalices,

---

[108] See Chapter 3, pp. 118–9.

[109] For the definition of the meaning in the Beazleyan vocabulary, see *BAdd*², M. Robertson, Preface, p. XVI–XVII.

[110] On **1603*** from Apollonia Pontica, it seems from the photograph that, at least below the rim, there is no decoration; but this does not exclude the possibility of pairs of lines futher down and on the floor.

[111] Seeberg, *Corinthian Komos*, 69. There is a Corinthian crater fragment with a komast scene from Phana in Lamb, Phana 162, pl. 37.34 and Seeberg, *ibid.*, 48 no. 238.

[112] *ABV* 27–37 for main bibliography; *GPP*², 74 and 78, and Boardman, *ABFH*, 18. Recently Brijder *SC I*, 25, slightly lowered the accepted dates, "from the first half of the 570's down to the middle of the century", and his note 19 with the various dates assigned by other scholars.

[113] *NC* 199, and Kilinski, *Boeotian black-figure vase painting of the Archaic period*, (Diss. Missouri-Columbia, 1975), 123–124.

[114] *NC* 123, and n.7; Lane, Lakonian, 160, n.1; J.D. Beazley and F. Magi, *La Raccolta Benedetto Guglielmi nel Museo Gregoriano Etrusco*, 1939–1941, pl. 1, no. 3.

1561* and **1562***. Sometimes they occur with women as on **1468*** from Emporio, **1487*** from Rizari, and fragments which have been classified either here or in the Chalice style. Thus, they are never crowded and the filling ornament, when existing, is also thinly used, even in Group F. The whole concept is that of a neat and clear picture which does not weigh down the onlooker with detail. The komast chalices are divided into six stylistic groups based on the following elements: the presence or absence of the filling ornament; the rendering of the band, turban and facial details, mainly of ears; inner decoration (only roughly) and the rim pattern, which has disappeared in the last group. Yet this last is not an altogether safe criterion, as a few late pieces still retain a rim pattern, whereas others which are early, do without it.[115]

The sadly fragmentary state of the material in hand and the fact that in many cases as a result all the above mentioned elements were not present renders the classification tentative at times and some of the groups are not altogether coherent because only one criterion was available.

Group A: This comprises **1487*** (FIG. 94) and **939*** of the Chalice style. They are in a mixed technique, i.e. outline for women, black figure for komasts. There is no filling ornament nor a rim pattern. They display some variety with the introduction of women, who are similarly rendered, especially their heads and elongated eyes.

The affinities between this group and that of the third group in the Chalice style[116] are obvious.

Group B: This consists of **1484**, **1489***, **1530***, **1546*** (FIG. 95) and **1620***. Some display a half rosette which looks like a wide arc from which sprout small bristles; on **1620*** these bristles are pendant from the rim pattern. A pattern on the rims is always encountered. The inside of **1620*** has an elaborate rosette with cogwheel petals, a motif favoured in other Chian styles. It is the device on Achilles' shield on the Troilos chalice from Pitane, **800***, and in a more complicated manner on two shield-devices in the Grand style, **698*** and **724***.

This group has a loose relation with Group B of the Sphinx and Lion style and in particular **1347***.

1496–1503, all very small fragments from Naucratis, could be placed here solely on the basis of the type of their rosette, which is similar to that forming the core of the group. It is a debased form of the Sphinx and Lion style type 3 rosette and relates to Group D of that style.

Group C: This contains **1468*** (FIG. 96), **1488*** (FIG. 96), **1489*** (FIG. 96), **1505*** (FIG. 96) and **1506*** (FIG. 96)—these two are either by the same hand or from the same vase—**1518**, **1520***, **1540***, **1545*** (FIG. 96) and **1574*** (FIG. 96). It is not an entirely coherent group, but the best komasts belong to it. Almost always a pattern exists on the rim; there is no filling ornament. Some variety is displayed, especially in details. Bands are either saw-edged as on **1488*** or across the chest in little parallel lines as on **1505***, **1506*** and **1545***. Turbans are quite carefully incised. Ears are carefully rendered and display variety: a kidney-shaped one is seen on **1505*** and **1506***, whilst another like a rough eight appears

---

[115] Cf. *Emporio*, 158. [116] See Chapter 3, p. 131.

THE BLACK-FIGURE CHALICES

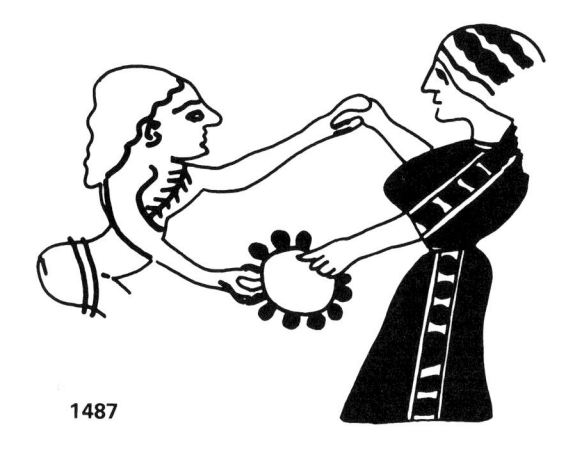

1487

Fig. 94   Komast Group A

1546

Fig. 95   Komast Group B

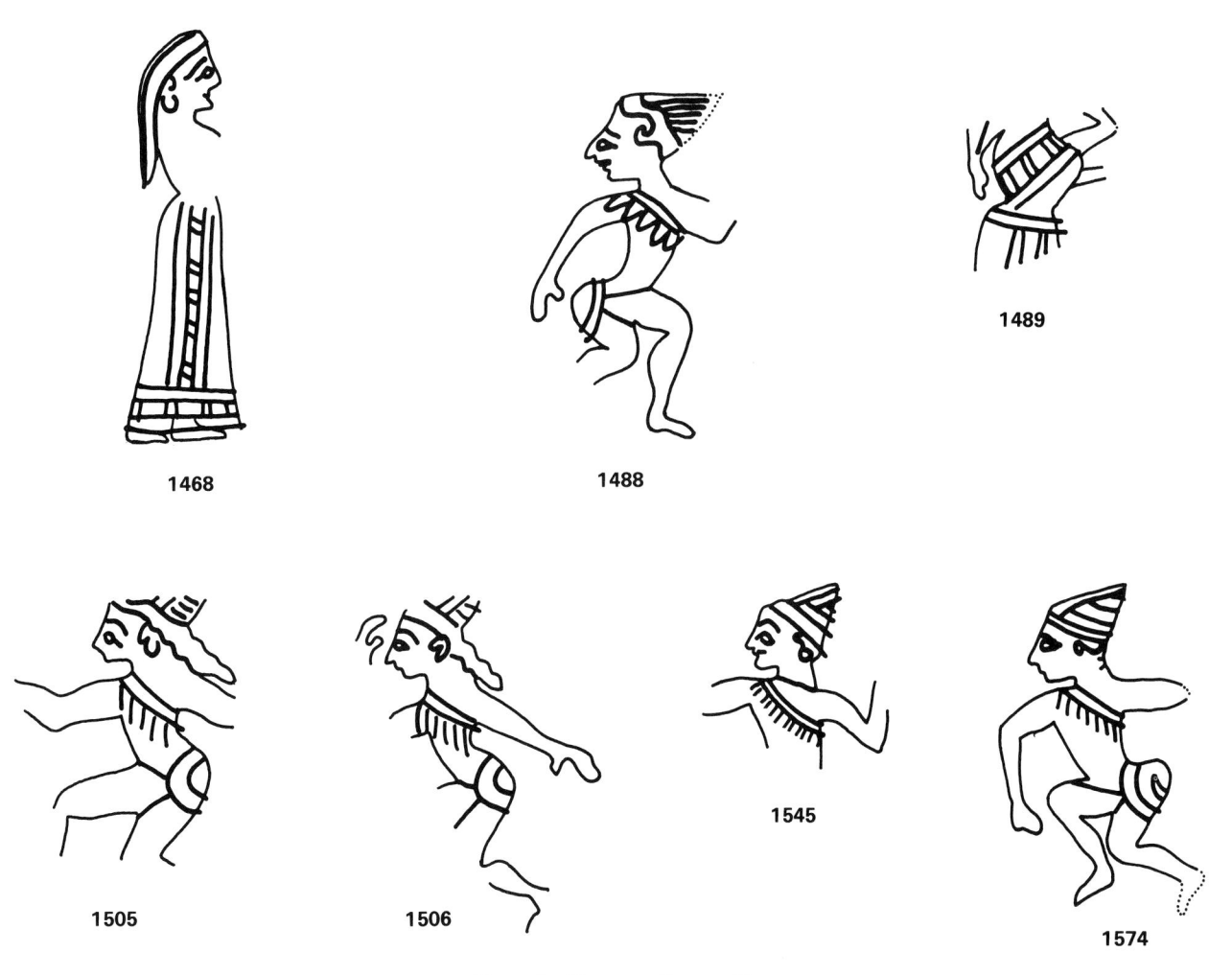

1468   **1488**   **1489**

1505   **1506**   **1545**   **1574**

Fig. 96   Komast Group C

Fig. 97 Komast Group D

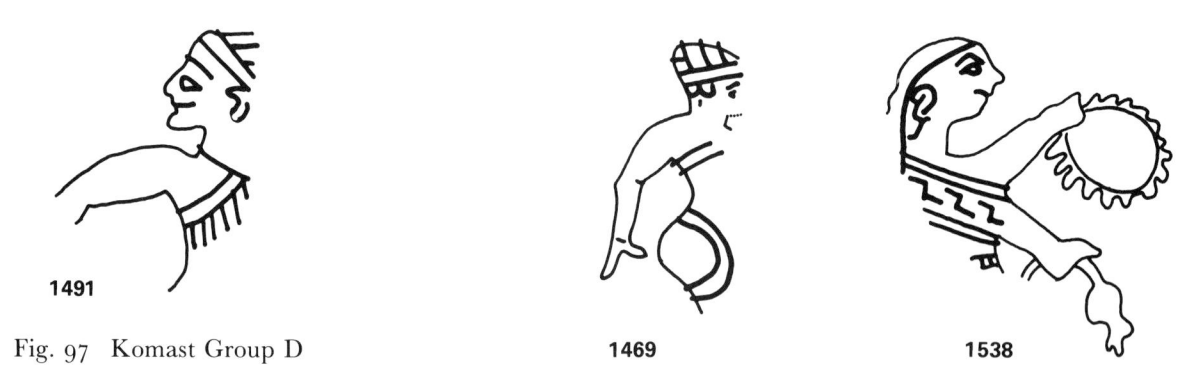

Fig. 98 Komast Group E

on **1545***. Inner decoration is of the finest quality: particularly on **1505*** and **1506*** with an elaborate chain of lotus and rosette in red and white. **1520*** has another elaborate pattern, which is why it has been classified here.

In conclusion, this group contains good and meticulous work. Incision is mostly careful and delicate.

Group D: **1470***, **1478***, **1482***, **1485***, **1491*** (FIG. 97), **1492**, **1534***, **1535***, and **1590*** are gathered here. Rim patterns exist. All the fragments have a disc for filling ornament which is carefully drawn with one or two incised concentric circles within. This is also a common feature on the Rhitsona chalice, **1602***, which brings it close to this group. On **1492** the komast wears a saw-edged band and his ear is rendered as that of the sphinx on **1347***. Except for this and **1491*** with a careful oblique band and a kidney-shaped ear, the other pieces show the first step towards the degeneration of the style.

Group E: This comprises the majority of the pieces. From Emporio: **1469*** (FIG. 98), **1471**, **1472**, **1474***, **1475***, **1476***, **1477***, **1479***, **1480***. From Phana: **1481***. From Naucratis: **1507**, **1531***, **1532***, **1533***, **1536***, **1537***, **1538*** (FIG. 98), **1539***, **1541***, **1547***, **1548**, **1549***, **1554***, **1555***, **1558***, **1560***. From Tocra: **1561***, **1562***, **1569***. From Old Smyrna: **1587*** and **1588*** and from Olbia: **1583***.

1481* and **1558*** are by the same hand, as are **1549*** and **1560***, with the extremely protruding buttocks and the identical placing of the incision.

The fragments are associated principally for three reasons: there is no filling ornament; bands, ears and turbans are of the simplest type, and inner decoration is elementary.

This group, as the previous one, contains pieces of a rather debased style; both drawing and incision are careless. Groups D and E are distinguished from one another here *only* by the presence or absence of discs and could conceivably be assimilated; they both lead to the final stage and with them the beginning of the end is clear.

Two strays do not fit into any of the groups. **1493*** has a rosette which could place it in Group B but band, turban and ear are of the simplest type. **1584*** has typically coarser rosettes, but incision on the band and facial details exist, even if cursorily drawn.

Fig. 99 Komast Group F

Group F: This contains **1485***, **1494***, **1495**, **1509***, **1510**, **1516***, **1552**, **1563***, **1565*–1568***, **1582*** (FIG. 99), **1585*** and **1591**. A coherent group, it clearly demonstrates the end of the style. Usually discs have become blobs with incision applied at random; occasionally there are fragments with no filling ornament. Komasts have become stick—or shadow—men. Paint is poor and diluted and incision is in the most careless manner of all Chian black figure. Bands on komasts' chests are now two hasty parallel lines; turbans are hardly reminiscent of what they once had been; ears are non-existent. In short, this is the worst hackneyed work produced in all Chian vase painting.

2. Animal chalices
The majority of the black-figure animal chalices, depicting cocks or cocks and hens, constitute a single stylistic group. Their style is coherent and has an intimate homogeneity. The drawing on the best pieces has a unique precision and incision is very careful and firm. This is the best black-figure Chian work, next to the black-figure Grand style.

The Poultry Group, named after the subjects employed, demonstrates an evolution: the gradual decline of the style can be traced step by step. Four stages can be discerned:

Stage A: The starting point with **1593**, **1595*** and **1596*** from Naucratis; **1607** and **1608** from Berezan and **1602*** (FIG. 100) from Rhitsona.

The careful discs with their incised circles on the Rhitsona chalice relate it to Group D of the komast chalices discussed above; it displays a unique rim pattern for this class (FIG. 91.7), which also appears as the chiton's hemline on **1462***. This is a link of a sort with black-figure Grand style.

Another element besides the filling ornament that suggests the placing of the Rhitsona chalice at the head of this group is the artist's slight uncertainty regarding the scale of his figures in that the cocks' crests overlap with the rim pattern. Whereas, on the rest, they are better placed and care is taken to achieve good proportions and balance.

Stage B: The second stage is that of **1600*** (FIG. 100) and **1601*** from Tocra, **1593–1596*** from Naucratis, **1613*** from Old Smyrna and **1605*–1606*** from Berezan. The composition is well balanced to judge by the vases from Tocra. The drawing is precise and

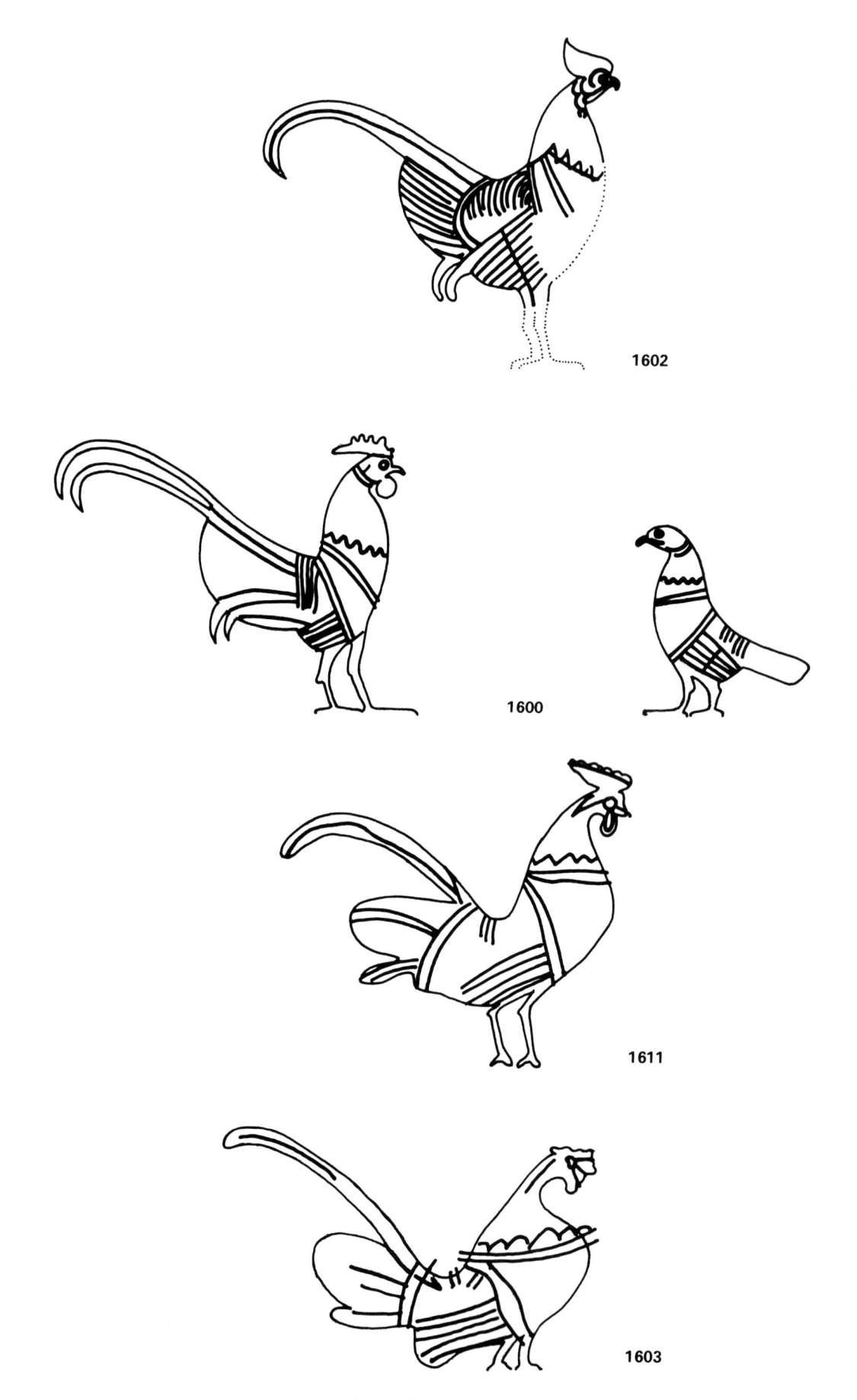

Fig. 100 Cocks and hens in the Poultry Group

almost identical on all; furthermore incision occurs unmistakably in the same places. All nine chalices of this stage can unreservedly be attributed to one hand.

Stage C: On the two chalices from Pitane, **1611*** (FIG. 100) and **1612**, the days of elaborate execution have passed. **1611*** looks slightly later than **1612**. The cock's crest is almost flat; the saw pattern on the neck is incised negligently; the incision on the body is hasty and careless; the back has become schematic with little incision and the feathers of the tail, especially the incised line separating them, are hastily executed.

Stage D: **1603*** (FIG. 100) must be placed at the very end of the style. There is no longer a rim pattern but the filling ornament returns. Two dreadfully drawn cocks facing each other over an even worse lotus flower—which has displaced their partner—are hardly reminiscent of the graceful Tocra chalices. Further the layout is ineffective: one cock is down on one side, then the lotus is set above the handle and on the other side is the other cock. The artist's intention is no longer to construct a well balanced antithetical "picture" but merely to fill up space as quickly as he can. The cocks are drawn in a perfunctory manner. The long, endless tail, the hasty semicircular necklace—purporting to be the old saw-edged pattern—together with the deplorable blobs speak for the total decline, or rather disappearance, of a style which in its heyday produced outstanding vases.

The Poultry group is the work of very few artists. The esoteric evolution of style suggests also that it was relatively shortlived.

Komast and black-figure animal chalices are probably the output of the same workshop which was producing the contemporary Chalice style, as the size of the vessels and ornamental decoration imply. Save for a few exceptions, e.g. the Tocra Poultry group chalices, **1600*** and **1601***, they bear the metope saw-edged handle pattern, thus betraying their common source. They take over the black-figure technique from the earlier Sphinx and Lion style and later on, bequeath it to the late black-figure kantharoi and other late groups of the second half of the century. The draughtsmen credited with the production of Group D, stage 2, and Group E in the Sphinx and Lion style are the source for Group D of the Komast chalices and the Rhitsona black-figure chalice (**1602***).

4. THE BLACK-FIGURE KANTHAROI

The shape, as well as the frequency and distribution, of the sixth-century kantharos has already been discussed in the previous chapter on the reserving styles, the most eminent example being **1625*** (FIG. 101), from Emporio. Under this heading, unslipped and slipped kantharoi[117]—those which bear some sort of figurative, or even patterned decoration—have been collected.

---

[117] For the unslipped black-figure kantharoi see *Emporio* 168 and for the slipped, *ibid.*, 161–2. The slipped black-figure kantharoi collected here are of Williams' type A, see *AA* 1983, 169.

Apart from the inscribed kantharoi, there are plain examples—all are again of type A—from Rizari (unpublished); Aegina town in *AA* 1983, 169, figs. 10 and 1; Delos in *Délos* X, pl. 20, nos. 119 and 120; Rhodes in *ClRh* VIII, 43, fig. 26 (right) and [probably] Naucratis in the Ashmolean in *CVA*, Oxford II, pl. 392.18 (bought in Paris).

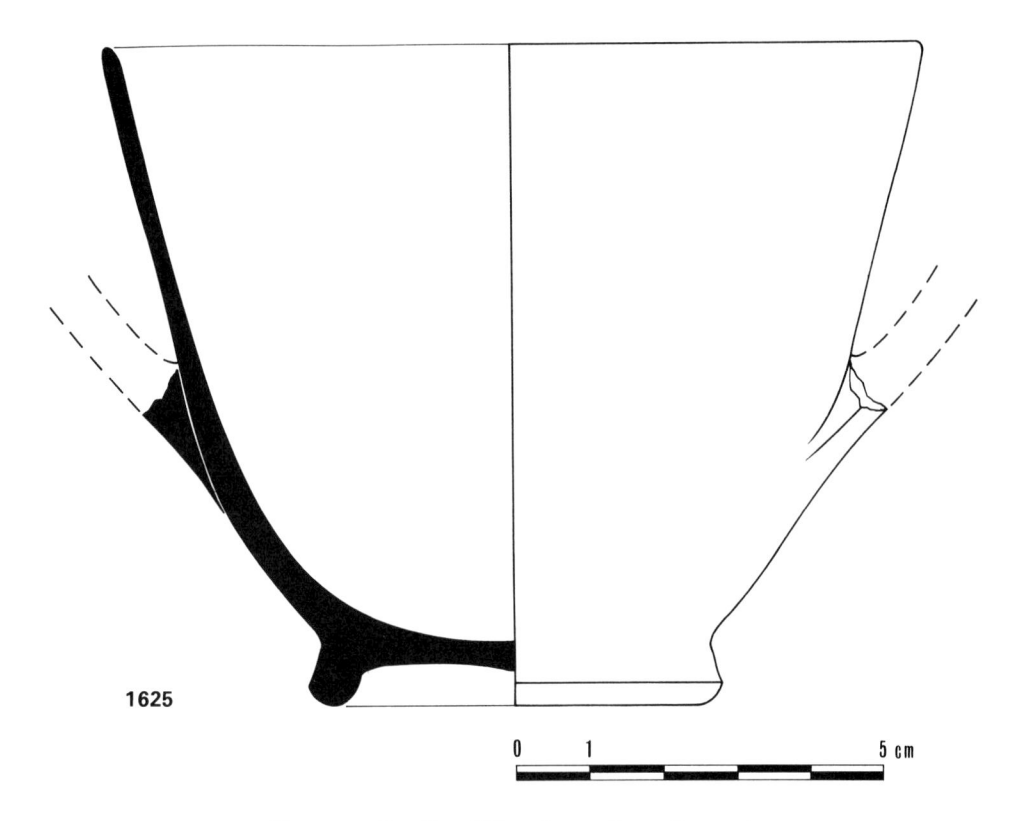

Fig. 101 Profile of Kantharos from Emporio

The decoration of these kantharoi consists of practically the same repertory as that of the black-figure animal chalices, i.e. cocks, hens, dolphins and geese or swans. Also a human figure on **1630** and an incised inscription ΣΥΜΦΟΡ[on **1629*** exist.[118] Composition on the kantharoi is of the simplest: an isolated animal is placed approximately at the centre of the "metope" which is flanked by palmettes. Inner decoration consists of bands in red and rarely white, first usually below the rim, then below the middle of the vase and lastly just above the centre. The absence of slip and the general use of palmettes mark an attempt by Chian vase painters to imitate Athenian practices,[119] which was of little avail because the class was small and shortlived.

In *style*, the cock on **1625*** approximates to that on the animal chalices,[120] specifically **1611*** and **1612** from Pitane: the crest is rendered more realistically on the kantharos, as is the rear part with the carefully incised feathers. However, the incision on the centre of the body, above and below, as well as the incised zigzag line separating the neck from body, is identical. The cock on the kantharos can be placed between stage B, with the Tocra chalices, and stage C, with the Pitane ones, of the Poultry group. A loose stylistic proximity exists between this kantharos (**1625***) as well as others, (**1626*–1628***), from Emporio,

[118] See *BSA* 5, 1898–9, 55 no. 42.
[119] *Emporio* 168 and *CGED* 85.
[120] The stylistic similarities of the cocks on the kantharoi and the black-figure animal chalices have been pointed out by Boardman in *CGED* 85.

with a few late komasts of Group E and specifically **1507** (the band on the neck which is almost rendered like a necklace), **1561*** and **1562***. A similar band to that on **1546*** is worn by the komast on **1507** and on the cock's collar (**1625***). The unslipped kantharos, (**1625***), has been stylistically compared with the unslipped chalice in Copenhagen,[121] (**1617***), and indeed, though not very close, affinities do exist: for example the absence of slip on both; the use of added white which in Chian black figure, in general, is an indication of a late date,[122] and finally the rough figure drawing. The inner decoration of the Copenhagen chalice, **1617***, with the spacing of the lotuses and cogwheel-rosettes speaks for a late date; the kantharos with the pair of lines within for an even later one.

It is evident, however, that the figure decoration on the outside of **1617***[123] is influenced by Clazomenian wares in the use of incision and the added white lines, the white dots on the paryphai of both chitons and himatia and finally in the five intervening rosettes consisting of dots in black and white.[124] This vase is still drawn in a careful and painstaking manner. The kantharoi are executed more hastily.

The distribution of this class at Locri Epizephyrioi (**1633***) and possibly Sinope (**1634**) shows that Chian fine pottery was still in demand during the third quarter of the sixth century, where the vases are to be dated from the stratigraphical evidence at Emporio[126] and from the stylistic comparisons.

5. LATE BLACK-FIGURE GROUPS

The end of black-figure on Chios has already largely been explored,[126] though further evidence is now available. A few vases and groups, most of which bear figure-decoration, have been collected in the Catalogue under the label "Miscellanea" in an eclectic manner.

1. The Lithi hydria (**1638***) was confiscated in 1984 and marks the first known appearance of the shape in the figured styles. It is a short hydriske, barely 20 cm in height, with a short neck and out-turned lip; the body is very near that of oenochoe **1433*** in the Sphinx and Lion style in that it narrows smoothly at the bottom and sits on a ring foot. The form is better-proportioned than the known plain examples from other parts of the island,[127] but has no connections with the much earlier linear-patterned hydriai from Rizari.[128]

---

[121] *Emporio* 168 and *CGED* 85.

[122] No added white is employed on the Sphinx and Lion style vases or the komast and animal black-figure chalices.

[123] Apart from the Copenhagen intact chalice, **1617***, Kinch in *Vroulia*, 151, refers to two more unslipped chalices: one fragmentary that he found at Vroulia (not illustrated in the publication) and another (unpublished) from Berezan in the Odessa Museum (**1618** and **1619**).

[124] Clazomenian influence can be traced on the inner decoration of a Grand style chalice (**806**) in the use of the white and red crescent as a decorative motif.

[125] *Emporio* 168.

[126] By Boardman in *Emporio* 169–70. Since the British School excavations in 1952–55 no systematic work has been taken up on the island. A few strays have turned up in salvage excavations, or have been confiscated, as the Lithi hydria, **1638***, but none have been properly published.

[127] *Emporio* 137 and note 4.

[128] A.A. Lemos in *Chios Conference*, 236 and fig. 8.

The birds on the Lithi hydria, be they geese or swans because of their long necks, are well drawn and even more carefully incised; also the blobs are placed in a triangular disposition in front of each of them. Had the general character been miniaturistic they could well have been classified within the Sphinx and Lion style. Indeed, they bear stylistic affinities, especially with members of Group E of the last, where too the rosettes have become mere blobs. However, the closest stylistic ties of the hydria geese are with those on the slipped kantharos **1635***, where even the posture of the bird with spread wings is kept. The birds on these two vases, the Lithi hydria and the Berezan kantharos, anticipate offspring first on the later black-figure chalice **1614*** with its poor drawing and haphazard incision and then the bird with the elongated body and tail on the two-handled amphoriskos **1647***.

Stylistically, this small group could be ordered thus, ultimately related to Group E of the Sphinx and Lion style: the Lithi hydria (**1638***), the Berezan slipped kantharos (**1635***), the Camirus black-figure animal chalice (**1614***) and finally the Olbia two-handled pot (**1647***).

2. The two-handled pots are a well defined, if small class. The shape is a miniature, oval amphoriskos ranging in height from 5 to 7.5 cm; although fragments **1642–4** from Cyrene seem to have been from taller vases to judge by their estimated diameter at the rim. The point of maximum diameter is in the middle on the Emporio (**1640**)[129] and Olbia (**1647***) examples, whilst later it has moved further down the body as on the Rizari (**1641***) and the Agora (**1645***) amphoriskoi; on the very last it is even more pronounced. They all sit on a ring foot. The handles are at first horizontally, and then slightly obliquely, placed above the middle of the body.

The decoration is composed of dashes on the lip, a meander running left on the shoulder on the better pieces, a metope on the handle zone, where a figure might appear, as on **1647***, and finally tongues on the lower body.

The manner in which the tongues, in some disorder, invade the handle zone metope on the Rizari amphoriskos (**1641***) is an eloquent witness to the last stage of this class, perhaps dating even later than the Olbia pot (**1647***) with its elongated bird. Both these vases point to a date slightly later than the middle of the century, within the third quarter.[130]

3. The ivy-patterned vases are assembled together only on grounds of their common decorative motif. They run beyond the turn of the century. Usually the ivy-pattern is in two rows of juxtaposed leaves, either as on the neck of the slim Emporio jug (**1648***) or as a rim pattern on a mug (**1653***) and a chalice (**1652***). Alternatively it may be spread all over the walls of a chalice (**1649***). The interpretation, on the basis of Strabo's evidence, of the man's head between the palm trees (**1648***) as Apollo at his nearby Phana sanctuary is ingenious and persuasive.[131] This and the fragmentary mug (**1653***) have been dated to "the very end of the sixth century".[132]

---

[129] See *Emporio* fig. 116 on p. 168.
[130] Cf. *Emporio* 169 and cf. Schaus in *Dem. Sanct., Cyrene* II, 79 who dates the Olbia amphoriskos to "the second quarter or the mid-sixth century".
[131] *Emporio* 169.
[132] *Ibid.* 169.

Of a still later date, perhaps the first half of the next century, but still archaic in spirit, is a class of small chalices recovered recently in Chios town from rescue excavations. These chalices have ivy or myrtle patterns either in rows or all over the walls in a careless and disorderly manner.[133]

Ivy and myrtle patterns are common in Archaic workshops in general[134] and have been used on Athenian vases at an earlier date. They are also encountered most frequently on the Ionian Little Master and plastic cups of the mid-century,[135] from where they could have been transplanted to the later examples on Chios.

4. Clazomenian influence can be traced sporadically on a few late strays. The most outstanding are three in number: a) the Copenhagen unslipped chalice (**1617***), reassuringly Chian because of its shape and inner decoration, b) the fragmentary basket-handled vase (**1654***) and c) the fragmentary column crater from Naucratis (**1656***).

The white and red dot rosettes on the first two vases have their counterparts on the similarly executed wreath held by women on **1656***. The figure drawing on the Copenhagen chalice has parallels perhaps in North Ionian works.[136] The origin of the column crater (**1656***) has been argued to be both Chian and Clazomenian. The shape of the vase and composition of the files of women holding hands and apparently dancing should make one sceptical about a straightforward classification as Chian.[137] On the other hand, the overwhelmingly white slip and the familiar subject of women proceeding in files and holding hands *and* wreaths, as for example on the superb Grand style chalice **717***, could perhaps rather encourage its classification as Chian—with a direct and strong influence from a scene admittedly more commonly encountered in Clazomenian iconography.[138]

5. A loose stylistic relation exists between the dancers' heads of the column crater, (**1656***), and the negro fragment (**1657***), about whose identity doubts have also been expressed.[139]

Indeed, a lack of parallels makes it difficult for **1657*** to be classified as Chian,[140] but since only a handful of quality black-figure Chian work involving human figures is known, this is not of itself a strong argument. The whiteness of the slip and the observed stylistic similarities between the heads on **1657*** and **1656*** may equally argue for a Chian identity.

The possible interpretation of the negro boy as one of Bousiris' attendants in the Heracles' episode[141] could then add another mythological theme to the Chian repertoire.

6. The inclusion here of the one-handled cup from Olbia (**1658***) is open to debate: it has been published as Rhodian;[142] claimed as Fikellura;[143] but might yet show Chian

---

[133] They were kindly shown to me by A. Tsaravopoulos, who has reported them in *Horos* 4, 1986, 130, pl. 28.3. a and d (here **1650–1**).

[134] Cook, Fikellura, 74.

[135] *Samos* VI.1, pls. 52.447b; 55.480b; 56.484b; 57.481, 482 and 483. Also *BSA* 60, 1965, pl. 32 a–k.

[136] See *Emporio* 168, where is the reference to a tiny male flute-player on a lid from "Larisa" in *Larisa am Hermos* III, pl. 40.22.

[137] However see R.M. Cook in *BSA* 47, 1952, 127 and note 20, where he states that it was Chian which first influenced Clazomenian.

[138] *BSA* 60, 1965, pl. 34.68 and *Samos* VI.1, pl. 127. 919 and 965. See also Boardman in CN 61 note 10.

[139] By Price 222.

[140] Observe the eyes of **1657***, which are close to those of **1460***, although they are also a generic Archaic trait.

[141] Hemelrijk, *Caeretan Hydriae* 173.

[142] Shtitelman, *Antique Art* 1977, no. 12.

[143] G.P. Schaus in *BSA* 81, 1986, 270 and note 56.

ancestry too. The shape is not only met in Samian but is very common in Chian plain wares;[144] the slip looks very white; and the decoration—the ivy pattern, discussed above, albeit certainly in a simpler manner—is met in the Chian repertoire. As a complete vase it finds no ready parallels in Chian, whilst the meander cross around the base does in Fikellura. On balance, then, its assessment as a Chian product must remain distinctly tentative.[145]

---

[144] *Emporio* 123, the first two types, nos. 284–345.

[145] A few vases, which have been classified as Chian in *Samos* VI.1, either have been rejected by other students involved in the study of East Greek pottery, or do not appear Chian to my eyes. Nos. 723 (pl. 99); 730 (pl. 99); 731 (pl. 97) and 732 (pl. 99) are North Ionian. No. 687 (pl. 98), an amphora, is Clazomenian, see *Samos* XIV, fig. 231. Nos. 838 a–b (pl. 100), 839 a–b (pl. 100), 840 and 841 are Boeotian imitating Athenian, see Boardman in *CGED* 288. No. 845 is a Samian hydria under heavy Chian influence, see *AM* 98, 1980, 188ff., Beil I and Kyrieleis in *Chios Conference* 194 and pl. III. No. 692 (pl. 92) is most probably Aeolian. And nos. 702 a–b (pl. 93) and 718 (pl. 92) are Chian, but are here considered products of a workshop established in Thrace, see Chapter 7.

5

DATING

The dating of Chian fine wares depends mainly on stylistic criteria, which are at times subjective. External evidence from stratified deposits does exist but the distinctions which are permitted are not fine enough for dating painted pottery. Quarter centuries are as far as it is possible to go. In these circumstances, tomb contexts are of the utmost help. Many important ones, however, are either unpublished, for example from Italy, Greece, and Turkey or they have passed unrecorded, for example Camirus on Rhodes, or the tombs in Etruria. Thus, the Würzburg chalices were found in all probability at Vulci, as they were once members of the Feoli collection.

Moreover, discoveries known to exist at some sites are proving somewhat disappointing too. In those where Chian painted pottery has been recovered in respectable quantity and in most of the styles, either excavation occurred last century and the beginning of the present, e.g. Naucratis, Camirus, Berezan and Olbia, or proper publication is awaited, e.g. Kavala, Ayia Paraskevi near Thessaloniki, Pitane and Erythrae.

Fortunately, competent excavations with a prompt record of publication, as at Emporio, Phana, Tocra and Cyrene, as well as tombs containing examples of the better-dated Corinthian and Athenian series are sufficient still to permit a comprehension to be gained of the rise and decline of each style; absolute dates can perhaps be assigned thereby to the various groups and workshops.

RESERVING STYLES

Mention is made first of the basic sites that have yielded Chian vases in ascending order of usefulness.

Naucratis is of no help. The reasons for this have been sufficiently explained elsewhere.[1]

Rizari, though excavated after the war, is of no value for dating purposes, as it was a hurriedly performed rescue excavation. The pottery sealed in the sarcophagi and the pithos-amphorae was all plain,[2] whilst the truly decorated vases and sherds, published here, were scattered in confusion on top of the burials.

Berezan and Olbia are not of much aid either. Excavations were, and it appears are, extensive. Here, however, as well as at sites on the Kerch peninsula, publication has been sparse.

Thasos and generally sites on the East Macedonian and Thracian coast both imported and it seems locally produced Chian pottery.[3] As regards the imported pottery, nothing

---

[1] Boardman in *GO*³, 118–9 with notes 33 and 34 for a detailed discussion on the conditions of excavating and the subsequent unsuccessful efforts to define stratification. Also, Austin, *Greece and Egypt*, 22 and 59, for chronology; on p. 25 and note 4 for Chian pottery.

[2] By plain is meant all pottery lacking distinctive figurative decoration. *PAE* 1952, 527–8 and A.A. Lemos in *Chios Conference*, 233–8 and figs. 4–8, touch on this material (see Preface).

[3] See Chapter 7.

more precise than that it roughly belongs to the first half of the sixth century can be deduced from the reports.

The recent publication of the pottery finds from the extramural sanctuary of Demeter and Persephone at Cyrene gives no fixed deposit dates. The sanctuary was founded roughly a generation after the first colonists established Cyrene. As regards Chian pottery it appears from the beginning, *c.* 600 B.C., and continues for approximately three generations to the middle years of the sixth and was mostly recovered in "largely undisturbed early occupation levels".[4]

The important excavations at Emporio and the exemplary publication of the material are significant. It has been pointed out[5] that although not much assistance for establishing precise dating for the sixth-century pottery can come from Emporio, Wild Goat fragments come from contexts basically of Period IV of the Harbour Sanctuary (630–600); Animal Chalice style fragments are mainly from Period I of the Athena Temple Terrace—a vast period, exceeding the span of a century and a half, but which terminates in the middle of the sixth;[6] and the following Chalice style is again of the same period, and of Period V of the Harbour Sanctuary (600–550). Therefore, Wild Goat pieces belong to the last third of the seventh century whilst the Chalice style is of the first half of the sixth century.

The same range is evident at Tocra. Chian squat chalices occurred in Deposit I of *c.* 620 – *c.* 590;[7] everything else is from Levels 8 (*c.* 590 – *c.* 565) and 7 (*c.* 565 – *c.* 520/10), that is of the first three-quarters of the sixth century. Only a few pieces, **925*** and **934***, survive the middle of the century: this is confirmed by stylistic analysis as well.

Five remaining sites give, with a varying degree of validity, further hints as to the dating of the reserving styles:

Catane: The group of Chian vases found in a Demeter deposit was stated in the preliminary report[8] to include vases not earlier than the beginning of the sixth century. This is also suggested by **624***, the biggest preserved fragment, because of the form of its shape at the transitional stage, the oldish "metope" decoration and the appearance of inner decoration.

Tarentum: Chalice **938***, with a sphinx, was found in a tomb together with a Middle Corinthian amphoriskos, a Samian undecorated lekythos and an Athenian cup of Ionian type (Pl. 244). The dating to the 570's was proposed because of the amphoriskos,[9] but is somewhat controversial. On grounds of style, as will be explained below, the chalice should be dated to about 560, or even later. A plain chalice, **1030***, was found in another tomb together with a Middle Corinthian amphoriskos, an Athenian plain skyphos and a spherical pyxis produced at Metapontum (Pl. 245). It has been dated by these associations to about 580–570;[10] this or the next decade would agree with the date proposed from the form of the chalice.

---

[4] Schaus *Dem. Sanct., Cyrene* II, 77 and 93. See also, D. White, *The Extramural Sanctuary of Demeter and Persephone at Cyrene, Libya. Final Reports I*, 1984, 114 and 119.
[5] *Emporio* 157 and note 3.
[6] *Emporio* 101 for the chronological tables.
[7] *Tocra* II, 3.

[8] By Rizza in *BolldArte* 1960, 251–5.
[9] *CGED* 111 and 135 dated to around 580; Cook, Distribution, 158, note 14, no. 1, who first dated it, writes "in company with a Corinthian amphoriskos of the 570's".
[10] Cook, Distribution, 158, note 14, no. 3; *CGED*, 135 (F.G. Lo Porto).

Caere: A plain chalice, **1031***, has been dated from the contents of the tomb to the second quarter of the sixth century;[11] perhaps it might be placed more precisely within the decade of 570–560 on the grounds of its shape.

Pitane: The Troilos chalice, **800***, was found in a stone sarcophagus[12] together with an Athenian komast cup, a clay lydion and a lekythos. The Athenian komast cup is referred to both as a work of the KX painter[13] and of the KY painter;[14] the attribution makes no great difference to its dating which must be from the 570's to the 560's.[15] The stylistic evidence of the chalice, perhaps of a decade later, roughly coincides.

The other chalice, **801***, in the Grand style, together with three vases in the Sphinx and Lion style and an Athenian band cup were found in a cremation tomb.[16] Mention is made further below on the Chian black-figure styles.

Old Smyrna: In the well-controlled excavations at Bayrakli, sherds of chalices of almost all types were found. **96*** was in an early seventh-century context.[17] Three more published fragments, **97*–99***, are from the late seventh century. All these derive from patterned chalices. **243***, of the same shape and period, is in the Wild Goat style. Of later pieces, **966***, with a lion, was found in a context dated *c.* 560; and **967***, with a sphinx and **1064***, plain, in a context of about the 540's. On grounds of style the two decorated chalices (**966*** and **967***) should not be dated by as much as fifteen or twenty years apart. The plea that **967*** had seen more use than the other is not justified, as no such indications of wear are obvious.

Turning now to the internal evidence, each style is considered individually.

The *patterned proto-chalices* have been dated according to their shape and its evolution to the second third of the seventh century from the evidence of the excavations at Emporio.[18] The classification has been confirmed by finds elsewhere, especially by the aforementioned **96***, from an early seventh-century context at Old Smyrna.

The better known squat type of the *early chalice* can with certainty be placed in the last third of the seventh century, first from the stage of the shape's evolution and secondly from the stratified examples, again found in abundance at Emporio and confirmed by the relevant material at Tocra and Old Smyrna. **77***, from a tomb near Cerveteri, "with nothing later than Early Corinthian pottery"[19], confirms this.

The group with the "two saw-edged patterns", repeated on each side of the handle zone,[20] might perhaps be a little later than the rest, though again possibly within the last quarter of the seventh century.

The Chian *Wild Goat style* cannot be fixed more accurately and safely than stylistic evolution suggests, even though a little external evidence does exist. The opening stages,

---

[11] Cook, Distribution 158, note 14, no. 4.

[12] "When the sarcophagus lid was removed, it collapsed and smashed the chalice" in C.H. Greenewalt Jr., *Lydian Pottery of the sixth century B.C.: The Lydion and marbled ware.* Ph.D. University of Pennsylvania 1966, 190.

[13] *CGED*, 29.

[14] In Greenewalt's Diss. 1966, 191: "Güven Bakir has attributed the Komast cup to the KY painter, and proposed the years customarily assigned to similar cups, 580–570".

[15] Brijder, *SC I*, 67 for the dating of painters in the manner of the KX Painter (first half 570's) and the KY Painter (mid-570's to mid-560's).

[16] *CGED* 29.

[17] *BSA* 50, 1965, 140, fig. 19a.

[18] By Boardman in *Emporio*, 119–120, also p. 101 and fig. 60 on p. 103.

[19] C.M. Lerici, *Nuove Testimonianze dell' Arte et della Civiltà Etrusca* 1960, 46.

[20] See Chapter 1, p. 12.

though an early date has been implied for **247***, **264*** and **273** on stylistic comparisons, seem "floating" and not well fixed. The group of "the Emporio Bull Oenochoe" can perhaps be placed in the Middle I Wild Goat style,[21] according to the stratified pieces from Emporio, where almost all come from Period IV of the Harbour Sanctuary, 630–600. Further, their style is directly comparable to other East Greek workshops of that date.[22] The advanced and detailed style of the most significant Chian pieces point to a late date within Middle I, possibly the 30's or even the 20's of the seventh century.

The stylistic groups of the Middle II Wild Goat phase have already been placed in chronological order in the relevant chapter;[23] the reasons for that evidence are given now.

The group of "the Emporio chalices", on the argument that NIKESERMOS also painted some, could date to around 620–610; not far removed from the Würzburg group, to which it bears close resemblances. Indeed, the group of the "Würzburg chalices" could occupy the last decade of the seventh century. It consists of members mainly from Naucratis, the date of the foundation of which is disputed, but from which the earliest pottery, alongside Transitional and Early Corinthian and a fragment of the Athenian Nessos painter's workshop,[24] also includes Chian.[25] Chronologically the group of "the Aphrodite bowl", though stylistically more advanced, cannot be distanced more than a decade at the most. The Aphrodite group could be dated to around 600, based wholly on stylistic criteria of the figure drawing and on the light on dark decoration of the tondo, which from now is established as a favourite practice for the inside of chalices.

The "Gela dinos" stands towards the end of the Wild Goat style (Middle II); for reasons that have already been explained, in the relevant paragraph on style, it might date just after 600. Late Wild Goat groups may run on down into the beginning of the sixth century. "In the style of the Würzburg chalices", members of which timidly demonstrate inner decoration, date perhaps to the first decade of the sixth century. Finally, another Late Wild Goat group from Rizari, on which patterns are of a debased nature, could have continued much longer and cannot be fixed with more certainty than in the first quarter of the sixth century.

The *Animal Chalice style* with its two trends clearly shows that it is the offspring of the Wild Goat style. The more conservative group of the "Catane and Tocra chalices" dates immediately after about 600. This is sustained by the Catane chalice, **624***, found in a deposit "with vases not earlier than 600."[26] At the end stands the Tocra chalice, **616** in which the degree of the degeneration of style implies a long duration for the group.

The renewed Animal style, best exhibited in the group of "the elaborate animal chalices" from Naucratis, might start at a slightly later date, *c.* 590, but does not last much longer than the end of the first quarter of the sixth century. The homogeneity and consistency of the style lead to the belief that it cannot have exceeded this span of time.

Its immediate descendant, the *Grand style* has been dated to the second quarter of the sixth century.[27] However, the recently published and very important chalice, (**799***),

---

[21] As defined and dated by Cook in *Gnomon*, 1965, 506, that is *c.* 640–625. See also *Emporio* 148.

[22] Especially Kardarda, *Rhodiake*, her Late Orientalising style 61 ff. and specifically her group A, 64–71 and her Arkades School, 91–4.

[23] See Chapter 2.

[24] *GO*³, fig. 142 and *CVA*, Toronto I, pl. 39.1.

[25] *JHS* 57, 1937, 288 and *GO*³, 117, 119 and 121.

[26] Rizza in *BolldArte* 1960, 251–5.

[27] Boardman, CN, 60.

which in ornamental decoration takes after Wild Goat more than the Animal Chalice style, might on merely stylistical reasoning extend the upper boundary to within the first quarter. Group A with the filling ornaments is very close to the Animal Chalice style too; all the others (B, C and D) follow on both stylistically and chronologically. The Pitane chalices, **800*** and **801***, from their contexts give a date within the second quarter of the sixth century, nearer to the 560's. The Troilos chalice (**800***) was found in company with an Athenian komast cup and must therefore be earlier than the Farewell chalice (**801***) recovered with an Athenian band cup. However, they cannot be much removed from each other as both their style and the association of the last with three vases in the Sphinx and Lion style would indicate. A date in the seventies for the Troilos (**800***) and a decade later for the Farewell chalice (**801***) would be consistent with both the external and internal evidence.

The Naucratis painter and the Aphaia painter and their work cannot be fixed more precisely than the later part of the second quarter of the century.

The *Chalice style* is the immediate successor to the Animal Chalice and the Grand styles, though the output of a different workshop than these two. Production would have continued for the undecorated chalices from the seventh century, but for the decorated categories it will have started at the beginning of the second quarter of the sixth century. Group A with "the Antithetical Sphinxes" is the earliest; the stratified chalices from Tocra, **927*** and **928*** (Deposit II, Level 8: *c.* 590–565), are in accordance with this dating. As regards the unpublished Ayia Paraskevi chalices (**953–955**), they cannot be appreciably earlier than the 570 upper limit given to the whole cemetery.[28]

Some disturbing discrepancies exist between external and internal evidence for three chalices in Group B. Ironically these three are amongst the few Chian vases that provide firm external evidence. **938***, from Tarentum has been dated to the 570's from the contexts of the grave, mainly the Middle Corinthian amphoriskos; but its degenerate style would indicate a later date. **966***, from Old Smyrna, on the other hand comes from a level of *c.* 560 and **967***, again from Old Symrna, from another deposit of the 540's. It is indeed difficult to accept the Tarentum sphinx with its more summary drawing as earlier than the Old Smyrna pieces. Though the Old Smyrna chalices might have been painted much earlier than they were deposited—a hypothesis which is not justified by the good state of preservation of the drawing, the Tarentum chalice (**938***) still seems to be dated very high on stylistic grounds; a proposed solution would have been to update the Old Smyrna chalices, to *c.* 570, and lower the Tarentum one to about 560.

The last stage of Group B, with the completely debased sphinxes, could be dated to the years around or a little after the middle of the sixth century. Stylistic observations here can be reinforced by **925***, from Tocra, a fragment of which was found in Level 7: "*c.* 565 – *c.* 520/510".

Finally, Group C: the "worshippers' group" is closely linked to Group A of the Komast chalices and can be placed towards the middle years of the century, rather before than

---

[28] K. Sismanidis in *Ametos*, 788 and 801.

after. This requires an updating of the example, **964***, from Berezan, which is from an inhumation burial dated by the excavators to the second half of the sixth century.[29]

As regards the *Plain, sixth-century chalices*, which are part of the Chalice style, they presumably start at around the 570's, and continue till well beyond the middle of the century. An early example in the series is the Tarentum plain chalice, (**1030***, Pl. 245), dated by the contexts of the tomb to *c*. 580–570. A date for the end of the series within the third quarter of the sixth century is suggested by **1062*** and **1063*** (FIG. 43) with the later squat chalice form and the lapse of inner, floral, decoration.

BLACK-FIGURE STYLES

External evidence is scanty for establishing the chronology of the Chian black-figure styles. Only two cemeteries, Rhitsona and Pitane, and the stratified settlement of Old Smyrna give indications from which approximate dates can be deduced.

At Rhitsona grave 50 was rich in pottery—Corinthian, Athenian, Boeotian and the black-figure animal chalice, **1602***. The grave was first dated from about 570 to the 540's and the chalice to about 570.[30] A recent study of the grave's contents has fixed a more precise date *c*. 560–550.[31] This does not necessarily mean that the chalice was manufactured in precisely that decade, but it could not be later and is unlikely to be much earlier, as stylistic evidence confirms.

It is a useful and important date; perhaps the only one on which the dating of Chian black figure can rely with adequate certainty, at present.

Excavations at Pitane are of even greater potential importance for Chian black figure since the vases were accompanied in the graves by the more securely dated Corinthian and Athenian. The unpublished nature of this material imposes severe limits on how it may be used: present mention is slight, scattered and inevitably incomplete.[32] Of the three intact vases in the Sphinx and Lion style it has been revealed that all three were found together with a Chian polychrome vase—presumably **801***—and an Athenian band cup. Athenian band cups span over thirty years from *c*. 560–530. The two black-figure animal chalices, **1611*** and **1612**, are associated with three black-figure Athenian plates, two kotylai and a Late Corinthian aryballos which are all collectively placed around the middle of the sixth century. The chalices, on grounds of style, might not be far removed from them.

The komast chalice from the cemetery of Ayia Paraskevi (**1580**) is known, although it has not yet been published.

Finally, Old Smyrna is of noteworthy significance. A fragment in the Sphinx and Lion style, **1457***, from the siege-mound[33] provides evidence for the beginning of the style by about 600. **1587*** and **1588*** are from komast chalices and were found in a well-stratified trench together with Athenian black-figure fragments; it was a level, lying immediately above the Burnt House, dated *c*. 560 or in the 550's.[34] Had the fragment from a black-

[29] Kocybala, Diss. 1978, 199, where she refers to the original sources.
[30] Cook, Distribution, 158, note 14 no. 2.
[31] *JHS* 87, 1967, 128–30 for a list of the graves of the Rhitsona cemetery with reference to their contents.
[32] Mainly, *CGED*, 27–30 and now Akurgal, *Türkei*, 25 and pls. 10b and c, 11, 20a and 21a.
[33] *Emporio* 166 note 4.
[34] *BSA* 60, 1965, 122 and 141, nos. 2–3, and recently J.M. Cook, *BSA* 80, 1985, 25–6.

figure chalice **1613*** been found in a datable context,[35] it would provide the relevant group with an even more accurate dating.

The remaining evidence is wholly stylistic. **1457***, in the *Sphinx and Lion style*, from the siege mound of Old Smyrna, is a starting point for the whole style; it might be dated at about the turn of the century or even a little earlier.[36] Influences from Early and Middle Corinthian, which have been discussed,[37] also imply this dating.

Group A of the Sphinx and Lion style, in which **1457*** has been placed, together with Group B, are the earliest on the grounds of their rosette type too. They emerged by about 600 and lasted for approximately twenty years; members of these groups are of unequal quality and this span of time seems necessary to account for this variety of standard.

Group C is the successor to Group A. Though it displays an almost identical form of rosette, the drawing of the figures is firmer. It could have started in the second or third decade, but perhaps lasted for fewer years than Group D. This last (Group D) appears from its filling ornament to be more in the tradition of Group B. It possibly started at about the same time as Group C, that is in the 580's, but might have outlasted it down to *c*. 560, as it represents an intermediate stage towards the final decline. These two groups, C and D, are correlated with the first komast groups and with the black-figure Grand Style. **1324***, with the komast rider, is the first evidence for the production of komast chalices as well as Group D of the Sphinx and Lion: this is shown by the shared type of rosette on the one hand, and their lively character on the other. The rendering of figures with their details have affinities with the komast Group C, e.g. the vivid komos scene on **1468***. Group D of the Sphinx and Lion style leads stylistically and chronologically to Group E, which probably starts in the 560's and does not last longer than a decade.

In conclusion, the Sphinx and Lion style undoubtedly did not survive as late as the komast chalices;[38] by the middle of the century it was definitely no longer in production.

All the fragments in the *black-figure Grand style*, save one, were found at Naucratis. Thus, external evidence is completely excluded; comprehension comes exclusively from stylistic comparisons. Since this category depends heavily upon Laconian, recourse must be had to this better studied material. The two Chian fragments, **1458*** and **1459**, have been connected with the work of the Boreads painter, who has been dated to the decade of 575–565.[39] Taking into consideration the elaboration of the Chian style—or, at least, features[40] held in common with good black-figure work in Laconian and Athenian, of an even much later date—it might not seem wholly unreasonable to lower the established dating which places them within the second decade of the century.[41] The lowering of their date would not contradict the stylistic affinities with other Chian pieces, e.g. **1407*** of the Sphinx and Lion Group C, dated *c*. 580–570, or **1468***, the komast chalice from Emporio,

---

[35] *BSA* 60, 1965, 141, no. 9.
[36] *Emporio* 166.
[37] See Chapter 4, p. 146.
[38] *Emporio* 166.
[39] Earlier considered as the Hephaistos painter by Lane, *Lakonian*, 186, who first distinguished the two fragments (**1458*** and **1459**). Then assigned to the output of the Arkesilas painter, see Boardman, *CN* 61 with notes 1–4, it finally ended up as the work of the Boreads painter, see Stibbe, *LV* 88–89, 234, no. 142 and notes 3 and 4, pl. 60.2–3.
[40] Even though only applied on isolated patterns, explored in Chapter 4.
[41] Lane, *Lakonian* 186 and Boardman, *CN*, 61 and note 1.

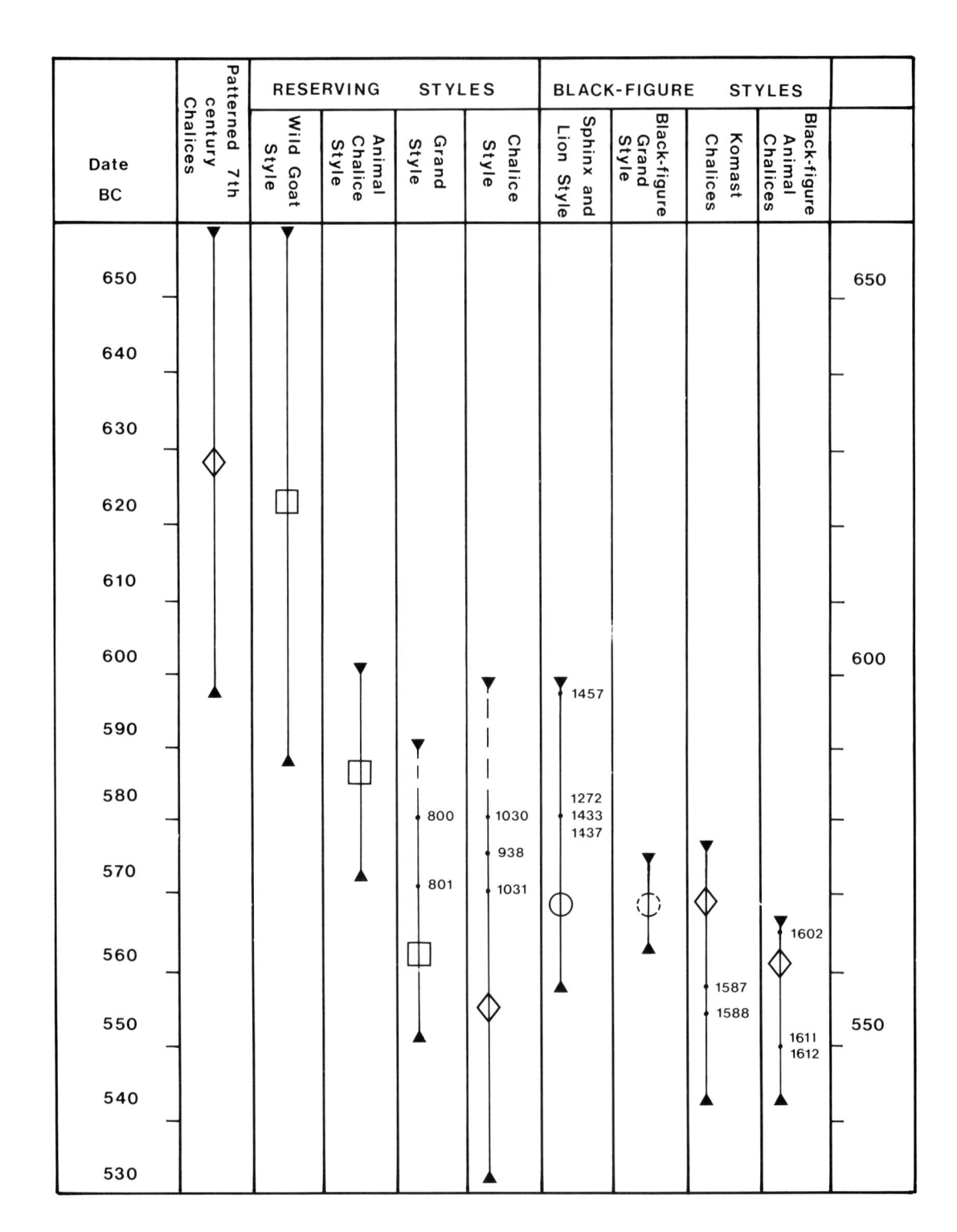

Fig. 102 Chronological Chart
Symbols denote related workshops; numbers individual vases; broken lines areas of doubt

DATING

dated in roughly the same period. For these reasons the date proposed for this style would be immediately after the beginning of the second quarter, approximately 570–560.[42]

The dating of *komast chalices* is for the most part dependent on stylistic comparisons. The only more accurate dates are from the excavations at Old Symrna in connection with **1587*** and **1588*** (*c.* 560 or the 550's). On **1587*** the simple band consisting of two oblique parallel lines with fringes sprouting from the lower end, and the absence of filling ornament on both fragments place them in Group E. The date of this group could be fixed between about 560 and 550, or slightly later.

Considering the komast groups as defined here,[43] it can be proposed that Group A in the mixed technique could not be placed more precisely than the second quarter of the sixth century. The absence of a rim pattern, the simpler inner decoration and above all the weariness of the komast's and woman's features and details on **1487*** point to a rather late date within this quarter, probably towards the middle of the century.

The loose affinities of Group B with other Chian styles, first with the Grand style and secondly with Group D of the Sphinx and Lion on the grounds of their filling ornament, imply a dating to about the beginning of the second quarter and a duration of approximately twenty years.

Group C might be of a slightly earlier date. Elaborate pieces, as **1468***, bring it nearer to Group B of the Sphinx and Lion which goes down to *c.* 580. This group might have already started by then and lasted for twenty years too.

Group D is closely related to Group E of the Sphinx and Lion style displaying the same filling ornament: a disc. The komast group seems to employ an earlier version of the disc, while in Group E of the Sphinx and Lion it looks as if the disc is bowing out. This same ornament unites both groups with the Rhitsona chalice, **1602***. There are other stylistic affinities among them, previously mentioned. The date proposed for all of them is *c.* 565–560 and for the komast group a possible duration of twenty years.

Group E is contemporary with Group D; they both lead to the final and by all appearances very shortlived Group F, which sees the end of the Chian komast chalice by around 540.

The *black-figure animal chalice* is strictly correlated to the komast chalice. In particular the life of the Poultry Group could not exceed thirty years; the available evidence covers all stages of the stylistic evolution: the early, then the most elaborate and its gradual and final decline. External evidence from the graves of Rhitsona for **1602*** and Pitane for **1611*** and **1612** has already been dealt with. This, together with the previously discussed affinities with other Chian black figure point to a date of about 565–560 B.C. for a starting point. The Tocra chalices (**1600*–1***) are a step further in the stylistic development and could be dated slightly later in the decade *c.* 560–550. External evidence from the stratified Deposit II at Tocra which goes down to *c.* 565[44] does not necessarily contradict these conclusions; besides, only **1600*** was found in that deposit.[45]

---

[42] Stibbe, *LV*, no. 142 on p. 234. Laconian imitations of Chian, in general, that is the inside of chalices and phialai in the reserving styles, are earlier. See Boardman, *CN*, 60–61 and especially *RDAC*, 1968, 13, on the pomegranate pattern and its eastern origin.

[43] See Chapter 4, pp. 170–3.
[44] *Tocra* I 59 and *Tocra* II 3–5.
[45] *Tocra* I 59 and 63.

A decadence is already present in **1611*** and **1612** from Pitane which could date them to the decade 550–540. This is in accordance with the dating of the tomb—if correct—to about the middle of the century.[46] **1603*** is at the very end of the style and could be placed about 545, or a little later.

This relatively worked out chronology for the Poultry group, based on both the internal evolution of the style and the dated graves from Rhitsona and Pitane, and the Tocra deposit, would run thus (FIG. 100):

c. 565–560   the Rhitsona chalice (**1602***) with stage A.
c. 560–550   the Tocra chalices (**1600*–1***) with stage B.
c. 550–540   the Pitane chalices (**1611*** and **1612**) with stage C.
c. 545–540   the Apollonia Pontica chalice (**1603***) with stage D.

This table leaves time for stylistic development. Black-figure animal chalices are proportionately a small class and the work of very few painters. It might have taken just less than a generation to reach its peak and soon afterwards became decadent.

The *black-figure kantharoi* and other *late black-figure groups* have already been assigned a rough dating, mainly on the evidence of the Emporio stratified finds and stylistic comparisons.[47] It looks as if nothing more precise and accurate about them can be said at present, beyond that they belong to the second half of the sixth century.[48]

A pattern of the stylistic evolution and the chronology of the various styles and workshops operating on Chios has been worked out here. This basically depends on the fixed points given by the contexts of tombs where Chian vases were found in company with Corinthian and Athenian. An overall impression of the length of time the various workshops were active and the extent to which they were contemporary may be gained readily from the Chronological chart (FIG. 102).

[46] *CGED* 29.
[47] *Emporio* 168–9.
[48] See Chapter 4, pp. 175–180.

6

DISTRIBUTION

The distribution of Chian fine pottery is traced in the present chapter and, for reasons of substance as well as convenience, has been divided into six geographical areas:

A. Egypt and Cyrenaica
B. The West
C. Mainland Greece and the Aegean Islands
D. North Greece and the Black sea
E. East Greece and Anatolia
F. The Eastern Mediterranean

The starting point is Naucratis for reasons more than self evident; then follows a clockwise movement around the littoral of the Mediterranean basin, including sporadically a few inland sites, where Chian pottery has been unearthed and reported, terminating in the coastal settlements of Cilicia and Phoenicia. This pattern is that used also in the Catalogue.

Chian fine pottery here comprises what has been discussed in the previous chapters: the patterned chalices of the seventh and sixth centuries, the Wild Goat style, vases in the reserving and black-figure styles. In addition, in certain instances plain vases not listed in the Catalogue are also included. Reference is also made to Chian amphorae of the Archaic period.[1] On the maps the evidence is presented by three different symbols so that a comprehensive picture of both the distribution and the volume of the material can be gained at a glance (FIGS. 103 and 104).

The manner of the dispersal of this pottery in modern times has proved occasionally both entertaining and instructive. For an example chosen at random, **109***: a chalice which had travelled from Chios to Al Mina some time within the third quarter of the seventh century B.C. was eventually recovered in the twentieth century A.D. and again moved further East to find its way at last into the Nicholson Museum at the University of Sydney in Australia. Subsequently, it received full publication by a Swiss scholar writing in English.

The first attempt in 1924 to trace the distribution of the then so-called "Naucratis ware" has today been superseded;[2] since 1949, when an article was written that was dedicated specifically to this topic, the volume of evidence has increased enormously.[3] The post-war increase in excavation has inevitably produced new material and as Chian is quite readily

---

[1] Wherever I had knowledge of them. They have not been subjected to closer scrutiny as amphorae and other plain wares will eventually constitute a separate study, see Preface. Dr A. W. Johnston is undertaking a major survey including Chian.

[2] Price 205–6.

[3] Cook, Distribution, 154–61 and especially his lists on pp. 159–61. His statement "the export of Chiot pottery was wide but generally small" still holds true.

recognisable, it has been generally reported or even published. Nevertheless, some significant material remains unpublished.[4]

Chian pottery and its export has been well treated in two books, which have formed the foundation for this chapter. *Greek Emporio* presented the known material with a wealth of supporting references;[5] *The Greeks Overseas* deals comprehensively with the whole question of Greek trade and influences, of which Chian is but one.[6]

Bibliographical references to vases mentioned here can be retrieved under the appropriate entry in the Catalogue.

A. EGYPT AND CYRENAICA

1. Naucratis: This Panionian trading centre was the major foreign market for Chian wares. Apart from the category of the undecorated inscribed kantharoi and other open vases, arguments for whose place of manufacture are perhaps weighted in favour of Naucratis,[7] all other figurative pottery is here believed to be imported, as has been argued in the relevant sections.[8] Chian pottery is present at Naucratis in all its techniques of decoration and almost all its shapes: the relative dearth of painted oenochoai could be due to the fact that this shape had already gone out of fashion in the full Wild Goat style of the last third of the seventh century, when Chian decorated pottery first started to appear at Naucratis. A little more than half of the listed material, 887 items of the 1659 catalogued, were unearthed in the prolific excavations of Naucratis. A detailed table would run thus:

6   items are of the patterned chalices of the seventh century: **64–9***.

197   items are of the Wild goat style: **125–235*, 248–258, 263*, 267*–8*, 280*–302*, 340*–345*, 355–366, 372*–416***.

185   items are of the Animal Chalice style: **433*–610*, 681*–3*, 685–6*, 688*** and **695***.

105   items are of the Grand style: **697*–792*, 802*–3*, 805*–7*, 810*–3***.

126   items are of the Chalice style (figure-decoration): **829*–923a*, 975–7, 979*–995, 1256–1261*** and **1266–9***.

72   items are of fragments of plain or nondescript chalices and other shapes: **1073–4*, 1084–1130b*, 1213–1234** and **1253–5***.

196   items are in the black-figure styles: **1287*–1308*, 1331*–1360a*, 1379*–1392*, 1402–3, 1406–1415*, 1418*, 1420*, 1426*–1430*, 1440*, 1443*–1453*, 1458–1466*, 1489–1560*, 1592–1599, 1615–6*, 1620*–1621, 1629*–32** and **1656*–7***.

To these numbers, at least two to three hundred more fragments in the collection of the British Museum must be added. They are basically fragments from: 1. Plain inscribed

---

[4] The material from Naucratis in the BM and the sherds from Naucratis dispersed in various museums and collections all over the world are dealt with here. There remains outstanding still the majority of the material from the old excavations in Berezan and Olbia and the new material from these and other sites in the present territory of the USSR; almost all—with very few exceptions—from the sites of Anatolia, e.g. Pitane, Phocaea, Dascylium, Erythrae and now Ainus; the material from Thasos, Kavala, Ayia Paraskevi, in the region of Thessaloniki, and Rizari on Chios and at least half of the finds in Italy.

[5] *Emporio* 120 notes 3–5; 157 notes 4–5; 158 notes 1–5 for the chalices and many more—passim—throughout the section on Pottery.

[6] I have also profited from an unpublished Oxford D. Phil. thesis on *The Archaeology and Early History of Chios* 1976, by E. Yalouris who kindly allowed me to consult it.

[7] Boardman in *Chios Conference* 254–8, champions their local manufacture, presenting fresh arguments.

[8] Grand style in Chapter 3 and the black-figure Grand style in Chapter 4.

Fig. 103 Distribution of Sites

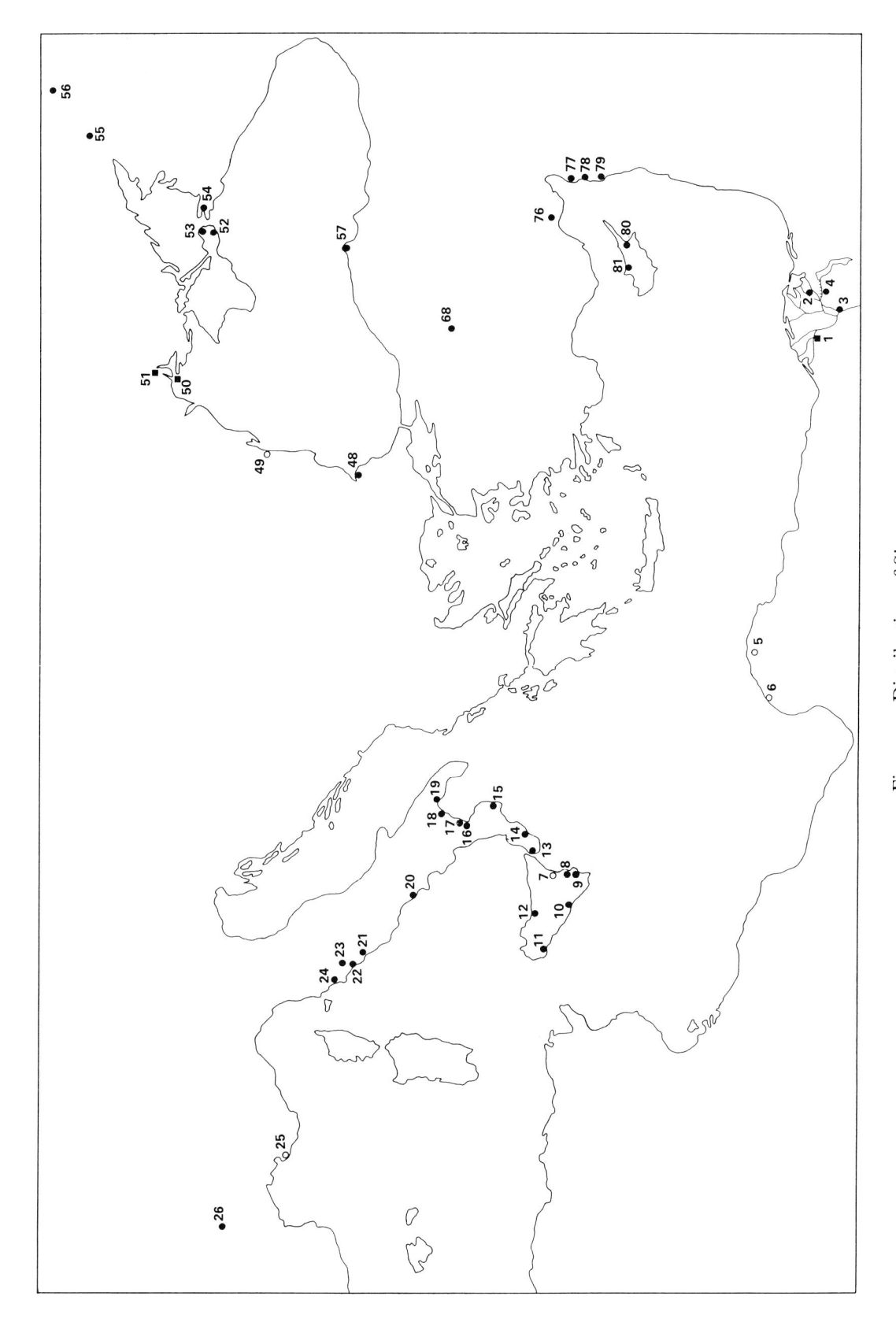

● Chian fine wares present;   ○ Chian fine wares present in respectable numbers;   ■ Chian fine wares present in abundance

kantharoi with an intact one in Oxford,[9] and other open shapes; 2. Bowls, rims and handles of, probably, plain sixth-century chalices and 3. Omphaloi from phialai, rims and handles from dinoi or spouts from kernoi.

Naucratis received consignments of Chian fine pottery from its first establishment as a trading port,[10] that is certainly earlier than the end of the seventh century until approximately the end of the third quarter of the sixth. Shortly after the middle of the century two basic factors combine to contribute to the gradual diminution and final disappearance of Chian pots: on the one hand, the increasing inundation of Athenian pottery which swamped all other, "provincial" wares—though Chians ineffectively tried to compete with a few Atticising products of their own;[11] and on the other hand, the decay of decorated pottery at home, possibly in reaction to Persian pressure on the island and its eventual submission to them. Chian trade with this cosmopolitan centre gradually decreases during the period 540 to 525/20, and finally fades away after the Persian invasion of Egypt about 525 B.C. The pottery from Naucratis is votive in intent, deriving mainly from the temple of Aphrodite which is considered to be a Chian foundation.[12]

The recovery of Chian amphorae of the early sixth century attests to the wine and olive trade of the island with Naucratis in exchange for corn from Egypt. It has been supposed that Chian merchants purchased corn in exchange for wine and silver, which products they acquired and transported from the North Aegean area—specifically from Maroneia, Chios' sole colony in the region, which had access to Mt. Pangaeum's mineral wealth.[13]

Thus, the site received large quantities of Chian decorated and plain pottery from around 620/10 to about 525/20. Chian pottery ranks second only to 'Rhodian' Wild Goat—and, on the argument that ceramics provides an accurate indication of the carriers of trade, it follows that the Chian merchants had a major share of this business, and that the chalice was the favoured trade item, destined for votive use.[14]

2. Tell Defenneh: A fragment [? in the Wild Goat style] has been mentioned.[15] The site need have no direct links with Chios[16] and the piece could have travelled from nearby Naucratis.

3. Abusir: The same holds true for Abusir from where a black-figure fragment in Bonn is recorded.[17]

4. Zagazig: A female head from a vase might be Chian, **1387***, and not Clazomenian on the grounds of the whiteness of the slip and the remnants of a dotted necklace. It was bought here, but, of course, could have come from Naucratis.

5. Cyrene: Three find spots have uncovered Chian pottery: the Artemision and the Agora in the town from the older Italian excavations, and the extramural sanctuary of Demeter,

---

[9] *CVA*, Oxford II, pl.392.18 (bought in Paris; probably from Naucratis).

[10] For the settling of Chians at Naucratis, Cook in *JHS* 57, 1937, 227–37. Also Roebuck in *ClPh*. 46, 1951, 213–4 and 217–8 who strongly argues for the probability of Chians being interested originally in the trading opportunities, and that only conseqently did their descendants populate the town; Austin, Greece and Egypt, 7–75 and especially for Chios and its pottery, 25 and note 4. For an up-to-date treatment with a critical summary of the evidence, *GO*³ 111–33.

[11] *Emporio*, 168–70 and *CGED* 85.

[12] Roebuck in *ClPh*. 45, 1950, 239 and 242.

[13] Roebuck in *Chios Conference* 82–4.

[14] Without trying to underestimate the great importance of Chian pottery at Naucratis. This site, however, is probably not unique: Chian is also found en masse at Berezan and possibly Olbia too, in so far as fine wares are concerned.

[15] *Tanis* II, 62.

[16] *GO*³ 134.

[17] Cook, Distribution 160 [= Bonn 2002.14]

from the recent American ones. All are scraps from debris. **617** is a piece of fine ware[18] with part of a red-spotted boar, classified here in the Animal Chalice style. Five more fragmentary chalices, **935** and **1009–1012** come from the Agora.

Of the now published sixty nine Chian fragments from the extramural sanctuary of Demeter and Persephone,[19] forty one have some decoration. A fragment from a closed vase might be of the Polychrome style (**794**).

Chian is represented in substantial quantities in almost all the styles of the sixth century and in a variety of shapes, including the ubiquitous chalices. There are nine more fragmentary chalices,[20] besides those catalogued here; also phialai mesomphaloi, bowls with lids, closed vases (presumably oenochoai), two-handled pots, cups, dishes, fruitstands, a plate, an oinochoe and a janiform female head from a lid, most of them are undecorated. A surprisingly wide range of shapes exceeded only at Naucratis and Berezan. Excluding Corinthian and Athenian, Chian ranges fifth in quantity out of eight provincial Archaic fabrics: a grade that speaks for the relative popularity of these wares and the commercial ties with the island.[21] Chian amphorae were not recovered at the extramural sanctuary, only at the Agora in Cyrene.[22]

6. Taucheira (modern Tocra): This provided another good market for Chian products. Out of the sixty one vases and fragments published,[23] the thirty eight decorated are listed here. Chian comes sixth in popularity, following Corinthian, "Rhodian", Athenian, Local and Laconian.[24] It appears in the late seventh century,[25] becomes frequent in the earlier part of the sixth and diminishes towards its middle. A remarkably high proportion are chalices of all types and styles, including one with a mythological scene, **793**, possibly of the Grand style. Only one late vase in the Sphinx and Lion style (**1271***) and an even later phiale mesomphalos (**1075***) exist. Of plain pottery, fragmentary band cups and perhaps a foot fragment of a fruit-stand as well as Chian wine amphorae have been found.[26]

It seems peculiar that Middle II Wild Goat is absent; **616***, though following the Würzburg chalices schemes, is certainly within the sixth century as are the rest of the animal chalices, **612*–615**. Both Cyrene and Tocra imported from Chios and there is no necessity to consider that **617** from Cyrene and **793** from Tocra were imported from Naucratis. The relative frequency of Chian pottery in Cyrenaica in the sixth century attests both to the preference of an "en vogue" votive ware, since the vases have been mainly recovered in sanctuaries and their debris, and to more ordinary trade ties with the region as the presence of the amphorae distinctly implies.

B. THE WEST

7. Catane: At least twenty fragmentary chalices, and pieces from a crater, a phiale

---

[18] *GO*[3] 157 considered as imported from Naucratis (of the Grand style).
[19] Schaus, *Dem. Sanct.*, *Cyrene* II, 77–85.
[20] Schaus, *Dem. Sanct.*, *Cyrene* II, 81–2, nos. 495–503.
[21] *Ibid.* 3–4 and 104–5 for a discussion on the trade ties between Chios and Cyrenaica.
[22] *Ibid.* 77 and note 6 for Chian amphorae found in Cyrene's agora.
[23] *Tocra* I and II, 57–63 and 24–28 respectively.
[24] *Tocra* II, 3–5 and figs. 1 and 2.
[25] It is apparent that the coastal sites of Cyrenaica were founded later than Cyrene but were receiving pottery consignments earlier than 600, see *GO*[3] 157–8.
[26] *Tocra* I, 137–9, nos. 1414–5, pl. 90 and perhaps 1418–21, fig. 67 and *Tocra II*, 62, nos. 2258–63, fig. 25 and pl. 32.

mesomphalos and cups were uncovered in a rich deposit at a Demeter sanctuary. This signficant find was reported[27] and some fragments illustrated. Of these all were from animal chalices with the transition from bowl to walls still perceptible but decorated inside; their patterns, especially above the handles, are in the manner of the Würzburg chalices.

8. Megara Hyblaea: Five scraps, **1144–8**, from plain sixth-century chalices,[28] which were votives, appeared amongst the plethora of other Archaic imported pottery.

9. Syracuse: Two fragments in Wild Goat style, **417*–8***, and two intact plain sixth-century chalices, **1019*–20***, come from Ortygia.

Nearby Camarina has yielded Chian amphorae from the old excavations.[29]

10. Gela: The intact dinos, **303***, and the fragmentary, **304**, derive from the old excavations in the Bitalemi sanctuary which have been recently resumed; from these last a few fragments of chalices have been recovered and reported.[30] Presumably, they are all votive.

11. Selinus: Rare chalice fragments have been reported from the old excavations including an interesting piece from an animal chalice, **631**. Again, they are votives at the local sanctuary of Malophorus.

12. Himera: A lid in the animal style of the sixth century has been published, **693**.

13. Rhegium: A komast chalice, **1574***, derives from the sacred area of the settlement.

14. Locri Epizephyrioi: A seventh-century chalice, **73**, and an animal chalice, **632**, have been reported and a late unslipped black-figure kantharos, **1633**, fully published. All are from the necropolis at Centocamere (Mannella).

15. Croton: At least one chalice has been reported, **1149**, from the Archaic settlement.

16. Sybaris: Eighteen fragments were reported and at least half of them published. The lot comprises scraps of seventh-century chalices, **74–5**; oenochoai, **346–7**; animal chalices, **633–4**; a simple figure chalice, **937**; and fragments of plain sixth-century chalices, **1021–8** and **1150–2**, and a dish.[31]

17. Francavilla Marittima: Fragments in both the Animal Chalice style, **635–9**, and apparently from plain sixth-century chalices, **1153–8**, were recovered at Motta.

18. Metapontum: A fragment apparently of a plain sixth-century chalice with inner decoration, **1029**, derives from a sanctuary.

19. Tarentum: The well-known intact chalices, one with a sphinx, **938***, and the other plain, **1030*** and a fragmentary phiale mesomphalos, **1242**, most probably Chian, came from tombs.

20. Cumae: A fragment of an animal chalice, **640**, is the single Chian import in Campania.

21. Caere (Cerveteri): From the tombs and the area nearby four plain and intact chalices have been found. Two, **76–7***, are seventh-century, (**76** is very early in form, and could date a little after the middle of the century) and two more, **1031*–2***, are of the sixth. All are funerary and, naturally, well-preserved.

Chian amphorae of the sixth century have been also found at Caere.[32]

---

[27] *BolldArte* 1960, 251–2 and fig. 14.

[28] Chian amphorae were also recovered and published in *Mégara Hyblaea* II, 83–4 and pls. 70–1.

[29] *MA* XIV, 1904, 861, fig. 69 and 865–6, fig. 71.

[30] *CGED* 95.

[31] *NSc* 23, 1969, Suppl. I, 89, no. 178, fig. 75.

[32] G. Colonna in *ArchCl* XIII, 1961 20 and note 9 where stated "frequenti a Caere", for the Ionian amphorae, including Chian. For the distribution of Chian amphorae in Etruria, see *CGED* 162–3.

22. Gravisca: Fragments from two plain sixth-century chalices have been reported, **1160–1**, which are from the debris of the Archaic sanctuary of Aphrodite; also Chian amphorae,[33] as expected in Etruria's main port.

23. Vulci: The two famous Würzburg chalices, **236*–7***, were probably recovered here in a tomb, as they once formed part of the Feoli collection, which was mainly put together from finds at Vulci.

24. Gavorrano, Grosseto: A wrongly restored footless chalice, with decoration that has peeled off, **1159***, derives from a tomb in the area of Poggio Pellicia.

25. Massalia (modern Marseilles): The proportions of pottery follow the norm of Ionian-founded colonies with Chian coming after "Rhodian". Specifically, around twelve chalices and fragments have been published of which the decorated include two figured ones, **641** and **939**, and scraps from lip and handle zone patterns from sixth-century chalices **1162 a** and **b***, **1163 a** and **b***. Together with Chian sixth-century wine jars, these attest to probable Chian trading activity with this Phocaean colony. Presumably they all are from debris of sanctuaries.

26. Agde: At Béssan, Herault, fragments of a plain sixth-century chalice, with a simple rim pattern, **1033**, together with four more fragments from Provence[34] imply that fashionable drinking cups could travel inland, perhaps as "curios".

The distribution of Chian fine pottery in the West is wide and likely to increase; however it is limited in quantity, apart from Marseilles and possibly Catane. Chian vases found their way here through the occasional travels of their owners, whether Chian or other Greek merchants, most often on pilgrimage to judge from their final resting places. The markets for decorated Greek pottery in Italy and further West, with the exception of Marseilles, were monopolized from the beginning of their colonization by Euboeans, then in the seventh century by the Corinthians and from the middle of the sixth onwards by the Athenians.

C. MAINLAND GREECE AND THE AEGEAN ISLANDS

27. Corcyra: A tiny fragment in the Sphinx and Lion style, **1454**, has been reported.

28. Ithaca: A plain kantharos is known.[35]

29. Corinth: Fragments of seventh-century patterned chalices, **81–93**, and of sixth-century plain ones with inner decoration, **1034–9**, have turned up periodically in the fruitful excavations at Corinth. The proportion of Chian is unimportant in comparison to other wares. It most probably derives from sanctuaries.[36]

30. Perachora: Three fragments of sixth-century, plain, chalices derive from the debris of sanctuaries.[37]

---

[33] *CGED* 228–30.

[34] Jully, *Languedoc*, 532.

[35] A dubious piece, as it is difficult to judge from the profile in *BSA* 43, 1948, 97, no. 586.

[36] L.J. Siegel, *Corinthian Trade in the Ninth through Sixth centuries B.C.* (Ph.D. Yale University, 1978). Chian pottery, mainly fragments from plain sixth-century chalices, is listed; mainly her third Chapter "Chiot Imports at Corinth", 64–114, nos. 37–307 and pls. 15–31. In all there are seventy one pieces, almost all undecorated. Also *Hesperia* 7, 1938, 608, no. 219.

[37] *Perachora* II, 375–6, nos. 4065–4065a and 4066, pl. 156.

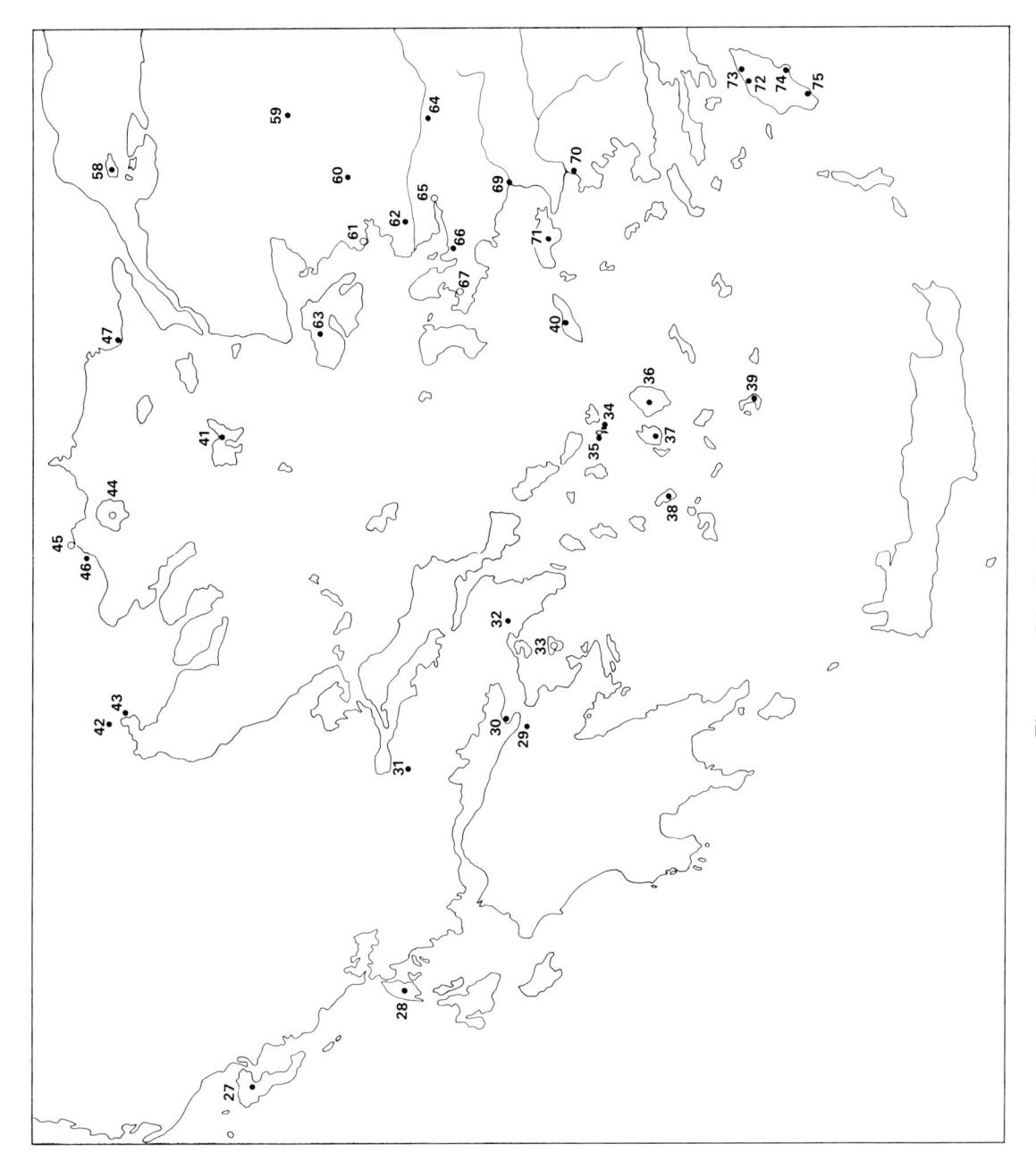

Fig. 104 Distribution of Sites

● Chian fine wares present; ○ Chian fine wares present in respectable numbers

31. Rhitsona in Boeotia: The nearly intact black-figure animal chalice, **1602***, was found in grave 50.

32. Athens: Chian sherds were recovered on the Acropolis and in the Agora. The Acropolis fragments consist of the dubious piece from a phallus cup, **367**; the famous Heracles piece in the Polychrome style, **797***; two fragments from animal chalices, **658*–9***, and another from a plain sixth-century one, **1182**.

The Agora material comprises two restored and one fragmentary plain seventh-century chalices, **78***, **79*** and **80**; pieces from four different figured chalices, **660–1** and **949–50** and a fragmentary amphoriskos, **1645***.[38] With a total of twelve to thirteen vases so far, an insignificant number, Athens definitely was not the market cherished by Chians. The sporadic finds suggest rather occasional pilgrimages to the Acropolis and visits to the Agora; to the latter, as early as the last quarter of the seventh century, as the squat chalice shape tells.

33. Aegina: The find places are the modern town which possesses an Archaic Apollo temple at Colonna, and the Aphaia temple. Old and new German excavations at both were promptly and efficiently published.[39]

Chian from the town numbers ten very significant fragments: a plate in Early Wild Goat style, **264***; oenochoai of Middle I, **348–9**; Animal chalices, **645–6**; a chalice in the Grand, **796*** and another in the Chalice style, **942**. Lastly, scraps of plain chalices have been found.

In the Aphaia temple over four hundred fragments of Chian pottery have been recovered of which a selective catalogue of a hundred and sixty-nine was published,[40] embracing sixth-century chalices of all styles, kantharoi,[41] cups, jugs and phialai: most drinking vessels and, of course, all votives. Thirty five fragments with figure decoration have been chosen for the purposes of the present work, to the exclusion of plain pottery and the inscribed kantharoi. The Grand style chalice (**795***) is here considered to be a direct import from Chios. However striking the numbers might be, yet Chian stands proportionately low in the list of imported wares to this island which had no pottery of its own.[42] It is perhaps reasonable to deduce from this that Aeginetans were trading with Chios during the sixth century[43] and even earlier, and held Chian fine pottery in great esteem as votives for their sanctuaries.

34. Delos: From the Heraion come two animal chalices, **643*** and **644**. **1040***, whose decoration has peeled off, might have been from an animal chalice as the shape and size indicate. Two plain kantharoi are not listed here.[44] From the three sanctuaries in the West bank were recovered two fragmentary chalices in Wild Goat style of a debased stage,

---

[38] The fragment in *Hesperia* 1946, 136, no. 34, pl. 24.6, is not, I think, Chian.

Chian amphorae are not infrequent in the Agora, though most are later than our period; and much has been published: in *Hesperia* 1934, 202, fig. 1 and pl. 1; 1935, 495–6, 514–6; 1937, 301 fig. 33 no. 202; 1938, 607, fig. 29, no. 213; 1946, pl. 28, nos. 27, 29; 1956, 12–14 no. 58 and 62–3 and 373, nos. 100–1; 1958, 175–8. Also in *Kerameikos* IX in contexts.

[39] *Aegina*, 455–6, pl. 129 and *Alt-Ägina* II.1, 14–16 and pl. 15.

[40] *AA* 1983, 154–186.

[41] The plethora of kantharoi enabled Williams to discern two main types of the shape with further subdivisions of type B.

[42] However, S.P. Morris, *The Black and White style*, 1984, 19–36, raises claims for a local workshop operating on Aegina and puts together vases which have been generally considered Middle Protoattic.

[43] Jeffery in *AG* 231 thinks the two islands had "a trade-link".

[44] *Délos* X, pl. 20, nos. 119 and 120.

238–9, another in the Chalice style, **941**; an omphalos from a phiale, **1243**; two komast chalices, **1576–7** and a two-handled pot, **1646**. These thirteen vases, all votives, make up a very minor proportion of the imported material on the island.

35. Rheneia: A seventh-century chalice, **94***; another in the Chalice style, restored, **940***, in the museum of Mykonos; fragments from sixth-century plain chalices and a tiny one in the Sphinx and Lion style, **1455**, all again votives, were recovered here. A total of eighteen Chian vases from this Panionian shrine and the Katharsis grave on Rheneia is not a considerable amount, but alongside the mass of the Cycladic wares Chians seemingly carried and dedicated their own.

36. Naxos: Three chalice scraps from the excavations at Aplomata, **1164–6***, suggest a visit of Chians to the nearby temple of Apollo.[45]

37. Paros: A fragment from an animal chalice, **642**, and feet from two plain sixth-century chalices, **1167–8**, come from the Delion, and had been used as votives. Two more undecorated fragments, make up the total of Chian imports.[46]

38. Siphnos: Few scraps from sixth-century chalices have been reported, **1169–71**.

39. Thera: A fragment of a Chian amphora has been published and a few pieces from handles, bowls and feet of plain sixth-century chalices from the Sellada cemetery at old Thera are stored at the Phyra museum.[47]

40. Icaria: Some sherds have been reported.[48]

41. Lemnos: Fragments of bowls and lids in the Sphinx and Lion style from the Italian excavations on the island are exhibited in the museum at Myrina.

The diffusion of Chian fine wares in Mainland Greece and the islands is wide, but again restricted to either very small quantities or isolated finds, with the exception of Aegina. The sites receiving Chian in this geographical area are fifteen in number, which is fewer than those in the West at twenty. The main reason for this disparity being that however fashionable Chian wares were in the foreign markets of the South and West, competition was too hard in the Aegean, where the produce of local pottery workshops was preferred. The distribution of Chian here indicates casual journeys or pilgrimages rather than organised trade. As regards the isolated Rhitsona chalice, it might have been the beloved drinking cup of an Ionian immigrant, which his relatives placed in his tomb to accompany him in his afterlife.

D. NORTH GREECE AND THE BLACK SEA

42. Thessaloniki: Three published sherds from undecorated sixth-century chalices, **1044*–6***, were unearthed at Karabournaki before the war and form part of the Archaeological collection at the University museum.[49]

43. Ayia Paraskevi (S.E. of Thessaloniki): A rich Archaic cemetery, in the region of ancient Anthemous, yielded three hundred and seventy seven graves of the period of

---

[45] They were found in unstratified levels.

[46] M.H. Bikakis, *Archaic and Classical Imported Pottery in the museums of Paros and Naxos* Ph.D. Cincinnati, 1985, 43–6, nos. 25–32.

[47] Kindly shown to me by Ch. Sigalas of the Ephoreia.

[48] *JHS* 64, 1944, 89. I was told that there are fragments in the Wild Goat style in the local storeroom from older excavations but do not know whether they are Chian.

[49] M. Tiverios in *To Archaiologiko Ergo sti Makedonia kai Thraki* 1, 1987, 1988, 257 and fig. 9.

around 570–500 B.C. Amongst the innumerable ceramic imports nine chalices were found, preserved in an excellent condition.[50] Eight are in the Chalice style, **952*–5** and **1047–50**, of which the last four are plain sixth-century chalices and a komast chalice, **1580**. This newly discovered Chian material might bring fresh dating contexts.[51]

44. Thasos: This extensively excavated island has yielded both imported Chian and vases of a category from a locally established workshop somewhere in the region. Leaving aside what is here considered of local manufacture,[52] it is sufficient to mention that seventeen pieces, inclusive of amphorae, have been published.[53] Fragments from plain sixth-century chalices have turned up pell-mell in the Archaic strata. Most are from sanctuary debris or the Artemision, with only a few coming from the settlement.

45. Neapolis (modern Kavala): From the sanctuary of a local deity, the Parthenos, both imported pieces and members of the local Chian workshop have been uncovered. **798***, **804*** and the restored phiale, presumably mesomphalos, **814***, all inadequately published, constitute a small but important group of Chian polychrome or perhaps more probably represent the impact made by it.[54]

Imported Chian vases comprise chalice-sherds with the head of a sphinx, **951**, plain ones, **1041–2**, or with komasts, **1579***: all of the usual Chian stock. Apart from these seven fragments more unpublished Chian material from the sanctuary is stored in the Kavala museum.[55] Maroneia which might be proved responsible for Chian trade with the region[56] is known only from literary sources, and so far no archaeological record for the Archaic period is attested. Chios' role in the North Aegean, wherever its headquarters,[57] seems to be an important one as is emphasised by recent abundant and repeated discoveries. Chian had a strong role to play in influencing Thasian pottery proper, in addition to the Cycladic. Indeed, this territory seems to be a stronghold of East Greeks of the North Aegean in general.

46. Oesyme (modern Nea Peramos): Chian sherds, from older excavations, of the category manufactured locally[58] are exhibited in the Oesyme showcase in the Kavala museum; from the recently resumed work two sherds have been illustrated in the report.[59] It is evident that Oesyme like Neapolis was importing, amongst other fabrics, pots of the category manufactured nearby.

47. Ainos (modern Enez): The Aeolian colony of Ainos on the mouth of river Hebros, where Turkish excavations have recently started,[60] has, it seems, revealed as its

---

[50] *Arch. Reports* for 1982–83, 41. Also, K. Sismanidis in *Ametos* 794, pl. 163.2 gives the first fuller report of the digs. The chalices will eventually be published by Mrs. E. Poulakie-Pandermalis.

[51] See Chapter 5.

[52] See Chapter 7.

[53] *Et. thas.* VII, 36–9. What has been illustrated in the *BCH* since 1956 is of the local category, but in the text there is mention of Chian proper as well. For Chian amphorae, see *BCH* 85, 1961, 934, fig. 34.

[54] See Chapter 3, pp. 113–4.

[55] This material will be published by Ch. Koukouli-Chrysanthaki, K. Rhomiopoulou, E. Yiouri and collaborators.

[56] A.J. Graham, *BSA* 73, 1978, 95 and note 328 where references to the ancient literary sources; *CAH* III2, 117.

[57] Roebuck's view in *ClPh.* 46, 1951, 212 ff. "on the organisation of Naucratis" emphasises Chios' leading role in the North Aegean, because of Maroneia and its access to the silver mines of Mt. Pangaeum. And now, Roebuck in *Chios Conference*, 82–4.

Ionian nondescript vases and mainly Ionian cups have been found in Abdera in *BCH* 91, 1967, 724, fig. 6 and 729, figs. 15–6 and *ADelt.* 20, 1965, pls. 540, 558. Also *ibid.* 444, pls. 512–4 from the ?Thracian town Nine Roads (Enneahodoi).

[58] See Chapter 7.

[59] *To Archaiologiko Ergo sti Makedonia kai Thraki* 1, 1987, 1988, 384, fig. 24.

[60] See Chapter 7, notes 4 and 26.

predominant ceramic ware an abundance of fragments from bowls and lekanai of the locally manufacturing Chian workshop; they are of a slightly earlier date than the Oesyme, Kavala and Thasos finds.

48. Apollonia Pontica:[61] An animal chalice, **662**, in the style of the Würzburg chalices has been mentioned, and a black-figure animal chalice, **1603***, has appeared in a guide of the Sozopol museum.

49. Istros: A squat chalice, **95**; an ambiguous fragment in Wild Goat style, **305**; two fragments from animal chalices, **663*–4***; fourteen from the Chalice style, **956*–8** and **1262***, of which ten are from plain sixth-century chalices, **1051*–8**, **1186–8**; four from phialai mesomphaloi, **1076*–9***; four in the Sphinx and Lion style, **1367*–70***, and a female head from a plastic vase, **1396***, of doubtful parentage,[62] are the published pieces from older and newer excavations. To these a fair number of Chian wine jars must be added.[63]

Apart from the seventh-century chalice, the bulk of Chian pottery, which was votive, is of the first half of the sixth century only; only a few are from beyond the middle of the century. The fruitful harvest of Chian vases points towards trading relations with this Milesian colony.

50. Berezan: More than 800 graves have been reported to have been excavated on Berezan.[64] Of the pottery uncovered only a very small selection has been published; among the unpublished Chian sherds 100 fragments in the Sphinx and Lion style, 200 fragments from komast chalices and 12 from black-figure animal chalices are mentioned.[65] These striking numbers approximate the quantities recovered at Naucratis and are certainly unequalled anywhere else. Reference, perforce only to the published material, is restricted to the following: six fragments of animal chalices, **665*–70**; seven in the Chalice style, **959–65*** and fourteen in the black-figure styles, **1312*–4***, **1371*–4***, **1439***, **1584*–6**, **1605*–6*** and **1635***. This is only a very small selection, and demonstrates that Chian consignments started reaching Berezan a little after the beginning of the sixth century and lasted till around the third quarter. From this extensive quantity and the vast variety of shapes, including amphorae,[66] arises the assumption that the greatest part of the trade with the Milesian colonies of the Black Sea was equally in the hands of Chians and of the other Ionians.[67] Chian vases admittedly come second on the list, following "Rhodian", many categories of which might perhaps now anyway be regarded as Milesian. This pattern is the norm for an East Greek colonized area, at least in the first part of the sixth

---

[61] Neighbouring Mesembria (Nesebar) yielded fragments of Chian amphorae. See *BCH* 84, 1960, 228. I owe the reference to M. Vickers who brought it to my attention.

[62] Possibly but not certainly Chian.

[63] *Histria* IV, 94ff and in particular no. 621, fig. 18.

[64] By L. Kopeikina in the summary of the *Acta XI Inter. Congr. Class. Arch.*, 1978, 198.

[65] *SovArch.* 1957, 138 and note 9. The more spectacular vases were transported to the Hermitage, see Kocybala, Diss. 1978, 209–210 and notes 226–233.

[66] A Chian wide-mouthed pointed pithos-amphora for funerary use was published in *SovArch.* 1960, 2, fig. 14; also *GO*³ 250, fig. 290. It is from the same "workshop of the concentric circles" that produced the Rizari pithoi-amphorae, see *Emporio*, pl. 44X and A.A. Lemos in *Chios Conference* 236–8 and fig. 7. Kocybala, Diss. 1978, 198 and note 154 refers to one more such pithos-amphora from Berezan: Hermitage inv. no. B120.

[67] *GO*³ 238–45 and especially p. 243 for Chios' role.

century, before the balance of the pottery trade passed to Athenian hands. The mass of Chian pottery derives from both tombs and sanctuaries of the settlement.

51. Olbia: Another very important market for Chian merchants; it ranges third after Naucratis and Berezan in significance and quantities received.

Again, published pottery is meagre: a fragmentary dish in Late Wild Goat style, **265**; fragments in the Sphinx and Lion style, **1456**; a female head from a plastic vase, **1397***; fragments from komast chalices, **1581–3**; from a black-figure animal chalice, **1604**; from a kantharos, **1636**; and finally, an intact two-handled pot, **1647***. The unpublished Chian fragments from Olbia, which derive from debris of sanctuaries, must form a much vaster corpus.[68] There are also Chian amphorae in Olbia.[69]

52. Tiritake: The site lies on the West bank of the straits entering the sea of Azov, 11 km. south of Panticapaeum. It has yielded at least a fragmentary black-figure kantharos, **1637**, and two more fragments from excavations undertaken after the war.

53. Panticapaeum: Two Late Wild Goat fragments, **306*** and **671**; scraps of sixth-century chalices, **1189–91** and a phiale, **1080**, are known. As usual, much more is unpublished.[70]

54. Kepoi: The settlement lies on the East bank of the straits. Two cup fragments of doubtful Chian parentage, **1609–10**, are from recent excavations. Chian amphorae were also recovered here[71] and at Hermonassa.[72]

55. Krivoroshie: The site lies inland, 250 miles from the sea up the river Donetz. From here comes the ram-oenochoe, **350***, which is probably Chian.

56. Choperskie: Over 100 miles further inland, it was from here that the bull-oenochoe, **351***, was recovered.

The presence of seventh-century vases in settlements that were colonized and populated only in the early sixth century has been fully explained by the theory of early pre-colonial contact and experimental penetration of alien territories with which East Greeks gradually became familiar.[73] Peculiarities, such as oenochoai with plastic heads, must have travelled amongst the natives who viewed them as "curios".

57. ?Sinope: A fragment from an unslipped black-figure kantharos might have been unearthed at Sinope, **1634**.

E. EAST GREECE AND ANATOLIA

58. Proconessus: A plain one-handled cup and a kantharos have been reported.[74]

---

[68] I owe knowledge of this material initially to drawings of Professor Boardman's and then to Miss Yulia Ilyina, of the Hermitage museum, who kindly guided me through the Chian material from the colonies of the North Sea under her supervison.

[69] *Samos* VI.1, 138, no. 688. For the Milesian colonization of Berezan and Olbia, see N. Ehrhardt, *Milet und seine Kolonien* 1983, 74–5 and 75–9 respectively.

[70] Kocybala, Diss. 1978, 324 and note 720. She was shown pottery material in many museums of the USSR, and in her thesis has summarised the reports and the rarer publications of material; however, she is not entirely reliable in her classification of pottery and the plates are totally unreadable in the xeroxed form.

[71] *Eirene* 1972, 617.

[72] *SovArch*. 1974, 70, pl. 2a and b. And Ehrhardt for the Milesian colonization of Panticapaeum, *ibid*. 80–1 and Kepoi, *ibid*. 81–2.

[73] See Boardman's "The Black Sea and its Approaches" in GO^3 238–44.

[74] *IstMitt* 22, 1972, pl. 21.2.5.

59. Dascylium: Chian pottery, possibly plain and in limited amounts, has been reported.[75]

60. Pergamum: Fragments of a Wild Goat dinos, **307**, are from debris.

61. Pitane: Excavations in the necropolis were fruitful in Chian vases, most of which were intact or nearly so, furnishing tombs which also contained Corinthian and Athenian vases. Thirty five contexts out of two hundred and fifty contained Chian decorated vases: that is 14%. The pottery from Pitane as well as that recovered at Erythrae, Phocaea, Dascylium and other sites in Anatolia has not been published so far. From the little that has been declared,[76] it was possible to distinguish twenty six vases,[77] though in inadequate detail. More analytically the list runs thus:

a) five fragmentary patterned seventh-century chalices, **100*–4**.
b) three Wild Goat chalices, **240–2**.
c) thirteen sixth-century chalices: three in the Animal Chalice style, **674*–5***; two in the Grand style, **800*–1***; four in the Chalice style, **968–71***; three plain, **1069** and **1198–9**; one floral, **1263**.
d) three vases in the Sphinx and Lion style: a stemmed skyphos crater, **1272***; an oenochoe, **1433***; and an incense vase, **1437***.
e) two black-figure animal chalices, **1611*–2**.

Both Pitane[78] and "Larisa" were Aeolian cities and imported fine pottery from various parts of Greece. The proportion of Chian in the former is perhaps high compared to other Aeolian sites and other East Greek centres generally; in the latter it is extremely sparse. Not surprisingly, taking into consideration the proximity of Chios to Pitane—in favourable weather it would hardly take more than six to eight hours—Pitane's inhabitants took a liking to this highly fashionable ware and made considerable use of it for their funerary purposes. The ties between Chios and Aeolis in general, as suggested from the impact in art that the former exercised on the latter, now are seen to have been strong.[79]

62. "Larisa": Three fragmentary chalices are catalogued here, **672–3** and **1197**, as well as a fragmentary lid in the Sphinx and Lion style, **1375**. The presence of Chian wares is insignificant.

63. Antissa (on Lesbos): A scrap from the handle zone of a sixth-century chalice, **1059**, is known.

64. Sardis: The foot from a late seventh-century chalice, **105**, was the only Chian presence.

65. Old Smyrna: Twenty three Chian vases are catalogued, more exist but are either plain or unpublished. The amount is not insignificant even when the volume of other products is taken into account. The variety displayed covers almost all styles and a number

---

[75] *CGED* 27.

[76] Mainly C. Bayburtluoğlu in *CGED* 27–30 where on pp. 28–9 on the Chian pottery from Pitane a few contexts are mentioned. Also, now Akurgal, *Türkei* 25 and pls. 10b and c and 11, 20a and b.

[77] I have seen, but not handled, the exhibited material in the Archaeological museums in Istanbul, Izmir and Bergama and at an exhibition at Ayia Eirene in Istanbul, see *Catalogue Istanbul*, 1983; Chian from Pitane B83 and B84.

[78] Brief summaries and accounts of the excavations have appeared annually in the *AJA* since 1961; also *Arch. Reports* for 1964–5, 35–6. Chian amphorae were also recovered, see *Emporio*, 137.

[79] E. Walter-Karydi, *Äol Kunst*, 3–18.

of shapes: apart from the ubiquitous chalice there are phialai, a mug, a dish, probably a plastic vase and amphorae.[80]

Chian fine wares reached Smyrna from around the middle of the seventh century with a scrap of a proto-chalice, **96***, continued with the squat patterned chalices, **97*–9***, and scraps of Wild Goat chalices, **243*–4* and a**. In the sixth century they were represented by fragmentary chalices in the Chalice style, **966*–7***, and plain ones, **1064*–8***;[81] furthermore, phialai, **1247*–9***; a sherd in the Sphinx and Lion style, **1457*** and chalices with komasts, **1587*–9***, and animals, **1613***, exist. This Chian pottery was found in debris or in the foundations of houses.

66. Clazomenae: Several undecorated fragments were reported.[82]

67. Erythrae: Excavations have been carried out on the Athena temple, and perhaps another to Apollo, on the Acropolis, almost annually since 1965. No pottery has yet been published,[83] but the frequency of Chian sherds seems to be so overwhelming—around one thousand fragments—as to suggest to one of the excavators a new birthplace for the ware.[84]

Only two pieces are catalogued here: an early squat chalice in Wild Goat style, **245**, and a fragmentary lid in the Sphinx and Lion style, **1376** (FIG. 81).[85]

68. Gordion: Three fragments of sixth-century chalices, **1200*–2**, were recovered in the old excavations.

69. Ephesus: Little Chian was found and published: a plain sixth-century chalice, **1070***,[86] a phiale, **1250**, and a mid sixth-century kantharos.[87]

70. Miletus: Not much Chian, as it seems, was found here either. Chalice fragments have been reported[88] and a phiale, **1251**. Recently, a few Chian amphorae[89] and plain kantharoi have been found.[90]

71. Samos: The German excavations at the Heraion recovered thirteen fragments, mostly chalices: in the Wild Goat style, **246** and **247***; plain sixth-century, **1192–6**; floral, **1264**; komast, **1590*** and feet, **1622–4**. Also recovered were fragments of a plate, **687** and a bowl.[91]

From the Greek rescue excavations at the Pythagoreion come a few unpublished sherds, mostly of mid-sixth century chalices; there are less than a dozen feet, handles and bowls.[92]

---

[80] *BSA* 53–4, 1958–9, 16, fig. 4 and *GO*³ 17, fig. 1 early in the series.

[81] The bowl of another sixth-century chalice was on exhibit in the Fuar Museum in 1982.

[82] Cook, *Distribution*, 159; I was unable to trace any and presumed that Professor Cook must have had oral information about them.

[83] Brief reports appear annually in the *AJA* and Professor Akurgal in his Foreword to C. Bayburtluoğlu's *Erythrai II, Terracottas in Erythrai*, 1977, announced the publication of the Orientalizing pottery in a forthcoming volume.

[84] *CGED* 30 but cf. Boardman's reply, *ibid.* 316–7, on the identification of local wares and against Bayburtluoğlu's claim for the proposed parentage, and for the warning that no proportional analyses are given.

[85] For this piece I am indebted to Professor Akurgal who kindly referred me to the Authorities of the Basmahane museum; they were very helpful but were in the course of moving to the new Archaeological museum. However, from what was still left were two drawers filled with approximately 100–150 fragments from sixth-century plain chalices, mainly from the bowls, feet and handles and the lid, **1376**, (FIG. 81).

[86] Exhibited at the Selçuk museum.

[87] Langmann in *Fest. Eichler*, 107, pl. 42.2.

[88] *JHS* 29, 1909, 333–4 from Cook, *Distribution*, 159.

[89] *IstMitt* 22, 1972, 72–4, fig. 2a, 2b, 3 and 4 and pl. 21.1.

[90] *Ibid.* fig. 5, pl. 21.2.3.

[91] *Samos* IV, 149, no. 524, pl. 69 and fig. 13.

[92] I am indebted to M. Marthari who brought them to my attention and subsequently helped me obtain a permit to see them.

The strong local tradition in pottery will have much reduced the need for imports. Moreover, the islands' relationship, though they were two major participants in the Ionian league, was poor.[93] Both these factors will naturally have tended to curtail the presence of Chian wares; thus the above pieces might be another instance of material left by pilgrims.

Rhodes

72. Camirus: Six almost intact chalices come from unrecorded tombs: two in the Chalice style, **972*–3***; two plain, **1062*–3***; one in black-figure animal style, **1614*** and an unslipped one, **1617***. All were recovered in Biliotti and Salzmann's excavations, therefore no archaeological record has survived.[94]

73. Ialysos: An intact plain sixth-century kantharos is from a grave.[95]

74. Lindos: Four sherds, again from kantharoi, are from debris.[96]

75. Vroulia: Sherds from nine vessels[97] have been published of which the following are listed here: fragments of a seventh-century plain chalice, **106**; of two sixth-century plain ones, **1060*–1***; of a phiale mesomphalos, **1252***; of a komast chalice, **1591**; and finally from two unslipped chalices like the Camirus-Copenhagen chalice, **1617***.

The proportion of Chian is not significant in this heavily excavated island. It is interesting that Chian penetrated an island with strong pottery production of its own, though admittedly the Chian examples from Rhodes, with the exception of **106**, all date after the end of the first quarter of the sixth century, when the heyday of "Rhodian" painted pottery was long gone.[98]

F. THE EASTERN MEDITERRANEAN

76. Tarsus: A fragment from a very early seventh-century chalice, **107**, denotes an isolated Chian contact.

77. Al Mina: Chian sherds found are two from squat seventh-century chalices, **108–9***, and perhaps a few more fragments from Wild Goat oenochoai, **352–4**. Further scrutiny of the Al Mina material, now much dispersed, ought to define better the early stages of Chian Wild Goat style.

78. Ras el Bassit: An oenochoe fragment in the Sphinx and Lion style, **1434***, was reported and there is much more unpublished:[99] amphorae, oenochoai, chalices and phialai mesomphaloi. They derive from the settlement.

79. Tell Sūkās: Eleven chalice fragments and two jugs have been published, of which here are listed: a plain chalice, **1072**, and chalice fragments, **1203–10**. The last have inner decoration, but are either very small or have not preserved their outer decoration: they cannot therefore be classified with certainty. These, in addition to four Chian amphorae, derive from the settlement.[100]

[93] Recently pointed out by Kyrieleis in *Chios Conference* 187 ff.
[94] C. Gates *From Cremation to inhumation: burial practices at Ialysos and Kameiros during the Mid-Archaic Period, ca. 625–525 B.C.*, Occ. Paper 11 of UCLA, 1984, 44 and notes 2 and 157, gives a resumation of the evidence.
[95] *ClRh.* VIII, 43, fig. 26 right and Cook, Distribution, 159.
[96] *Lindos* I, no. 973 a–d and Cook, Distribution, 159.
[97] Kinch, *Vroulia*, 149–151.
[98] Currently many categories of Rhodian vase painting, especially of the Wild Goat, are believed to be Milesian.
[99] *CGED* 42.
[100] *Sūkās* II, pl. 16.322–5 and fig. d.

80. Salamis on Cyprus: There are two probable Chian candidates in Wild Goat style, **308*–9***.

A fair number of Chian amphorae have been recovered at Salamis,[101] also at Kition,[102] Lefka,[103] Amathous[104] and other places on Cyprus[105] which indicates that trading relations with Chios in wine, and probably olive products, were active during the sixth century.

81. Marion on Cyprus: Two intact chalices— one decorated, **974***, the other plain, **1071***—and an intact phiale mesomphalos with exquisite inner decoration, **1081***, are, presumably, from graves, though no archaeological record is given. Chian amphorae are also found at Marion.[106]

With the exception of the amphorae which betray a systematic wine trade, Chian vases are found in the Eastern Mediterranean as strays, and could be the personal belongings of traders.

To recapitulate, a few conclusions can be drawn. First, the distribution of Chian fine pottery is extremely wide, if often sparse. Secondly, it follows the general distribution pattern of East Greek wares. And thirdly, it attests, from its occasional abundance, the pressure of Chian trade.[107]

Close long-distance ties based on trade existed both to the north in the Black Sea colonies (Berezan and Olbia), and also to the south with Naucratis, perhaps to a degree too with Cyrene and Tocra. The mechanics of these may be different: in the first, the Chians seem to be associated with the colonizing activities of Miletus, even though they themselves had no role outside that of traders, whilst in Egypt a Chian community might have been established and flourishing for two to three generations. Broadly speaking, the island of Thasos and the coastal settlements of Macedonia and Thrace also show evidence of considerable activity and influence: this may have emanated from Maroneia, Chios' only colony, as much as from the mother island.

In the West, with the exception of Marseilles and perhaps Catane, contacts are extremely restricted, even casual. Much the same holds true for Mainland Greece and the islands of the Central Aegean. It is suggested that individual pilgrimages to Panionian shrines of Delos and Naxos may account for the finds at such places; there may be similar reasons for the material on, for example, the Athenian Acropolis.

In home waters, Chian fine pottery was favoured generally in the North area—at Pitane, Old Smyrna, Erythrae; but in the Southern region, e.g. Samos, Rhodes, Ephesus, and Miletus, the demand was extremely restricted as they had to face strong competition. In the settlements of Tarsus in Cilicia and Al Mina in Syria, Chian is present only as strays and, of course, very early.[108] Chian merchants did not transport pottery, at least their

---

[101] Gjerstad, *Cyprus*, 18, nos. 96–8, 99, 100–5.
[102] *Ibid*. 63, no. 10, pl. 2.5.
[103] *Belleten* 86, 1962, 336, fig. 11.
[104] Gjerstad, *Cyprus*, 73–4, nos. 96–8, pls. 6.3–5.
[105] *Ibid*. 77, nos. 183–7, pls. 21.5, 6 and 22.1, 3.
[106] *Arch. Reports for 1965–6*, 34, fig. 12.
[107] *JdI* 74, 1959, 123. Whatever caution is drawn on special grounds for the distribution of Laconian pottery, in *JHS* 99, 1979, 153–4, this cannot apply to Chian pottery, however much stress Williams in *AA* 1983, 155–86, puts on Aeginetan trading or transportation.

[108] The destruction of Tarsus is placed *c.* 696 and Al Mina did not receive much Greek pottery until later in the century.

own, in this region either at this time or later. A completely different story can be told with respect to the considerable wine trade with Cyprus and all round the Mediterranean to judge from the frequency of Chian amphorae from early in the sixth century.[109]

[109] The distribution of Chian amphorae is not systematically dealt with here, but will occupy a future work based on the Rizari wide-mouthed linear examples which, I think, head the whole series.

7

A CHIAN WORKSHOP IN THRACE?

A category of Chian figurative pottery,* which has been and is still being recovered on Thasos,[1] at Kavala (ancient Neapolis),[2] New Peramos (ancient Oesyme)[3] and Enez (ancient Ainos)[4] on the Thracian coast, does not form part of the main corpus of Chian pottery. Although it shares certain essential features of the style, it differs from Chian proper in many aspects.

Pending the publication of the Orientalizing and Archaic Pottery from Thasos[5] we are restricted to articles and annual reports; naturally the discussion and remarks are still provisional.[6] However, they are presented because this category poses stimulating problems leading to the ultimate question of whether Chian workshop(s) operated outside the limits of the island and where. Could it have been after all "a most interesting example of Chian enterprise overseas"?[7]

The history of this study goes back to the sixties when L. Ghali-Kahil published the pottery finds from the older excavations on Thasos; in her section on the Chian material, apart from the obviously imported pieces, she singled out a group of fragments which lacked the characteristic distinctive white slip and suggested that they were of local manufacture.[8]

It seems that the quality of the drawing of this category was esteemed by art dealers long before the first publication was produced; some sherds from Thasos had travelled abroad and I recognised a sherd of a plate from this category (Pl. 231.1). It had been wrongly united with an Athenian black-figure fragment; both mounted on a support, en vogue in

---

* I have presented a more detailed version with a corpus in a paper delivered at the Table Ronde Internationale on "Les ateliers de potiers dans le monde grec aux époques géométrique, archaïque et classique" at the French School of Archaeology in Athens in October 1987, which will appear in a *BCH* Supplement (ed. J. Perreault), forthcoming.

[1] L. Ghali Kahil has published the pottery in *La Céramique grecque (fouilles 1911–1956)*, Et.thas. VII, 1960. In the *BCH* a number of articles on pottery and the annual reports of the excavations are published by the French excavators and scholars.

[2] Apart from annual reports in the *PAE* and *ADelt* (see below), Mrs Ch. Koukouli-Chrysanthaki, K. Rhomiopoulou, E. Yiouri and collaborators will publish the material deriving from the sanctuary of Parthenos at Neapolis.

[3] I have seen at least two fragments of the category under discussion here in the showcase of Oesyme in the museum of Kavala and there must be more in the storerooms. For the identification of the site with ancient Oesyme, see G. Bakalakis in *PAE* 1938, 101 with notes 2 and 3. Oesyme was colonized together with Neapolis from Thasos, c. 650–625, see *CAH* III, 3², 117. For the excavation at Nea Peramos (ancient Oesyme), see *ADelt* 20, 1965, 447–451 and for the more recent ones, resumed two years ago, in *Arch. Reports* for 1987–1988, 54–55. See now E. Yiouri & Ch. Koukouli, "Excavation at ancient Oesyme" in *To Archaiologiko Ergo sti Makedonia kai Thraki* I, 1987, 1988, where fragments of the category under discussion appear on p. 384, fig. 24.

[4] Enez (ancient Ainos) is being excavated at the moment by Professor Afif Erzen of Istanbul University and has produced a respectable amount of sherds from our category. These are illustrated in the annual excavation reports, in *Kazi Sonuçlari Toplantisi*.

[5] *BCH* 95, 1971, 177 and *BCH* 105, 1981, 924.

[6] I am grateful to Mrs. K. Rhomiopoulou who asked me to contribute to the publication on this specific category and Mrs. Ch. Koukouli and E. Yiouri, who kindly permitted me to handle it.

[7] Boardman in *Chios Conference*, 258.

[8] *Et.thas*. VII, 35. From Lekanai, pls. 13 nos. 13–14 and 18–23 A+B and 14 nos. 7 and 8 and possibly pl. 7 nos. 33 and 34 (as Salviat claimed in *CGED* 89).

those days, fortunately with the rather helpful label "Thasos 1932".[9] This category has been mainly recovered at the Artemision and other sanctuaries of Thasos; very few pieces only come from other parts of the ancient city.[10]

Meanwhile, in 1959–61, the Greek Archaeological Service performed rescue excavations at Kavala on the spot where G. Bakalakis in 1936 had identified the sanctuary of the Parthenos, a local deity.[11] From his excavations only three Chian fragments appeared in the reports: a rather large piece of a plate[12] and two fragments possibly from lekanai.[13] On the other hand from the work resumed by Lazaridis the most important pieces were mentioned in his Guide to the Kavala Museum and also exhibited; the best known of these are the spectacular column-crater[14] (Pls. 221–5), a nearly complete oenochoe[15] (Pl. 226), and two plate fragments[16] (Pl. 227.1 and 2). There is much more material in the storerooms, mostly fragments of lekanai.

Boardman at a very early stage[17] distinguished this group from Chian proper and after personal examination of the earlier excavated material from Thasos adopted the view that there must have been a workshop established locally.[18] Akurgal held the same opinion.[19] Robert Cook was reluctant in accepting the view of immigrant artists competing in a centre with a strong artistic pottery tradition of its own.[20] Walter-Karydi does not discriminate between Chian proper and this category in her classification of Chian proper; however, she had very little of the material available to her at the time so that only two vases appear in her Catalogue.[21]

F. Salviat, both in his early reports in the *BCH* and chiefly in his article "La céramique de style chiote à Thasos" in *CGED* 84–92 and pls. 45–52, recognised the peculiarity of these vases. Apart from presenting presumably the most significant pieces, he makes a few attributions to painters and singles out the special features of the category in a general manner. He proposed a workshop established in the North Aegean, hinting at Maroneia, Chios' colony, but with the evidence at hand he confines himself to Thasos, which he argues would also provide for its colonies on the Peraia.

---

[9] I would like to thank Dr. V. Solomonidis of the Greek Embassy, London, who had shown me the piece and also kindly allowed me to photograph and publish it. Cf. *Et.thas.* VII, Avant Propos (G. Daux) 5 note 1: "les fouilles clandestines, qui longtemps ont fait passer dans le commerce tant d'objets archéologiques (notamment sur le marché de Salonique), sont devenues tout-à-fait exceptionnelles".

[10] The sanctuary of Artemision was identified by Macridy and Reinach at the beginning of this century; the main excavations by F. Salviat and N. Weill took place in the years 1957–60 and after a long pause were restarted in 1975 and have continued ever since.

[11] G. Bakalakis, *Arch. Eph* 1936, 1ff; *Arch. Eph* 1938, 106ff; *PAE* 1937, 45–81; *PAE* 1938, 45ff and his article "Naucratite sherds from Kavala" in the *Aphieroma Eis Amanton*, 1940, 155–62.

[12] *PAE* 1937, 62–63, figs. 4 and 5. A piece definitely by the same painter, probably from the same vase, turned up years later in Lazaridis' excavations, see *BCH* 85, 1961, 833, fig. 4 upper row. (Kavala Museum A645, 646 on exhibit, and Lazaridis, *Guide* 107).

[13] *PAE* 1938, 78, fig. 4 no. 6 and 9 (in the middle).

[14] Kavala Museum A 985–6, on exhibit. Lazaridis, *Guide* 106, pl. 36 and see *Samos* VI. 1, pl. 93. 702 a–d.

[15] Kavala Museum A 1100, on exhibit. Lazaridis, *Guide* 109.

[16] Kavala Museum A 645, 646. Lazaridis, *Guide* 107 (see note 11, here). It is from the same vase, or Painter as *PAE* 1937, 62–63, figs. 4 and 5.

[17] *Emporio* 157 note 2. *Greek Emporio* was published in 1967 but most of it was written by 1960.

[18] Also in *CGED* 326 and *GO*[3] 232 and recently in *Chios Conference* 258 n. 14.

[19] Salviat quotes him in *CGED* 91 note 20.

[20] *GPP*[2] 141. Professor Cook, who kindly read an earlier draft of this chapter and made helpful comments, remains reluctant to accept the view of an immigrant pottery workshop established in a colony wherever that might be.

[21] *Samos* VI.1 69, and nos. 702 and 718.

Finally, D. Williams in his publication of the Chian material from the Aphaia temple on Aegina,[22] rightly gives precedence to style, draws parallels with unslipped vases unearthed on Chios, admittedly of a later date,[23] and tentatively puts forward a proposal for experimental workshop(s) on Chios.

From recent Turkish excavations at the modern town of Enez (or Enoz) on the right hand bank at the mouth of the Hebros river,[24] where the ancient Aeolian colony of Ainos[25] was identified, the majority of fragments recovered are of our category; some sixty of them have appeared up to now in the annual reports.[26] They are mostly, as expected, from open vases, plates and lekanai, and from their abundance amongst the pottery finds one can infer that they are the predominant ware.

The excavations of Ainos are continuing and full publication of the material is not yet expected; and that goes for the other sites of Thasos, Neapolis and Oesyme. It would have been very useful to learn first whether the vases uncovered at all four use the same clay, and second whether this clay is Chian, Thasian or from another source. A chemically tested uniformity and consequent clay source identification might have confirmed the stylistic analysis put forward here.

Clay analyses for Chian vases from Naucratis, Emporio and modern clay beds both on the island and in Chios town have confirmed their uniformity;[27] however, clay analyses of this particular ware have not been undertaken,[28] or at least have not been reported. It would also be necessary to test the clay of this category against local Thasian clays in order to determine whether it was manufactured there.

If one relies on more traditional ways, that is visual inspection combined with the use of the Munsell Chart,[29] one would conclude that the clay looks Chian both from its texture and because the Munsell measurements fall in the centre of the chromatic range of Chian clays, which are 5 YR 7/3 and 7/4 "pink", at least for the majority of the Kavala fragments.

---

[22] *AA* 1983, 155 ff.

[23] *Ibid.* 182. The unslipped black-figure kantharoi from Chios (*Emporio*, 168 nos. 838–841) and from Aegina (*AA* 1983, 170) and the unslipped black-figure chalice from Camirus in Copenhagen (**1617***), are of the third quarter of the sixth century or even later.

[24] *GO*³ 230.

[25] Ainos was colonized by inhabitants of Mytilene and Kyme in the seventh century, as *Strabo* VII, Fr. 51 informs us. Mentioned in the Homeric poems, *Il.* IV.520. See J Bérard, *L'expansion et la colonisation grecques jusqu'aux guerres médiques*, 1960, 94 and 95 with n. 6.

[26] Afif Erzen "Yili Enez Kazisi Çalişmalari" in:
   V   *Kazi Sonuçlari Toplantisi* 1983, 297–300, pls. 537–547. Sherds from our category, pl. 17 on p. 544 (9 sherds) and pl. 18 on p. 545 (1 sherd, bottom right).
   VI   *Kazi Sonuçlari Toplantisi* 1984, 213–234, pl. 1. 1–15 (15 sherds) on p. 225.
   VII   *Kazi Sonuçlari Toplantisi* 1985, 603–617, pl. 9 on p. 612 (11 sherds), pl. 10. 1, 2 on p. 612 (2 sherds) and pl. 11 on p. 612 (4 sherds).
   VIII   *Kazi Sonuçlari Toplantisi* II, 1986, 273–290, pl. 8. 2, 3, 5 on p. 281 (3 sherds).
   IX   *Kazi Sonuçlari Toplantisi* II, 1987, 279–297, pl. 3 on p. 286 (10 sherds).

Professor Boardman drew my attention to Vol. VII, 1985. See also, *AnatSt.* 1986, 190–3 and *ibid.* 1987, 187–8 for the excavations at Enez.

[27] See Introduction, p. 2 and notes 7–10.

[28] P. Dupont in *Dacia* 27, 1983, 24 refers to the stylistic analyses of L. Kahil in *Et.thas.* VII and F. Salviat's articles, which suggest "l'existence d'un atelier d'imitation sur l'île de Thasos". For figure-decorated pottery it is reasonably clear that chemical analyses only confirm what has been determined already by eye.

[29] The measurements in the Munsell chart were performed on sherds of the Kavala material. For the presence or absence of the slip or the use of a thin wash, apart from what I have observed for the Kavala vases myself, I use Salviat's description for the vases from Thasos.

The fine white *slip*, an indispensible element in all Chian vases of the first half of the sixth century, is a criterion of primary importance. However, in this category it cannot be viewed as a determining factor: sometimes because it is not used at all, or appears only as a rather thin wash. For yet others it is present in its canonical colour and texture. Three types of use can be distinguished:

To the first, with no slip at all, belong the Kavala column crater (Pls. 221–5) and the fragment of a lekane (Pl. 227.3): both from the sanctuary of the Parthenos at Neapolis.

To the second, where a thin wash is used, belong the following: *Et.thas*. VII, pl. 14. nos. 7 and 8 (Pl. 239.8 and 9) and pl. 13. nos. 18–23A and B (Pls. 234.2 and 239.3–7); *CGED* pl. 49.11 (Pl. 228.3–5), pl. 50.12 (Pl. 232.4), 13, 14 (Pl. 233.1 and 2), pl. 51.15 (Pl. 234.1) and pl. 52.18 and 19 (Pl. 230.1 and 2).

Finally in the third, with the characteristically fine white Chian slip,[30] are the Kavala oenochoe A1100 (Pl. 226), the plate fragments from both Bakalakis' and Lazaridis' excavations (Pl. 227.1 and 2) and *CGED* pl. 47.5 and 6 (Pls. 228.1 and 231.2) and pl. 48.8–8a and 9 (Pl. 232.1 and 2).

This factor of *fabric* could prove decisive and further research in this field is a sine qua non. However, Boardman's theory of the transport of Chian clay and slip could prove applicable in this case.

The *shapes* of the category do not all accord with the usual Chian repertoire. The column crater is a shape unknown to Chian proper.[31] The oenochoe is common to both; however the Kavala oenochoe (Pl. 226) does not find a ready parallel in Chian proper for two reasons: first, most Chian oenochoai are in a fragmentary condition and thus do not give profiles, and second, the only two intact Chian oenochoai from Rizari in the Wild Goat style (**324***) and from Pitane in the Sphinx and Lion style (**1433***) bear no close resemblance.[32] The profile of the Kavala vessel (Pl. 226) is widest two thirds up the body; the form of the neck and lips cannot be judged because they are lost. It is more elegant and slender and can be characterised as more piriform in contrast to Pitane (**1433***), which has a more globular body.

Plates are fairly common in both wares and start early in the case of Chian proper.[33] Lekanai and especially bowl-craters with offset lip and conical foot are not encountered in Chian, whereas they are quite common in contemporary Thasian, especially in the black-figure technique.[34] Finally, a terracotta statuette base from the Artemision of Thasos[35] painted in the style of this category finds no parallels in Chian pottery.

The absence of the lekane and bowl-crater from the range of Chian forms and their presence in local Thasian black figure form the basis for the argument that they were locally manufactured on Thasos.[36]

---

[30] I can confirm the presence of Chian slip on the Kavala vases of the third division.

[31] The example from Phana listed in *Samos* VI. 1, no. 701 = *ADelt* II, 1916, 204, fig. 23, which has not survived removal into the new Museum, looks late and of a different make.

[32] See FIG. 10 for the profile of the Rizari oenochoe (**324***).

[33] *Alt-Ägina* II. 1, pl. 5 no. 74.

[34] Salviat in *CGED* 89 note 10; 90 note 14 and 15 and 92 note 22 gives examples, to which add *BCH* 101, 1977, 690 fig. 47; *BCH* 103, 1979, 656, fig. 29; *BCH* 105, 1981, 945, fig. 32 and *BCH* 107, 1983, 838, fig. 26.

[35] Now fully published in N. Weill, *La Plastique archaïque de Thasos. Figurines et statues de terre cuite de l'Artemision. I. Le haut Archaïsme*, *Et.thas*. XI, 1985, 117–8, no. 109, pl. 27 a–e.

[36] *CGED* 91–2.

Fig. 105 Griffins, deer and cock

The *decoration* can be divided into figurative and ornamental. The former comprises a mythological scene, the first as yet in this category, and of course the usual animal world; the last closely resembles the Chian Wild Goat style, though the two are not contemporary. A few remarks point to certain differences which are perhaps not fortuitous.

1. The frequency of wild goats at a time—first half of the century—when they have fallen out of fashion in Chian proper.[37]
2. The preference for griffins (FIG. 105) demonstrated in the Kavala column crater and a plate from Artemision inv. 3997,[38] whereas their occurrence in Chian pottery is relatively rare. The fragmentary state of the certain Chian pieces—chalice fragments from Naucratis[39]—does not permit any stylistic comparisons.
3. The fallow deer (FIG. 105) on the Kavala column crater do not resemble the rare

---

[37] Mentioned in *CGED* 91.
[38] *CGED* pl. 47.5, (here Pl. 228.1).
[39] *CVA* Oxford II, pl. 396.4 and BM 1888.6–1.199 and BM 1888–6–1.472k. Here **218***, **437***, **456***. But if we are to compare them with the griffin on the Old Smyrna oenochoe (Izmir Museum 3333 = Akurgal, *Alt-Smyrna* I, 1983, 48, pl. 38–9 and Text-plates B and C; also, *Catalogue Istanbul* 1983, 29, B65) once considered Chian and now most probably from the pottery workshop of Old Smyrna, it is at once evident that it is of a different type from the ones in the category under discussion.

examples on Chian pots. However fallow deer are more frequent in Thasian reserving styles.[40]

4. The siren is completely unknown to the category, though Chian reserving styles of the time do not ignore it.

5. The existence of the cock (FIG. 105) on lekane no. 2141 from the Artemision[41] and probably on two other fragments from Thasos.[42] The creature is unprecedented on Chian pots of the reserving styles in general. Chian cocks are a completely different breed, restricted to the black-figure "Poultry group", which is of a much later date.[43]

The grouping and stances of animals display a wider variety than in Chian Wild Goat style; apart from the standardised processional, sometimes the antithetical, the back to back position is also much used. Sphinxes and boars populate the friezes more commonly. Playful attitudes are not abandoned; an example is on the bowl-crater, inv. no. 2143, from Thasos,[44] where a lion raises its right foreleg perhaps to tease the preceding bull on the upper frieze of the vessel, and the last goat on the left is rearing ready to jump over a floral on the lower frieze.

However, the processional goats—heading always to the right and occupying an entire frieze, usually the lower as is usual in Wild Goat—are an inherent Chian habit, or rather a general practice in this style.[45]

The sole mythological scene is displayed on the upper frieze of the Kavala column crater (Pls. 223 and 225) and identified generally as the Calydonian boar hunt.[46] According to Schnapp's recent study of scenes in Corinthian and Athenian black figure of the sixth century[47] this example presents only one of his iconographical criteria: the dogs attacking the boar from the front, behind and beneath. A large piece of the vase is missing and one cannot judge therefore whether there was a dog on the back of the beast. The lack of symmetry[48] could be forgiven in a provincial workshop, which would not always obey the canons set by Corinth and Athens. The iconographical element of the dogs' disposition and the hunters' offensive weapons, spears and tridents,[49] could perhaps persuade one of the scene's identification, but uncertainty on this point has already been indicated.[50]

The *ornamental decoration* of this category comprises mainly dividing bands (FIG. 106) and filling ornament (FIG. 108). Many are either wholly Chian or very close to them, though

---

[40] See *Samos* VI.1, pl. 101.862, 863 and 874 and pl. 102.865.

[41] *CGED* pl. 49.11, (here Pl. 228.3–5).

[42] *BCH* 87, 1963, 854, fig. 13.8 (*CGED* 90 and note 17) and also *Et.thas.* VII, pl. 2 no. 22 (noted by Salviat in *BCH* 87, 1963, 853).

[43] See pp. 173–5.

[44] *CGED* pl. 52.18, (here Pl. 230.1).

[45] Examples are the Kavala oenochoe (Pl. 226); *BCH* 83, 1959, 785, fig. 14; *CGED* 90, pl. 51.17.

[46] Lazaridis, *Guide* 106; Salviat in *CGED* 91 and Hemelrijk, *Caeretan Hydriae* 185.

[47] Schnapp in *RA* 1979, 195 ff. See also G. Daltrop, *Die Kalydonische Jagd in der Antike*, 1966 and *LIMC* II.1 s.v. Atalante 940–942 and 948.

[48] See P. de la Coste-Messelière, *La Musée de Delphes*, 1936, 132, but cf. p. 144 on the intentional asymmetry.

[49] Tridents figure in many Athenian Calydonian boar hunt scenes, for example the band cup by Archikles and Glaukytes, in Munich, Antikensammlungen 2243, from Vulci, see *ABV* 163.2 and *BAdd*² 47 and M. Ohly-Dumm, *Attische Vasenbilder der Antikensammlungen in München nach Zeichnungen von Karl Reichhold*, Band I, 1975, pl. 3, p. 13. And on side B of a merrythought cup from Sardis, N.H. Ramage, *AJA* 87, 1983, pl. 65, fig. 6. There are many more examples.

[50] See F. Brommer, *Vasenlisten zur griechischen Heldensage* 1973³, 315 no. 17, where the scene is classified amongst those whose meaning is dubious.

others are of uncertain nature. The clearly Chian ornaments are the SS bands vertically or horizontally disposed, the bands of squares with dotted blanks, the bands with filled squares flanked by two lines, the tongues, the rays with dotted rosettes between—an ornament excessively used in Chian, the friezes of lotus and bud,[51] the complex double meander alternating with squared crosses, the simple guilloche with either eyes in the centre or spikes at the corner and the double guilloche.

Ornamental decoration in this category is not restricted to the usual set. It employs also a few new ornaments, such as:

a) Bands with alternating bars

b) Bands with alternating bars and dots between

c) Bands with opposed bars and dots

Fig. 106 Dividing bands

All these are well attested on Athenian black figure vases of at least a generation before and are practised by painters of the Nessos workshop, the master himself and the Panther painter;[52] but one need not go so far afield. All three are variations of the same pattern, which derives from the Chian *step pattern with bars in the bays*; this is not encountered on vases, but found on bronze belts (FIG. 107) at Emporio.[53] The pattern is simple and can be varied easily. Since it can be traced on Chian works, even in a slightly different form and use, it might well be considered Chian, or Chianising in the extreme.

Fig. 107 Bronze belts from Emporio (*Emporio* pls. 88.279 and 90.314. Courtesy of Professor Sir John Boardman)

[51] Mainly of *GPP*² fig. 19 type C: Late Wild Goat style: early 6th cent. BC.; but now many of the Ainos fragments display friezes of lotus and bud, *GPP*² fig. 19 type A: Middle Wild Goat *c.* 630–600 BC. and it seems that from this and other ornamental features the Ainos material is slightly earlier.

[52] See A.A. Lemos in *BCH* Suppl. (ed. by J. Perreault), forthcoming.

[53] *Emporio* 104 and 214 and fig. 140. Also, cf. Polyxena's paryphe-pattern on the Troilos chalice **800***.

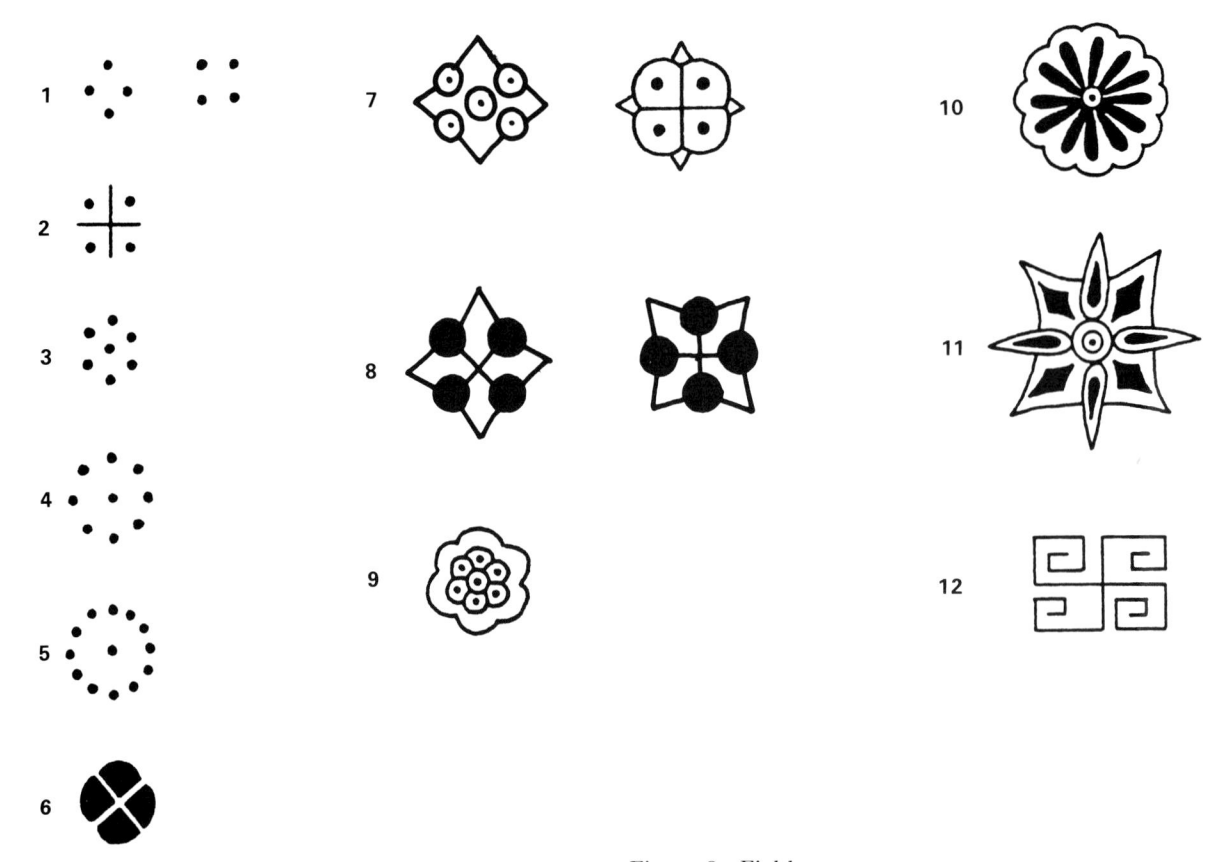

Fig. 108 Field ornaments

In the filling ornament, pendants are exactly the same in both wares[54] and retain the scheme of triangles below the forelegs and roundels below hindlegs of goats. All vases in this category, even the mythological scene on the upper frieze of the Kavala column crater, use field ornaments. Most are dotted circles and various forms of rosettes. The swastika appears rarely. They are collected in FIG. 108. They are fundamental to the differentiation of the two stylistic groups.

Types 1–6 of the rosette and **type 12**, the swastika, are universally found in all Archaic workshops.

Types 7–9, either as illustrated or in slightly different variations, are used in Chian Wild Goat from the Middle I phase.

Type 10 could be considered as a more slender translation of the Würzburg chalice rosette, or the floral ornament below the Emporio tripod bowl (**259***) and is more frequently met in North Ionia.[55]

---

[54] Examples picked at random:
  a) Triangles: compare *CGED* pl. 48.9 to **236***, **237***, **252***.

  b) Roundels: compare *CGED* pl. 48.9 to **1286***.

[55] *Samos* VI.1, pl. 111. 914.

Type 11 is a creation of the workshop and is not encountered in Chian in exactly the same form. Nevertheless, it could be considered a transformation of the central floral on the inside of the Aphrodite bowl (**252***).

Salviat attributed certain vases to individual hands.[56] With the material not properly published[57] and yet more to come,[58] any stylistic groups suggested here are of a provisional character. However with the material at hand two stylistic groups can be distinguished.

Group A: The Kavala column crater group consists of:
1. The Kavala column crater, (Pls. 221–5).
2. Lekane inv. no. 2141 from Thasos, (*CGED* pl. 49.11), (Pl. 228.2–5).
3. Bowl crater inv. no. 2056, with an incised dedicatory inscription to Athena, from the Athenaion on Thasos, (*CGED* pl. 51.16 and also *Et.thas*. XI, 1985, 117, fig. 52), (Pl. 229.1).[59]
4. Bowl-crater inv. no. 4020 from Thasos, (*CGED* pl. 51.17), (Pl. 229.2).
5. Bowl-crater inv. no. 2143 from Thasos, (*CGED* pl. 52.18), (Pl. 230.1).
6. Bowl-crater inv. no. 2144 from Thasos, (*CGED* pl. 52.19), (Pl. 230.2).
7. Plate fragment from Thasos in London, (Pl. 231.1).

Stylistically very close to the group are:
1. The Kavala oenochoe A1100, (Pl. 226).
2. Plate fragments A645, 646 from Lazaridis', (Pl. 227.1 and 2) and
3. Bakalakis' excavations (*PAE* 1934, 62–3, figs. 4–5). (If not same vase, then same painter).
4. Lekane fragment from the Artemision on Thasos, (*BCH* 101, 1977, 690, fig. 48), (Pl. 238.1).
5. Plate from Thasos, (*CGED* pl. 47.6), (Pl. 231.2).
6. Lekane from Thasos, (*CGED* pl. 48.8–8a), (Pl. 231.1).
7. Lekane inv. no. 3993 from Thasos, (*CGED* pl. 48g), (Pl. 232.2).

The drawing of figures, both human and animal, is very elaborate and bears a close resemblance to figures in both the Animal Chalice and the Grand styles. The warrior on **724*** is a good parallel but not the only one. Other figures, on **702***, **727***, **763**, **772***, **797*** and **830*** approximate in facial details to the hunters of the Calydonian boar hunt scene, especially in the receding foreheads, the curved line for the nostril and the summary rendering of arms and hands. The whirligig pattern as a shield device on the last hunter's shield is the same as that used for the warrior's shield on **732***. The border of the shield—dotted squares alternating with black squares—is shared by the first hunter on the column crater and the warrior on **761***. In the filling ornament, **type 7**, common to this group, is

---

[56] Salviat *CGED* 89–91, attributed pl. 49.11 and pl. 52.19 to one hand, and together with the Kavala column crater to a single group.

[57] See p. 209.

[58] In all four sites, Kavala, Thasos, Nea Peramos and Enez excavations are continuing.

[59] *Et. thas* XI, 1985, 117, fig. 52 and J. Boardman in *The Classical Review* 1987, 323 (local, though Chios inspired).

met on the Grand style chalices. Examples picked at random are **698*** and **769***. **Type 9**, again common in the group, is also well-attested on vases of the Grand style. Examples are **768*** and **774***. **Type 11** has evolved from Chian Wild Goat Middle II and from rosettes figuring as shield devices, as on **698*** and **724*** from Naucratis and **800*** from Pitane. Animals need not be compared with the contemporary Chian vases, as they are so similar in style, especially the lions, sphinxes, bulls,[60] and boars.

This group is interesting, because it mixes conservative—or at least, old fashioned—elements with new, or even unknown, ones. On the one hand, it still makes use of wild goats: on the Kavala oenochoe (Pl. 226), on the bowl craters from Thasos[61] in rows, and elsewhere isolated, while retaining the Middle II practice of dotted bellies on most animals, especially on sphinxes which by this time are rarely dotted in the Chian reserving styles.[62] On the other hand, the frequency of griffins and the appearance of the cock are new.

Group B: The Thasos lekanai group:
1. Lekane from Thasos, (*Et.thas.* VII, pl. 13.19.), (Pl. 232.3).
2. Lekane from Thasos, (*CGED* pl. 50.12.), (Pl. 232.4).
3. Lekane from Thasos, (*CGED* pl. 50.13.), (Pl. 233.1).
4. Lekane from Thasos, (*CGED* pl. 50.14.), (Pl. 233.2).
5. Lekane from Thasos, (*CGED* pl. 51.15.), (Pl. 234.1).

Stylistically very close:
1. Plate from Thasos, (*CGED* pl. 47.5.), (Pl. 228.1).
2. Lekane from Thasos, (*Et.thas.* VII, pl. 13.18.), (Pl. 234.2).
3. Lekane from Thasos, (*CGED* pl. 49.10.), (Pl. 234.4).
4. Fragment, possibly from a lekane from Thasos (road to the theatre), (*BCH* 105, 1981, 949, fig. 41 (upper row)), (Pl. 234.3).

In this group the use of rosette **type 8** is a trademark. Also the frequent use of **type 6**, which is encountered also in variations, on the very fragmentary material from Ainos.[63]

The drawing of the animals is slightly less meticulous; overlapping of figures with bands might perhaps betray a more aged or tired hand. The stylistic unity of the first five pieces is so close in both the details of the animals and in the placing of the filling ornament that I think they are the work of one painter, whose "signature" is this type (**8**) of rosette. The other four pieces are closely connected.[64]

The *dating* of this category depends only on style and comparisons drawn with the not altogether safely dated Chian proper. The excavators, both French and Greek, mention

---

[60] Venit, *Egypt. Museums* 35–6, attributes to the same painter her no. 127, pl. 32 (here **606***) and two fragments from Thasos in this category—*CGED* pl.48, figs. 8–8a (here Pl.232.1) and *CGED* pl. 50, fig. 13 (here Pl.233.1). All bulls in Chian painted pottery have a superficial resemblance, closer study is needed to tell them apart stylistically. In addition, the two pieces from Thasos do not belong to the same stylistic group. For Venit's book, see now the review by Boardman in *Gnomon*, forthcoming.

[61] *CGED* pl. 51 nos. 16 and 17, (here Pl. 229.1 and 2).

[62] This practice recurs only periodically on some late and degenerate examples, e.g. **938***.

[63] See V. *Kazi Sonuçlari Toplantisi* 1983, pl. 17.2 on p. 544. This very same **type 6** rosette with a cross in the middle appears on another fragment, see, *ibid.* 1984, pl. 1.10 on p. 225.

[64] See *BCH* 89, 1965, 956, fig. 15 for a Thasian lekane in reserving style with a lion's head, a dotted rosette and a **type 6** rosette which looks influenced in style by this group.

that vases of this category were found in Archaic strata:[65] a general term that covers a wide span of time and is unprofitable for our purposes. One has to content oneself, at present, with stylistic parallels, a few of which have been mentioned. Comparisons have also been drawn with the Troilos chalice (**800***), which was found in a tomb at Pitane together with an Athenian Komast cup.[66] This internal evidence points to a date within the first quarter of the sixth century and probably towards its end: that is, the decade 580 to 570 B.C. with a possible margin of error either way of another decade.[67]

The *general character of the style*, as distinguished by the specific deviations discussed above, should make anyone sceptical of production on the island of Chios. Even Williams' conjecture that "it is really the unslipped pieces that are unusual" and his proposal "but these could always represent the products of a rather more experimental workshop or workshops",[68] which seem prima facie ingenious as a middle position, cannot be sustained because closer examination of the material makes its premise untenable. Leaving aside the island of Chios, fragments of this category have been recovered only in the coastal sites of East Macedonia and Thrace and not as yet on the numerous sites overseas[69] where Chian figurative pottery is distributed. If an experimental workshop existed on Chios, was it just producing "bespoke" vases exclusively for export to a specific area?

The arguments that speak for the category's independence are to my mind stronger and lead to the opinion that a group of immigrant Chian potters and painters established themselves in the region and produced vases of this category. Vases not only of the reserving technique but, as will be shown in black figure were also manufactured. The factors that argue for this view are in brief: first, the proveniences: limited to three coastal sites in East Macedonia and Thrace (Oesyme, Neapolis, Ainos), and to the island of Thasos, in combination with their complete absence in the wide distribution of Chian figurative pottery elsewhere.

Secondly, the shapes: some are unknown in the canonical Chian output, others either have closer ties to Thasian black figure, as evidenced by the lekanai and bowl-craters, or are influenced by Corinthian and Athenian, as in the case of the column crater.

Thirdly, slight differentiations and peculiarities in the decoration outside the Chian norm, described above in full detail.

Fourthly, style, which, to a certain extent, permits groupings, and even the very probable identification of painters.

The argument based on fabric cannot be conclusive; not merely because Chian clay and slip could be transported, but also because the absence of slip, or the use of a thin wash, is not a definitive feature for distinguishing the stylistic groups.

---

[65] Though the ex-voto finds from the Artemision on Thasos are generally dated from the second half of the seventh century to the second quarter of the sixth in the first reports, see *BCH* 52, 1958, 808.

[66] See Bayburtluoğlu in *CGED* 20 (KX Painter) and also Greenewalt Diss. 1966, 190–1, pl. IX A.C.D. For the Athenian Komast Cups, see now H.A.G. Brijder, *Siana Cups I and Komast Cups* 1983. Unfortunately, the tombs from Pitane are not yet published; however Bakir has attributed the Athenian Komast cup, which was found with the Troilos chalice, to the KY Painter: see G. Bakir, Pitane, Daskyleion, ve Phokaia' da bulunmus, Alti Attika Kyliksi ni 1963–64, *Bitirume Tezi*, no. 7166, pp. 3–4. Bayburtluoğlu, however, refers to this cup as by the KX Painter in *CGED* 29.

[67] As suggested now by the fresh material from Ainos, which displays quite frequently the Middle II Wild Goat style lotus and bud frieze.

[68] *AA* 1983, 182.

[69] See Chapter 6, on Distribution.

A fifth and valid argument could be drawn from the very strong impact that this workshop had in the whole area. It is, of course, better understood on Thasian black-figure vases, because of the volume of material excavated and published. Arguably this Chian workshop produced vases in the black-figure technique as well. They are as yet very few, not well known and can be easily confused with what is considered Thasian:[70]

1. Plate from Artemision on Thasos, (*CGED*, pl. 46.3.), (Pl. 235.1).
2. Stand inv. nos. 2688 and 2689 from Artemision on Thasos, (*CGED* pl. 46.4), (Pl. 235.2).
3. Lekane fragment from Thasos, (*Et. thas.* VII, pl. 13.24.), (Pl. 236.1).
4. Lekane fragment from Thasos, (*Et. thas.* VII, pl. 13.25.), (Pl. 236.2).
5. Lekane fragment from Thasos, (*Et. thas.* VII, pl. 13.25 bis.), (Pl. 236.3).
6. Lid from the Sanctuary of the Parthenos at Neapolis, (Kavala Museum inv. no. 1094, Lazaridis, *Guide* 108), (Pl. 236.4). The animals on it approximate in style to Group A of the Kavala Column crater.
7. Plate 80.575.23 + 579.15, (*BCH* 105, 1981, 944, fig. 27.), (Pl. 237).

The last is an important fragment which was found at the Artemision of Thasos in the excavations of 1980 and I think it reinforces our view. A wholly Chian komast is drawn with the characteristically saw-edged band across his chest and is associated with a sphinx and other animals amidst a field filled with Chian rosettes of very meticulous execution. In front of the komast there is a dinos, with a stand, on top of which are placed on the right an oenochoe and on the left a drinking cup, whose resemblance to the sixth-century type of the Chian chalice is undeniable. This clearly Chian picture with its purely native elements—komast, rosettes, chalice—supports most strongly the view that Chians were at work *somewhere* in East Macedonia and Thrace fabricating and selling their vases to the neighbouring towns.[71] The close interrelation of shapes has suggested influence from Thasian black-figure wares and the place of manufacture has already been claimed to be Thasos,[72] but I doubt whether the workshop was established there. The connection with Thasian pottery has been overestimated, perhaps owing to the statistically overwhelming quantities of fine ware from Thasos. Why would a group of immigrant Chian craftsmen choose a place with good quality pottery of its own, where resistance might have been considerable?[73]

In the light of this objection can any other centre(s) be proposed? A suitable starting point would be somewhere with strong Chian connections—a colony, par excellence. There is one to hand, indeed the only one ever credited to Chian enterprise, in Maroneia. The evidence for this, it is admitted, is literary and historical and does not touch on pottery production; direct supporting archaeological confirmation is yet to appear, for though

---

[70] The first five fragments were singled out by Salviat in *CGED* 88. However, *Et.thas.* VII, 37–38, 14 bis and 14 ter, (Istanbul, nos. 5284 and 5285), here **1311***, is in the Sphinx and Lion style proper.

[71] The vases of this category in the reserving technique are still called, not unjustifiably, by their excavators *pseudochiotes*. The black-figure vases of the Chian East Macedonian-Thracian workshop are very easily confused with Thasian black figure; in fact, it is hard to distinguish Thasian black figure, which is influenced by Chian styles in general, and the products of our workshop, which as it seems adopts certain Thasian features. With so limited available material the interrelation is yet difficult to define.

[72] *CGED* 91–92.

[73] *GPP*[2] 141, R.M. Cook writes: "It seems unlikely that several distinct and competing styles were being practised without serious contamination in a single place, even if the practitioners were immigrant craftsmen who arrived with their styles already formed".

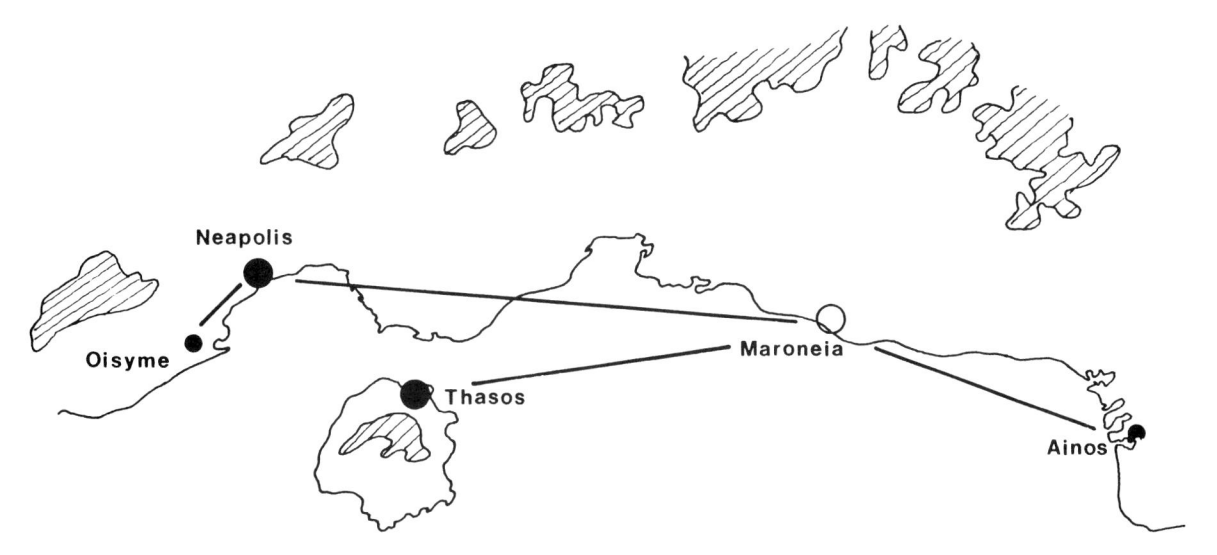

Fig. 109 Distribution map

excavation has enabled the identification of the site as ancient Maroneia,[74] it has not yet reached any Archaic levels. This prosperous city[75] with arable land and access to the silver mines of Mount Pangaeum[76] was founded in the seventh century by Chians, who would have undoubtedly imported their ceramics from home at first. Later a pottery workshop is quite likely to have been established with its craftsmen—potters and painters—drawn from Chios. It seems probable that they brought with them both material (clay and slip) and the style they had been trained in, as the black-figure pieces explicitly indicate. However, they had to adjust to the demands of the local market. The presence at Ainos of the pottery of this workshop as the predominant ware is a crucial link in the discussion, and it might reasonably be argued to attest a Chian "daughter factory" in the region. A ready candidate for such would be the Chian colony of Maroneia, in an area encircled by sites known to be using this ware (FIG. 109).

Older excavations at the beginning of the century at Maroneia[77] had brought to light a few pieces of sculpture of mediocre quality and late date, amongst which was a votive relief in the form of a Kybele naiskos.[78] Kybele's cult[79] and her naiskoi are well attested on

---

[74] See *PAE* 1971, 101–118 to *PAE* 1983, 27–9. The excavations have uncovered a theatre of the third century B.C., a sanctuary of the second half of the fourth century B.C., a Hellenistic edifice and a cemetery which is dated from the fourth century B.C. to the Roman times and finally various ruins of the late Roman and Byzantine era. See also, D. Lazaridis, *Maroneia and Orthagoria* in *Ancient Greek Cities, Athens Centre of Ekistics*, 16, 1972, p. 10 with figs. 21 and 22 for the Archaic period. Several stamped amphora handles with ΘΑΣΙΩΝ were recently found at Maroneia, see *PAE* 1982, 1984, 30 and *Supplementum Epigraphicum Graecum*, 1988, 225 no. 815.

[75] Σκύμνος ὁ Χῖος, Ἡ Περιήγησις 678 on the foundation of Maroneia. Maroneia is referred to in the Homeric poems and the Lyrics, *Il.* IX.71–2; *Od.* IX.126–8; Archil *F2D* and Philochorus *FGH* 328 F43; also Hdt. VII, 109 refers to it, and later on Strabo VII, 331, Frg. 44 ff. and Diod I 18.20. See J. Bérard, *L'Expansion et la colonisation grecques jusqu'aux guerres médiques*, 1960, 95 and n. 4 and *GO*³ 230.

[76] Roebuck, *Ionian Trade* 136 and recently Roebuck in *Chios Conference*, 83–4 for the trading of Chians with Egypt and Thrace and specifically access to the silver mines through Maroneia, but cf. Austin, *Greece and Egypt*, 40, who finds the evidence incomplete for the triangular trading relations between Egypt, East Greece and Thrace in general.

[77] *AA* 33, 1918, 34–47.

[78] *Ibid.* 39 fig. 45.

[79] F. Graf, *Nordionische Kulte, Religionsgeschichtliche und epigraphische Untersuchungen zu den Kulten von Chios, Erythrai, Klazomenai und Phokaia*, 1985, 107 ff.

Chios[80] and generally in East Greece from the late Archaic period, of the late sixth and early fifth century B.C. Conceivably, then, there is an echo here of an earlier attachment in the colony's history.

The proposal is speculative; but Maroneia is the only plausible candidate for the place where a Chian workshop could have been established towards the end of the first quarter of the sixth century, roughly two to three generations after the first colonists had settled. However, adjustments had to be made to the demands of a local market, by which certain Thasian characteristics were absorbed. From the centre of Maroneia, traces of a trading network may be detected in the sites in its neighbourhood.

Archaeological excavation and clay analyses are required to confirm this line of approach and convert these points from plausible to more secure.

[80] F. Naumann, *Die Ikonographie der Kybele in der phrygischen und griechischen Kunst*, 28 Beih. *IstMitt.* 1983, 129 and Cat. nos. 56 and 56a and p. 150–2 and Cat. No. 119. See also Graf, *ibid.* 108 and note 8 and recently V.v. Graeve in *Archaische und Klassische griechische Plastik*, ed. H. Kyrieleis, 1986, Band I, 21.

8

THE CHARACTER OF CHIAN VASE PAINTING

The general impression of the character of Chian vase painting that emerges after the detailed discussion and analysis of the various fine-ware styles is that of a severe and strictly disciplined school. The mannerisms, and indeed virtues, of its pioneer painters in their prime lie mainly in their predilection for a refined line in figure drawing and in their preference for ornament which ultimately contributes to a *painterly manner* in their work. Linear and at times angular contours bestow a degree of rigidity to the figures, which yet coexists with a deliberate and more relaxed attitude towards their decorative embellishment. A love for colourful and at times even vivid representation, ultimately expressed in the polychrome vases, might be considered a quality native to their approach—the outcome of a long tradition traceable in embryo as far back as Geometric times.[1] This trait finds particular expression in the interior decoration of all open sixth-century vessels. Here the stiffness of the figure drawing is combined and balanced against a highly ornamented background to produce the especial character of the overall Chian approach to vase painting in the Archaic period.

On present evidence, Chian vase painting can be divided into four *mainstream workshops on the island*, and two potential *external ones*.

Of the island centres, the *first* undoubtedly derives from the Geometric period. It involves too the production of plain wares in general and the well-defined seventh-century patterned chalices in particular. At around the turn of the seventh/sixth centuries, the fundamental evolution of the chalice shape took place. Production then continues for the greater part of the sixth century with the Chalice style, within which the plain chalices are a class. The reason for including the undecorated chalices here was their inseparable connection with the finer wares, to which they seem to have been companion pieces in the market-place and elsewhere. The saw-edged handle zone pattern is the constant trademark of this workshop.

The *second* centre began production around the middle of the seventh century: it expressed an East Greek style highly en vogue in those days—the Wild Goat style. Late Wild Goat groups and the revamped Animal Chalice style follow on. From the periphery of this workshop's sphere of activity, albeit under the inspiration of a more creative mind, the Grand style then appears. This derivation is supported specifically by points like handle zone and inner decorative patterns being shared between the styles and the comparable mixing of humans with animals (as on **458***).

---

[1] For some early examples, see *Emporio* 119 and pl. 32.200–1 kantharoi, (here Pl. 240.3); 123 and pl. 37.298–302 group A of tall cups; and pl. 47.537 oenochoe (here Pl. 240.2).

The *third* workshop is that producing the Sphinx and Lion style, under definite influence from Corinthian vase painters and also involving shapes new to the Chian ceramic tradition.

The *fourth* took up the last's technique of decoration, and developed a further series of black-figure categories—all, in fact, except the Komast and black-figure Animal Chalices, which are argued in Chapter 4 to be part of the first workshop's output. This was perhaps the longest tradition to survive, running approximately on down to the end of the Archaic era: its last gasp, translated into broader Archaic mannerisms, is on the ivy-patterned vases, mainly chalices, of the early fifth century.

The above-mentioned four workshops were all active on the island of Chios. It seems additionally probable that two more Chian centres were established outside these limits.

The *first*, in business in the earlier part of the sixth century, operated from somewhere in the region of the North Aegean. Unpublished, yet very significant, material both from Kavala and from the recently opened excavations at Enez render Thasos, despite its artistic links with North Ionia, an unlikely candidate. It is here tentatively proposed, wholly on literary and historical evidence, that the workshop's headquarters be sought in Maroneia.[2] The *second* external production centre of the second quarter of the sixth century would perhaps be that argued to have been established at Naucratis, turning out the well-known and much discussed class of the inscribed kantharoi. The view[3] that considers these last as made at Naucratis with imported Chian clay and slip is founded on three arguments. First, that such pieces were not found on Chios; second, that the bespoken inscriptions of their dedicators' names makes more plausible the local production of a cheap, votive class, which was in great demand, as it seems, including by the local pious hetairai; amongst these last—significantly—is the ethnic, Aigyptis. Lastly, from the fact that Aegina, although on hostile terms with Chios, has yet produced an abundance of this material. The two associates, Aristophantos and Damonidas (apparently Aeginetan merchants), the argument goes, would have found this trade easier to conduct with—say—Naucratis than directly with Chios. At present, this bespoke class of vases appears to offer the best support for the argument that a workshop existed in Egypt.

These two ventures overseas must represent considerable enterprise by Chian emigrants. Later, known instances of emigrant potters establishing workshops, though perhaps for rather different reasons, can be found in those various Ionian wares in Italy in the second half of the sixth century.[4]

Chian painted pottery has been found mainly associated with sanctuaries and in more limited quantities from cemeteries. Sure examples from settlements, as at Old Smyrna, are relatively rare. This weighting in their provenance and the argued functions of these vases give the impression that Chian *fine* pottery was not primarily used as an everyday commodity, but rather was restricted to the milieu of the temple, as a *votive*, or of the grave, as a gift or the like. Their potential usefulness as tableware at symposia cannot be ruled out completely, yet their good surface preservation in general might not be consistent with

---

[2] See Chapter 7.
[3] J. Boardman in *Chios Conference* 253–8 with fresh arguments after the publication of the material from Aphaia on Aegina; see also D. Williams, *AA* 1983, 155–86.
[4] Eg. the Caeretan hydriai, the Campana dinoi and the Northampton group.

such lively use. If this role as votive and funerary accessory is accepted, then it is the coarser, plain or linear-decorated wares that will have answered the daily needs.

Chian painted pottery was not made merely for home-consumption. Its presence at eighty-one sites around the Mediterranean world, and beyond, exactly matches the *distribution pattern* of other leading East Greek wares, and leads to the conclusion that it was an admired and desirable 'international' commodity.[5] The amounts recovered in some places, in relation to other wares, argue the existence of considerable trading contacts to support such demands.

Overall *dating* has been gleaned from stratified deposits first—mainly at Emporio, Tocra, Cyrene and Old Smyrna, and, more importantly, from the contexts of tombs, basically at Tarentum, Rhitsona and Pitane, where the better-understood Athenian and Corinthian series is of assistance in establishing relative associations. Such provide the stable points from which is deduced the interrelated web of relationships on which, in turn, matters concerning the evolution for the various styles, categories, groups and painters are all ultimately based.

During this particular period the *external impact* of the Chian school was not to be despised. The extreme case of the exquisite, polychrome hydria of the Samian artist who, between *c.* 590–80, worked under heavy Chian influence is indeed isolated.[6] More usual is a more selective response: for Thasos such occurred, arguably, from the category believed to have been made at Maroneia, of which examples have turned up at Thasos, Kavala, Oesyme and Ainus. Similar circumstances should account for the finds at Aeolian and other North Ionian centres, though here the contact was with Chios direct. Later, at the end of the sixth century, a return brought North Ionian, basically Clazomenian, traits to bear on the late black-figure Chian vases, of which a striking example is the Copenhagen chalice from Camirus (**1617***).

Even the southern East Greek region did not escape altogether. Thus, an isolated sherd from Labraunda, with a lion fighting a bull (Pl. 243.1),[7] directly imitates the Sphinx and Lion style. More indirectly, an as yet not well-known group, perhaps from near Miletus,[8] stands witness.

Chian vase painting is, it has to be admitted, the product of an undoubtedly provincial school—not only if compared to the obviously greater and more innovative centres of Corinth and Athens, but even with those at Laconia or on the various Cycladic islands. Nonetheless, as the leading centre of North Ionian art during the Archaic era it developed an individual and well-defined character. The interest in establishing a more natural and realistic standard of portrayal, evident—if hesitantly—in the attempts at foreshortening seen in human limbs in the Grand style, and the especially refined line for attempting such

---

[5] *GO*³ 158.
[6] H. Kyrieleis in *Chios Conference* 194.
[7] *Labraunda* II.3, 12 and 29, pl. 39.42 (here Pl. 243.1).
[8] A list of this group is given by R.M. Cook in *Festschrift Akurgal, Anadolu (Anatolia)* xxi 1978/1980, 1987, 74 note 8, to which the oenochoe that recently appeared on the London market, Charles Ede Ltd. *Corinthian and East Greek Pottery* VII, 8.3.1990, no. 29, can now be added. For discussions of this newly-recovered group, see Cook, *ibid.* 72–3; G.P. Schaus, *BSA* 81, 1986, 290–1 and E.A. Hemelrijk, *BABesch* 62, 1987, 33–55. Schaus and Hemelrijk independently reached the same conclusion of a provincial Carian workshop imitating East Greek Orientalising pottery.

work, represent the outward manifestation of the essential core of the painters' artistic endeavour. Thus, Chios makes its own modest contribution towards the creation of the artistic splendours achieved in the subsequent Classical Age of Greece.

The fact that the findspot of a Chian plain sixth-century chalice, from tombs near Miletus in Caria, is probably held in common with the above—see the same lot on the London market, Charles Ede Ltd., *ibid.* no.25—could lead to two conclusions of value: first, that the dating of this provincial West Anatolian group belongs to the mid-sixth century, and that it was influenced by Chian fine pottery.

CATALOGUE

EXPLANATORY NOTE

The Catalogue is arranged with bibliographical references for vases and fragments published or for some, occasionally, illustrated or even reported in periodicals. For the hitherto unpublished material, deriving mainly from Naucratis, Rizari in Chios town and certain sites in Anatolia a short description is given; also for all vases and fragments in the Grand style; and whenever, for various reasons, a new description was thought to be needed. I have also listed such vases and sherds, Chian in my eyes, that I have observed in certain museums and which still await publication: most of them accordingly lack inventory numbers, dimensions, description or illustration.

The material is presented first by the technique of decoration, next by style, then by shape and finally by sites, working in a clockwise direction around the Mediterranean. Concerning vases and sherds from Naucratis, the scheme followed opens with those from the British Museum and other museums in Great Britain, secondly museums in the United States, thirdly those in Germany, fourthly in the rest of Europe and lastly museums in Egypt and Australia.

The criterion for the classification is the decoration on the outside of the vase. To give an example: **1075*** from Tocra is classified in the Chalice style: B. Patterned Phialai Mesomphaloi, on account of its external decoration. Had it on the other hand been wished to order it according to its inner decoration, it would have gone to the Chalice style: D. with floral decoration.

All dimenstions are in centimetres; usually, they record unless otherwise stated, the greatest width of the fragment when correctly positioned. As regards most of the vases exhibited in the Archaeological museums of Istanbul, Bergama, Izmir and Selçuk dimensions are roughly estimated by eye.

The items illustrated in the Plates of Volume II are indicated with an asterisk *.

ABBREVIATIONS

Alexandria	Graeco-Roman Museum of Alexandria, Egypt
BM	British Museum
Chios Mus.	Archaeological Museum of Chios
Dec.	decoration
Diam.	diameter
Est. Diam.	estimated diameter
fig.	figure
fill. orns.	filling ornaments
fr.	fragment
frs.	fragments
H.	height
inv. no.	inventory number
l.	left
MMA	Metropolitan Museum of Art, New York
Oxf.	Oxford, Ashmolean Museum
pl.	plate
r.	right
ROM	Royal Ontario Museum, Toronto
sph.	sphinx
sphs.	sphinxes
UCD	University College, Dublin
UCL	University College, London
UM Philadelphia	University Museum, Philadelphia
W.	width

CONTENTS

Chapter 1: The Patterned chalices of the seventh century	1*–109*
Chapter 2: The Wild Goat style	110*–418*
I. CHALICES	110*–247*
II. BOWLS	
A. *Bowls*	248–251*
B. *Open bowls with out-turned sides*	252*–258
C. *Tripod bowl*	259*
III. DISHES	260*–265
IV. PLATES	266*–268*
V. LEKANAI	269*–272*
VI. VOTIVE SHIELD	273
VII. DINOI	274*–309*
VIII. OENOCHOAI	310*–354
IX. RING VASES	355–364*
X. PHALLUS VASES	365*–367
XI. FRAGMENTS	368*–418*
Chapter 3: The Reserving styles of the sixth century	419*–1269*
1. THE ANIMAL CHALICE STYLE	419*–696*
I. CHALICES	419*–676*
II. KANTHAROI	677*–680*
III. PHIALAI MESOMPHALOI	681*–683*
IV. PLATES AND DISHES	684*–687
V. LIDS	688*–694
VI. CLOSED VASES	695*–696*
2. THE GRAND STYLE	697*–807*
I. CHALICES	697*–801*
II. PHIALE MESOMPHALOS?	802*
III. PLATES	803*–804*
IV. DINOI	805*–806*
V. CLOSED VASE	807*
2A. LIGHT ON DARK DECORATION	808*–814*
3. THE CHALICE STYLE	815–1269*
A. VASES WITH NO FILLING ORNAMENTS	815–995
I. CHALICES	815–974*
II. KANTHAROI	975–978*
III. PHIALAI MESOMPHALOI	979*–995
B. PATTERNED VASES	996–1083*
I. CHALICES	996–1072
II. PHIALAI MESOMPHALOI	1073–1081*
III. PLATES	1082–1083*

	C.	FRAGMENTS FROM EITHER A OR B CATEGORIES OR WITH DECORATION LOST	1084–1255*
	I.	CHALICES	1084–1210
	II.	PHIALAI MESOMPHALOI	1211–1252*
	III.	OTHER SHAPES	1253–1255*
	D.	VASES WITH FLORAL DECORATION	1256–1269*
	I.	CHALICES	1256–1265*
	II.	PHIALAI MESOMPHALOI	1266–1269*

Chapter 4: The Black-Figure styles of the sixth century

1.	THE SPHINX AND LION STYLE		1270*–1457*
	I.	BOWLS WITH LIDS	1270*–1271*
	II.	STEMMED SKYPHOS CRATER	1272*
	III.	Fragments of I or II	1273*–1398
		A. *Lower part*	1273*–1314*
		B. *Upper part*	1315*–1376
		C. *Plastic heads*	1377*–1398
	IV.	TRIPOD BOWLS	1399*–1400
	V.	DINOI	1401*–1403
	VI.	KOTHON	1404
	VII.	PLATES	1405*–1416
	VIII.	DISHES	1417*–1418*
	IX.	OPEN VASES	
		A. *?Lekane*	1419*
		B. *Lekane with wide offset rim*	1420*
	X.	OENOCHOAI	1421*–1434*
	XI.	INCENSE VASES	1435*–1437*
	XII.	BASKET-HANDLED CYLINDRICAL VASE	1438*
	XIII.	?BASKET	1439*
	XIV.	RING VASE	1440*
	XV.	FRAGMENTS	1441–1457*
2.	THE BLACK-FIGURE GRAND STYLE		1458*–1467*
	I.	CUPS	1458*–1460*
	II.	CHALICES	1461*–1465
	III.	BOWL	1466*
	IV.	FRAGMENT	1467*
3.	THE BLACK-FIGURE CHALICES		1468*–1624
	1.	Komast chalices	1468*–1591
	2.	Animal chalices	1592–1614*
	3.	Chalices with floral decoration	1615*–1616*
	4.	Unslipped chalices	1617*–1619
	5.	Chalices with indiscernible or unpreserved decoration	1620*–1624
4.	THE BLACK-FIGURE KANTHAROI		1625*–1637
	1.	Unslipped kantharoi	1625*–1634
	2.	Slipped kantharoi	1635*–1637
5.	MISCELLANEA		1638*–1659
	I.	HYDRIA	1638*
	II.	TWO-HANDLED POTS	1639–1647*
	III.	IVY-PATTERNED VASES	1648*–1653
	IV.	VARIA	1654*–1659

CATALOGUE

Chapter 1: The Patterned chalices of the seventh century

1*–5*	Emporio	*Emporio* 121, nos. 217–221, pl. 33.
6*–17*	Emporio	*Emporio* 121, nos. 222–233, pl. 33.
18	Emporio	*Emporio* 121, no. 234, pl. 33.
19–20	Emporio	*Emporio* 121, nos. 235–236.
21*	Emporio	*Emporio* 121, no. 237, pl. 33.
22*–23*	Emporio	*Emporio* 121, nos. 238–239, pl. 33.
24	Emporio	*Emporio* 121, no. 240.
25*	Emporio	*Emporio* 121, no. 241, pl. 33.
26*–27*	Emporio	*Emporio* 121, nos. 242–243, pl. 33.
28	Emporio	*Emporio* 121, no. 244, pl. 34.
29*	Emporio	*Emporio* 121, no. 245, pl. 34.
30–33	Emporio	*Emporio* 121, nos. 246–249, pl. 34.
34*	Emporio	*Emporio* 121, no. 250, pl. 34.
35*	Emporio	*Emporio* 121, nos. 251, pl. 34 and no. 614, pl. 97; *Chios Conference* 233–4, fig. 1.
36*	Emporio	*Emporio* 121, no. 252, pl. 34.
37–40	Emporio	*Emporio* 121, nos. 253–256.
41–43	Emporio	*Emporio* 121, nos. 257–259, pl. 34.
44*	Emporio	*Emporio* 121, no. 260, pl. 34.
45*–47*	Emporio	*Emporio* 121, nos. 261–263, pl. 34.
48*	Emporio	*Emporio* 121, no. 264, pl. 35.
49*–51*	Emporio	*Emporio* 121, nos. 265–267, pl. 35.
52–57	Emporio	*Emporio* 121, nos. 278–283, pl. 36.
58	Phana	*BSA* 35, 1934–5, 159, pl. 32 no. 19.
59	Phana	*BSA* 35, 1934–5, fig. 12.8.
60–63	Chios town, Kofiná Ridge	*BSA* 49, 1954, 134, pl. 6.1 a–d.
64	Naucratis	BM 1886. 4–1.786 = 1924.12–1.640. *Naukratis* I, pl. 10.1; *Emporio* 120 note 4.
65	Naucratis	*Naukratis* I, pl. 10.3; *Emporio* 120 note 4.
66*	Naucratis	BM 1886.4–1.1042. *Saw pattern at the handle zone; inside: grey.* W: 0.093

67*	Naucratis	*CVA* Reading I, 37, pl. 550. 5.a.b.
68*	Naucratis	Wiel, *Leiden*, pl. 1.1; Prins de Jong, *Scherben* pl. 1.1.
69*	Naucratis	Cambridge, Museum of Classical Archaeology, NA 274. *Part of the bowl with the handle zone. Saw pattern at the handle zone.* *Max. Pres. W: 0.104.*
70*	Tocra	*Tocra* I, no. 771, pl. 39 and fig. 30; *Emporio* 120 note 4.
71	Tocra	*Tocra* I, no. 772; *Emporio* 120 note 4.
72*	Tocra	*Tocra* II, no. 2042, pl. 14.
73	Locri	*CGED* 108 and note 23.
74	Sybaris	*NSc* 1970, 3 suppl., 155, fig. 159, no. 377; *CGED* 108 and note 21.
75	Sybaris	*NSc* 1970, 3 suppl., 155, fig. 159, no. 326; *CGED* 112 and notes 82–88.
76	Cerveteri	*StEtr.* 45, 1977, 443, pl. 61a; *CGED* 161 no. 3.
77*	Cerveteri	C.M. Lerici, *Nuove Testimonianze dell' arte et della civiltà etrusca*, 1960, 46; *Emporio* 120, note 4; *CGED* 161 no. 4, pl. 79. 21.
78*	Athens, Agora	*Hesperia* 30, 1961, 357, G54, pl. 86; *Agora* VIII, 58, pl. 13, 230; *Emporio* 120 no. 4.
79*	Athens, Agora	*Hesperia* 30, 1961, 357, G55, pl. 86.
80	Athens, Agora	*Hesperia* 30, 1961, 357, inv. nos. Agora P 24077 a and b.
81	Corinth	C 73–131 *Hesperia* 43, 1974, 20, no. 20, pl. 4.
82	Corinth	C 73–132 *Hesperia* 43, 1974, 20, no. 21, pl. 4.
83	Corinth	C 73–133 *Hesperia* 43, 1974, 20, pl. 4.
84–93	Corinth	C 73–121; 124–126; 128–130; 134–136. *Hesperia* 43, 1974, 20.
94*	Delos, Rheneia	*Délos* XVII, 77–78, no. 2, pl. 52A.2.
95	Istros	*Histria* II, cat. 377, pl. 20; *Histria* IV 52, no. 150, fig. 6; *Emporio* 120 note 4.
96*	Old Smyrna	*BSA* 60, 1965, 140, fig. 19a; *Emporio* 120 note 3.
97–99*	Old Smyrna	*BSA* 60, 1965, 140, fig. 19.c.d.e.
100*	?Pitane	*CGED* 28, pl. 6.7. *Early chalice: Emporio fig. 60B.* *Walls: two rows of concentric circles; handle zone: metopes of four horizontally disposed zigzags done with a multiple brush of nine members, flanked by nine vertical lines done in the same way; below horizontal lines.*
101*	?Pitane	*CGED* 28, pl. 2.8 upper row. *Part of the walls and handle zone of an early chalice. Decoration: crossed square.*

102*	?Pitane	*CGED* 28, pl. 7.8 middle. *Part of the walls and handle zone of an early chalice. Decoration: vertical lines ?flanking saw patterns.*
103*	?Pitane	*CGED* 28, pl. 7.8 lower row. *Part of the walls and handle zone of an early chalice. Dec: saw patterns flanked by vertical lines. All done with a multiple brush of nine members.*
104	Pitane	*CGED* 29, pl. 7.9.
105	Sardis	Greenewalt in *Stud. Hanfmann*, 48.
106	Rhodes, Vroulia	Kinch *Vroulia*, 149, no. 3. pl. 41. 18.3.
107	Tarsus	*Tarsus* III, fig. 101, 1499; *Emporio* 120 note 3.
108	Al Mina	*JHS* 60, 1940, 9, fig. 4k; *Emporio* 120 note 4.
109*	Al Mina	Nicholson Museum, Sydney, inv. no. 49.105. *Eretria* VI, 11, no. 36, pl. 2.

Chapter 2: The Wild Goat style

I. CHALICES

110*–111*	Emporio	*Emporio* 121, nos. 268–9, pl. 35.
112	Emporio	*Emporio* 121, no. 270, pl. 98 and p.244, no. 615.
113*	Emporio	*Emporio* 121, no. 271, pl. 35.
114*	Emporio	*Emporio* 120, 121, no. 272, pl. 35. *Wrongly restored in the walls and without a foot.*
115*–119*	Emporio	*Emporio* 121, nos. 273–277, pls. 35–36.
120–122	Phana	*BSA* 35, 1934–35, 159, pl. 37.9, 10 and 14.
123	Phana	*BSA* 35, 1934–35, 159, pl. 37.16.
124*	Rizari, Chios town	Chios Mus. nos. 3311 a–c. *Three frs. from the same vase. Brown paint on creamy slip.* *1. Frieze with meander.* *2. Frieze with goats grazing to the r. amidst fill. orns.* *3. Frieze of lotus and bud* *Inside: two parallel double lines.*
125	Naucratis	BM 1886.4–1.1076. *Naukratis* I pl. 5.17. *Rim pattern: broken cable then two parallel lines. Inside: black paint on slip.* *W: 0.041.*
126	Naucratis	BM 1886.4–1.1077. *Naukratis* I pl. 5.18. *Head of a goat to the r. Inside: black.* *W: 0.026.*

| 127 | Naucratis | BM 1886.4-1.1550.
Naukratis I pl. 5.11.
Rim pattern: chequer with dots, then broken meander between two parallel lines. On the walls: fill. orns. and dividing band.
W: 0.067. |
|---|---|---|
| 128 | Naucratis | BM 1886.4-1.1552.
Naukratis I pl. 5.13.
Rim pattern: row of chequers with dotted blanks then row of dotted squares. Part of the muzzle of a goat to the r. Fill. orns.
W: 0.044. |
| 129 | Naucratis | BM 1886.4-1.1556.
Naukratis I pl. 5.16.
Rim pattern: broken meander. Part of the head of a goose to the r. Fill. orns.
W: 0.020. |
| 130 | Naucratis | BM 1886.4-1.1554.
Naukratis I pl. 5.15.
Rim pattern: broken meander. Fill. orns.
W: 0.030. |
| 131 | Naucratis | BM 1886.4-1.1553.
Naukratis I pl. 5.14.
Rim pattern: chequers with dotted blanks then dotted squares. Fill. orns.
W: 0.030. |
| 132* | Naucratis | BM 1886.4-1.1560.
Naukratis I pl. 5.27.
Vertical dividing bands of meander and chequers with dotted blanks, then hindlegs of a goat with a shoehorse pendant between them.
W: 0.066. |
| 133* | Naucratis | BM 1886.4-1.1562.
Naukratis I, pl. 5.31.
Part of a handle zone with handle root. Handle zone: horizontal tongues and then dotted concentric circles. On the walls: zigzag below meander running r. On the bowl: band above broken meander.
W: 0.065. |
| 134 | Naucratis | BM 1888.6-1.468c.
Broken meander, band, line and then lotus and bud frieze.
W: 0.086. |
| 135 | Naucratis | BM 1888.6-1.469F.
Meander, then broken meander between lines and bands and then rays.
W: 0.061. |
| 136 | Naucratis | BM 1924.12-1.467.
Same patterns and disposition as the last.
W: 0.067. |
| 137 | Naucratis | BM 1924.12-1.511.
Double guilloche, then band between lines and then rays.
W: 0.049. |

138	Naucratis	BM 1888.6–1.468g: 1924.12–1.533. *Handle zone: double guilloche, then meander running l. between bands and lines. Then lotus and bud frieze.* *W: 0.105.*
139	Naucratis	BM 1888.6–1.471p: 1924.12–1.108. *Goose to the r.* *W: 0.063.*
140*	Naucratis	BM 1888.6–1.473a. *Rim pattern: diagonal strokes, above meander running l. Goat walking to the r. Fill. orns.* *W: 0.084.*
141*	Naucratis	BM 1888.6–1.473c: 1924.12–1.86. *Frieze of goats walking and grazing on the r. amidst fill. orns. Handle zone: broken meander above double meander running r.* *W: 0.042.*
142*	Naucratis	BM 1888.6–1.473a: 1924.12–1.91. *Rim pattern: dots. Goat to the r. turning its head to the l.* *W: 0.038.*
143*	Naucratis	BM 1888.6–1.473g : 1924.12–1.195. *Rim pattern: meander running l. between two parallel lines. Part of the neck and horn of a goat to the r. amidst fill. orns.* *W: 0.064.*
144*	Naucratis	BM 1888.6–1.473h : 1924.12–1.104. *Rim pattern: diagonal strokes above meander running l. Part of the head of a goat to the r. and then neck of a goose to the r. amidst fill. orns.* *W: 0.050.*
145*	Naucratis	BM 1888.6–1.473k : 1924.12–1.150. *Goat to the r. turning its head to the l. then dividing band of vertical broken meander.* *W: 0.055.*
146*	Naucratis	BM 1888.6–1.473l : 1924.12–1.447. *Rim pattern: diagonal strokes then broken meander between two parallel lines. Goat to the r. then dividing band of vertical chequers with dotted blanks.* *W: 0.055.*
147*	Naucratis	BM 1888.6–1.473l and m: 1924.12–1.285. *Rim pattern: meander running l. Squares with meanders, dividing bands and hindquarters of a goat to the r.* *W: 0.138.*
148*	Naucratis	BM 1888.6–1.475c : 1924.12–1.107. *Goose to the r. Handle zone: meander to the l. between two parallel lines.* *W: 0.067.*
149*	Naucratis	BM 1888.6–1.475b : 1924.12–1.105. *Frieze of geese to the r. amidst fill. orns.* *W: 0.047.*

150*	Naucratis	BM 1888.6–1.475a. *Rim pattern: chequer with dotted blanks above broken meander between two parallel lines. Spiral volutes, dotted at the outer row, and then head and neck of a goose to the l. amidst fill. orns.* *W: 0.068.*
151*	Naucratis	BM 1888.6–1.475d : 1924.12–1.110. *Head of a goose to the r., then preceding goose to the r. but with head turned back towards its partner, amidst fill. orns.* *W: 0.035.*
152*	Naucratis	BM 1888.6–1.475c : 1924.12–1.113. *Head of a goose to the r. Inside: ?lotus* *W: 0.032.*
153*	Naucratis	BM 1888.6–1.475f : 1924.12–1.118. *Two geese to the r. amidst fill. orns.* *W: 0.059.*
154*	Naucratis	BM 1888.6–1.475g : 1924.12–1.119. *Head of a goose to the r. then a rosette. Inside: black.* *W: 0.062.*
155*	Naucratis	BM 1888.6–1.477b. *Rim pattern: meander to the l. between two rows of chequers with dotted blanks. Lion with dotted belly to the l. amidst fill. orns.* *W: 0.052.*
156*	Naucratis	BM 1888.6–1.477c. *Dividing band: vertical meander flanked by two vertical rows of chequer with dotted blanks; then, hindleg of a lion to the r. amidst fill. orns.* *W: 0.057.*
157*	Naucratis	BM 1888.6–1.477e : 1924.12–1.159. *Handle zone with handle root: double guilloche. Hindlegs of a panther to the l.* *W: 0.073.*
158*	Naucratis	BM 1888.6–1.478a. *Rim pattern: meander running l. between two rows of chequer with dotted blanks. Dividing band: vertical dotted chequer, broken meander between lines and then squares with meander.* *W: 0.065.*
159*	Naucratis	BM 1888.6–1.478c : 1924.12–1.446. *Fill. orns. and dividing band of broken cable. Handle zone: simple guilloche and tongue pattern near handle.* *W: 0.035.*
160*	Naucratis	BM 1888.6–1.478L : 1924.12–1.455. *Rim pattern: broken meander above row of dots between two parallel lines. Dividing band of vertical meander and then squares with meanders.* *W: 0.046.*
161*	Naucratis	BM 1888.6–1.478F : 1924.12–1.460. *Rim pattern: double meander running l. between two rows of chequer with dotted blanks. ?Mane of a lion to the r. and fill. orns.* *W: 0.042.*

162* Naucratis BM 1888.6–1.478i : 1924.12–1.508.
Legs of goats to the l. amidst fill. orns. Handle zone: dotted concentric circles then lines and band above meander.
W: 0.053.

163* Naucratis BM 1888.6–1.478j : 1924.12–1.513.
Handle zone: dotted concentric circles then two parallel lines. Bowl: Two parallel lines.
W: 0.064.

164* Naucratis BM 1924.12–1.88.
Rim pattern: meander running l. Part of the forepart, ear and horn of a goat to the r. amidst fill. orns.
W: 0.047.

165* Naucratis BM 1924.12–1.100.
Rim pattern: meander running l. Hindquarters of a ?goat to the r. amidst fill. orns. Incised inscription: ΟΧΙΟΣ
W: 0.044.

166* Naucratis BM 1924.12–1.106.
Goose to the r.
W: 0.033.

167* Naucratis BM 1924.12–1.109.
Squares with meander, dividing band: vertical dotted squares, goose to the r. amidst fill. orns. Inside: rosette.
W: 0.044.

168* Naucratis BM 1924.12–1.112.
Neck and head of a goose turning l. amidst fill. orns. Rim pattern: meander running l.
W: 0.033.

169* Naucratis BM 1924.12–1.111.
Rim pattern: zigzag line between parallel lines. Head of a goose to the r. amidst fill. orns.
W: 0.035.

170* Naucratis BM 1924.12–1.115.
Rim pattern: chequer with dotted blanks above meander running l. Head of a goose to the l. amidst fill. orns.
W: 0.038.

171* Naucratis BM 1924.12–1.114.
Rim pattern: broken meander. Part of a goose to the r. amidst fill. orns.
W: 0.035.

172* Naucratis BM 1924.12–1.117.
Goose to the l. amidst fill. orns.
W: 0.039.

173 Naucratis BM 1924.12–1.116.
Geese to the l. amidst fill. orns.
Inside: wheel rosette above two parallel lines.
W: 0.040.

174 Naucratis BM 1924.12–1.309b.
Meander running l. above goat's horn to the r.
W: 0.024.

175*	Naucratis	BM 1924.12–1.419. *Legs of goats to the r. amidst fill. orns. Handle zone: simple guilloche with eye and broken meander above. On the bowl: double meander running l. between two parallel lines.* *W: 0.078.*
176*	Naucratis	BM 1924.12–1.421. *Goat with dotted belly walking to the r. amidst fill. orns. Handle zone: double guilloche.* *W: 0.046.*
177*	Naucratis	BM 1924.12–1.423. *?Hindleg of a goat to the r. amidst fill. orns. Handle zone: double meander to the l., alternating with crossed squares, then tongue pattern near missing handle. On the bowl: two bands.* *W: 0.077.*
178	Naucratis	BM 1924.12–1.436. *Dividing bands: broken meander and chequer with dotted blanks, then fill. orns.* *W: 0.063.*
179	Naucratis	BM 1924.12–1.439. *Dividing bands: broken meander between two rows of chequer with dotted blanks. Handle zone: meander to the l. alternating with squares filled with cross squares and meander.* *W: 0.041.*
180	Naucratis	BM 1924.12–1.440. *Dividing bands: broken meander between two rows of chequer with dotted blanks; then squares with meander.* *W: 0.037.*
181	Naucratis	BM 1924.12–1.448. *Dividing band: vertical chequer with dotted blanks and then broken meander. Incised inscription:*]HI *W: 0.030.*
182	Naucratis	BM 1924.12–1.468. *Goose to the r. amidst fill orns. Handle zone: zigzag above triple meander running l.* *W: 0.061.*
183	Naucratis	BM 1924.12–1.469. *Rays. Handle zone: tongues near handle root.* *W: 0.053.*
184	Naucratis	BM 1924.12–1.471. *Triple meander running l., then band, then broken meander and then band between lines.* *W: 0.026.*
185	Naucratis	BM 1924.12–1.472. *Broken meander between two bands.* *W: 0.037.*
186	Naucratis	BM 1924.12–1.473. *Handle zone: tongues and then ?meander to the l. Below band and then broken meander.* *W: 0.057.*

187	Naucratis	BM 1924.12–1.481. *Rim pattern: meander running l. between lines. Dividing band: vertical meander and then lotus and ?tendrils.* *W: 0.049.*
188	Naucratis	BM 1924.12–1.430. *A daisy-like rosette with alternate red and white petals.* *W: 0.034.*
189	Naucratis	BM 1924.12–1.470. *Lower part of a chalice. Friezes of broken meander and rays.* *W: 0.079.*
190	Naucratis	BM 1924.12–1.531. *Meander running l. between lines and bands, then frieze of lotus and bud.* *W: 0.058.*
191	Naucratis	BM 1924.12–1.548. *Rim pattern: broken meander, then chequer with squares in the blank. Incised inscription:*]ΘHKE[*W: 0.027.*
192	Naucratis	BM 1924.12–1.555. *Broken meander between bands, then lotus and bud frieze.* *Incised inscription:*]ΘHKEN[*W: 0.044.*
193	Naucratis	BM 1924.12–1.643. *Triple meander running l. then band. Incised inscription:* ANEΘ[*W: 0.094.*
194	Naucratis	BM 1924.12–1.496. *Rim pattern: broken meander above chequer with dotted blanks. Horn of a goat amidst fill. orns.* *W: 0.042.*
195	Naucratis	BM 1924.12–1.492. *Rim pattern: chequer with dotted blanks. Dividing bands: broken meander between lines and then squares filled with dotted squares.* *W: 0.026.*
196	Naucratis	BM 1924.12–1.507. *Handle zone: dotted concentric circles between two parallel lines.* *W: 0.037.*
197	Naucratis	BM 1924.12–1.512. *Handle zone: tongues near handle then dotted concentric circle.* *W: 0.035.*
198	Naucratis	BM 1924.12–1.515. *Goose to the r. amidst fill. orns. Handle zone: dotted concentric circles.* *W: 0.055.*
199	Naucratis	BM 1924.12–1.514. *Fill. orns. Handle zone: double guilloche.* *W: 0.048.*
200	Naucratis	BM 1924.12–1.516. *Handle zone: double guilloche and band.* *W: 0.039.*

201	Naucratis	BM 1924.12–1.521. *Handle zone: dotted concentric circles and tongues near missing handle.* W: 0.055.
202	Naucratis	BM 1924.12–1.551. *Rim pattern: zigzag between two parallel lines. Goose to the r. amidst fill. orns., then dividing band: broken meander between two vertical lines, then squares with meanders. Inside: lotus above two parallel lines.* W: 0.090.
203	Naucratis	BM 1924.12–1.677. *Dividing bands: vertical meander between lines, then chequer with dotted blanks and then squares with meanders.* W: 0.035.
204	Naucratis	BM 1924.12–1.676. *Swastika with angular edges. Inside: traces of ?buds.* W: 0.036.
205*	Naucratis	BM 1924.12–1.1248 or 1266. *Rim pattern: double meander running l. between two parallel lines. Neck and head of a goose amidst fill. orns.* W: 0.060.
206	Naucratis	BM 1924.12–1.1251. *Neck and head of a goose to the r.* *Incised inscription:*]ΟΔΙΤΗΙ[W: 0.056.
207	Naucratis	BM 1924.12–1.1249. *Neck and head of a goose turned l. Rim pattern: dots between ?lines. Inside: lotus.* W: 0.039.
208	Naucratis	BM 1924.12–1.259. *Rim pattern: chequer above broken cable between two parallel lines. Head of a goose to the r. amidst fill. orns.* W: 0.069.
209	Naucratis	BM 1924.12–1.437. *Lion's paws to the l. amidst fill. orns.* W: 0.030.
210	Naucratis	*Naukratis* I, pl. 5.25. *Rim pattern: chequer with dotted blanks above a row of squares with dots in the middle. Squares with meanders, then dividing bands: broken meander between two vertical lines and chequer with dotted blanks, then hindquarters of a goat to the r. amidst fill. orns.* W: 0.072.
211*	Naucratis	BM 1886.4–1.1078. *Naukratis* I, pl. 5.22 *Meander running l. above two parallel lines then a goat to the r. with its head turned back. Inside: black* W: 0.082.

212*	Naucratis	BM 1886.4–1.1079. *Naukratis* I, pl. 5.32 *Goat grazing to the r. amidst fill. orns. Below: tongues. Inside: black* *W: 0.038.*
213*	Naucratis	BM 1886.4–1.1064. *Naukratis* I, pl. 5.30 *W: 0.049.*
214	Naucratis	BM 1886.4–1.1561. *Naukratis* I, pl. 5.29 *W: 0.062.*
215	Naucratis	BM 1924.12–1.152. *Deer to the r. Inside: traces of decoration.* *W: 0.030.*
216*	Naucratis	*CVA* Oxford II, 81, pl. 396.7.
217*	Naucratis	*CVA* Oxford II, 81, pl. 396.2.
218*	Naucratis	*CVA* Oxford II, 81, pl. 396.4.
219*	Naucratis	*CVA* Oxford II, 81, pl. 396.6; Jones, *Review*, pl. 8.11.a.
220*	Naucratis	*CVA* Cambridge II, 33, pl. 496.16.
221	Naucratis	*CVA* Cambridge II, 33, pl. 496.17 (now lost).
222*	Naucratis	*CVA* Cambridge II, 33, pl. 496.18 and 20.
223*	Naucratis	*CVA* Cambridge II, 33, pl. 496.19.
224*	Naucratis	*CVA* Cambridge II, 33, pl. 496.24.
225*	Naucratis	*CVA* Cambridge II, 34, pl. 496.41.
226*	Naucratis	*CVA* Cambridge II, 34, pl. 496.43; Jones, *Review*, pl. 8.11.a.
227*	Naucratis	*CVA* Cambridge II, 34, pl. 496.32.
228*	Naucratis	Cambridge, Museum of Classical Archaeology, NA 70. *Part of the handle zone: guillloche.* *W: 0.036.*
229*	Naucratis	UCL 755. *Part of a goose to the r. amidst fill. orns. Handle zone: double guilloche.* *H: 0.052 W: 0.027.*
230	Naucratis	*CVA* Reading I, 37, pl. 549.27. *Part of a handle zone with handle root.* *W: 0.064.*
231	Naucratis	*Naukratis* I, pl. 5.26. *Goats walking to the r. amidst fill. orns. Handle zone: dotted concentric circle.* *W: 0.046.*
232*	Naucratis	*CVA* Heidelberg I, pl. 437.8.
233*	Naucratis	Alexandria inv. no. 17220. Venit, *Egypt. Museums*, no. 136, pl. 33 and drawing on p. 168. *Rim pattern: broken cable between two parallel lines.*

234*	Naucratis	Alexandria inv. no. 9497. Venit *Egypt. Museums*, no. 128, pl. 32 and drawing on p. 167. *Part of a goose to the r.*
235*	Naucratis	Alexandria inv. no. 9307. Venit, *Egypt. Museums*, no. 124, pl. 32 and drawing on p. 167. *A pendant.*
236*	Vulci	*CVA* Würzburg I, 30–32, fig. 15, pls. 1904. 1 and 2 and 1906.1, *where all previous bibliography resumed, drawing of the profile appears for the first time and excellent new photographs*; *Chios Conference* 238 and fig. 9.
237*	Vulci	*CVA* Würzburg I, 32–33, fig. 16, pls. 1905. 1 and 2 and 1906.2, *as the last.*
238	Delos	*Délos* XX, 37, fig. 33.6.
239	Delos	*Délos* XX, 37–38, fig. 33.5.
240	Pitane	*CGED* 29, pl. 7.10.
241	Pitane	Istanbul Archaeological Museum, inv. no. 8234 (on exhibit). *Small chalice, put together from many frs. Almost intact but for one big part at the back. Est. H. and Diam. c. 0.10. Slip: white to creamy beige. Foot and handles painted in a diluted brown paint. Two white parallel lines on the foot above the base. Decoration: Rim pattern: meander to l. On the walls: Goat with dotted belly and very thin legs walking to the r. Fill. orns.: a triangle between the forelegs; a horseshoe roundel between the hindlegs. Above the handles: Four square meanders flanked by two parallel lines decorated with vertical meander. Handle zone: meander running l. Inside: Chain of three lotus and three buds in red and white, then two parallel lines, then again two parallel lines, then again two parallel lines, and at the centre: two parallel lines and a flower with four petals in red and four in white.*
242	Pitane	Istanbul Archaeological Museum, inv. no. 8547 (on exhibit). *Almost intact, put together from many frs. and foot restored. Transition from bowl to walls obvious. Slip: white. Decoration: Rim pattern: meander running l. On the walls: Two geese walking to the r. in front of the spirals and squared meanders then on the l. dividing bands: chequer with dotted blanks, and vertical meander flanked by two vertical lines. Fill. orns.: 1. dotted rosettes 2. crosses filled with squares and 3. spiky rosettes.*
243*	Old Smyrna	*BSA* 60, 1965, 140, fig. 19.b.
244*	Old Smyrna	*BSA* 60, 1965, 141, pl. 43 no. 7.
244a	Old Smyrna	*BSA* 80, 1985, 27, fig. 3.
245	Erythrae	*CGED* 29, pl. 7.11.
246	Samos, Heraion	*Samos* IV, 147, pl. 67. 509.
247*	Samos, Heraion	*Chios Conference* 192 and fig. 4.

II. BOWLS

A. Bowls

248   Naucratis   BM 1888.6–1.477d.
Part of a ?panther to the r. Inside: lotus
W: 0.033.

249   Naucratis   BM 1924.12–1.954.
Rim pattern: vertical strokes above lines. Chain of lotus and palmette.
W: 0.081.

250   Naucratis   BM 1924.12–1.1265.
Rim pattern: three parallel lines. Dividing band: rays and meander.
W: 0.061.

251*   Naucratis   Wiel, *Leiden*, pl. 1, no. 4.

B. Open bowls with out-turned sides

252*   Naucratis   BM 1888.6–1.456.
Naukratis II, pl. 6. 1 and 2; Price 216–7; *Emporio* 149 note 3; A. Lane, *Greek Pottery*, 1971, pl. 17b; *BSA* 44, 1949, 158 and note 11; *Samos* VI.1, 138, fig. 139, pl. 90. 715 a and b; R.M. Cook and R.J. Charleston, *Masterpieces of Western and Near Eastern Ceramics*, Vol. II, *Greek and Roman Pottery*, 1979, no. 53.

253*   Naucratis   BM 1888.6–1.460k and 1924.12–1.84.
GPP[2] pl. 31c; *Samos* V 127, pl. 125. 615 (wrongly stated from Chios); *Chios Conference* 239 and fig 11.
Inside: Hindquarters of a lion to the l. and then a goat walking to the r. amidst fill. orns. Above and below meander running l. between two lines. Outside: Goats grazing to the r. amidst fill. orns. Above and below meander running l. between two lines. Further below, broken meander.
W: 0.194.

254*   Naucratis   BM 1888.6–1.460j.
Inside: bulls to the r. amidst fill. orns. Outside: Goat grazing to the r. amidst fill. orns. Below: meanders running l.
W: 0.066.

255*   Naucratis   UCL 754.
Johnston, *Exhibition* 1978, no. 66; *Chios Conference* 239 and fig 12.
Brown paint on white slip. Inside: Rim pattern: meander running l. Goat to the l. in front of a floral with dotted spiral and amidst fill. orns. Outside: Rim pattern: meander running l. Goat to the r. amidst fill. orns.
H: 0.103   W: 0.089.

256*   Naucratis   *CVA* Cambridge II, 34, pl. 496.57; *Samos* VI.1, 139, no. 716.

257*	Naucratis	Alexandria inv. no. 9492. Venit, *Egypt. Museums*, no. 123, pl. 31 and drawing on p. 167. *Outside: Goat to the r. amidst fill. orns. Inside: Goose to the r. amidst fill. orns.*
258	Naucratis	Edgar, *Catal. Caire*, 13, no. 26159.

C. Tripod Bowl

259*	Emporio	*Emporio* 151, no. 652, pl. 56; *Samos* VI.1, 139, pl. 91.740.

III. DISHES

260*–262*	Emporio	*Emporio* 180–1, nos. 648–650, pl. 55.
263*	Naucratis	*Naukratis* I, pl. 5.33; Fairbanks, *Catal.* 101, no. 305.4; *Samos* VI.1, 139, no. 241.
264*	Aegina, Old town	*Alt-Ägina* II.1, 15, pl. 5.74; *BSA* 44, 1949, 154, pl. 41a; *Emporio* 149 and n. 5.
265	Olbia	*SovArch* VII, 1941, fig. 4.1; Kocybala, Diss. 1978, 230, fig. 13a. *Two frs. of ?dishes.*

IV. PLATES

266*	Rizari, Chios town	Chios Mus. no. 3356. *Inside: Frieze of meander alternating with squares. Then frieze of a panther to the r. amidst fill. orns. and dividing band of vertical meander and line. Outside: Rim pattern: strokes, then lines and bands.* *W: 0.091.*
267*	Naucratis	BM 1888.6–1.499a and c and Boston 88.1085 (= Fairbanks, *Catal.*, pl. 34, no. 319.8). *Rim pattern: dots then band. Frieze of concentric circles united with strokes and horizontal lines then rays.* *W: 0.104 and W: 0.064.*
268*	Naucratis	Leipzig, sent from Oxford in 1928 (lost during the war). *Rim pattern: double meander running l. Then two rows of meander running l. and then rays.*

V. LEKANAI

269*	Rizari, Chios town	Chios Mus. no. 3376. *Inside: Bands in black paint and white. Outside: Rim pattern: ivy pattern. Slip: very white.*
270*	Rizari, Chios town	Chios Mus. no. 3408. *Inside: Rays and fishbone. Outside: Rim pattern: broken meander above squares. Then semi-circles and rays. Slip: very white.*

271*	Rizari, Chios town	Chios Mus. no. 3407. *Inside: Strokes at the border. Outside: Frieze with palmettes above strokes arranged in a circle. Slip: very white.*
272*	Rizari, Chios town	Chios Mus. no. 3406. *Inside: hatched double broken meander alternating with flowers. Outside: Frieze of lotus and bud below hatched pattern. On the disks: rosette. Slip: very white.*

VI. VOTIVE SHIELD

273	Phana	*BSA* 35, 1934–35, 159, pl. 37, nos. 23 and 30; *JHS* 54, 1934, 197, fig. 8.

VII. DINOI

274*	Emporio	*Emporio* 148, 151, no. 651, pl. 55; *AJA* 1956, pl. 99, fig. 7; *Samos* VI.1, 138, no. 698; *AntK* Beiheft 7, 1970, 5.
275*	Rizari, Chios town	Chios Mus. no. 3326. *Chios Conference* 238 and fig. 10. *Brownish paint on creamy slip peeled off in many parts. Hindquarters of a ?lion to the l. and then a goose to the r. turning her head back, then floral with spirals: the outer dotted, amidst fill. orns. Above: tongues: Added red. Thickness: 0.009.*
276*	Rizari, Chios town	Chios Mus. no. 3421. *Rim of a dinos. Broken meander and strokes.*
277*	Rizari, Chios town	Chios Mus. no. 3353. *Rim of a dinos. Double guilloche. Brown paint on creamy slip. Added red on the dots and lozenges of the guilloche.*
278*	Rizari, Chios town	Chios Mus. no. 3352. *Part of a dinos with a four-reeded handle. Below handle: guilloche. Right of the handle: dividing bands.*
279*	Rizari, Chios town	Chios Mus. no. 3354. *Part of a dinos. Fill. orns. and dividing bands of chequer with dotted blanks and broken cable flanked by two parallel lines.*
280*	Naucratis	BM 1886.4–1.1003. *Part of a dinos and rim. Rim pattern: simple cable with eyes. Sph. with her foreleg raised, and touching the floral in front of her, to the r. Fill. orns.* *W: 0.084.*
281*	Naucratis	BM 1886.4–1.1122. Price 215, pl. 10.3; *Samos* VI.1, 138, pl. 98. 695. *Rim pattern: double guilloche. Dotted squares above tongue pattern then the head of a lion to the l. amidst fill. orns.* *W: 0.069.*
282*	Naucratis	BM 1888.6–1.458. Price 216, pl. 10.1; *Samos* VI.1, 138 no. 691. *Three rows of grazing goats to the r. amidst fill. orns.*

283	Naucratis	BM 1888.6–1.459. Price 216, pl. 10.2 and fig. 41; *Samos* VI.1, 138 no. 693. *Two rows: upper row: goat to the r. amidst fill. orns. Lower row: deer amidst fill. orns. Paint: brown fired red. Inside: unslipped.*
284*	Naucratis	BM 1888.6–1.460e. Price 213, fig. 48; Homann-Vedeking, *Vasenornamentik* 29, fig. 3; Schiering, *Werkstätten* 68 and note 489; *Samos* VI.1, 138, pl. 92. 690; Cook, *Claz. Sarc.*, 102 note 50. *Ram with dotted neck to the r. amidst fill. orns. Above meander running l.* *W: 0.073.*
285	Naucratis	BM 1888.6–1.457 : 1924.12–1.1255. *Four friezes of goats to the r. amidst fill. orns. Paint: black and in parts fired light brown. Inside: unslipped.*
286	Naucratis	BM 1888.6–1.499d. *Rim of a dinos. Rim pattern: double guilloche.* *W: 0.056.*
287	Naucratis	BM 1888.6–1.461. *Big dinos. Rim diam. c.0.18 Rim pattern: guilloche. Walls: wild boar, panther, an indiscernible animal, and bull to the r. Inside: plain.*
288	Naucratis	BM 1888.6–1.499f. *Four-reeded handle of a dinos. Inside: plain.* *W: 0.061.*
289	Naucratis	BM 1888.6–1.499g. *Four-reeded handle of a dinos. Below: meander running l. On the right: vertical meander. Inside: plain.* *W: 0.060.*
290	Naucratis	BM 1924.12–1.2. *Rim and part of a dinos. Rim pattern: double guilloche. Below: chequer and dotted blanks. Head and horn of a goat to the r. amidst fill. orns. and a dividing band of chequer with dotted blanks. Inside: plain.* *W: 0.062.*
291	Naucratis	BM 1924.12–1.23. *Rim of a dinos. Rim pattern: flat side: simple guilloche with eyes. Outside: double meander running l.* *W: 0.061.*
292	Naucratis	BM 1924.12–1.911. *Rim and part of a dinos. Rim pattern: double guilloche, below it: broken meander and then tongues.* *W: 0.129.*
293	Naucratis	BM 1924.12–1.912. *Rim of a dinos. Rim pattern: simple cable with eyes. Inside: plain.* *W: 0.089.*
294	Naucratis	BM 1924.12–1.519. *Rim of a dinos. Rim pattern: ?double guilloche. Inside: paint gone.* *W: 0.042.*

295	Naucratis	BM 1924.12–1.939. *Rim and part of a dinos. Rim pattern: double guilloche. Below it: dotted squares above tongue pattern.* *W: 0.062.*
296*	Naucratis	UCD 309. *JHS* 91, 1971, 113, pl. 13B; Johnston, *Ireland*, 430, no. 942; *CGED*, 160; Johnston, *Exhibition* 1978, no. 67.
297*	Naucratis	Fairbanks, *Catal.*, 102, pl. 30, no. 307.3; *Samos* VI.1, 138, pl. 98. 697.
298*	Naucratis	MMA inv. no. 55.71.8; acquired by exchange with the University of Pennsylvania in 1955 (ex-Philadelphia E5.175.16). *Rim and part of a dinos. Rim pattern: double guilloche. Bull to the r. amidst fill. orns. and dividing bands behind it.*
299	Naucratis	*CVA* Heidelberg III, 109, pl. 1331.6.
300	Naucratis	München (lost during the war). *Rim and part of a dinos. Pattern: simple cable with eyes.*
301	Naucratis	München (lost during the war). *Rim of a dinos. Pattern: guilloche.*
302*	Naucratis	Cairo inv. no. 26136. Edgar, *Catal. Caire*, 5, no. 26136, pl. 2; Venit, *Egypt. Museums*, no. 137, pl. 33.
303*	Gela	Palmero Mus. inv. no. N.I. 1653 (on exhibit). *MonAnt* 17, 1906, 250, fig. 188; *BSA* 44, 1949, 155 and 160; *Enc. dell'Arte Antica* VI, 758, fig. 880; Schiering, *Werkstätten*, 39; *Emporio*, 149, note 7; *CGED* 95 and note 19, pl. 55, fig. 17.
304	Gela	*MonAnt* 17, 1906, 249, fig. 187.
305	Istros	*Materiale* 8, 400, fig. 4.3; *Histria* II, cat. 60, pl. 5; *Histria* IV, 42, no. 60, pl. 6. *(Tentatively classified as Chian).*
306*	Panticapaeum	*MIA* 103, 1962, 122, fig. 8; *Histria* IV, 26 and note 43. *Rim of a dinos. Rim pattern: double guilloche.*
307	Pergamum	*AA* 1979, 326, fig. 17.
308*	Cyprus, Salamis	BM 1891.8–6.72 : A 722. Gjerstad, *Cyprus*, 13–15, no. 54, pl. 6; *CGED* 46, pl. 21.3; *JHS* 12, 1891, 141–142 and fig. 5.
309*	Cyprus, Salamis	Inv. no. 69/7394. Gjerstad, *Cyprus*, 15, no. 57, pl. 6. *?Crater.*

VIII. OENOCHOAI

310*	Emporio	*Emporio* 148–9, 150, no. 634, figs. 99–101, pls. 53 and 54.
311*–323	Emporio	*Emporio* 148–9, 150, nos. 635–647, fig. 102 and pls. 53, 54 and 55.

324*	Rizari, Chios town	Chios Mus. nos. 3314, 3314 bis, 3315 bis, 3316, 3318, 3321, 3325, 3333 and 3350: 10 sherds. *PAE* 1952, 523, fig. 9. (13 sherds); *Samos* VI.1, 137, no. 685. *Ten sherds of a trefoil oenochoe. Panel decoration flanked by dividing bands below it. Frieze of goats grazing to the r. amidst fill. orns.*
325*	Rizari, Chios town	Chios Mus. no. 3317. *Hindlegs of a lion to the l. with a horseshoe petal between its legs.*
326*	Rizari, Chios town	Chios Mus. no. 3322. *Neck and part of the head of a doe grazing to the r.*
327*	Rizari, Chios town	Chios Mus. no. 3328. *Frieze with grazing goat to the r. with pendant. Below: rays.*
328*	Rizari, Chios town	Chios Mus. no. 3329. *Grazing goat to the r. amidst fill. orns.*
329	Rizari, Chios town	Chios Mus. no. 3344. *Brown to orange paint on white slip. Part of the head and horn of a goat to the r. amidst fill. orns.*
330*	Rizari, Chios town	Chios Mus. no. 3357. *Two friezes: upper: triangle and ? a running animal to the r.; lower: goats walking to the r.*
331*	Rizari, Chios town	Chios Mus. no. ?3333. *Part of the neck of an oenochoe. Double guilloche and below it strokes.*
332*	Rizari, Chios town	Chios Mus. no. 3333. *Part of the neck of an oenochoe. Double guilloche. Perhaps same vase as the last, but not joining.*
333*	Rizari, Chios town	Chios Mus. no. 3362. *Part of an oenochoe. Meander running r. and below it, tongue pattern.*
334*	Rizari, Chios town	Chios Mus. no. 3350. *Two-reeded handle of an oenochoe. Stripes of black and white with added red on them.*
335*	Rizari, Chios town	Chios Mus. no. 3332. *Three-reeded handle of an oenochoe. Stripes and then spirals with added red on them.*
336*	Rizari, Chios town	Chios Mus. nos. 3330. *Three-reeded handle of an oenochoe and disc decorated with dotted concentric circles.*
337*	Rizari, Chios town	Chios Mus. no. 3331. *Disc from an oenochoe with concentric circles and dots around them.*
338*	Rizari, Chios town	Chios Mus. no. 3409. *Neck of an oenochoe. Band and line; lotus and bud; battlement pattern between two parallel lines; strokes between lines and bands.*
339*	Rizari, Chios town	Chios Mus. no. 3349. *Three-reeded handle and part of an ?oenochoe. The handle is striped. Fill. orns. and dividing bands.*

340*	Naucratis	BM 1888.6–1.460c. *Two friezes: upper: fill. orns. and dividing bands; lower: goat to the r. with fill. orns.* *W: 0.057.*
341	Naucratis	BM 1888.6–1.499b. *Meander running r. between two parallel lines. Below dividing band of vertical meander.* *W: 0.056.*
342	Naucratis	BM 1888.6–1.468j: 1924.12–1.529. *Chain of lotus and bud below band and lines.* *W: 0.076.*
343	Naucratis	BM 1924.12–1.443. *Legs of a goat to the r. amidst fill. orns.* *W: 0.051.*
344*	Naucratis	*CVA* Cambridge II, 34, pl. 496.31.
345*	Naucratis	Boston 88.970. Fairbanks, *Catal.*, no. 321.13, pl. 34.
346	Sybaris	*NSc* 1972, Suppl., 100 no. 154, fig. 91; *AttiMGrecia* 1972–73, pl. 50c; *CGED* 109 note 27.
347	Sybaris	*NSc* 1971, Suppl., 89, no. 151–152, fig. 89; *CGED* 108 and note 21.
348	Aegina, Old town	*Alt-Ägina* II.1, 15, pl. 5. 72.
349	Aegina, Old town	*Alt-Ägina* II.1, 15, pl. 5. 73.
350*	Krivoroshie	*Bull. Inst. Arch. Bulg.* XXII, 1959, 57–59, fig. 3 a and b; *Arch. Reports* for 1962–3, 41, fig. 17; *Emporio* 148 and note 1; *GO³*, 244 fig. 284 and note 92. *Plastic head as mouth of an oenochoe.* *(Tentatively classified as Chian).*
351*	Choperskie	*Arch. Reports* for 1962–3, 41, fig. 18; *Emporio* 148 and note 1. *Plastic head as mouth of an oenochoe.* *(Tentatively classified as Chian).*
352	Al Mina	Oxford 1954. 290. 293. 294 (*same vase*). *JHS* 60, 1940, 10, pl. 1. f. h. j; Kardara. *Rhodiake* 68–69, nos. 12. 15. 16; *GO³*, fig. 18. *(Tentatively classified as Chian).*
353	Al Mina	*JHS* 60, 1940, 10, pl. III t. *(Tentatively classified as Chian).*
354	Al Mina	Oxford 1954. 284. *JHS* 60, 1940, 10, pl. IIp; Kardara, *Rhodiake*, 67 no. 5. *(Tentatively classified as Chian).*

IX. RING VASES

355	Naucratis	BM 1888.6–1.152a. *Part of a ring vase. Decoration: chequer with dotted blanks.*
356	Naucratis	BM 1888.6–1.154a. *Part of a ring vase with two spouts; back: white.*

357	Naucratis	BM 1888.6–1.154b. *Spout of a ring vase.*
358	Naucratis	BM 1888.6–1.154c. *Part of a ring vase with spout.*
359	Naucratis	BM 1888.6–1.155. *Part of a ring vase with spout. Outside: triple guilloche. Round the neck of the spout: tongues.*
360	Naucratis	BM A 954: 1888.6–1.1526. *Part of a ring vase with two spouts and two bases of protomes. Outside: guilloche. Round the neck of the spout: tongues.*
361	Naucratis	BM A 954.1. *Two spouts and the base of a protome.* *W: 0.146.*
362	Naucratis	*CVA* Oxford II, 84, pl. 396.59.
363*	Naucratis	UCL 756. *Decoration: guilloche. Spout or base of a protome.* *W: 0.091.*
364*	Naucratis	Fairbanks, *Catal.*, 104, no. 311, pl. 30; *Naukratis* II, pl. 7.3.

X. PHALLUS CUPS

365*	Naucratis	BM 1888.6–1.496 a and b. *BSA* 44, 1949, 158 note 12.1, pl. 41b; *AA* 1976, 288 no. 25. *Meander running l, broken meander, tongues red alternating with white and the hindleg of a goat to the r. amidst fill. orns.* *Pres. length: 0.146.*
366	Naucratis	BM 1888.6–1.496 bis. *BSA* 44, 1949, 158 note 12.2 *Fr. of underside of similar but larger cup.*
367	Athens, Acropolis	Acropolis Mus. no. 5043. *BSA* 44, 1949, 158, note 12.3; E.D. van Buren, *Greek Fictile Revetments in the Archaic Period*, 1926, 16 and 184, no. 7, figs. 49–50.

XI. FRAGMENTS

368*	Rizari, Chios town	Chios Mus. no. 3351. *Meander running l. above a row of spirals.*
369*	Rizari, Chios town	Chios Mus. no. 3313. *Fill. orn.: a cross with spikes and spirals at its edge.*
370*	Rizari, Chios town	Chios Mus. no. 3312. *(?same vase as the last). Hindleg of a goat to the r. amidst fill. orns. Inside: two parallel lines.*
371*	Rizari, Chios town	Chios Mus. no. 3401. *Black paint on very white slip. Two rows: upper: lotus and bud; lower: rays.*

372*	Naucratis	BM 1886.4–1.1284. *Naukratis* I, pl. 5.52 *Goats grazing to the r. amidst fill. orns.* *W: 0.058.*
373*	Naucratis	BM 1886.4–1.1564. *Naukratis* I, pl. 5.47 *Body of a feline to the l., with a rosette.* *W: 0.044.*
374	Naucratis	BM 1888.6–1.4681 : 1924.12–1.524. *Lotus* *W: 0.49.*
375	Naucratis	BM 1888.6–1.468i : 1924.12–1.528. *Chain of lotus and bud and then rays.* *W: 0.104.*
376*	Naucratis	BM 1888.6–1.473d : 1924.12–1.89. *Head of a goat grazing to the r. and of another to the l. in an antithetical composition amidst fill. orns.* *W: 0.065.*
377*	Naucratis	BM 1888.6–1.473f : 1924.12–1.92. *Goat to the l. and rosette in front of it. Inside: lotus.* *W: 0.041.*
378*	Naucratis	BM 1888.6–1.473i : 1924.12–1.122. *Head of a dog to the r.* *W: 0.023.*
379*	Naucratis	BM 1888.6–1.473j : 1924.12–1.123. *Head of a dog to the r. amidst fill orns.* *W: 0.030.*
380*	Naucratis	BM 1888.6–1.478b : 1924.12–1.445. *Goose to the r. in front of floral with palmettes and spirals.* *W: 0.074.*
381	Naucratis	BM 1924.12–1.20. *Hindleg of a lion to the r. and horseshoe pendant.* *W: 0.053.*
382*	Naucratis	BM 1924.12–1.85. *Goat to the r. amidst fill. orns.* *W: 0.043.*
383*	Naucratis	BM 1924.12–1.87. *Goat grazing to the r. amidst fill. orns.* *W: 0.043.*
384*	Naucratis	BM 1924.12–1.93. *?Chimaera to the r. amidst fill. orns.* *W: 0.048.*
385*	Naucratis	BM 1924.12–1.96. *Goat to the l.* *W: 0.033.*
386*	Naucratis	BM 1924.12–1.94. *Legs of a goat to the r. amidst fill. orns.* *W: 0.035.*

387*	Naucratis	BM 1924.12–1.99. *Hindquarters of a goat to the r. amidst fill. orns.* *W: 0.035.*
388*	Naucratis	BM 1924.12–1.128. *Siren with scaly body.* *W: 0.028.*
389*	Naucratis	BM 1924.12–1.151. *Head of a goat to the r.* *W: 0.022.*
390	Naucratis	BM 1924.12–1.178. *Goat walking to the r. amidst fill. orns.* *W: 0.034.*
391	Naucratis	BM 1924.12–1.203. *Feline seated to the r. Below: meander running l. above row of chequer and then strokes.* *W: 0.055.*
392	Naucratis	BM 1924.12–1.302. *Hindquarters of a goat to the r. amidst fill. orns.* *W: 0.048.*
393	Naucratis	BM 1924.12–1.309a. *Meander running l. above frieze with goat to the r. amidst fill. orns.* *W: 0.036.*
394	Naucratis	BM 1924.12–1.475. *Goat to the r. above roundel.* *W: 0.044.*
395	Naucratis	BM 1924.12–1.495. *Rim pattern: strokes above chequer with dotted blanks, then meander and ?dividing band.* *W: 0.032.*
396	Naucratis	BM 1924.12–1.1028. *Goat to the r. and the horn of another to the l. in an antithetical composition amidst fill. orns. Above simple guilloche with eyes. Incised inscription:*]ΗΣΑΝΕ[*W: 0.061.*
397	Naucratis	BM 1924.12–1.1026. *Frieze with fill. orns. above elongated strokes and then meander running r.* *W: 0.044.*
398	Naucratis	BM 1924.12–1.1027. *Fill. orns.: semi-circles and swastika.* *W: 0.048.*
399	Naucratis	BM 1924.12–1.1036. *Horn of a goat and goose to the r.* *W: 0.033.*
400	Naucratis	BM 1924.12–1.1029. *Two friezes: Upper: Fill. orns. Lower: guilloche with eyes.* *W: 0.032.*

401	Naucratis	BM 1924.12–1.1032. *Rays above two parallel lines, then broken meander.* *W: 0.079.*
402	Naucratis	BM 1924.12–1.1127. *Tongue pattern above battlement and then chain of lotus and palmette.* *W: 0.057.*
403	Naucratis	BM 1924.12–1.1141. *Head of a ?man to the r. between rays.* *W: 0.073.*
404*	Naucratis	BM 1924.12–1.1240. *Hindquarters of an animal to the l.* *W: 0.021.*
405	Naucratis	BM 1924.12–1.517. *Guilloche above three parallel lines.* *W: 0.034.*
406	Naucratis	BM 1924.12–1.522. *Frieze of lotus and bud.* *W: 0.029.*
407*	Naucratis	BM 1888.6–1.466c. *Guilloche* *W: 0.055.*
408	Naucratis	BM 1924.12–1.476. *Pendant.*
409*	Naucratis	*CVA* Oxford II, 81, pl. 396.10.
410*	Naucratis	Fairbanks, *Catal*, 110, no. 321.5, pl. 34.
411*	Naucratis	Fairbanks, *Catal*, 98, no. 302.5, pl. 32, upside-down.
412*	Naucratis	*CVA* Brussels III, 1–2, pl. 104.2
413*	Naucratis	Leipzig, sent from Oxford in 1928 (lost during the war). *Goat to the r. amidst fill. orns.*
414*	Naucratis	Leipzig, sent from Oxford in 1928 (lost during the war). *Hindquarters of a goat to the r. with swastika.*
415*	Naucratis	Leipzig, sent from Oxford in 1928 (lost during the war). *Feet of a ?bull to the r.*
416*	Naucratis	Leipzig, sent from Oxford in 1928 (lost during the war). *Head of a goat to the r.*
417*	Syracuse from Ortygia	Syracuse Museum. *Forelegs of a goat to the r. amidst fill. orns.*
418*	Syracuse from Ortygia	Syracuse Museum. *Triple meander running l. below frieze with fill. orns.*

Chapter 3: The Reserving styles of the sixth century

1. THE ANIMAL CHALICE STYLE

I. CHALICES

419*–429	Emporio	*Emporio*, nos. 724–734, pls. 58–59, figs. 106–107.
430	Phana	*BSA* 35, 1934–35, 159, pl. 37.15.
431*	Chios town, Kofiná Ridge	*BSA* 49, 1954, 134, pl. 6.2.
432*	Naucratis	BM 1886.4–1.1075. *Naukratis* I, pl. 5.21. *Boar's head to the r. Inside: two white parallel lines.* *W: 0.032.*
433*	Naucratis	BM 1886.4–1.1065. *Naukratis* I, pl. 5.20 *Lion's head to the l. Fill. orns.* *W: 0.043.*
434	Naucratis	BM 1886.4–1.1548. *Naukratis* I, pl. 5.5, inside. *Rim pattern: two parallel lines with vertical strokes in between. Fill. orn.: a rosette. Inside: lotus and rosette with pomegranates.* *W: 0.044.*
435	Naucratis	BM 1886.4–1.1565. *Naukratis* I, pl. 5.48 *Feline to the l. Fill. orns.* *W: 0.055.*
436	Naucratis	BM 1886.6–1.181. *Lion to the r. Fill. orn. Rim pattern: strokes; then, meander. Incised inscription on the animal's body boustrophedon:*]EPMO[ ]ΘHKE[O[*Inside: two white lines* *W: 0.037.*
437	Naucratis	BM 1888.6–1.199. *Rim fr. Griffin's head to the l. Fill. orn.: Triangle. Inside: lotus and white line.* *W: 0.038.*
438*	Naucratis	BM 1888.6–1.466a. Price, pl. 10.7; Johnston, *Exhibition* 1978, no. 77. *Wall and handle zone. Brown paint on creamy slip. Lion v. bull to the l. Fill. orns. Handle zone: guilloche.* *W: 0.162.*
439*	Naucratis	BM 1888.6–1.466d, f, e. Price, pl. 10.9; *Samos* VI.1, pl. 92. 751 *Wall and part of the handle zone. Brown paint diluted yellow on*

THE ANIMAL CHALICE STYLE

the mane of the lion, on very white slip. Added red on boar's body. Lion v. boar to the r. Fill. orns. Handle zone: guilloche. Inside: white lines and dotted rosettes.
W: 0.241.

440*   Naucratis   BM 1888.6–1.466g and a: A791; (same vase).
Black paint diluted brown for the wings on white slip. Added red. Frieze of sphs. to the l. Fill. orns. Inside: chain of palmettes and rosettes then two white parallel lines then buds alternating with concentric circles.
BM 1888.6–1.466g: W: 0.141.
BM 1888.6–1.466a: W: 0.105.

441*   Naucratis   BM 1888.6–1.471b: 1924.12–1.412.
Brown paint diluted yellow on the outline on white slip. Frieze of bulls to the r. Fill. orns. Rim pattern: two parallel lines with vertical strokes in between. Inside: chain of lotus and rosettes, then three lines.
W: 0.171.

442*   Naucratis   BM 1888.6–1.471a.
Lion with bull in an antithetical composition. Fill. orns. Inside: lotus and two white lines.
W: 0.064.

443*   Naucratis   BM 1888.6–1.471b: 1924.12–1.139.
Part of a bull's head to the r. Fill. orns. Inside: lotus and two white lines.
W: 0.028.

444*   Naucratis   BM 1888.6–1.471c: 1924.12–1.136.
Part of a bull's head to the r. Inside: lotus and two white lines.
W: 0.035.

445*   Naucratis   BM 1888.6–1.471e: 1924.12–1.142.
Bull's head to the r. then dog standing. Fill. orns. Inside: grey
W: 0.059.

446*   Naucratis   BM 1888.6–1.471f: 1924. 12–1.138.
Bull to the r. Fill. orns.
W: 0.032.

447*   Naucratis   BM 1888.6–1.471g: 1924.12–1.137.
Bull and lion in an antithetical composition. Fill. orns. Inside: two white lines.
W: 0.058.

448*   Naucratis   BM 1888.6–1.471h: 1924.12–1.130.
Boar's head to the r. Inside: three white and two red lines.
W: 0.048.

449*   Naucratis   BM 1888.6–1.471i: 1924.12–1.131.
Boar's head to the r.
W: 0.029.

450*   Naucratis   BM 1888.6–1.471j: 1924:12–1.132.
Boar and lion in an antithetical composition. Fill. orn.: dotted rosette. Handle zone: guilloche. Inside: two white lines.
W: 0.052.

451*   Naucratis   BM 1888.6–1.471k : 1924.12–1.129.
Samos VI.1, pl. 92. 749; Bernard, *Le Delta égyptien*, pl. 45.2 top row; Johnston, *Exhibition* 1978, no. 70.
Boar's head to the r. Fill. orn.
W: 0.037.

452*   Naucratis   BM 1888.6–1.471b : 1924.12–1.1247.
Part of boar's body to the r. Fill. orns. Inside: two white lines.
W: 0.037.

453*   Naucratis   BM 1888.6–1.471m : 1924.12–1.143.
Price fig. 46.
Dog to the r. above volute-palmette. Inside: two white lines and then two white lines.
W: 0.062.

454*   Naucratis   BM 1888.6–1.471n : 1924.12–1.147.
Price 211, fig. 46; *Samos* VI, 1, pl. 92. 752
Dog's head to the r.
W: 0.028.

455*   Naucratis   BM 1888.6–1.471o : 1924.12–1.121.
Dog's head to the r.
W: 0.025.

456*   Naucratis   BM 1888.6–1.472k.
Griffin's head to the r. Inside: two white lines.
W: 0.022.

457*   Naucratis   BM 1888.6–1.472l : 1924.12–1.1236.
Two rows: upper: feet of feline in an antithetical composition; lower: lion to the l. Fill. orn.
W: 0.069.

458*   Naucratis   BM 1888.6–1.464.
Two joining sherds of a very big chalice. Brown paint diluted yellow for the outlines on white slip. Decoration: outside: rim pattern: two parallel lines with vertical strokes in between; on the walls: woman in black chiton and red himation to the l., then two antithetical sphs. amidst fill. orns. Inside: lotus and rosette frieze, then battlement pattern between two white lines, then two parallel lines and lower down three white parallel lines.
W: c. 0.15 for smaller fr.
W: c. 0.22 for bigger fr.

459*   Naucratis   BM 1888.6–1.474e : 1924.12–1.157.
Johnston, *Exhibition* 1978, no. 82
Sph. to the r. Fill. orns. Inside: traces of lotus and lines.
W: 0.085.

460*   Naucratis   BM 1888.6–1.474g : 1924.12–1.249.
Sph. to the l. amidst fill. orns. Inside: rosette and two white lines.
W: 0.054.

461*   Naucratis   BM 1888.6–1.474n : 1924.12–1.267.
Sph. to the r. amidst fill. orns.
W: 0.042.

462*	Naucratis	BM 1888.6–1.474r : 1924.12–1.280. *Sph. to the l. amidst fill. orns.* *W: 0.082.*
463*	Naucratis	BM 1888.6–1.474s : 1924.12–1.286. *Sph. to the l. amidst fill. orns. Inside: lotus and two white lines.* *W: 0.036.*
464*	Naucratis	BM 1888.6–1.474t : 1924.12–1.282. *Rim pattern: two parallel lines with vertical strokes in between. Sph's wing to the l. amidst fill. orns. Inside: lotus.* *W: 0.034.*
465*	Naucratis	BM 1888.6–1.476d : 1924.12–1.257. *Sph's head to the l. amidst fill. orns. Rim pattern: two parallel lines with strokes in between. Inside: lotus.* *W: 0.033.*
466*	Naucratis	BM 1888.6–1.476b : 1924.12–1.263. *Head of a sph to the l. amidst fill. orns. Rim pattern: two parallel lines with vertical strokes in between.* *W: 0.029.*
467*	Naucratis	BM 1888.6–1.476l : 1924.12–1.401. *Head of a sph. to the r. amidst fill. orns. Inside: two white lines.* *W: 0.021.*
468*	Naucratis	BM 1888.6–1.476m : 1924.12–1.449. *Head of a ?sph. to the l. amidst fill. orns. Inside: lotus.* *W: 0.040.*
469*	Naucratis	BM 1888.6–1.478g : 1924.12–1.482. *Rim part of a chalice. Rim pattern: strokes, meander running l. and then chequers. Fill. orns. Inside: lotus and rosette.* *W: 0.082.*
470*	Naucratis	BM 1888.6–1.480. *Two sphs. in an antithetical composition. Fill. orn.: dotted circle. Inside: lotus and two white lines.* *W: 0.080.*
471*	Naucratis	BM 1924.12–1.425 + 97. *Rim patterns: strokes, meander and parallel lines. Hindquarters of an animal amidst fill. orns. Inside: lotus and rosette.* *W: 0.085.*
472*	Naucratis	BM 1924.12–1.98. *Hindquarters of a goat to the r. amidst fill. orn. Inside: lotus and white lines.* *W: 0.032.*
473*	Naucratis	BM 1924.12–1.101. *Goat to the r. Rim pattern: two parallel lines with broken meander in between. Inside: lotus bud.* *W: 0.029.*
474*	Naucratis	BM 1924.12–1.120. *Hindquarters of a ?dog amidst fill. orns. Inside: lotus.* *W: 0.046.*

258   THE ANIMAL CHALICE STYLE

475*   Naucratis   BM 1924.12–1.135.
Foreleg of a lion on the hindleg of a bull to the r. amidst fill. orns.
W: 0.044.

476*   Naucratis   BM 1924.12–1.141.
Hindquarters of a feline to the l. amidst fill. orns.
W: 0.054.

477   Naucratis   BM 1924.12–1.133.
Rim pattern: two parallel lines with broken cable in between. Boar's head to the r. amidst fill. orns. Inside: lotus.
W: 0.040.

478   Naucratis   BM 1924.12–1.127.
Siren to the l. Inside: rosette and two white lines.
W: 0.036.

479   Naucratis   BM 1924.12–1.134.
Rim pattern: two parallel lines with vertical strokes in between. Siren to the r. amidst fill. orns. Inside: tendril and rosette.
W: 0.046.

480*   Naucratis   BM 1924.12–1.186.
Sph. to the l. amidst fill. orns. Inside: lotus and white lines.
W: 0.050.

481   Naucratis   BM 1924.12–1.239.
Lion to the r. amidst fill. orns. Inside: white and red lines.
W: 0.082.

482   Naucratis   BM 1924.12–1.244.
?Sph. to the l. amidst fill. orns. Inside: rosette.
W: 0.069.

483   Naucratis   BM 1924.12–1.241.
Lion to the r. amidst fill. orns. Inside: white and red lines.
W: 0.053.

484   Naucratis   BM 1924.12–1.240.
Lion to the r. Handle zone: double guilloche.
W: 0.052.

485   Naucratis   BM 1924.12–1.242.
?Sph. to the l. amidst fill. orns. Inside: two white lines.
W: 0.055.

486   Naucratis   BM 1924.12–1.252.
?Boar to the r.
W: 0.045.

487   Naucratis   BM 1924.12–1.251.
Sph. to the r. amidst fill. orns.
W: 0.048.

488*   Naucratis   BM 1924.12–1.277.
Naukratis I, pl. 5. 39.
Sph. to the l. amidst fill. orns. Inside: white lines.
W: 0.040.

489*   Naucratis   BM 1924.12–1.255.
Sph. to the l. amidst fill. orns.
W: 0.051.

490*	Naucratis	BM 1924.12–1.281a. *Sph. to the r.* *W: 0.025.*
491*	Naucratis	BM 1924.12–1.264. *Head of a ?sph. to the l. amidst fill. orns. Rim pattern: two parallel lines with broken cable in between.* *W: 0.072.*
492*	Naucratis	BM 1924.12–1.281. *Head of a ?sph. to the l. amidst fill. orns. Rim pattern: two parallel lines with broken cable in between.* *W: 0.072.*
493*	Naucratis	BM 1924.12–1.283. *Sph. to the l. Inside: two white lines.* *W: 0.034.*
494*	Naucratis	BM 1924.12–1.295. *Bull to the r. Inside: white and red lines.* *W: 0.044.*
495*	Naucratis	BM 1924.12–1.296. *Bull to the r. amidst fill. orns.* *W: 0.038.*
496*	Naucratis	BM 1924.12–1.308. *Sph. to the l.* *W: 0.037.*
497*	Naucratis	BM 1924.12–1.290. *Sph. to the r. amidst fill. orns. Inside: lotus and white lines.* *W: 0.035.*
498*	Naucratis	BM 1924.12–1.297. *Bull to the r. Inside: palmette, chequers and lines.* *W: 0.030.*
499*	Naucratis	BM 1924.12–1.299. *Hindquarters of a feline to the l. amidst fill. orns. Inside: lotus and lines.* *W: 0.056.*
500*	Naucratis	BM 1924. 12–1.298. *Indiscernible objects amidst fill. orns. Inside: lotus and lines.* *W: 0.030.*
501*	Naucratis	BM 1924.12–1.301. *Hindquarters of a bull to the r. Inside: rosette.* *W: 0.032.*
502*	Naucratis	BM 1924.12–1.303. *Lion to the l. Inside: lines and vertical strokes.* *W: 0.052.*
503*	Naucratis	BM 1924.12–1.304. *Bull to the r. amidst fill. orns. Inside: rosette and lines.* *W: 0.027.*
504*	Naucratis	BM 1924.12–1.305. *Lion to the r. amidst fill. orns. Inside: rosette.* *W: 0.053.*

THE ANIMAL CHALICE STYLE

505*   Naucratis   BM 1924.12–1.313.
Dog to the l. Inside: white lines.
W: 0.039.

506   Naucratis   BM 1924.12–1.308.
Bull to the l. amidst fill. orns. Inside: two white lines.
W: 0.036.

507   Naucratis   BM 1924.12–1.317.
Rim pattern: chequer, double meander running l., two parallel lines, chequers with dotted blanks and two parallel lines. Inside: lotus.
W: 0.063.

508   Naucratis   BM 1924.12–1.314.
Rim pattern: as the last. Inside: lotus.
W: 0.063.
(?same vase as the last).

509   Naucratis   BM 1924.12–1.316.
Rim pattern: chequer, two parallel lines, meander running l. and two parallel lines. Fill. orns. Inside: lotus.
W: 0.065.

510   Naucratis   BM 1924.12–1.318.
Rim pattern: chequers with dotted blanks, parallel line, broken meander to the l. and two parallel lines. Dividing vertical bands. Inside: lotus.
W: 0.056.

511   Naucratis   BM 1924.12–1.323.
Rim pattern: chequers with dotted blanks, two parallel lines, cable and two parallel lines.
W: 0.020.

512   Naucratis   BM 1924.12–1.325.
Rim pattern: two parallel lines with vertical strokes in between. Dividing vertical bands.
W: 0.044.

513   Naucratis   BM 1924.12–1.328.
Rim pattern: two parallel lines with diagonal strokes in between.
W: 0.023.

514   Naucratis   BM 1924.12–1.331.
Rim pattern: chequer with dotted blanks and then squares with dots in the middle.
W: 0.022.

515   Naucratis   BM 1924.12–1.333.
Rim pattern: two parallel lines, double meander running l. and two parallel lines. Inside: lotus.
W: 0.036.

516   Naucratis   BM 1924.12–1.343.
?Boar to the r. amidst fill. orns. Inside: horizontal dividing band with squares.
W: 0.040.

THE ANIMAL CHALICE STYLE

517*　　Naucratis　　BM 1924.12–1.420.
Naukratis I, pl. 5.28
Two felines in an antithetical composition amidst fill. orns. Handle zone: guilloche.
W: 0.072.

518*　　Naucratis　　BM 1924.12–1.424.
Part of the wall and handle zone with handle root. ?Boar to the r. amidst fill. orns. Inside: white lines.
W: 0.083.

519　　Naucratis　　BM 1924.12–1.422.
Bulls to the r. amidst fill. orns. Inside: white lines.
W: 0.060.

520　　Naucratis　　BM 1924.12–1.431.
Forelegs of an animal to the r. amidst fill. orns. Inside: lotus and rosette.
W: 0.043.

521　　Naucratis　　BM 1924.12–1.427.
Rim pattern: two parallel lines with diagonal strokes in between. Fill. orn. Inside: lotus and rosette.
W: 0.046.

522　　Naucratis　　BM 1924.12–1.426.
Rim pattern: two parallel lines with SS in between. Fill. orn. Inside: rosette and two white lines.
W: 0.035.

523　　Naucratis　　BM 1924.12–1.434.
Fill. orns. Handle zone: broken meander to the l. Inside: lotus and rosette.
W: 0.046.

524　　Naucratis　　BM 1924.12–1.432.
Fill. orn. Inside: lotus and white lines.
W: 0.023.

525　　Naucratis　　BM 1924.12–1.477.
Rim pattern: parallel lines with dots in between, simple meander running l. and two parallel lines. ?Bull to the r. amidst fill. orns.
W: 0.058.

526　　Naucratis　　BM 1924.12–1.484.
Rim pattern: two parallel lines with double meander in between. Inside: lotus and horizontal chequers.
W: 0.055.

527　　Naucratis　　BM 1924.12–1.483.
Rim pattern: chequer, two parallel lines with SS in between. Tail of an animal amidst fill. orns. Inside: lotus.
W: 0.048.

528　　Naucratis　　BM 1924.12–1.497.
Rim pattern: strokes, two parallel lines and guilloche.
W: 0.034.

529	Naucratis	BM 1924.12-1.499. *Rim pattern: chequer, two parallel lines, double guilloche and chequer with dotted blanks. Inside: lotus.* *W: 0.052.*
530	Naucratis	BM 1924.12-1.501. *Rim pattern: as the last.* *W: 0.069.*
531	Naucratis	BM 1924.12-1.487. *Rim pattern: broken meander to the l. then chequer with dotted blanks. Part of the neck and ear of a bull to the r.* *W: 0.033.*
532	Naucratis	BM 1924.12-1.489. *Rim pattern: vertical strokes, double meander to the l, and triple meander to the r.* *W: 0.025.*
533	Naucratis	BM 1924.12-1.538. *Rim pattern: chequer with dotted blanks, double meander to the l., chequer with dotted blanks. Inside: lotus and rosette.* *W: 0.034.*
534	Naucratis	BM 1924.12-1.542. *Rim pattern: two parallel lines with SS in between. Fill. orn. Inside: lotus and rosette.* *W: 0.027.*
535	Naucratis	BM 1924.12-1.547. *Rim pattern: strokes, then broken cable. Part of the mane of a lion to the r. Inside: lotus.* *W: 0.037.*
536	Naucratis	BM 1924.12-1.558. *Rim pattern: chequer, double meander to the l. and chequers with dotted blanks. Fill. orns. Inside: lotus and palmette.* *W: 0.096.*
537	Naucratis	BM 1924.12-1.574. *Rim pattern: as the last. Inside: lotus.* *W: 0.053.*
538	Naucratis	BM 1924.12-1.555. *Rim pattern: two parallel lines with broken cable in between. Fill. orns. Inside: lotus.* *W: 0.038.*
539	Naucratis	BM 1924.12-1.575. *Rim pattern: chequer and double meander running l. Inside: lotus and bud.* *W: 0.037.*
540	Naucratis	BM 1924.12-1.673. *?Sph. to the l. amidst fill. orns. Inside: white line.* *W: 0.032.*
541	Naucratis	BM 1924.12-1.1245. *Part of a bull to the r.* *W: 0.034.*

THE ANIMAL CHALICE STYLE

542   Naucratis   BM 1924.12–1.509.
Rim pattern: two parallel lines with diagonal lines in between. Fill. orns. Inside: lotus and rosette then two white lines.
W: 0.033.

543   Naucratis   BM 1924.12–1.438.
Rim pattern: two parallel lines with broken cable in between. Fill. orn. Inside: rosette.
W: 0.046.

544*   Naucratis   BM 1924.12–1.1287.
Naukratis I, pl. 5. 44
Boar to the r.
W: 0.055.

545   Naucratis   BM 1924.12–1.474.
Sph. to the r. amidst fill. orns.
W: 0.032.

546*   Naucratis   BM 1888.6–1.463.
Naukratis II, pl. 5.7.
Heavy chalice. Brown paint diluted yellow for the outlines on white slip. Rim pattern: two parallel lines with meander alternating with square crosses in between. Lion v. bull and a feline to the r. amidst fill. orns. Handle zone: two parallel lines with broken meander to the l. in between and then double guilloche. Part of the bowl: four bands. Inside: frieze of lotus and rosette, then chequers, then rosettes, then meander to the l., then three parallel lines and then tongues in red and white.
W: c. 0.22.

547   Naucratis   *Naukratis* I, pl. 5.24.
Rim pattern: chequers with dotted blanks. Sph. to the l. amidst fill. orns. and dividing band.
W: 0.084.

548   Naucratis   *Naukratis* I, pl. 5.50.
?Bull to the r. amidst fill. orns.
W: 0.042.

549   Naucratis   BM 1924.12–1.580.
Rim pattern: two parallel lines with chequer in between. Tail of an animal amidst fill. orns. Inside: rosette.
W: 0.044.

550   Naucratis   BM 1924.12–1.579.
Rim pattern: chequers with dotted blanks. Fill. orns. Inside: lotus and rosette.
W: 0.052.

551   Naucratis   BM 1924.12–1.616.
Sph. to the l. amidst fill. orns. Inside: chain of pomegranates.
W: 0.032.

552*   Naucratis   BM 1888.6–1.465a : 1924.12–1.537.
? joins Boston, Fairbanks, *Catal.* 302.7
[same vase: BM 88.6–1.465d; BM 88.6–1.465e; BM 88.6–1.465b; now in the J. Paul Getty Museum, in

exchange] (*BM Occ. Pap.* 22, 1981, 32ff.) and BM 88.6–1.465c.
Rim pattern: two parallel lines, tongues, zigzag and two lines. Lion and then sph. to the l. amidst fill. orns. Inside: chain of lotus and rosette then strokes and lines.
W: 0.192 for the bigger fr.

553	Naucratis	BM 1888.6–1.472a : 1929.12–10.10. *Light chalice. Brown paint on very white slip. Lion to the r. amidst fill. orns.* *W: 0.175.*
554*	Naucratis	BM 1888.6–1.475h : 1924.12–1.126. *Scaly body of a siren to the r. amidst fill. orns.* *W: 0.036.*
555*	Naucratis	BM 1888.6–1.475i : 1924.12–1.160. *Scaly body of a siren to the l. amidst fill. orns. Inside: lotus.* *W: 0.046.*
556*	Naucratis	BM 1886.4–1.1074. *Naukratis* I, pl. 5.23. *Rim pattern: two parallel lines with vertical strokes in between. Neck and head of a deer to the l. Inside: lotus.* *W: 0.037.*
557	Naucratis	BM 1924.12–1.461. *Rim pattern: chequers, then meander running l. and then two parallel lines. Fill. orns. Inside: lotus.* *W: 0.041.*
558*	Naucratis	*CVA* Oxford II, 82, pl. 396.12.
559*	Naucratis	*CVA* Oxford II, 82, pl. 396.20.
560*	Naucratis	*CVA* Oxford II, 82, pl. 396.27.
561*	Naucratis	Oxf. 1925. 608c. *Rim pattern: two parallel lines with simple cable in between. Mane of a lion to the r. amidst fill. orns.* *W: 0.051.*
562	Naucratis	Oxf. G114.43. see: Boardman CN, 60 note 5. *Hindquarters of an animal, ?dog. Handle zone: double guilloche.* *W: 0.053.*
563	Naucratis	*CVA* Oxford II, 82, pl. 396.24. *The inside of a chalice.*
564*	Naucratis	*CVA* Cambridge II, 33, pl. 496.22.
565*	Naucratis	*CVA* Cambridge II, 33, pl. 496.25.
566*	Naucratis	*CVA* Cambridge II, 33, pl. 496.29.
567*	Naucratis	*CVA* Cambridge II, 34, pl. 496.39. *A siren.*
568*	Naucratis	Cambridge, Museum of Classical Archaeology, NA 66. *Rim pattern: SS between lines. Fill. orns.* *W: 0.034.*

THE ANIMAL CHALICE STYLE

569*   Naucratis   Cambridge, Museum of Classical Archaeology, NA 69.
Rosette, two bands and then a lotus.
W: 0.026.

570*   Naucratis   Cambridge, Museum of Classical Archaeology, NA 71.
Animal's leg to the l. amidst fill. orns. Handle zone: triple meander running l.
W: 0.029.

571*   Naucratis   Cambridge, Museum of Classical Archaeology, NA 72.
Goat to the r. amidst fill. orns.
W: 0.027.

572*   Naucratis   Cambridge, Museum of Classical Archaeology, NA 73.
Boar to the r. amidst fill. orns.
W: 0.041.

573*   Naucratis   Cambridge, Museum of Classical Archaeology, NA 74.
Part of a white-spotted boar to the r.
W: 0.034.

574*   Naucratis   UCL 798.
Johnston, *Exhibition* 1978, no. 68
Goat to the l. and perhaps another animal on the l. amidst fill. orns.: rosettes and dotted rosette. Inside: tongues.
W: 0.058 H: 0.050.

575*   Naucratis   UCL 757.
Johnston, *Exhibition* 1978, no. 71
Thin-walled chalice. Rim pattern: chequer with dotted blanks, broken meander to the l., two parallel lines. Head of a goose to the r. Inside: lotus.
W: 0.021 H: 0.035.

576*   Naucratis   UCL 749.
Johnston, *Exhibition* 1978, no. 89
Thin-walled chalice. Rim pattern: two parallel lines with SS in between. Fill. orns.: triangle, tendril, swastika. Inside: lotus.
W: 0.069 H: 0.027.

577   Naucratis   UCL 767.
Thin-walled chalice. Back of an animal Inside: elaborate complex of lotus and palmette.

578*   Naucratis   *CVA* Reading I, 37, pl. 550.5 a and b.

579*   Naucratis   Liverpool 56–21–525.
Leg of a lion to the l. and below handle zone pattern: guilloche. Inside: two pairs of white lines.
H: 0.027 W: 0.019.

580*   Naucratis   Liverpool 56–21–529.
Rim pattern: broken meander and below a roundel. Inside: rosette.
H: 0.024 W: 0.013.

581*   Naucratis   Liverpool 56–21–532.
Handle zone pattern: guilloche. Inside: orn.
H: 0.026 W: 0.017.

582*	Naucratis	Boston 88.830, 7. Fairbanks, *Catal.* 99, no. 302.7, pl. 32 *Perhaps from the same vase as BM 1888.6–1.465, here* **552***. *A sph. to the l. amidst fill. orns.*
583*	Naucratis	Fairbanks, *Catal.* 99, no. 302.8, pl. 32.
584*	Naucratis	Fairbanks, *Catal.* 99, no. 302.9, pl. 32.
585*	Naucratis	MMA inv. no. 26.211.2 (Gift of Elinor R. Price, 1926). *Part of a bull to the r.*
586*	Naucratis	UM Philadelphia E 175 A8. *Sph. and fill. orn.* H: 0.021 W: 0.041.
587*	Naucratis	UM Philadelphia E 175 B2. *Lion to the l. amidst fill. orns.* H: 0.050 W: 0.043.
588*	Naucratis	UM Philadelphia E 175 E5. *?Bull to the r. and roundel.* H: 0.026 W: 0.038.
589*	Naucratis	UM Philadelphia E 175 G7. *Patterns.* H: 0.048 W: 0.054.
590*	Naucratis	UM Philadelphia E 175 L12. *Spiked rosette.* H: 0.026 W: 0.042.
591*	Naucratis	ROM 910 x 234.8. Hayes, forthcoming.
592*	Naucratis	ROM 910 x 234.6. Hayes, forthcoming.
593	Naucratis	ROM 910 x 234.7. Hayes, forthcoming.
594*	Naucratis	Berlin Antiquarium (lost during the war). *Part of a siren to the l. and below a pendant.*
595*	Naucratis	Berlin Antiquarium (lost during the war). *Naukratis* II, 63, pl. 21.728 and *BSA* 47, 1952, 165 n. 37. *End of the tail of a feline.* *Inscription:*]TYXΩ[
596*	Naucratis	Bonn. *Part of a ?siren and part of a pendant.*
597*	Naucratis	Bonn. *Part of a ?feline to the r. and part of a pendant.*
598*	Naucratis	*CVA* Heidelberg I, 13, pl. 437.7.
599*	Naucratis	*CVA* Heidelberg I, 13, pl. 437.9 and 12.
600*	Naucratis	*CVA* Heidelberg I, 13, pl. 437.10.
601*	Naucratis	*CVA* Heidelberg I, 14, pl. 437.18.
602*	Naucratis	*CVA* Heidelberg I, 13, pl. 437.13.
603*	Naucratis	*CVA* Musée Scheurleer II, pl. 69.4; Wiel, *Leiden*, pl. 1.2; Prins de Jong, *Scherben*, pl. 1.5.

604*	Naucratis	Cairo inv. no. 26158. Edgar, *Catal. Caire*, 12, no. 26158; Venit, *Egypt. Museums*, no. 126, pl. 32.
605	Naucratis	Cairo inv. no. 26157. Edgar, *Catal. Caire*, 12, no. 26157; Venit, *Egypt. Museums*, no. 125, pl. 32.
606*	Naucratis	Alexandria, inv. no. 9376. Venit, *Egypt. Museums*, no. 127, pl. 32 and drawing on p. 167. *Bull's head to the r. Inside: lotus and then two parallel lines.*
606a*	Naucratis	Alexandria, inv. no. 9374. Venit, *Egypt. Museums*, no. 133, pl. 33 and drawing on p. 168. *Lotus.*
607*	Naucratis	Nicholson Museum, Sydney, inv. no. 46.43/1, presented by J.D. Beazley. A.D. Trendall, *Handbook to the Nicholson Museum*,[2] 1948, 253, fig. 53.d. *Part of a rim pattern with SS between lines and then a pendant and a rosette. Inside: strokes between lines and then a lotus.*
608*	Naucratis	Nicholson Museum, Sydney, inv. no. 46.43/2, presented by J.D. Beazley. A.D. Trendall, *Handbook to the Nicholson Museum*,[2] 1948, 253, fig. 53e. *Part of a rim pattern: chequer with dots and then meander running left; part of a fill. orn. Inside: lotus.*
609	Naucratis	Nicholson Museum, Sydney, inv. no. 46.43/3, presented by J.D. Beazley. A.D. Trendall, *Handbook to the Nicholson Museum*,[2] 1948, 253, fig. 53f. *Inside: part of a rosette and lotus.*
610*	Naucratis	Nicholson Museum, Sydney, inv. no. 46/43.5, presented by J.D. Beazley. A.D. Trendall, *Handbook to the Nicholson Museum*,[2] 1948, 253, fig. 53g. *Part of the rim pattern with dots between lines. Inside: strokes between lines and then a rosette.*
611*	Tocra	*Tocra* I, 60, pl. 40.773.
612*	Tocra	*Tocra* I, 60, pl. 40.774.
613	Tocra	*Tocra* I, 60, pl. 41.776.
614*	Tocra	*Tocra* I, 60, pl. 41.777.
615*	Tocra	*Tocra* I, 60, pl. 41.778.
616*	Tocra	*Tocra* I, 60, pl. 41.779.
617	Cyrene, Artemision	Pernier, *Africa Italiana* IV, 1931, 200, no. 12, pl. 3; *BSA* 51, 1956, 61 note 7.
618	Cyrene, Demeter Sanct.	Schaus, *Dem. Sanct., Cyrene* II, 80, no. 479, pl. 28.

619	Cyrene, Demeter Sanct.	Schaus, *Dem. Sanct., Cyrene* II, 80, no. 480, pl. 28.
620	Cyrene, Demeter Sanct.	Schaus, *Dem. Sanct., Cyrene* II, 80, no. 481, Ill. 7.
621	Cyrene, Demeter Sanct.	Schaus, *Dem. Sanct., Cyrene* II, 80, no. 482, pl. 28.
622	Cyrene, Demeter Sanct.	Schaus, *Dem. Sanct., Cyrene* II, 80, no. 483, pl. 28.
623	Cyrene, Demeter Sanct.	Schaus, *Dem. Sanct., Cyrene*, II, 80, no. 484, pl. 28.
624*	Catane	*BolldArte* 45, 1960, 255, fig. 14, nos. 13. 18. 19. 20; *Emporio* 157 note 4; *Samos* VI. 1, pl. 94.744.
625*	Catane	*BolldArte* 45, 1960, 255, fig. 14.4.
626*	Catane	*BolldArte* 45, 1960, 255, fig. 14.5.
627*	Catane	*BolldArte* 45, 1960, 255, fig. 14.6.
628*	Catane	*BolldArte* 45, 1960, 255, fig. 14.8.
629*	Catane	*BolldArte* 45, 1960, 255, fig. 14.1.
630*	Catane	*BolldArte* 45, 1960, 255, fig. 14.3.
631	Selinus	*MonAnt.* 32, 1921, pl. 83.4; *Emporio* 157 note 4.
632	Locri	*CGED* 114 and note 111.
633	Sybaris	*NSc* 1969, 1: suppl., 94, fig. 81 no. 212; *CGED* 112 and note 84.
634	Sybaris	*NSc* 1969, 1: suppl., 94, fig. 81, no. 213; *CGED* 112 and note 84.
635	Francavilla Mma, Motta	*AttiMGrecia* 15–17, 1974–76, 144, pl. 67.1a.
636	Francavilla Mma, Motta	*AttiMGrecia* 15–17, 1974–76, 144, pl. 67. 2a, 2e (and 1b).
637	Francavilla Mma, Motta	*AttiMGrecia* 15–17, 1974–76, 144, pl. 67. 2b and 1c.
638	Francavilla Mma, Motta	*AttiMGrecia* 15–17, 1974–76, 145, pl. 67. 2c.
639	Francavilla Mma, Motta	*AttiMGrecia* 15–17, 1974–76, pl. 67, 2h.
640	Cumae	*CGED* 138.
641	Marseilles	Vasseur, *Marseille*, pl. 5.8; *Emporio* 157 note 4.
642	Paros	O. Rubensohn, *Das Delion von Paros*, 1962, 113, no. 2, pl. 21: inv. no. 308, Delion. *Rim pattern: two parallel lines with broken cable in between. Inside: lotus.*
643*	Delos	Delos Museum B. 6230.208. *Délos* X, 55–57, pl. 19, 61, 62.121; Price pl. 9.11; *Emporio* 157 note 4; *Samos* VI.1, 139, pl. 94.745.
644	Delos	*Délos* X 57, pl. 20, no. 122 a and b.

645	Aegina	*Alt-Ägina* II.1, 16, pl. 5.75.
646	Aegina	*Alt-Ägina* II.1, 16, pl. 5.76.
647	Aegina	*Alt-Ägina* II.1, 16, pl. 5.77.
648*	Aegina, Aphaia Temple	*AA* 1983, 163, fig. 7.2 a–d.
649*	Aegina, Aphaia Temple	*AA* 1983, 163, fig. 7.3.
650*	Aegina, Aphaia Temple	*AA* 1983, 164, fig. 7.4.
651*	Aegina, Aphaia Temple	*AA* 1983, 164, fig. 8.9.
652	Aegina, Aphaia Temple	*AA* 1983, 164, fig. 8.10.
653*	Aegina, Aphaia Temple	*AA* 1983, 164, fig. 8.12.
654*	Aegina, Aphaia Temple	*AA* 1983, 164, fig. 8.15.
655*	Aegina, Aphaia Temple	*AA* 1983, 164, fig. 8.22.
656	Aegina, Aphaia Temple	*AA* 1983, 164, fig. 8.23.
657	Aegina, Aphaia Temple	*AA* 1983, 164, fig. 8.25.
658*	Athens, Acropolis	Graef-Langlotz, 47, 451, pl. 15.
659*	Athens, Acropolis	Graef-Langlotz, 47, 452, pl. 16; *Emporio* 157 note 4.
660*	Athens, Agora	*Agora* VIII, 106, pl. 41. 654a; *Emporio* 157 note 4.
661*	Athens, Agora	*Agora* VIII, 106, pl. 41. 654b; *Emporio* 157 note 4.
662	Apollonia Pontica	Bonn, Akademisches Kunstmuseum, inv. no. 20025. *Histria* IV, 25 and note 34.
663*	Istros	Lambrino, *Vases*, 302, fig. 290; *Emporio* 157 note 4; *Histria* IV, 51, pl. 13.139.
664*	Istros	*Histria* I, 392, fig. 242; *Emporio* 157 note 4; *Histria* IV, 51, no. 138, fig. 5.
665*	Berezan	Hermitage, inv. no. B191. *SovArch.* 1957.4, 132, fig. 4.1; *Emporio* 157 note 4; Kocybala, Diss. 1978, 209 and note 229.
666*	Berezan	Hermitage, inv. no. B470. *SovArch.* 1957.4, 132, fig. 4.2; *Emporio* 157 note 4; *Samos* VI.1, 139, pl. 92.754; Kocybala, Diss. 1978, 209 and note 229.
667*	Berezan	Hermitage, inv. no. B57. (Ex-coll. Skadovsky no. 13265). *MIA* 50, 1956, fig. 3; *SovArch.* 1957.4, 132, fig. 5; *Emporio* 157 note 4; *Samos* VI.1, 139, pl. 92; Kocybala, Diss. 1978, 196, 209 note 229; Kinch, *Vroulia*, 229, fig. 117.

668*	Berezan	Hermitage, inv. no. B468. *SovArch.* 1957.4, 132, fig. 4.3; *Emporio* 157 note 4; Kocybala, Diss. 1978, 209 and note 229.
669	Berezan	Fabritsius, *Arch. Karta* I, pl. 12.2; *Emporio* 157 note 4.
670	Berezan	Fabritsius, *Arch. Karta* I, pl. 12.3; *Emporio* 157 note 4.
671	Panticapaeum	*MIA* 103, 1962, 121, fig. 7.1; *Emporio* 157 note 4; Kocybala, Diss. 1978, 323 and note 710.
672	"Larisa"	*Larisa am Hermos* III, 171, pl. 57.23; *Emporio* 157 note 4.
673	"Larisa"	*Larisa am Hermos* III, 171, pl. 57.24; *Emporio* 157 note 4.
674*	Pitane	Istanbul Archaeological Museum, inv. no. 2267. Perrot-Chipiez IX, 409, fig. 202; *Emporio* 157 note 4. *Sph. to the l. amidst fill. orns. Handle zone: double guilloche.*
675*	Pitane	Bergama Museum. *TürkArkDerg.* 10, 1960, pl. 2.4; *Emporio* 157 note 4; *Samos* VI.1, pl. 95.753.
676*	Pitane	Istanbul Archaeological Museum. *CGED* pl. 5.5. *Frieze with four does to the r. Rim pattern: two parallel lines with broken cable in between. Handle zone: double meander to the l.*

II. KANTHAROI

677*–679	Aegina, Aphaia Temple	*AA* 1983, 169, nos. 57–60, fig. 12.
680*	Aegina, Aphaia Temple	*AA* 1982, 66, fig. 6 left; *AA* 1983, 169, no. 62, fig. 12. Inscription:]THIΦAIH[

III. PHIALAI MESOMPHALOI

681*	Naucratis	*CVA* Oxford II, pl. 396.1; *Samos* VI.1, 138, no. 719.
682*	Naucratis	UCL 751. Johnston, *Exhibition* 1978, n. 90. *Rim pattern: tongues and below zigzag between lines. Inside: lotus. H: 0.029 W: 0.055.*
683*	Naucratis	Berlin inv. no. 3150. *Naukratis* II, pl. 21.739; *BSA* 47, 1952, 165, no. 16, pl. 34.1. Inscription:]N AΦOΔITHI[*Lion to the r. and rosette.*

IV. PLATES AND DISHES

684*	Emporio	*Emporio* 163–164, no. 785, pl. 60.
685	Naucratis	BM 1924.12–1.312. *Foot of a dish. Decoration: cable above frieze of double meander. W: 0.128.*

THE GRAND STYLE

686*	Naucratis	Fairbanks, *Catal.*, 113, pl. 35, no. 323.7; *Samos* VI.1, 139, pl. 92.728.
687	Samos, Heraion	*Samos* VI.1, 138–9, pl. 98.721, a and b, and fig. 138.

V. LIDS

688*	Naucratis	Cambridge, Museum of Classical Archaeology, NA 102. *Goat to the r. amidst fill. orns.* *W: 0.067.*
689–692	Cyrene, Demeter Sanct.	Schaus, *Dem. Sanct., Cyrene* II, 85, nos. 533–536, pl. 31.
693	Himera, Sicily	*Himera* I, pl. 17.1
694	Apollonia Pontica	Bonn inv. 2000.35 Cook, Distribution 160.

VI. CLOSED VASES (OENOCHOAI OR HYDRIAI)

695*	Naucratis	Cambridge, Museum of Classical Archaeology, NA 106. *Two friezes with fill. orns. separated by a band between two lines.* *W: 0.051.*
696*	Chios town	Chios Mus. inv. no. B.M. 1433. *Chiaka Meletemata* I, 72, fig. 29. *Lion's head and mane to the r. amidst fill orns. Dividing bands with SS, rays, vertical strokes and chequer. Inside: unslipped.* *W: 0.059 H: 0.051.*

2. THE GRAND STYLE

I. CHALICES

697*	Naucratis	BM 1886.4–1.1549. *Naukratis* I, pl. 5.9, inside only. *Brown paint on yellow slip. Head and arm of a figure to the r. Rim pattern: two parallel lines with diagonal strokes in between.* *W: 0.030.*
698*	Naucratis	BM 1888.6–1.468m : 1924.12–1.195. Price pl. 6.5; *Samos* VI.1, 140, pl. 96.795. *Brown, red and diluted yellow on creamy slip. Shield and device. Fill. orn.: rosette with spikes.* *W: 0.063.*
699*	Naucratis	BM 1888.6–1.576c : 1924.12–1.189. Price pl. 6.3. *Woman to the r. Inside: rosette.* *W: 0.031.*

700*   Naucratis   BM 1888.6–1.479.
Naukratis II, pl. 5.2; Price pl. 6.1; Johnston, *Exhibition* 1978, no. 83.
Black, brown, red, yellow on the outlines and white. Row of sphs. to the l. Rim pattern: vertical strokes between two parallel lines. Inside: chain of lotus and palmette.
W: 0.093.

701*   Naucratis   BM 1888.6–1.482a.
Brown and diluted yellow. Bearded man to the r.
W: 0.039.

702*   Naucratis   BM 1888.6–1.482b.
Price 218, no. 5, pl. 6.6; *BSA* 51, 1956, 60; Bernard, *Le Delta égyptien*, pl. 42.3; Johnston, *Exhibition* 1978, no. 75.
Black, yellow and white. Female left arm to the r. Bearded man to the r. Indiscernible figure to the l. Inside: ?tendrils, then squares, then two parallel lines.
W: 0.044.

703*   Naucratis   BM 1888.6–1.482c.
Price 215, fig. 56.
Brown and yellow on very white slip. Bearded man to the r. with left arm raised. Rim pattern: diagonal strokes between two parallel lines. Fill. orn.: rosette. Inside: lotus and palmette.
W: 0.069.

704*   Naucratis   BM 1888.6–1.483.
Price 219, fig. 63.
Brown to orange and yellow on very white slip. Bearded man to the r. with left arm raised and holding a lotus. Rim pattern: as the last. Inside: lotus and rosettes.
W: 0.052.

705*   Naucratis   BM 1888.6–1.489.
Light brown on creamy slip. Head of a spear in silhouette and hand in outline to the r. Rim pattern: as the last. Inside: lotus and palmette.
W: 0.037.

706*   Naucratis   BM 1888.6–1.484.
Price pl. 10, last row, right; *Samos* VI. 1, 140, pl. 96. 799.
Black, red and yellow on white slip. Horse and rider to the l. Rim pattern: as the last. Inside: lotus and palmette.
W: 0.036.

707*   Naucratis   BM 1888.6–1.486 : A 768.
Price 208, pl. 10.4; *Samos* VI.1, 140, no. 784.
Brown and diluted yellow on very white slip. Figure to the r. amidst fill. orns.
W: 0.092.

708*   Naucratis   BM 1888.6–1.485.
Price 215, fig. 57.
Brown, red and yellow on very white slip. Archer drawing his bow to the r. Fill. orns.: triangle and dotted rosette. Rim pattern: broken meander to the l. between two parallel lines.
W: 0.046.

THE GRAND STYLE

709*   Naucratis   BM 1888.6–1.487.
Price 213, fig. 49.
Black and brown on very white slip. Horse and rider to the r. Fill. orns.: rosette and swastika.
W: 0.038.

710*   Naucratis   BM 1888.6–1.490.
Price pl. 6.4; *Samos* VI.1, 140, pl. 96.796; Johnston, *Exhibition* 1978, no. 85.
Black, brown, red and yellow. Shield with bull's protome as device to the l. Bull's head in outline. Inside: two white lines.
W: 0.043.

711*   Naucratis   BM 1888.6–1.491.
Price 213, fig. 50; *Samos* VI.1, 139, pl. 92.750; Johnston, *Exhibition* 1978, no. 69.
Owl on a tendril. Rim pattern: chequer. Inside: two white lines.
W: 0.036.

712*   Naucratis   BM 1888.6–1.493i : 1924.12–1.378.
Price pl. 9.1, inside only; *AA* 1983, 160; *Emporio* 169, note 9.
Light chalice. Black, brown and yellow on creamy slip. Lower part of two men wearing chiton and himation to the r. Inside: komast to the l. and then two parallel lines.
W: 0.042.

713*   Naucratis   BM 1888.6–1.497.
Light chalice. Black, red and diluted yellow on creamy slip. Horse's head and the tail of a preceding horse to the r. Inside: tendrils, zigzags and two parallel lines.
W: 0.048.

714*   Naucratis   BM 1888.6–1.493d : 1924.12–1.193.
Price pl. 6.2; *Samos* VI.1, 140, no. 807, but not together with Price, pl. 6.7.
Light chalice. Black, brown and yellow on creamy slip. Woman wearing chiton and lifting her himation to the r. Inside: figure in white.
W: 0.030.

715*   Naucratis   BM 1888.6–1.493n : 1924.12–1.386.
Light chalice. Black, brown and yellow on creamy slip. Figure wearing chiton to the r. Inside: figure in white.
W: 0.030.

716*   Naucratis   BM 1888.6–1.493h : 1924.12–1.377.
Light chalice. Black, brown and yellow on creamy slip. Figures wearing chiton and himation to the r. Inside: figure in white.
W: 0.054.

717*   Naucratis   BM 1888.6–1.493a.
Naukratis II, pl. 5.5; Price pl. 6.9; *Samos* VI.1, 140, no. 804.
Light chalice. Black, red and yellow on creamy slip. Row of women wearing chitons with dotted paryphai and holding wreaths to the l. Then vertical strokes between parallel lines and then guilloche. Inside: dotted concentric circles and buds between parallel lines.
W: 0.060.

718*   Naucratis   BM 1888.6–1.493k : 1924.12–1.404.
Heavy chalice. Black, brown and red on creamy slip. Part of a chiton and himation with dotted paryphe. Inside: lotus and dotted concentric circle.
W: 0.059.

719*   Naucratis   BM 1888.6–1.493c : 1924.12–1.192.
Price pl. 6.8.
Black, brown and yellow on creamy slip. Part of a chiton and himation decorated with crosses and dots on the paryphe. Inside: fishbone between two parallel lines.
W: 0.038.

720*   Naucratis   BM 1888.6–1.493b : 1924.12–1.191.
Price pl. 6.25.
From the ?same vase as the last. Part of a chiton and himation decorated with crosses and dots on the paryphe. Inside: bud, then two parallel lines.
W: 0.028.

721*   Naucratis   BM 1888.6–1.493j : 1924.12–1.385.
Part of a chiton and himation with dotted paryphe.
W: 0.032.

722*   Naucratis   BM 1888.6–1.493g : 1924.12–1.372.
Black, brown and red on white slip. Bearded man wearing chiton and himation to the r. Inside: lotus and bud and then two parallel lines.
W: 0.030.

723*   Naucratis   BM 1888.6–1.493m : 1924.12–1.383.
Light chalice. Black and brown to red paint. Part of a himation with dotted paryphe.
W: 0.041.

724*   Naucratis   BM 1888.6–1.504.
Naukratis II, pl. 5.6; Price pl. 6.11; *BSA* 47, 1952, 166, no. 59, pl. 34.5; *Samos* VI.1, 140, pl. 96.797.
Light chalice. Brown, very light brown and white on grey slip. Bearded man holding a shield with a seven-petal rosette as device to the l. In front of him two ?spears. Inside: tendrils and dotted concentric circles above bands and zigzags. Inscription: EHΘOI
W: 0.062.

725*   Naucratis   BM 1888.6–1.500.
Price pl. 11, third row, left; *Samos* VI.1, 140, pl. 96. 793.
Brown, light brown for the skin and yellow on white slip. Man holding a wreath in his l. raised arm to the r. Rim pattern: vertical strokes between two parallel lines. Inside: lotus.
W: 0.021.

726*   Naucratis   BM 1888.6–1.503.
Price pl. 6.12; *Samos* VI.1, 140, pl. 96.791.
Light chalice. Brown, light brown, white for eye-ball, on light beige slip. Bearded man wearing a turban to the r. Inside: lotus and dotted concentric circle.
W: 0.022.

727*	Naucratis	BM 1888.6–1.501. Price 219, no. 6, pl. 6.23; *Samos* VI.1, 140, pl. 96.788. *Light chalice. Brown and light brown on beige slip. Bearded man to the r. Rim pattern: vertical strokes between two parallel lines.* *W: 0.043.*
728*	Naucratis	BM 1888.6–1.788 + 507. Price pl. 6.13; Buschor, *Satyrtänze*, 62, fig. 21; *Samos* VI.1, 140, pl. 96.798; Johnston, *Exhibition* 1978, no. 74; *AA* 1983, 162 note 8. *Light chalice. Black, brown, light brown for skin, yellow and white on beige slip. Bearded man wearing a hat and a chequered band on his chest; his l. arm raised to the r. Behind him: a wreath. Inside: chain of lotus and pomegranates above two parallel lines with zigzag in between.* *W: 0.057.*
729*	Naucratis	BM 1888.6–1.502. *AA* 1983, 162 note 8. *Light chalice. Brown, light brown and yellow on creamy slip. Part of a wreath. Rim pattern: diagonal strokes between two parallel lines. Inside: lotus and rosette.* *W: 0.039.*
730*	Naucratis	BM 1888.6–1.506. Price 219, no. 6, pl. 6.22; *Samos* VI.1, 140, pl. 96.786. *Light chalice. Brown, light brown and yellow on beige slip. Man in chiton and himation with dotted top border; his left arm holding folds of his garments to the r. Inside: lotus above a chain of bands and zigzag.* *W: 0.042.*
731*	Naucratis	BM 1888.6–1.505. *Light chalice. Brown, light brown and yellow paint. Part of a chiton and himation. Inside: lotus and dotted concentric circle.* *W: 0.030.*
732*	Naucratis	BM 1888.6–1.512. Price pl. 6.15; *Samos* VI.1, 140, pl. 96.790. *Heavy chalice. Dark brown, light brown and yellow on light beige slip. Bare footed men holding spears and shields with a whirliging device to the l. Handle zone: guilloche. Inside: rosette and volutes between two parallel lines.* *W: 0.084.*
733*	Naucratis	BM 1888.6–1.510. Price 219, no. 6, pl. 6.21; *Samos* VI.1, 140, pl. 96. 787; *Naukratis* II, pl. 5.4; Johnston, *Exhibition* 1978, no. 76. *Black, brown, light brown for male skin, and white for female skin, on light beige slip. Woman wearing chiton and himation with dotted paryphai holding in her l. hand the head of a man from a lock. Inside: lotus above a chain of bands and zigzags.* *W: 0.042.*

734*   Naucratis   BM 1888.6–1.511.
Price pl. 6.26.
Man in a short chiton to the l. Inside: two parallel lines.
W: 0.028.

735*   Naucratis   BM 1888.6–1.508.
Brown, yellow and white on grey slip. Woman to the r holding two pomegranates in her raised hand. Inside: lotus and palmettes.
W: 0.059.

736*   Naucratis   BM 1888.6–1.509.
Price pl. 6.10; Johnston, *Exhibition* 1978, no. 86.
Black, brown, light brown for skin and white on white slip. Man wearing short chiton and holding spear with an eye as a device to the l. Inside: vertical long strokes above horizontal bands.
W: 0.045.

737*   Naucratis   BM 1888.6–1.513.
Price pl. 6.28; *Samos* VI.1, 140, no. 806.
Brown, light brown, yellow and white on beige slip. Sandalled alternating with bare footed men in long chitons to the r. Handle zone: double guilloche. Inside: chain of buds and dotted concentric circles below a band.
W: 0.112.

738*   Naucratis   BM 1888.6–1.517.
Price pl. 6.17; *Samos* VI.1, 140, no. 810.
Light brown for male skin and dark yellow for satyr. Hairy fat satyr-like figure lying on the ground behind a male leg to the r. Inside: vertical strokes between parallel lines and then rays.
W: 0.060.

739*   Naucratis   BM 1888.6–1.518.
Light chalice. Black and light brown on white slip. Horse and tail of the preceding one to the r. Rim pattern: broken cable between two parallel lines. Inside: lotus and palmette.
W: 0.038.

740*   Naucratis   BM 1888.6–1.514.
Price pl. 6.14; *Samos* VI.1, 140, pl. 96.789; Johnston, *Exhibition* 1978, no. 73.
Heavy chalice. Brown, light brown for skin, white and yellow. Bare footed man holding a shield with a dotted band as device to the r. Then a l. foot wearing a greave. Inside: zigzag, two parallel lines, vertical strokes, two parallel lines and then rays between parallel lines.
W: 0.083.

741*   Naucratis   BM 1888.6–1.519.
Price pl. 6.19; *Samos* VI.1, 140 no. 808.
Light chalice. Brown, light brown, diluted yellow and white for dots, on beige slip. An archer in short dotted chiton holding a bow to the r. and wearing the lion skin: Heracles. Inside: lotus above a chain of dotted squares. W: 0.040.

THE GRAND STYLE

742*   Naucratis   BM 1888.6–1.515 and 516.
Price pl. 6.27; *Samos* VI.1, 140, no. 801; Johnston, *Exhibition* 1978, no. 72.
Heavy chalice. Brown, light brown and yellow on creamy slip. Bare footed men dancing to the r. with kantharoi in between. Handle zone: double guilloche. Inside: two parallel lines.
W: 0.110.

743*   Naucratis   BM 1924.12–1.190.
Price pl. 9.2, inside only; *Emporio* 169 note 9.
Brown, light brown and yellow on creamy slip. Man in chiton and himation with dotted paryphe to the r. Inside: part of a komast playing the double flute to the l. in white with yellow and red for details and incisions for the knee-caps. Below: two white parallel lines.
W: 0.054.

744*   Naucratis   BM 1888.6–1.194.
Price pl. 6.24.
Light chalice. Brown and yellow on creamy slip. Bearded man in chiton and himation with dotted paryphe with his l. arm raised to the r. Inside: zigzag between two parallel lines.
W: 0.033.

745*   Naucratis   BM 1888.6–1.375.
Light chalice. Light brown for male feet. Part of a chiton and himation with dotted paryphe. Inside: part of a leg to the r. then parallel lines with dotted squares in between.
W: 0.035.

746*   Naucratis   BM 1924.12–1.370.
Light chalice. Brown, light brown and yellow on creamy slip. Lower part of a figure in long chiton, bare footed, to the l. Inside: two parallel lines.
W: 0.035.

747*   Naucratis   BM 1924.12–1.391.
Foot to the r. in light brown paint. Handle zone: double guilloche.
W: 0.021.

748*   Naucratis   BM 1924.12–1.384.
Light chalice. Brown and light brown on creamy slip. Part of a figure's chiton to the l. Inside: part of lotus and then parallel lines.
W: 0.033.

749*   Naucratis   BM 1924.12–1.390.
Brown and light brown on creamy slip. Part of a chiton with dotted paryphe. Inscription:]ΜΟΣΑ[*Inside: two parallel lines with zigzag in between.*
W: 0.029.

750*   Naucratis   BM 1924.12–1.392.
Man's leg to the l.
W: 0.029.

751*	Naucratis	BM 1924.12-1.396. *Light chalice. Orange to yellow on creamy slip. Rim pattern: simple guilloche between two parallel lines. Head of a woman wearing wreath and earring to the r. Inside: rosette.* *W: 0.033.*
752*	Naucratis	BM 1924.12-1.402. *Light chalice. Brown, light brown and yellow on white slip. Man in chiton and himation to the r. Inside: lotus above parallel lines.* *W: 0.027.*
753*	Naucratis	BM 1924.12-1.415. *Left leg of a man to the r. Handle zone: vertical strokes.* *W: 0.042.*
754*	Naucratis	BM 1924.12-1.408. *Light chalice. Brown and yellow for outlines, on creamy slip. Legs of a ?man to the l. Inside: dotted squares, two parallel lines, a row of pomegranates and two parallel lines.* *W: 0.023.*
755*	Naucratis	BM 1924.12-1.406. *Light chalice. Brown and yellow for outlines, on creamy slip. Part of a chalice with rim. Rim pattern: vertical strokes, then three parallel lines. Dividing band: broken meander vertically placed between two parallel lines. Part of a shield with concentric circles as a device and chequer at the border and part of a ?helmet.* *W: 0.047.*
756*	Naucratis	BM 1924.12-1.412. *Horse and rider in short chiton to the r. Inside: tendril and lotus.* *W: 0.036.*
757	Naucratis	BM 1924.12-1.413. *Part of a horse to the r. Inside: tendrils and then zigzag between two parallel lines.* *W: 0.044.*
758*	Naucratis	BM 1902.6-20.1. *Men bare footed and in short chitons striding to the r. Handle zone: double guilloche. Inside: bud above three parallel lines.* *W: 0.069.*
759*	Naucratis	BM 1902.6-20.2. Price pl. 6.20. *Woman in long hair wearing a chiton with her r. arm raised and her l. holding an indiscernible object to the l. Inside: lotus and then zigzag between parallel lines.* *W: 0.047.*
760*	Naucratis	BM 1902.6-20.3. Price pl. 6.16. *Men bare footed and in short chitons striding to the r. Behind them part of a hairy figure. Inside: tongues.* *W: 0.022.*

761*   Naucratis   BM 1888.6–1.480b.
Price pl. 9.7.
Heavy chalice. Walking lion to the r. Below triple meander running l.
W: 0.131.

762*   Naucratis   BM 1888.6–1.460d : 1924.12–1.187.
Johnston, *Exhibition* 1978, no. 79.
Heavy chalice. Two confronted warriors: the l. is bare footed; the r. one is wearing greaves and holding a shield which has chequers with dotted blanks as a border. No fill. orns. Double meander running l.
W: 0.079.

763   Naucratis   *Samos* VI.1, 140, pl. 96.803.
Bearded man wearing earrings and holding ?spears to the l.

764*   Naucratis   *CVA* Oxford II, 82, pl. 396.15.
Rim pattern: broken cable between two parallel lines. Bearded man in long hair wearing chiton and himation with dotted paryphe to the r.
W: 0.022.

765*   Naucratis   *CVA* Oxford II, pl. 396.18.
The left leg of a warrior to the l. overlapping the right leg of another warrior carrying a shield to the l.
W: 0.013.

766*   Naucratis   *CVA* Oxford II, pl. 396.19.
Part of the chiton and himation of a woman to the r.
W: 0.009.

767*   Naucratis   Price pl. 10.6; *CVA* Cambridge II, 32, pl. 496.1 and 54; *BSA*, 47, 1952, 166, no. 30.
Light chalice. Light brown on creamy slip. Rim pattern: broken cable between two parallel lines. ?Figure bearing two spears overlapping the rim pattern. Inscription: ΠΟΔΑΝΙΚΟΣ *Inside: lotus.*
W: 0.061.

768*   Naucratis   *CVA* Cambridge II, 32–4, pl. 496.3 and 55 and 9 and 53. (Cook: same chalice).
Hands holding reins to the r. Fill. orns. Inside: chain of lotus and palmette.
W: 0.106.

769*   Naucratis   *CVA* Cambridge II, 32, pl. 496.2 and 56.
Light chalice. Brown paint on creamy slip. Four rivet-holes. Rim pattern: broken cable between two parallel lines. Part of the upper body of a man holding reins to the r. Fill. orns. Inside: chain of lotus and rosette.
W: 0.092.

770   Naucratis   *CVA* Cambridge II, 32, pl. 496.5.
Rim pattern: vertical strokes between two parallel lines. Then an indiscernible object. Inside: lotus and circle with dots around it.
W: 0.048.

771*   Naucratis   Price 215, fig. 54; *CVA* Cambridge II, 32–33, 34, pl. 496.6 and 40.
Light chalice. Brown, red and white on creamy slip. Woman wearing earrings and playing the double flute to the r. Inside: palmette.
W: 0.030.

772*   Naucratis   *CVA* Cambridge II, 33, 34, pl. 496.13.38 (Not from the same vase as Price pl. 6.23).
Light chalice. Brown and light brown for skin, on creamy slip. Rim pattern: vertical strokes between two parallel lines. Head of a man to the r. Inside: lotus and rosette.
W: 0.029.

773*   Naucratis   *CVA* Cambridge II, 33, pl. 496.14 and 46; Price fig. 55.
Black, brown, red, yellow, white and lighter brown for skin, on creamy slip. Man wearing chiton and himation to the r. and a woman's toe opposite him to the l. Inside: tongue above two parallel lines then chequer below line.
W: 0.033.

774*   Naucratis   *CVA* Cambridge II, 33, pl. 496.15 and 48.
Light chalice. Brown and yellow on creamy slip. Rim pattern: broken cable between two parallel lines. Head of a horse in bridle to the r. and rosette in front of it. Inside: lotus and palmette.
W: 0.060.

775*   Naucratis   *BSA* 5, 1898–9, 58, pl. 5.2; Price, 214, 215, fig. 58; *CVA* Cambridge II, 34, pl. 496.42.
Light chalice. Black, brown and diluted yellow for the crest, on creamy slip. Rim pattern: broken cable between two parallel lines. Part of the head and helmet of a woman to the r., presumably Athena. Inside: lotus.
W: 0.037.

776*   Naucratis   *BSA* 5, 58, pl. 5.3; *CVA* Cambridge II, 44, pl. 496.44.
Brown and yellow for outlines, on creamy slip. Part of a face and a hand holding a phiale to the l. In front, an indiscernible object. Inside: palmette.
W: 0.023.

777*   Naucratis   Price 212, 213, fig. 51: *NC* 174, note 1; *CVA* Cambridge II, 34, pl. 496.45.
Brown paint on white slip. Lower part of a bird, ?partridge, walking up the steps of a chequered altar. Inside: zigzag then lines and rosette.
W: 0.031.

778*   Naucratis   Price pl. 10, third row, middle; *CVA* Cambridge II, 34, pl. 496.50.
Light chalice. Brown on white slip. Part of the head of a goat to the r. confronting the head of a bearded man to the l. Inside: lotus.
W: 0.019.

779*	Naucratis	*CVA* Cambridge II, 34, pl. 496.51; *BSA* 47, 1952, 165, no. 25.
Light chalice. Brown to reddish on creamy slip. Inside: red background. Hand and part of a himation to the r. Above inscription:]IΣ *On the right: a stripe. Inside: rosette.*
W: 0.032.
780*	Naucratis	Cambridge, Museum of Classical Archaeology, N 85.
Outside: chequer pattern, perhaps an altar. Inside: palmette, three parallel lines and then palmettes above two parallel lines.
W: 0.035.
781*	Naucratis	UCL 744.
Johnston, *Exhibition* 1978, no. 95; *BICS* 29, 1982, 39, pls. 4. d. e and 5. a.
Three preserved heads of horses, from a quadriga, two of which in bridle to the r. In front of them ?the arm of a female figure. Inside: chain of spiral and palmette.
H: 0.048 W: 0.048.
782*	Naucratis	Liverpool 56–21–528.
Golden brown, black and red on creamy slip. Rim pattern: SS between lines. Head to the r. Inside: leaves, lines and below rosette.
H: 0.036 W: 0.013.
783*	Naucratis	Fairbanks, *Catal.*, 99, no. 302.10, pl. 32.
Head and upper part of a woman to the r. below a network band. Inside: lotus.
H: 0.056 W: 0.046.
784*	Naucratis	Fairbanks, *Catal.*, 98, no. 302.6, pl. 32; *Samos* VI.1, 140, no. 812.
Lower part of a chalice. Bowl: two bands. Handle zone: double guilloche, then tongue near handle root. On the walls: left foot and lower part of the chiton of a woman to the r. and in front of her the left foot and lower part of the chiton of a woman running to the r. Fill. orns. Dotted paryphai on their chitons. Incised inscription:]OΔIT[*Inside: white lines separating a band of spiky rosettes, then a band of small squares and the beginning of an elaborate pattern.*
H: 0.121 W: 0.078.
785*	Naucratis	UM Philadelphia E175 A1.
Human figure to the r. Handle zone: guilloche.
H: 0.047 W: 0.052.
786*	Naucratis	Berlin Antiquarium (lost during the war).
A woman to the r. Inside: lotus.
787*	Naucratis	Berlin Antiquarium (lost during the war).
Two rows with double guilloche. Inside: upper row: lotus and rosette; lower row: a spiked rosette and a lotus leaf.
788*	Naucratis	Bonn.
Leg of a warrior with shield to the r. before a dressed human figure.

789*	Naucratis	Athens, British School. Price 215, fig. 58; *Samos* VI.1, 140, pl. 96.800. *Female head wearing a helmet to the l.; presumably, Athena.* *W: 0.050.*
790*	Naucratis	Athens, British School. *BICS* 29, 1982, 39, 42 note 16, pl. 5c. *Head of a horse in bridle to the r. Rim pattern: diagonal strokes between two parallel lines.* *W: 0.049.*
791*	Naucratis	Athens, British School. *Two human figures wearing chitons and himatia to the l. Fill. orns.: rosette and dotted square.* *W: 0.053.*
792*	Naucratis	Athens, British School. *Rim pattern: dots between two parallel lines. Rosette and an indiscernible object, perhaps an eye.* *W: 0.042.*
793	Tocra	*Tocra* I, 60 no. 775, fig. 31; *Samos* VI.1, no. 814.
794	Cyrene, Demeter Sanct.	Schaus, *Dem. Sanct., Cyrene* II, 78, no. 470, pl. 28. *It might be of the Grand style.*
795*	Aegina, Aphaia Temple	*AA* 1983, 156–160. no. 1, figs. 1–5, where previous frs. and bibliography resumed; *Chios Conference* 196, fig. 7. *Thirty five frs. of the bowl, walls and rim of a chalice. Rim pattern: diagonal strokes between two parallel lines. Below it inscription:* ΚΑΛΗΕΙΜ[*On the walls: Figured zone divided into two scenes.* *Side A: Left: Two standing figures – most likely male – in chitons and boots to the r. One wears a himation on top of the chiton. Two ?spears between them. Right: Part of the himation of a figure to the r. then right arm and thigh of a figure in short chiton to the r. then a large hairy monster to the l. down on his left knee and behind it a figure, most likely female, in chiton and himation with a battlement pattern decorating the paryphe.* *Side B: Left: Legs of a woman striding to the r. Right: Sandalled foot to the r. then lower part of a figure – most likely male – in chiton, himation and sandals to the r. and then sandalled feet of a figure to the l. In all ten figures.* *Inside: Chain of lotus and palmettes united with tendrils above fishbone between two parallel lines. Then figured scene with ?eight komasts, in long hair, wearing earrings and buttock-pads and holding wreaths to the l. Then two parallel lines above zone of buds.* *Pres. H: 0.23. Thickness of wall: 0.04–0.075. Est. Diam. at the rim: 0.34.*
796*	Aegina, Old town	*Alt-Ägina* II.1, 16, pl. 5.78. *First fr. from the rim: Rim pattern: chequer then diagonal lines between two lines. Fill. orns. Inside: lotus and palmette.* *H: 0.030.* *Second fr. from the wall: Part of the mane of a horse and the body*

of a rider to the l. Inside: lotus above network between parallel lines.
H: 0.041.

797*   Athens, Acropolis   Graef-Langlotz, 47, no. 450 a and b, pls. 14 and 25; Buschor, *Gr. Vasen*, fig. 107; Martin-Charbonneaux-Villard, *La Grèce archaïque*, fig. 39; *Samos* VI.1, 140, no. 809; Pfuhl, *MuZ*, 145, pl. 27.119.
Fr. a.: Bearded man wearing the lion skin, sword and a short chiton to the r.: Heracles. Inside: lotus above squares and then tongue pattern.
Diam.: 0.040 × 0.070.
Fr. b.: Part of a panther. Inside: Spirals
Diam.: 0.038 × 0.030.

798*   Kavala   Kavala Mus. no. A1889.
Lazaridis, *Guide*, 108.
Winged horse – presumably Pegasus – to the l. Mane in mauve with white dots. Fill. orns.: rosettes.

799*   Berezan   Kornysova, *Olbia*, 45, fig. 18.

800*   Pitane   Istanbul Archaeological Museum, inv. no. 8904.
AJA 69, 1965, 148; Greenewalt, Diss. 1966, 190–1, pls. IX A.C.D; *JdI* 85, 1970, 48, figs. 14 and 15; *CGED*, 29, pl. 7.12; *Catalogue Istanbul, 1983*, 34, B 84; *LIMC* i s.v. Achilleus 77, no. 254; Chr. Zindel, *Drei vorhomerische Sagenversionen in der griechischen Kunst*, 1974, 107 Nr. 8.
For the inside: E. Akurgal, *Orient und Okzident*, 1966, 203, fig. 63; *Samos* VI.1, pl. 95.782; Akurgal, *Türkei* pl. 21a.
Complete, but slip and paint have flaked off in large areas. Rim pattern: broken meander between two lines. On the walls: A man riding one horse and leading another to the r. In front of him a man to the l. in short chiton pours water from an oenochoe into a basin. Between them a tree. Behind a prostyle building with chequered wall, an Aeolic column capital and foliate acroteria and behind it, a bearded man in an Ionian helmet holding spear and shield. Behind him a woman in long chiton with a decorated paryphe holds in her left hand a hydria and carries a bigger one on her head. Behind her come five male figures, two wearing striped hoods, carrying a sack, a branch and two of them spears. In all, eleven figures, including the two horses. Mythological scene: Achilles in ambush for Troilos. Handle zone: double guilloche and tongue pattern near handles. Bowl: Five broad parallel stripes. Foot: Three double bands in matt white.
Inside: Dark paint over slip with decoration in white and red. Chain of lotus and palmette united with tendrils of spiral above network between parallel lines, then a frieze of lions to the l. alternating with round flowers above network between parallel lines, then a frieze of dotted circles and then central rosette.
H: 0.297.
Diam. at the rim: 0.303–0.306.
Diam. at the foot base: 0.147.

801*   Pitane   *Arch. Reports* for 1964–65, 3; *CGED* 29; Akurgal, *Türkei*, pl. 11.
Very big chalice, c. 0.45 in height and diameter.
Shape: The transition from bowl to the walls of the vase is still apparent. Slip: dazzling white.
Decoration: Rim pattern: battlement pattern below chequers. On the walls: Seven horsemen and a standing woman to the r., then a worn out figure, who holds a shield, presumably, a warrior, below him a dog, then a warrior, then a woman who unveils herself and then at a distance a ?kneeling figure, above one handle. The two warriors to the l. in characteristically dotted garments. Chitons in mauve colour. Thirteen figures, in all. Handle zone: double guilloche.
Inside: Chain of tendrils uniting lotuses and palmettes.

II. PHIALE MESOMPHALOS?

802*   Naucratis   *CVA* Cambridge II, 33, pl. 496.8 and 52.

III. PLATES

803*   Naucratis   BM 1886.4–1.1281 : A990.
Samos VI.1, pl. 96.802; Johnston, *Exhibition* 1978, no. 65.
A figure on a couch; two legs emerge from the drapery, the right one looks as if rendered from above.
Diam: c. 0.27.

804*   Kavala   Lazaridis *Guide* 93, no. A1103; Hemelrijk, *Caeretan Hydriae* 178 and note 754.

IV. DINOI

805*   Naucratis   *CVA* Oxford II, pl. 397.5; Cook, *Fikellura*, 53, pl. 10 a and b. (Part of Cook's Flautist Dinos).
Man in long hair with a flute to the l. Behind him man in silhouette with stretched arms.
W: 0.052.

806*   Naucratis   Cambridge, Museum of Classical Archaeology, NA 107.
BSA 47, 1952, 144, fig. 7 lower row.
Crescents.
W: 0.027.

V. CLOSED VASE

807*   Naucratis   Price pl. 10, third row, left; *CVA* Cambridge II, 34, pl. 496.47.
Brown for reins and yellow for horse's outline on white slip. Part of the head of a horse in bridle to the r. Inside: plain.
W: 0.030.

2A. LIGHT ON DARK BACKGROUND

808*   Emporio   *?LEKANE FR.*
Emporio 169–70, no. 848, fig. 117, pl. 64; *Samos* VI.1 69, 141 no. 846.
Within, a kid suckled by his dam, in creamy white on dull black paint.

809*   Emporio   *?KANTHAROS FR.*
Emporio 169–170, no. 849, fig. 117, pl. 64; *Samos* VI.1, 69, 141 no. 847.
Within, a dolphin in white with a red eye.

810*   Naucratis   outside of a CHALICE.
JHS 25, 1925, pl. 5.1; *CVA* Oxford II, 82, pl. 396.28 a and b; *Samos* VI.1, 69, 140, pl. 95.781; *Emporio* 169, note 9.
Two riders on white horses in an antithetical composition. Fill. orns.: dotted circles.

811*   Naucratis   outside of a CHALICE.
Price pl. 9.6; *CVA* Oxford II, 82, pl. 396.16; *Emporio* 169 note 9.

812*   Naucratis   outside of a CHALICE.
CVA Oxford II, 82, pl. 396.17; *Emporio* 169 note 9.

813*   Naucratis   CHALICE
outside: plain.
inside: light on dark technique.
Price pl. 9.3; *Emporio* 169, note 9; *CVA* Cambridge II, 33, pl. 496.7; *Samos* VI.1, 69, 140, no. 783.
Beak of a griffin to the l. above chequer pattern between white parallel lines.

814*   Kavala   *PHIALE ?MESOMPHALOS.*
Kavala Mus. nos. A 1069–1072.
Lazaridis, *Guide*, 107.
Put together from many frs. Decoration in white, red and orange paint on black ground.
Inside: Frieze of lotus and palmette united with tendrils above squares between two white parallel lines. Then, the figured zone with six animals in an antithetical composition: bull, panther and boar to the r.; griffin, deer and lion to the l. amidst triangles. Then squares between two white parallel lines and then the centre which is not preserved.
Outside: Frieze of white and round rosettes on dark background and then the rest of the vase slipped.

3. THE CHALICE STYLE
A. VASES WITH NO FILLING ORNAMENTS
I. CHALICES

815–820	Emporio	*Emporio* 157-8, 159, nos. 735–740, pl. 59 and fig. 107.
821*	Phana	*ADelt* II, 1916, 193–5, pl. 2, figs. 7 and 8; *Emporio* 157 note 5; *Chios Conference* 242 and fig. 15. *Sph. to the l. Handle zone: saw pattern. Inside: lotus and ?buds then parallel lines.*
822*	Phana	*ADelt* II, 1916, 193, pl. 2.7, left.
823*	Phana	*BSA* 35, 1934–35, 159, pl. 37.7; *Emporio* 157 note 5.
824*	Phana	*BSA* 35, 1934–35, 159, pl. 37.12; *Emporio* 157 note 5.
825	Phana	*BSA* 35, 1934–35, 159, pl. 37.13; *Emporio* 157 note 5.
826*	Rizari, Chios town	Chios Mus. no. 3299. *Dark brown paint on white slip. Part of the head of a sph. to the l. Rim pattern: broken cable between two parallel lines. Inside: rosette with spikes.* *W: 0.032.*
827*	Rizari, Chios town	Chios Mus. no. 3301 a–d. *Four pieces made up from several frs.* *Dark brown paint on white slip. On one of the frs. part of a sph. to the l. Handle zone: Metope pattern. On the bowl: bands. Inside: chain of lotuses.* *Est. Diam.: c. 0.20.*
828*	Rizari, Chios town	Chios Mus. no. 2634. *Wing of a sph. to the l. Inside: lotus above two parallel lines.*
829*	Naucratis	BM 1888.6–1.476g: 1924.12–1.380. *Woman's head to the l. Rim pattern: dotted squares between two parallel lines. Inside: rosette.* *W: 0.024.*
830*	Naucratis	BM 1924.12–1.403. *Bearded men's head and bust to the l. Inside: parallel lines.* *W: 0.020.*
831*	Naucratis	BM 1924.12–1.397. *Rim pattern: chequer, two parallel lines with SS in between. Head of a woman to the l.* *Inscription:*]HI *W: 0.023.*
832*	Naucratis	BM 1924.12–1.407. *Rim pattern: dots between lines. Head of a woman to the r.* *W: 0.030.*
833*	Naucratis	BM 1924.12–1.409. *Part of a figure in long chiton to the r. Fill. orns.: rosette and triangle.* *W: 0.052.*

834	Naucratis	BM 1924.12–1.410. *Part of a chiton with vertical meander on the paryphe. Inside: meander running l. between parallel lines.* *W: 0.027.*
835*	Naucratis	BM 1886.4–1.1285. *Naukratis* I, pl. 5.38. *Head of a woman or sph. to the l. Rim pattern: chequer. Inside: lotus above two parallel lines.* *W: 0.021.*
836*	Naucratis	BM 1888.6–1.472b : 1924.12–1.1230. *Part of the head of a lion to the r.* *W: 0.025.*
837*	Naucratis	BM 1888.6–1.472c : 1924.12–1.1232. *Head of a lion to the r. Inside: lotus above parallel lines.* *W: 0.032.*
838*	Naucratis	BM 1888.6–1.472d : 1924.12–1.153. *Head of a lion to the l.* *W: 0.023.*
839*	Naucratis	BM 1888.6–1.472e : 1924.12–1.1283. *Part of a lion to the r. Inside: lotus* *W: 0.037.*
840*	Naucratis	BM 1888.6–1.472h : 1924.12–1.1231. *Part of a lion to the r. Inside: lotus* *W: 0.054.*
841*	Naucratis	BM 1888.6–1.472g : 1924.12–1.1234. *Part of a lion to the r. Inside: rosette.* *W: 0.019.*
842*	Naucratis	BM 1888.6–1.472f : 1924.12–1.1229. *Head of a lion to the l.* *W: 0.025.*
843*	Naucratis	BM 1888.6–1.477d : 1924.12–1.19. *Part of a sph. to the l. Inside: rosette above pattern of chequers with dotted blanks.* *W: 0.036.*
844*	Naucratis	BM 1888.6–1.474l : 1924.12–1.265. *Head of a sph. to the l. Rim pattern: diagonal strokes between two parallel lines.* *W: 0.023.*
845*	Naucratis	BM 1888.6–1.474i : 1924.12–1.18. (now in the J. Paul Getty Museum, in exchange) *BM Occ. Pap.* 22, 1981, 32ff. *Sph. to the l. Inside: lotus above two parallel lines.* *W: 0.057.*
846*	Naucratis	BM 1888.6–1.474j : 1924.12–1.245. (now in the J. Paul Getty Museum, in exchange) *BM Occ. Pap.* 22, 1981, 32ff. *Sph. walking to the l. Inside: traces of parallel lines.* *W: 0.044.*

847*	Naucratis	BM 1888.6–1.474p : 1924.12–1.271. *Sph. walking to the l. Inside: two parallel lines.* *W: 0.049.*
848*	Naucratis	BM 1888.6–1.474g : 1924.12–1.274. *Part of a sph. to the l. Inside: two parallel lines.* *W: 0.034.*
849*	Naucratis	BM 1888.6–1.476f : 1924.12–1.285. *Spiral and wing of a sph. to the l. Inside: lotus above parallel lines.* *W: 0.045.*
850*	Naucratis	BM 1888.6–1.476i : 1924.12–1.398. *Head of a sph. to the l. Inside: lotus above parallel lines.* *W: 0.029.*
851*	Naucratis	BM 1888.6–1.476j : 1924.12–1.399. *Head of a sph. to the r., possibly from an antithetical composition. Inside: as the last.* *W: 0.024.*
852*	Naucratis	BM 1888.6–1.475j : 1924.12–1.258. *Head of a sph. to the l. Inside: lotus* *W: 0.039.*
853	Naucratis	BM 1888.6–1.476k : 1924.12–1.400. *As the last.* *W: 0.022.*
854	Naucratis	BM 1924.12–1.140. *Lion to the r. Inside: traces of parallel lines.* *W: 0.044.*
855	Naucratis	BM 1924.12–1.156. *Part of a sph. to the r. Inside: lotus above two parallel lines.* *W: 0.045.*
856	Naucratis	BM 1924.12–1.238. *Hindquarters of a ?sph. to the l. Inside: lotus above two parallel lines.* *W: 0.032.*
857	Naucratis	BM 1924.12–1.247. *Part of a sph. to the l. Inside: lotus.* *W: 0.023.*
858	Naucratis	BM 1924.12–1.243. *Hindquarters of a ?sph. to the l. Inside: parallel lines.* *W: 0.036.*
859	Naucratis	BM 1924.12–1.246. *Part of a sph. to the r. Inside: parallel lines.* *W: 0.056.*
860*	Naucratis	BM 1924.12–1.262. *Part of the head of a sph. to the l.* *W: 0.031.*
861*	Naucratis	BM 1924.12–1.270. *Part of the spiral and hair of a sph. to the r. Inside: parallel lines.* *W: 0.026.*

862*   Naucratis   BM 1924.12–1.269.
Part of a sph. to the l. Inside: ?buds and parallel lines.
W: 0.033.

863*   Naucratis   BM 1924.12–1.272.
Part of a sph. to the l. Inside: parallel lines.
W: 0.031.

864*   Naucratis   BM 1924.12–1.273.
Part of a sph. to the l.
W: 0.035.

865*   Naucratis   BM 1924.12–1.276.
Part of a sph. to the l. Inside: parallel lines.
W: 0.029.

866*   Naucratis   BM 1924.12–1.261.
Part of a sph. to the l.
W: 0.048.

867*   Naucratis   BM 1924.12–1.275.
Part of a sph. to the l.
W: 0.026.

868*   Naucratis   BM 1924.12–1.288.
Part of a sph. to the l. Inside: parallel lines.
W: 0.019.

869*   Naucratis   BM 1924.12–1.293.
Part of a sph. to the r. Inside: parallel lines.
W: 0.032.

870*   Naucratis   BM 1924.12–1.294.
Part of the head of a sph. to the l.
W: 0.033.

871*   Naucratis   BM 1924.12–1.291.
Part of the wing of a sph. to the l. Inside: tendrils above parallel lines.
W: 0.046.

872*   Naucratis   BM 1924.12–1.289.
Part of the wing of a sph. to the r. Inside: ?bud above parallel lines.
W: 0.026.

873*   Naucratis   BM 1924.12–1.307.
Part of the wing of a sph. to the l. Inside: lotus above chequers with dotted blanks.
W: 0.029.

874   Naucratis   BM 1924.12–1.320.
Part of a sph. to the l. Inside: parallel lines.
W: 0.036.

875*   Naucratis   BM 1924.12–1.1237.
Part of a lion to the r.
W: 0.032.

876*	Naucratis	BM 1924.12–1.1235. *Head of a lion to the r.* *W: 0.031.* [Cook in *BSA* 47, 1952, 166 note 41 thinks that this is Heracles wearing the lion skin].
877*	Naucratis	BM 1924.12–1.1239. *Part of a lion to the r. Inside: parallel lines.* *W: 0.027.*
878	Naucratis	BM 1924.12–1.462. *Part of the head of a sph. to the l. Rim pattern: SS between two parallel lines.* *W: 0.019.*
879	Naucratis	BM 1924.12–1.393 and 388. *Part of a sph. to the l.* *W: 0.019.*
880	Naucratis	BM 1924.12–1.329. *Rim part of a chalice. Rim pattern: SS between two parallel lines.* *W: 0.016.*
881	Naucratis	BM 1924.12–1.330. *Rim part of a chalice. Rim pattern: diagonal strokes between two parallel lines.* *W: 0.037.*
882	Naucratis	BM 1924.12–1.327. *Rim part of a chalice. Rim pattern: diagonal strokes between two parallel lines. Inside: lotus.* *W: 0.017.*
883	Naucratis	BM 1924.12–1.124. *Head of a lion to the r. Rim pattern: SS between two parallel lines. Inside: lotus.* *W: 0.036.*
884	Naucratis	BM 1924.12–1.855. *Tail of a ?sph. to the l. Inscription:*]THI *W: 0.026.*
885	Naucratis	BM 1924.12–1.630. *Part of the wing of a sph. to the l. Inside: rosette.* *W: 0.026.*
886	Naucratis	BM 1924.12–1.541. *Part of the head of a sph. to the l. Rim pattern: chequers with dotted blanks, then broken cable between two parallel lines. Inside: lotus and dotted concentric circles.* *W: 0.039.*
887*	Naucratis	BM 1888.6–1.467. *Naukratis* II, pl. 5.3; Price pl. 10.8; *Samos* VI.1, 139, pl. 92.348. *Boar hunted by dog to the r. Handle zone: double guilloche.*

THE CHALICE STYLE

888*   Naucratis   BM 1886.4–1.1286.
Naukratis I, pl. 5.44; Price pl. 6.18; *Samos* VI.1, 140, no. 805.
Woman in chiton with dotted paryphe holding a wreath in her right hand to the r. Inside: ?legs of a komast, then diagonal strokes between two parallel lines.
W: 0.036.

889*   Naucratis   BM 1888.6–1.493f: 1924.12–1.371.
Woman in chiton with dotted paryphe holding a pomegranate to the r. Inside: part of a ?rosette and then zigzag between two parallel lines.
W: 0.038.

890*   Naucratis   BM 1888.6–1.481.
Samos VI.1, 140, pl. 96.794
Woman in chiton and ?himation with dotted paryphe, holding a pomegranate in her l. hand to the l. Inside: lotus and rosette above two parallel lines.
W: 0.047.

891*   Naucratis   BM 1924.12–1.373.
Woman in chiton and ?himation with dotted paryphe holding a wreath in her left hand and her right arm raised to the l. Inside: lotus above two parallel lines.
W: 0.034.

892*   Naucratis   BM 1924.12–1.374.
Woman in chiton and ?himation with dotted paryphe with her arms extended, as if receiving something, to the l. Inside: bud.
W: 0.034.

893   Naucratis   BM 1924.12–1.376.
Lower part of a chiton with dotted paryphe.
W: 0.022.

894   Naucratis   BM 1924.12–1.382.
Wreath handed over by a woman to the l. In front of her an indiscernible figure, probably a komast. Inside: lotus above two parallel lines.
W: 0.040.

895*   Naucratis   BM 1924.12–1.376.
Woman in chiton with dotted paryphe holding a wreath to the l. Inside: zigzag between two parallel lines.
W: 0.044.

896*   Naucratis   BM 1924.12–1.381.
Woman in chiton with dotted paryphe holding a pomegranate with her right hand and extending her left hand towards a komast's right arm. Inside: bud above two parallel lines.
W: 0.038.

897   Naucratis   BM 1924.12–1.411.
Lower part of a chiton with dotted paryphe to the ?r.
W: 0.037.

898   Naucratis   BM 1924.12–1.414.
As the last. Inside: zigzag between two parallel lines.
W: 0.015.

899*   Naucratis   BM 1888.6–1.493e.
Price pl. 6.7 and pl. 9.5; *Samos* VI.1, 140, no. 807; Johnston, *Exhibition* 1978, no. 84; *Emporio* 169 note 9.
Bare footed woman in long chiton with her paryphe in the middle decorated with a vertical battlement pattern flanked by two vertical parallel lines and carrying shield with strokes as a device and dots on the border, to the l.; presumably she is goddess Athena. Inside: Hands and arms of a ?female figure to the l. above two parallel lines and then chain of lotus and bud.
W: 0.048.

900*   Naucratis   BM 1924.12–1.202.
Lower part of a woman's chiton with paryphe decorated with strokes to the l. Inside: parallel lines.
W: 0.053.

901*   Naucratis   *Samos* VI.1, 140, pl. 96.792.
Two confronting sphs. Rim pattern: diagonal strokes between parallel lines.

902*   Naucratis   *CVA* Oxford II, 81, pl. 396.9.
Sph. to the r.
W: 0.018.

903*   Naucratis   *CVA* Oxford II, 81, pl. 396.11.
Lion to the r. Handle zone: metope pattern.
W: 0.015.

904*   Naucratis   *CVA* Oxford II, 82, pl. 396.13.
Sph. to the l. Rim pattern: diagonal strokes between two parallel lines.
W: 0.016.

905*   Naucratis   *CVA* Oxford II, 82, pl. 396.14.
Lion to the l. Rim pattern: SS between two parallel lines.
W: 0.018.

906*   Naucratis   *CVA* Cambridge II, 32, pl. 496.4 and 37.

907*   Naucratis   *CVA* Cambridge II, 34, pl. 496.36.

908*   Naucratis   Cambridge, Museum of Classical Archaeology, NA 75.
Sph. to the l.
W: 0.032.

909*   Naucratis   Cambridge Museum of Classical Archaeology, NA 77.
Part of the handle zone and walls of a chalice. Lion to the r. Handle zone: saw pattern.
W: 0.024.

910*   Naucratis   UCL 753.
Johnston, *Exhibition* 1978, no. 81.
Two confronting sphs. Rim pattern: dots. Inside: lotus.
W.: 0.029 H.: 0.025.

911*   Naucratis   *CVA* Reading I, 38, pl. 550.14 a and b.

912*   Naucratis   *CVA* Reading I, 37, pl. 550.4 a and b.

913*	Naucratis	Liverpool 56–21–533. *Wing of a sph. Inside: black with a reserved band at the rim.* *H: 0.023 W: 0.016.*
914*	Naucratis	MMA inv. no. 262.11.8 (Gift of Elinor R. Price, 1926). *Tail of a ?sph. to the l.*
915*	Naucratis	MMA inv. no. 262.11.7 (Gift of Elinor R. Price, 1926). *Part of the head of a lion to the r. Rim pattern: broken cable between two parallel lines.*
916*	Naucratis	UM Philadelphia E 175 C3. *Animal's foot to the l., below two parallel lines.* *H: 0.058 W: 0.030.*
917*	Naucratis	ROM 910 × 234.9. Hayes, forthcoming.
918*	Naucratis	*CVA* Heidelberg I, 13, pl. 437.10 and 14.
919	Naucratis	Leipzig, sent from Oxford in 1928, (lost during the war). *Lion to the r.*
920*	Naucratis	Wiel, *Leiden*, pl. 1.3; *CVA* Musée Scheurleer II, pl. 69.1; Prins de Jong, *Scherben*, pl. 1.3.
921*	Naucratis	Wiel, *Leiden*, pl. 1.1; *CVA* Musée Scheurleer II, pl. 69.5; Prins de Jong, *Scherben*, pl. 1.2.
922*	Naucratis	Athens, British School. *Sph. to the l.* *W: 0.043.*
923*	Naucratis	Alexandria inv. no. 17162. Venit, *Egypt. Museums*, no. 129, pl. 32 and drawing on p. 167. *Sph. to the l. Inside, lotus.*
923a*	Naucratis	Alexandria inv. no. 9490. Venit, *Egypt. Museums*, no. 134, pl. 33 and drawing on p. 168.
924*	Tocra	*Tocra* I, 59, 62, no. 780, pl. 41; *Emporio* 157 note 5.
925*	Tocra	*Tocra* I, no. 781 and *Tocra* II, 26, pl. 14. no. 781.
926*	Tocra	*Tocra* I, 59, 62, no. 782, pl. 41; *Emporio* 157 note 5.
927*	Tocra	*Tocra* I, 59, 62, no. 783, pl. 42; *Emporio* 157 note 5.
928*	Tocra	*Tocra* I, 59, 62, no. 784, pl. 42; *Emporio* 157 note 5.
929*	Tocra	*Tocra* I, 59, 63, no. 792, pl. 44; *Emporio* 157 note 5.
930*	Tocra	*Tocra* I, 59, 63, no. 793, pl. 45; *Emporio* 157 note 5.
931*	Tocra	*Tocra* I, 59, 63, no. 794, pl. 45; *Emporio* 157 note 5.
932*	Tocra	*Tocra* I, 59, 63, no. 795, pl. 45; *Emporio* 157 note 5.
933*	Tocra	*Tocra* II, 25, 26, no. 2044, pl. 14.
934*	Tocra	*Tocra* II, 26, no. 2045, pl. 14.
935	Cyrene	Stucchi, *Cirene 1957–1966*, fig. 163.
936*	Catane	*BolldArte* 1960, 155, fig. 14.2. *Head of a lion to the r.*
937	Sybaris	*NSc* 1969, 1: suppl., 120, no. 86, fig. 106; *CGED* 112 and note 85.

938*	Tarentum	*BSA* 44, 1949, 158 note 14; *ASAtene* 37–38, 1959–60, 126, figs. 98d and 99a and c; *NSc* 21–22, 1959–60, 125, figs. 98 + 99; *Emporio* 157 note 5; *Tocra* II, 59 note 2; *Samos* VI.1, no. 758, pl. 94; *RA* 1975, fig. 1c; *CGED* 111, 135 and pl. 66.14.
939*	Marseilles	Villard, *Marseille*, 38, pl. 19.3; *Emporio* 158 note 1.
940*	Delos, Rheneia	*Délos* XVII, 77, pl. 52A.1.
941	Delos	*Délos* XX, 37, fig. 33.4. *Sph. to the l. Rim pattern: chequer.*
942	Aegina, Aphaia Temple	*Aegina*, no. 243, pl. 129.1 middle; *Emporio* 157 note 5.
943	Aegina, Aphaia Temple	*Aegina*, no. 240, pl. 129.1 middle and right upper middle; *AA* 1983, 164, no. 16.
944*	Aegina, Aphaia Temple	*AA* 1983, 164, no. 7, fig. 8.
945*	Aegina, Aphaia Temple	*AA* 1983, 164, no. 8, fig. 8.
946*	Aegina, Aphaia Temple	*AA* 1983, 164, no. 11, fig. 8.
947	Aegina, Aphaia Temple	*AA* 1983, 164, no. 13, fig. 8.
948*	Aegina, Aphaia Temple	*AA* 1983, 164, no. 14, fig. 8.
949*–950*	Athens, Agora	*Agora* VIII, 105–6, pl. 41.653 a and b; *Emporio* 157 note 5.
951	Kavala	*AE* 1938, 119, no. 82; *Aphieroma Amantou* 155, figs. 1.1 and 2.1 and 3; *Emporio* 157 note 5.
951a*	Kavala	Unpublished. *Two fragments: a) Part of a sph. to the l. b) rim pattern: squares between lines; then part of the wing of a sph.*
952*	Thessaloniki, Ayia Paraskevi	Thessaloniki Museum inv. no. 14305. From Ayia Paraskevi cemetery, tomb 221. *Ancient Macedonia, Catalogue*, no. 121. *Lion to the r. Diluted paint for facial details. Inside: floral designs in red and white.* H: 0.14 Diam. at the rim: 0.153.
953	Thessaloniki, Ayia Paraskevi	*Ametos* 794, pl. 163.2 upper row: middle. *Two confronting sphs. with dots on the inner feathers. Rim pattern: dots between lines. Handle zone: a double saw edged pattern in the front and rear executed with a sixtuple brush. Inside: chain of lotus and rosette in red and white.*
954	Thessaloniki, Ayia Paraskevi	*Two confronting sphs. Handle zone: front, guilloche and rear, double meander.*
955	Thessaloniki, Ayia Paraskevi	*Two confronting sphs. Handle zone: front, guilloche and rear, double meander.*

956*	Istros	Lambrino, *Vases*, figs. 286b, 288, 287 and 286a and pl. 2 (Lambrino separates the sherds in to two chalices but Alexandrescu publishes them as from one chalice); *Emporio* 157 note 5; *Histria* IV, 51, pl. 13.141.
957*	Istros	Lambrino, *Vases*, 302, fig. 289; *Emporio* 157 note 5; *Histria* IV, 51–52, no. 142.
958	Istros	*Histria* II, no. 338, pl. 20; *Histria* IV, 52, no. 149.
959	Berezan	*SovArch.* 7, 1941, 315, fig. 3.4; *Emporio* 157 note 5; Kocybala, Diss. 1978, 394 and note 230.
960*	Berezan	Hermitage no. B187. *SovArch.* 1957.4, 135, fig. 7.1; *Emporio* 157 note 5; *Tocra* I, 59 note 14; Kocybala, Diss. 1978, 209 and note 230.
961*	Berezan	Hermitage no. B196. *SovArch.* 1957.4, 135, fig. 7.2; *Emporio* 157 note 5; Kocybala, Diss. 1978, 209.
962*	Berezan	Hermitage no. B186. *SovArch.* 1957.4, 135, fig. 7.3; *Emporio* 157 note 5; Kocybala, Diss. 1978, 209.
963*	Berezan	Hermitage no. B471. *SovArch.* 1957.4, 132, fig. 6; *Emporio* 157 note 4; *Samos* VI.1, 139, pl. 92.755.
964*	Berezan	Hermitage no. B55, on exhibit. *Bull. comm. imp. arch.* 40, 1911, 142–8, figs. 1–4; *MIA* 103, 1962, 229; *SovArch.* 1957.4, 135; *Tocra* I, 59 note 9; Price 210, 218; *Chios Conference* 242 and fig. 16.
965*	Berezan	Hermitage no. B63–102, on exhibit. *Chalice put together from many frs. Rim pattern: diagonal strokes between two lines. Sph. walking to the l.*
966*	Old Smyrna	*BSA* 60, 1965, 141, pl. 44.1 and fig. 1; *Emporio* 157 note 5.
967*	Old Smyrna	*BSA* 60, 1965, 141, pls. 42.10 and 44.10; Akurgal, *Bayrakli*, pl. 16; *Emporio* 157 note 5; *Tocra* I, 59, note 15; *BCH* 74, 1950, 314, fig. 17; Greenewalt, Diss. 1966, 16 and note 11; Akurgal, *Alt-Smyrna* I, 55, pl. 45a.
968	Pitane	Istanbul Archaeological Museum, inv. no. 8546, on exhibit. *An almost intact chalice put together from many frs. Dark black paint on white slip. Transition from walls to bowl non existant. Decoration: Rim pattern: SS between two parallel lines. On the walls: two confronting sphs. seated on their hindlegs. At the contours of the faces and necks the paint is diluted to yellow. Handle zone: double guilloche. Inside: chain of four lotuses alternating with four rosettes.* Est. H. and Diam.: 0.20
969	Pitane	Istanbul Archaeological Museum, inv. no. 9004, on exhibit. *Intact chalice. Black paint diluted into yellow on the outline of face and neck on white slip. Decoration: Sph. couchant to the l. Handle zone: Metope pattern. Foot and handles on the exterior are painted*

with brown paint. Inside: first row: chain of three lotuses alternating with three buds; second row: two parallel white lines at equal distances; third row: two more parallel lines; at the centre: flower with four petals in white and four in red.
Est. H. and Diam.: c.0.15.

970 Pitane Istanbul Archaeological Museum, inv. no. 8544, on exhibit.
Intact chalice put together from many frs. Non existant transition from bowl to walls. Slip and paint are worn out in many places, but decoration discernible. Decoration: lion couchant to the r. The tail is placed high up on the buttocks. Head in outline: diluted yellow. Handle zone: metope pattern.
Est. H. and Diam.: c.0.12.

971* Pitane Izmir Museum, no. 5050, on exhibit.
Intact chalice. Dark brown paint on white slip. Decoration: Lion couchant to the r. Tail placed high up on the buttocks. Head and mane outlined with diluted yellow paint. Handle zone: metope pattern executed with a quintuple brush. Outside of foot and handles painted brown.
Est. H. and Diam.: c.0.15.

972* Rhodes, Camirus Louvre A330, 1.
Zervos, *Rhodes*, fig. 38, 117; Longpérier, *Musée*, pl. 12.1; Pottier, *Vases*, 165, A 330, 1; Salzmann, *Camiros*, pl. 38; Pfuhl, *Muz*, 145, pl. 20.120; *Emporio* 157 note 5; *GPP*² 127, fig. 20; *Samos* VI.1, 139, pl. 94.756. R.M. Cook and R.J. Charleston, *Masterpieces of Western and Near Eastern Ceramics*, Vol. II, *Greek and Roman Pottery* 1979, no. 54.

973* Rhodes Florence no. 79244.
Brought in the Museum in 1901.
BSA 47, 1952, 159; *Emporio* 157 note 5
Sph. to the l. Rim pattern: chequer. Handle zone: front, vertical lines and rear, metope pattern. Two white lines on the edge of the foot.

974* Cyprus, Marion Gjerstad, *Cyprus*, 34, no. 157, pl. 16.56, where bibliography resumed; in addition: *JHS* 66, 1946, 5, pl. 1 a and c; *Emporio* 157 note 5; *Samos* VI.1, 139, pl. 95.757; *AM* 77–78, 1962–63, Beil. 15.3.

II. KANTHAROI

975 Naucratis BM 1924.12–1.390.
BSA 47, 1952, 166, no. 61, pl. 34.7; *BSA* 51, 1956, 57 note 3.
Inscription:]ΜΟΣΑ[
Woman

976 Naucratis *CVA* Cambridge II, 33, pl. 496.10; *BSA* 47, 1952, 165, no. 24.
Inscription:]ΩΙΛΟΣΕ[
Back of an animal.
W: 0.021.

977	Naucratis	*CVA* Cambridge II, 34, pl. 496.51; *BSA* 47, 1952, 165, no. 25. *Inscription:*]IΣ *Hand and part of a himation to the r.*
978*	Aegina, Aphaia Temple	*AA* 1983, 169, fig. 12.57.

III. PHIALAI MESOMPHALOI

979*	Naucratis	BM 1888.6–1.472j : 1924.12–1.17. *Rim pattern: chequers with dotted blanks then SS between two parallel lines. Lion to the r.; no fill. orns. W: 0.058.*
980*	Naucratis	BM 1888.6–1.474k : 1924.12–1.256. *Sph. to the r.; no fill. orns. Inside: lotus.* *W: 0.044.*
981*	Naucratis	BM 1888.6–1.476h : 1924.12–1.394. *Woman with her r. arm raised to the l. Inside: row of dots between lines and then row of strokes.* *W: 0.052.*
982	Naucratis	BM 1924.12–1.125 and uninvertoried *BSA* 47, 1952, 166, no. 60, pl. 35.26; *BSA* 51, 1956, 57 note 1. *Inscription:*]ΚΟΣΜΕΑΝΕΘ[*Horse to the r.*
983	Naucratis	BM 1924.12–1.144. *Rim pattern: zigzag between two lines. Lion to the r. Inside: lotus and rosette above tongue pattern.* *W: 0.068.*
984*	Naucratis	BM 1924.12–1.310. *Lion to the right, above row of dots between parallel lines. Inside: traces of ?buds above two lines, then tongue pattern.* *W: 0.038.*
985*	Naucratis	BM 1924.12–1.311. *Lion to the r. above chequer between two parallel lines. Inside: row of dots and then tongues between two parallel lines.* *W: 0.057.*
986*	Naucratis	BM 1924.12–1.365. *Komast holding ball to the r. then SS between two parallel lines. Inside: buds above dots between two parallel lines, then tongues and then again dots between lines.* *W: 0.076.*
987*	Naucratis	BM 1924.12–1.395. *Hand of a komast holding wreath to the l. Rim pattern: two parallel lines. Inside: bud above tendrils between two parallel lines.* *W: 0.047.*
988	Naucratis	BM 1924.12–1.397 and 848. *BSA* 47, 1952, 166, no. 62, pl. 34. 13–14. *Inscription:*]ΣΕΑΝ----ΗΙ[*Human head.*

989	Naucratis	BM 1924.12–1.520. *Lion to the r. above chequer row.* *Inside: traces of parallel lines above tongue pattern.* *W: 0.044.*
990	Naucratis	BM 1924.12–1.583. *Naukratis I, pl. 5.3, inside, only.* *Rim pattern: two parallel lines. Head of a lion to the r. above two parallel lines. Inside: two rows of buds with lines in between.* *W: 0.035.*
991	Naucratis	BM 1924.12–1.585. *Lion to the r. above chequer row. Inside: chain of lotus and rosette above two parallel lines, then tongue pattern.* *W: 0.047.*
992	Naucratis	BM 1924.12–1.590. *Rim pattern: SS between two parallel lines. Sph. to the l., above chequer row. Inside: frieze of buds between two rows of dotted squares.* *W: 0.097.*
993	Naucratis	BM 1924.12–1.593. *Sph. to the l. above chequer row. Inside: buds above dotted squares then tongues.* *W: 0.054.*
994	Naucratis	BM 1924.12–1.633. *Lion to the r. above chequer row.* *Inside: two parallel lines above elongated triangles.* *W: 0.025.*
995	Naucratis	Oxf. 1888.218, V186n, 862, (unpublished, in the *CVA*). *BSA* 47, 1952, 169, no. 201. Inscription:]ΗΙΦΑ[*Hindquarters of an animal.*

B. PATTERNED VASES

I. CHALICES

996–1002	Emporio	*Emporio* 158, 159–60, nos. 741–747, pl. 59.
1003*	Rizari, Chios town	Chios Museum no. 3303. *Parts of walls and foot. Outside: black paint on white slip. Inside: same.*
1004	Chios town	*Horos* 4, 1986, 130, pl. 28.3b.
1005	Chios town	*Horos* 4, 1986, 130, pl. 28.3c.
1006*	Tocra	*Tocra* I 59, 63, no. 797, pl. 45; *Emporio* 158 note 2.
1007	Tocra	*Tocra* I 63, no. 798, fig. 30.
1008	Tocra	*Tocra* I 63, no. 799, fig. 30; *Emporio* 158 note 2.
1009–1010	Cyrene	Pernier, *Africa Italiana* IV, 1931, 199, pl. 2.10 and 11; *Emporio* 158 note 2.
1011	Cyrene, Agora	Stucchi, *Agorà di Cirene* I, pl. 10.5.

1012	Cyrene, Agora	Stucchi, *Agorà di Cirene* I, pl. 14.1.
1013–1018	Cyrene, Demeter Sanct.	Schaus, *Dem. Sanc., Cyrene* II, 81, nos. 489–494, pl. 29.
1019*	Syracuse	Syrac. Mus. "P. Orsi" no. 53810. *Rim pattern: chequer. Handle zone: metope pattern.* H: 0.13. Diam at the rim: 0.149.
1020*	Syracuse	Syrac. Mus. "P. Orsi" no. 53811. *Slip flaked off in most parts. Handle zone: metope pattern.* H: 0.13. Diam. at the rim: 0.148.
1021–1025	Sybaris	*NSc* 1969, 1: suppl., 129–130, nos. 142–146, fig. 111; *CGED* 112 and note 87.
1026–1027	Sybaris	*NSc* 1970, 3: suppl., 92, 107, fig. 76, nos. 40 and 90; *CGED* 119–120, notes 215–216.
1028	Sybaris	*NSc* 1970, 3: suppl., 255, fig. 265, no. 129; *CGED* 119–120 note 214.
1029	Metapontium	Antiquarium di Metaponto, inv. no. 31923. *CGED* 112 and note 77.
1030*	Tarentum	Taranto Mus. no. 52105. *BSA* 44, 1949, 158, note 14, no. 3; *ASAtene* 37–38, 1959–60, 188, fig. 160; *Emporio* 158 note 2; *Tocra* I 60 note 3; *CGED* 111 and 135, pl. 67.15.
1031*	Cerveteri	Museo di Villa Giulia, inv. no. 20789–90. *MonAnt.* 42, 1955, 278, fig. 37.3; *BSA* 44, 1949, 158 note 14 no 4 and p. 160; Helbig, *Führer*, III, 577 no. 2615; *Emporio* 158 note 2; *StEtr.* 1927, 162, pl. 38c; *Tocra* I, 60 note 2; *CGED* 161 no. 5.
1032*	Etruria, unknown prov.	Florence inv. no. 3702. *Emporio* 158 note 2; *CGED* 161, pl. 79.23.
1033	Bessan, Hérault, Agde.	*RA* 1975, 13, pl. 1 a and b; Jully, *Languedoc*, Partie I, 1982, 44 and note 226; Jully, *Caesarodunum* 12,1, 1977, 168 and note 1.
1034	Corinth	C 73-152. *Hesperia* 43, 1974, 16, no. 12, pl. 4.
1035	Corinth	C 73-96. *Hesperia* 43, 1974, 161, pl. 4.
1036	Corinth	C 73-110. *Hesperia* 47, 1974, 16, pl. 4.
1037–1039	Corinth	C 73-149, 150, 152. *Hesperia* 43, 1974, 16.
1040*	Delos	*Délos* X, 57, pl. 20.123; *Emporio* 158 note 2.
1041–1042	Kavala	*AE* 1938, 118, nos. 80 and 81; *Aphieroma Amantou*, 155, figs. 1.2, 3 and 2.2, 3; *Emporio* 158 note 2.
1043*	Thessaloniki, Karabournaki	Thessaloniki, University Museum inv. no. 341. *Epitymbion Tsountas*, 371. fig. 6.1; *Emporio* 158 note 2; *To Archaiologiko Ergo sti Makedonia kai Thraki* 1, 1987, 1988, 257, figs. 9a and 10.

1044*–1046*	Thessaloniki, Karabournaki	Thessaloniki, University Museum inv. nos. 356–358. *To Archaiologiko Ergo sti Makedonia kai Thraki* 1, 1987, 1988, 257, fig. 9.
1047–1050	Thessaloniki, Ayia Paraskevi	*Arch. Reports* for 1983–84, 41; *Ametos* 794.
1051*–1053*	Istros	B724; B725; B722. Lambrino, *Vases*, 303 fig. 291; *Histria* IV, no. 143.
1054*–1055*	Istros	B726; B727. Lambrino, *Vases*, 303–4, fig. 292 a + b; *Histria* IV, no. 144.
1056*	Istros	B1048a. Lambrino, *Vases*, 304, fig. 293; *Histria* IV, no. 145.
1057	Istros	V9552A. *Histria* II, cat. 336, pl. 20; *Histria* IV, 52 no. 151.
1058	Istros	V9449a. *Histria* II, cat. 335, pl. 20; *Histria* IV, 52, no. 152.
1059	Lesbos, Antissa	*BSA* 32, 1931–2, 59, pl. 23.31; *Emporio* 158 note 2.
1060–1061	Rhodes, Vroulia	I 34 and I 19. Kinch, *Vroulia*, 149–150, pl. 28.3 a and b and 4; *Emporio* 158 note 2.
1062*	Rhodes, Camirus	Louvre A 330,2. Pottier, *Vases*, 165, no. 330, 2; *Emporio* 158 note 2; *Chios Conference* 235 fig. 3.
1063*	Rhodes, Camirus	Berlin F 1646. Neugebauer, *Führer* II, 28; *Emporio* 158 note 2; *CVA* Berlin IV, pl. 171.2.
1064*	Old Smyrna	*BSA* 60, 1965, 140, pl. 42.11 and 44.11; *Emporio* 158 note 2.
1065–1067	Old Smyrna	*BSA* 60, 1965, 140, nos. 4–6, pl. 43.
1068*	Old Smyrna	*BSA* 60, 1965, 140, no. 12, pl. 43.
1069	Pitane	Istanbul Archaeological Museum, on exhibit. *Almost intact chalice put together from many frs. Slip mostly worn out. Rim pattern: dots between two parallel lines. Handle zone: metope pattern executed with a sixtuple brush. Brown paint on the outside of bowl and handles. Inside: chain with lotus alternating with dotted rosettes 3×3. The transition from bowl to walls is slightly discernible.* *Est. H. and Diam.: c. 0.25.*
1070*	Ephesus	Selçuk Museum, on exhibit. Langmann in *Festr. Eichler*, 105, 107, pl. 42.1. *Intact chalice. Rim pattern: wide band; handle zone: saw pattern.* *H: 0.17 W: 0.17.*
1071*	Cyprus, Marion	*JHS* 66, 1946, 6, pl. 1.b; *Emporio* 158 note 2; Gjerstad, *Cyprus*, 34, no. 158, pl. 16.7 and 8; *Chios Conference*, 233 fig 2.
1072	Tell Sūkās	*AASyrie* 13, 1963, 220, fig. 23; *Emporio* 158 note 2; *Sūkās* II, 72, fig. d and pl. 16.312.

II. PHIALAI MESOMPHALOI

1073   Naucratis   BM 1886.4–1.1073.
Part of a phiale. Outside: band on the edge, then line and then four parallel lines. Inside: dots between two parallel lines, then buds, then three parallel lines and then tongues in white and red.
W: 0.104.

1074*   Naucratis   UCL 748.
Two bands on white slip. Inside: white band and below rays.
W: 0.039 H: 0.05.

1075*   Tocra   *Tocra* II, 25, 26, no. 2051, pl. 16 and fig. 10.

1076*   Istros   Lambrino, *Vases*, 305–6, no. 12, fig. 295–6, pl. 3; *Histria* IV, 51, pl. 13.134.

1077*   Istros   Lambrino, *Vases*, 306, no. 13, fig. 297 and pl. 7.8; *Histria* IV, 51, pl. 13.135.

1078*   Istros   Lambrino, *Vases*, 307, no. 14, pl. 7.6; *Histria* IV, 51, no. 136.

1079*   Istros   Lambrino, *Vases*, 307, no. 15, fig. 292c.

1080   Panticapaeum   *MIA* 103, 1962, 124, fig. 7.6; Kocybala, Diss. 1978, 324 and note 720.

1081*   Cyprus, Marion   Dikaios, *A Guide to the Cyprus Museum*[3], 1961, 79, pl. 39.3; *RDAC*, 1968, 12ff., pl. 4; *Tocra* II, 25 and note 4; Gjerstad, *Cyprus*, 30, no. 103, pl. 10. 1–2.

III. PLATES

1082   Phana   *BSA* 35, 1934–35, 159, pl. 37.20; *Samos* VI.1, 139, no. 738.

1083*   Phana   Chios Mus. no. 2821.
BSA 35, 1934–35, 159, pl. 37.21; *Samos* VI.1, 139, no. 739.

C. FRAGMENTS OF EITHER A OR B CATEGORIES OR WITH DECORATION LOST

I. CHALICES

1084   Naucratis   BM 1886.4–1.1551.
Naukratis I, pl. 5.12.
Rim pattern: chequer with dotted blanks above line. On the walls: two united triangles forming a clepsydra. Inside: parallel lines.
W: 0.052.

1085   Naucratis   BM 1924.12–1.161.
Rim pattern: two parallel lines. Inside: bud above line.
W: 0.032.

1086   Naucratis   BM 1924.12–1.163 and 162.
Naukratis I, pl. 5.6, inside, right.
Rim pattern: chequers. On the walls: dotted circles. Inside: lotus and bud.
W: 0.107.

1087	Naucratis	BM 1924.12–1.315. *Rim part of a chalice: chequer with dotted blanks.* *W: 0.039.*
1088	Naucratis	BM 1924.12–1.332. *Rim part of a chalice: dots between lines.* *W: 0.030.*
1089	Naucratis	BM 1924.12–1.464. *Part of handle zone and bowl. Metope pattern. Inside: two parallel lines.* *W: 0.032.*
1090	Naucratis	BM 1924.12–1.480. *Rim part. Rim pattern: dots between lines.* *W: 0.039.*
1091	Naucratis	BM 1924.12–1.488. *Rim part. Rim pattern: chequers with dotted blanks.* *W: 0.072.*
1092	Naucratis	BM 1924.12–1.546. *As the last.* *W: 0.035.*
1093	Naucratis	BM 1924.12–1.576. *Rim part, as the last. Inside: bud.* *W: 0.069.*
1094	Naucratis	BM 1924.12–1.612. *Rim part. Rim pattern: diagonal strokes between two parallel lines. Inside: lotus and dotted circle.* *W: 0.037.*
1095	Naucratis	*Naukratis* I, pl. 5.53.
1096	Naucratis	*Naukratis* I, pl. 5.55.
1097	Naucratis	*Naukratis* I, pl. 5.19. *Rim pattern: dots between lines.* *Inscription:*]ΕΑΝΕΘ[*and a dotted circle.*
1098	Naucratis	BM 1924.12–1.568. *Part of the bowl of a small chalice.*
1099	Naucratis	BM 1924.12–1.571. *Part of the bowl, handle and walls of a small chalice. Handle zone: triple meander running l. Below broken meander and then rays.*
1100	Naucratis	BM 1888.6–1.774. *Foot and part of the bowl of a small chalice. Broken meander and then rays.*
1101	Naucratis	BM 1924.12–1.598. *Handle and part of the bowl and walls of a small chalice. Broken meander and then rays.*
1102	Naucratis	*CVA* Oxford II, 84, pl. 396.62.
1103*–1108*	Naucratis	Cambridge, Museum of Classical Archaeology, NA 60, 81, 82, 86, 87 and 89.
1109	Naucratis	UCL 748. *Plain*

1110*	Naucratis	Liverpool 56–21–527. *Rim pattern: dots between lines. Inside: black paint with a reserved band on the rim* H: 0.024 W: 0.029.
1111*	Naucratis	Liverpool 56–21–530. *Rim pattern: dots. Inside: dotted rosette.* W: 0.046.
1112*	Naucratis	Liverpool 56–21.534. *Plain. Inside: rosette.* H: 0.026 W: 0.029.
1113*	Naucratis	*CVA* Reading I, 37, pl. 550.2 a and b.
1114*	Naucratis	*CVA* Reading I, 37, pl. 550.9 a and b.
1115*	Naucratis	*CVA* Reading I, 37, pl. 550.3 a and b.
1116*	Naucratis	*CVA* Reading I, 37, pl. 550.7 a and b.
1117*	Naucratis	*CVA* Reading I, 38, pl. 550.11 a and b.
1118*	Naucratis	MMA inv. no. 26.211.6. (Gift of Elinor R. Price, 1926). *Inside: Tendrils and lotus.*
1119*	Naucratis	MMA inv. no. 26.211.11. (Gift of Elinor R. Price, 1926). *Inside: Part of a lotus.*
1120*	Naucratis	MMA inv. no. 26.211.12. (Gift of Elinor R. Price, 1926). *Inside: Parallel lines.*
1121*	Naucratis	UM Philadelphia E175 D4. *Part of the handle zone. Saw edged pattern.* H: 0.028 W: 0.042
1122*	Naucratis	UM Philadelphia E175 F6. *Inside: two white lines and below petals of a rosette.* H: 0.040 W: 0.031
1123*	Naucratis	UM Philadelphia E175 N14. *Part of the bowl. Bands.* H: 0.035 W: 0.042
1124*	Naucratis	ROM 910 × 234.10. Hayes, *forthcoming*.
1125*	Naucratis	*CVA* Heidelberg I, 14, pl. 437.19.
1126*	Naucratis	Bonn. *Part of the handle zone with a saw edged pattern.*
1127*	Naucratis	Bonn. *Part of the wall with two parallel lines.*
1128*	Naucratis	Bonn. *Part of the bowl with two bands.*
1129*	Naucratis	Bonn. *Part of the handle zone and the root of the handle.*
1129a*	Naucratis	Alexandria inv. no. 17161. Venit, *Egypt. Museums*, no. 130, pl. 32 and drawing on p. 168.

1130*	Naucratis	Alexandria inv. no. 17181. Venit, *Egypt. Museums*, no. 131, pl. 33 and drawing on p. 168. *Part of the handle zone with saw edged pattern.*
1130a*	Naucratis	Alexandria inv. no. 17257. Venit, *Egypt. Museums*, no. 132, pl. 33 and drawing on p. 168.
1130b*	Naucratis	Alexandria inv. no. 17195. Venit, *Egypt. Museums*, no. 135, pl. 33 and drawing on p. 168.
1131*	Tocra	*Tocra* II 26, no. 809, pl. 15.
1132*	Tocra	*Tocra* II, 26, no. 2043, pl. 15.
1133	Cyrene, Demeter Sanct.	*LA* 13–14, 1976–7, pl. 85b top right; Schaus, *Dem. Sanct., Cyrene* II, 81–2, no. 495, pl. 29.
1134	Cyrene, Demeter Sanct.	*LA* 13–14, 1976–7, pl. 85b top right; Schaus, *Dem. Sanct., Cyrene* II, 82, no. 496, pl. 29.
1135–1141	Cyrene, Demeter Sanct.	Shaus, *Dem. Sanct., Cyrene* II, 82, nos. 497–503, pl. 29 and fig. 9.
1142	Himera	*Himera* II, 268 no. 2. (inv. H73. 132, 3c)
1143	Gela, Bitalemi	*CGED* 95. *Several frs. of Chian chalices from the new excavations.*
1144–1147	Megara Hyblaea	*Mégara Hyblaea* II, 84, pl. 70.3. *Four undecorated frs.*
1148	Megara Hyblaea	*Mégara Hyblaea* II, 84, pl. 70.4.
1149	Croton	*CGED* 114 and note 106.
1150	Sybaris	*NSc* 1972, suppl., 95, no. 138, fig. 71; *CGED* 112 and note 83.
1151	Sybaris	*NSc* 1972, 112, no. 398, fig. 434 on p. 412; *CGED* 112 and note 86.
1152	Sybaris	*NSc* 1969, suppl. 3, 137, fig. 115, no. 184.
1153–1158	Francavilla Mma, Motta	*AttiMGrecia* 15–17, 1974–76, pl. 67. 2d, f, g, i, j, k.
1159*	Gavorrano, Grosseto	Florence inv. no. 29463. *CGED* 161, pl. 79.22.
1160–1161	Gravisca	*CGED* 222. *Two undecorated chalices from the Archaic sanctuary of Aphrodite.*
1162*	Marseilles	Vasseur, *Marseille*, 43, pl. 17.2.
1162a*	Marseilles	Vasseur, *Marseille*, 35, pl. 5.9 and 10.
1162b*	Marseilles	Vasseur, *Marseille*, 36, pl. 5.11.
1163	Marseilles	Vasseur, *Marseille*, 42, pl. 6.8; Villard, *Marseille*, 38, no. 5.
1163a*	Marseilles	Vasseur, *Marseille*, 36, pl. 5.12.
1163b*	Marseilles	Vasseur, *Marseille*, 38, fig. 19.1.
1164	Naxos, Aplomata	Naxos Mus. inv. no. 1404. *Foot of a chalice.* *Diam. at the base: 0.06.*

1165	Naxos, Aplomata	Naxos Mus. no. inv. no. *Part of the handle zone and walls with the handle root. Metope pattern.*
1166*	Naxos, Aplomata	Naxos Mus. inv. no. B1237. *Part of the handle zone and walls. Metope pattern.* *W: 0.05.*
1167–1168	Paros, Delion	Paros Mus., Delion no. 307 and no. 538. O. Rubensohn, *Das Delion von Paros*, 1962, 113, pl. 21.2. *Feet of two chalices.* *no. 307: Inside: two parallel lines and a cross with three petals.*
1169–1171	Siphnos	*BSA* 44, 1949, 50. *1. Metope pattern on handle zone.* *2. Rim pattern: dots between lines.* *3. Foot.*
1172	Aegina, Aphaia Temple	*Aegina*, pl. 124.1 middle right; *AA* 1983, 166, no. 26.
1173*–1178*	Aegina, Aphaia Temple	*AA* 1983, 166 nos. 28–33, figs. 8 and 9.
1179–1181	Aegina, Old town	*Alt-Ägina* II.1, 16, nos. 79–81, pl. 5.
1182	Athens, Acropolis	Graef-Langlotz, no. 453; *Emporio* 158 note 2.
1183–1185	Perachora	*Perachora* II, 375–6, nos. 4065–4066, pl. 156.
1186–1188	Istros	*Histria* IV, 52, nos. 146, 147, 148, fig. 6.
1189	Panticapaeum	*MIA* 103, 1962, 120, fig. 7.2; Kocybala, Diss. 1978, 324 and note 719.
1190	Panticapaeum	*MIA* 103, 1962, 120, fig. 7.3; Kocybala, Diss. 1978, 324 and note 719.
1191	Panticapaeum	*MIA* 56, 1957, 186, fig. 2b, 3; *MIA* 103, 1962, 120, fig. 7.4 a and b; Kocybala, Diss. 1978, 324 and note 719.
1192	Samos, Heraion	*Samos* VI.1, 129, pl. 98.746.
1193	Samos, Heraion	*Samos* VI.1, 140, pl. 98.775.
1194	Samos, Heraion	*Samos* VI.1, 140, no. 779, fig. 142.
1195	Samos, Heraion	*Samos* VI.1, 140, no. 780, fig. 144.
1196	Samos, Heraion	H. Kyrieleis, *Chios Conference*, 192. "One [fragment] comes from a chalice of the familiar Chian type with red and white lotus decoration on the white interior."
1197	"Larisa"	*Larisa am Hermos* III, 171, pl. 57.22.
1198	Pitane	*CGED* 29. *Datable to the second quarter of the sixth century.*
1199	Pitane	*CGED* 29. *Datable to the third quarter of the sixth century.*
1200*–1202	Gordion	Körte, *Gordion*, 185–186, nos. 41, 42 and 45, fig. 169.
1203–1204	Tell Sūkās	*Sūkās* II, 71, nos. 310 and 311, pl. 16.
1205	Tell Sūkās	*Sūkās* II, 72, no. 313, pl. 16; *AASyrie* 10, 1960, 127–8, fig. 16.
1206	Tell Sūkās	*Sūkās* II, 72, no. 314, pl. 16.

306   THE CHALICE STYLE

1207   Tell Sūkās   *AASyrie* 13, 1963, 216, fig. 25; *Emporio* 157 note 5; *Sūkās* II, 72, no. 315, pl. 16.

1208–1210   Tell Sūkās   *Sūkās* II, 72, nos. 316–8, pl. 16.

II. PHIALAI MESOMPHALOI

1211–1212   Phana   *BSA* 35, 1934–5, 159, pl. 37.4 and 6; *Samos* VI.1, 139, nos. 736–7, only.

1213–1216   Naucratis   BM 1888.6–1.498 a. b. c. and d.
                                   Omphaloi painted with chequers and broken cable patterns outside. Inside: flowers with petals in red and white on black.
                                   W: 0.058 498c: 0.044.

1217   Naucratis   BM 1924.12–1.589.
                                   Rosette. Rim pattern: two parallel lines. Inside: tongue pattern.
                                   W: 0.032.

1218   Naucratis   BM 1924.12–1.586.
                                   Part of a small phiale. Outside: chequer between two parallel lines. Inside: chequer, lotus bud and chequer.
                                   W: 0.061.

1219   Naucratis   BM 1924.12–1.606.
                                   Part of a small phiale. Outside: three parallel lines. Inside: rosettes, band and lozenges.
                                   W: 0.063.

1220*   Naucratis   *CVA* Oxford II, 82, pl. 396.25.

1221*   Naucratis   Cambridge, Museum of Classical Archaeology, NA 67.
                                   Part of a phiale. An indiscernible object and a rosette above a band of chequers.
                                   W: 0.065.

1222   Naucratis   Cambridge, Museum of Classical Archaeology.
                                   Part of a phiale. Lion to the r. above a band of chequers.
                                   W: 0.049.

1223*   Naucratis   Cambridge, Museum of Classical Archaeology, NA 95.
                                   Face of a figure to the r. Inside: dots between lines and below a rosette.
                                   W: 0.069.

1224*   Naucratis   Cambridge, Museum of Classical Archaeology, NA 96.
                                   Plain. Inside: dots and then tongues.
                                   W: 0.050.

1225*   Naucratis   *CVA* Reading I, 37, pl. 550.8 a and b.

1226*–1228* Naucratis   *CVA* Reading I, 38, pl. 550.10 a and b; 12 a and b; 13 a and b.

1229*   Naucratis   Liverpool 56–21–524.
                                   Broken meander and above ?feet of a feline. Inside: dotted rosette.
                                   H: 0.035 W: 0.030.

1230*   Naucratis   Liverpool 56–21–526.
                                   Rim pattern: zigzag between lines Inside: lotus.
                                   H: 0.030 W: 0.018.

1231*	Naucratis	Fairbanks, *Catal.*, 100, no. 305.1, pl. 32.
1232*	Naucratis	UM Philadelphia E175 J10. *Tongues.* *H:0.025 W:0.018.*
1233*	Naucratis	Berlin Antiquarium (lost during the war). *Parallel lines. Inside: a row of pomegranates, then lines and tongues.*
1234	Naucratis	*CVA* Brussels III, pl. 105.3 a and b.
1235–1241	Cyrene, Demeter Sanct.	Schaus, *Dem. Sanct., Cyrene* II, 83, nos. 509–515, pl. 30.
1242	Tarentum	*BolldArte* 1962, 161, no. 9, fig. 14b; *CGED* 116 and note 148.
1243	Delos	*Délos* X, 57, pl. 8 B, no. 125.
1244*–1245*	Aegina, Aphaia Temple	*AA* 1983, 180–1, nos. 168–9, fig. 20.
1246	Thasos	*Et. thas.* VII, 39, pl. 13.15.
1247*–1249*	Old Smyrna	*BSA* 60, 1965, 141, nos. 13–15, pls. 43 and 44.
1250	Ephesus	in Vienna University. Cook, Distribution, 159.
1251	Miletus	*IstMitt* 9–10, 1959–60, pl. 64.2.
1252*	Rhodes, Vroulia	Kinch, *Vroulia*, 150, pl. 46.2 and 3.

III. OTHER SHAPES

1253	Naucratis	*CVA* Brussels III, pl. 105.6.
1254*	Naucratis	*CVA* Brussels III, pl. 105.7.
1255*	Naucratis	*CVA* Brussels III, pl. 105.9.

D. VASES WITH FLORAL DECORATION

I. CHALICES

1256	Naucratis	BM 1924.12–1.428. *Outside: lotus. Inside: rosette above two parallel lines.* *W: 0.027.*
1257	Naucratis	BM 1924.12–1.451. *Outside: Rim pattern: chequers above line. Lotus and bud. Inside: lotus.* *W: 0.019.*
1258	Naucratis	BM 1924.12–1.527. *Outside: bands and lines and then lotus.* *W: 0.044.*

1259	Naucratis	BM 1924.12–1.550. *Outside: Rim pattern: dots between lines, then chain of single alternating with double meander running l. between two parallel lines. On the walls: chain of lotus and bud. Inside: lotus and cross with looped edges.* *W: 0.059.*
1260*	Naucratis	*CVA* Oxford II, 81, pl. 396.5 (upside-down).
1261*	Naucratis	Wiel, *Leiden*, pl. 1 no. 5; *CVA* Musée Scheurleer II, pl. 69.2; Prins de Jong, *Scherben*, pl. 1.6. *Outside: chain of lotus and bud then broken meander.*
1262*	Istros	Lambrino, *Vases*, 304–5, fig. 294; *BSA* 44, 1949, 158, note 14; *Emporio* 157 note 4; *Histria* II, cat. 335, ref., *Histria* IV, 51, no. 140, pl. 13.
1263	Pitane	Istanbul Archaeological Museum, inv. no. 8545 on exhibit. *Not complete; put together from many frs. Est. H.: c.0.12. Decoration: lotus, upside down, between the handles and dotted rosettes flanking it. Above the left handle: the beginning of another lotus. Above the right handle: meander running l. Foot: restored, not the original.*
1264	Samos, Heraion	*Samos* VI.1, 139, pl. 98.747.
1265*	Rhodes, Vroulia	Kinch, *Vroulia*, 149, piece I.2.

II. PHIALAI MESOMPHALOI

1266	Naucratis	BM 1924.12–1.26. *Chain of lotus and bud between two parallel lines, then a bud flanked by two dotted circles.* *W: 0.039.*
1267	Naucratis	BM 1924.12–1.145. *Lotus and bud chain. Inside: traces of lotus and bud.* *W: 0.048.*
1268	Naucratis	BM 1924.12–1.525. *Rim pattern: two parallel lines. Chain of lotus and bud.* *W: 0.049.*
1269*	Naucratis	UCL 752. Johnston, *Exhibition* 1978, no. 88. *Rosette. Inside: white dots and then tongues.* *W: 0.041 H: 0.028.*

Chapter 4: The Black-Figure styles of the sixth century

1. THE SPHINX AND LION STYLE

I. BOWLS WITH LIDS

1270*	Emporio	*Emporio* 166, no. 824, figs. 114–5, pl. 60.
1271*	Tocra	*Tocra* II 26, no. 2052, fig. 10, pl.17.

II. STEMMED SKYPHOS CRATER

1272*   Pitane   Istanbul Archaeological Museum, on exhibit.
AJA 66, 1962, 378, pl. 103.31; *Emporio* 166 note 6 and 194 no. 18; *CGED* 29, pl. 5.3; *AntK* Beiheft 7, 1970, 7 (Aeolian).
Put together from many frs. Knob and below it four female heads. On the lid: five friezes. 1. tongues. 2. sphs. to the l. amidst rosettes. 3. lions to the r. amidst rosettes. 4. sphs. to the l. amidst rosettes. 5. geese to the r. amidst rosettes. Short rays at the end of the rim of both lid and the bowl.
On the bowl: five friezes. 1. lions to the r. amidst rosettes. 2. simple guilloche. 3. geese with open wings to the l. amidst rosettes. 4. lions to the r. amidst rosettes. 5. lotus and bud.
On the stem of the vase: four friezes. 1. triangles alternating with inverted triangles. 2. tongue pattern. 3. double meander running l. 4. sphs. to the r. amidst rosettes. Rays at the edge of the ring foot.
Est. H.: c. 0.50–0.55.

III. Fragments of I or II:

A. Lower Part

1273*	Pyrgi Cem., Chios	*Emporio* 166, no. 830, pl. 63.
1274*	Emporio	*Emporio* 168, no. 831, pl. 63.
1275	Emporio	*Emporio* 168, no. 832, pl. 63.
1276	Emporio	*Emporio* 168, no. 833, fig. 115, pl. 63.
1277*	Phana	Chios Mus. no. 2936. *BSA* 35, 1934–5, 160, pl. 37. 1,3; *Emporio* 166 note 6.
1278*	Chios, unknown provenance	Chios Mus. no. 3870. *Two friezes: Upper: a triangle; Lower: a man to the r. but facing left. Rosettes and half-rosettes.* *W: 0.04 H: 0.059.*
1279*	Rizari, Chios town	Chios Mus. no. 3383. *Two friezes: Upper: bull to the r. Rosette and half-rosette. Lower: lotus and bud.* *W: 0.049 H: 0.047.*

1280*	Rizari, Chios town	Chios Mus. no. 3384. *On both sides decoration. Exterior: Sph. to the l. and rosettes. Interior: Sph. to the l., rosette and half-rosette. Below: meander running l.* *W: 0.10 H: 0.061.*
1281*	Rizari, Chios town	Chios Mus. no. 3363. *Two friezes: upper: lion to the r. and ? half-rosette Lower: lotus and bud.* *W: 0.057 H: 0.086.*
1282*	Rizari, Chios town	Chios Mus. no. 3377. *Short rays at the rim. Lion to the r. Red paint on creamy slip.* *W: 0.039 H: 0.042.*
1283*	Rizari, Chios town	Chios Mus. no. 3385. *Short rays at the rim. Lion to the r. Added red on the triangles of the mane.* *W: 0.033 H: 0.035.*
1284*	Rizari, Chios town	Chios Mus. no. 3391. *Decorated on both sides. Exterior: two friezes of sphs. to the l. Rosettes. Interior: sph. to the l. Rosettes.* *W: 0.091.*
1285*	Rizari, Chios town	Chios Mus. no. 3394. *Short rays at the rim. Lion to the r. and blobs.* *W: 0.063.*
1286*	Rizari, Chios town	Chios Mus. no. 3364. *Broken meander at the rim. Lion to the l. Fill. orns.: horseshoe roundel, rosette and a small circle.* *W: 0.035 H: 0.028.*
1287*	Naucratis	BM 1888.6–1.547c. Price pl.12.9 *Short rays at the rim. Frieze of lions to the l. Rosettes and half-rosettes. Below a frieze of broken meander and below lotus and bud. White slip inside.* *W: 0.081.*
1288*	Naucratis	BM 1886.4–1.1071. Price pl. 12.10. *Short rays at the rim. Lion to the l. Rosettes and half-rosette.* *W: 0.031.*
1289	Naucratis	BM 1924.12–1.337. *Two friezes: Upper: ?sph. to the l. and half-rosette. Then broken meander between two parallel lines. Then chain of lotus and bud above meander.* *W: 0.072.*
1290	Naucratis	BM 1924.12–1.345. *Foreleg of a ?bull to the l. Rosettes.* *W: 0.047.*
1291	Naucratis	BM 1924.12–1.338. *Two friezes: Upper: lions to the r. Lower: sph. to the l. Rosette.* *W: 0.058.*

THE SPHINX AND LION STYLE

1292*   Naucratis   Oxf. G120.24, V188j.
CVA Oxford II, 83, pl.396.31, (wrongly stated G129.9 in the *CVA*).
Short rays at the rim. Sphs. to the l. Rosettes.
W: 0.044.

1293*   Naucratis   Oxf. G120.7 1888.185a, V188a.
CVA Oxford II, 83, pl.396.39; Price pl.12.3; *Samos* VI. 1, pl.97.705 (wrongly stated G120.17 in the *CVA*).
Two friezes: Upper: sph. to the l. Lower: lion to the r. Rosettes.
W: 0.062.

1294*   Naucratis   Oxf. G120.14.
CVA Oxford II, 83, pl. 396.35, perhaps joins *CVA* Musée Scheurleer II, pl. 69.3.
Short rays at the rim. Lion to the r. Rosettes.
W: 0.044.

1295*   Naucratis   Oxf. G120.36.
Rays at the rim. Lion without mane to the r. and the tail of another. Red paint.
W: 0.042.

1296*   Naucratis   Oxf. G120.5.
Short rays at the rim. ?Panther to the l. and bull to the r. with their tails entangled. Rosettes and half-rosettes.
W: 0.057.

1297*   Naucratis   Oxf. G120.15.
Short rays at the rim. Lion to the l. with his paw raised.
W: 0.039.

1298*   Naucratis   *CVA* Cambridge II, 34, pl. 496.58.

1299*   Naucratis   *CVA* Cambridge II, 34, pl. 496.59.

1300*   Naucratis   *CVA* Cambridge II, 34, pl. 496.60.
Two friezes: Upper: sphs. to the l. Rosettes. Lower: lions to the r. Rosettes and half-rosettes.

1301*   Naucratis   UCD 68.
JHS 91, 1971, 115, pl. 13c; Johnston, Ireland, 430, no. 943.

1302*   Naucratis   Fairbanks, *Catal.*, pl. 32, no. 310.3; *Samos* VI.1, 140, pl. 97.774; Cook, *Claz. Sarc.*, 103 note 61.

1303*   Naucratis   *CVA* Heidelberg I, 13, pl. 437.17.

1304*   Naucratis   Leipzig, sent from Oxford in 1928 (lost during the war).
Two friezes: Upper: sphs. to the r. Lower: lotus and bud.

1305*   Naucratis   Hague inv. T2902, now in Leiden.
Prins de Jong, *Scherben*, 36, 81, pl.1.10; *CVA* Musée Scheurleer II, pl. 69.3; Wiel, *Leiden*, 3, pl. 1, n. 8.

1306*   Naucratis   Alexandria inv. no. 950.2
Venit, *Egypt. Museums*, no. 141, pl. 34, drawing on p. 169 (wrongly positioned).
Sph. to the r. and half-rosette.

1307*	Naucratis	Alexandria inv. no. 17102. Venit, *Egypt. Museums*, no. 138, pl. 34 and drawing on p. 169. *Short rays at the rim. Lion to the r. and half-rosette. Inside: slipped.*
1308*	Naucratis	Alexandria inv. no. 16904. Venit, *Egypt. Museums*, no. 82, pl. 23 and drawing on p. 156. *Short rays at the rim. Sph. to the r. Rosette. Inside: slipped.*
1309	Cyrene, Demeter Sanct.	Schaus, *Dem. Sanct., Cyrene* II, 79, no. 473, pl. 28.
1310	Cyrene, Demeter Sanct.	Schaus, *Dem. Sanct., Cyrene* II, 79, no. 474, pl. 28.
1311*	Thasos	Istanbul no. 5284 and 5285. *Et. thas.* VII, 37–38, figs. 1.2; *Emporio* 166 note 6, and 194 no. 4; *Samos* VI.1 pl.97.703; Cook, *Distribution* 159.
1312*	Berezan	*MIA* 50, 1956, 223, fig. 1.7; Kocybala, Diss. 1978, 196 and note 136.
1313	Berezan	*MIA* 50, 1956, 223 fig. 1.9; Kocybala, Diss. 1978, 196 and note 138.
1314*	Berezan	*MIA* 50, 1956, 223 fig. 2.6; Kocybala, Diss. 1978, 196 and note 137.

B. Upper Part

1315*	Emporio	*Emporio* 166, no. 825, pl.62.
1316*	Emporio	*Emporio* 166, no. 826, pl.63.
1317*	Emporio	*Emporio* 166, no. 827, pl.63.
1318*	Emporio	*Emporio* 166, no. 829, fig.115, pl.63.
1319*	Rizari, Chios town	Chios Mus. no. 3381. *Animal's feet to the l. Rosette. Short rays at the edge of the lid and a flange beneath.* *W: 0.026.*
1320*	Rizari, Chios town	Chios Mus. no. 3366. *Lions to the r. Rosettes and half-rosette. Short rays at the edge of the lid and a flange beneath.* *W: 0.082 Est. Diam.: c. 0.146.*
1321*	Rizari, Chios town	Chios Mus. no. 3367. *Lions to the r. Rosettes. Short rays at the edge of the lid and a flange beneath.* *W: 0.052 Est. Diam.: c. 0.124.*
1322*	Rizari, Chios town	Chios. Mus. no. 3368. *Sphs. to the l. Blobs. Short rays at the edge of the lid and a flange beneath.* *W: 0.035 Est. Diam.: c. 0.154.*
1323*	Rizari, Chios town	Chios Mus. no. 3365. *?Sph. to the l. Rosettes and half-rosettes. A row of dots and then short rays at the edge of the lid and a flange beneath it. Slipped within.* *W: 0.104 Est. Diam.: c. 0.26.*

1324*	Rizari, Chios town	Chios Mus. no. 3369. *Two friezes: Upper: goose and bull to the r. Lower: tail of a horse, horse with komast-rider and siren to the l. Rosettes and half-rosettes. A row of dots and then short rays at the edge of the lid and a flange beneath. Slipped within.* *W: 0.143 Est. Diam.: c. 0.28.*
1325*	Rizari, Chios town	Chios. Mus. no. 3392. *Half-rosettes and dashes at the edge of the lid.*
1326*	Rizari, Chios town	Chios Mus. no. 3388. *?Four friezes: 1. and 2. animals not distinguishable. 3. Lion to the r. 4. Sph. to the r. Rosettes.* *W: 0.073.*
1327*	Rizari, Chios town	Chios Mus. no. 3371. *Lions to the r. Rosette and half-rosettes.* *W: 0.052.*
1328*	Rizari, Chios town	Chios Mus. no. 3374. *Two frs. Animal's feet and blobs. Short rays at the edge of the rim and a flange beneath.* *W: 0.042 W: 0.048.*
1329*	Rizari, Chios town	Chios. Mus. no. 3378. *Sph. to the l. Rosettes. Slipped within.* *W: 0.033 H: 0.037.*
1330*	Rizari, Chios town	Chios Mus. no. 3379. *Tongues. Sph. to the l.* *W: 0.056.*
1331*	Naucratis	BM 1886.4–1.1296. *Naukratis* I, pl.5.56. *Two friezes: Upper: two antithetical sphs. and between them a rosette. Lower: bull to the r.* *W: 0.095.*
1332*	Naucratis	*Naukratis* II, pl. 7.2; Price pl.12.5; *Samos* VI.1, pl.97.704. *Tongues in alternating red and white at the centre of the lid. Two friezes: Upper: feet of a feline, lion to the r. but facing l., sph. to the l., siren to the l., lion to the l. and sph. to the l. amidst rosettes. Lower: lion to the l., sph. to the l., lion to the l., siren to the l., lion to the l. but facing r., lion to the r. amidst rosettes. Rays at the edge of the lid.*
1333*	Naucratis	BM 1888.6–1.547b. *Two rows of tongues. A frieze of geese, some with open wings to the l. amidst rosettes and half-rosettes. Rays at the edge of the lid. White slip inside.* *W: 0.105.*
1334	Naucratis	BM 1886.4–1.1095. Price pl.12.12. *Decorated on both sides. Outside: lion to the r. Rosettes and half-rosettes. Inside: lotus and bud.* *W: 0.066.*

1335	Naucratis	BM 1886.4–1.1135. Price pl.6.31 and 12.7. *Lion to the r. Rosettes and half-rosettes. Rays at the edge of the lid.* *W: 0.108.*
1336	Naucratis	BM 1911.6–6.74. Price pl. 12.4. *Lions to the r. Rosettes. Dashes at the edge of the lid. White slip inside.* *W: 0.030.*
1337	Naucratis	BM 1924.12–1.336. *Sphs. to the l. Rosettes. Short rays at the edge of the lid.* *W: 0.066.*
1338	Naucratis	BM 1886.4–1.998. Price pl. 12.1. *Decorated on both sides. Outside: two friezes, both with sphs. to the r.; rosettes and half-rosettes. Between the friezes dividing band with a row of dots. Inside: two rows of tongues. Frieze of lions to the r. Rosettes and half-rosettes.* *W: 0.093.*
1339	Naucratis	BM 1924.12–1.168. Price pl. 12.11 and 6.30. *Bull to the l. Rosette. Rays at the edge of the lid.* *W: 0.078.*
1340	Naucratis	BM 1886.4–1.1208. *Two friezes: Upper: animal's feet to the r. Lower: sph. to the l. Rosettes. Slipped inside.* *W: 0:059.*
1341	Naucratis	BM 1888.6–1.1068. *Naukratis* I, pl. 5.36; Price, pl. 12.6. *Row of dots. Sph. to the l.* *W: 0.040.*
1342*	Naucratis	*CVA* Oxford II, 83, pl. 396.36 (wrongly G.120.15). *Sph. to the l. Rosette. Rays at the edge of the lid.* *W: 0.039.*
1343*	Naucratis	Oxf. G120.6, G120.8, G120.20 (Boardman joined three frs.). *Plastic head as a knob; step pattern. Two friezes: Upper: sirens with scale bodies to the l. Rosettes. Dividing band with chequer pattern. Lower: bull to the r. Half-rosettes.* *W: 0.103 G120.6* *W: 0.039 G120.8* *W: 0.082 G120.20*
1344*	Naucratis	*CVA* Oxford II, 83, pl.396.32. (Boardman thinks that it might be from the same vase as **1351*** of this Catalogue, but it does not join). *Tongues. Lion attacking a bull. Half-rosette.* *W: 0.038.*

THE SPHINX AND LION STYLE

1345*   Naucratis   *CVA* Oxford II, 83, pl.396.40.
Two friezes: Upper: feet of a feline and half-rosette. Lower: bull to the r. and rosette.
W: 0.039.

1346*   Naucratis   *CVA* Oxford II, 83, pl.396.37.
Lion to the r. Rosettes.
W: 0.069.

1347*   Naucratis   Oxf. G120.17, V187a, 1889.215a.
Price pl. 12.8; *CVA* Oxford II, 83 pl. 396.38 (wrongly 1885.215); *Samos* VI. 1, pl.97.714.
Two friezes: Upper: sphs. to the l. Rosettes and half-rosettes. Dividing band with dots. Lower: sphs. to the r.
W: 0.067.

1348*   Naucratis   Oxford 1912.32a.
Price pl.12.13.
Lion and ?siren to the r. Rosettes.
W: 0.042.

1349*   Naucratis   Oxf. G120.11.
Geese with open wings to the l. Rays at the edge of the lid and a flange beneath.
W: 0.062.

1350*   Naucratis   Oxf. G120.10.
Sph. to the l. Half-rosette. Rays at the edge of the lid and a flange beneath.
W: 0.055.

1351*   Naucratis   *CVA* Cambridge II, 35, pl.496.62.
(Boardman thinks that it might be from the same vase as **1344*** of this Catalogue.)
Tongues. Bull to the r.

1352*   Naucratis   *CVA* Cambridge II,35, pl.496.61.
Two friezes: Upper: sirens to the l. Blobs. Lower: ?sirens and blobs. Dividing band with dots.

1353   Naucratis   *CVA* Reading I, 37, pl. 549.28.

1354*   Naucratis   National Museums of Scotland, Edinburgh 1886.518.2j.
CVA, Edinburgh, 5, pl. 720.23
Brown paint on creamy slip: Pink brown clay. Two friezes: Upper: sph. to the l. Rosette and half-rosette. Lower: lions to the r. Rosette and half-rosette. Brown paint. No paint inside. Red on mane and rosette-centre.
W: 0.047

1355*   Naucratis   Fairbanks, *Catal.* no. 309; pl.32.
Knob of a lid.

1356*   Naucratis   *CVA* Heidelberg I, 14, pl. 437.21.

1357*   Naucratis   Leipzig, sent from Oxford in 1928, (lost during the war).
Two friezes: Upper: siren to the l. and half-rosette. Lower: tail of a ?bull to the r. and half-rosette.

1358*   Naucratis   Leipzig, sent from Oxford in 1928, (lost during the war).
Sph. to the l. and rosettes.

1359*	Naucratis	*CVA* Brussels III, 2, pl.105.5.
1360*	Naucratis	Alexandria inv. no. 9501. Venit, *Egypt. Museums*, no. 140, pl. 34 and drawing on p. 169, (wrongly positioned). *Feline's feet to the r. Rays at the edge of the lid.*
1360a*	Naucratis	Alexandria inv. no. 17248. Venit, *Egypt. Museums*, no. 139, pl. 34 and drawing on p. 169. *Lion to the r.*
1361	Cyrene, Demeter Sanct.	Schaus, *Dem. Sanct., Cyrene* II, 85, no. 527, pl. 30.
1362	Cyrene, Demeter Sanct.	Schaus, *Dem. Sanct., Cyrene* II, 85, no. 528, pl. 31.
1363	Cyrene, Demeter Sanct.	Schaus, *Dem. Sanct., Cyrene* II, 85, no. 529, pl. 31.
1364	Cyrene, Demeter Sanct.	Schaus, *Dem. Sanct., Cyrene* II, 85, no. 530, pl. 31 and fig. 10.
1365	Cyrene, Demeter Sanct.	Schaus, *Dem. Sanct., Cyrene* II, 85, no. 531, pl. 31 and fig. 10.
1366	Cyrene, Demeter Sanct.	Schaus, *Dem. Sanct., Cyrene* II, 85, no. 532, pl. 31.
1367*	Istros	*Histria* IV, 43, pl.8. no. 67; Lambrino, *Vases* 259, fig. 226, no. 17.
1368*	Istros	*Histria* IV, 44, pl.8, no. 70; Lambrino, *Vases* 310, fig. 301; *Emporio* 166 note 6.
1369*	Istros	*Histria* IV, 44, pl.8, no. 71.
1370*	Istros	*Histria* IV, 44, pl.8, no. 72.
1371*	Berezan	Hermitage B456. *SovArch.* 1957.4, 137, fig.10.4; *Emporio* 166 note 6.
1372*	Berezan	Hermitage B464. *SovArch.* 1957.4, 137, fig.10.1; *Emporio* 166 note 6.
1373*	Berezan	Hermitage B462. *SovArch.* 1957.4, 137, fig.10.3; *Emporio* 166 note 6.
1374*	Berezan	Hermitage B460. *SovArch.* 1957.4, 137, fig.10.2; *Emporio* 166 note 6.
1375	"Larisa"	*Larisa am Hermos* 111, pl.57.21; *Emporio* 166 note 6.
1376	Erythrae	Basmahane Mus. in Izmir no. 930 *Two rows: Upper: sph. to the l. Rosettes. Lower: lions to the r. Rosettes and half-rosettes. Rays as rim pattern. The manes of the lions, with added red, do not have the two incised parallel lines to divide them from the saw edged mane. From the old excavations of Akurgal.* *W: 0.14 H: 0.081.*

C. Plastic Heads

1377*	Emporio	*Emporio* 194 no. 3 and 200, no. 115, pl. 81. *Possibly from the same vase as* **1270*** *of the Catalogue.*
1378	Phana	*ADelt.* II, 1916, pl.3 fig.20.21; *Enc. World Art* VII, pl. 19 top right; *Emporio* 194, no. 2. *Same vase as* **1438*** *of the Catalogue.*
1379*	Naucratis	BM 1886.4–1.1218. *Female head.*
1380*	Naucratis	BM 1886.4–1.1300. *Emporio* 194 no. 5? *Female head.*
1381	Naucratis	BM 1888.6–1.497. Price 217 fig.62; *Emporio* 194, no. 6. *Female protome. It could be from a ring vase.*
1382	Naucratis	BM 1886.4–1.1399. *Female head.*
1383	Naucratis	BM 1886.4–1.1429. *Two female heads, back to back.*
1384	Naucratis	BM A 954 : 1888.6–1.1526. *A ring vase which has preserved two spouts, one female protome and the beginning of another. Catalogued as* **360** *for the decoration.*
1385*	Naucratis	*CVA* Oxford II, pl.396.58; *Emporio* 194, no.7.
1386*	Naucratis	Oxford 1886.469. *Emporio* 194, no. 8 *Female head.*
1387*	Naucratis	Oxford 1921.1204. *CVA* Oxford II, pl. 404.22; *Emporio* 194 no. 9. *Female head.*
1388*	Naucratis	Cambridge, Museum of Classical Archaeology, NA 110. *Emporio* 194, no. 10. *Two heads, back to back pierced vertically; a narrow orifice at the top.*
1389*	Naucratis	UCL 750. Johnston, *Exhibition* 178, no. 80. *Female head with dotted necklace.*
1390*	Naucratis	Leipzig, sent from Oxford in 1928, (lost during the war). *Emporio* 194, no. 14. *From the leg of a vase. The features are broken away.*
1391*	Naucratis	Boston 88.926. *Emporio* 194, no. 12. *From the foot of a vase.*
1392*	Naucratis	Boston 88.978. Price pl. 12.15; Fairbanks, *Catal.* pl.30 no. 308.5; *Emporio* 194 no. 11.
1393	Cyrene, Demeter Sanct.	Schaus, *Dem. Sanct., Cyrene* II, 85, no. 537, pl. 31.

1394	Thasos	Istanbul 5284. *Et. thas.* VII, 38, fig. 2; *Emporio* 194 no. 4. *Same vase as* **1311*** *of this Catalogue.*
1395	Chios town	Unpublished, seen in Chios museum
1396*	Istros	*Dacia* VI, 1962, 155 fig. 19; *Emporio* 194, no. 15; *Histria* IV, 62, no. 252, pl. 25.
1397*	Olbia	*SovArch.* 1957.4, 308, fig. 1; Shtitelman, *Antique Art*, 1977, pl. 10; Kocybala, Diss. 1978, fig. 12. *Female head.*
1398	Pitane	*AJA* 66, 1962, pl. 103.31; *Emporio* 194, no. 13. *From the same vase as* **1272*** *of the Catalogue.*

IV. TRIPOD BOWLS

1399*	Rizari, Chios town	Chios Mus. no. 3382. *Part of the bowl and one leg of a tripod bowl. Patterns: chequer, meander and tongues.*
1400	Naucratis	Coulson and Leonard, *Naucratis* 53–54, inv. no. 80-119, pl. 6.4; Boardman in *Chios Conference*, 251 note 3. *Light brown paint on flaky white slip. Pattern: chequer, dots between two parallel lines and tongues.*

V. DINOI

1401*	Rizari, Chios town	Chios Mus. no. 3361. *Cable on the lip. Boar to the right. Rosettes. Added red on the body of the boar, (red-spotted boar), at the centre of the rosettes and the eyes of the cable.* *W: 0.059 Est. Diam.: c. 0.11.*
1402	Naucratis	BM 1924.12-1.3. *Cable on the lip. Lions to the r. Rosette. Inside: plain.* *W: 0.065.*
1403	Naucratis	Manchester III D.12. *Memoirs and Proceedings of the Manchester Literary and Philosophical Society*, 77, 1932-33, 2, pl. 1.3; *BSA* 47, 1952, 144, note 105, fig. 7 (Part of Cook's b.f. dinos); *Samos* VI.1, 138, no. 694.

VI. KOTHON

1404	Emporio	*Emporio* 168, no. 837, pl.63.

VII. PLATES

1405*	Phana	*ADelt.*II, 1916, 201 fig. 19; *Emporio* 166 note 1. *Est. Diam.: c. 0.246.*

1406	Naucratis	BM 1924.12–1.16. *Meander at the rim. Lion to the r. Rosette and half-rosettes.* *W: 0.060.*
1407*	Naucratis	BM 1886.4–1.1278. Price pl.12.12; *Samos* VI.1, 141 no. 837. *Chequer near the rim. Sph. to the l. Rosette.* *W: 0.075.*
1408*	Naucratis	*CVA* Oxford II, 83, pl.396.34, now missing.
1409*	Naucratis	Oxford 1925.608e. *Sph. to the l. Rosettes.* *W: 0.062.*
1410	Naucratis	Oxford G119.46. *Lions to the r. Half-rosettes.* *W: 0.042.*
1411*	Naucratis	Cambridge, Museum of Classical Archaeology, NA 98. *Rim pattern: double meander running l. Head of a lion to the r. and half-rosette.* *W: 0.071.*
1412*	Naucratis	München (lost during the war). *Rays and then chain of lotus and bud. At the centre: ?siren amidst rosettes and half-rosettes.*
1413*	Naucratis	inv. no. 2044. *CVA* Brussels III, 2, pl.105.4.
1414*	?Naucratis	no. A 1774, perhaps unknown prov. *CVA* Brussels III, 2, pl. 104.4. *Double meander running left at the rim above chequer with dotted blanks and then half-rosette and a feline to the r.*
1415*	Naucratis	Alexandria inv. no. 9486. Venit, *Egypt. Museums,* no. 78, pl. 22 and drawing on p. 156. *Sph. to the l. and rosette.*
1416	Cyrene, Demeter Sanct.	*LA,* 13–14, 1976–77, 302, no. 2, pl. 86b; Schaus, *Dem. Sanct., Cyrene* II, 84, no. 526, pl. 30.

VIII. DISHES

1417*	Emporio	*Emporio* 168, no. 835, pl.63.
1418*	Naucratis	Alexandria inv. no. 9491. Venit, *Egypt. Museums,* no. 142, pl. 34 and drawing on p. 169. *Outside: slipped. Inside: Feet of feline to the r. amidst rosette and half-rosette, then broken cable between lines and bands and then lotuses.*

IX. OPEN VASES

A. ?Lekane

1419*	Chios, unknown provenance	*ADelt.* I, 1915, 89f., figs. 33 and 34; *Emporio* 166 note 6.

B. Lekane with wide offset rim

1420*	Naucratis	*CVA* Oxford II, 82, 84, pls. 396. 29 and 60; *Samos* VI.1, pl. 97.717.

X. OENOCHOAI

1421*	Phana	Lamb Phana 160, pl. 37.2; *Emporio* 166 note 6.
1422*	Chios town, Kofiná ridge	*BSA* 49, 1954, pl. 6.12; *Emporio* 166 note 6. *W: 0.066.*
1423*	Chios town, Kofiná ridge	*BSA* 49, 1954, pl. 6.13; *Emporio* 166 note 6. *W: 0.075.*
1424*	Rizari, Chios town	Chios Mus. no. 3386. *Dashes at the rim; double meander running l., two parallel lines and then lion to the r. Half-rosette.* *W: 0.035.*
1425*	Rizari, Chios town	Chios Mus. no. 3362. *Dashes at the rim; double meander running l.* *W: 0.021.*
1426*	Naucratis	*CVA* Oxford II, pl. 396.41. (Not aryballos but from a close vase). *Siren to the l.* *W: 0.032.*
1427*	Naucratis	Vermont 85–152 (loan from Boston). *Goose to the l. Rosettes and half-rosettes.*
1428*	Naucratis	Leipzig, sent from Oxford in 1928, (lost during the war). *Dashes. Head of a lion to the r.* *Rosettes.*
1429*	Naucratis	Leipzig, sent from Oxford in 1928, (lost during the war). *Head of a lion to the l. Rosette.*
1430*	Naucratis	Athens, British School. *Samos* VI.1, pl. 97.706. *Perhaps from an oenochoe.*
1431	Abusir	Bonn 2002.14 Cook, Distribution 160
1432	Sybaris	*NSc* 1971, Suppl., 91, fig. 91, no. 150; *CGED* 112 and note 90.

1433*   Pitane   Istanbul Archaeological Museum, inv. no. 8904, on exhibit.
Almost intact trefoil oenochoe with two discs and a three-reeded handle put together from many frs.
On the neck: Two rows of tongues, one short the other long. Then: double guilloche. On the shoulder: Two rows of dashes. On the belly: Five friezes 1. Lions to the r. 2. Sphs. to the l. 3. Lions to the r. 4. Sphs. to the l. and the bust and head of a bearded man to the l. amidst the sphs. 5. Lotus and bud. Above the ring foot a row of short rays. Rosettes and half-rosettes in the field. Added red.
Est. H.: c. 0.30–0.35.

1434*   Ras el Bassit   *CGED* 42, pl. 18.16.

XI. INCENSE VASES

1435*   Emporio   *Emporio* 166, no. 828, pl. 62.

1436*   Rizari, Chios town   Chios Mus. no. 3389.
?Sph. to the l. Rosettes. Below a row of short rays. Rest not distinct.
W: 0.035.

1437*   Pitane   Istanbul Archaeological Museum, inv. no. 8580.
CGED 29, pl. 5.4; *Catalogue Istanbul* 1983, 33, B83.
The vase has a large opening on one side and sieve-like holes at the bottom inside.
On the handle, crowning the vase: double meander. On the upper part: sphs. to the r. Rosettes. On the body of the vase between the two flanges: lions to the r. Rosettes. Below: a lotus and bud frieze. Around the opening: vertical row of chequers. On the flanges: dashes.
H: 0.25 Diam.: 0.215.

XII. BASKET-HANDLED CYLINDRICAL VASE

1438*   Phana   *ADelt.* II, 1916, 202f., pl. 3.20–22; *Emporio* 166 note 6 and 194 no. 2; *Enc. World Art* VII, pl. 19 top right.

XIII. ?BASKET

1439*   Berezan   *MIA* 50, 1956, 223, fig. 1.10; Kocybala, Diss. 1978, 196 and note 135.

XIV. RING VASE

1440*   Naucratis   BM 1888.6–1.763.
Price pl. 6.29; *Samos* VI.1, pl. 97.844.
On the top of the vase: lion to the l. On the side: sph. to the l. and man to the r. holding branches. Half-rosettes. On the spout: tongues.

XV. FRAGMENTS

1441	Pyrgi Cem., Chios	*Emporio* 168, no. 834, pl. 63.
1442	Emporio	*Emporio* 168, no. 836, pl. 63.
1443*	Naucratis	BM 1924.12–1.205. *Lion to the r. In front of the lion an indiscernible object.* *W: 0.038.*
1444*	Naucratis	BM 1924.12–1.208. *Sph. to the l. Rosette.* *W: 0.032.*
1445	Naucratis	BM 1886.4–1.1297. *AA* 1983, 169: a kantharos. *Two friezes: Upper: hindquarters of ?sph. and ?tail of another animal. Lower: lion to the r. Rosettes.* *W: 0.072.*
1446	Naucratis	BM 1886.4–1.1101. *A goose heading r. but facing l. and the tail of an animal. Rosettes.* *W: 0.052.*
1447*	Naucratis	Oxford 1948.298g. *Two friezes: Upper: feet of a feline to the l. Lower: lion to the r. Half-rosette in a shape imitating the Wild Goat horseshoe roundel.* *W: 0.042.*
1448	Naucratis	Oxford G119.46. *Lions to the r.* *W: 0.041.*
1449*	Naucratis	LID. Cambridge, Museum of Classical Archaeology, NA 103. *Goat walking to the r. amidst rosettes. On the flange: rays.* *W: 0.064.*
1450*	Naucratis	LID. Cambridge, Museum of Classical Archaeology, NA 104. *Two friezes: lower: felines to the l. Upper: ?lion to the r. amidst rosettes.* *W: 0.047.*
1451*	Naucratis	Price pl. 12.4; Fairbanks, *Catal.* pl. 32, no. 310.1.
1452*	Naucratis	Fairbanks, *Catal.* pl. 32, no. 310.2.
1453*	Naucratis	Fairbanks, *Catal.* pl. 34, no. 320.6.
1454	Corcyra	*PAE* 1961, 125, pl. 76B.
1455	Delos, Rheneia	*Délos* XVII, pl. 63 B4.
1456	Olbia	Kocybala, Diss. 1978, 285 and note 381.
1457*	Old Smyrna	Athens, British School. *Emporio* 166 note 4. *Two friezes: Upper: lion to the r. Half-rosette. Lower: sph. to the l. and the tail of another in front. Rosettes.* *W: 0.031.*

2. THE BLACK-FIGURE GRAND STYLE

I. CUPS

1458*   Naucratis   Oxford G133.2 and 6.
CVA Oxford II, pl. 396.33; Boardman, CN 61 note 1; Lane, Lakonian 186; *RA* 1907, I, 379 and 407, fig. 19, pl. III,1; *RA* 1907, II, 52, no. 39; Stibbe, *LV*, 89 note 1, pl. 60.2.3; Samos VI.1, pl. 99.836; *Chios Conference* 254 and fig. 3.
Outside: From rim to the centre: 1. Two parallel lines. 2. A band of rays flanked on both sides by two parallel lines. 3. A band of tongues flanked on both sides by two parallel lines, then 4. Parallel lines.
Fr. G133.6 gives part of the handle palmette.
Tondo: at the border: pomegranate motif. Lane, Lakonian: *Type 2, fig. 21.2. Siren wearing a polos to the l. with open wings.*
Est. Diam: c. 0.18.

1459   Naucratis   Lane, Lakonian 186, fig. 26.
Outside: the end of a handle-palmette. Tondo: at the border: part of a pomegranate motif.

1460*   Naucratis   BM 1886.4–1.1283.
Price pl. 12.16; Boardman, CN 61 note 1.
Outside: bands of stripes and lines. Inside: two heads, the one next to the other, the one behind protruding to show its profile, wearing poloi and heading left.
W: 0.053.

II. CHALICES

1461*   Naucratis   Price pl. 9.10; *CVA* Cambridge II, pl. 496, 67; Boardman, CN 61 note 1; *Chios Conference*, 254 and fig 4.
Outside: legs wearing winged boots. Below them, a siren. Inside: lotus above two parallel lines.

1462*   Naucratis   BM 1924.12–1.206.
Price pl. 12.17; Boardman, CN 61 note 1.
Outside: The lower part of the long chiton of a ?seated figure to the l. In front of this figure to the l. an indiscernible object, ?a cock or hen, with a saw edged collar. Inside: a very elaborate rosette in red and white.
W: 0.043.

1463*   Naucratis   BM 1888.6–1.550a.
Price pl. 12.18; Boardman, CN 61 note 1.
Outside: Rim pattern: broken cable flanked by two parallel lines. Then two female heads, one after the other, heading l., wearing poloi. Inside: a very elaborate rosette in red and white.
W: 0.045.

1464*   Naucratis   BM 1924.12–1.204.
                               Price pl. 12.19; Boardman, CN 61 note 1.
                               Outside: The lower part of a long chiton with a border, paryphe with a chequer pattern, heading l. In front of this figure to the l. an indiscernible object, ?a cock or a hen, with a saw edged collar. Inside: ?black paint on white slip.
                               W: 0.034.

1465   Naucratis   BM 1888.6–1.550b.
                               Sph. to the l.
                               W: 0.042.

III. BOWL

1466*   Naucratis   BM 1886.4–1.1070.
                               Johnston, *Exhibition* 1978, no. 96.
                               A bull to the r.
                               W: 0.043.

IV. FRAGMENT

1467*   Berezan   Hermitage B263.
                               Brown paint over slip. Lower part of a long chiton rendered in the same manner as **1462*** *and* **1464***. *Female, figure to the r. At her l. a dog.*

3. THE BLACK-FIGURE CHALICES

1. Komast chalices

1468*	Emporio	*Emporio* 160, no. 748, fig. 108, pl. 59; *Samos* VI.1, 140, no. 760; *Chios Conference* 196, fig.6.
1469*	Emporio	*Emporio* 160, no. 749, pl. 59; *Samos* VI.1, 140, no. 761.
1470*	Emporio	*Emporio* 160, no. 750, pl. 60; *Samos* VI.1, 140, no. 762.
1471	Pyrgi Cem., Chios	*Emporio* 160, no. 751, pl. 60; *Samos* VI.1, 140, no. 763.
1472	Emporio	*Emporio* 160, no. 752, fig. 108; *Samos* VI.1, 140, no. 764.
1473	Emporio, Anemonas	*Emporio* 160, no. 753, pl. 60; *Samos* VI.1, 140, no. 765.
1474*	Emporio	*Emporio* 160, no. 754, pl. 60; *Samos* VI.1, 140, no. 766.
1475*	Emporio	*Emporio* 160, no. 755, pl. 60; *Samos* VI.1, 140, no. 767.
1476*	Emporio	*Emporio* 160, no. 756, pl. 60; *Samos* VI.1, 140, no. 768.
1477*	Emporio	*Emporio* 160, no. 757, pl. 60; *Samos* VI.1, 140, no. 769.
1478*	Emporio	*Emporio* 160, no. 758, pl. 60; *Samos* VI.1, 140, no. 770.
1479*	Emporio	*Emporio* 161, no. 759, pl. 60; *Samos* VI.1, 140, no. 771.
1480*	Emporio	*Emporio* 161, no. 760, pl. 60; *Samos* VI.1, 140, no. 772.
1481*	Phana	*ADelt* II, 1916, 195, pl. 2, fig. 10; *Emporio* 158 note 3.

1482*	Phana	*ADelt* II, 1916, 195, fig. 11. 1–3; *Emporio* 158 note 3; Price pl. 11, middle.
1483*	Phana	*ADelt* II, 1916, 197, fig. 11. 4–5; *Emporio* 158 note 3.
1484	Phana	*ADelt* II, 1916, 197, pl. 2.12; *Emporio* 158 note 3.
1485*	Phana	*ADelt* II, 1916, 198, pl. 2.13; *Emporio* 158 note 3.
1486	Phana	*BSA* 35, 1934–5, 160, pl. 37.11; *Emporio* 158 note 3.
1487*	Rizari, Chios town	Chios Mus. no. 3296. Villard, *Marseille* pl. 43.4; *Emporio* 158 note 1. *Put together from many frs. and foot restored. Decoration: On the wall: A komast on the l., who stretches his hands to a woman on the r. She wears only a chiton and the paryphe at her side is reserved and dotted. With her l. hand she handles a wreath, while she stretches her r. hand, which might have been holding an object. Slip and paint have flaked away on that part. Handle zone: Metope pattern, flanked by stripes. No rim pattern and no filling ornament. Dark brown paint on white slip. Inside: lotus flowers and rosettes in white and red just below rim; then, pairs of white lines; at the centre, on the floor, white cross with red dots.* *H: 0.151 Diam.: 0.143.*
1488*	Rizari, Chios town	Chios Mus. no. 3297 a–d. *Chios Conference* 248, fig. 19. *(Four frs. put together from many pieces).* *Decoration: On two frs: two komasts walking to the r. and turning their heads to the l. Rim pattern: chequers. No pattern is preserved on the handle zone. Inside: lotus flowers and rosettes in white and red just below rim; then, pairs of white lines; at the centre, on the floor, white cross with red dots.* *Diam.: 0.139.*
1489*	Naucratis	BM 1886.4–1.1072. *Naukratis* I, pl. 5. 45. *Woman to the l. wearing a belted chiton. Cogwheel-rosette. Inside: two white parallel lines.* *W: 0.035.*
1490	Naucratis	BM 1924.12–1.342. *Lower part of a woman's chiton.* *W: 0.039.*
1491*	Naucratis	BM 1886.4–1.1067. *Naukratis* I, pl. 5. 40; Price pl. 11.10. *Komast to the r. but facing l. Blob-rosette. Rim pattern: chequer. Inside: lotus flower below rim; then two white parallel lines.* *W: 0.033.*
1492	Naucratis	BM 1888.6–1.548k. Price pl. 11.3. *Komast to the r. Blob-rosette. Rim pattern: a dotted band.* *W: 0.033.*
1493*	Naucratis	BM 1888.6–1.548n. *Komast to the l. Rosette. Rim pattern: chequer. Inside: lotus flower.* *W: 0.048.*

1494*	Naucratis	BM 1886.4–1.1069. *Naukratis* I, pl. 5. 47. *Komast to the r. Blob-rosettes. Inside: lotus flower; then two white parallel lines which are repeated below.* *W: 0.033.*
1495	Naucratis	BM 1888.6–1.548p. *Komast to the r. Rosettes.* *W: 0.046.*
1496	Naucratis	BM 1924.12–1.346. *Komast to the l. holding a ball in his l. hand. Cogwheel-rosette.* *W: 0.037.*
1497	Naucratis	BM 1924.12–1.358. *Komast's hands. Rosettes.* *W: 0.031.*
1498	Naucratis	BM 1924.12–1.359. *Komast's hand. Rosette.* *W: 0.032.*
1499	Naucratis	BM 1924.12–1.348. *Komast's hands. Rossete.* *W: 0.029.*
1500	Naucratis	BM 1888.6–1.548j. *Komast's leg. Rosette.* *W: 0.036.*
1501	Naucratis	BM 1888.6–1.548d. *Komast's leg. Rosette and half-rosette.* *W: 0.025.*
1502	Naucratis	BM 1924.12–1.362. *Half-rosette. Rim pattern: chequer.* *W: 0.030.*
1503	Naucratis	BM 1924.12–1.350. *Komast's leg. Half-rosette. Handle zone: meander running l.* *W: 0.025.*
1504	Naucratis	BM 1924.12–1.360. *Komast's hand. Rosettes.* *W: 0.026.*
1505*	Naucratis	BM 1888.6–1.548n. *Komast to the l. No fill. orn. Inside: lotus and rosette in red and white.* *W: 0.023.*
1506*	Naucratis	BM 1888.6–1.548c. *Komast to the l. No fill. orn. Inside: lotus and rosette in red and white.* *W: 0.023.*
1507	Naucratis	BM 1888.6–1.548g. Price pl. 11.1. *Komast to the l. The ?foot of another at the l. No fill. orn.* *W: 0.051.*

THE BLACK-FIGURE CHALICES

1508   Naucratis   BM 1888.6–1.548f.
Komast to the l. No fill. orn.
W: 0.033.

1509*   Naucratis   BM 1888.6–1.1066.
Naukratis I, pl. 5.42.
Komast to the r. but facing l. No fill. orn. Inside: two white parallel lines.
W: 0.029.

1510   Naucratis   BM 1924.12–1.344.
Komast's head to the r. Rim pattern: two lines. Inside: lotus flowers and below two white parallel lines.
W: 0.040.

1511*   Naucratis   BM 1888.6–1.548b.
Komast to the l. Rim pattern: chequer. Inside: lotus in red and white.
W: 0.026.

1512   Naucratis   BM 1924.12–1.351.
Komast's cap to the l.
W: 0.023.

1513   Naucratis   BM 1924.12–1.355.
Komast's left hand and part of his buttocks. No fill. orn.
W: 0.038.

1514   Naucratis   BM 1924.12–1.347.
Komast's left hand and buttocks. No fill. orn.
W: 0.038.

1515   Naucratis   BM 1924.12–1.357.
Komast's ?right leg.
W: 0.025.

1516*   Naucratis   BM 1888.6–1.548m.
Komast's left leg. Inside: red and white rosette.
W: 0.027.

1517   Naucratis   BM 1888.6–1.548i.
Komast's buttocks and left leg to the r. No fill. orn.
W: 0.032.

1518   Naucratis   BM 1888.6–1.548o.
Komast's legs to the r.
W: 0.015.

1519   Naucratis   BM 1924.12–1.356.
Komast's leg to the l.
W: 0.031.

1520*   Naucratis   BM 1888.6–1.548e.
Komast's ?legs. Handle zone: cable. Inside: two white parallel lines, then tongues then two white parallel lines and then, tongues and a line.
W: 0.035.

1521   Naucratis   BM 1924.12–1.366.
Komast holding a wreath.
W: 0.049.

1522	Naucratis	BM 1924.12–1.349. *Komast's buttocks to the r. Inside: red and white lotus and then two white parallel lines.* *W: 0.019.*
1523	Naucratis	BM 1924.12–1.341. *Komast's hand holding a ball.* *W: 0.036.*
1524	Naucratis	BM 1924.12–1.367. *Komast to the r. Rosette.* *W: 0.036.*
1525	Naucratis	BM 1888.6–1.548h. *Komast's head and bust to the l.* *W: 0.027.*
1526	Naucratis	BM 1924.12–1.570. *Part of the interior of a chalice.* *W: 0.054.*
1527	Naucratis	BM 1924.12–1.566. *Part of the interior of a chalice At the centre: rosette with eight petals alternating in red and white.* *W: 0.083.*
1528	Naucratis	BM 1924.12–1.352. *Part of the rim and wall of a chalice. Rim pattern: SS between two parallel lines. Then, rosette. Inside: lotus.* *W: 0.024.*
1529	Naucratis	BM 1924.12–1.544. *Part of the rim and wall of a chalice. Rim pattern: diagonal strokes between two parallel lines. Incised inscription:]ΑΦΡΟ[* *Inside: lotus and palmette.* *W: 0.042.*
1530*	Naucratis	*CVA* Oxford II, 83, pl. 396.46.
1531*	Naucratis	*CVA* Oxford II, 83, pl. 396.47.
1532*	Naucratis	*CVA* Oxford II, 83, pl. 396.49, (where wrong number G115.6).
1533*	Naucratis	*CVA* Oxford II, 83, pl. 396.50. (where numbers are wrong).
1534*	Naucratis	*CVA* Oxford II, 83, pl. 396.51. inv. no. G115.6.
1535*	Naucratis	*CVA* Oxford II, 83, pl. 396.52.
1536*	Naucratis	*CVA* Oxford II, 83, pl. 396.53a.
1537*	Naucratis	*CVA* Oxford II, 83, pl. 396.53b.
1538*	Naucratis	*CVA* Oxford II, 83, pl. 396.54b.
1539*	Naucratis	*CVA* Oxford II, 84, pl. 396.54a; *BSA* 5, 1898–9, pl. 6.5, part.
1540*	Naucratis	*CVA* Oxford II, 84, pl. 396.55.
1541*	Naucratis	*CVA* Oxford II, 84, pl. 396.56.
1542	Naucratis	Oxford 1933. 435e. *Komast's hand. Blob-rosettes. Rim pattern: chequer.*

1543	Naucratis	Oxford 1912. 32a. *Komast's leg.*
1544	Naucratis	Oxford G115.9. *Komast's buttocks and hand.*
1545*	Naucratis	Price pl. 11.4; *CVA* Cambridge II, 35, pl. 496.63.
1546*	Naucratis	*BSA* 5, 1898–9, 58, pl. 6.4; Price pl. 11.4; *CVA* Cambridge II, 35, pl. 496.64.
1547*	Naucratis	*CVA* Cambridge II, 35, pl. 496.65.
1548	Naucratis	*CVA* Cambridge II, 35, pl. 496.66, (missing since the war).
1549*	Naucratis	*CVA* Cambridge II, 35, pl. 496.68.
1550*	Naucratis	Cambridge, Museum of Classical Archaeology, NA 83. *Left arm and head of a komast to the r. and then right arm of another to the r.* *W: 0.043.*
1551*	Naucratis	Cambridge, Museum of Classical Archaeology, NA 84. *Lower part and right leg of a komast to the r.* *W: 0.019.*
1552*	Naucratis	Cambridge, Museum of Classical Archaeology, NA 79. *Part of the rim and walls of a chalice. Rim pattern: diagonal strokes between two parallel lines. A pomegranate.* *W: 0.055.*
1553*	Naucratis	Cambridge, Museum of Classical Archaeology, NA 80. *Part of the rim and walls of a chalice. Rim pattern: as the last. Frieze of lotus and bud and then tendril.* *W: 0.044.*
1554*	Naucratis	Fairbanks, *Catal.* pl. 32, no. 310.4.
1555*	Naucratis	Fairbanks, *Catal.* pl. 34, no. 321.14.
1556*	Naucratis	MMA inv. no. 26.211.3 (Gift of Elinor R. Price, 1926). *Komast to the l. above handle zone double guilloche and tongues near handle.*
1557*	Naucratis	MMA inv. no. 26.211.9 (Gift of Elinor R. Price, 1926). *Rosette.*
1558*	Naucratis	*CVA* Heidelberg I, 14, pl. 437.15 and 16.
1559*	Naucratis	Berlin Antiquarium (lost during the war). *Komast to the l. and rosette. Inside: two pairs of white parallel lines.*
1560*	Naucratis	Athens, British School. *Komast to the r.* *W: 0.023.*
1561*	Tocra	*Tocra* II, addenda to *Tocra* I, 26, no. 807, fig. 10, pl. 14.
1562*	Tocra	*Tocra* I, 63, no. 787, fig. 30, pl. 44; *Emporio* 158 note 3.
1563*	Tocra	*Tocra* I, 53, no. 788, pl. 44; *Emporio* 158 note 3.
1564*	Tocra	*Tocra* I, 63, no. 789, pl. 44; *Emporio* 158 note 3.
1565*	Tocra	*Tocra* I, 63, nos. 790–1, pl. 44; *Emporio* 158 note 3.
1566*	Tocra	*Tocra* II, 26, no. 2046, pl. 15.
1567*	Tocra	*Tocra* II, 26, no. 2047, pl. 15.

1568*	Tocra	*Tocra* II, 26, no. 2048, pl. 15.
1569*	Tocra	*Tocra* II, 26, no. 2049, pl. 15.
1570	Cyrene, Demeter Sanct.	*LA*, 13–14, 1976–77, pl. 85b bottom right; Schaus, *Dem. Sanct., Cyrene* II, 81, no. 485, pl. 28.
1571	Cyrene, Demeter Sanct.	Schaus, *Dem. Sanct., Cyrene* II, 81, no. 486, pl. 28.
1572	Cyrene, Demeter Sanct.	Schaus, *Dem. Sanct., Cyrene* II, 81, no. 487, pl. 29.
1573	Cyrene, Demeter Sanct.	Schaus, *Dem. Sanct., Cyrene* II, 81, no. 488, pl. 29.
1574*	Rhegium	Museo Reggio di Calabria, inv. no. 19148. *CGED* 114 and note 114; E. Lattanzi, *Il Museo Nazionale di Reggio Calabria* 1987, 81 and illustr. on p. 82.
1575	Himera	*Himera* II, 268, pl. XLIII, 5. *Chalice fragments.*
1576	Delos	*Délos* XX, 37, fig. 33.2.
1577	Delos	*Délos* XX, 37, fig. 33.3.
1578*	Aegina, Aphaia Temple	*AA* 1983, 164, no. 17, fig. 8.
1579*	Kavala	*AE* 1938, 119, no. 83; *Emporio* 158 note 3.
1580	Thessaloniki, Ayia Paraskevi	*Ametos* 794, pl. 163.2 upper row, right. *Paint fired red. Three komasts to the r. wearing turbans. Inside: chain of lotus and rosette.*
1581	Olbia	Kocybala, Diss. 1978, 259 and note 299; *AGSP* 361, fig. 5.
1582*	Olbia	Kiev Historical Museum. V.D. Blavatsky, *History*, 1953, 259; Knipovič, *Ancient Cities* I, 1955, 361, fig. 5; D. Scheloff, *Die antike Welt im nördlichen Schwarzmeerraum* russ. 1956, 51, fig. 14; *Emporio* 158 note 3; Ballu, *Olbia* pl. 28.2; *Samos* VI.1, pl. 95.759; Shtitelman, *Antique Art*, pl. 13.
1583	Olbia	*SovArch.* VII, 1941, 315, fig. 4.3; *Emporio* 158 note 3; Kocybala, Diss. 1978, 230, fig. 3c.
1584*	Berezan	Hermitage B465. *SovArch.* 1957.4, 135, fig. 7.4; *Emporio* 158 note 3; Kocybala, Diss. 1978, 209 and note 231; *Histria* IV, 26 and note 41: B461.
1585*	Berezan	Hermitage B461. *SovArch.* 1957.4, 135, fig. 7.5; *Emporio* 158 note 3; Kocybala, Diss. 1978, 209 and note 231; *Histria* IV, 26 and note 41: B465.
1586	Berezan	Fabritsius, *Arch. Karta* I, pl. 12.1; *Emporio* 158 note 3.
1587*	Old Smyrna	*BSA* 60, 1965, 141, no. 2, pl. 43.2; *Emporio* 158 note 3.
1588*	Old Smyrna	*BSA* 60, 1965, 141, no. 3, pl. 43.3; *Emporio* 158 note 3.
1589*	Old Smyrna	*BSA* 60, 165, 141, no. 8, pl. 43.8.
1590*	Samos	*Samos* VI.1, 70 and 140, fig. 143, pl. 98, no. 773.
1591	Rhodes, Vroulia	Kinch, *Vroulia*, 150, no. 2, pl. 46.4, and pl. 28.2 a, b; *Emporio* 158 note 3.

2. Animal chalices

1592   Naucratis   BM 1924.12–1.340.
Outside: bull to the r. Rosette. Inside: lotus and below two white parallel lines.
W: 0.038.

1593   Naucratis   BM 1888.6–1.549.
Johnston, *Exhibition* 1978, no. 87.
Lower part of a cock to the l.; the r. leg steps forward.
W: 0.033.

1594*   Naucratis   BM 1886.4–1.1563.
Naukratis I, pl. 5.43.
Lower part of a cock to the l. Handle zone: metope with saw pattern.
W: 0.030.

1595*   Naucratis   *CVA* Oxford II, 82 and 83, pl. 396.43 and 22.
Outside: Rim pattern: chequer. Cock's head to the r. Inside: rosette in red and white.

1596*   Naucratis   *CVA* Oxford II, 83, pl. 396.44.
Outside: Rim pattern: chequer. Cock's head to the r. Inside: black with red lotus in white outline and two white bands.

1597*   Naucratis   *CVA* Oxford II, 83, pl. 396.42; Price fig. 52.
Fish and blob-rosettes. Handle zone: metope with saw pattern.

1598*   Naucratis   *CVA* Oxford II, 83, pl. 396.45.
The heads of two antithetical swans and part of the necks. Blob-rosettes.

1599   Naucratis   Oxford 1912.32a.
A tail of a bird.

1600*   Tocra   *Tocra* I 59, 63, no. 785, pl. 42 and 43; Boardman, *GA*² 87, fig. 80; *Emporio* 158 note 4; *Samos* VI.1, pl. 100.815 and 95.815.

1601*   Tocra   *Tocra* I 59, 63, no. 786, pl. 43; *Emporio* 158 note 4.

1602*   Rhitsona   Museum of Thebes, inv. no. 50.257.
JHS 29, 1909, 332ff., fig. 15, pl. 25; *Emporio* 158, note 4; *Tocra* I 59 and note 4; *BSA* 44, 1949, 158, n. 14.

1603*   Apollonia Pontica   Museum of Bourgas.
G. Gorov et al., *Musée Archéologique de Bourgas* 1967, fig. 19.
Two confronted cocks with a lotus between them. Blob-rosettes. Rim pattern: ?band, worn off. Handle zone: metope with saw pattern. Bowl: two parallel bands. Black paint on the outside of handles.
H: 0.066 Diam. at the rim: 0.098.

1604   Olbia   Kocybala, Diss. 1978, 259, fig. 29.
Rim part of a chalice. Bull to the r. No fill. orns.

1605*–1606*   Berezan   Hermitage.
SovArch. 1957.4, 136, fig. 8; *Emporio* 158 note 4.
Two frs. On one fr.: Rim pattern: chequer. Cock to the r. On the other fr.: cock to the l.
1: W: 0.051; 2: W: 0.039.

1607	Berezan	Fabritsius, *Arch. Karta* I, pl. 12.4; *Emporio* 158 note 4. *Hen to the l. Added red on plumage.*
1608	Berezan	Fabritsius, *Arch. Karta* I, pl. 12.5; *Emporio* 158 note 4. *Rim pattern: chequer. On the wall: cock to the l. Rosettes. Handle zone: metope with saw pattern.*
1609	Kepoi in Kertsch	Kocybala, Diss. 1978, 343, fig. 47. *Sph. to the l. No fill orns.* *(It might be from a cup).*
1610	Kepoi in Kertsch	Kocybala, Diss. 1978, 347, fig. 48. *Head of a ?boar to the l.* *(It might be from a cup).*
1611*	Pitane	Istanbul Archaeological Museum, inv. no. 8906. *CGED* 29, pl. 6.6; *Catalogue Istanbul* 1983, 35, B85; Akurgal, *Türkei* 1987, pl. 20a (on the right). *An intact chalice, restored from many frs. Rim pattern: chequer. On the wall: cock to the r. Handle zone: metope with saw pattern. On the bowl: two parallel lines. Foot and outside of handles painted ?black.* *H.: 0.14.*
1612	Pitane	*CGED* 29; Akurgal, *Türkei*, 1987, pl. 20a (on the left).
1613*	Old Smyrna	*BSA* 60, 1965, no. 9, pl. 44.9 and 43.9; *Emporio* 158 note 4. *Outside: part of the upper front of a cock to the l. No fill. orn. Inside: lotus and rosette in red and white and below a band of chequer-dots.*
1614*	Rhodes, Camirus	BM 1867.5–6.42. Price pl. 9.9; *Emporio* 158, note 4. *Rim pattern: two parallel lines. On the wall: a goose to the l. Blob-rosettes. Handle zone: metope with saw pattern. On the bowl: two parallel bands. Foot painted dark brown.*

3. Chalices with floral decoration

1615*	Naucratis	*CVA* Oxford II, 81, pl. 396.8.
1616*	Naucratis	Oxford G115.17. *CVA* Oxford II, pl. 396.30 and inside pl. 396.23. *Wrong inv. no. G115.7.*

4. Unslipped chalices

1617*	Rhodes, Camirus	Copenhagen, inv. no. 5612. Kinch, *Vroulia* 151, pl. 46.1; *CVA* Copenhagen II, pl. 81.2; *Emporio* 158 and note 5; *Samos* VI.1, pl. 100.818.
1618–1619	Rhodes, Vroulia	Kinch, *Vroulia* 151; *Emporio* 158 and note 5. *Two fragments of unslipped chalices.*

5. Chalices with indiscernible or unpreserved decoration

1620*   Naucratis   Oxford 1925.608e.
CVA Oxford II, pl. 396.48 and inside pl. 396.26.
not revellers.

1621   Naucratis   Oxford 1966.1027.
Fr. from a miniature chalice. Blob-rosettes incised. Added red on the centre of rosette.

1622   Samos, Heraion   *Samos* VI.1, 140, pl. 98.777. *Foot of a chalice.*

1623   Samos, Heraion   *Samos* VI.1, 140, pl. 98.778.

1624   Samos   *Samos* IV, 148, inv. no. 510, K4241.

4. THE BLACK-FIGURE KANTHAROI

1. Unslipped kantharoi

1625*   Emporio   *Emporio* 168, no. 838, fig. 116, pl. 63; *JHS* 74, 1954, 164, fig. 12b; *Samos* VI.1, 141, no. 826.

1626*   Emporio   *Emporio* 168, no. 839, pl. 63.

1627*   Emporio   *Emporio* 168, no. 840, pl. 63.

1628*   Emporio   *Emporio* 168, no. 841, pl. 63.

1629*   Naucratis   BM 1911.6–6.12.
Incised inscription:]ΣΥΜΦΟΡ[

1630   Naucratis   Oxf. G1009.
Emporio 168 note 1.

1631   Naucratis   Oxf. 1912.37.
Emporio 168 note 1.
Dolphins.

1632   Naucratis   Oxf. 1925.608d.
Emporio 168 note 1.
A cock.

1633   Locri   *Locri Epizefiri* I, 88, no. C30, pl. 26.

1634   ?Sinope   Münster, inv. no. 771.
Boreas I, 1978, 178, pl. 24.3.

2. Slipped kantharoi

1635*   Berezan   Hermitage B 189.
SovArch. 1957.4, 136, fig. 9.1,2,3; *Emporio* 162 note 1; Kocybala, Diss. 1978, 200 and note 166.
Three frs. from the same vase.
Fr. 1: Decoration in two rows: Upper: cock's feathers to the r. Lower: goose with open wings to the l. amidst blob-rosettes.
Fr. 2: Decoration in two rows: Upper: geese with open wing to the r. Lower: antithetical dolphins amidst blob-rosettes.
W: 0.118.
Fr. 3: A hen to the l., then dividing band.
W: 0.069.

1636	Olbia	*SovArch.* VII, 1941, 315, fig. 4.2; Kocybala, Diss. 1978, 230, fig. 13.b. *(where wrongly classified as an oenochoe; it has a double-reeded handle and is from a kantharos of type A: see AA 1983, 169).*
1637	Tiritake	*MIA* 25, 1952, 236, fig. 6; Kocybala, Diss. 1978, 311 note 645.

5. MISCELLANEA

I. HYDRIA

1638*	Lithi on Chios	Chios Mus. inv. no. 3739. (Confiscated by the Archaeological Service in March 1984). *Brown to red over very white slip. Decoration: Frieze on the shoulder: Four geese with open wings to the l. with blob-rosettes forming a triangle in front of them. Handle zone: Dots below tongues. Lower part: Four bands.* *H: 0.191.* *Diam. on the handle zone: 0.15.* *Diam. on the lips: 0.091.*

II. TWO-HANDLED POTS

1639	Emporio	*Emporio* 169–170, no. 843, pl. 64.
1640	Emporio	*Emporio* 169–170, no. 844, fig. 116.
1641*	Rizari, Chios town	Chios Mus. no. 3285. *Emporio* 169. *Dark brown paint on a creamy-yellowish slip. On the rim: two parallel lines and in between zone with vertical, parallel lines. On the belly: double lines above and below handle zone and in between a "metope" with vertical and wavy lines. Below, a zone of parallel lines and on the base of the vase a band.* *H: 0.05 Diam. at the rim: 0.039.*
1642	Cyrene, Demeter Sanct.	Schaus, *Dem. Sanct.*, *Cyrene* II, 79, no. 476, pl. 28.
1643	Cyrene, Demeter Sanct.	Schaus, *Dem. Sanct.*, *Cyrene* II, 79, no. 477, fig. 9.
1644	Cyrene, Demeter Sanct.	Schaus, *Dem. Sanct.*, *Cyrene* II, 79, no. 478, pl. 28.
1645*	Athens, Agora	*Agora* VIII, 59, no. 244, pl. 13.
1646	Delos	*Délos* XV, pl. L6.
1647*	Olbia	Hermitage o.1913.350, on exhibit. *AA* 1914, 231f., figs. 45, 46; *Emporio* 169 and note 1; Ballu, *Olbia* pl. 28.4 (where wrongly classified as Samian); Skudnova, *Olbia* 1988, 141, KAT. 222.

III. IVY-PATTERNED VASES

1648*	Emporio	JUG. *Emporio* 169–170, no. 842, fig. 116, pl. 64.
1649*	Emporio	CHALICE, fragmentary. *Emporio* 158, 161, no. 762, pl. 60.
1650–1651	Chios town	CHALICES. *Horos* 4, 1986, 130, pl. 28.3. a and d.
1652*	Naucratis	Oxf. G114.34. CHALICE, fragmentary. *CVA* Oxford II, pl. 396.3; Boardman, CN 62 note 2.
1653*	Old Smyrna	MUG, fragmentary. *BSA* 60, 1965, 142, pl. 43.16; *Emporio* 169 and note 3.

IV. VARIA

1654*	Emporio	*Emporio* 169–170, no. 846, pl. 64.
1655	Chios town, Kofiná ridge	OENOCHOE, fragmentary. *BSA* 47, 1954, 134, no. 3, pl. 6.3.
1656*	Naucratis	BM 1888.6–1.520. *Naukratis* II, pl. 13; Pfuhl, *MuZ* fig. 123; Price 204; *BSA* 47, 1954, 127 note 20 and 139 note 64; Boardman, CN 61 note 10; *Samos* VI.1, pl. 100. 700.
1657*	Naucratis	*Naukratis* I pl. 5.41; Pfuhl, *MuZ*, fig. 124; Price 222; Buschor, Das Krokodil des Sotates, *MüJb*, 35; *Samos* VI.1, pl. 100. 819.
1658*	Olbia	ONE-HANDLED CUP. Kiev Historical Museum. Shtitelman, *Antique Art*, pl. 12; G.P. Schaus, *BSA* 81, 1986, 270 note 56 (Fikellura). *One-handled cup with trefoil mouth and eyes under the rim. Upper row: pattern of a branch with interchanging ivy and vine leaves. Middle row: dots arranged in two rows. Lower row: double meander running to the r.* *H: 0.115.*
1659	"Larisa"	LID, fragmentary. *Larisa am Hermos* III, 93, pl. 40.22.